Dear Appalachia

Dear Appalachia

Readers, Identity, and Popular Fiction since 1878

EMILY SATTERWHITE

UNIVERSITY PRESS OF KENTUCKY

Copyright © 2011 by The University Press of Kentucky
Paperback edition 2015

Scholarly publisher for the Commonwealth,
serving Bellarmine University, Berea College, Centre College of Kentucky,
Eastern Kentucky University, The Filson Historical Society, Georgetown
College, Kentucky Historical Society, Kentucky State University, Morehead
State University, Murray State University, Northern Kentucky University,
Transylvania University, University of Kentucky, University of Louisville,
and Western Kentucky University.
All rights reserved.

Editorial and Sales Offices: The University Press of Kentucky
663 South Limestone Street, Lexington, Kentucky 40508-4008
www.kentuckypress.com

Maps by Dick Gilbreath.

The Library of Congress has cataloged the hardcover edition as follows:

Satterwhite, Emily, 1972-
  Dear Appalachia : readers, identity, and popular fiction since 1878 / Emily Satterwhite.
      p. cm.
  Includes bibliographical references and index.
  ISBN 978-0-8131-3010-1 (hardcover : acid-free paper) —
  ISBN 978-0-8131-3011-8 (ebook)
  1. American literature—Appalachian Region—History and criticism.
  2. Appalachian Region—In literature. I. Title.
  PS286.A6S28 2011
  810.9'974--dc23   2011037216

  ISBN 978-0-8131-6110-5 (pbk. : alk. paper)

This book is printed on acid-free paper meeting
the requirements of the American National Standard
for Permanence in Paper for Printed Library Materials.

Manufactured in the United States of America.

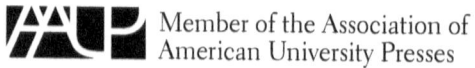 Member of the Association of
American University Presses

In memory of Jamie Bishop
and all the faculty and students
who lost their lives at Virginia Tech
on April 16th, 2007.

In gratitude to survivor Derek O'Dell.
When some resisted being defined by the event,
he countered: "Let your response define you."

In kinship with all of us haunted in ways
recognized, unnamed, and unknown.

For what is knowable is not only a function of objects—
of what is there to be known. It is also a function of subjects,
of observers—of what is desired and what needs to be known.
—Raymond Williams, *The Country and the City*

Everywhere has to be somewhere.
—Chris Offutt, *Kentucky Straight*

Contents

List of Illustrations   xi

Acknowledgments   xiii

Introduction: Best-Selling Appalachia   1

1. Charm and Virility, circa 1884   27

2. Tonic and Rationale, circa 1908   55

3. Country to City, circa 1949–1954   89

4. City to Country, circa 1967–1970   131

5. A Sweet Land That Never Was, circa 1994–2001   177

Conclusion:
The Production of Region and the Romance
with Whiteness   211

Appendix:
Methodological Essay   229

Notes   249

Selected Bibliography   331

Index   353

Illustrations

Figures

Mary Noailles Murfree at eleven   35
Postcard from a Charles Egbert Craddock fan, 1884   43
Mary Noailles Murfree among Boston literati, 1885   50
Advertisement for *The Trail of the Lonesome Pine*, 1908   58
John Fox Jr., circa 1894   64
"I'm afraid this is the kind of a dinner you describe in your book": from John Fox Jr., "On the Trail of the Lonesome Pine," 1910   69
Illustration from *The Trail of the Lonesome Pine*, 1908   79
Advertisement for *Hunter's Horn*, 1949   101
Advertisement for *The Dollmaker*, 1954   103
Harriette Simpson Arnow, circa 1954   107
Advertisement for *Christy*, 1967   137
Advertisement for *Deliverance*, 1970   159
"Experience the Real Cold Mountain": tourism Web site for Asheville, North Carolina, 2010   190
"Find Your Way Home": advertisement for the film adaptation of *Cold Mountain*, 2003   191
Readers saw in Appalachia their familial histories and their own best simple selves   223

Maps

All fan mail to Charles Egbert Craddock/Mary Noailles Murfree, 1883–1928   46
Fan mail to John Fox Jr., 1903–1919   74
Fan mail to John Fox Jr. from migrant fans and fan-acquaintances   76
Fan mail to Harriette Arnow regarding *Hunter's Horn*, 1949–1961   96

All fan mail to Harriette Arnow regarding *The Dollmaker*,
    1954–1978   98
Fan mail to Harriette Arnow regarding *Hunter's Horn* from migrant fans
    and fan-acquaintances   114
Fan mail to Harriette Arnow regarding *The Dollmaker* from migrant
    fans and fan-acquaintances   116
Fan mail to Catherine Marshall regarding *Christy*, 1967 and 1968   140
Fan mail to Catherine Marshall from migrant fans, 1967–1973   146
Fan mail to James Dickey regarding *Deliverance*, 1970 and 1971   154
Fan mail to James Dickey from migrant fans and fan-acquaintances,
    1970–1980   162
Fan mail from tourists to Catherine Marshall, 1967–1973   168
Big Stone Gap fans who mention migrations, 2000–2003   198

Acknowledgments

This project received generous financial support from many institutions. At Emory University, the Graduate Institute of the Liberal Arts (ILA) and the Graduate School of Arts and Sciences provided research travel grants, a Woodruff Fellowship, a Brown Southern Studies Research Grant, a Brown Southern Studies Research Fellowship, a Dean's Teaching Fellowship, and a Quadrangle Research Fund Fellowship in Post-national American Studies. At Virginia Tech, the Department of Interdisciplinary Studies (now the Department of Religion and Culture) and the College of Liberal Arts and Human Sciences (CLAHS) at Virginia Tech provided travel funding, a Humanities Summer Stipend, a departmental teaching release, a South Atlantic Humanities Center Fellowship, and a South Atlantic Studies Initiative award, thanks to department chairs Betty Fine and Peter Schmitthenner and college deans Jerry Niles and Sue Ott Rowlands. Additional travel and research funds were provided by the Appalachian Studies Program, thanks to program director Anita Puckett, and by the Center for Instructional Development and Educational Research, thanks to faculty study group mentors Dan Thorpe and Mark Barrow. The Appalachian Studies Association and the National Endowment for the Humanities funded a Wilma Dykeman Faces of Appalachia Post-doctoral Research Fellowship for the Study of Race, Ethnicity, and Gender, which made it possible to write during the summer after my daughter Maryn was born. Additional financial support was provided by a research fellowship sponsored by the Smithsonian Center for Folklife and Cultural Heritage and the Emory Center for the Study of Public Scholarship.

 I owe a great debt to countless librarians. The Interlibrary Loan Offices at Emory University, King University (Bristol, Tennessee), and Virginia Tech were essential to my research. Thanks goes to Kathy Shoemaker, Naomi Nelson, and Randy Gue at Emory University; Claire McCann, Jason Flahardy, Matt Harris, and especially Kate Black at the University of Kentucky; Delinda Buie, Sue Finley, Rachel Howard, and Ann Collins at the University of Louisville; Patrick Kerwin and Marilyn Ibach at the Library of Congress; Shannon Wilson at Berea College; Faye Harkins and Gina Claywell at Murray State University; Donna Baker at Morehead State University; Elizabeth Dunham at the University of Tennessee at Knoxville; and Elizabeth Bagley and especially Marianne Bradley, as well as students Victoria Belarde and Zijia Sun, at Agnes Scott College. Research trips were made possible by my friends and hosts: Jennifer Meares and Amy Viar in Atlanta; Leslie and Ryan Bates in Louisville; and Marsha Ford in Washington, DC. Additional assistance with images was provided by Thomas Wells at the University of Tennessee Press.

Undergraduate students at Virginia Tech have made invaluable contributions to this project. In spring 2007, students in my course Critical Issues: Popular Appalachia in Film and Fiction (Kate Andrukonis, Kim Berkey, Morgan Cain, Kathryn Drumwright, Rebecca Farthing, Mark Gregory, Grant Harris, Jason Luke, Kristen McFeeley, and Katie Paxton) helped me clarify my thinking and prepared projects on best sellers that directed me to useful resources. Work-study students Syeda Kutub, Michelle Pac, Mackenzie D'Assis, Kareli Arce, and Jessica Edwards helped with library runs, deciphering and typing fan letters, distilling demographic data on the fans, and mapping the origins of the fan mail. CLAHS ambassadors volunteered their time to assist in my research and analysis, including Ashley Ferguson, Jarryd Mushatt-Valery, and Kerry Kaleba. The Undergraduate Research Institute sent me angels by the names of Jason Ramsey, Meagan Watson, Blair Knight, Jared Rowan, Ryan McLaughlin, and especially Kevin Gillispie and Karen Spears. They created maps, completed and standardized citations, and pursued images and permissions. Kevin checked for errors of attribution in secondary and primary sources (often with a much sharper eye for fans' handwriting than mine) and helped me bounce ideas around. Graphic design major Amanda Kubista created the striking cover illustration. Additionally, graduate students Scott Tate and Dana Cochran in the Alliance for Social, Political, Ethical, and Cultural Thought (ASPECT) doctoral program did a brilliant job as teaching assistants, enabling me to write.

I would like to thank my dedicated professors and mentors in the ILA and in the departments of history and English at Emory University, including Cristine Levenduski, Amy Schrager Lang, Jonathan Prude, Jim Roark, Allen Tullos, and especially Michael Elliott—who has spent even more hours advising me after my graduation than before. I am immensely grateful to my writing group members at Emory: Amy Wood, Brian Luskey, Marni Davis, Molly McGehee, and especially Jennifer Meares, who saved the day near the end; and at Virginia Tech: Nikol Alexander-Floyd, Carlos Evia, and especially Gena Chandler. Thanks also goes to the Spaces of Identity Research Group at Virginia Tech, organized by women's and gender studies program director Barbara Ellen Smith: Katy Powell, Gena Chandler, Maria-Elisa Christie, Minjeong Kim, and Laura Gillman. My most steadfast and long-standing writing adviser, Mary Lynn Satterwhite, read multiple chapters for the clarity and correctness of my prose. What follows is much improved thanks to her keen eye.

Additional readers, interlocutors, colleagues, teachers, advocates, and friends who deserve special mention for nurturing my thinking and my career include H. D. Satterwhite, Virginia Shadron, Katherine Skinner, Steve Fisher, Tal Stanley, David Whisnant, Elizabeth Engelhardt, Darlene Wilson, Cece Conway, June Howard, Janice Radway, Jack Furlong, Chad Berry, Barbara Hochman, Barbara Ryan, Amy Blair, Jean Haskell, Neal King, Mark Barrow, Heather Diamond, Jen and Steve Daskal, Erika Meitner, Anita Puckett, and Katherine Ledford. Thank goodness for the support of the Lane Hall mafia; those people know how to get things done around here. University Press of Kentucky acquisitions editor Laura Sutton's belief in the project reinvigorated me for the final stretch, which Steve Wrinn, Allison Webster, and a skillful UPK staff saw me through. Stephanie Foote, Chris Green, Chad Berry, and an anonymous reviewer helped me see my work and what was at stake in new ways; I cannot fully express my gratitude to them for their careful reading and grappling with the manuscript. I cherish the friendship and mentoring of Barbara Ellen Smith; our many conversations shaped and improved immeasurably the ideas herein. Emory, Virginia Tech, the Appalachian Studies Association, and the Reception Studies Society have introduced me to many more brilliant collaborators than I can mention individually.

To Phil Olson, who made this book possible in more ways than I can count, I owe much more than gratitude alone. Thank you for being my sweetheart, my best friend, and a doting dad. I love you.

Parts of this book were initially published as "Reading Craddock, Reading Murfree" in *American Literature*, reprinted by permission of Duke University Press; "'That's What They're All Singing About'" and "Objecting to Insider/Outsider Politics and the Uncritical Celebration of Appalachia," reprinted by permission of *Appalachian Journal*; "Imagining Home, Nation, World," reprinted by permission of the *Journal of American Folklore*; and "Romancing Whiteness" in *At Home and Abroad*, reprinted by permission of the University of Tennessee Press.

Introduction

Best-Selling Appalachia

> Appalachia—read-about Appalachia, personally experienced Appalachia, laughed-at Appalachia, inspired-by Appalachia—is just as much a social construction as is the Cowboy or, for that matter, the Indian.
> —Allen Batteau, *The Invention of Appalachia*

> Most of contemporary life is presented as acultural; the real "culture" must be represented as belonging to the past, something that isn't quite dead yet but exists only in scraps and traces.
> —Benjamin Feinberg, *The Devil's Book of Culture*

For many Americans, Appalachia conjures up toothless hillbillies in overalls on sagging front porches. Coal mining. Poverty. Moonshining. Incest. And of course, the strains of "Dueling Banjos" from the film *Deliverance*. For other Americans, however, a far less grim set of associations overtakes these impressions. Scenic mountains and close ties to nature. The Appalachian Trail. Bluegrass music. Quilts. The simple life. Salt-of-the-earth country people. Pioneer fortitude and self-sufficiency. As novelist Silas House has aptly put it, "People have one of two stereotypes about this place: they think it's either 'beautiful and simple' or 'stupid and simple.'"[1]

In mass media's visual representations of the region, the negative images ("stupid and simple") have predominated. Movies in particular, from silent films through the opening of the twenty-first century, used Appalachia as a cautionary tale. Recent manifestations of this trend include horror movies that warn young white viewers against venturing into dead zones for cell phone service. In popular fiction, however, wretchedness and gothic barbarism have almost always been outweighed by the "beautiful and simple"—a hefty dose of pastoralism and even utopianism. Both sets of images—the wretched and the redemptive—presume the region's rurality and lack of refinement. But in popular fiction these qualities have suggested Appalachia's welcome difference from the perils of metropolitan America. Stories and novels have proffered readers an invitation to a more communal, interconnected, and vibrant way of life—sustained in Appalachia, purportedly, thanks to its isolation from the vagaries of consumer capitalist society.[2]

Dear Appalachia examines fan mail written in response to best-selling fiction set in Appalachia to understand how readers imagined the region and what purposes these imagined geographies served for them. Fan mail shows us that, from 1878 to 2003, readers who embraced best-selling fiction set in Appalachia conceived the region as a rooted, rural place populated by simple whites with a rich and colorful heritage protected from mass culture. Despite vast historical changes affecting each generation of readers (and the nation, the world, and the region itself), over the course of a century and more, readers embraced a surprisingly static view of Appalachia. While different sets of readers made best sellers out of different kinds of Appalachian stories under very different historical circumstances, every generation produced an American audience hungry for a romantic version of Appalachia and eager to consume it in the form of popular stories and novels.[3]

The precise reasons for readers' embrace of what might be called "Authentic Appalachia" have varied over time, but in most instances the ideal is wielded, at least in part, as a means to criticize "business as usual" in modern industrial or postmodern postindustrial U.S. society.[4] Some best sellers emphasize rough-and-tumble life in a primitive near wilderness, and others emphasize peaceful if arduous agrarianism, but fans found in each a promise of the persistence of Appalachia as a place sheltered from both the ills and the advantages of "civilization." Central to the motivations for, and the representations of, recurring images of romanticized Appalachia was its appeal as a place and a culture deemed "authentic but not threatening in its difference."[5] The notion of authenticity itself rested upon what David Hsiung has noted as the twin pillars of enduring images of the region: associations of Appalachia with isolation and community.[6] Although Authentic Appalachia figured at times as a rough place littered with elements of the wretched or barbaric (violent feuding, nauseating filth, murderous rapists), it simultaneously offered readers a glimpse of or a visit to a more vibrant way of life in tightly knit communities.

Authentic Appalachia dates at least to the years immediately following the Civil War. Indeed, according to Henry Shapiro's landmark *Appalachia on Our Mind*, Appalachia would not exist as a concept at all were it not for the region's starring role in popular fiction during what is known as the local-color movement.[7] During the Gilded Age (circa 1865–1890s), local-color writing reigned as a fashionable literary mode in national periodicals. Magazine publishers, in their thirst for new material, welcomed stories about all the "little corners" of a reuniting post–Civil War United States and thereby kindled the national imagination of region. This imagination of region promised to preserve in fiction rural ways of life that, supposedly, would soon be superseded by industrialization, urbanization, and corporatization.[8] Although local-color writing featured various places across the United States (for example, New England, the West, the South, the Midwest, and the Louisiana bayou), the genre's legacy has been more powerful for Appalachia than perhaps any other region. Appalachian stereotypes ranging from violent primitivism to picturesque beauty coalesced during this period.

Since the invention of Appalachia in the late 1800s, any number of attempts have been made to define the region and mark its boundaries.[9] The most agreed-upon geographic definition of "core Appalachia" includes West Virginia and the upland counties of Virginia, Kentucky, Tennessee, North Carolina, and Georgia.[10] Beyond that, there is surprisingly little agreement among scholars regarding what makes something "Appalachian." Increasingly, regional scholarship recognizes that Appalachia is not all white or native-born, not entirely rural or agrarian, not completely poor or unworldly, nor even uniformly mountainous. Appalachia in the national geographic imaginary, however, has largely remained an essentialist vision of the region—white, rural, poor or working-class mountain people with highly specific cultural traditions that range from quilts and handmade crafts to moonshining and snake handling.[11] Appalachia, like other regions, is a concept as much as a place.

While the image of Authentic Appalachia in best-selling fiction has remained a remarkably consistent contrast to "mainstream" America, the popularity of regional fiction, including that set in Appalachia, has waxed and waned. I speculate that readers' interest in region as a site of authentic culture rose and fell in part in relation to the rise and fall of U.S. imperialism and neo-imperialism and attendant concerns about racial difference, anxieties about geographic and upward mobility, and fears about the alienating effects of modernity and postmodernity. The local-color movement occurred during the Gilded Age, an era that provoked anxieties about urbanization and homogenization and witnessed a masculinist, nationalistic, and racialized drive for empire, exemplified in part by the war against Spain that resulted in territorial acquisitions in the Philippines, Guam, Puerto Rico, and (briefly) Cuba. A resurgence in the popularity of local-color fiction occurred during what commentators have called the Neo–Gilded Age, the years from about 1985 to 2008 when once again the gap between rich and poor widened, concerns about immigration fueled nativist movements, imperialistic projects expanded overseas, and Americans expressed dizzied alarm over their sense of distance from "real life."[12] In the 1990s and early 2000s, the presence of a steady and growing base of upper-middle-class enthusiasts for Appalachia was evident not only in best-selling fiction but also in the revival of bluegrass music; the wild popularity of Charles Frazier's best-selling novel *Cold Mountain* and its film adaptation; and the embrace of roots music festivals, independent films like *The Songcatcher* (2000), and televised documentaries such as PBS's *Appalachia: A History of Mountains and People* (2009), narrated by actress Sissy Spacek; Diane Sawyer's *A Hidden America: Children of the Mountains* (2009); and the History Channel's *Hillbilly: The Real Story* (2008), narrated by country singer Billy Ray Cyrus. Chapters 1 and 5 examine the role of Appalachian-set fiction in ameliorating the concerns of the Gilded Age and the Neo–Gilded Age.

The Appalachian-set best sellers that emerged between the two Gilded Ages may signal moments of heightened need for reassurance regarding the consequences of modernization and the propriety of nationalism and imperialism that dominated the Gilded Ages themselves. Chapters 2, 3, and 4 examine best sellers that spoke to readers' needs during the Progressive Era, the post–World War II era, and the Vietnam War era, respectively. Appalachia, imagined since at least 1873 as folksy and isolated, seems at first glance to have little to do with the glitz of the Gilded Ages or the reach of American imperialism. Yet, I suggest, it is precisely because Appalachia has been associated with simple innocent white Americans that it has soothed white readers' concerns about conspicuous wealth and global ambitions.

The Functions of Popular Regional Fiction

Fiction that extols rather than mocks mountain whites is understandably a breath of fresh air for Appalachia's advocates. Those of us weary of tired old negative stereotypes about mountain residents are often tempted to react by investing in an ideal of Appalachia that highlights its most progressive, admirable, and underappreciated aspects. But in my research for *Dear Appalachia*, I have had to confront the fact that the places I care about are sometimes appropriated for personal and political projects with which I cannot sympathize.

My examination of fan mail indicates that best-selling Appalachian-set fiction met white readers' needs and eased their cultural anxieties in at least three ways: it produced Appalachia as an authentic place, offered readers a means of establishing a sense of identity and belonging, and facilitated the circulation of power across geographic scales. Viewed as a case study, my research suggests that all popular regional fiction, regardless of where set, may serve to satisfy readerly cravings for a sense of place, identity, and power. As I discuss below and in the conclusion, however, assumptions about race, ethnicity, and class that are particular to Appalachia allowed it to function, uniquely, as a touchstone for purportedly pro-white but nonracist Americanness.

First and foremost, best-selling Appalachia produced the region as an authentic place.[13] It fed what Jeff Karem calls readers' "fascination with and desire for texts and authors" that readers "believed distilled the exotic essences of the nation's cultural margins."[14] The stories offered solace to readers who hoped for the persistence of a place characterized by unalienated relations among people, between people and the land, and between people and the vibrancy of "real life" purportedly missing from modern and postmodern life. Readers found in best-selling fiction locales where a sense of place was seemingly preserved from standardization and homogenization. In Foote's formulation, readers were drawn to fiction's "presentation of people and places that seemed to have 'escaped' the dubious improvements of a stronger and more integrated urban economy."[15] Key to readers' faith in the region's authenticity was the books' representation of Appalachian residents as simple country denizens: people classed as peasants/farmers and/or laborers whom middle- or upper-middle-class readers found appealing for their presumptively "honest industry . . . independence . . . frank spirit of equality, and . . . ability to produce and enjoy a simple abundance."[16] As Brodhead notes, the "paradox" of local-color writing "is that it purports to value a culture for being intactly other at the very time that it is offering outsiders the chance to inhabit it and enjoy its special 'life.'" Perversely, in their longing for the colorful vitality of an imagined Appalachia, readers sometimes saw their own middle- and upper-middle-class geographies and identities as somehow impoverished, as if their class status were an impediment to wholeness, liveliness, and happiness.[17]

The second way in which best-selling Appalachian-set fiction eased the concerns of white readers was by providing them with a means to carve out a sense of identity and belonging. Appalachia's ability to assuage readers' concerns regarding identity and belonging has been wholly dependent upon the aforementioned notion of its authenticity.[18] First, as an authentic place, Appalachia was endowed with a unique cultural identity purportedly missing from "mainstream" white America. Appalachianness therefore offered some readers, especially in later eras, the promise of ethnic belonging in the face of disquietude about generic whiteness. Second, as an authentic place, Appalachia was supposedly home to community in the old-fashioned sense of a neighborly face-to-face way of life rooted in place. Readers of best-selling Appalachian-set fiction exhibit what Gunnar Almgren describes as a "nostalgic attachment to the idealized notion that the existence of community is embodied in the village or small town where human associations are characterized" by relations "that are intimate, familiar, sympathetic, mutually interdependent, and reflective of a shared social consciousness."[19] Readers felt a connection to a fictional community that served as an imagined home place replete with "salt-of-the-earth" characters whom readers claimed as friends or even kin. Imagining themselves as kin to culturally distinct mountain whites in turn allowed some middle- and upper-middle-class white readers to experience vicariously the sense of community that they presumed common among localities populated by the lower classes. Especially for descendents of relatively recent out-migrants from the region, regional fictions operated as fables of identity grounded upon the assumption that we are where we came from.

Finally, popular regional fiction promoted U.S. readers' sense of power and status vis-à-vis their locales, regions, nation, and the globe. This dynamic worked in multiple ways. Reading itself enhanced prestige, especially when the reading material was associated with highbrow or high middlebrow outlets (for example, periodicals like the *Atlantic Monthly* and trade fiction formats popular from the 1990s).[20] Readers also established status by claiming association with, and projecting themselves into, a translocal assemblage of literati.[21] Some regional elite readers appropriated a distinguished role within national print culture by asserting an intimate familiarity with, yet sophisticated appreciation of, quaint rural denizens whom they held themselves above. In some cases, regional fiction trained readers to imagine supposedly primitive peoples (foreign as well as domestic) as in need of guidance. It promoted readers' confidence in their knowledge about, superiority over, and obligation toward supposedly place-bound subjects raced as nonwhite or not-quite-white and classed as lower class or "primitive."[22]

Appalachian-set fiction's ability to address these three sets of readerly needs depended first and foremost upon readers' deep-set belief in the region as a static and rooted place buffered from the currents of globalism that they felt destabilized their own lives. Indeed, fan mail suggests that readers' physical mobility may have been fundamental to the success of all literary regionalism. Certainly in the case of Appalachian-set best sellers, highly mobile and cosmopolitan readers—out-migrants and in-migrants, tourists and missionaries, and regional elites, all of whom feared the costs of upward and geographic mobility—played a critical role in constructing an idealized version of Appalachia.

From the 1870s to the 2000s, metropolitan readers outside Appalachia sought to imagine it as a rural place free of the problems of urban heterogeneity and as an antidote to their anxieties about geographic mobility. Henry Shapiro observed that Mary Noailles Murfree's literary success during the local-color movement arose in part from her affirmation of the existence of Appalachia "independent of" tourists' observations of it.[23] The evidence I found in fan mail confirms Shapiro's speculation that while regionalism imagines rural places as rooted, its appeal in various eras was dependent upon the movement of readers. In the twentieth century, the popularity of Appalachian-set fiction remained linked to touristic desire but also to migrations into and out of the region.[24] Metropolitan consumers turned to Appalachian-set novels as travel guides for escape, adventure, or personal mission or quest. Onetime residents of Appalachia consumed comforting constructions of "home" even (or especially) when they had little desire for an actual return. When newcomers to the region were members of what Wendy Griswold calls "the reading class," such "educated, mobile people" paradoxically "work[ed] hard at putting down cultural roots" and "demonstrate[d] their cosmopolitanism through an intense localism" that included reading regional fiction.[25]

Cosmopolitan readers from Appalachia participated equally in consuming romantic depictions of the region. Some expressed patronization toward Appalachian characters and places while others expressed a powerful identification with them, but all sought affirmation in mass-mediated representations of familiar places. Just as Hsiung found that cosmopolitan residents of Upper East Tennessee contributed to constructions of their neighbors as backwards in the revolutionary and antebellum eras, I find that physically and upwardly mobile residents of the region from the first Gilded Age to the second lent crucial credibility to the essentialist notions of Authentic Appalachia in national best sellers.[26]

All the readers examined in this book, from professional reviewers to working-class out-migrants from the South, shared a need for an imagined geography of Authentic Appalachia in order to bolster their own status, appease fears of placelessness, and confirm a vision of the nation and the world as one wherein whites of a certain class should appreciate but must manage cultural difference. Sadly, the Authentic Appalachia embraced by fans of best sellers may help reinforce simplistic versions of the region that celebrate whiteness, glorify Americanness, and figure primitive peoples the world over as in need of the expert guidance of well-to-do Americans. In the conclusion, I discuss the role of regional fiction in creating regional identity, and I share my concern that a region I hold dear may be commodified in ways that have the potential to undermine Appalachia as a tool to critique dominant assumptions.

Dear "Appalachian" Author

To return to Jeff Karem's quote, readers desired not only "texts" but also or especially "authors" whom readers supposed "distilled the exotic essences of the nation's cultural margins." Fans of best sellers believed in the authentic nature of Appalachia in part because they believed in the authenticity of the authors. Not all fictional genres demand that authors have a personal relationship to the story they tell; indeed, inherent in the idea of literature is the notion that authors exercise their artistic imagination to create places, characters, and plots. Yet fans, critics, and scholars of regional and ethnic literatures have demanded that authors write from personal experience. Fans of Appalachian-set fiction wanted to believe that it was "true to life." The authorial persona therefore became key to the success of the fiction. The best-selling authors examined here successfully produced Appalachia as an authentic place partially because their readers were convinced—by authorial voice, by promotion and marketing, and/or by reviews—that they had an inside scoop.

The title *Dear Appalachia*, then, refers not only to the fact that the region was dear to its readers. It also implies that when fans addressed letters to regional authors, they believed that they were in some way writing to the region itself. (As nineteenth-century author and literary critic Hamlin Garland describes it, in local-color fiction the land expresses itself: "the cotton-boll has broken into speech.")[27] Fans demanded that authors act as regional representatives who stood for, and stood *in* for, the region. Fans frequently engaged with the authors as characters from their works of fiction, and were sometimes surprised (particularly in the cases of Mary Noailles Murfree and Harriette Simpson Arnow) that the authors did not resemble their earthy protagonists. In the chapters that follow, I attend to the disjunctions between authors' romanticized reputations among critics and fans and their actual biographies in order to track the ways in which those authors came to personify Appalachia for their readers.

Despite the fact that best sellers' success depended in part upon readers' belief in the author's authentic relationship to the place fictionalized, the very acts of writing and publishing fundamentally require some degree of "outsiderness." As Lee Smith, a well-loved author of Appalachian-set novels, observed in 2006, "The position of any serious writer is always that of an outsider." Smith noted that "we have to put ourselves a little bit outside to get the necessary distance to write. . . . The people who write are always the ones who feel a little different. . . . You're a writer because you're interested in looking *at* your community."[28] While familiarity or affiliation with a place perceived as "peripheral" may have enabled a writer to produce local-color fiction, even so-called insiders necessarily engaged highbrow literary traditions and anticipated national audiences. Conceptualizing authorship required above all a sophisticated acquaintance with *nonlocal* audiences and their perspectives on the local. The act of publishing one's work inevitably inserted a writer into a translocal, cosmopolitan network that included editors, publishers, journalists, and readers. To paraphrase Ross Posnock, it is naive to believe that the necessary distance that constitutes writers as writers can be erased.[29] As Jennifer Rae Greeson notes about southern literature, its authors "always work within the preconceptions and demands of a national audience and the centralized publishing industry that creates and serves it." She argues that "representations of 'the South' in United States culture are always, in some measure, not about the southeastern United States at all but, rather, about the needs and expectations of a broader American imaginary."[30]

Dear Appalachia contends that it makes little sense to consider any author an "insider" or an "outsider" to what is, after all, a fictional world of his or her own creation. With Catherine Jurca, I am concerned with the ways best-selling novels "enter into the popular consciousness [and] construct imaginative and yet influential worlds to which they frequently claim to be referring" as though they were real places populated with accurately documented people.[31] The popular local-color texts that I examine were all released by publishing companies with national or international audiences. Even authors with the closest relationships to the places they fictionalized had intervening experiences—for example, Harriette Arnow's years in Louisville and Cincinnati—that surely shaped their perspectives on the local. All were exposed to, and in conversation with, constructions of Appalachia available in the national imagination.

Dear Appalachia therefore argues for a different understanding of the relationship between regional writing and reality. Following Raymond Williams, this book demonstrates that fiction does not simply and accurately reflect the world around it (if and when it is crafted by an appropriately authentic representative reporting upon real-life experiences). Fiction constructs the realms it represents. It actively shapes readers' desires, attitudes, and lenses for interpreting and acting upon the world. Even as it shapes readers, published fiction also necessarily anticipates and responds to readers' needs and desires. Understanding the relationship between fiction and reality in this way reminds us that the medium is always already shaped by capitalist production and marketing. This approach helps demystify all literature, sometimes pedestaled as supposedly "universal," as if it is above or outside economic considerations. At the same time, this approach affirms the prominence that literary studies accords literature by attending to fiction's broad social significance beyond the classroom and library. Once we recognize more fully the ways in which fiction shapes and is shaped by the institutions and values surrounding it, we can see more clearly how literary production and reception are central to the study of social history.

Critics' and readers' assumptions about the mimetic accuracy of regional fiction written by authentic insiders notwithstanding, local-color fiction—then and now—tells us less about rural people and places than it does about the tastes and anxieties of well-to-do readers, about "what is desired and needs to be known," to reference the Williams quote in one of the epigraphs to this book. Fans, in the words of reception scholar Amy Blair, responded "in highly personal ways that say more about reader needs than about the text itself or [the] authorial project."[32] Best-selling fiction about Appalachia offers less a transparent window onto the region than it does a means for understanding the political, economic, and social needs of its consumers and the economic imperatives of national publishing firms. For this reason, I avoid the label "Appalachian literature," which encourages the assumption that fiction about the region is also fiction *of* the region (or even somehow *by* the region, as Hamlin Garland proposed). Instead, I prefer to use the more unwieldy phrase "Appalachian-set fiction" to describe the popular texts I discuss.

All of this is to say that this book is about readers from within and beyond the Appalachian region more than it is about the region itself. You will find in it few judgments as to what authors got "right" or "wrong" in their depictions of Appalachia. Such an undertaking would require a book in its own right. Furthermore, such determinations are ultimately beside the point I want to make, which is that readers of best sellers set in Appalachia sought out essentialized notions of the region that they could consume as accurate.

On Methodologies and Anachronisms

Fan mail is a heretofore untapped source for ascertaining how and why certain representations of Appalachia appealed to readers during different historical moments, and with what consequences. My approach draws on the work of Steven Mailloux, who advocates constructing the "reception histories" of texts. I reconstruct reception histories in order to determine what "cultural work" (in Brodhead's formulation, what "emotional and conceptual service") they performed for their audiences. As Janice Radway observes, "Interpretation and textual meaning . . . are as dependent on who the reader is, on how she understands the process of reading, and on the cultural context within which she operates, as they are on the text's verbal structure itself."[33]

I chose to concentrate on the cultural work performed by popular works of fiction. I was interested not in books that best captured Appalachian realities necessarily, nor necessarily in books of high literary repute, but in books embraced by relatively large numbers of readers and therefore likely influential in the construction of the nation's imagined geography of Appalachia. One of the most convenient ways of assessing the popularity of books published after the turn of the twentieth century is their presence on best-seller lists based upon sales figures reported by bookstores or distributors. Despite the manifest problems with the accuracy of best-seller lists (which I discuss in the appendix), they provide a starting point for generating a body of popular Appalachian-set fiction. Throughout the majority of the book I refer to the texts that I include as *best sellers*, though this term is anachronistic to the first Gilded Age, for which period popularity is established by the number of editions printed. While my arguments are based on best sellers, I sometimes generalize to "popular" fiction for the sake of variation.

Conventions for the scholarship of reception are not well established. Despite the fact that neither the label *fan* nor *fan mail* was common until the 1930s, I chose to use both terms throughout the book. The term *fans* allows me to distinguish between those correspondents who wrote in response to a given text and those correspondents who had additional reasons to write, whom I cite in the notes as *fan-acquaintances* or *acquaintances*. Frequently I invoke "readers," though technically my findings are based only upon critics, readers who wrote letters to authors who archived them, and readers who wrote customer reviews. (See "Appendix: Methodological Essay" for a discussion of these terms.) When citing fan mail or customer reviews, I reproduce the writer's words and punctuation just as I found them, even when this means replicating errors or nonstandard uses. I avoid marking such places with *sic*, which is distracting and, arguably, patronizing, though on occasion I have added text in brackets where the meaning might not otherwise be clear.

I use the terms *local color* and *regionalism* interchangeably to refer to fiction "*about* the representation of difference," fiction that "culturalizes" difference, to borrow from Stephanie Foote. This decision involves the anachronistic use of each term, since the concept of "local color" dates to the Gilded Age and is generally reserved for fiction published during that era, while "regionalism" was adopted in the early twentieth century, largely to refer to fiction set in rural places and oppositional in its stance toward centralization and nationalization. I understand "local color" to refer not to a work's content, its quality, or its political valence, but to its tools for representation and its attitudes about the value of the local. Local color's formal qualities include representation of dialect, representation of characters as somehow unassimilated or nonstandard (Foote's terms), and an ambition to reach middle-class and upper-class audiences across the nation.[34]

I frequently refer to *highbrow readers* or *high middlebrow readers*. The fans I study read best sellers targeted to readers with upper-middle-class and elite interests, but they were not always of the middling or elite classes. I define high middlebrow cultural products as those that do not meet the standards of "high art" but that aim for respect exceeding that ascribed to middlebrow products.[35] For the earliest works by Mary Murfree and John Fox, the stories' appearances in highly regarded "quality" journals prior to their publication in book form suggest the types of audiences that authors and editors imagined Appalachian-set fiction would find. All the best sellers I examine were pitched as high middlebrow or highbrow.

Because I found that the cultural work a local-color story performed often depended upon readers' geographic affiliations, I mapped the places from which fan letters were mailed. To revise Mailloux's term, my work reconstructs the "reception geographies" of popular fictions in order to show how they meant different things for readers of different social positions living in different places at different historical moments. Whereas scholars of the late nineteenth century suggest that pastoral regionalism appealed primarily to metropolitan elites, the maps provide empirical evidence that fans of regionalism lived in and near the region being represented and in a wide range of rural and metropolitan locales. Appalachia, the maps tell us, is not solely "a creature of the urban imagination."[36] The introduction of a regional readership demonstrates how reception history can reveal the status aspirations of readers who recognized that to be identified with a region was to be placed low in a hierarchy of place value that somehow everyone understood.[37] Furthermore, it advances David Hsiung's argument regarding the role played by regional "insiders" in the creation of Appalachian stereotypes. Conversely, the maps help demonstrate the broad distribution of admirers of Appalachian-set stories, repudiating some observers' assumption that regionalism has been of mere provincial interest and draws almost solely upon a region's inhabitants for its audiences. It should be self-evident that best sellers necessarily must have appealed to wider national audiences in order to become best sellers.

Additionally, a second set of maps illustrates the migration narratives provided by fans in their letters to demonstrate the extent to which regionalism that imagined Appalachia as rooted and static appealed to mobile readers' felt senses of dislocation and uprootedness. These maps indicate that Authentic Appalachia captivated not only geographically mobile consumers everywhere but especially charmed readers who felt themselves once removed from the region—sometimes by virtue of their upward class mobility and usually by virtue, too, of their own or their family's physical migration away from it.

Each era and each book generated its own sets of readers with their own sets of concerns. Mary Murfree's admiring correspondents, for example, fall into two groups: metropolitan elites and regional (or rural) elites. John Fox's readers are more usefully understood as nationally identified, locally identified, or transitional readers with loyalties to both home and highbrow ambition. Harriette Arnow's best sellers appealed in distinctive ways to metropolitan-identified readers, midwestern professionals, regional and rural elites (from Kentucky and elsewhere), and out-migrants from the upland South. Catherine Marshall and James Dickey drew largely nationally identified metropolitan readers but also southerners and out-migrants. For best sellers published after 1985, the three largest sets of fans were "touristic cosmopolitans," "nostalgic cosmopolitans," and "charmed Appalachians." The most important commonality across the eras is the extent to which familiarity with the region and movement into, within, or away from it heightened fans' emotional attachments to their vision of an Authentic Appalachia.

Scholars have argued long and hard about the consequences of literary regionalism's emphasis upon the peculiarities of regional places and people. Richard Brodhead argues that local-color writing allowed elite readers of highbrow periodicals to shore up power by using their common highbrow culture to project themselves into a "translocally incorporated social elite" supposedly superior to rural places and regionalized people.[38] Meanwhile, Nancy Glazener claims, based on reviews in populist journals, that "less privileged" rural readers drew on local-color writing to resist the dominant hierarchies found in highbrow culture.[39] Feminist revisionist scholars contend that although some writing of this era reinforced elites' power, other writing sided with the marginalized. Judith Fetterley and Marjorie Pryse recommend distinguishing between "local color fiction," which denigrates or mocks regional people, and "regional fiction," which invokes readers' "empathy and respect"—the latter, they claim, is written by authors marginalized by, for example, their sex, race, or region of origin.[40]

Fetterley and Pryse's distinction rightly acknowledges that not all fiction has the same consequences. But how do we know whether a particular story prompts mirth or empathy? For most literary scholars, the answer lies in a close reading of the story itself (which will reveal the author's sympathies and/or the best interpretation) or in an assessment of whether the author was an "insider" or an "outsider" to the culture depicted. The problem is that scholars using these strategies have argued opposite conclusions. Mary Murfree's stories, for example, have been denounced as insulting by Appalachian studies scholars and praised as empathetic by feminist revisionists.

In *Dear Appalachia*, I demonstrate that readers' reactions are a crucial additional resource for assessing the consequences of any given story. I argue that texts cannot be considered inherently hegemonic simply because they were written by "outsiders" or by authors astutely engaged in the literary marketplace. Because a creative product is financially profitable doesn't mean it will have a hegemonic effect. Nor are texts intrinsically counter-hegemonic merely because they are written by "insiders" of one stripe or another. As I show through my analysis of archival sources, the documented reactions to a text by contemporary readers can show us whether readers mobilized that text to underwrite impulses and projects that bolstered or challenged dominant ideologies. Furthermore, my findings challenge regionalist scholarship that too readily correlates "elite" with "urban" (like Brodhead's) or "rural" with "less privileged populations" (like Glazener's), particularly through my discovery of the major role played by regional elites in the construction of regional imaginaries.

I do not envision the fans I study as pawns crassly manipulated by the hegemonic forces of capitalist authors, publishers, and booksellers. Nor do I imagine them, in the vein of much "fan studies" scholarship, as entirely proactive agents and resistant readers who make their own counter-hegemonic readings of the materials before them. Instead, I interpret the admiring readers of best sellers as embedded within particular historical moments that helped shape individual needs, desires, and interpretive possibilities. Reception studies offers an avenue out of the impasse between arguments regarding the resistant or dominant valences of popular representations in the mass media by showing how a single reader or set of readers might embrace both revolutionary and counterrevolutionary meanings within the same texts. Furthermore, reception methodologies admit to always incomplete and revisable assessments depending upon the sources uncovered and analyzed.[41]

Appalachia offers particularly fertile ground for the study of fans' attachments to regionality. The region is distinct in that it has operated as both an ancestral homeland for white Americans and, unlike the "cradle" of New England, as an "arrested civilisation," whose white inhabitants somehow seem not quite white. As Dunaway points out, Americans since Frederick Jackson Turner have viewed Appalachia as having pioneer conditions long after the frontier had marched past in its westward journey. Belief in a persistent frontier in turn permitted widespread faith that the region sustained a populace of Jefferson's beloved yeoman farmers shunted from more "civilized" quarters of the nation.[42] Though the Appalachian region competes for "Americanness" with the "heartland" of the Midwest and the Yankees of New England, its association with pioneers lends it the aura of "home" and "homeland" in opposition not only to large U.S. cities but also to foreign places that seem to threaten "home."[43] Representations of southern Appalachia also differ from those of other U.S. regions in class inflection, including a misleading identification of Appalachia as the primary site of U.S. poverty. (The Black Belt, Tex-Mex border, and Native American reservations, among other areas, have persistent rural poverty rates as high as the poorest sections of Appalachia, which include the coal fields of eastern Kentucky, southern West Virginia, Southwest Virginia, and East Tennessee.) In the early 2000s, commentators described Appalachia as a safe haven for the perpetuation of cultural practices ranging from traditional music and handicrafts to subsistence farming and moonshining, all famously featured in the 1970s in the *Foxfire* series and persistently promoted by tourism officials and folk festivals. The region looms large in readers' imaginations in part because it seems relatively nearby and accessible, the "backyard" of the metropolitan eastern seaboard.[44]

Appalachia has held an appeal for readers that is distinct from the appeal of "the South," though the two places are often conflated in the popular imagination. This distinctive appeal is partly due to Americans' belief in Appalachians as "racially innocent" by virtue of their presumed isolation from slavery and therefore presumptively free from either hating or being influenced by African Americans—despite decades of scholarship demonstrating the pervasive influence of slaveholding, pro-Confederacy sentiment, and racial violence in parts of the Appalachian South. Readers caught up in a romance of Appalachia, then, frequently imagined it as whiter than the South, and imagined mountain whites as simple, working-class, "down-home," salt-of-the-earth, small-farm, and woodland people, in contrast to either "white trash" or greedy, pompous, and slave-exploiting plantation aristocrats of the tropical Deep South.[45]

Appalachia, Locally Colored, 1865–2003

The pastoral impulse in literature can be traced to as early as the ninth century BCE, and the nineteenth-century shift into industrial and urban work intensified the romanticization of rural landscapes. According to Raymond Williams, pastoral novels provided British readers with "knowable communities" they found less intimidating than the atomistic cities they experienced as too complex, too opaque, too chaotic, too materialistic, and too threatening. The countryside promised to alleviate modern suffering by providing readers a much-anticipated, even if rarely *actual*, return to rural green landscapes.[46]

The earliest representations of mountain settlers in the American backcountry contained little of the romanticization of rural places; in the late 1700s, travelers depicted backwoods people in the mountains as poor, savage, and primitive people. By the early 1800s, however, Americans considered the countryside the repository of the moral worth of the agrarian Republic. The white mountaineer stereotype emerged slowly as a distinct type from the more generalized figures of frontiersmen, hunters, settlers, and "ruffians" dominant in early Republic travelogues.[47]

The popularity of Appalachian-set fiction reached its height during the local-color literary movement, which featured regions across the United States. From 1865 to 1895, publishers of periodicals like *Harper's Weekly* and the *Atlantic Monthly* reached beyond the literary establishment to debut authors outside the metropolitan Northeast.[48] Such authors provided new settings populated by characters whose nonnormative speech, dress, and manners were attributed to their presumed geographic or chronological distance from northeastern, urban, middle-class readers.

Readers gave local-color stories a warm reception. Debates about literary regionalism during the past decade have emerged from attempts to understand its tremendous appeal, particularly for metropolitan elites.[49] For elites confronted with massive urbanization, industrialization, and foreign immigration, local-color fiction seemed to ensure the "preservation" and "memorialization" of regional and local cultures whose passing readers mourned. As Richard Brodhead argues, local-color writing served not only to sacralize supposedly dying rural lifeways but to make their eclipse by the modern order seem inevitable and justifiable. Local-color fiction provided urban elites proof of the victory of homogenization and nationalization, proof of "the pastness of the past," and proof of the impossibility of viable alternatives to dominant development patterns.[50] Furthermore, according to some accounts, middling Americans' fears of social instability, including labor strife and perceived threats to traditional patriarchal authority, family structure, and sexual mores, heightened their need to shore up white middle-class respectability through reassuring depictions of less respectable others.[51]

Scholars also attribute the appeal of local-color fiction to a sense of "weightlessness" or alienation among Americans anxious about the rapid pace of change, who then sought to ameliorate their self-estranged condition by seeking "some experience or place that seemed more real or more 'authentic' than the conditions of modern life." Foote revises this thesis by suggesting that fiction serves not as a simple "antidote" to alienation and self-estrangement but a means for wrestling with and negotiating the anxieties that arise from such sensations. She argues that local-color sketches in highbrow magazines met the needs of Gilded Age readers "whose freedom from the constraints of provincial communities made them vulnerable to the isolation and alienation of urban life at the turn of the century." As Foote observes, narrators like Sarah Orne Jewett's in *The Country of the Pointed Firs* express longing to be incorporated as authentic residents of the quaint places they visit, demonstrating an urban impulse to project onto "regional" people the potential for an intact, unitary identity compared to the fragmented self experienced in the metropolis. Brodhead argues that readers of local-color fiction presumed that people who live in "backward" locales are "more fully alive" and that their lives could be appropriated for highbrow readers' psychic well-being. Indeed, Brodhead offers as the very definition of regionalism "literature that posits that someone else's way of living and talking is more 'colorful' than one's own (culturally superior) way, . . . [and] that a primary vitality absent from the refined is present in the backward *and* that this other life can be annexed for the cultivated class's leisured recreation, made pleasurably inhabitable in print." As Lucinda MacKethan speculates (and as the cover image captures so beautifully), local-color readers wanted to see "something of themselves, or at least something of their own roads not taken, in characters whose lives had remained more deeply rooted in place and community than their own."[52]

Numerous authors achieved literary success thanks to the popularity of local color. The names of a few are illustrative. Some scholars date the advent of local color to Brett Harte's 1868 "Luck of the Roaring Camp," set in the gold rush West. Jewett's stories feature New England, and Joel Chandler Harris became famous for his "Uncle Remus" stories romanticizing southern plantation life. George Washington Cable's stories deliver New Orleans to national audiences, while Hamlin Garland's stories feature the Midwest. The number of fiction authors who benefited from the popularity of the southern mountains is impressive, including Rebecca Harding Davis, Frances Hodgson Burnett, John Esten Cooke, and Constance Fenimore Woolson, to name just a few of the early short story authors. According to Henry Shapiro, between 1870 and 1890, dozens of writers had published at least ninety sketches and 125 short stories that portrayed the southern mountain region as a discrete and homogenous cultural entity.[53]

Even before 1878, the year Mary Noailles Murfree's first mountain story was published (and hence the start date of this study), most of the conventions of mountain fiction were already in place, including beautiful, half-wild, illiterate, and quick-learning young mountain girls in homemade dresses; exhausted mountain women old before their time; swarthy and taciturn mountain men carrying guns; and drunken ne'er-do-wells, moonshiners, and revenuers. While local-color fiction promoted simplified images of rural people everywhere, its consequences have been, arguably, more reductive, more profound, and longer lasting for Appalachia than for any other region. Audiences came to view Appalachia as whiter than the South but more questionably white than New England or the Midwest, less foreign and more rural than "Cajun" New Orleans, and poorer and more downtrodden than the West. Readers seem to accept that, in most regions, "standard," "normal" Americans coexisted side by side with the quainter citizens featured in local-color writing. National readers imagined southern mountain folk, on the other hand, as anachronistic anomalies, locals bypassed by (or locals who had resisted) the natural progression from pioneer to civilized citizen. Appalachia was increasingly seen as uniformly populated with unruly denizens living out of time, out of step with national norms, and out of the bounds of standard behavior and blood lines—although the exact dimensions of the national imagination of Appalachia varied over time, depending upon the needs of the nation's high middlebrow publishers, authors, and readers.

In chapter 1, I examine the reception of Mary Noailles Murfree, one of the most influential writers in the early construction of the idea of Appalachia. Murfree's *Atlantic Monthly* stories, published under the pseudonym Charles Egbert Craddock and reprinted in book form as *In the Tennessee Mountains* in 1884, are widely regarded as having solidified and popularized an image of the southern mountaineer that remained dominant for a century or more.[54] As Lorise Boger notes, Murfree's collection triggered "a flood of novels using and misusing the southern mountaineer."[55] By analyzing reviews, articles, and archived correspondence, I show that readers imagined "Craddock" as an author from the mountains who traded on his rugged Appalachian background to build his career—until Craddock revealed "himself" to be the genteel Miss Murfree. I argue that the national reaction to the revelation of Murfree's true identity renders tangible the ways in which her writing served the needs of multiple readerships. Print reviews indicate that metropolitan elites used Murfree's persona and stories to negotiate their anxieties about perceived threats to their power, including immigration and the feminizing effects of overcivilization; their worries over the supposed urbanization and homogenization of the United States; and their investments in nativism, nationalism, and imperialism. I use archived correspondence from Murfree's admirers to demonstrate that, unlike metropolitan readers, local elites throughout North America rightly intuited the class and social status of the unknown Craddock, even though they, too, had been fooled into believing "him" to be a man. Local elites saw Murfree's fiction as a resource for promoting the prominence of their domains and believed the author's acceptance into highbrow circles boded well for their own advantageous incorporation into a national highbrow network.

Literary regionalism's popularity waned somewhat during the Progressive Era (1900–1920), though a number of local-color novels set in Appalachia emphasized possibilities for uplift.[56] *The Little Shepherd of Kingdom Come* (1903), set partly in the mountains, and the Appalachian-set *The Trail of the Lonesome Pine* (1908), by Kentuckian John Fox Jr., were among the first American books to make the new "best-seller" lists at a time when reformers were eager to promote modern civilization yet avoid the twinned pitfalls of urban materialism and poverty. Fox shared the spotlight with novelists like Harold Bell Wright, whose 1907 Ozarks-set *Shepherd of the Hills* has echoed into the twenty-first century in the form of an outdoor play cum tourist attraction (as has Fox's *The Trail of the Lonesome Pine*). Chapter 2 contributes to our understanding of the

Progressive Era by illuminating the anxieties of a swath of middle-class Americans whose pursuit of schooling and professional work compelled their social and geographical movement away from the people and places of their childhood. The exponential growth in literacy rates and new mechanisms for production and distribution at this time allowed the novels of John Fox Jr. to become "almost synonymous with the words 'best seller'" and thereby participate in the solidification of imagined community fortified by an expanding print culture.[57]

According to Appalachian scholar Dwight Billings, "No literary figure more widely influenced national perceptions" of the southern mountain region than did Fox, who "set into play many of the most enduring and pejorative images of the Appalachian mountaineer."[58] In particular, Fox's *Lonesome Pine* and the many films it inspired fueled a caricature of hillbilly feuding that persists today. Appalachian studies scholars have argued that Fox's fiction justified industrial exploitation and affirmed readers' nationalism, racism, and imperialism. Yet for over a century, boosters hoping to increase the prominence of Kentucky and Virginia venerated Fox's "sympathy" for mountaineers and his promotion of mountain locales. My reader-centered approach acknowledges the ways the novel served the needs of nationally identified readers while offending locals who objected to Fox's fictional treatment of their lives. But archived letters also uncover the presence of readers transitioning between the local and the national who deeply identified with what Fox depicted as his characters' wrenching ambivalence regarding the relative benefits of the supposedly savage mountain world versus the apparently refined but environmentally and emotionally costly industrial world.

Around the time of the First World War, demand for Appalachian local-color fiction had dwindled somewhat—perhaps dampened first by preoccupation with wartime concerns and later, in the 1920s, by a degree of acceptance of the metropolitan character of the nation.[59] The development in the 1920s and 1930s of a fully self-conscious regionalist movement informed a number of influential literary works set in Appalachia but did not produce best sellers.[60] Lorise Boger notes that mysteries set in the region were popular in the 1920s and early 1930s, though these apparently did not capture large enough audiences to make the best-seller lists. In the 1940s and 1950s, humorous fiction set in the mountains was popular, though only Jesse Stuart's *Taps for Private Tussie* (1943) was on the *New York Times* best-seller list and only for three weeks.[61]

Indeed, just five Appalachian-set best sellers, including Stuart's, appeared between John Fox's last (*Heart of the Hills* in 1913) and the resurgence of local-color fiction beginning in the 1980s. The Great Depression witnessed a wave of consumer interest in media representations of the mountain "hillbilly" as either a threatening or a welcome dissident from modernity. Throughout the economic and social distress of the Great Depression, the hillbilly image pervaded country music, cartoons, and motion pictures. Other visual representations of the region emphasized the noble rather than the comedic mountaineer, including Works Progress Administration (WPA) photography, WPA documentary writing, and regional material productions such as crafts.[62] Yet, the iconic figure was largely absent from popular fiction.

As Tom Lutz notes, "Local color literature fared quite badly" by the 1950s, when "the fate of farmers was not a key concern for the general culture, and suburbia became the milieu that seemed richest for displaying the culture's fault lines."[63] Fan responses to the second and third of the five midcentury best sellers, Harriette Arnow's agrarian *Hunter's Horn* (1949) and her migration-themed *The Dollmaker* (1954), illustrate white American concerns about mobility and "roots" that stemmed from mass suburbanization and the Southern Diaspora. In chapter 3, I argue that readers' post–World War II era experiences of the dislocations of suburbanization and rural-to-urban migration instilled in them a profound nostalgia for a lost sense of place, roots, and home. Migrants expressed anguish over their constrained choices between staying home and pursuing economic opportunity. Meanwhile, midwestern social workers, journalists, and commentators insisted that the rural poor would be better off if they could be kept from flooding midwesterners' hometowns. Arnow's depictions of communal life in Kentucky in *Hunter's Horn* appealed predictably to readers on the eastern seaboard and West Coast. *The Dollmaker* succeeded spectacularly where other regional fiction did not, perhaps because it represented movement between country and city in ways that vast numbers of white readers were experiencing or witnessing between the 1920s and 1950s. I argue that the long-term future of Appalachian-set fiction was secured in part by white out-migrants of the Southern Diaspora, thanks to their descendants' sense of nostalgia regarding white rural worlds lost. By examining Arnow's readers, we see the formation of a pattern of readership for Appalachian-set fiction that would become endemic to the 1990s and early 2000s.

The "media hillbilly" returned in the 1960s and 1970s but was still generally absent from best-selling fiction. *The Beverly Hillbillies, The Andy Griffith Show*, and *The Waltons* provided Appalachian foils to the excesses of civilization. The Appalachian poor also received a flood of attention in the national press and in social commentaries like Michael Harrington's *The Other America* (1962) and Harry Caudill's *Night Comes to the Cumberlands* (1963). As Anthony Harkins observes, the hillbilly figure "reemerged in the 1960s at a time of widespread questioning of the price of 'progress' and the social equity of the 'affluent society.'" According to Harkins, the hillbilly became a means for whites to appropriate the language of identity politics but in reaction against the achievements of the civil rights movement, the countercultural movement, and the women's movement of the era.[64]

At the close of the decade, with the intensification of the conflict in Vietnam, two more midcentury Appalachian-set novels made the national best-seller lists. In chapter 4, I demonstrate the ways that regional fiction of this era affirmed and compelled touristic and missionary perspectives, each of which relied upon an assumption of interchangeability among authentic rural primitives nationally and globally. I compare fans of Catherine Marshall's pastoral novel *Christy* (1967), which features a missionary to the mountaineers in 1912, to fans of James Dickey's gothic novel *Deliverance* (1970), whose 1972 movie adaptation continues to be the single most prominent pop cultural reference to Appalachia. *Christy* sold almost 8 million copies in ten years. *Deliverance* sold 1.8 million copies in just three years.[65] The reception of both novels illuminates white high middlebrow readers' reinvocation of home, place, and innocence during U.S. imperialist militarism and civil rights activism. I examine two dominant strains among Marshall's readers as found in her fan mail: those who found affirmation for their missionary outlook toward rural people everywhere and those whose reading of *Christy* compelled them to vacation in the novel's East Tennessee setting. A surprising number of Dickey's readers were either outdoor enthusiasts who saw in Appalachia "a geography of hope" (a phrase Wallace Stegner used to describe the American West) or out-migrants from the South whose homesickness was soothed by Dickey's depiction of what one fan referred to as "grass roots" people.[66] Both Marshall's and Dickey's novels address a local-color fascination with a passing or lost order and reinforce local-color strategies for imagining place, self, and empire via projections of Appalachia as both a romantic and a nightmarish departure from the normative.

Shortly after the successes of Marshall and Dickey, the United States began to enter a Neo–Gilded Age, or Second Gilded Age (circa 1985–2008), as observers have dubbed it.[67] The Neo–Gilded Age had its origins in the presidency of Ronald Reagan (1981–1989). Like its earlier counterpart, the Neo–Gilded Age witnessed burgeoning wealth disparities, the reinvigorated power of corporations, and the escalation of U.S. empire. As Stephanie Foote argues, the "global ambition of the late-twentieth-century United States [bore] a striking resemblance to its late-nineteenth-century incarnation."[68]

Dear Appalachia argues that the resurgence in popular local-color fiction, which I date from the 1985 publication of Garrison Keillor's *Lake Wobegon*, occurred when it did because of social and economic dislocations and anxieties parallel to those of the Gilded Age. After the initiation of Keillor's *A Prairie Home Companion* franchise, local-color representations of supposedly backward or simple people and places gained in numerical preponderance and popularity, organized under rubrics like Barnes and Noble's "Settings and Atmosphere" category on its Internet site.[69] Partly as an outgrowth of multiculturalism of the 1960s and 1970s, "marginal texts and authors" became, in Jeff Karem's words, "objects of desire for American reading publics."[70] Just as the late-1800s demand for highbrow periodicals promoted an unprecedented surge in regional authorship, the market expansion of contemporary trade paperback novels beginning in the mid-1980s and 1990s opened up a new venue for regional writing by marketable newcomers.[71] The resurgence of popular literary regionalism highlighted settings across the United States, from the healing power of African American women in the South in *The Secret Life of Bees* (2002) to the healing power of cowboys in the West in *The Horse Whisperer* (1995), but the concentration of popular novels set in Appalachia since the 1980s is striking.[72] I examine the resurgence through 2002–2003—the year designated by the U.S. Congress as the "Year of Appalachia"—though at that juncture it showed no signs of slowing.[73] It may be that time will show that the close of the Second Gilded Age arrived with the "great recession" that began in December 2007.

In chapter 5, I show how white readers during this Second Gilded Age turned to best-selling Appalachian-set novels as if they are reliable, true-to-life ethnographies of rural white mountain cultures. I examine online customer reviews of four best sellers— Jan Karon's *At Home in Mitford* (1994), Charles Frazier's *Cold Mountain* (1997), Adriana Trigiani's *Big*

Stone Gap (2000), and Silas House's *Clay's Quilt* (2001)—to reveal the range of interpretations available to readers depending upon their geographic affiliations. Metropolitan readers found in the novels an "escape from our too hurried world" or access to the authentic roots of a wayward America or to their own peripatetic familial pasts.[74] Appalachian residents participated in the romantic construction of the region for their own purposes of self-affirmation—either through pride in their own Appalachian identity or gratification that a nationally embraced conception of the region was so in keeping with their own sense of being charmed by their Appalachian neighbors. For readers who had migrated out of the region, memories of Appalachia recalled and shaped by best-selling Appalachian-set fiction served as a foil against which they measured their new homes. Appalachian-set best sellers borrowed multiculturalism's emphasis on the value of difference in a way that offered white readers from each of these groups a means to participate in the era's search for roots and heritage.

Dear Appalachia examines not only the way that authors and publishers produced and marketed an imagined geography of Appalachia but also the ways in which various readers in cities and towns across the United States consumed and relied upon a particular vision of Appalachia they found comforting for reasons that varied not only depending upon their social location (for example, their class, sex, and race) but also upon their physical location and geographic affiliations. For some white readers, Appalachia is eccentric, a site for negotiating difference that is not as threatening as the racial otherness they attribute to African Americans or the incommensurable religious difference they attribute to Muslims.[75] For others, rural white Appalachia is "home quarters" in a dangerous world, offering the familiar and familial, the comforting and homey. Still others seek usable pasts, revolutionary nostalgia. Their belief in the existence of a simple quaint Appalachia is a means to critique the underside of American capitalism because readers project onto it their desires for a less commercial, less market-driven, less virtual, less manufactured, less falsified place. *Dear Appalachia*, then, acknowledges and illuminates the ways in which regions are socially constructed. Nonetheless, it also argues and demonstrates that we must take seriously the very real consequences of the ways people imagine place.

Chapter 1

Charm and Virility, circa 1884

A LITERARY SURPRISE
Feminine Author Discovered Under Male Pseudonym.
Charles Egbert Craddock is Miss Murfree.
Boston Literary Circles Greatly Astonished.
—*Boston Herald*, 5 March 1885

You see it had never occurred to any of us that "Craddock" was not a man, and I had often given free rein to my fancy in imagining how he would look and act.
—William Dean Howells, *Literary News*, April 1886

On 4 March 1885, *Atlantic Monthly* editor Thomas Bailey Aldrich was shocked to discover that longtime contributor "M. N. Murfree" was not, as he had assumed, a man, but the "delicate looking lady" standing before him in his Boston offices. The *Boston Herald*'s account of the meeting claimed that Aldrich "would have been better prepared" to learn that the popular local-color writer was "a Strapping Six-foot Tennessean" than Miss Mary Noailles Murfree (1850–1922), a young-looking woman who walked with a slight limp. The *Herald* reported that Aldrich "could hardly have been more astounded had the roof fallen in, and he turned and ran several steps under the pressure of the shock."[1]

Readers had known Murfree as Charles Egbert Craddock, the nom de plume under which she had published her stories in the *Atlantic Monthly* and then, with Aldrich's support, in the popular collection *In the Tennessee Mountains* (1884). "No one," remarked the anonymous writer for the *Herald*, "can have suspected that the master of a style so strikingly masculine as that in these mountain tales was not a man." Murfree had signed her correspondence to publishers and editors with the name M. N. Murfree, and they had taken it upon themselves to address the writer "as Mr. M. N. Murfree, or M. N. Murfree, Esq."[2]

The "Literary Surprise," as the *Herald*'s headline dubbed it, was purportedly the discovery that "Craddock" was a woman. Certainly, readers' gender biases led them to believe that only a man would be capable of presenting an "inside" view of a Tennessee mountain world they assumed demanded rugged strength and manly fortitude to traverse. Yet when Murfree presented herself to Aldrich she unwittingly upset other, equally substantial, assumptions. While some editors had thought Murfree deserving of the honorific "Esquire," the image of a "strapping six-foot Tennessean" suggests that a number of readers had pictured the author as an unrefined mountaineer akin to his lowly characters. Aldrich himself, the *Herald* reported, "used to muse considerably over the personality of the author, and he once wrote asking how the latter could have become so intimate with the strange, quaint life of the mountaineers."[3]

The "intimacy" Aldrich perceived between "M. N. Murfree" and mountaineers in fact bordered on a mistaken conflation of the two; according to the *Herald*, "Mr. Aldrich told Miss Murfree that he used to suppose that she wrote with one of those 'dip' brushes, which the mountaineers use in their habit of 'dipping snuff'!"[4] In a letter to Murfree, Aldrich expressed curiosity as to "how you picked up so rich and varied a vocabulary," perhaps indicating his bewilderment about the author's means of obtaining an education if—as many readers assumed—the author had been raised in the place "he" had convinced readers was wholly absent of schools and uniformly populated by ignorant and illiterate residents.[5] When the *Herald* article pronounced that "the development of this author is proof, not only of the wealth of the literary material that lies hidden throughout the United States, in obscure regions, but also that the conditions there existing may produce the genius to utilize them," it allowed Murfree to retain the benefit of one of the most important and longest-lasting suppositions about her, that she was native to the "obscure region" that supposedly produced her genius.[6] Given widespread assumptions about the documentary nature of local-color fiction, the author's apparent familiarity with and, to use a phrase from a Houghton Mifflin letter to her, "apparent fidelity" to the lives of mountaineers suggested that "Craddock" was a product of an obscure region distant from nationally recognized centers of elite society. At the same time, the writer's skill with language and refined sensibility seemed to indicate to highbrow readers like Aldrich that perhaps "he" was of their social station nonetheless.[7]

By some combination of conscious design and fortuitous accident, Murfree had successfully negotiated the contradictory demands placed on local-color writing in this era by projecting a masculine persona of ambiguous class and geographic status.[8] Her appearance in Boston as a "fragile, pale-faced, lame girl" six years after the 1878 publication of her first mountain story disrupted readers' illusions of Craddock as a rough-and-ready rambler of ambiguous social station.[9] In this chapter, I examine reviews of Murfree's stories and reactions to the "literary surprise" of Murfree's unveiling to illuminate readers' assumptions and desires regarding Charles Egbert Craddock. Metropolitan-based elite readers like Aldrich clearly had seen in Craddock a brawny "insider" to the region he depicted as homogenous and frontierlike. Like Aldrich, these readers traced literary authority to the author's presumed authenticity, an authenticity that guaranteed, they thought, the documentary accuracy of local-color writing. Metropolitan readers used Murfree's persona and stories to negotiate their anxieties about perceived threats to their power (including immigration, racial diversity, and overcivilization), their worries over the supposed urbanization and feminization of the United States, and their investments in nativism, nationalism, and global power at the close of the nineteenth century.[10]

While national periodicals dramatized metropolitan reviewers' reactions to Murfree's unveiling, archival research reveals that some readers assumed all along that Craddock was refined rather than a rough-and-tumble rogue. Letters and postcards written by members of a geographically dispersed local gentry point to an audience that wrought its own set of meanings from Craddock's stories. Nonmetropolitan readers were far less likely than reviewers for New York– or Boston-based periodicals to confuse the Tennessee author with his characters. They might have been as dazzled as Aldrich to discover that Murfree was not a man, but they would not have shared in the metropolitan press's wonder that Murfree was not a rugged mountaineer writing with a dip brush. For these readers, Murfree's nationally embraced depictions of rural mountain places conveyed evidence not of her marginal class status but rather her literary stature—and hence the potential for her acceptance, and by extension *their* acceptance, into a national network of elites.

Nonmetropolitan highbrow readers may have shared metropolitan readers' interest in maintaining their authority as elites, but they likely felt less threatened than their urban counterparts by urbanization, feminization, and immigration. They interpreted Craddock's identity according to a distinct set of experiences, anxieties, and desires. With the consolidation of economic, social, and political power occurring in postbellum America, members of the local gentry in small towns and cities across the United States—despite their immense influence at home—registered the possibility that they might each be marked as a "person from 'nowhere.'" It thus became increasingly urgent for local elites either to protect their domains from translocal incorporation or to strategically assert their locales as significant "somewheres" and themselves as cosmopolitan "someones."[11] I use fan mail to show how these particular needs and concerns played out in local elites' investments in Charles Egbert Craddock.

Even today, readers assess the value of Murfree's work based upon their understanding of her identity and biography. Revisionist scholarship in the feminist tradition argues that Murfree's marginalization as a woman who walked with a limp allowed her to identify with the socially oppressed.[12] Through a logic that grants Murfree "insider" status to the mountains because she holds "insider" status in terms of gender and disability, revisionists claim that Murfree's stories invite readers to feel empathy for mountain characters. Appalachian studies scholars, on the other hand, rely on Murfree's biography to count her as a privileged "outsider" who, despite having the perspective of a disabled female, wrote stereotypical and exploitive portrayals of marginalized mountain people whom she condescended to find enthralling.[13] Though some recent scholars have attempted to convey a more nuanced view of Murfree's relationship to the people represented in her fiction by calling her a respectful or "familiar outsider," even these terms flatten the complexity of Murfree's social position and authorial stance.[14]

We might attempt to resolve these differences by determining which set of scholars has a better understanding of the way Murfree's biography shaped her intentions. But even if Murfree *intended* to rouse readers' empathy rather than their prurient curiosity, as some scholars claim, her readers' interpretations were not entirely within her control. Biographical research and close readings of fictional texts are necessary but not sufficient tools for uncovering the meanings local-color writing held for its contemporaries. The publication context also mattered, including the reputations of the journals or presses in which Murfree's work appeared or was reviewed, but this also is not the whole story.[15] To understand whether Murfree's fiction had a positive or negative effect upon readers' attitudes toward nonelite mountain residents and other marginalized people, we need a different approach. The meaning of her stories depended not just upon Murfree's social position and geographic history, but on her readers' as well. By contrasting metropolitan readers' reactions in national periodicals with nonmetropolitan readers' assumptions in archived fan mail, I offer a clearer sense of how these two audiences made use of Craddock's mountain stories in their everyday lives. By paying attention to differences in interpretation according to where fans lived and what their relationships were to the mountains, I chart a geography of fan reception.

Various scholars have tried to take into account readers' reception of local-color writing. As Susan Belasco observes, the *Atlantic Monthly*, where Craddock's stories initially appeared, was an "elite magazine read by a small but loyal audience." In *Cultures of Letters*, Richard Brodhead argues that elite readers of highbrow periodicals like the *Atlantic* read local-color writing in order to project themselves into a national highbrow culture and thereby bolster their sense of superiority over "locals" and transform themselves into a single translocal social elite. Nancy Glazener demonstrates that local-color stories had different meanings for readers whose interpretations were shaped by reviews in populist journals geared toward farmers, which saw local-color stories as resisting dominant hierarchies that placed metropolitan life and people above rural life and people.[16] Where Brodhead sees local color as a tool of elites' self-creation and self-preservation, Glazener sees potentially emancipatory purposes.

Reception studies offers a way out of the impasse between revisionist feminists' celebratory assessments and others' cynical interpretations of local-color writing's ideological commitments. My research into the geographies of reader reception adds to Brodhead and Glazener by allowing a more nuanced and empirically based investigation of the ways in which fans' class status and geographic affiliations affected their interpretations. Though the number of extant letters is quite small, they document a significant contrast in readers' assumptions compared to those published in the print reviews and articles that circulated in highbrow periodicals and metropolitan newspapers. (For more on my methodological choices and sources, see "Appendix: Methodological Essay.")

Although feminist revisionist interpretations focus on counter-hegemonic readings of Murfree's texts, the ways in which metropolitan reviewers celebrated the author's purported marginality indicate that her fiction tended to preserve rather than challenge metropolitan elites' sense of their own power and privilege. Indeed, I would argue that it was precisely because so many local-color writers were, like Murfree, neither metropolitan nor entirely marginalized from highbrow culture that their works were able to appeal to multiple audiences that were in the process of coalescing into a single national elite. Ultimately, my investigation into the reception of Murfree's stories questions the usefulness of "insider" and "outsider" labels as literary credentials and rejects the romance of "authenticity" from which those labels arise. As we shall see in chapter 5, notions of authenticity tied to marginalization according to social class and geography are still used to praise and market regional authors today. But as I argue in the conclusion to this chapter, authors published by national publishers should be understood as part of a translocal network of readers and writers. Regardless of whether they are native to the places they represent, they are almost always cosmopolitans attuned to audience, almost always engaged in literary conversation with other published fiction, and almost always savvy about the publishing industry.

From Murfree to Craddock and Craddock to Murfree

From the time that the American literary public was first introduced to Charles Egbert Craddock in the May 1878 *Atlantic Monthly*, admiring readers eagerly sought more information about the "habitat and habits" of the story's author.[17] Aldrich, after taking over the editorship of the *Atlantic* from William Dean Howells, himself wrote Murfree to express curiosity about her background. Closely guarding the biographical information that Aldrich tactfully sought to uncover, Murfree replied evasively: "I struck upon the mountaineers as a topic at hap-hazard. . . . I used to spend much time in the mountains long before I knew of the existence of such a thing as 'literary material.' . . . I have, however, passed most of my life, so far, in Middle Tennessee, where I was born and educated." Aldrich, likely not aware of the distinction between the plantation-rich Middle Tennessee and mountainous East Tennessee, was left to imagine for himself the exact nature of the shadowy M. N. Murfree.[18]

In 1884, reporters mistakenly identified Murfree's father as the author of the popular Tennessee Mountain stories, and by January 1885, when Murfree's serial novel *The Prophet of the Great Smoky Mountains* began to appear in the *Atlantic*, newsmen and admirers had traced the Murfrees to their home in St. Louis. Murfree, her father, and her sister Fanny, deciding that the author should introduce herself to Aldrich, who could then reveal her identity to the public as he thought best, traveled to Boston.[19]

The precise manner of Charles Egbert Craddock's unveiling was reported excitedly in literary periodicals and major newspapers around the country. Upon meeting Aldrich at the *Atlantic Monthly* offices, Murfree said, "Mr. Aldrich, I have had some correspondence with you, and being in Boston, I decided to come to see you." "Beg pardon," Aldrich responded politely. "What name is it?" When Murfree replied, "I am M. N. Murfree—Charles Egbert Craddock," Aldrich exclaimed, "Why, what *are* you telling me? But this is impossible, impossible!" The shocked editor began to back out of the room, unconvinced until Murfree produced his letters to her as proof. When Aldrich recovered, he and his wife organized a dinner for Murfree the following evening at which they introduced her to several members of the Boston literati, including Howells and Oliver Wendell Holmes. Throughout the meal, Mrs. Aldrich referred to Murfree as "Miss Craddock" and the bewildered Annie Fields, wife of publisher James T. Fields, could never muster more than a vague "they" in Murfree's direction.[20]

The extent of the literary circle's astonishment, to paraphrase the *Boston Herald*'s headline, indicates the degree to which Murfree's readers found their construction of Craddock necessary to their sense of themselves and the world. The Craddock persona heavily relied upon a particular construction of the Appalachian region just coming into being in the late 1800s. Although Murfree had become familiar with the Tennessee mountains during her stays at an establishment that depended upon traffic from urban places, her fiction represented the mountains as inaccessible wilderness whose mountain "settlements" had little to no contact with "valley towns."[21] Reviewers and readers who had not themselves lived in or near the mountains almost necessarily imagined Craddock as an adventurer in unknown territory. An anonymous reviewer for the *Independent* wrote, "*In the Tennessee Mountains* guides us suddenly into what must be to many a new, unexplored, secluded strip of territory. . . . Mr. Craddock will do well to continue in the wild track he has struck into." Such emphasis upon the role of fiction as a "guide" into an "unexplored . . . territory" and a "wild track" conflated composing fiction about Appalachia with physical adventure. Reviews portrayed local-color writing as a sort of romanticized bushwhacking and painted Craddock as "an active fearless man accustomed to every phase of a wild out-of-door life" who had "a mountaineer's familiarity" with the landscape.[22] Believing as they did that Craddock was from the mountains, reviewers assumed that he was a self-taught and untrained writer whose natural "genius" was spontaneously and organically "produced" by the "obscure region" itself. A writer for the *Critic*, for example, wondered "in what secret hiding-place, what secure literary workshop, this artist has learned his trade and mastered his art, so that he can appear before us with perfection as his first public effort."[23]

While the author may have *seemed* to appear out of nowhere, in reality Murfree did in fact have a "secure literary workshop." When the *Atlantic Monthly* introduced Craddock in 1878, Murfree had already experimented with pseudonyms, shrewdly studied the literary market, learned how to pitch her writing to national publishers, and even, in two stories that had been accepted but not yet published by *Appleton's*, practiced the mountain-story formula that would make her famous.[24]

A number of factors converged to make what might otherwise have been the unspectacular life of a southern belle into one of a literary celebrity. Mary Murfree was raised at her family's plantation, Grantland, two miles outside of Murfreesboro, Tennessee, a town named for a grandfather who had fought in the Revolutionary War. Because Murfree's parents were distantly related to one another, they inherited much of the extended family's wealth accumulated over several generations, including property in Nashville and three plantations in Mississippi. Murfree spent her summers at Beersheba Springs, a fashionable resort at the far western fringe of the Cumberland Mountains, so she had met firsthand the types of locals who would soon become—thanks partly to her own success—darlings of the literary set who fictionalized and often sensationalized them.[25] After the Civil War, Murfree lived at Grantland until she was thirty-one, when her father abandoned the no-longer-profitable plantation and moved the family to St. Louis, where he took up a law career.[26] Murfree, then, like many local-color writers, was from a genteel background; she pursued authorship in part because of her commitment to highbrow culture and in part because of postbellum financial necessity.

Like other local-color writers, Murfree found entrée into literary circles through representations of "nonstandard" people and places, though this was not an element of her first literary endeavors: two satirical portrayals of elite social circles published in *Lippincott's* magazine. These

Mary Noailles Murfree at eleven, circa 1861. Courtesy of Special Collections Library, the University of Tennessee, Knoxville.

were perhaps inspired by her experiences in the late 1860s at boarding schools in Nashville and Philadelphia. Perhaps sensing that the nom de plume she had used for these first stories, R. Emmet Dembry, was too effete for her mountain tales, Murfree chose the name of a character from one of her unpublished mountain stories, prefixing "Charles" "to add a more masculine touch," according to her sister.[27] After she turned from the subject of high society to mountain society, she gained entrance into that hallowed organ of highbrow literature, the *Atlantic Monthly*, with William Dean Howells's 1878 acceptance of "Dancin' Party at Harrison's Cove." In the next five years, Craddock published seven more tales about rustic mountaineers in the prestigious highbrow periodical as well as six stories commissioned by *Youth's Companion*. In 1884, the *Atlantic Monthly*'s parent firm, Houghton, Mifflin, published Murfree's *Atlantic* stories as *In the Tennessee Mountains*.

The stories are wide ranging in topic and character, from "Dancin' Party's" soldier cum preacher's intervention in a love triangle to a lawyer's "*mésalliance*" with a young girl after he is banished to the mountains in "The Romance of Sunrise Rock" (*TM*, 199). Many of the stories depend for drama on the question of whether a wrong will be righted. "Driftin' Down Lost Creek," for example, features a mountain lass who braves the "valley country" to petition for the pardon of her innocent lover, only to find upon his release from prison that he had chosen not to return to the mountains and her (*TM*, 57). Remarkably well received, the collection sold nine thousand copies in its first year alone and went through seventeen printings within two years.[28] As local-color writing came into vogue, Murfree translated the charm she found in mountain people into a lucrative cottage industry: all told, from 1878 to 1899 she published almost thirty short stories (most also collected in volumes) and eight novels (in serial and book form) set in the Tennessee mountains.

Metropolitan Readers Imagine Craddock as Marginal, Other

Charles Egbert Craddock's readers speculated enthusiastically and unrestrainedly about the nature of the unknown author. Happily unburdened by biographical facts, thanks to Murfree's pseudonym, metropolitan-based elite readers constructed the author as a virile, self-taught adventurer in the rugged mountains. The intensity of their desire for a virile frontiersman who would nonetheless deserve the honorific "Esquire" underscored their anxieties. White middle- and upper-class Americans in the late 1800s were preoccupied with the supposed decline of masculinity and the rise of "overcivilization," both of which were understood as problems resulting from urbanization and industrialization. Cities supposedly coddled men instead of demanding that they be tough, as the trials of frontier living were said to do. General Horace Porter, for example, warned that urban life could cause a boy to lead an "unambitious, namby-pamby life, surrounded by all the safeguards of civilization."[29] Furthermore, readers' fabrication of Craddock as a manly gentleman mountaineer gestured toward their less explicit concerns about immigration, imperialism, and white racial superiority.

Highbrow readers' reactions to Craddock's stories indicate that they saw literature as part of the problem of overcivilization. A review in the *New York Times* the autumn after Murfree's revelation praises her for writing in a masculine manner and mocks writers who provoke anguished handkerchief wringing. As if in reply to Porter, the article is emphatically titled "Not Namby-Pamby." Unlike the male authors of romances who write in an "effeminate way," the columnist asserts, Murfree writes with reassuring masculine energy: "She fires off a pistol in your face and never flinches herself over flash or report. . . . She, like her . . . 'mounting' [mountain] blacksmith, hammers away until her book clangs in your ears and the reader's eyes see the sparks 'hizz' and scatter." This review contains perhaps the most lengthy, explicit, and imaginative celebration of Murfree's "masculine" style, but other reviews also remarked upon the "vigor," "power," and "virility" of her stories and characters. Even after Murfree revealed her identity, reviewers persisted in their preferred vocabulary, calling her writing replete with "force" and "masculinity," describing her male characters as "virile creations."[30]

Murfree's efforts to convey a masculine persona had apparently worked, given one critic's stunned amazement that the "writer whose name of the crushing consonants always suggested a nut-cracker" was "not Nutcracker after all, but Sugardolly."[31] A masculine name and mysterious identity likely benefited Murfree as the author of "mountaineer" stories, given the preoccupations of metropolitan-based readers. Such devices would not have provided the same help for a writer of local-color fiction set in a region like New England, imagined as a domestic space depleted of masculine energy. Appalachia, as the southern mountains would be termed by the turn of the century, served a highly gendered role as a masculine and masculinizing frontier in an urbanizing—and supposedly feminizing—nation. As one of Murfree's contemporaries put it in a short story in 1888, the lives of the "peculiar people" in the mountains seemed to offer an "unconscious . . . Spartan protest against the enervating influences of our civilization."[32]

Reviews that tied Murfree's writing to a protest against civilization linked her to a particular version of "primitive masculinity" coming into vogue in the final decades of the century, when urban men increasingly pursued—and were urged to pursue—camping, hunting, and fishing.[33] (In this regard, they credited her with anticipating the upcoming literary trend of naturalism, which would soon eclipse the seemingly more domestic local-color writing.) The primitive masculinity ideal, in turn, fit neatly with emerging imperialist ideals. When Theodore Roosevelt advocated the "strenuous life," he meant that white people ought to be strong leaders for nonwhite nations—in other words, he meant that America (imagined as "white") ought to be imperialist.[34] But the "strenuous life" came to mean not just bearing the so-called white man's burden around the world but being an active and strong white man in everyday life. American males tried to fall in step not only by spending time outdoors but also by reading adventure stories. The public's eager embrace of such tales likely influenced *Youth's Companion* to commission stories from Murfree, since the magazine promoted "boy culture" as one cure for the feminization Americans feared was overtaking U.S. society. Such stories of boyhood adventures were precisely the fare that "strenuous life" proponent Roosevelt devoured as a youth.[35] As an adult, Roosevelt was a huge admirer of Murfree's writing and wrote to her on more than one occasion to encourage her to visit him in the White House. Once, years after the author was widely known as "Miss Murfree," President Roosevelt stopped at the railway station in her hometown and called out, "Where's Craddock? She's the person I want to see."[36]

Murfree's fiction, particularly her native white mountaineers living on family farmland "nigh on ter a hundred year," appealed especially to readers like Roosevelt and Aldrich who were concerned with Anglo-Saxon supremacy and nativism in an era of intensive immigration from eastern Europe (*TM*, 111). Aldrich, the most vigorous promoter of Murfree's work, expressed "alarm" at the seeming disappearance of a "relatively homogenous, small-town, socially stable America." Aldrich's infamous 1892 poem, "Unguarded Gates," despairs of "the wild motley throng" that "presses" into the United States, bringing "accents of menace alien to our air." For someone like Aldrich, a lifetime member of the Anti-immigration League, part of Murfree's appeal lay in her portrayal of a more tractable, more naive, whiter, and less menacing lower order native to the United States. Plantation local color featured docile, loyal slaves or former slaves, but Murfree's white mountaineers surely held particular potency for a poet who admonished the "white Goddess" of "Liberty" to guard her gates. The racist nativism of some Murfree readers is also suggested in the eager reporting of her "Brilliant Line of Ancestry" after her identity became known.[37]

Murfree's characters promised readers not only mountain strongholds where native whites lived untouched by immigration but, paradoxically, a titillating sense of vitality that readers linked to authentic lives they associated with racial or ethnic minorities. As late as 1894, critic Henry Vedder described Murfree's literary skills as being as natural and untrained as those of a "negro kalsominer," or whitewasher, rather than those of an artist. Howells (reportedly prior to Murfree's revelation) and later Vedder praised Murfree's work as having a "raciness of the soil," suggesting a process of racialization by which her earthy characters reinvigorate a nation perceived as threatened by standardization and ennui.[38] Furthermore, readers' enchantment with the earthiness of her characters suggests her stories participated in a kind of "blood and soil" nationalism that identified so-called pioneer blood as the one true indication of rightful citizenship. Gendered as male and classed as both ruffian and literary lawyer, Craddock was raced paradoxically as "colored" by a locale deemed safely white. His persona thereby injected American nationalism with a vigorousness simultaneously raced both Anglo-Saxon and authentically, nongenerically, not-quite-white. The idea of Appalachia—as replete with pure white pioneer stock but also energized by authenticity, rootedness, and vitality—offered highbrow metropolitan readers a perfect balance between fear of standardization and fear of racial difference.

That Murfree's fiction could—and did—serve the racist, sexist, nationalist, and imperialist interests of metropolitan elites might surprise readers familiar with Murfree solely through recent anthologies. Even though most of Murfree's *Tennessee Mountains* stories take the region's "local-color" eccentricity for granted and portray the region as hermetically sealed from all outsiders, local-color collections tend to republish those few Murfree stories that feature tourists or other "outsiders" who call attention to the nature of the local-color enterprise. "The Star in the Valley," one of Murfree's most frequently anthologized stories, offers an explicit critique of city tourists' assumptions about mountain people. As recent anthologies note, "The Star in the Valley" resists dominant assumptions of metropolitan superiority through its city character Reginald Chevis, who admires the denigrated mountain girl Celia as the moral center of the story. But even in his recognition of Celia's moral worth, Chevis responds to her bravery as if it were an aesthetic object like a play, a poem, or a painting. Despite (or because of) his repeated nostalgic remembrance of Celia as "that star in the valley," the narrator suggests, Chevis fails to comprehend his and Celia's "common humanity" or to realize that his departure has left her heartbroken and on her deathbed (*TM*, 154, 150). Chevis and the story's sympathetic readers alike are implicated by their failure to recognize Celia's action and experience as anything other than a moral lesson and by their failure to recognize the "suffer[ing] unheeded in those mountains." In their very appreciation of rural mountain people, the story implies, readers are complicit in the aestheticization of mountain people's lives that the story condemns (*TM*, 154).

Of all Murfree's *Tennessee Mountains* stories, only "The Star in the Valley" is so overtly self-reflexive about the danger of being enthralled by and detached from the harsh realities of life in the mountains. The story closely resembles earlier mountain stories, including "Louisiana" by Frances Hodgson Burnett and "The Yares of Black Mountain" by Rebecca Harding Davis, in which tourists and the objectification of mountain people are central themes. Indeed, Murfree's success may have been attributable largely to the fact that, consciously or not, she moved away from the sort of self-examination apparent in such earlier works. Five of eight stories in *Tennessee Mountains* contain no "cultivated" visitors at all. They give the appearance that the world of the mountains exists unseen by outsiders. Even in the three stories that do feature cultivated "outsiders," the means of their coming and going to and from the mountains is not specified, including when the characters arrive or leave in the course of the story. No railroad, stagecoach, or other conveyance makes an appearance. As Henry Shapiro observes, Murfree's stories likely helped persuade nineteenth-century readers that the "peculiarity" of mountain life existed "independent of its observation from a train window or a hotel's veranda."[39]

Reviewers seem to have drawn their assumptions about Craddock from characters featured in the stories that are largely forgotten in the recent recovery of Murfree's work. "A-Playin' of Old Sledge at the Settlemint," for example, features a "roistering blade" whose depiction must have influenced readers' images of Craddock. The roustabout rides "a wiry gray mare without a saddle, and carrie[s] a heavy rifle." He is one of two local men who "rides thar horses . . . ter the Settlemint . . . ter play kyerds . . . jes' a-drinkin' of apple-jack [whisky], an' a-bettin' of thar money" (*TM*, 90, 80). The outline of "Craddock" ingrained in the metropolitan imagination derived from the assumption that regional authors write based on firsthand experience and from readers' acceptance of Murfree's depiction of the region as entirely cut off from the wider world. Given these conventions, Murfree left metropolitan readers with little choice but to imagine that the author must be an "authentic" product of the mountain world she constructed. An 1885 columnist remarked that it was little wonder that "reviewers and all the rest . . . thought for a while, at least, that Charles Egbert Craddock really wore . . . suspenders, played poker, and rode a horse—not with a sidesaddle."[40] As this review and Aldrich's earlier observation that he thought Murfree wrote with a dip brush suggest, readers sometimes mistook Craddock for one of his own characters.

Metropolitan-based reviewers and editors were so keen on the idea of Craddock as a self-taught, rough-and-ready rambler akin to his male characters (even though this image did not quite fit with their assumption that he was deserving of the honorific "Esquire") that they were bitterly disappointed by the author who appeared in Boston. Murfree was a genteel lady unlikely to be confused with a rough-hewn character. A New Orleans columnist sighed: "It is such a pity to be obliged to give up Craddock, he was such a charming man." The journalist bemoaned the loss of the Craddock who had "roamed constantly . . . stopping in frequently for rest at the rude, isolated cabins" and had exhibited "comprehension of these strange, rough, honest mountaineers."[41] Despite the fact that Murfree wasn't the rogue they'd imagined, most reviewers seemed reluctant to relinquish their faith in the mountain world Murfree had offered them. They continued to commend Craddock's stories for their bracing and salutary effects on American civilization. For them, the revelation of Murfree's gender changed little more than the pronouns in their prose.

Nonmetropolitan Readers Imagine Craddock as Prominent, Like Themselves

If readers in metropolitan cities seemed to confuse Murfree with her characters, other readers seem to have picked up on cues that "crude, 'low down, no 'count,'" as one reviewer called Murfree's characters, did not describe their author.[42] Elites from small towns and cities easily identified Murfree as a member of their own social circle. Although such landed gentry, merchants, new professionals, and rising industrialists may have thought of Murfree as someone thoroughly familiar with rural mountain life, this did not suggest to them that she was somehow marginal or underprivileged. Nonmetropolitan elites themselves were neither natives (speaking or behaving in the manner of regionalized characters) nor tourists (mere visitors to the places regionalized in local-color fiction). They may have assumed the author was a visitor like her tourist characters. Or they may have assumed the author was someone like them. From fan mail written to Charles Egbert Craddock before and after the March 1885 revelation of Murfree's identity, we get a picture of a geographically dispersed but ideologically and socially linked set of readers who imagined the unknown author as a familiar peer sharing their affection for and indulgent patronization of less privileged whites.

A February 1884 postcard to Craddock demonstrates that nonmetropolitan readers recognized the author as a peer rather than an uncouth mountaineer. The Reverend Hamilton Wilcox Pierson, considered an expert on the Cumberland Mountains of Kentucky and the author of *In the Brush; or, Old-time Social, Political, and Religious Life in the Southwest* (1881), wrote: "Dear Sir—I knew and was accustomed to visit Mr. Craddock near Louisville Ky. before the war? Are you of that family? I have just read with great interest 'Drifting Down Lost Creek,' and 'reckon' you must be to the 'manner born'—yours, H. W. Pierson, Author of '*In the Brush*,' Toledo, Ohio." The original Shakespearean sense of the phrase "to the 'manner born'"—to have been born into certain "native" customs—was still in use in 1884. Pierson's speculation that Craddock was to the manner born may indicate that he assumed Craddock came by his knowledge of mountain people honestly, as one born into the area. Or perhaps Pierson found Craddock a "natural," untrained writer, as a later meaning of the phrase might indicate.[43] The homonyms *manner* and *manor* might also have been at play, with Pierson imagining Murfree to be genteel because born to the manor. In any case, Pierson clearly believed that he

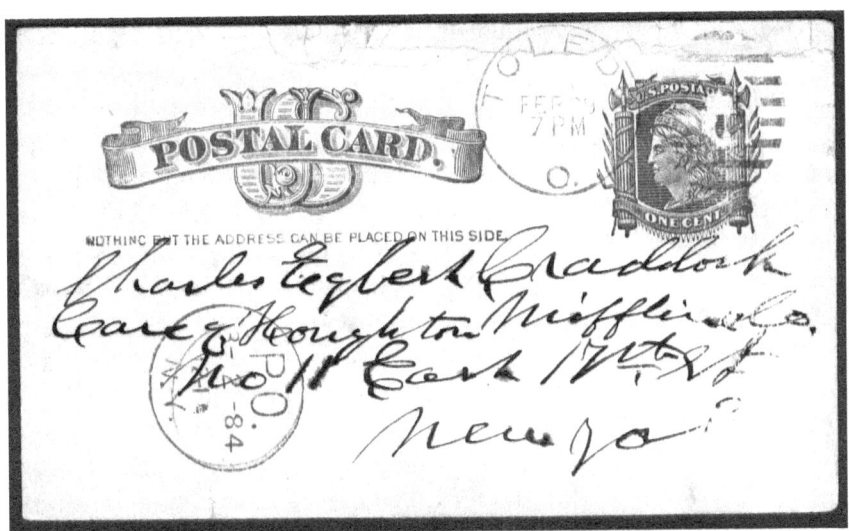

Postcard from a Charles Egbert Craddock fan, 1884. H. W. Pierson imagined Craddock as a peer and credited "him" as being "to the 'manner born.'" Courtesy of Manuscript, Archives, and Rare Book Library, Emory University, Atlanta, GA.

and the author occupied similar social positions, and perhaps were even former friends or acquaintances.

Other fan mail demonstrates the chord Murfree struck with readers who had known "mountaineers" but believed themselves to be part of a more elite set. Lucy D. Laighton, writing from Petersburg, Virginia, on the heels of Murfree's unveiling, conveyed to "My dear Miss Murfree" her thanks for Murfree's "having contributed to my mental pleasure, when I thought Emerson's death had closed the world of books to me." Laighton's reference to the highbrow Emerson reveals the prestige she attributed to Murfree's fiction as well as the status she accorded herself as a reader of literature. Laighton wrote admiringly, "I have lived in communities where some of the inhabitants spoke precisely the jargon that y[ou]r characters do, the wonder to me, is how you caught it, all that I c[oul]d do, was to comprehend it." In 1886, William Glyndon assured Murfree of her popularity among "the cultured circles of Canadians": "To me your portrayal of the grave, sombre, superstitious lives of the Cumberland Mountaineers is a reminiscence rather than a revelation. Years ago I was among them, and with them." George K. Grant, writing decades later from Chattanooga, an industrial center in the southern Tennessee mountains, proudly attested that "it has been my privilege to live much among the mountains." He had found "no fault" in her depictions of life there.[44] Here were readers who had "lived in communities" of rural mountain people, had been "among them," but did not dream of identifying themselves as being one of them or speaking their jargon. Glyndon's comments "Your characters are so new. Their idiom so quaint" emphasize this distance he felt between himself and the mountaineers. Murfree's observations meshed neatly with these genteel readers' own perceptions of the "peculiar" people they had encountered. Her patronizing sympathy for her characters mirrored genteel readers' sense of their higher class standing and their perceived detachment from unsophisticated mountaineers. These admirers saw themselves in Charles Egbert Craddock and registered Craddock's mountaineers as types they recognized but did not themselves resemble.

As suggested by Pierson's postcard, many of Craddock's nonmetropolitan fans were writers or aspiring writers who shared her interest in translating local lifeways for national readerships. W. H. Peck wrote to Murfree's publisher on letterhead from the the *Spectator* in St. Louis to express curiosity about the author of *In the Tennessee Mountains*, noting, "I am from Tennessee and have half written out a story located in the Apalachian range." Perhaps with his own "half-written-out" story in mind, Peck inquired of Houghton "what success" the book had "met with in sale?" Like Murfree, Peck was a reader of national highbrow magazines and was conscious of the market value for stories set in "that part of the state." His comment that he could "testify to the Exactness" of Mr. Craddock's "portraitures" suggests that he shared Murfree's desire to comprehend and represent rural mountain people while at the same time accentuating his own distinctive difference from them.⁴⁵

Murfree also received friendly and congratulatory letters addressed to Charles Egbert Craddock from such esteemed authors as Sarah Orne Jewett and Celia Thaxter. The poet and nature writer Thaxter wrote to Craddock: "Did you get the photograph I sent, and the two notes, my dear Mr. Craddock? I am sure you would have replied and sent the picture of yourself you promised me, had you done so—Will you not let me know?" She was writing after Murfree's unveiling, but if Thaxter had not yet learned Craddock's identity, her coy tone (that of a would-be sweetheart?) might indicate that in addition to acknowledging Craddock as part of a fellowship of writers, Thaxter assumed that he was not so far removed from polite society that he wouldn't be a potential suitor.⁴⁶

Whereas metropolitan readers like Aldrich wondered how Murfree could have such a "rich and varied vocabulary," coming as she did from a mountain world supposedly cut off from modern civilization, Murfree's nonmetropolitan admirers apparently discerned that she shared the attitudes and cultural references of highbrow readers. Murfree's stories emphasize the contrast between the narrator's elevated diction and the mountain characters' dialogue, which she represents in phonetically spelled dialect that exaggerates differences between standard and mountain pronunciations. In Murfree's fiction, the narrator's sophisticated perspective always carries more weight than an opinion expressed by a mountain character, especially when the mountain character offers a superstitious explanation. References to figures in classical and European culture and occasional French words or phrases imply the narrator's genteel education, as in an "arrogant *hauteur* worthy of Coriolanus" (TM, 165). Readers who picked up on these cues to the author's social station may have found their interpretation reinforced by the message her narrators frequently emphasize—that only a cultivated observer of mountain life had the appropriate tools to sufficiently appreciate it. Nonmetropoli-

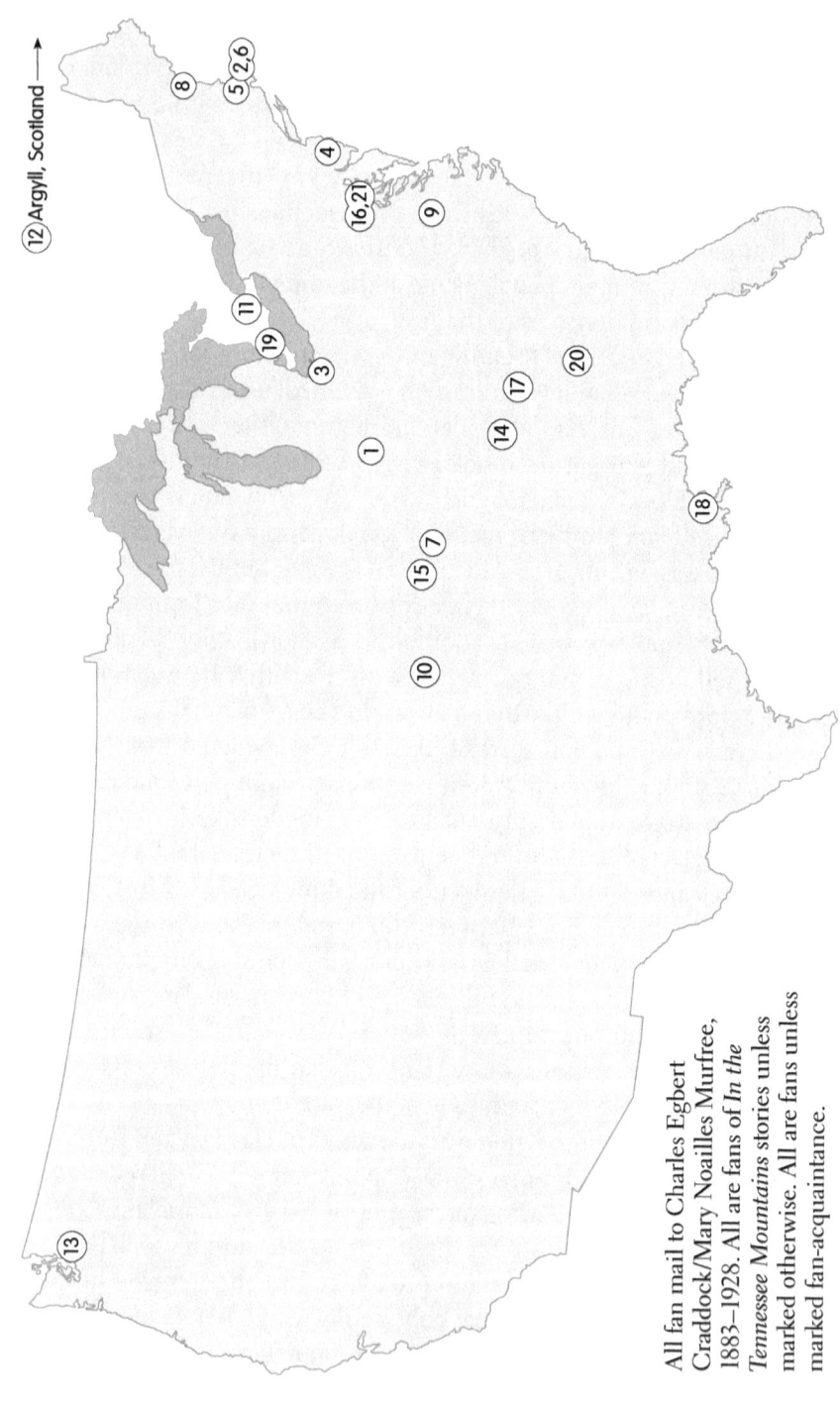

1. Mary Hannah Krout, fan-acquaintance, *Saturday Evening Journal*, Crawfordsville, Indiana
2. T. B. Aldrich, fan-acquaintance, *Atlantic*, Boston, Massachusetts
3. Hamilton Wilcox Pierson, author, Toledo, Ohio
4. Oscar Fay Adams, fan-acquaintance, author, Plainfield, New Jersey
5. W. M .D., Cambridge, Massachusetts
6. Sarah Orne Jewett, author, Boston, Massachusetts
7. W. H. Peck, *Spectator*, St. Louis, Missouri
8. Celia (Laighton) Thaxter, author, Kittery Point, Maine
9. Lucy D. Laighton, Petersburg, Virginia
10. Charles Sumner Gleed, author, Topeka, Kansas
11. William Glyndon, Hamilton, Ontario, Canada
12. Colin Lietch, Argyll, Scotland
13. Charles Cooper Nott, Chambers, Washington
14. G. H. Baskette, *Banner*, Nashville. Tennessee
15. Richard Henry Jesse, fan of Missouri-set fiction, Columbia, Missouri
16. Theodore Roosevelt, president of the United States, Washington, DC
17. George K. Grant, Chattanooga, Tennessee
18. John McLaren McBryde Jr., New Orleans, Louisiana, retired from the University of the South, Sewanee, Tennessee
19. Andrew Stevenson, London, Ontario, Canada
20. Ralph W. Barnette, fan of *Despot of Broomsedge Cove*, East Point, Georgia
21. Mabel Hatch, Washington, DC

tan readers assumed the author was just such a refined interpreter, and envisioned themselves as similarly adept.

Local elites must have found Murfree's fiction so compelling partly due to their concern about their status relative to national power during an era of translocal consolidation and incorporation. For elites who faced a loss of local control, Murfree's delight in local particularities may have helped justify their resistance to incorporation into a national network of railroads, faster communication, and increased trade. Many local elites must have accepted metropolitan elites' assumption that modernity required the extinction of local cultures.[47] At the same time, local elites may have been, like Murfree, genuinely saddened at the prospect of losing local folkways and dialect. Some local elites apparently felt patronizing pleasure in local qualities—perhaps because their own elite training and education were so different from local custom, and because they were trained by the *Atlantic Monthly* and other highbrow magazines to recognize locals as charming. In any case, seeing pieces of their own worlds in print generated in far-off places must have engendered great excitement and pride.

Despite the possibilities for resistance to national control that local gentry may have found in Murfree's fiction, her stories also enabled them to fulfill needs and desires they shared with their metropolitan counterparts. The stories denied capitalism's presence in the mountains, permitting mountain elites a willed ignorance of the incursion of industrialized labor and a view of local residents as a quaint and quiescent underclass. At the same time that they felt sincere pride in the attention paid to their homes, nonmetropolitan elites with national ambitions for their locales must have felt themselves advantageously integrated into a national highbrow network, their status enhanced, as "their" places were incorporated into highbrow fiction.

Certainly, the genteel elite were eager to claim Murfree as one of their own as a means to augment the national prominence of their own locales. Readers in St. Louis and Tennessee sent hundreds of excited telegrams to the *Boston Herald* in response to Murfree's revelation. And upon Murfree's return to St. Louis after her Boston tour, "a desperate effort was made by a number of society ladies to bring her out." In 1885 some "prominent Knoxvillians" who had met Murfree at a resort in the Smokies adopted her title character in the novel *The Prophet of the Great Smoky Mountains* as the mascot for their carnival.[48]

Even when local elites had no opportunity to associate the celebrity author with themselves or their places, reading Murfree's stories in the prestigious *Atlantic Monthly* undoubtedly enabled them to join a national circle of highbrow readers. Whether Murfree was herself a sympathetic "insider" or a condescending "outsider" to the mountains, her stories aided "an American upper class coming together as a social entity in the late nineteenth century." In this sense, local-color writing permitted metropolitan and nonmetropolitan elite readers alike to partake in a kind of "literary tourism" that replicated the purpose of actual tourism in resorts where elites met one another and recognized each other as peers.[49]

As the attitudes and postures of Murfree's correspondents show, her readers identified themselves as observers of quaintly primitive people from whom they thought themselves distant socially and culturally. When they found that geographically they were not distant from "primitive" peoples, these readers reached out to connect with others whom they felt were more nearly their social peers. Elite readers in places perceived as peripheral to the highbrow cultural life of the country—like Murfree's correspondents in Toledo, Petersburg, and Chattanooga—were confident that the famed Charles Egbert Craddock was one of their own class. Like Murfree, they had learned to regard local people and places as good "literary material."

Murfree was a central figure in highbrow literary circles largely because she was perceived as marginal—as the authentic voice of a rural mountain way of life peripheral to seats of elite culture and power.[50] After the sensational revelation that Craddock was a refined lady rather than a rough-and-ready mountaineer, commentators continued to consider Murfree a mountain "insider"—even as her success allowed her to travel in refined circles with some of the biggest celebrities and socialites of her day. During the famed trip to Boston in March 1885, for example, the Murfree sisters were houseguests at the Aldriches'; spent time with William James, Mark Twain, and Nathaniel Hawthorne's daughter; and visited Emerson's grave with his son. Socialite Mrs. Royal E. Robbins opened her oceanfront house to the Murfree sisters and a dozen ladies from Boston.[51]

Yet although Murfree's social success suggests her eminence among Boston elites and the most powerful literati of her time, her reception during the two months she spent in New England also bears a striking resemblance to that accorded to Zuni Indians in 1882 (accompanied by the Smithsonian anthropologist Frank H. Cushing). Bostonians proudly

Mary Noailles Murfree among Boston literati, 1885. *Standing:* Edwin Booth, Fanny N. D. Murfree, James M. Bugbee; *sitting:* Mary Noailles Murfree, Thomas Bailey Aldrich, Lilian Woodman Aldrich, Miss Houghton. From Edd Winfield Parks, *Charles Egbert Craddock (Mary Noailles Murfree)* (Chapel Hill: University of North Carolina Press, 1941), 127.

showed their Zuni visitors the ocean and invited them to visit with students at Wellesley College. Images of the incongruity of the traditionally garbed Zuni guests in these locations were circulated in *Century Illustrated* as curiosities of an "Aboriginal Pilgrimage."[52] Even—or especially—in the graciousness of her hosts' gestures, then, Murfree was marked as a visitor from a place apart. Her prominence at home notwithstanding, metropolitan elites continued to make distinctions between their social set and hers.

Like readers in Murfree's time, readers today often label regional writers as "insiders" or "outsiders" in order to decide whether their fiction is an "authentic" representation of a place. Most Appalachian scholars have labeled Murfree an outsider and dismissed her perspective as that of a tourist. Feminist revisionist scholars, on the other hand, insist on the value women writers from "marginal" places brought to their subject matter. They have argued that Murfree, who was "briefly paralyzed from a childhood illness that left her lame," "appeared to understand people who were 't'other' and differently abled." They contend that Murfree's stories demonstrate her "decentered" perspective and her sympathy for the oppressed, both of which they attribute to her sex and her visible difficulty in walking.[53] Both Appalachian studies and feminist revisionist scholars rely on their textual interpretations of the stories (as either hopelessly stereotypical or subtly subversive) to support their claims about the ways authors' social identities shape their fiction. For example, revisionist scholars read Murfree's "The 'Harnt' That Walks Chilhowie" in such a way as to argue that Murfree's stories elicit readers' empathy for mountain people. Yet a contrarian close reading shows that textual interpretation can readily support the opposite conclusion.

"The 'Harnt'" features a disabled character, a one-armed fugitive named Reuben Crabb, who is thought to have been shot and killed by the sheriff. The hungry "ghost" prevails upon the mountain girl Clarissa to bring him food. Simon Burney, an elderly widower enamored of Clarissa, fears the girl will be charged with abetting a criminal and so convinces Reuben to turn himself in by promising to feed and shelter him once he is acquitted of murder. Some revisionists note that Murfree gives her lead female character, Clarissa, "a voice to speak out . . . in defense of herself, the 'harnt,' and the principle of feeding those who are hungry."[54] But Clarissa feeds the starving Reuben just once. It is the unrewarded "Old Simon Burney," whose interest in Clarissa provokes her mirth and disgust, who shelters Reuben for the rest of Reuben's "no-'count" days (TM, 320). The "voice" that "speak[s] out" for the "harnt" and the "principle of feeding . . . the hungry" is not that of the female protagonist. Furthermore, the story privileges and legitimates Simon Burney as a virtuous caretaker through the crude stereotyping of a minor crippled character.[55] Finally, the story's pathos turns on the narration's flattery of cultivated readers, its insistence that they can appreciate the nobility of Simon's "prince[ly]" sacrifice, although none of the ignorant mountaineers can (TM, 321).

Does "The 'Harnt'" empower disabled people and deserve admiration for its strong female character? Or does it flatter elite readers' sense that their artistic sensibilities grant them authority over those for whom they condescend to feel sympathy? Does the story's effect stem from the writer's class, sex, race, or geographical affiliation—or the reader's? Revisionist and Appalachian studies scholars want to answer these questions by close readings filtered through literary biography. This can be useful. As one contemporary of Murfree asserted in 1930, the fact that Murfree was a young girl who walked with a limp may have afforded her unusual access to mountain people's kindness and to their homes.[56] The consequences of Murfree's ensuing observations of mountain people, however, are more complicated. Indeed, revisionist scholars themselves acknowledge that their students are not swayed by a text's or an author's attempt to arouse empathy for regionalized characters.[57]

Murfree was a woman, and lame. She was the well-educated daughter of a wealthy slave owner and considered Middle Tennessee home. These facts shaped her life immeasurably and influenced the content of her writing, but they did not determine either the substance or the reception of her fiction. Designating a writer as insider or outsider cannot take the place of assessing the ways different sets of actual readers (whose reactions are often guided by such labels) make meaning of a text. For a fuller picture of those consequences in Murfree's own time, we have to perform the archival work and historical investigation embraced by methodological innovations in reception scholarship.

Through genius, luck, persistent practice, or some combination of these, Murfree's fiction succeeded with two distinct but coalescing audiences. Her choice of pseudonym and her fusing of rough characters and cultivated narrators satisfied the readerly desires of both. As letters to Murfree demonstrate, local-color stories reinforced for nonmetropolitan elites their proud affiliation to places with considerable national cachet, places whose embrace by highbrow literary circles seemed to promise local elites a seat at the new national table. Even as the stories promoted local gentry's pride in those places, they reinforced a sense of superiority over less privileged locals. Metropolitan elites, by contrast, appropriated local-color stories out of a sense of the superiority of the modern city over supposedly premodern rural places, and out of a sense of their superiority over rural people (including local gentry). Local-color writing reassured metropolitan elites of their self-preservation as elites through its delight in rural white Americans and its promise to promote the strenuous life at home and abroad. Local-color writing also served for both sets of elites as a kind of vicarious tourism that allowed them to feel connected to others with highbrow tastes. For metropolitan readers, literary tourism provided exotic habitats that offered relief from a seemingly sterile and mundane urban life.[58]

Murfree's familiarity with a place perceived as peripheral may have enabled her to produce local-color fiction, but conceptualizing authorship required above all her familiarity with *nonlocal* audiences and their perspectives on the local. The point is not to dismiss Murfree as an "outsider" to the mountains or extol as virtuous her marginality arising from her being an "insider," but to suggest that fiction always has more complex consequences than such binary labels imply.

Chapter 2

Tonic and Rationale, circa 1908

"It must be very agreeable to her to be settled within so easy a distance of her own family and friends." . . .

"I should never have considered the distance as one of the *advantages* of the match," cried Elizabeth. "I should never have said Mrs. Collins was settled *near* her family. . . . The far and the near must be relative, and depend on many varying circumstances. Where there is fortune to make the expense of travelling unimportant, distance becomes no evil. But that is not the case *here*." . . .

Mr. Darcy drew his chair a little towards her, and said, "*You* cannot have a right to such very strong local attachment. *You* cannot have been always at Longbourn."

—Jane Austen, *Pride and Prejudice*

In 1917, author John Fox Jr. (1862–1919) received a handwritten letter from a student at Stonewall Jackson College for Young Women in Abingdon, Virginia.[1] The topic of Una M. Crawford's fan mail was Fox's second best seller, published almost ten years earlier and set in southwestern Virginia. "Ever since Ive read your book 'Trail of the Lonesome Pine' I've felt there was some one who really understood my feelings of my mountain home," Miss Crawford wrote. A self-proclaimed "mountain girl of North Carolina," Crawford identified with Fox's Pygmalion-like character June. She saw in *The Trail of the Lonesome Pine* (1908) recognition of her anguish over what she described as "the pain that comes after being with cultured refined people and then going back to the 'old life.'"[2]

Crawford's missive represents one of a handful of letters Fox received from readers who were drawn into the circles of translocal elites yet discerned, and felt keenly, those elites' disdain for childhood homes they held dear. Her letter offers us a new way to comprehend the sensational popularity of Fox's *The Trail of the Lonesome Pine*. Previously, interpretations of Fox have fallen along two lines. Scholars who criticize Fox argue that the author bungled his representations of mountaineer characters. They accuse him of promoting imperialism by caricaturing feuding moonshiners as an inferior but potentially redeemable "peculiar mountain-race."[3] Conversely, Fox's promoters—from Fox's day to the present—have praised his "intimate knowledge" of mountain residents, whom they believed Fox captured accurately and sympathetically.[4]

I agree for the most part with Fox's detractors. Print reviews suggest that much of his audience was comprised of metropolitan-based *nationally identified* readers who turned to Fox's novel as an antimodernist tonic that celebrated mountain quaintness, rationalized industrial interventions, and affirmed readers' nationalism, racism, and imperialism. Nationally identified readers were trained into the high middlebrow perspectives of print culture offered by the periodicals in which Fox published, including *Harper's Weekly* and *Scribner's*. Meanwhile, *locally identified* readers in Appalachia saw themselves fictionalized as the stereotypical buffoons who comprised the majority of Fox's characters, and were rightly offended.

Fan mail like Una Crawford's, however, reveals that Fox's depiction of the mountain girl June's loyalty to two different worlds struck a chord that resonated with *transitional* readers whose pursuit of schooling, professional work, or—in the case of regional elites—advantageous matrimonial matches compelled their social and geographical movement away from the people and places of their childhood. Fox's correspondence illuminates the anxieties of a broad swath of Americans on the make and points to the ways that *The Trail of the Lonesome Pine* expressed, constructed, and helped them negotiate the pangs of joining the rising middle class. Crawford's divided allegiances appeared among a larger set of letter writers: shopkeepers, bankers, timber agents, preachers, and other members of the still-consolidating middle class who cherished so-called backwater places but participated eagerly in a bureaucratic, rational, and modern nation.[5] Though Fox's admiring letters are largely from readers with regional ties, his dramatic national success suggests that newly professional middle-class readers across the country also felt deeply ambivalent about their experiences of professionalization and bureaucratization. Though they did not always have mountain roots like Crawford, transitional readers from every corner of the nation may have shared her sense of dislocation and loss of home. Merchants, clerks, salesmen, and other members of the consolidating professional classes, whatever their region, may have picked up on themes in the novel that appear to have touched mountain residents most keenly and urgently.⁶ Even for regional elites whose financial stature seemed secure, widespread migration intensified the sensation of feeling torn between home and a worldly cosmopolitanism.

Unlike locally identified readers, transitional readers were ensconced in the high middlebrow perspectives of national print culture and had learned to share in the antimodernism, white nationalism, and sense of imperial duty of nationally identified readers.⁷ These readers' identifications transitioned back and forth between a national imagined community and local loyalties; they still had one foot in a place marked by the larger culture as irrelevant. Fox's promoters are mistaken when they identify him, a loyal partisan of the central Kentucky Bluegrass region, as a "native" interpreter of mountain people. Nonetheless, the ambitious Kentucky-born author did serve—if only inadvertently—as a native interpreter of the desires and anxieties of upwardly and geographically mobile readers from areas considered the nation's "hinterlands."

Fox's popularity among nationally identified readers alone might have accounted for *Lonesome Pine*'s appearance as the third-best seller in 1908 and fifth-best seller in 1909.⁸ Readers responded to the novel's primitive setting on the mountainous Virginia-Kentucky border with fascinated enchantment. Fox's earlier Civil War best seller, *The Little Shepherd of Kingdom Come* (1903), which opens in the mountains and moves to the Bluegrass, attracted readers charmed by the hill country and thrilled by its pro-Southern but pro-Union stance.⁹ Both novels were so popular that they became, in the words of Alice Payne Hackett, "almost synonymous with the words 'best seller'" just as the term came into existence.¹⁰ Between 1885 and 1920, Fox published at least twelve books and more than forty-five articles and short stories in magazines as prominent as *Harper's* and as popular as *Ladies' Home Journal*.¹¹

Of all Fox's works, it was *The Trail of the Lonesome Pine* that remained among all-time best sellers for at least half a century after its publication. Indeed, it inspired so many musical, theatrical, and cinematic crossovers—including two popular songs, two plays, and three movies (1916, 1922, and 1936—the last starring a young Henry Fonda)—that it qualifies as a proto-blockbuster.¹² Fox's success had much to do with new trends in the book industry, where ever larger investments in advertising resulted in ever larger payoffs in a growing marketplace, thanks partly to the expansion of literacy.¹³ Nevertheless, *Lonesome Pine*'s phenomenal popularity

Advertisement for *The Trail of the Lonesome Pine*, 1908, as it appeared in the *New York Times*, 24 October 1908.

and longevity suggest that the novel hit a nerve in a way that cannot be explained by its conventional insider-outsider romance alone.

The heart of this chapter is the transitional readers whose presence I unearth through examination of Fox's fan mail. In order to understand how their discovery expands our knowledge about early twentieth-century literary audiences I outline the other types of readers Fox's novel attracted. My reading of *The Trail of the Lonesome Pine* points to its tension, often unacknowledged, between boosterism and melancholy over the consequences of industrialism. I show how print reviews evince antimodernist, nationalist, and imperialist readings of the novel that rarely acknowledged the gloomier messages pulsing through it. These nationally identified reviews support T. J. Jackson Lears's argument about the antimodernist impulses that emerged when late-nineteenth-century changes provoked a sense of "weightlessness" or alienation among middle-class Americans, who then sought to ameliorate their self-estranged condition by seeking experiences or places that seemed more "real" than modern life.[14] I note the irony of print reviews' falsely casting Fox as an authentic representative of mountain people, as previous scholars have shown and as locally identified readers' responses highlight.

I then turn to fan mail to uncover the more complicated meanings transitional readers found in Fox's fiction. (For more on my methodological choices and sources, see "Appendix: Methodological Essay.") Readers' geographic and class mobility made the place-bound culture represented in *Lonesome Pine* seem particularly attractive but also particularly doomed, highlighting the extent to which the popular success of regional fiction was tied to the movement of readers. Finally, I return to Fox's biography to illuminate how he was able to speak to those readers caught up in the contradictory impulses of the professionalizing middle class. I argue that the tremendous popularity of regional fiction like *Lonesome Pine* can be traced to migratory readers' ambivalence regarding the relative benefits of the supposedly rooted but barbaric hinterlands versus the supposedly refined but environmentally and emotionally costly industrial world.

Industrialism: Triumph and Sorrow

Fox's scholarly critics have painted *The Trail of the Lonesome Pine* as presenting the industrialization of the mountains as a triumph, an interpretation supported by reviews published in the months following the novel's release. Yet the novel provides a darker picture of modernization than either scholarly or professional critics have acknowledged. *The Trail of the Lonesome Pine* describes the intervention of coal-boom industrialists in a feud-ridden territory on the border of Kentucky and Virginia and follows a love interest between John (Jack) Hale, an outsider and engineer "gone native," and June Tolliver, the barefooted mountain girl he sends to finishing school. As Fox scholar Darlene Wilson has noted, *The Trail of the Lonesome Pine* tries to hew to the party line of Fox family friends and business partners: development will bring schools, churches, civilization, and law and order to unruly violent mountaineers. Moreover, the novel credits the coal boom for a truce between feuding factions. As multiple reviews noted, "Nobody had time . . . for deviltry and private vengeance—so busy was everybody picking up the manna" from the sky.[15] When the coal industry bust comes, however, the feudists are idle, and moonshining and quarreling flourish once more.

Industrialization in the novel is indeed portrayed as a necessary process, even a good process, carried out by honorable men like Jack Hale. But it is also ugly and alarming. The novel dwells on that ugliness and alarm in a way that exceeds a basic antimodernist nod toward the sadness of losing the primitive. Even as the novel attempts to back the inevitability and rightness of "progress," it portrays mining's presence in June's home, Lonesome Cove, as a jolting, devastating foreignness, racially coded as black. When June returns home from school, she finds that "the cruel, deadly work of civilization had already begun." The "crystal" stream is polluted by sawdust, and the water is "black as soot" and full of dead fish. The saw, to June's ears, is a "buzzing monster" that bites "a savage way through a log, that screamed with pain as the brutal thing tore through its vitals." June's fright at the alien presence in her cove intensifies when "two demons" appear, "sooty, begrimed, with black faces and black hands." June tries to reassure herself that "it was all very wonderful . . . Jack Hale was doing it all and, therefore, it was all right." The novel's narration defends June's ill-placed faith by condescendingly pointing out her naïveté about the extent of the destruction: "The ugly spot on the great, beautiful breast of the Mother was such a little one after all and June had no idea how it must spread" (*TLP*, 201–2). Boom times supposedly bring a welcome respite from feuding, but they also bring "uptorn earth," unsightly mining shacks, bottles and cans strewn around the lovely cove, and a river devoid of life (*TLP*, 415–16). Capitalism's busts eventuate not only in the return of feuding but also in a deserted town, with the hero's options limited by his tremendous debt.

Despite the novel's acknowledgment of the damage done by industrialization, and despite June's urging that Jack "leave old Mother Nature to cover up the scars," *Lonesome Pine* refuses to endorse a preindustrial mountain way of life as a viable alternative (*TLP*, 416). Gone are the novel's opening observations about the productivity of the cove—the orchard and the outbuildings that marked its owner as well-to-do. Instead, Lonesome Cove becomes June and Jack's retreat from failed industrialization when the disappointingly small size of the coal seam on June's family's land becomes a blessing in disguise. Jack promises June he will repair the damage: "I'll take away every sign of civilization, every sign of the outside world" (*TLP*, 416). The cove consequently provides the best of nature and civilization but appears to remain outside the local or national economy. Its appeal requires the presence of refinement in the form of gifts Jack has given to June, including a cultivated garden, a "modern" bedroom, and that quintessential symbol of middle-class status, the piano. *Lonesome Pine*—like Frances Hodgson Burnett's "Louisiana" and Grace MacGowan Cooke's *The Power and the Glory* before it—reaches for a bit of refinement in the wilderness, for Leo Marx's middle pastoral, as a solution.[16] Unfortunately for the dead fish, blackened stream, and the now-unemployed miners, the industrial moment is purportedly required to save the wilderness from ignorance and grime, to drag it out of the "benighted . . . Middle Ages" into the "greed of the Twentieth Century" to arrive at that middle ground (*TLP*, 96, 39).

Print reviewers avoided mention of the novel's grimmest moments. No review in any national periodical lingered on *Lonesome Pine*'s representation of cyclical boom-and-bust capitalism or its consequences for people's lives. Reviewers neglected to comment upon the creeks black with coal dust, ominously black-faced miners and their shacks, or even Jack's promise to bury the trash and allow the earth to heal. Far from mentioning (much less sanctioning) the gloomy picture of industrial development proposed by portions of Fox's novel, most reviewers went only so far as to say reassuringly (in the case of the *New York Times Saturday Review of Books*) that the "moonshiners and their feuds [were only] slightly disturbed by the encroachment of industrial enterprise."[17]

Instead, reviewers for the most part interpreted *Lonesome Pine* as supportive of "development" in a land of "arrested civilisation." The *Washington, D.C., Star*'s review professed that the book "ends on a note of pure joy." After all, despite Jack's financial ruin, he has accomplished "the end of the old barbaric order" and "faces the future, prepared for greater achievements." Critics acknowledged that Jack Hale comes up short in his enterprises but never doubted his heroism. Reviewers described him as a "cultivated, educated, brave, resourceful" man who "arous[es] . . . a mountain village to a realization of law and order through [his] pluck and determination." He is "the type of American life of which we are most proud, the vigorous, brave, energetic man of flesh and blood, who 'does things.'"[18] Jack Hale embodied the national hero, with all the boyish "pluck" of a Horatio Alger upstart heading out of the city and all the virility of a Rooseveltian white patriarch leading the strenuous life in the wilderness. The anonymous critic for the *Independent* described *Lonesome Pine* as "a thrilling demonstration of the way civilization in the forms of law and order is advancing up the mountain sides to the fastnesses of medieval humanity still to be found there." Dozens of reviews very much like this one, in both national and local periodicals, make clear that critics cast civilization as the necessary arrival of "law and order" imposed upon feuding, "semi-savage" mountain "tribes," whose racialized primitive status required outsiders' intervention.[19] If the stakes are civilization versus the "Middle Ages," then civilization must win.

If reviews downplayed the negative consequences of capitalism, they nonetheless registered the novel's sense that the arrival of "law and order" is a somewhat disappointing transformation. *Lonesome Pine*'s narrator half mockingly bemoans the fact that mountaineers must begin to follow the new Police Guard's regulations in town: "The wild centaurs no longer allowed to ride . . . with their reins in their teeth and firing . . . and, Lost Spirit of American Liberty!—they could not even yell" (*TLP*, 142). Magazine critics suggested wistfully that mountaineers lived "a wild, free life, governed only by such laws as it pleased them to observe." While "tribes" stuck in the "Middle Ages" surely need civilizing, the *Independent*'s reviewer romantically observed that Fox transforms feuding "into something like rude knight errantry." Reviews instructed high middlebrow readers that there was something valuable to be retained and learned from "rude" folk, even if they must be introduced to "justice" and "civilization." The novel assures readers that "the world is still the right sort of a place, and that love and honor" persist much as they were "in the most . . . chivalrous of ages."[20]

Reviews, then, embraced Fox's fiction as a "tonic" and a "breath of inspiration" "fresh from the wilds" that offered relief for "modern men and women."[21] Perhaps the most pointed review in this vein was written by Sinclair Lewis for the *New York Times Saturday Review of Books*. Lewis explored the proposition made by *Lonesome Pine* "that the world would be better off without machinery." Fox's story makes it "deplorable that so exquisite an elf as June Tolliver should be dragged out into the world; . . . a degenerate place." Lewis demanded, "Didn't Mr. Fox mean it when he gently hinted that exquisite Junes must stay in the mountains, away from forged steel, if they are not to become blasé Novembers?"[22]

The Construction of the Authentic: Appalachia and Fox

The antimodernism evident in the reviews was accompanied by and propelled by a hunger for the authentic. A review in *Outlook*, written by perhaps the only female critic to evaluate *Lonesome Pine*, described the mountains as a place "where no sane person would willingly abide." For most critics, however, the world delivered up by *Lonesome Pine* appealed greatly. They found the "delightful country" of the Cumberlands and its people "charming" and "vigorous."[23] Reviewers relished the "spirit of freedom" among the "wild inhabitants" of the mountains.[24] Readers' hunger for authenticity fed a desire to visit the primitive. *The Trail of the Lonesome Pine* inspired readers to travel to eastern Kentucky to witness for themselves the "real" people about whom, they assumed, Fox wrote.[25] Train conductors even pointed out for tourists a tree that they assured their passengers was the one of *Lonesome Pine* fame.[26]

The allure of authenticity is underscored by critics' insistence upon Fox's right relationship to the "primitive folk" he "knows so well" and whom he describes with "intimate knowledge and love."[27] Promotional materials for Fox's earlier lecture tours marketed and praised the author's credentials. Fox, author James Lane Allen claimed, "has lived several years among the native folk, has talked with them, studied them." Thomas Nelson Page echoed these encomiums, stating that Fox "understands the dialect of the mountaineers . . . as few people in this country do." A flyer claimed that Fox was "at home in the cabins of moonshiners. . . . The people of whom he writes he knows thoroughly."[28] On occasion, reviewers claimed that Fox's stories validated earlier accounts of the mountains, including Murfree's *In the Tennessee Mountains*, though Fox was credited with a far more scientific mode of observation.[29] Fox planned to deliver purportedly nonfiction speeches about mountain people, replete with pretensions of sociological, anthropological, and scientific analysis and objectivity, at Harvard and at the Anthropological Society of Philadelphia. He was invited to present at the International Folk Lore Association alongside other local colorists like Joel Chandler Harris.[30]

Scholars have pointed out that Fox's presumed knowledge about the mountains was bogus. He was raised about thirty miles outside Lexington, Kentucky, in the state's Bluegrass region. Fox spent little time in the mountains even after his family moved to Big Stone Gap, Virginia, in search of coal, timber, and real-estate profits when Fox was twenty-eight.[31] Like many central Kentuckians, Fox had no exposure to the mountainous portions of the state growing up. Indeed, as he once admitted, "I never saw a mountain until I started for Harvard in my seventeenth year and through those I passed at night."[32] It was Fox's experiences in Boston and New York, where he was able to "see a man who had painted a

John Fox Jr., circa 1894. Courtesy of Special Collections and Digital Programs, University of Kentucky Libraries, Lexington.

picture, carved a statue, or written a book," that convinced him that he could become a writer. Like Murfree before him, he began his fiction career with pithy sketches of upper-class characters.[33] It was not until an 1882 summer break from Harvard that Fox first visited the mountains to work with his half brother James for the Proctor Coal Company near Jellico, Tennessee. According to his later recollections, it was there that he, "without knowing it," first began "gathering material" for his mountain fiction.[34]

Fox and his advisers nonetheless understood that his success depended upon audiences accepting him as an accurate interpreter of mountain people. James Lane Allen encouraged him, "I believe a lecture on the Cumberland mountaineers would fetch you in a good sum of money, if you lectured so far away that no one knew anything about them. Miss Murfree's audience in New England ought to be ready for you."[35] Fox carefully crafted his persona to represent himself as intimately familiar with mountaineers yet relied on his familiarity with high middlebrow audiences in order to make a living representing Appalachia. His representations succeeded because many Americans of his day shared his perspective that "the word 'mountaineer' and the look of it in print" always held "a singular fascination."[36] In short order, Fox became a well-connected author whose racialized theories about mountain people were drawn less from observation and more from such powerful figures as his great admirer Theodore Roosevelt, Berea College president William Frost, popular Kentucky local-color author James Lane Allen, and prominent Virginia plantation local-color author Thomas Nelson Page.

Nationally Oriented Readers

For nationally identified readers who interpreted Fox through the lens of national periodicals, Fox's "authentic" white mountaineers therefore offered antimodernist tonic and respite. As one reviewer noted, Fox represents the "primitive folk" as "our pioneer forefathers" otherwise "lost out of our times." The *Baltimore Sun* observed, "Interest is stirring the country . . . concerning the 'mountain whites,' descendants of Revolutionary ancestors."[37] Another reviewer called mountaineers an "unmodernized and unassimilated remnant of the old Scotch and English stock which . . . sings the old ballads of the Motherland."[38] Perhaps it was thanks to the representation of mountaineers as children "of the soil" that, reviewers argued, "The tale is American to the backbone" and strikes "an intensely national note."[39] Because "half-civilized" mountain residents were "a race and a type standing apart" and a "remnant of the last individuality extant, North or South, East or West, in the United States," they reassured nationally identified readers that the country could withstand the assimilation and standardization that threatened to dilute the pioneer blood.[40] For readers concerned with the effects of immigration from eastern and southern Europe, the "unassimilated remnant of the old Scotch and English stock" promised nothing less than the preservation of Anglo America.[41]

Mountaineers' closeness to the soil spoke to their importance to the nation, but it simultaneously pegged them as a racially marked tribal people, "an alien population" that required intervention and uplift.[42] Many national reviews quoted at some length the "anthropological" explanation of the mountaineers' character given by Sam Budd in the novel ("You see, mountains isolate people. . . ." [*TLP*, 97]).[43] June, explained one critic, is a "justification" of Berea president William Goodell Frost's "faith in the blood of mountain people and their capacity for growth."[44] In a published interview, Fox linked for readers the parallel capacity for growth among worthy yet racially suspect mountaineers, on the one hand, and Cuban objects of imperial duty on the other. Asked about "the capacity of the Cubans for self-government," Fox called Cubans "an irresponsible lot," but claimed the "Cuban war was nothing in comparison with" the experience of corralling mountaineers as a member of the Volunteer Police Guard that protected industrialists' interests in southwestern Virginia.[45] If fiction about taming the South made imperialist intervention seem necessary, reviewers nonetheless held onto their concern for what might be lost by bridling the "magnificent," wild, free "ruffians." As one observed, "It is hard to forgive" Hale for sending the "passionate young savage" June "off to school and civilization" when the "uncivilized mountaineer is—in fiction at least—the finer article."[46]

Fan mail from Murfree's *Atlantic* editor Thomas Bailey Aldrich, *Clansman* author Thomas Dixon, and future presidents Theodore Roosevelt and Howard Taft, plus friendly correspondence from Joel Chandler Harris, Thomas Nelson Page, Jack London, Owen Wister, and Frederic Remington, suggest the racist, nationalist, and imperialist sensibilities to which Fox's fiction appealed. Remington, for example, wrote about Cuba: "Its hot and a d—— mean place—not worth saving."[47] Other nationally identified readers unearthed through the fan mail shared Fox's belief in the need to uplift potentially redeemable mountain whites for the sake of the nation. Arthur William Barber of New York City linked the Progressive Era's impulse for uplift with nationalist and nativist fervor for preserving in Appalachia what contemporaries considered a reservoir of true Anglo-Saxon Americans. He wrote to Fox in 1910 to underscore the need for patriotic efforts at education in "this splendid, uncultivated nursery of American manhood and womanhood." Barber understood Fox's "message to the American people" as an instruction to "give our care" to the "neglected heritage at our doors." An 1895 recipient of the National Society of the Sons of the American Revolution medal, Barber urged, "If the stock of these mountaineers be the stock of [the *Little Shepherd*] Chad and [*Lonesome Pine*'s character] June, here are undeveloped resources" for "the republic."[48] Nationally identified fans like these found in Fox's fiction an affirmation of the value of mountaineers as "resources" for a supposedly Anglo-Saxon nation.

Nationally identified readers, as steeped as they were in both print culture and *The Trail of the Lonesome Pine*'s nationalism and imperialism, were nonetheless more likely than reviewers to acknowledge the novel's mixed messages about the promises and perils of industrialization. Critics' rosy descriptions cast *Lonesome Pine* as a "happily ever after" narrative, but a letter from one admirer reveals that the gloom of *Lonesome Pine* may have touched more readers than were able to articulate or acknowledge it. Henry Whitehead, assistant editor of the *Port Chester Record*, a newspaper based northeast of New York City, claimed to be "a hardened reader," reviewer, and editor, but confessed to having "an obsession" with *Lonesome Pine*. He told Fox he had "never known anything like the haunting grip of your portrayal of the element of sadness,—in the . . . heart-breaking paradox of little June Tolliver's development . . . , while Hale correspondingly 'degenerates.'" Whitehead asserted that a "weight of onerous sadness . . . settles down like a pall over the reader."[49] Whitehead recognized the despondency at the novel's emotional core that professional critics failed to acknowledge. Perhaps no reviewer wanting to keep his or her job would mention anything like a "pall," as it would have been bad form to dwell on negativity that might discourage potential buyers. In any case, Whitehead's letter illuminates the darker lessons of *Lonesome Pine* and highlights readers' frequent concern for June's growing worldliness.

Locally Oriented Readers

Locally oriented readers in the mountains had little use for expressions of either regret or relief regarding industrialization or June's worldliness. In contrast to nationally oriented and transitional readers, locally oriented readers were not educated into presumptions about the quaintness and inevitable extinction of mountain life. They nonetheless understood themselves as the inspiration for Fox's mountain characters, finding themselves "regionalized," or stereotyped according to geography, by nationally identified readers. Fox's supposedly authentic representations of them as redeemable American whites fell flat.

Because locally oriented readers rarely committed their opinions to print, it is not possible to gauge the full extent of their hostility toward or embrace of Fox's fiction. We will probably never know if John Fox Jr. received any hate mail. Certainly his personal archive, edited by his sisters, contains not a scrap of it.[50] In the absence of evidence from letter writers, I draw the contours of locally oriented readers' opinions from anecdotal reports of local reception.[51]

Observations made by contemporaries indicate that some mountain residents were gravely offended by, and challenged, the way Fox represented them. According to the 1950 recollections of Tom Wallace, a Lexington, Kentucky, newspaper editor, when Fox visited the eastern Kentucky town of Jackson, a group of boys "rejoiced in reading [Fox's] books aloud in the courthouse yard" in order "to ridicule the quaint speech he put in mouths of mountain folk." As the editor observed the local boys' merriment, one turned to him and demanded indignantly, "Do I talk like that?"[52] A western North Carolina man had a similar reaction when *Our Southern Highlanders*' author Horace Kephart showed him one of Fox's stories. The man exclaimed, "Why, that feller *don't know how to spell!*" and resisted Kephart's explanation of the dialect convention. His reply, ironically captured by Kephart in dialect, was: "That tale-teller then is jest makin' fun of the mountain people by misspellin' our talk. You educated folks don't spell your own words the way you say them."[53] In a third instance, Fox's performance before an audience that included the Berea College choir enraged some of the students: "Several male mountain-born members of the choir threatened to thrash [Fox,] suggesting tar and feathers for emphasis. The protesting students . . . promised that . . . Fox would be a most unwelcome guest" in their neighborhoods.[54]

Other locally identified readers reacted with less indignation, though it is possible this was out of politeness toward a guest. Fox reported feeling great relief when during a 1910 trip in the mountains his host in the mountain town of Whitesburg, Kentucky, said "Lots of us over here who have read your books think you are all right." Later on his journey, when he gave his name to "an old lady" sitting on a porch, "she looked at me afresh with mild curiosity. 'I've heerd o' you,' she said simply."[55] On another foray into eastern Kentucky on the heels of *Lonesome Pine*'s publication, Fox stopped for dinner at a cabin. Apparently in shock that his hostess had read his novel and guessed who he was, Fox "almost gasped" when she apologized for the simple dinner she had to offer by saying, "I'm afraid this is the kind of a dinner you describe in your book."[56]

"I'm afraid this is the kind of a dinner you describe in your book." Original caption from John Fox Jr., "On the Trail of the Lonesome Pine," *Scribner's*, October 1910, 427. Illustration by George Wright. Mountain residents' familiarity with Fox's best seller indicates that they were not as isolated and illiterate as Fox made them out to be in his fiction. Fox's surprise at their familiarity with his work suggests he believed his fictional representations of them were accurate.

In addition to suggesting that perhaps some residents took Fox's fiction with a grain of salt, these last two accounts tell us something else. Some readers in mountainous eastern Kentucky may have expressed little interest in joining the "polite society" beyond their locales, but clearly they evinced far more familiarity with that "cultured" world than Fox and his elite readers gave them credit for. When Fox recounts that his hostess "was my character June in 'The Trail of the Lonesome Pine'! She wasn't quite as pretty . . . but she was as keen, alert, and intelligent," he indicates that meeting her affirms for him how true to life he felt his fictional characters were.[57] Yet his hosts' detailed knowledge of Fox's stories reveals just how inaccurate were his depictions of complete illiteracy and isolation in the mountains. Indeed, Fox's admission that mountain residents had read *Lonesome Pine* highlights the fallacy of one of the novel's central tenets—that only with outside intervention might mountaineers be led to literacy and education, culture and cosmopolitanism.

It would seem that Fox was either blithely unaware of such contradictions or astutely savvy in portraying the mountains as he did for his national audience. He wrote in 1908 that his stories almost landed him "into serious trouble . . . for when [they] began to penetrate the mountains, they were naturally and bitterly resented. There is no people but resents being pointed out as different and peculiar."[58] Clearly Fox was at some point forced to recognize that texts published in New York circulated even in places accessible only by horseback—though the success of his fiction depended upon concealing that fact.

Transitional Readers

As we have seen, nationally oriented readers turned to *The Trail of the Lonesome Pine* largely out of antimodernist and nationalist impulses, though some of them registered the grim picture of industrialization that the novel conveys far more than did contemporary reviewers or recent scholars. The best-selling novel served little use for locally oriented readers, although we know from published anecdotes that readers in the mountains of Kentucky and North Carolina were familiar with it. Some locally oriented readers expressed disgust while others did not, but certainly none expressed great admiration for the novel or affection for its mountain characters.

It is only thanks to Fox's fan mail that we can unveil the novel's special power for transitional readers whose allegiances moved back and forth between the local and the national. Of the twenty-eight fans and fan-acquaintances who wrote to Fox, twenty-one can be understood as transitional readers. This high proportion suggests that Fox's fiction appealed most forcefully to those who, metaphorically, had one foot in a place identified as hinterland and the other in the national print culture realm and its assumptions about civilization and refinement.

There was vast class variation among transitional readers who cherished both regional and national ties, from regional elites to members of the professionalizing class. Most viewed the mountain characters in Fox's novel as emblematic of home but not of themselves. Just two identified deeply with June's liminal status between worlds. I also include here one so-called outsider passionate about the beauty of the mountain realm he encountered while employed by a timber firm in North Carolina. For all of them, *The Trail of the Lonesome Pine* articulated—and helped shape—their sense of the opportunities and the emotional costs of mobility and modernization.

One set of transitional readers was comprised of local and regional elites who wielded a great deal of power in their domains. They embraced Fox's fiction as a means of gaining recognition from the highbrow world of translocal elites. Though in some senses they belonged to that translocal world, they felt anxiety about their position in it.[59] Kentucky elites craved inclusion in national highbrow circles, and—like Murfree's fans in earlier years—found in local-color fiction a resource for promoting the prominence of their own realms. They felt Fox's successes brought literary prestige to themselves and their hometowns.

Moreover, regional elites grasped for evidence of their region's significance to the project of nation building. B. A. Logan, a school principal in Shelbyville, Kentucky, shared in the sense that Fox was proving Kentucky's significance to the American national story. He wrote in 1909 to share with Fox the text of his school's Arbor Day ceremony, which praised Fox for capturing "the richness of mountain vintage" and the "folk-lore of a mighty people." The ceremony recognized Fox for "the high place to which he has helped to bring the literature of our people." The grandson of Kentucky abolitionist Cassius Clay also saw Kentucky as a resource for the nation; he thanked Fox for giving "American literature one of its few chapters that are distinctively American" and urged him to "stick to your policy of writing literature that smacks of the native soil."[60] Though Francis Clay wrote from Pittsburgh, his notation following his signature, "Formerly of Whitehall, Kentucky," suggested the ongoing importance of his geographic history to his identity. Despite their seeming pride in the native folk, regional elites allied themselves with assumptions that such folk were in need of uplift. A *Little Shepherd* fan in favor of mountain interventions wrote, "When I think of what you have done for our Appalachian neighbors I wonder that you do not 'blow a bugle' for Berea College," which serves poor mountain students.[61]

Like Clay, regional elites who found themselves living away from their hometowns seemed if anything even more anxious for the literary attention and prestige wrought by Fox's fame. In 1908, Fox received a letter from Mrs. Jackson Hendrick, who reported that she had once given a commencement address in Lexington, Kentucky, in which she predicted that "the Walter Scott of America must come from the foot hills of the Cumberland. . . . I see him in you." A Kentucky native living in New York City, Hendrick encouraged Fox: "Now, having struck the trail, don't desert it. . . . There are many *people* there you have not yet introduced to polite society."[62] Like local elites back home, Hendrick felt gratitude to Fox for explaining "our" folk to the rest of the nation and praised him for raising the profile of "our" literature. For elites living away from home, Fox's novels became a tonic not only for their confrontation with the supposedly numbing effects of civilization but also for their homesickness. Letters from migrants implied readers relied on fiction in order to remain connected to a home identity.[63] The Reverend R. W. Cleland, who wrote from Long Beach, California, had served as Presbyterian pastor in Paris, Kentucky, outside of Lexington. "I am a Kentuckian of the Kentuckians," Cleland pronounced proudly.[64]

Even when they moved in increasingly cultured circles in more cosmopolitan locales, elite transitional readers clung to their former homes—perhaps missing the unique sense of place or missing the special status that had been afforded them in their hometowns. For example, the privileged daughters of General Basil Duke of Louisville, despite their pedigree, had little control over their geographic destinies. Both were wed to men who sought their fortunes away from Kentucky. Fox visited one of Duke's daughters in Hawaii in 1894 on his way to cover the Russo-Japanese War. She and her husband "were glad to see someone from home. . . . They talked of . . . things in America, of Kentucky . . . and when he took his leave of them, they were more than a little homesick and lonesome at his leaving." General Duke's other daughter, Currie Duke Mathews, to whom Fox dedicated *The Little Shepherd*, wrote proudly about the popularity of Fox's first best seller in her social circles in Lenox, Massachusetts: "So many have spoken to me here of the little Shepherd and with much interest and enthusiasm."[65]

At the other end of the scale were readers who saw themselves in Fox's character June. If the passion of letters like Miss Una Crawford's quoted at the opening of the chapter is any indication, Fox's novel spoke most profoundly to transitional readers of modest origins. Indeed, the articulate reactions of Crawford and former Kentuckian William Connelley extensively quoted below may point to reasons for Fox's vast popularity among upwardly mobile white Americans during an era of urbanization, industrialization, and bureaucratization. Fox received formally composed mail from erudite readers, but overall the prose of Fox's correspondents featured far more irregular grammar and spelling than had that of Mary Murfree's. The wider variation of writing skills perhaps illustrates Fox's appeal to readers across the highbrow/lowbrow continuum, including adoring adolescents. It also reminds us of the era's new mechanisms for the production and distribution of books and the tremendous expansion of literacy occurring across the United States.[66] Though most of our evidence comes from transitional readers who had ties to Kentucky or to the mountains, *Lonesome Pine*'s extraordinary popularity suggests that it may have appealed to readers of the middling classes across the country who found themselves with loyalties to their childhood homes but ambitions for status that required their conceptual and often their physical movement away from those homes.[67] Such readers may have found Fox's representation of modernization poignantly in keeping with their own proud cosmopolitanism and their own metaphorical and literal homesickness.

Whereas Murfree's readers of a quarter century earlier traveled for leisure, for Fox's readers upward mobility often required geographic mobility. For middle-class readers from Kentucky, Tennessee, West Virginia, and Virginia, Fox's story of the Pygmalion-like June struck home. Migration may have heightened professionalizing readers' identification with June as they found themselves torn between cosmopolitanism and their native province. The sense of community that migratory readers associated with intensively local places seemed something they might be forced to leave behind to pursue their careers. Unlike the Currie Dukes of the

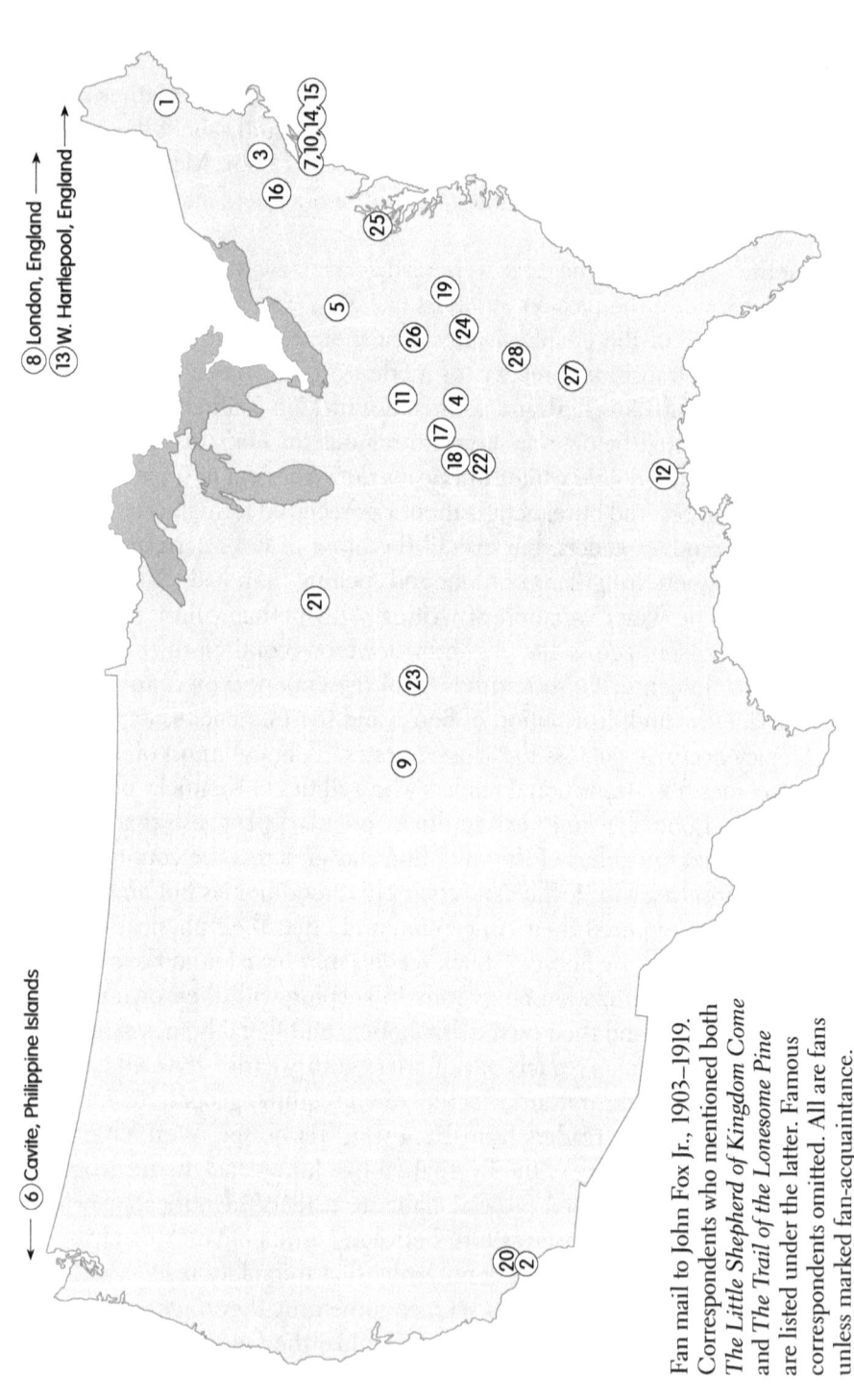

⑧ London, England →
⑬ W. Hartlepool, England →

⑥ Cavite, Philippine Islands

Fan mail to John Fox Jr., 1903–1919. Correspondents who mentioned both *The Little Shepherd of Kingdom Come* and *The Trail of the Lonesome Pine* are listed under the latter. Famous correspondents omitted. All are fans unless marked fan-acquaintance.

***The Little Shepherd of Kingdom Come* (1903)**
1. Charles E. Hamlin, fan-acquaintance, composer and playwright, Bangor, Maine
2. R. W. Cleland, Long Beach, California
3. Currie Duke Wilber, fan-acquaintance, Lenox, Massachusetts
4. Unknown name, Berea, Kentucky
5. Francis W. H. Clay, Pittsburgh, Pennsylvania
6. W. S. Hughes, U.S. naval station, Cavite, Philippine Islands
7. Kent Brooklyn Stiles, Brooklyn, New York
8. F. M. Scoone, London, England
9. George B. Bechem Jr., Mankato, Kansas
10. Arthur William Barber, fan-acquaintance, author, New York, New York
11. Alexander Hill, Cincinnati, Ohio

***The Trail of the Lonesome Pine* (1908)**
12. Rita Parker, Mobile, Alabama
13. Fred Brewster, West Hartlepool, England
14. Louis E. Van Norman, fan-acquaintance, *American Monthly Review of Reviews*, New York, New York
15. Mrs. Jackson Hendrick, New York, New York
16. Henry S. Whitehead, author, Chester, New York
17. B. A. Logan, Shelbyville, Kentucky
18. Ann Blakley, Valley Station, Kentucky
19. S. S. Burch, Roanoke, Virginia
20. Louis Neson, Los Angeles, California
21. Unknown name, banker, Eldora, Iowa
22. W. P. Matheney, Elkton, Kentucky
23. William E. Connelley, author, Topeka, Kansas
24. Una M. Crawford, Abingdon, Virginia
25. James Beauchamp "Champ" Clark, fan-acquaintance, Speaker of the House of Representatives, Washington, DC
26. W. H. Witten, St. Albans, West Virginia

"On Horseback to Kingdom Come" (1910)
27. E. D. Bostick, Atlanta, Georgia
28. S. B. Chapman, fan-acquaintance, Andrews, North Carolina

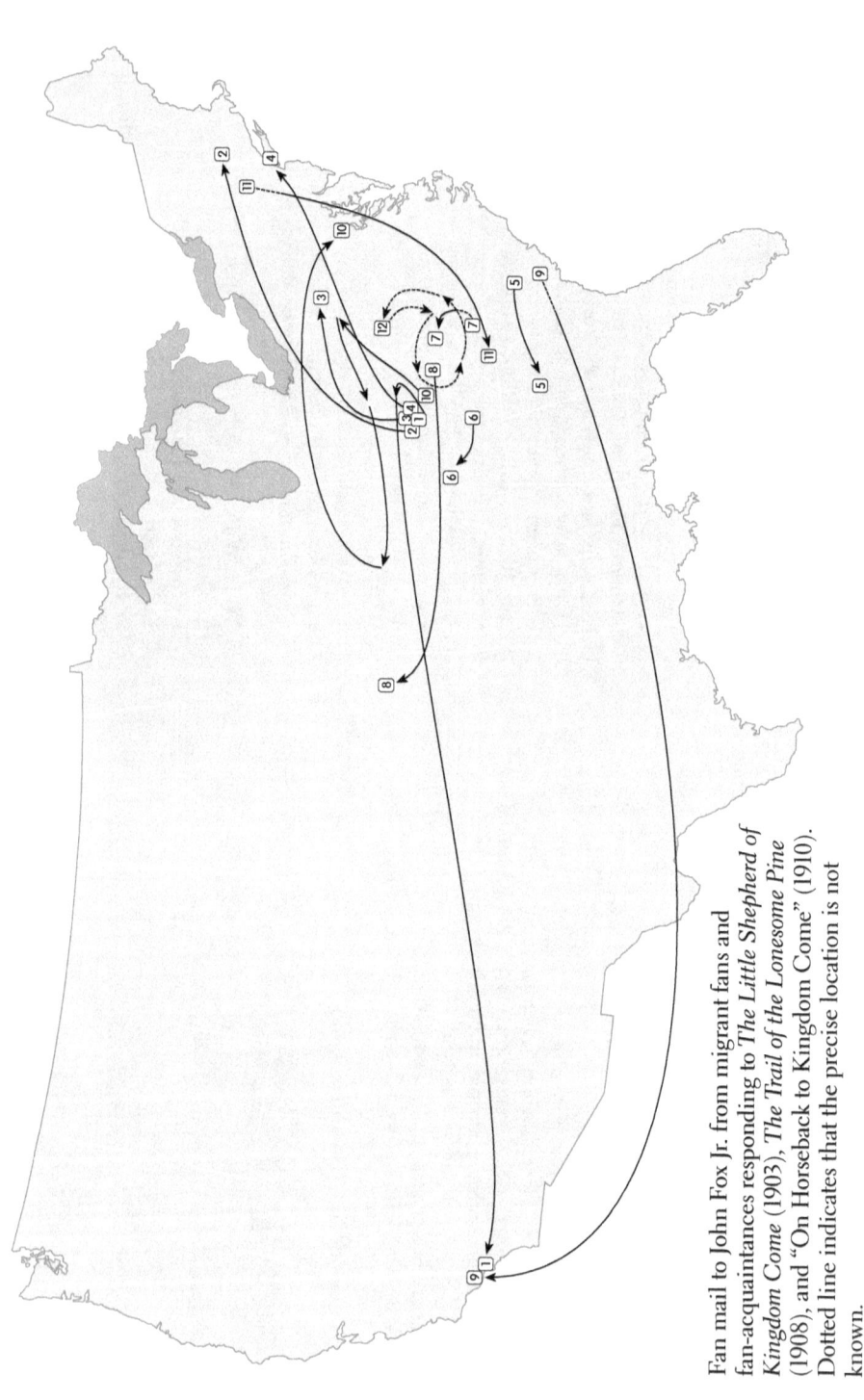

Fan mail to John Fox Jr. from migrant fans and fan-acquaintances responding to *The Little Shepherd of Kingdom Come* (1903), *The Trail of the Lonesome Pine* (1908), and "On Horseback to Kingdom Come" (1910). Dotted line indicates that the precise location is not known.

1. R. W. Cleland, Lebanon, Kentucky → Paris, Kentucky, → Long Beach, California
2. Currie Duke Matthews, fan-acquaintance, Louisville, Kentucky → Lenox, Massachusetts
3. Francis W. H. Clay, Whitehall, Kentucky → Pittsburgh, Pennsylvania
4. Mrs. Jackson Hendrick, Lexington, Kentucky → New York, New York
5. E. D. Bostick, Camden, South Carolina → Atlanta, Georgia
6. W.P. Matheney, Putnam County, Tennessee → Vanderbilt Training School, Elkton, Kentucky
7. Una M. Crawford, North Carolina mountains → Abingdon, Virginia
8. William E. Connelley, Wolf Pen, Kentucky → Topeka, Kansas
9. Louis Nesom, South Carolina → Los Angeles, California
10. James Beauchamp "Champ" Clark, fan-acquaintance, Lawrenceburg, Kentucky → Bethany College, Bethany, West Virginia → Cincinnati Law School, Cincinnati, Ohio → Bowling Green, Missouri → Washington, DC
11. S. B. Chapman, fan-acquaintance, ? → Andrews, North Carolina
12. W. H. Witten, West Virginia → Virginia → Kentucky → Tennessee → North Carolina → St. Albans, West Virginia

world, they lacked the wherewithal to visit home, amplifying their sense of distance.

While elite transitional readers tended to react to highbrow snobbery by distancing themselves from local lifeways even as they insisted upon their utility for the nation, Crawford and Connelley expressed greater affection for mountain characters and expressed less interest in national literary approbation. For these two middling readers who had received elite educations or held professional positions that incorporated them into middle-class and national spaces, *Lonesome Pine* dramatized and sensationalized the angst they felt at being taught to see "home" in new ways. Whereas locally identified readers took offense because they felt Fox characterized them as recalcitrant mountain men, Crawford and Connelley identified with the educable June.

The most touching letter from a transitional reader who embraced *The Trail of the Lonesome Pine* as a powerful and therapeutic transcription of her own life came from the student whose letter opens this chapter. Una Crawford identified wholly with Fox's heroine June and wrote to Fox with poignant gratitude. She explained, "From a mere child I've dreamed big dreams of the world and of what *my* part was to be in it." Crawford found in Fox's novel affirmation that she could "do something to make my Country proud of me. Mountain boys and girls *can*[,] for *all along* they've been doing it." Crawford's anguish over "the pain that comes after being with cultured refined people and then going back to the 'old life'" recalls June's despairing lament, "Why laboriously climb a hill merely to see and yearn for things that you cannot have, if you must go back and live in the hollow again?" (*TLP*, 271). Crawford thanked Fox "for the inspiration and sympathy" June gave her and said she hoped that "some day" she could "help other mountain girls, as you . . . by your *wonderful* books, have helped me and others."[68]

Even more remarkable, given the cross-gender identification it required, was transitional reader William E. Connelley's claim to kinship with the feminine young June. Writing in 1912 from Topeka, Kansas, the fifty-seven-year-old Connelley proudly explained to Fox that he knew something "of the mountaineer" because "I am one of them." Connelley, born at Wolf Pen Branch near Paintsville in eastern Kentucky, thought Fox had "mastered the character of the mountaineers." As a child, Connelley was schooled by Thomas J. Mayo, member of the local elite and father of future millionaire John C. C. Mayo. At age seventeen Connelley

Illustration from *The Trail of the Lonesome Pine*, 1908. Readers identified with the character June, who felt torn between the mountain ways of home and the sophistication into which she was trained.

taught school himself (John Mayo was one of his pupils) before moving west in 1881. By the time he wrote to Fox, he had published several volumes on Kansas history.[69]

Connelley wanted Fox to know that he had roots in Southwest Virginia, "knew the Tollivers," and was cousin to the McCoys (about whom he astutely noted, "There is a fine story in that feud.") "Out in the world," Connelley wrote, "I had many experiences such as you attribute to June. I could give you material for more than one novel." As evidence that "a mountaineer can hold his own against all comers if he will," Connelley boasted that he was elected to public office in Kansas within three years of his arrival. Being of mountain blood and a descendent of Revolutionary War soldiers, Connelley explained, made him "fitted to become a crusader or revolutionist of the most radical sort." Connelley claimed his life was proof that mountain boys could participate in a modern nation. At the same time, his identification with June spoke to his continued sensitivity to patronizing assumptions about his background.[70]

In seeing themselves in June, Crawford and Connelley are unique among Fox's fans. It might perhaps seem natural for readers to identify with the hero or heroine of a novel, but these were the only two to explicitly do so. A wide array of readers fell somewhere in between the status of regional elites striving for national prominence and Crawford and Connelley, who identified wholly with the angst of the transitioning June. Despite attachments to home, most transitional readers favored metropolitan standards in a way that distinguished them from the locally oriented readers who took great offense at Fox's depictions of them.

Fan letters demonstrate that many of Fox's transitional readers shared the nationally oriented imperatives found in print reviews. Readers like Rita Parker participated in their era's antimodernism and fascination with "primitive" people. Parker, a self-described "small and unknown writer" in Mobile, Alabama, wrote to tell Fox, "There is a fascination, almost a spell, in such scenes and lives."[71] The touristic impulse is evident in a letter from a seventeen-year-old boy writing from Brooklyn, who confessed that Fox's first best seller "makes me wish I had been born in Kentucky instead of New Hamp[shire]. I'll always have a longing to visit Bluegrass State, now."[72] The desire to escape to a place imagined as vibrant and replete with opportunities for self-improvement was articulated in a letter to John Fox from a young man on the make in England. Fred Brewster, a nineteen-year-old clerk in a timber merchant and ship owner's office who was reading *Lonesome Pine* serially in *Scribner's,* wrote to ask Fox how the characters "get their livings?" Brewster explained to Fox that he "would not mind 'roughing it,' as they call it, and if I knew that I would be able to make a living out there, I would 'chuck' this and go."[73]

A 1911 fan letter from Iowa is suggestive of *Lonesome Pine*'s appeal to the increasing numbers of middle-class Americans who shared in the national concern over the anesthetization of lively experiences in modern workaday life. This Iowa admirer reported that "in my travels about the state . . . as one of the state bank examiners, I find that your 'Trail of the Lonesome Pine' to be one of the most popular books which bankers read. . . . I saw that novel in the banks, in the homes of bankers and in the reader's hands more than any other volume of fiction." The bank examiner articulated his own enthusiasm for the novel in terms of its success as an American "blood and thunder" thriller when he linked it to Theodore Roosevelt: "No wonder that Roosevelt praises your work, you do what he likes and write what he likes. So do . . . we humble mortals like your stuff."[74] Roosevelt provides a link between Fox's antimodernist appeal and the appeal of authentic white mountaineers for those desirous of promoting white American nationalism and imperialism.

Transitional readers aligned themselves with dominant ideals of refinement and civilization even as they defended and rationalized mountain people by insisting that they could adapt to a superior, modern way of life if given the opportunity. For example, in 1911, Fox received a letter from W. P. Matheney, a co-principal of Vanderbilt Training School, who claimed the eastern Tennessee mountains as his "native home." Matheney praised Fox for understanding the mountaineer "as few men do" and offered to help the author by providing material for a story from moonshiners' point of view, which he felt ought to be "given to the world." He claimed that the mountaineer simply lacked the benefit of "civilization," which thankfully would soon arrive "by the penetrations of railroads, mills and mines into his coves and valleys." People like Matheney assumed, as Fox did, that a mountain way of life must inevitably recede before the advance of modernity. Like other transitional readers, Matheney demonstrated empathy for mountaineers, yet he also evinced condescending wisdom about the foreordination of a process he was helping to enact. He trusted in fiction to help preserve pieces of the "old ideals" for future generations.[75]

As Matheney's offer to help with a story suggests, readers of the day believed that their own stories deserved to be published. Like nationally identified readers, transitional readers were persuaded by translocal discourses that authentic white pioneer "roots" were crucial to the construction of the nation. Cassius Clay's grandson asked Fox to write a historical novel about his grandfather, which he himself would have written "if I had half your skill." He had "full faith" in the story's success, because the "heroic period of our national history is fast passing away" and "such men can never come again, nor can the conditions that produce such men."[76] Louis Nesom wrote from California with the seeds of a story set in South Carolina and Louisiana during the Revolutionary War. He apologized for the presumption of writing the famous author but explained, "I have in mind the plot of a story that I have in vain tried to write up, but I am not clever enough." His promise, "The story is entirely true," suggests that it was perhaps the story of his own family.[77] Whereas readers like Crawford and Connelley felt Fox had *already* written their story, and readers like Matheney, Clay, and Nesom offered to provide material to Fox, other transitional readers begged Fox for help with publishing theirs.

Indeed, the national popularity of regional narratives like Fox's seems to have invited just about everyone to try his or her hand at writing one. Some of these would-be writers were from very high-profile families, like Cassius Clay's grandson. Other supplicants were part of the up-and-coming middle class, such as the two fans who wrote to Fox on their respective companies' stationery. S. S. Burch wrote from Roanoke, Virginia, on Brand Shoe Company letterhead to ask advice regarding publishers for his wife's manuscript about the Civil War in Shenandoah Valley.[78] W. H. Witten, proprietor of the Colonial Hotel in St. Albans, West Virginia, near Charleston, petitioned Fox: "I would like to have you to assist me in writing up a History of my life[.] I was in the Revanew department for eight years [and worked] all through . . . the Cumberland Mountain from one end to the other." Witten promised "a thousand pages of hair raising stuff." "I think a true History of my life would be a money make[r.] Just make it a true History of a bad man." He sought to cash in on the national fervor for moonshiners and feuds in the "rough, wild lands" where "life is lived . . . , not evaded."[79]

Ironically, a reader poised to take advantage of the industrialization of the southern mountains expressed a special urgency about what Richard Brodhead calls the memorial function of Fox's writing.[80] S. B. Chapman credited regionalist authors with capturing in print a way of life that would otherwise, he assumed, soon be lost completely. In 1910, Chapman wrote to Fox in response to his just-published essay, "On Horseback to Kingdom Come," which muses over the changes industrialization had wrought in eastern Kentucky.[81] Chapman told Fox that, in a county adjacent to his, "there is still a 'Chunk' of nature uninjured by the desecrating hand of unhallowed man, where life is still one long happy dream." Chapman wrote on company stationery for Kanawha Hardwood Company, Manufacturers of Lumber (with mills at Andrews and Snowbird, North Carolina), and explained that he found himself "engaged at work for these people" who were complicit in ravaging places he described with great intensity: "the grandeur of the mountains the clearness of the streams and the quaintness of the people." Chapman's sense of Appalachia as antimodernist tonic seems to have been accelerated by his firsthand experience of it; he exhibited the torn allegiances between local and national expressed by transitional readers like Crawford and Connelley. Chapman's heartache for the mountains is evident in his begging Fox, "I therefore conjure you by all the ties that bind an Author to his profession, that you come and visit this wilderness and place upon paper an everlasting impression of its people before it is too late."[82]

Transitional readers like Chapman and Vanderbilt principal Matheney looked to Fox's fiction as a means to document what they feared was a doomed way of life without acknowledging their own agency in bringing about these changes, which they assumed were inevitable, necessary, and even beneficial to mountain residents. *Lonesome Pine* enabled national readers' accommodation *and* protest without prompting any change in the pace or direction of industrial modernization. As late as the 1949 dedication of the John Fox Jr. Memorial Library in Paris, Kentucky, funded by the Daughters of the American Revolution, the state historian spoke of Fox as a portrayer of "a way of life that is vanishing." Her use of the present tense points to the persistence of the notion of an ever-receding good life that somehow continued even though the dire predictions of its cultural demise had not come true half a century after Fox's novels were published.[83]

As the reference to the Fox Memorial Library suggests, his legacy has been protected and promoted by regional elites in Kentucky and Virginia throughout the twentieth century and into the twenty-first. It is precisely the kinds of readers found on the more elite end of the transitional scale who made significant investments in perpetuating Fox's fame. As Sharon Hatfield notes regarding Wise County, Virginia, "residents were proud of the advances that had been made, yet they loved to dip into the well of collective memory, to talk of their colorful and fractious past as imagined in" Fox's work. In time, "folklore surrounding *The Trail of the Lonesome Pine*" became "a linchpin of tourist attraction in Wise County."[84] Transitional readers who felt pride in their hometowns and wanted national recognition may be the precursors of those who hoped national recognition could be translated into tourist dollars via outdoor dramas and the designation of state highways as "The Trail of the Lonesome Pine."

Despite important class differences between local elites and middling professionals, transitional readers from across the spectrum shared a craving for inclusion in highbrow circles, a sense of injury from snobbery directed toward their home places, and often a history of migration in search of better opportunity or class station. This last commonality, which fomented transitional readers' sensation of displacement, is crucial to understanding Fox's sensational popularity. As the professional classes began to consolidate in the period between the 1880s and the First World War, their new status led, among other things, to the rise in planned suburbs and an identity based on consumption, including the consumption of the "right" literature. Beginning with Fox, Appalachian-set fiction enabled upwardly mobile readers who associated their newfound class privilege with placelessness to identify with characters like June and Jack as uprooted sufferers.

Fox as Native Interpreter of Middle-Class Ambition and Homesickness

By the time John Fox was in the process of composing *The Trail of the Lonesome Pine*, he was in a position to capture the genuine pain and the hypocrisy of a "diaspora" whose participants may have seen themselves as victims of geographic and upward mobility. Like other middling and elite Kentuckians, Fox participated in a movement away from the state that, though it paled in comparison to the mass migrations of working-class southerners that would soon follow, had tremendous consequences for the romanticization of Appalachia and the South.[85]

Fox was born in central Kentucky into a struggling middle-class family with a self-important sense of its privileged Virginia ancestry and grand aspirations for self-improvement in terms of both education and class.[86] When Fox matriculated at Harvard on a scholarship from a Fund for Poor Boys, it was the beginning of a complicated relationship with "home" that would persist for the rest of his life. While in Cambridge Fox associated largely with "the Kentucky boys." The expense of travel made his trips back to Kentucky rare and Fox regretted he could not afford a trip home to "cleanse him of the city."[87] After graduating, according to Fox biographer Bill York, "John grasped at his friends from home like a drowning man at straws. He was homesick most of the time now." His brother James forcefully discouraged Fox from moving to help their father run his school in Paris, Kentucky, twenty miles outside Lexington, cautioning him, "Paris means mere existence, stagnation." Indeed, when Fox did manage to get home, he found it to be a place of bleak prospects, few friends, and no satisfying work. Still, long periods away would make Fox forget his disdain and allow him to idealize country over city. In 1887, Fox wrote to a former Harvard classmate, waxing nostalgic and explaining his acceptance of a job at Proctor Coal Company: "I want to be in Kentucky. . . . I don't want to write about anything else than Kentucky."[88]

Transitional readers from more humble origins were not wrong, then, to sense Fox's deep appreciation of being torn between two worlds. True, Fox had not grown up in the mountains and at times seemed to have absolutely no sympathy for the locals. He would have insisted upon the inferiority of Miss Crawford's mountain upbringing compared to his own in central Kentucky. Yet still, Fox felt a painful pull between his "old life" and the "cultured refined people" he met in Cambridge and in his travels as a celebrity author. Fox's complicated nostalgia toward small towns and economic allegiance to the metropolis mirrored the experiences of readers of his day.[89] Though Fox did not ever explicitly address his alienation from home in his fiction, and indeed may have undergone little self-reflection about feeling torn between home and the success that depended upon his relationship to metropolitan places, his fiction nonetheless tapped into a widespread sense of loss and dislocation. This loss was felt by well-to-do as well as middle-class readers, though the Darcys of the world had far more resources with which to maintain ties to home than the Elizabeth Bennets or Mrs. Collinses.

If we were to read the print reviews alone, we might be content to chalk up *Lonesome Pine* as an antimodernist paean to the primitive. There is abundant evidence that it served this role for readers familiar with the region solely through the discourses of national literary periodicals. Nationally identified readers were enchanted with the apparent authenticity of the characters, setting, and author. *Lonesome Pine* served for them not only as a tonic to soothe the pains of modernism's disjunctions but also as a rationale for the exploitation of natural resources in Appalachia, the logic of white nationalism, and the pursuit of racialized imperialism overseas. On the other hand, published anecdotes suggest that locally identified readers, at least in the mountainous portions of Kentucky and North Carolina, had little interest in or need for Fox's fiction or its tonic and rationale for modernity and imperialism.

A reader-centered approach serves as an important corrective to literary historians, Fox admirers, and Appalachian scholars who have focused on close reading and selective biographical data in order to make claims about *Lonesome Pine* as purely "sympathetic" or wholly "exploitive." Through careful analysis of fan mail, combined with print reviews, close reading, and author biography, we uncover the presence of transitional readers and understand how Fox captivated them with his story about the tensions between industrialism and local lifeways. For these upwardly and geographically mobile readers with loyalties to both home and metropolis, Fox's novel offered the tonic of seeming empathy.

As with Mary Murfree, we see that our attempts to fix local-color authors as "insiders" or "outsiders" fail to capture either the complexity of their relationship to their literary material or the nature of their readers' personal attachments and political projects. Fox's perspective on mountain people was shaped by longing for the supposedly simpler life down home, even if it was ultimately dominated by a Bluegrass Kentucky–bred fascination with rural mountain people, his Ivy League eastern seaboard training, and the industrialist lenses—nationalist, racist, and imperialist—available to him when he first encountered mountain residents. Fox was not as intimately knowledgeable about mountaineers as many of his contemporaries assumed. But as an interpreter of class ambition and homesickness among nonmetropolitan readers from "hinterland" places like Kentucky, Fox told a story that rang authentic. Intentionally or not, *The Trail of the Lonesome Pine* conveyed Fox's discomfort over his own displacement from small-town Kentucky. The novel expressed and constructed for readers what it meant to have a "very strong local attachment" while being educated away from home. In doing so, it captured the imaginations of upwardly and geographically mobile readers who felt buffeted by the dislocations they had experienced. Such readers—alternating between honoring ties to the "old life" and commitments to the world of "cultured refined people"—negotiated feelings of loss by accepting a national high middlebrow consensus about the nobility, backwardness, and inevitable extinction of tradition-bound mountaineers.

The Trail of the Lonesome Pine—torn as it is between fashion, education, worldliness, and refinement on the one hand and simplicity, wildness, home, and freedom from social constraints on the other—tells two contradictory stories about "progress." The novel helped readers negotiate their scarcely acknowledged fears about industrialization and offered them a brief respite from modernity through the vicarious experience of a rough-and-ready backcountry, the provisional failure of the hero's industrial project, and a final scene of pastoral middle ground. A century later, as we will see in chapter 5, popular fiction about Appalachia would omit industrialization almost entirely in order to focus on a revised fantasy of the middle landscape—the small, neighborly town with the benefits of modernity, yet wholly protected from the dislocations and politics of the postmodern age.

Chapter 3

Country to City, circa 1949–1954

> High ways, high consumption of products . . . all . . . create employment—but [not] security—nor many of the lasting satisfactions—simple farm living offers—. . . Anyway—please take "Gertie" home—resell rural America to Americans—. . . This was the American Way—It still can be a secure, rich, warm, satisfying American Way.
> —Martha Henes to Harriette Arnow, 1954

> Please write another book sometime, and get poor Gertie Nevils out of Detroit, and back to Kentucky where she belongs.
> —Mrs. Delbert Moore to Harriette Arnow, 1954

Harriette Simpson Arnow (1908–1986) once said that she envisioned her first three novels—*Mountain Path* (1936), *Hunter's Horn* (1949), and *The Dollmaker* (1954)—"as a record of people's lives in terms of roads." "At first," Arnow recounted, there was "only a path, then a community at the end of a gravel road that took men and families away, and finally, where gravel led to a highway, the highway destroyed the hill community." Arnow had been "aware that nothing had been written on the Southern migrants" who left the South in search of work, "of what was actually happening to them and to their culture" in the early twentieth century. Then, during World War II, Arnow reported, "I witnessed the permanent move the men made by bringing their wives and children with them to the cities." Arnow's impression that a "permanent move" had taken place affected her dramatically. "With that last migration," she felt, "hill life was gone forever, and with it, I suppose, a personal dream of community I'd had since childhood and have been trying ever since to recapture in my writing." Arnow believed that out-migration from the rural South had "twisted, and possibly wrecked, my old dream."[1]

The success of Arnow's novels about "lives in terms of roads" suggests that her fervent attachments to a rooted "hill community" were widely shared among American audiences. True, her first novel reached a relatively small audience despite the fact that, at her editor's suggestion, Arnow "put in every kind of action you could: moonshining, murder, romance." (Arnow later conceded, "I wish now I'd left it alone but, my, I was happy when it was published.")[2] Perhaps her second and third novels fared so much better commercially because they eschewed these local-color conventions, as well as *Mountain Path*'s conventional "outsider" narrator, in a way that permitted readers to revel in the idyll of community that Arnow located in hill life.[3] Long and bleak, the novels were unlikely best sellers. Arnow's dense prose and heart-wrenching scenes could not easily be misconstrued as inviting either adventure or carefree escape to a pastoral retreat. (Joyce Carol Oates rightly referred to *The Dollmaker* as a "brutal, beautiful story.") Yet *Hunter's Horn* appeared on the *New York Times* best-seller list for five weeks in 1949, and *The Dollmaker* lingered on that list for thirty-one weeks beginning in May 1954 and appeared on the *Publishers Weekly* list for eighteen weeks.[4] Critics, too, liked Arnow's first novel but raved over *Hunter's Horn* and *The Dollmaker*.[5] Scholars point out that southerners' migrations were not ever "permanent," as Arnow surmised.[6] And the version of community about which Arnow dreamed appears to fall into what Gunnar Almgren has called an "idealized notion" of relationships that are "intimate, familiar, sympathetic, mutually interdependent," and grounded in one geographic place.[7] Nonetheless, fan letters to Arnow indicate that her readers passionately shared her grief over a dream seemingly "twisted" and "wrecked" by the upheavals of the twentieth century.

It seems likely that scholars, too, have been powerfully affected by the dream of hill community treasured by Arnow and her readers. Certainly, of all authors of best-selling Appalachian-set fiction, Harriette Simpson Arnow has achieved far and away the highest regard from Appalachian scholars, who have embraced her as the genuine article. According to Glenda Hobbs, for example, Arnow "avoids the passionate yearning for identification with the rural poor that betrays insecurity and condescension." Hobbs argues that "Arnow alone has rendered Kentucky highlanders fully and fairly, rescuing them from the literary stereotype of the lazy, suspicious, ignorant, manically violent hillbilly." Though the claim that "Arnow alone" captured Kentucky highlanders fairly is recognizable hyperbole, few Appalachian literary scholars would refute Arnow's special status as an empathetic interpreter of Appalachia, rivaled perhaps only by James Still, whose *River of Earth* (1940) is a longtime favorite (but not a best seller).[8]

Scholars are right that Arnow is unique. Unlike Mary Noailles Murfree and John Fox Jr. (see chapters 1 and 2), or Catherine Marshall and James Dickey (see chapter 4), Arnow grew up in the upcountry places she fictionalized. More than other best-selling authors, Arnow wrote in a nuanced and layered way about the pains and pleasures of rural people. More than other Appalachian-set best sellers, Arnow's *Hunter's Horn* and *The Dollmaker* acknowledge modernity's benefits even as they register the pull of antimodernism. And more so than any other author examined in this book, including Fox, Arnow reached readers who felt their lives paralleled those of her characters and who identified with them, rather than patronized or exoticized them. Indeed, alone among the best-selling authors considered here, Arnow singularly failed to attract letter writers motivated by a touristic impulse.

However justified scholars', critics', and readers' claims regarding Arnow's accuracy and sympathy for her hill characters, Arnow's achievement necessarily involved turning a supposedly nonmaterialistic, authentic place into a commodity that promised genuine community. As significant as Arnow's Wayne County upbringing must have been for her literary representations of the hills, her success nonetheless relied in part on readers' celebration of her rooted authenticity based upon selective impressions of her biography.[9] Whereas Arnow has long been admired as a progressive champion of Appalachian people, I point out some of the potentially conservative impulses that her fiction may have drawn upon and reinforced.

My analysis of print reviews and fan mail demonstrates that *Hunter's Horn* and *The Dollmaker* became best sellers in part because they fed the same readerly needs that best-selling regionalism has historically met: the production of authentic place, the construction of imagined community, and the circulation and augmentation of power among readers. Whatever tendencies readers had to mourn white rural worlds lost—white agrarian America lost—Arnow's books anticipated, affirmed, articulated, and amplified.[10] Fans, somewhat unfairly, interpreted Arnow's regional fiction as narrating above all else the possibility of an inward-looking, rooted community of belonging in rural hill country. Readers who regretted, in the words of one New York City fan, "the disappearing closeness to the soil, the uprootedness of human beings" inadvertently endorsed a kind of white nationalism that viewed a pastoral Appalachia as both *home* and as *national homeland*.[11] Furthermore, white readers' insistence upon imagining Americans as, at heart, simple unassuming country folk just trying to get by may have helped them both ignore and justify the country's dominance on the world stage.

Arnow's tales of the joys and tribulations of rural-born southern whites may have become best sellers because they tapped into a ready market of white readers trying to make sense of their experiences and observations during the height of the twentieth century's "Southern Diaspora."[12] The term *Southern Diaspora*, coined by historian James Gregory to refer to the multiracial wave of migration from the U.S. South during "the first three-quarters of the twentieth century," is inclusive of the Great Migration of African Americans as well as the mass migration of whites. By the time Arnow's best sellers were published, nearly 5 million southern-born whites and 3 million southern-born African Americans were living outside the South. Between 1950 and 1960 alone, in the wake of continued unemployment and low wages, 3 million more whites migrated out of the South.[13]

Arnow's timing could not have been better. Not only did she corner the market on the fictional representation of what millions experienced and witnessed, she released her novels just after a sea change in midwesterners' sentiments regarding the Southern Diaspora. The Great Depression had seen tremendous hostility to migrants competing for scarce jobs. But the bombing of Pearl Harbor, and the consequent need for industrial production to fuel World War II, softened anti-hillbilly sentiments.[14] Furthermore, a postwar boom brought higher standards of living, new mass-media technology, and suburbanization that generated as many fears as hopes for a prosperous new society.[15] Millions of white out-migrants mourned what they had lost in the way of communal agrarian life by a turn to industrial and consumer society. Millions more observers worried about what the nation was losing in the rise of new ways of life. Arnow offered a critique that spoke to readers' anxieties about consumerism without motivating them to eschew the rapidly consolidating consumer culture (of which book buying and reading were integral components).

Fan mail written in response to *Hunter's Horn* and *The Dollmaker* provides an important and heretofore unexamined glimpse into the emotional responses of these migrants and their observers. Arnow received letters from four primary groups of readers: metropolitan-identified readers from across the United States but especially from the eastern seaboard; professional midwesterners affected by the arrival of white migrants; elite Kentuckians, urban and rural, eager for the glare of the national literary spotlight, as well as rural elites from elsewhere; and a striking number of white migrants themselves. Indeed, the fact that at least one-fifth of Arnow's extant fan letters are from rural-to-urban migrants further sets her apart from other authors of best-selling Appalachian-set fiction. (For more on my methodological choices and sources, see "Appendix: Methodological Essay.")

Mapping Arnow's fan mail shows us how many of her admiring readers were caught up in the upheaval of the Southern Diaspora and demonstrates the critical role of readers' mobility in securing the popularity of regional texts that figure rural places as static and rooted. Perhaps the fact that *Hunter's Horn* and *The Dollmaker* emerged from Arnow's misgivings about urbanization and mass migration, and spoke to readers in the throes of negotiating their own misgivings, explains why Arnow stood out as a nearly lone figure in the literary scene able to publish best-selling Appalachian-set fiction between John Fox's *Heart of the Hills* (1913) and Catherine Marshall's *Christy* (1967).[16]

In this chapter, I first elaborate upon Arnow's four groups of fans and then give an overview of *Hunter's Horn* and *The Dollmaker* that illuminates what readers had to ignore in the two works in order to embrace them as unequivocal invitations to romantic pastoralism. I explain how, for each set of readers and to varying degrees, Arnow's best sellers met desires for authenticity (including that of the author), identity and belonging, and the circulation of power. I then argue that the novels' ability to meet all three of these needs is best illuminated by the convergence of these themes in perhaps the most common reader response, which I shorthand as: "Get Gertie home." Finally, one naysayer illustrates what we might consider the hypocrisy of a "Get Gertie home" stance for Arnow's readers—and for Arnow herself, for that matter—who thrived financially in the urban (and, in time, suburban) North. The author made tragic for her characters—and nearly unbearable for her readers—a path that Arnow herself chose to follow with great success.

Arnow's Fans

Fan mail preserved by Harriette Arnow elucidates the reasons for her novels' popularity among her most ardent admirers. The majority of letters were written by married women and mothers in their thirties and older. A plurality of fans could be identified as part of the "culture class," composed of teachers, journalists, librarians, authors, and critics. These readers likely earned middle-class incomes but held high middlebrow to highbrow tastes. Fans' self-described life histories indicate that a majority had ties to Kentucky and/or to common destinations for out-migrants. For example, nearly half of all *Hunter's Horn* correspondents had ties to Kentucky, Detroit, and/or Cincinnati. Of all fan letters about *The Dollmaker* (many of which mention *Hunter's Horn* as well), fully one out of every three came from someone who clearly shared a tie to Arnow's childhood (Kentucky) or adult (Michigan) home state, including one out of five with a tie to Kentucky.

Despite these commonalities among many of Arnow's fans, four divergent reader groups emerge if we map the geographic histories that fans recounted in their correspondence and link them to readers' socioeconomic backgrounds and class attitudes. First, Arnow corresponded with metropolitan-identified highbrow readers, largely based on the eastern seaboard, who generally held patronizing views of mountain people. Given the composition of the U.S. reading public historically and the fact that Arnow's novels appeared on the *New York Times* best-seller list, it is likely that Arnow attracted many more highbrow readers than the archives reveal. One postcard is suggestive; a friend serving as a chaperone on a luxury ocean liner to Europe reported that she had seen eight people reading *The Dollmaker* during the journey.[17]

A second major group of Arnow readers consisted of professionals in the Midwest, including librarians, principals, and journalists, who were trying to make sense of the large influx of white migrants from the rural South. Their attitudes ranged from condescension to compassion, with all the class privilege that such sentiments imply. A third group of fans included rural and urban elite Kentuckians and rural elites from other states. Though they expressed admiration for Arnow's Kentuckians, these readers kept her characters at arm's length with a hefty dose of pity and condescension. These readers found in Arnow's fiction a resource for regional or rural pride and self-aggrandizement; they were far more invested in the status that they felt Arnow's best sellers bestowed upon them than they were in the difficulties confronted by the people Arnow fictionalized.

Finally, and most notably, Arnow heard from a remarkable number of migrants who had moved from the rural South to work in the Midwest. Twenty percent or more of Arnow's admiring correspondents were rural-to-urban migrants. *Hunter's Horn* and especially *The Dollmaker* are the Appalachian-set best sellers most likely to have been read by readers whose experiences initially paralleled those of the fictional characters. George Latham, for example, "was brought up in [the] shadow [of the mountains] in Virginia. . . . Now, far from all that, I am a chemist for DuPont—still with a heart for the hills and its people."[18] About half of these migrants were in some ways indistinguishable from the first three groups in terms of their patronizing attitudes toward Arnow's characters and their enthusiasm for uplift. These condescending migrant readers expressed affection for working-class hill people but saw themselves as different from them and reported that Arnow had gotten those quaint people just right.

The other half of the migrant fan mail correspondents, however, represent a unique group among readers of regional fiction. They were nonelite, rural-identified readers, mostly out-migrants from the South. These readers' geographic and class identities aligned wholly and unabashedly with Arnow's characters. These empathizing migrant readers included Mrs. Delbert Moore, who wrote from Ohio, "I am a Kentuckian, and my wish is that I get back there sometime. I mean to stay. I told my husband if I should die up here, I want to at least be buried in Kentucky."[19] R. L. Cassell claimed identification with the novels' characters by his statement that "Cassie was doomed and the whole family was doomed . . . I know; I was a 'hillbilly' who came north." It is difficult to determine from fan mail the extent to which there were actual class differences between the migrants who read Arnow's novels as being about "those people" versus about "us." The empathetic Cassell, for example, included among his hillbilly credentials the fact that he still ate squirrel, and yet he had attended Eastern Kentucky State Normal School, had an occupation back home that involved an "office in Somerset," Kentucky, and, when he inquired as to whether he and Arnow shared any acquaintances, mentioned an optometrist, two judges, a principal, and a "doctor's wife."[20] Regardless of the extent of class differences between condescending and empathizing migrants, clearly their social postures were strikingly dissimilar. The wide range of responses to Arnow's novels suggests there was no typical response to the experience of migration, nor to the socioeconomic transformations that frequently accompanied the move.[21]

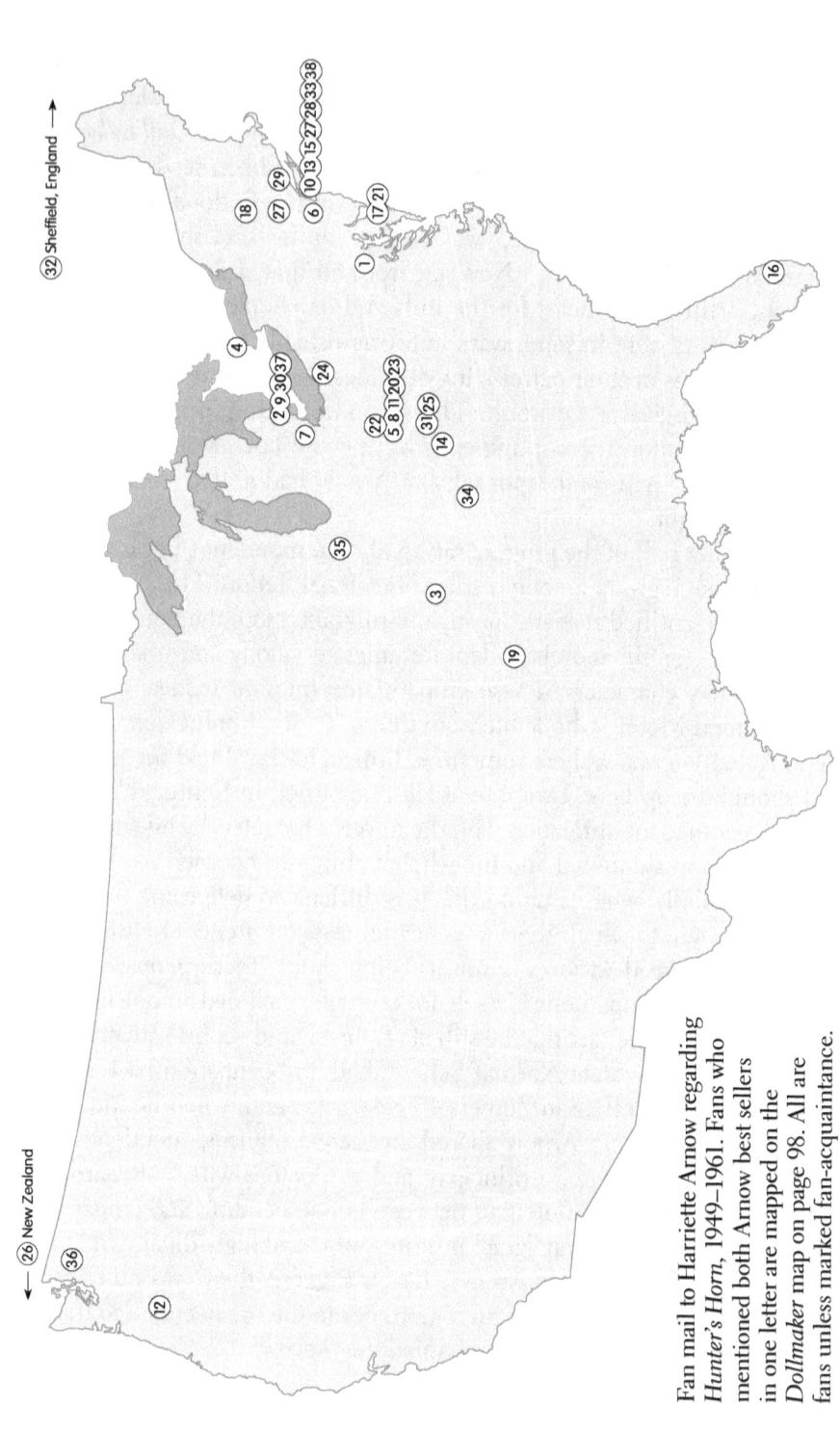

Fan mail to Harriette Arnow regarding *Hunter's Horn*, 1949–1961. Fans who mentioned both Arnow best sellers in one letter are mapped on the *Dollmaker* map on page 98. All are fans unless marked fan-acquaintance.

1. Frank Baldwin Darcy Jr., Rockville, Maryland
2. Dorothy J. Howes, Richmond, Michigan
3. William J. Hutchins, fan-acquaintance, former president of Berea College, St. Louis, Missouri
4. Phyllis McKishnie Kribs, Toronto, Ontario, Canada
5. E. J. Weeks, fan-acquaintance, Cincinnati, Ohio
6. Margaret McAndrew, Morristown, New Jersey
7. Mrs. Everdean Johnson, Trenton, Michigan
8. Alma B. Weber, fan-acquaintance, Blue Ash, Ohio
9. Mrs. W. C. Bishop, Detroit, Michigan
10. Margaret W. Vanderhook, New York, New York
11. Helen C. Little, fan-acquaintance; Cincinnati, Ohio [letter addressed to Arnow's sister]
12. Mrs. Harold V. Koontz, Portland, Oregon
13. J. Donald Adams, fan-acquaintance, *New York Times Book Review*, New York, New York
14. John Wilson Townsend, author, Lexington, Kentucky
15. Mrs. Hans Zinsser, New York, New York
16. Mrs. Clarence Parshall Bynes, Ft Lauderdale, Florida
17. Jennie Broujos, Wilmington, Delaware
18. L. Ramsay, Burnt Hills, New York
19. Everett Webber, author, Eureka Springs, Arkansas
20. Mildred Schulze, Cincinnati, Ohio
21. George H. Latham, Wilmington, Delaware
22. Leah T. Jones, Lebanon, Ohio
23. Mary Jane White, Cincinnati, Ohio
24. Frank B. Hines, Cleveland, Ohio
25. Elisabeth Ewen, fan-acquaintance, Morehead, Kentucky
26. J. McSkimming, New Zealand
27. Helen Wolfert, Lake Hill, New York, and New York, New York
28. Ernest Fred Manfred, New York, New York
29. Ruth E. Wilton, Bridgeport, Connecticut
30. Unknown name, fan-acquaintance, Detroit, Michigan
31. Lena Wells Voiers, Vanceburg, Kentucky
32. W. W. Duck, Sheffield, England
33. Helen K. Taylor, fan-acquaintance, New York, New York
34. Dolly (Reed) Gilmore Barmann, author, Trammel Fork Creek area, western Kentucky
35. Mrs. Clyde Burnette, Peoria, Illinois
36. Mrs. Charles S. Stowell, Seattle, Washington
37. Elmer C. Adams, fan-acquaintance, Detroit, Michigan
38. E. J. Joell, New York, New York

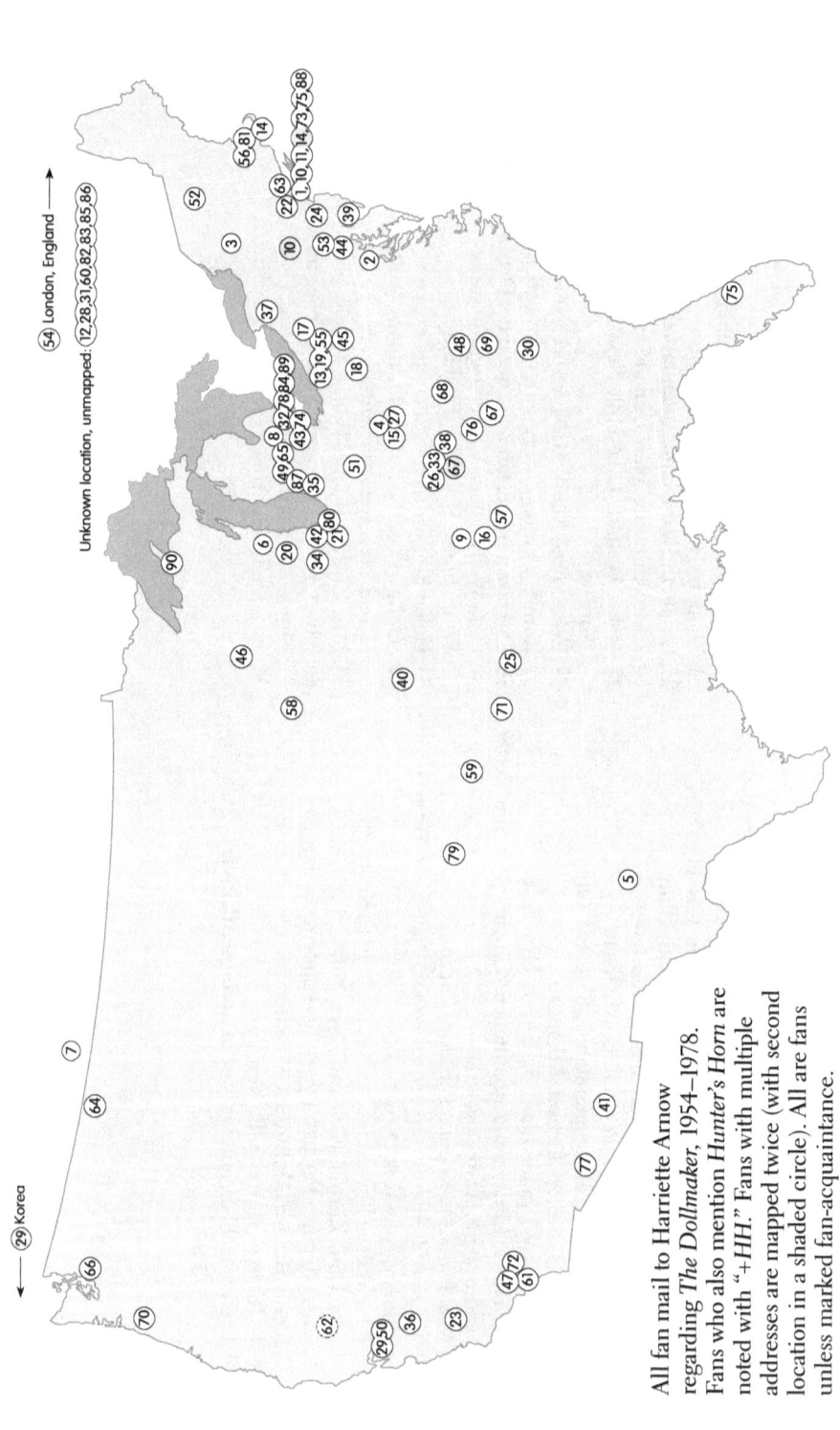

1. Helen Wolfert +*HH*, New York, New York [2nd letter; also on page 96]. 2. Claudine Lewis +*HH*, Washington, DC. 3. Elizabeth Whiting +*HH*, Dolgeville, New York. 4. Alma Weber, fan-acquaintance, +*HH*, Blue Ash, Ohio [2nd letter; also on page 96]. 5. Katherine Green +*HH*, Midland, Texas. 6. Hattie Abner +*HH*, Taycheedah, Wisconsin. 7. Marian L. Williams +*HH*, Calgary, Alberta, Canada. 8. Thelma A. Jarvis, fan-acquaintance, +*HH*, Lapeer, Michigan. 9. Fowler Curtis +*HH*, Rosiclare, Illinois. 10. Katherine Wolbarst, New York, New York, and Lake Como, Pennsylvania. 11. Therese Oppenheimer, New York, New York. 12. Marian Trainer +*HH*, unknown location. 13. Hazel E. Osterhouse +*HH*, Fairview Park, Ohio. 14. Doris Nash Wortman, fan-acquaintance, +*HH*, Vineyard Haven, Massachusetts, and New York, New York. 15. Rana Vaught +*HH*, Cincinnati, Ohio. 16. Winnie D. Moorman, Fulton, Kentucky. 17. Marian Potter, Warren, Pennsylvania. 18. R. L. Cassell +*HH*, Cadiz, Ohio. 19. Martha Henes, Wellington, Ohio. 20. Tom Watson, Edgerton, Wisconsin. 21. Sidney Ernestine Warfel +*HH*, Plainfield, Illinois. 22. Donald MacDonald, Newburgh, New York. 23. Ozro F. Grant, author, Tulare, California. 24. Blanche Balfour, Sewaren, New Jersey. 25. Marianna Hubbell, Fayetteville, Arkansas. 26. Mariam S. Houchens +*HH*, Louisville, Kentucky. 27. Mrs. Delbert Moore, Blanchester, Ohio. 28. Lili P. Segal, unknown location. 29. Unknown, San Francisco, California, and Korea. 30. Unknown, Duncan, South Carolina. 31. Unknown +*HH*, unknown location. 32. Alice Mary Hynes, Grosse Pointe, Michigan. 33. Dorothy K. Wilke, Louisville, Kentucky. 34. Ina Bushnell Johnson +*HH*, Polo, Illinois. 35. Antoinette Floritz +*HH*, Three Rivers, Michigan. 36. Erwin Jost, Visalia, California. 37. Elizabeth Van Lise, Cowlesville, New York. 38. Ferne Denney, fan-acquaintance, Berea, Kentucky. 39. Margaret Spado, fan-acquaintance, Penns Grove, New Jersey. 40. Minnie Holt +*HH*, Lee's Summit, Missouri. 41. Ruth Nye, fan-acquaintance, Tucson, Arizona. 42. Gertrude Snodgrass, Elgin, Illinois. 43. Mary Grindstaff, fan-acquaintance, Ann Arbor, Michigan. 44. Grace Evans, Coatesville, Pennsylvania. 45. Margaret Ogrey, Gibsonia, Pennsylvania. 46. Kathryn S. Ring, Minneapolis, Minnesota. 47. Alice Hodel +*HH*, Glendale, California. 48. R. A. Roberts, Galax, Virginia. 49. William Caverly, Howell, Michigan. 50. Frances Noe Prince, San Francisco, California. 51. Glenna H. Stiffler, Dunkirk, Indiana. 52. Esther Grover, Vergennes, Vermont. 53. Elizabeth Nuff, Telford, Pennsylvania. 54. D. Newland +*HH*, London, England. 55. Jessie M. Reaves +*HH*, Oberlin, Ohio. 56. Alice Lloyd +*HH*, Dedham, Massachusetts. 57. Dorothy Brooks, Camden, Tennessee. 58. Edith Graf Pylman, Sheldon, Iowa. 59. Vivian Spangler, Mayfield, Kansas. 60. Thorn N. Gale, unknown location. 61. Helen G. Tompkins, Beverly Hills, California. 62. Edna Candy, unknown location (California?). 63. Unknown, Noroton Heights, Connecticut. 64. Alice Banister +*HH*, Thompson Falls, Montana. 65. Donna Johnson, Williamston, Michigan. 66. Georgia Sealoff, Seattle, Washington. 67. Mrs. O. W. Johnson +*HH*, from Tennessee, stationed in Fort Knox, Kentucky. 68. Unknown +*HH*, Zebulon-on-Coon, Kentucky. 69. Martha H. Morehead, Hudson, North Carolina. 70. Mary Frances Parrott +*HH*, Portland, Oregon. 71. Reba Blankenship, Tulsa, Oklahoma. 72. Audrey Arellenes +*HH*, Alhambra, California. 73. Irving and Freda Weissman, New York, New York. 74. Irene Watt, Ypsilanti, Michigan. 75. Micki Davis, Cocoa Beach, Florida. 76. Lamoin Dalton, Monticello, Kentucky. 77. Hilah Simmons +*HH*, Ajo, Arizona. 78. Mary Reitenour, Farmington, Michigan. 79. Mary Ellen Clark, Lakin, Kansas. 80. Adele A. Graber, Chicago, Illinois. 81. Winifred Carr Jensen, Cambridge, Massachusetts. 82. Susanna Wise, unknown location. 83. Joyce Spragins, unknown location. 84. Florence Ogden Monaghan, Birmingham, Michigan. 85. Debbi Walter, unknown location. 86. Bella R. Rosner, unknown location. 87. Helen Neff, Kalamazoo, Michigan. 88. Ruth Martin +*HH*, Spring Valley, New York. 89. Helen McColgin, Detroit, Michigan. 90. Phyllis Matlok, Houghton, Michigan.

Qualified Pastoralism in *Hunter's Horn* and *The Dollmaker*

Hunter's Horn and *The Dollmaker* both tell complicated stories about the joys and sorrows of rural life. Subsistence farming is in Harriette Arnow's fiction clearly a hard, sometimes vicious, life. The novels frequently insist on uncomfortable and anguishing outcomes for their characters. *Hunter's Horn*, for instance, evinces a complex pastoralism, one that celebrates living off the land and yet concedes its hardships, especially for girls, as it recounts the story of subsistence farmers Nunn and Milly Ballew. Nunn, having escaped from working in the coal mines, is living out his dream of farming his ancestors' land. He expends tremendous resources that his family can hardly afford in order to raise foxhounds and pursue his obsession of capturing King Devil, a livestock-hunting fox. In a letter defending Nunn, Arnow emphasized to her editor the positive outcomes of roads and government agencies. "King Devil," Arnow wrote, "sent [Nunn] to the AAA office and he learned to grow grass and clover." Thanks to his obsession with King Devil, Nunn bought fencing and "started to become a real farmer."[22] The narrator observes that once the Works Progress Administration had "built a gravel road from the highway to Tuckerville," the farmers who lived there "were seeing good times."[23] *Hunter's Horn* acknowledges the desirability of the nonagrarian in other ways as well. Nunn's daughter Suse, an endearing character whom Arnow admitted was her favorite, dreams rapturously of trains, planes, "Town," and "the bright, ever calling North" (*HH*, 255).[24] The novel questions Suse's captivation with modernity when a neighbor returns from Cincinnati in possession of a fabulous radio but poor health and starving children (*HH*, 242), yet reaffirms it when Suse becomes trapped in a loveless, toilsome marriage.[25] *Hunter's Horn* refuses to romanticize the Ballews' desperate need for food and clothing and Suse's lack of opportunity, educational or otherwise.

Like *Hunter's Horn*, *The Dollmaker* relates a complicated story about agrarian life. Told through the eyes of the homesick Gertie Nevels, the novel exudes a sustained nostalgia for rural community, yet nonetheless recognizes the attractions of city life. Gertie, forced to follow her husband, Clovis, to Detroit with their five children during World War II, despises tenement living. The husky, capable protagonist is well suited to farm life, and dreams of buying the farm once owned by her ancestors. Clovis, on the other hand, loves machines. A skillful mechanic, he is delighted to find work in the industrial city, where wartime production demands have drawn masses of blue-collar Irish, Polish, and southern whites into fac-

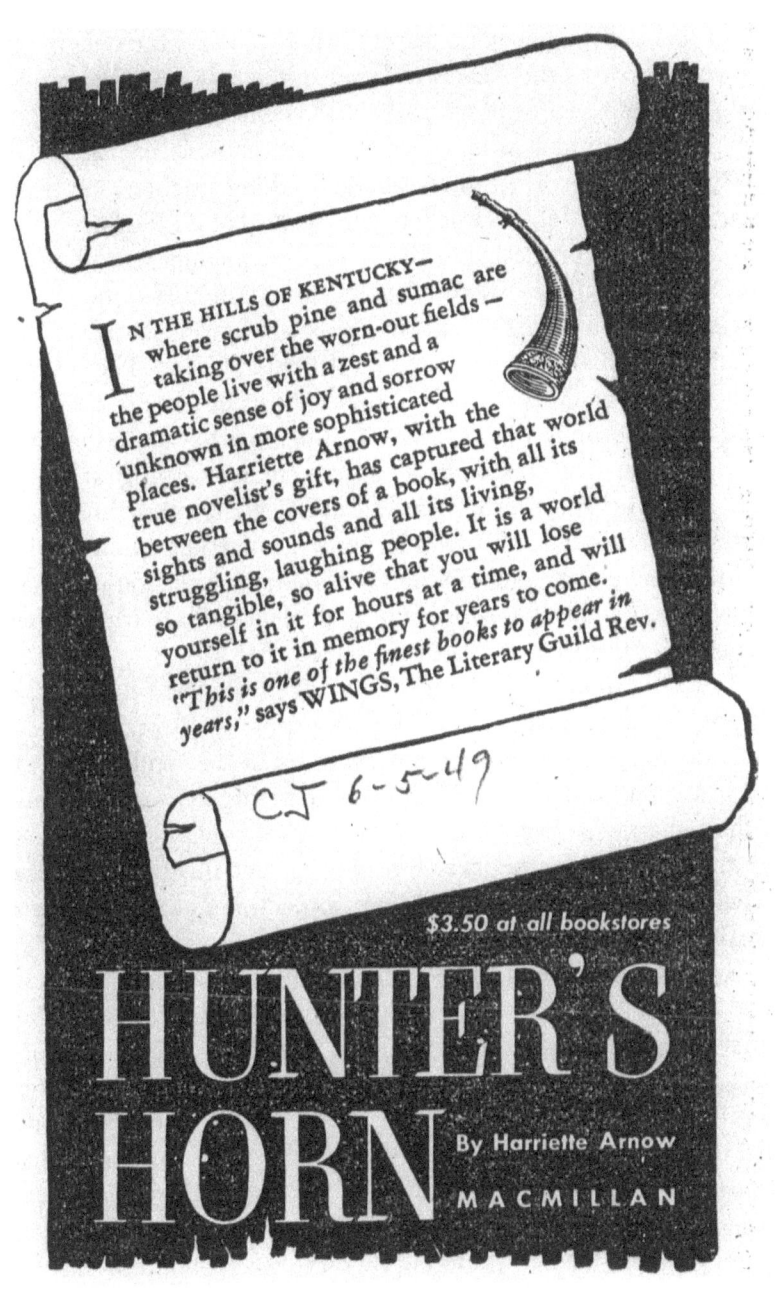

Advertisement for *Hunter's Horn*, 1949. Fans' interpretations of hill country were conventional and romantic. Courtesy of Special Collections and Digital Programs, University of Kentucky Libraries, Lexington.

tory jobs and crowded alley housing.[26] Arnow portrays the delight taken by Clovis and two of the Nevels children in the new world of consumer goods. Yet Arnow even more sympathetically conveys Gertie's desperation in her small apartment, where Gertie's claustrophobia intensifies when Clovis's splendid Christmas gifts—a large washing machine and hulking Icy Heart refrigerator in her kitchen—physically cut off the large woman from her children in the living room. Gertie's attempt to embrace the maxim that her children should "adjust" to city life drives her still further from her farm-loving elder son, Reuben, who runs away, and from her gentle imaginative wood sprite of a daughter, Cassie. The horrors of Detroit reach new levels when Cassie dies after her legs are cut off by a passing train. Gertie is unable to save Cassie in part because the menacing noise from an airplane overhead drowns out her warning shouts. Still, the neighborliness that Gertie experiences and offers in wartime housing rivals the "community" she left in Kentucky, where her mother's conservative fundamentalist views limited Gertie's free association with neighbors like John Ballew, the owner of the Old Tipton Place who refuses to contravene Gertie's mother by selling it to Gertie.

Reviews of *Hunter's Horn* and *The Dollmaker* missed the intricacies of the novels' lessons about rural life and urbanity. Reviewers did not highlight complexity but conventionality, even as they endeavored to set Arnow off from local-color writers by emphasizing her novels' grimness over their charm.[27] They insisted approvingly that *Hunter's Horn* avoids "quaintness piled on for the sake of mere color" and that the novel instead acknowledges the "agony of undernourishment, ignorance, bigotry and disease" and the "run-down farm overrun with scrub growth."[28] Yet even when reviews leaned toward a gothic rather than a pastoral interpretation of the two best sellers, they repeatedly affirmed a litany of conventional mountain associations for their readers: "hunting companions, moonshiners, midwives, school teachers," "molasses making," "Bible-quoting, hard-drinking" "mountain men," and "canned stuff . . . the work on the farm . . . parties and funerals." They emphasized the character Suse, who had no shoes and "a bastard child under her ragged dress."[29] As further indication of their folk authenticity, the Kentucky hill people appear in reviews to live outside of time and beyond the reach of industrial activity. Very few reviews acknowledged rural industrialization, although *Hunter's Horn*'s Nunn had worked in the coal mines and *The Dollmaker*'s Clovis had earned a living with his truck, hauling coal and other goods.[30]

Advertisement for *The Dollmaker*, 1954. The readers who catapulted Arnow's books to the national best-seller lists assumed her hill characters belonged to a simple, pastoral, and quaint world apart from their own. Courtesy of Special Collections and Digital Programs, University of Kentucky Libraries, Lexington.

Unqualified Pastoralism and Fans' Romance with Authenticity

While reviewers' interpretations were conventional and bleak in their emphasis on ignorant moonshining mountain men on run-down farms, fans' interpretations of the hill country were conventional and romantic. Fan mail demonstrates the extent to which many of Arnow's readers—despite the novels' warts-and-all depictions of rural life—almost exclusively felt the pull of romantic pastoralism and the desire for authenticity. Like critics, fans perceived the hill country as isolated and timeless. Unlike critics, few fans emphasized squalor, grimness, poverty, or pathetic tragedy. Despite Arnow's difficult prose and often painful, sorrowful fiction, most of her fans eschewed references to rural poverty and instead expressed great delight at the opportunity to either revisit or glimpse what they perceived to be a wholly different way of life lost to them.[31]

Indeed, readers from every set of Arnow's fans—elites who knew about Kentucky only through print culture; professional midwesterners who witnessed southern out-migration with a mix of pity and concern; and Kentuckians and out-migrants—embraced a romance of authenticity that constructed rural Appalachia as a place distant from modern society. The readers who catapulted Arnow's books to the national best-seller lists assumed her hill characters belonged to a simple, pastoral, and quaint world apart from their own—even if they themselves had once lived in a rural area. They yearned for the beauty and authenticity of pioneerlike conditions outside mass society that they found in Arnow's fiction. Midwesterner Hattie Abner praised the "old log house . . . its good clean home life, . . . and the live and let live," while for Mrs. Reaves in Ohio *Hunter's Horn* captured "a former time."[32] Just one couple took gentle exception to Arnow's rustic characterization of her home by observing, "We both feel that you have given a wonderful picture of this part of the county but for a period fifteen years or so before you wrote about. . . . There were many radios, newspapers & magazines all over, and no long full skirted dresses, except in the very old women."[33] Arnow's readers believed that separation from modernity was key to establishing not only an authentic, immediate, and rewarding way of life but also to establishing what Arnow called the "dream of community." In an important departure from fans of other Appalachian-set best sellers, many Arnow readers resisted exoticizing the people they deemed able to achieve such community. But fans nevertheless romanticized the conditions they believed contributed to the viability of community.

As part of their faith in the authenticity of Arnow's depiction of Kentucky hill country, correspondents affirmed (as did critics) the supposed documentary accuracy of *Hunter's Horn* and *The Dollmaker*. Arnow's level of detail in her descriptions, like that in literary realism dating to the 1870s, was so overwhelming that Helen Wolfert told Arnow that her "hunger . . . for reality was so satisfied in your book that for once I feel that my ignorance of a place and a people unknown to me has been completely annihilated." Readers expressed an intense interest in the characters, who seemed to them to be real people living in the world. Leah Jones reported that she did not have a "county map of Kentucky but [felt] sure the Ballews must live below Somerset to the East." When Jones traveled from her home in Ohio to Florida on route 27 through Kentucky, she heard "hounds and voices from below" and "now I know Nunn was out on Cows Horn Road . . . with Millie Crooksey!"[34]

For Arnow's readers, regardless of background, their sense of Arnow as an authentic representative of the people in her novels was absolutely key to their appreciation of her fiction as an authentic depiction of an authentic way of life unmediated by modernity. As far as they knew, Arnow was a Kentuckian and a migrant, writing about Kentuckians and migrants.

Harriette Simpson Arnow did indeed live for most of her formative years in the area she wrote about, unlike other authors of best-selling Appalachian-set fiction. She grew up in Wayne County in southern Kentucky, on the westernmost fringe of the Appalachian region and not far from the Tennessee border town of Jellico, where John Fox Jr. first tried his hand at representations of mountaineers. After attending Berea College and graduating in 1931 from the University of Louisville, she taught in a one-room school near Wayne County and for a brief time in Louisville, Kentucky's largest city. In 1934, at the age of twenty-six, Harriette Simpson moved to Cincinnati, Ohio (although at times she lived across the Ohio River in Covington, Kentucky), to devote herself to writing. In 1936 she published her first novel, *Mountain Path*. In 1939 she married former Chicagoan Harold Arnow, and the couple moved to the Cumberland National Forest (now Daniel Boone National Forest) south of Burnside, Kentucky, in Pulaski County (one county northeast of her birthplace) to become subsistence farmers and writers. The Arnows read the *New York Times* and wrote when they weren't raising chickens, tending a vegetable garden, canning, or, in Harriette's case, teaching school to bolster their depleted savings. In 1945, the Arnows moved after Harold found work as a reporter for the *Detroit Times*. Though Arnow was working on her second novel in her head during her years in Kentucky, it was not until she lived in Detroit that she was able to write *Hunter's Horn* (published in 1949). In 1950 the Arnows bought a forty-acre farm outside nearby Ann Arbor, where Arnow continued to write; *The Dollmaker* was published in 1954. Her later works of fiction and history achieved little popularity or acclaim among her contemporaries. Arnow attributed two awards she received in 1983 to anticipation of the film version of *The Dollmaker* (1984) starring Jane Fonda, who won an Emmy for the role.[35]

Published reviews of *Hunter's Horn* and *The Dollmaker* participated in authenticating and credentialing Arnow's authority to write through their selective interpretation of her biography. Macmillan's press releases for *Hunter's Horn* emphasized that the Arnows thought of their "farm in the Cumberland National Forest" as "home," but they also acknowledged that Arnow "was educated at Berea College and the University of Louisville," lived in Detroit, and worked as a waitress, cashier, clerk, and a writer with the Federal Writers Project.[36] Reviewers, however, chose to highlight only Arnow's closeness to her subjects. Of nine reviews of *Hunter's Horn* in papers based in New York, Los Angeles, Chicago, and Louisville, only one failed to assert that Arnow had, in the words of one, "recorded" Kentucky hill country "with authentic skill." Others attributed to Arnow "earthy reporting," a "familiarity" with her setting, and a gift for "close observation of the ways of *her* mountain people" [emphasis added]. Arnow at one point in her life combined farming and writing, explained one. Another stretched the truth slightly to describe her as "having lived all her life among the people about whom she writes."[37] For the most part, reviews of *The Dollmaker*, which is set partly in Kentucky but largely in working-class urban Detroit, were less insistent upon her rural Kentucky upbringing; they were more liable to authenticate her credentials by mentioning her time working as a cashier and waitress in Cincinnati.[38] But even when praising the vividness of *The Dollmaker*'s Detroit, reviewers noted that the author "draws from the roots of her native Kentucky" and claimed that Arnow "knows and loves the hillbillies of the remote Kentucky backwoods."[39]

As a child, Arnow thought of herself as living in a place distinct from that she would in time fictionalize. From above the town of Burnside,

Harriette Simpson Arnow, circa 1954. Published reviews of *Hunter's Horn* and *The Dollmaker* participated in authenticating and credentialing Arnow's authority through their selective interpretation of her biography. Courtesy of Special Collections and Digital Programs, University of Kentucky Libraries, Lexington.

she saw "the other world" of "hills to the east" and "wondered on the life there." Her own upbringing was "shaped by town life . . . within hearing of train and steamboat whistles" and "most of the time" she "looked toward" cities like Nashville and Cincinnati, "of which they spoke." But "the hills," Arnow mused, "were a first love."[40]

Other elements of Arnow's life that allowed her to write for a national audience but that did not quite fit the image of her as an authentic representative of Appalachia received little attention (for example, her college education and teaching experience in Kentucky's largest city). Furthermore, reviewers did not remark upon the wry names the Arnows gave their homes (Submarginal Manor in Kentucky and Bedlam in Ann Arbor), which suggest a sense of ironic distance likely not shared by many of their neighbors. Reviewers and scholars have rarely explored the effects of Arnow's migrations within Kentucky: her family's move from Bronston to Burnside when she was six for her father's job in a veneer factory, the move to Torrent when Arnow was twelve for her father's job in the oil fields, Arnow's time at boarding school thirty miles from Torrent in the following fall, and the family's move back to Burnside after the oil was exhausted.[41] Whatever familiarity Arnow had with rural Kentucky, she clearly did not lead a rooted agrarian life. In fact, mobility may have been key to Arnow's tendency to mythologize her "dream of community," just as readers' mobility aroused their enchantment with the hill country that they deemed static and pure.

Whatever role reviews played in convincing fans of Arnow's authority to write about hill characters, readers assumed as a matter of convention that regional fiction was written by a regional representative. Assumptions of correspondence between reality and regional fiction were so widely held that Arnow's mother despaired at the publication of Arnow's first novel: "Everybody will think you fell in love with a moonshiner down there"—just as Arnow's main character does.[42] Arnow's mother's concern was not misplaced. Like fans who assumed Mary Murfree was one of the roughriding mountaineers about whom she wrote, fans of Arnow wanted to interpret her work as autobiographical. One fan admitted in a letter, "I realize I think of you in many ways as [your protagonist] Gertie but an articulate Gertie." Claudine Lewis wrote, "We have enough people like you in the Mississippi Valley part of Kentucky for me to understand *you* thoroughly."[43]

Arnow was alternately bemused and perturbed by readers' tendency to mistake her for her characters. She reported that when her editor, the author and former Communist Granville Hicks, came to Detroit to meet her, "He just stood at the screen door gaping" and then said, "'Oh, I thought you would be a big woman.' He apparently thought I was Gertie." Arnow's feelings were hurt when someone "wrote to tell me, 'if I had a husband like you've got, wasting all that time hunting, I would take a skillet to his head.' And here's poor old Harold who never owned a foxhound in his life." Arnow complained, "The only trouble is some readers, judging from their letters, they never give me credit for imagination. They think all these are real people, and that I was Gertie."[44] Arnow's frustration, though surely genuine, is somewhat naive, if not disingenuous. Readers' assumptions about the documentary and autobiographical nature of regional writing historically ensured stronger approbation and better sales—though they also, as Arnow noticed, limited readers' appreciations of authors' artistry.[45]

Readers in Arnow's day sought authenticity and vibrancy in the urban slum as well as the pastoral farm. Arnow offered a glimpse into a teeming white ethnic tenement world—an immigrant, Catholic, Polish, Irish, and hillbilly slum—that held its own charm at a time when Detroit and other urban centers were becoming identified with black poverty during postwar white flight.[46] As whites, including out-migrants from the South, purchased suburban homes and as the inner city began to metamorphose into what came to be seen as the black ghetto in the late twentieth century, the downtrodden but high-spirited ethnic white slum may have appealed to readers repeatedly exposed to observers' disdain for the uniformity of the suburbs.[47]

Belonging and Identity

Readers' belief in the authenticity of Arnow, of her depictions, and of the organic way of life of primitive hill folk contributed to the ability of Arnow's fiction to fulfill a second set of readerly needs and desires. Fans found in *Hunter's Horn* and *The Dollmaker* reassurance that, despite their fears of atomistic, bureaucratic alienation, they belonged somewhere. The sense of belonging that Arnow's novels nurtured occurred at multiple levels.

First, the novels bolstered the imagined community of American nationalism. Print reviews resounded with nationalist themes that linked Arnow's characters to "blood and soil" assumptions about the rightful claimants to Americanness. American critics praised the good stock of Arnow's sturdy Kentuckians and emphasized their earthiness and vigor. Reviewers invited readers to think of *Hunter's Horn* as offering them a peek at "lives lived close to the soil." They pointedly mentioned that Nunn Ballew's farm and the Old Tipton farm that Gertie longed for had belonged to their ancestors, implicitly endorsing whites' ancestral claims to homeland.[48] The *Saturday Review* described *The Dollmaker*'s setting as "one of the few remaining sections of the country in which the native American [that is, the native-born—white]' has remained untouched for two centuries by our mechanical civilization."[49] Print reviews suggest that Arnow's novels reached a set of readers for whom a white "native America" of "pioneer" descent was crucial to imagining a Jeffersonian nation in the face of the massive industrialization of the World War II era. The fact that British reviewers panned *The Dollmaker*—which American reviewers enthusiastically embraced—indicates that the novel struck a peculiarly American chord.[50]

Critics' approval of the harsh and primitive conditions that they presumed persisted in some remote areas of the United States is reminiscent of the relief expressed by Murfree's and Fox's contemporaries who hoped to avoid the "namby-pamby" effects of civilization upon Americans. Appropriately vivacious "native" Anglo stock, critics implied, could be counted upon to reinvigorate Americans grown too soft through exposure to city life and "mechanical civilization." *Hunter's Horn* reviewers often cribbed from Macmillan's press releases and ads, which rejoiced that Kentucky hill people "live with a zest and a dramatic sense of joy and sorrow unknown in more sophisticated places." One reviewer somewhat callously described the story of "half-starved, hill-country farmers" as "wonderfully vital."[51] Reviews of *The Dollmaker* also insisted upon imagining Arnow's hill country as a world apart, fortuitously bracing in its primitive contact with nature and happily protected from society's ills. Such reviews suggested that critics identified rural Kentucky with the community, belonging, and vivacity they feared was being lost in contemporary Americans' rush to suburbanization.[52]

Fans' appreciation of Arnow, even more so than critics', was explicitly linked to concerns over migration's effects upon the nation and its supposedly agrarian soul. Readers across the nation experienced a need for rooted Americanness with heightened intensity because they were themselves highly mobile or because they witnessed—personally or through periodicals—the massive migration threatening their vision of an agrarian homeland.[53] Arnow's novels held out the tantalizing promise that her "dream of community" persisted somewhere, enabling seaboard elites and midwestern professionals to feel that they might one day find themselves wrapped in its comfort; in the meantime, they felt calmed that "simple" rural people continued to preserve the possibility for future belonging. For eastern seaboard elites, midwestern professionals, and other nationally identified readers, *Hunter's Horn* and *The Dollmaker* reinforced a national imagined community at the same time that they held out the promise that the "dream of community" lived on in some quiet corner of the country. Fan letters suggest that white midwestern observers who witnessed the Southern Diaspora experienced the dollmaker Gertie's loss as America's loss. In their belief in white hill people as the real America lost, they perpetuated an assumed correlation of nation with whiteness. Awareness or concern regarding African Americans' dislocation from the rural South, on the other hand, registered not at all in readers' letters.

Martha Henes, a columnist for the *Wellington Enterprise*, which she co-owned with her husband, spoke for many readers when she articulated her desire that white southerners maintain a rural agrarian national homeland. In 1954, the year of *The Dollmaker's* release, Henes wrote to thank Arnow. Henes explained to "my dear Mrs. Arnow" that the town of Wellington (outside Cleveland) "has not been happy over the influx of 'hillbillies' who came up to work in nearby industrial plants . . . *The Dollmaker* gives the other side." Despite Henes's interest in "the other side" of the story regarding the "forced move" of "hillbillies" because of wartime labor needs, she was not reconciled to the change. She chided Arnow: "Now—please—and at once—write a sequel—do get 'Gertie' back home—back where she can raise food—prepare for winter." As we saw in the epigraph to this chapter, she argued that modern ways like "high ways, high consumption of products" may "create employment" but not "security—nor many of the lasting satisfactions—simple farm living offers." "Anyway," Henes wrote in conclusion, "please take 'Gertie' home—resell rural America to Americans—and family unity—a home base—from which the young go—and to which they may return." Henes was so thoroughly steeped in the consumer culture she purported to criticize that she missed the irony of urging the author to "resell" rural America to those whom she believed should eschew consumerism. From her decidedly nonagrarian vantage point as a newspaper owner and professional journalist, Henes enthused that farming had been and should be "the American Way."[54] Other readers also took urgent issue with Arnow's fictional decisions, as if a different outcome in the novel would somehow improve the state of affairs in the real world as well. One fan reprimanded Arnow, insisting that she "just can't let [the Old Tipton Place] go to ruin waiting for some one to bring it back to life again."[55] The fate of the country seemed to rest on whether the character Gertie was able to live an agrarian life on ancestral farmland.

Fans emphasized genealogy and ancestry in expressing their appreciation for Arnow's fiction. Gertrude Snodgrass reported, "Your book has filled me with a pioneer spirit that I thot had gone with my girl-hood. . . . My own ancestors were among those early settlers."[56] L. Ramsay wrote that his and his wife's enjoyment of *Hunter's Horn* was due to "blood and atmosphere" since their family had for five generations had roots in Virginia and North Carolina but had migrated to Lawrence County, Indiana, via Jessamine County in central Kentucky.[57] The ancestral farms of protagonists Nunn Ballew and Gertie Nevels were a touchstone for fans, as for reviewers, who believed that America rightfully belonged to white "pioneers," even—or especially—in the face of teeming multicultural wartime housing like that featured in *The Dollmaker*. For readers with close personal ties to rural places, the sense of identity and belonging the novels evoked and provoked was far less abstract than it was for readers who felt that the essence of Americanness was at stake. Readers with personal ties could be found in all four of Arnow's reader groups—metropolitan-identified, midwestern professional, regional/rural elites, and migrants. Indeed, even fans who had no ties to Appalachia per se sometimes laid claim to close personal ties to the novels based upon memories of rural places significant during their childhoods. Occasionally this sense of connection engendered a sense of affinity and even alliance, as for a fan who wrote from England that he and his wife had to live in Sheffield due to his work but were "from the country" and "go back" home "whenever we can. . . . *Hunter's Horn* has moved us deeply." More often, however, fans with personal ties tended to romanticize and distance themselves from the rural places and people of their recollections. Mrs. Hans Zinsser of New York City, for example, appreciated Arnow's setting thanks to her devotion to what may have been a summer home; she had "known every hill and meadow, in my childhood, on the Hudson [River]."[58]

Many readers with personal ties belonged to the migrant readers group. Of the eighteen self-identified *Dollmaker* fans who migrated within the United States, usually as children or young adults, about half distanced themselves from Arnow's characters by describing them as curiosities, eccentrics, or unusually good and simple people. Through their distancing, these fans emphasized their sense of belonging to a social circle of high middlebrow readers even as they claimed a more privileged insight than most readers thanks to their firsthand familiarity with the countryside. Migrant readers who professed intimacy with simple rural ways but held themselves apart wrote to Arnow as if she shared their supercilious attitudes. A Wayne County native was "glad to find someone who can capture the charm and courage of these mountain folk." Another observed, "We grew up in the backwoods of Arkansas and I was struck many many times by the attitude of the people there. . . . I know full well the fantastic pride of the mountain man."[59] Phrases such as "these mountain folk" and "the people there" indicate the letter writers' disassociation from and detached contemplation of people whom they had observed but had not, they believed, embodied.

Sometimes migrants in this group walked a fine line between identifying with "the mountain people" and maintaining distance from them. Mrs. Fowler Curtis found commonality with Arnow because she was reared in the Kentucky hills, and readily identified a close relative as "like the [people] you write of," but in the end refused to include herself in that number, calling them "uneducated & poor but with a heart of gold & they had humility." She insisted proudly, "Nowhere else in the world will you find good people like the Ky. Mountain people." Curtis's stance toward "those good people" points to her own sense of superiority and authority over them—her good opinion indicates her affection and appreciation for them but also suggests that she saw herself as positioned to see them more clearly than they saw themselves.[60] Such readers found Arnow's fiction shared their own sociological postures toward mountain folk, simultaneously claiming familiarity and distance. The well-meaning appreciative comments by this half of the migrant readers with personal ties bordered on indulgent patronization.[61]

The other half of the migrant readers with personal ties to Arnow's settings represent a highly unusual group. Mostly from the South, these migrants were nonelite, rural-identified readers whose geographic and class identities aligned them wholeheartedly with Arnow's characters. Often, though not always, the difference in their stance was signaled by a willingness to refer to Arnow's characters as "our people" or "us" rather than "those good people" or "the mountain man." For this second half of migrant fans, Arnow's novels fulfilled a readerly desire for identity, belonging, and community in an intensely personal manner. Mrs. Charles Stowell of Seattle, for example, wrote to say that "as a young girl we lived on the edge of a locality similar . . . to your Kentucky Hill people . . . I loved the rolling hills and the Whip-Poor Wills & sometimes get home-sick for them & the paw paws."[62] Unbridled expressions of homesickness like Stowell's suggest that Arnow's fiction enabled fans to resist what Susan Matt calls the internalization of "dictates that require[d]" the middle class to "conquer homesickness" due to a "new orthodoxy, made clearest in wartime . . . that a cosmopolitan sensibility, rather than a homebound one, was necessary for the modern individual."[63]

It would be difficult to overestimate the significance of the legitimi-

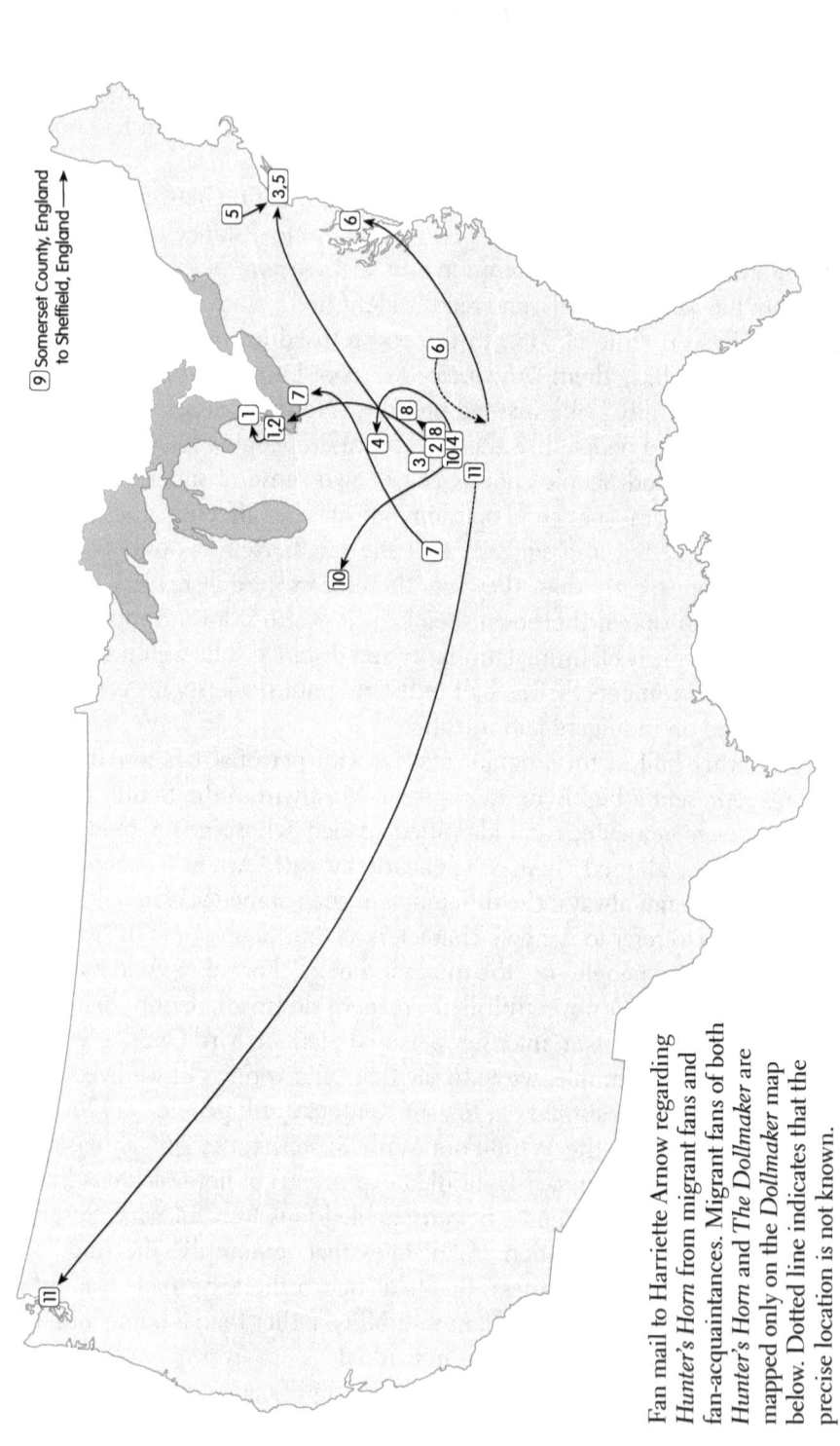

Fan mail to Harriette Arnow regarding *Hunter's Horn* from migrant fans and fan-acquaintances. Migrant fans of both *Hunter's Horn* and *The Dollmaker* are mapped only on the *Dollmaker* map below. Dotted line indicates that the precise location is not known.

1. Dorothy J. Howes, Detroit, Michigan → Richmond, Michigan
2. Mrs. W. C. Bishop, Pulaski County, Kentucky → Detroit, Michigan
3. Margaret W. Vanderhook, Kentucky → New York, New York
4. Helen C. Little, fan-acquaintance, Sloans Valley, Kentucky → Cincinnati, Ohio
5. Mrs. Hans Zinsser, Hudson River, New York → New York, New York
6. George L. Latham, western Virginia → Tennessee → Wilmington, Delaware
7. Frank B. Hines, Union/Jackson County, Illinois → Cleveland, Ohio
8. Elizabeth Ewen, fan-acquaintance, Stanton, Kentucky → Morehead, Kentucky
9. W. W. Duck, Somerset County, England → Sheffield, England
10. Mrs. Clyde Burnette, Monticello, Kentucky → Peoria, Illinois
11. Mrs. Charles S. Stowell, "a locality similar…(tho not in that state)" → Seattle, Washington

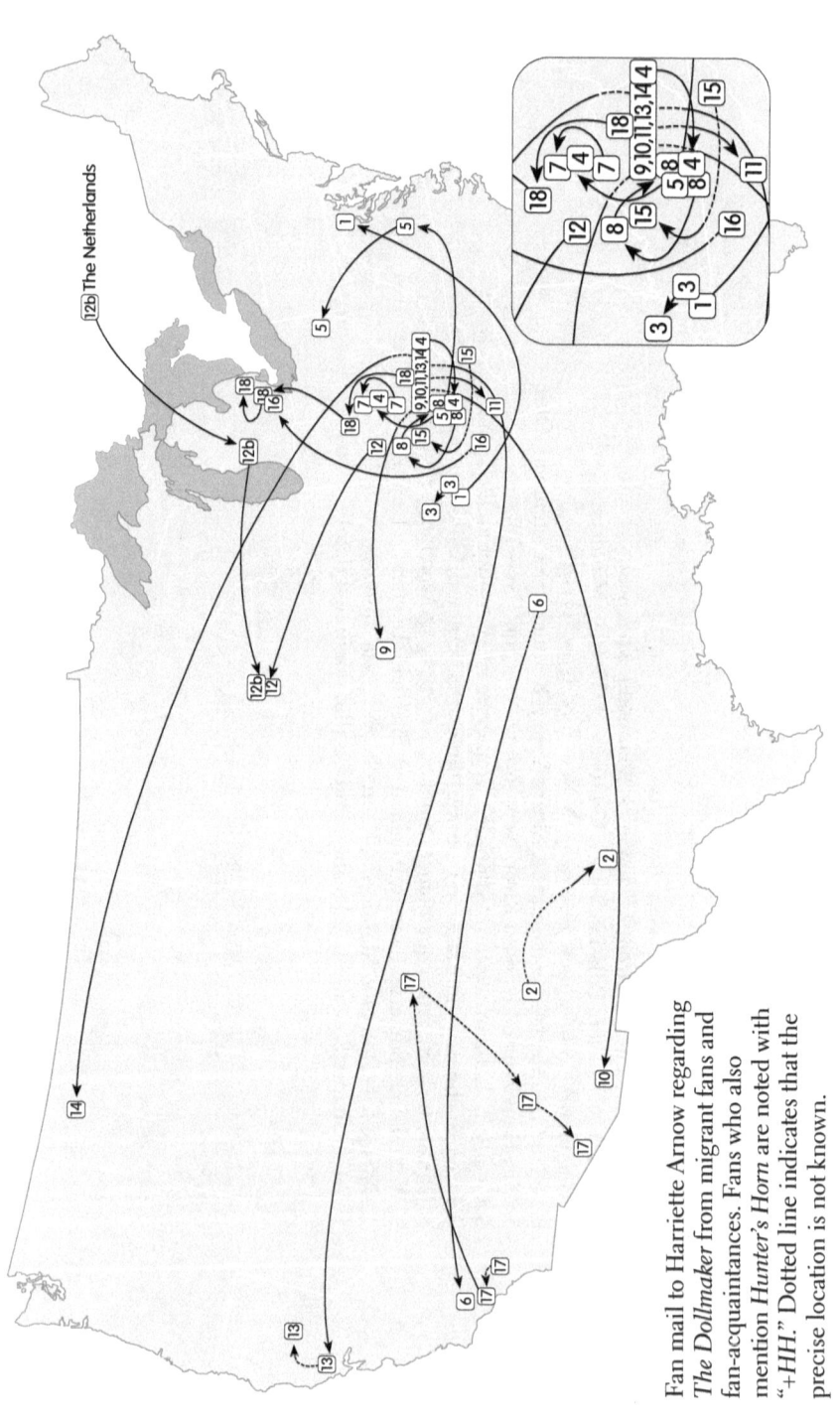

Fan mail to Harriette Arnow regarding *The Dollmaker* from migrant fans and fan-acquaintances. Fans who also mention *Hunter's Horn* are noted with "+*HH*." Dotted line indicates that the precise location is not known.

1. Claudine Lewis +*HH*, Mayfield, Kentucky → Washington, D.C.
2. Katherine Green +*HH*, New Mexico → Midland, Texas
3. Mrs. Fowler Curtis +*HH*, Livingston County, Kentucky → Rosiclare, Illinois
4. Rana Vaught, Floyd County, Kentucky → Somerset, Kentucky → Cincinnati, Ohio
5. R. L. Cassell +*HH*, Eubank, Kentucky → school in Richmond, Virginia → Cadiz, Ohio
6. Orzo F. Grant, rural Arkansas → Tulare, California
7. Mrs. Delbert Moore, northern Kentucky → Blanchester, Ohio
8. Ferne Denney, fan-acquaintance, Wayne County, Kentucky → Palmyra, Indiana → Berea, Kentucky
9. Minnie Holt +*HH*, Kentucky → Lee's Summit, Missouri
10. Ruth Nye, fan-acquaintance, Kentucky → Tucson, Arizona
11. Dorothy Brooks, Kentucky → Camden, Tennessee
12. Edith Graf Pylman, Spraytown, Indiana → Sheldon, Iowa
12b. husband: Netherlands → Grand Rapids, Michigan → Sheldon, Iowa
13. Edna Candy, eastern Kentucky → Richmond, California → California
14. Alice Banister +*HH*, Kentucky → Thompson Falls, Montana
15. Mrs. O. W. Johnson +*HH*, East Tennessee → stationed in Fort Knox, Kentucky
16. Irene Watt, Carthage, Tennessee → Ypsilanti, Michigan
17. Hilah Simmons +*HH*, California → Pomona College, Claremont, California → Colorado → Arizona → Ajo, Arizona
18. Mary Reitenour, Morehead, Kentucky → Muncie, Indiana → Detroit, Michigan → Farmington, Michigan

zation Arnow's novels offered rural-identified readers in nonrural places where their values and associations were poorly understood by those around them. In particular, out-migrants from the South to the Midwest, like John Fox Jr.'s readers torn between worlds, felt a pressing need to reflect upon their experiences and to have their experiences reflected back to them. For these out-migrants, the novels helped construct and affirm a rural identity as they moved through urban, industrial, and suburban landscapes. Minnie Holt, born in Kentucky but a resident of Missouri since she was twelve, remarked that "there are people without roots that live where they live, but this is not true of Kentuckians. It [Kentucky] is dear to my heart always." Irene Watt wrote speculatively, "I was one of those women from the hills of Tennessee who came with husband and children, to a place like the one to which the Dollmaker went." Watt thought it a shame that, though she was surrounded by "a lot of our people here," they did not "seem to remember what poke greens cooked with hogs jowl and served with corn pone and little green onions and buttermilk tastes like!" R. L. Cassell, quoted earlier as claiming identification with the novel's events —"I know; I was a 'hillbilly'"—had moved from Kentucky to Ohio in 1914. Forty years later he was still furious at the notion, questioned in *The Dollmaker,* that migrants must "adjust" to the Midwest.[64] These readers found in Arnow's fiction a cultural resource to affirm their sense of themselves, the importance of their homes, their memories of belonging, and the worth of what they saw as their unique cultural heritage, in stark contrast to those who viewed it as a resource for graciously appreciating that heritage in others.

Geographically mobile white readers, whether patronizing toward or identifying with hill characters, craved a way to understand their relationships to the seemingly atomizing mass culture that newly surrounded them. Perhaps more so than did the neighbors and kin they left behind, out-migrant readers sought out artifacts of consumer society like novels (and radio) that focused upon agrarian lifeways.[65] Living in dense urban areas with access to libraries and proximate friendship circles, they likely came into greater contact with fictional representations of themselves than they would have if they had remained in the rural South. According to one Detroit librarian, so many former Kentuckians wanted *Hunter's Horn* that there was a waiting list. She recounted a story about a man who had checked the book out but was frequently out of town for business; his wife secretly allowed four neighbors to borrow *Hunter's Horn* as long as they hurried it back before her husband's return.⁶⁶ Reading Arnow's novels helped such readers reaffirm rural identity and belonging at the same time that it linked them to new networks in their out-migrant destination.

Circulation of Power

As we have seen, whatever Harriette Arnow's intentions, her best sellers manifestly spoke to and reinforced readers' desires for authenticity and community. For all Arnow's fans—eastern seaboard elites, midwestern professionals, local elites, and migrants—these needs overlapped additionally with desire for the augmentation of personal power. Reading promoted readers' sense of status and enhanced their cultural capital—as demonstrated in part by numerous readers' mention of book clubs or requests for help with reading-group reports. As with other best-selling regional fiction in the nineteenth and twentieth centuries, Arnow's novels promoted the circulation of power across geographic scales in at least two additional ways. First, elites in the places (and kinds of places) featured in the novels embraced the best sellers for promoting their homelands to national visibility. Second, readers' sense of themselves as compassionate connoisseurs linked them, at times, to the politics of uplift and, by extension, imperialism.

Regional elites and members of the middle class in Kentucky welcomed the national attention that admiration for rural places garnered for their home state. For them, valuation of the local as an ideal was a tool of self-promotion rather than a means to address the economic or emotional crises of less privileged Kentuckians. On a postcard mailed from the city of Lexington, Kentucky, in 1949, John Wilson Townsend wrote, "If the rest of Kentucky is not proud of you, I am and have been for a long time and I make haste to say so."⁶⁷ Helen Little, a friend of Arnow's sister Elizabeth, wrote to the latter to say, "Here's hoping that your sister wins the Pulitzer Prize and puts the Kentucky Mountains on the map," making it clear what was at stake for her and for other Kentuckians with aspirations for status. She mused, "In a way I am one of them—my formative years were spent among them." Yet Little, the daughter of a lumber mill owner, seemed to hold herself apart when she said she had been among *them* and when she wrote, "Mother and father passed along to me the tales of the mountain folk."⁶⁸

Arnow's best sellers invited readers' compassion. Arnow's readers—

professional critics and fans alike—often expressed how "aroused by sympathy" they were by "those mountain people," whether the hardscrabble Ballews in *Hunter's Horn* or, especially, the out-of-their-element Nevels family in *The Dollmaker*.[69] Mrs. Clyde Burnette, raised in rural Kentucky but writing from Peoria, Illinois, praised Arnow's vision of "the hill people" yet held herself above them with the pitying remark that "these people didn't have a chance."[70] Sentiments of compassion and dismay were particularly pronounced among readers from the eastern seaboard. Elizabeth Neff of Pennsylvania wrote of *The Dollmaker* that she was "so shocked and grieved that I wept."[71] "The book is shattering," wrote construction worker, former Communist, and labor activist Irving Weissman, and "it is an anguish to pick it up again and reread portions."[72]

Letters from midwestern professionals who found themselves forced to confront out-migration in person (rather than simply in their armchairs, like Henes) demonstrate that Arnow's books may have increased their understanding of, and outreach to, newcomers from the South. Principal Mary Jane White wrote from Cincinnati, a popular destination for rural Kentuckians, to tell Arnow, "Our school is the center of the rooming house area where the mountain people locate." She hints at great frustration with new students who, "after leaving Old Andy's School," do not understand "that we must have regular attendance." White says that Arnow captures the mountain students' "warmth of understanding among themselves, the willingness to share their meager supply, the sudden bursts of anger we see each week." When Principal White told Arnow, "I consider your book most enlightening," she suggested that Arnow's fiction could be used to confirm, explain, and even partly affirm—though not wholly forgive—mountain distinctiveness.[73] Mildred Schulze, a librarian in Cincinnati, wrote that she was using *Hunter's Horn* to get "natives of Kentucky . . . into the library. So you see," Schulze wrote confidingly, "besides helping Kentucky, you are helping Elmwood Branch to win readers."[74] Gertrude Snodgrass was "consumed with grief over . . . Gertie's failure to return to her beloved Kentucky." Her belief that Gertie belonged back in Kentucky apparently did not keep her from cofounding a food pantry in the common out-migrant destination of Chicago.[75]

These comments all indicate the positive social change that Arnow's novels clearly helped advance. Some reception scholars, however, argue that more complicated consequences can emerge from fiction's elicitation of sympathy. The widespread popularity of what Lauren Berlant refers to as the "documentary realness about the pain of strangers" may have benefited Arnow (whose readers acknowledged that their appreciation of her excruciatingly painful novels could by no stretch be described as "enjoyment"). Berlant argues that "compassion is a term denoting privilege." Those who feel compassion do so privately and at a distance, enthralled by the "pain of strangers" who "live somewhere" else, "sharing an everyday life." For Berlant, "Private responses are not only insufficient but a part of the practice of injustice" because to be taught to feel "*appropriately* compassionate" is to be "trained in stinginess, not in caring." Representations of "the pain of strangers" may be popular, Berlant cautions, but it is rare for them to evoke appropriate public responses.[76]

Phyllis McKishnie Kribs of Toronto provides one example of a response to *Hunter's Horn* that Berlant might find problematic. "So real have you made these people," she wrote, "that one weeps with them when crops fail and food is scarce, or perhaps I should say for them, for they do not weep themselves, and joys with them when times are less hard. Above all, one loves them, for their big-hearted simplicity, for their humaneness, for themselves."[77] On the one hand, Kribs's desire to weep "with" Arnow's characters marks her as simpatico rather than pitying. Yet her "love" for "their big-hearted simplicity" makes painfully clear her sense of difference from them, and the fact that they do not weep for themselves may release her from any obligation. While the characters evoked pity and required compassion, they did not suggest the existence of a structural problem for all of Arnow's readers.

The link between compassion and patronizing attitudes of uplift is suggested by the fact that some Arnow fans reminisced to her about their past missionary ventures. When reading *Hunter's Horn*, Mrs. Everdean Johnson was reminded of her "exhilarating days" as a "nurse 'on horseback'" in eastern Kentucky, "50 miles from the L&N Railroad." She thought Arnow would appreciate the fact that Johnson had been inspired to write stories with such typical local-color titles as "In Saddle Bag Land," "Hannibal of the Hills," and "Baptizin."[78] Other fans steeped in the privilege of compassion and uplift wrote of past experiences evoked by reading Arnow's novels in such as way as to suggest equivalencies among plain folk everywhere. "I've never been in Kentucky," admitted Mariane Williams, "but I taught school during the thirties in the dustblown prairies here and have witnessed poverty and illiteracy and a certain courage of people all mixed up together."[79]

Though scholars have celebrated Arnow's work as representing a significant departure from conventional local-color fiction, some of Arnow's readers felt her books replicated their perspectives about quaint and wily mountain people deserving of compassion and uplift. *Hunter's Horn* and *The Dollmaker* appear to have helped some readers see themselves as benevolent aficionados and overseers of difference, perhaps not only domestically but also internationally.

"Get Gertie Home" (but Not Arnow or Her Readers)

Readers' romance with authenticity, desire for imagined community, and sense of their own status came out most fully in their expressions of dismay that Arnow had not returned her protagonist Gertie to her rightful home in Kentucky at the conclusion of *The Dollmaker*. In this regard, Ohio newspaper owner Martha Henes was far from alone in her reproach of Arnow. Fully one in five readers made it clear that they believed Gertie belonged back on her ancestral farm.[80] Katherine Green, missing her home state of New Mexico, told Arnow: "I am homesick for some mountains, myself, and I thought I simply could not bear it if that poor woman didn't get to go home, and," she continued with disgust, "sure enough, you left her there. I hope you write a sequel and redeem yourself."[81] Seventeen-year-old Stephen W. Harvey in Seattle wrote, "I wanted Gertie to go back to Kentucky, and instead she stayed in the dirt, debt, and radio screaming world she was not use to."[82] Out-migrant readers who identified with Arnow's characters scolded her passionately. Mrs. Delbert Moore, the working-class migrant featured in the epigraph, wrote from outside Cincinnati to plead, "Get poor Gertie Nevils out of Detroit, and back to Kentucky where she belongs with her son and other kinfolk. Please don't leave her stalled up there the rest of her life."[83]

The reason Gertie needed to go home, Arnow's fans and detractors alike implicitly argued, was to escape a soulless, urban, industrial, "radio screaming" Midwest for a supposedly happy, whole, organic, face-to-face rural way of life. Reviewers focused on the central contrast drawn in *The Dollmaker* between the Nevelses' "folk" way of life in Kentucky and their circumstances in Detroit.[84] A *Los Angeles Times* headline, for example, touted Gertie as a "Creature of Fresh Air, Freedom and Good Food" who "Survives Toxic Urbanity." Another reviewer asserted that when in Kentucky, Gertie "was living in paradise . . . for there in the Cumberlands" they had clean air, sweet-tasting water, and food that had flavor. The Old Tipton place was Gertie's "promised land." One could count on food "to be taken from the earth" and neighbors "to share trials but not to make living a nightmare of lack of privacy."85 Whereas reviews highlighted the supposed security, self-sufficiency, and community available in farming locales, the city offered a "barren existence" in the housing project, "social and economic disintegration," and a "congested" "asphalt jungle."86

Like reviewers, fans, too, expressed anti-urbanism and anti-industrialism. Alma Weber wrote to Arnow from the outskirts of Cincinnati, where she read *Hunter's Horn* "while riding the bus with radio blaring." She asserted, "If only [the character] Lureenie could have realized how fortunate she was not to have to cope with those" modern drawbacks. Outmigrant R. L. Cassell fumed at Arnow, "I hated that goddamn book, and the whole goddamn industrialism out of which it came." Claudine Lewis, in the Washington, DC, offices of a Kentucky politician, conflated midwestern living with materialism, insisting to the fictional Gertie that life in "this modern-living hell" would only worsen. "You know people were not supposed to live that way," Lewis chided Arnow's protagonist. "And who cares whether you have the biggest Icy Heart refrigerator?"87 Perhaps disillusioned with aspects of their own urban ways of life, these fans may have overly romanticized life without buses, radios, and large refrigerators.

Only three out of ninety-one fans of *The Dollmaker* resisted bemoaning the loss of agrarian ways. Sidney Ernestine Warfel reported that some members of her readers' group outside Chicago felt that the novel's ending was "constructive" because it represented Gertie's "setting aside her nostalgia, and longing for home. Now she was going to be practical and live for her family, only."88 Ozro F. Grant and his wife, themselves the authors of a novel that had sold 130,000 copies, "grew up in the backwoods of Arkansas." Writing from California, Grant noted unsentimentally, "We all have our 'Detroits' and we all long for the security of the old Tipton Place." "But," he insisted severely, "the Old Tipton Place was gone for Gertie and it does not exist for any of us."89

The third writer to dismiss nostalgia for the agrarian world was Edna Candy, who moved as a child from "the Kentucky mountains . . . to live in war housing" in Richmond, California. She wrote to tell Arnow that until reading *The Dollmaker* she "had put all the old hurtful things [from that period of her life] way back somewhere." Candy's letter contradicted other fans on two fronts. First, despite her painful memories of wartime housing, Candy implied that the tenements were endowed with a dense neighborliness that she had not experienced prior to her move from the mountains. In fact, the tenement provided a support network that outlasted the neighborhood itself; Candy told Arnow that the migrant families had all moved away and that the buildings themselves were gone, but that the couples still wrote to each other. Although Arnow acknowledged in a 1983 interview that Gertie encountered more kindliness in her Detroit alley than she had at home, Arnow's readers and Arnow herself situated the "dream of community" in rural places. Second, Candy focused upon out-migration as a success story. She "taught for six years in a state nursery school" for migrant families and, at the time of her writing, was attending university, "so," Candy admonished Arnow, "there really is a sequel to *The Dollmaker*." "Beat Gertie was . . . I know," she continued, "but you forgot the strength of her! I believe she made a come-back!" For Edna Candy, the sequel did not involve a return to the farm but building upon opportunities migrants had in cities.[90]

Edna Candy's sequel may have been more historically accurate than the one most readers begged Arnow to deliver. As historian Chad Berry documents, migration to the Midwest was not an experience of "weakness, misery, and victimization" but rather one of "success, . . . of finding a job and keeping it, of . . . overcoming the prejudices and adjustments . . . of buying a home and eventually burning the mortgage." By the time of *The Dollmaker*'s publication in 1954, southern out-migrants had begun to commit themselves to staying in the Midwest, buying houses and putting down roots in local churches.[91] Unlike African American migrants of the same era, white southerners were able to assimilate into the suburban developments that proliferated after the end of World War II. Furthermore, while readers' understanding of what befell out-migrants was misleadingly negative, their imagination of what came before was often misleadingly positive. Berry quotes Adolph Lacy's recognition that moving back home was nicer as an idea than as a reality: "I think why most people want to go back, see, they remember how it was when you left . . . but that's not there anymore . . . they've forgot that it's a new world." Out-migrant Nellie Austin noted that fondness for home required selective memory: "The hard work part . . . see, I don't remember that, and if I had to work real hard on the farm I would not have wanted to go back."[92] Yet for Arnow's readers, Gertie belonged back on the farm. Arnow's character—never one to shy away from hard labor—helped readers vicariously make the move home.

While Arnow's fiction acknowledges the pulls of both country and city, it registers this ambivalence through characters at odds with one another (for example, the land-loving Gertie versus her machine-loving husband, Clovis) rather than by a single character torn both ways. As Berry observes, Gertie and Clovis "represent emotional poles," with Clovis finding Detroit "Hillbilly Heaven" and Gertie finding it "Hillbilly Hell." Berry's research shows that it was more common for individual migrants to have a "divided heart." Being in the North was emotionally difficult but financially beneficial, as white "southerners who stayed in the North achieved an impressive economic status compared with that of native midwestern whites and native whites who remained in the South."[93]

Arnow, more privileged socioeconomically than most out-migrants, nonetheless resembled the vast majority who experienced a "divided heart" rather than simply "Hillbilly Hell" like her character Gertie. Indeed, there had always been tension between Arnow's "personal dream of community," which she linked to the Kentucky hill country, and her dream of professional success as an author. As a young adult she longed to hit the highway, first to Louisville, and then to Cincinnati. In 1982, Arnow avowed that she admired cities: "I like to live near a city. A city is, or was, supposed to be man's greatest achievement." She claimed it was her husband who had insisted upon living on farms in southern Kentucky and central Michigan, telling the *Nation* in 1976 that it was Howard "who dreamt of that simple life. . . . I'd never wanted to leave the city." And for good reason. Arnow wrote *Mountain Path* in Cincinnati and *Hunter's Horn* in Detroit; she readily identified her most urban residences as her most productive writing periods.[94]

On the one hand, Arnow had a strong love of the land and rural life, and the author's public persona emphasized her working-class hill country roots. On the other hand, Arnow embraced the cosmopolitan offerings of cities and scorned the narrow sexist roles prescribed for women in rural counties. Her fiction vacillates between the pleasures of agrarianism and urbanity's promise of expanded horizons and opportunities. But the path that the divided Arnow took—giving up on the hard life of teaching and subsistence farming in Kentucky and moving to Detroit where she had more time to write—she made agonizingly tragic for her characters, despite her own happy ending as a successful author on a suburban Ann Arbor farm.

Arnow and her readers nursed homesickness for a rural past despite the fact that, as Berry tells us, "already by 1960," southern white out-migrants' financial position "was becoming indistinguishable from that of their blue-collar white midwestern neighbors."[95] Arnow's readers, in feeling sorry for themselves, often failed to acknowledge their racial privilege and the upward mobility (and outward mobility to the suburb) that it generally afforded them. Catherine Jurca observes that fiction that conceptualizes suburban life as a problem of displacement allows readers to link "being white and middle class" with "subjugation" rather than "social dominance." Commentaries on corporate and suburban culture published in the 1950s identified members of the professional middle class as "the preeminent victims of postindustrialization and suburbanization" due to the postwar experience of dislocation, alienation, "insecurity, instability, and maladjustment" as well as "dehumanizing" and underpaid white-collar work. Once-maligned but eventually well-established white out-migrants began to imaginatively "convert the rights and privileges" of suburban life into a problem, "evidence of . . . alienation." Jurca contends that we must acknowledge "instances when the experience of white middle-class alienation has had more to do with self-pity than profound or even trite resistance to capitalist culture."[96] Readers embraced *The Dollmaker* as a critique of materialism and consumer culture. For Arnow's fans, the sense of dislocation and the sense of being forced to choose between a "vibrant" life and a comfortable one was real and often acute. Following Jurca, we must consider whether, in the end, readers' reactions to Arnow's best sellers promoted self-pity as well as resistance.

For almost all the out-migrant fan mail correspondents—the affirming identifiers and the patronizing distancers alike—Arnow's novels provided a nostalgic trip to the golden years of their own childhoods. But country living was to them a way of the past, unsustainable or undesirable in the present. Reading fiction allowed these fans to visit an imagined home place without having to give up their upwardly mobile urban or suburban lives. As Henry Shapiro notes, Appalachia offers Americans the "peace . . . of going home"—"something one liked better to think about than to do."[97] Arnow's readers, like Arnow, wanted for Gertie what they perhaps thought they should want but in fact did not really want for themselves. Readers shared Arnow's "dream of community" and the simple life, yet like most out-migrants and like Arnow herself, they chose to remain in the Midwest, where they found greater economic opportunities, had greater access to consumer goods (including novels), and sent their children to college. Reading became for them a means of assuaging homesickness while they pursued paths at odds with the values of *Hunter's Horn's* Nunn Ballew or *The Dollmaker's* Gertie Nevels.

Harriette Arnow, whom scholars often credit with having captured an accurate vision of mountain lives, attracted readers who identified with her characters more so than those of any other best-selling author, including John Fox Jr. *Hunter's Horn* and *The Dollmaker* were integral to out-migrants' understanding of their own experiences, often in the face of ridicule and the maxim that they must assimilate seamlessly into their new hometowns.

Whatever special purposes it served for migrants, Arnow's fiction also fed conventional readerly desires for authentic places, belonging, and a sense of power. However complicated a picture of rural life Arnow tried to present, readers seized upon a romanticized pastoral dream of belonging—even or especially out-migrant readers who had themselves experienced rural life and rural-to-urban migration with consequences far more nuanced than such pastoralism could express. Perhaps more than that of any other author discussed in this book, Arnow's work demonstrates the relationship between the mobility of readers and the popularity of regional fiction that readers interpret as figuring rural places as static and rooted. Readers whose fan letters expressed solidarity with Arnow's characters, as well as readers whose letters exhibited patronization of them, found in Arnow an affirmation of a pastoral vision made increasingly dear as millions of white Americans deserted the rural South. As did other Appalachian-set best sellers, Arnow's novels offered fans a place with a more genuine face-to-face connection among people, a place where residents experience a deeper bond to nature and the land, and a place where life is lived with a greater sense of immediacy than is supposedly possible in the bureaucratically and technologically mediated modern world. Fans' embrace of that pastoral vision belied their own life choices and failed to acknowledge the novels' ambivalence about agrarianism.

Fans in all four groups identified rural Kentucky as a site of community and belonging even though it was often their own involvement with close social networks in urban neighborhoods, libraries, or women's groups that provided them with access to Arnow's vision of it as such. Just as radio programming in preceding decades "packaged and sold rural identity" to listeners, as Lisa Krissoff Boehm argues, Arnow's best sellers constructed, packaged, and sold rural identity as authentic, connected, and protected from consumer culture for white readers across the nation.[98] Arnow's novels allowed readers to consume an Appalachia imagined as simple white America, an alternative to mass consumerism and rootlessness and the foundation for national identity and missions of uplift. The responses of many of Arnow's readers indicate their belief that eschewing modernity was key to establishing not only a meaningful and vibrant way of life but also to preserving and promoting "the American Way." The value of the local was its presumed function of safeguarding the simple, unpresuming people who provided the bedrock of the nation.

Arnow's novels augmented some readers' sense of status across multiple scales—as proud regional elites, as literary connoisseurs, as compassionate observers of others' misfortunes, and as citizens of a white, agrarian-at-heart nation deserving of dominance on the world stage. The value of the local was its seeming interchangeability with other "primitive" places whose people and culture, connoisseurs felt, should be appreciated and managed in the name of humanitarianism, mission, or imperialism. As with regionalism more generally, Arnow's novels upheld for her contemporaries a vision of an interior white homeland that provided support for white American nationalism and for high middlebrow notions of knowing what's best for others domestically and internationally. The "good war" had emboldened a sense of the United States as a selfless actor on the world stage. Arnow's novels may have enabled readers to retain a sense of innocence even as the country engaged in the long cold war. Furthermore, starting with John Fox Jr.'s work and continuing into the Second Gilded Age, regional fiction like Arnow's likely permitted some white readers to identify as casualties of out-migration, suburbanization, and the "Affluent Society" even as they were beneficiaries of them.[99]

Mapping the migrant readers of *Hunter's Horn* and *The Dollmaker*, and understanding those novels' popularity in the context of massive out-migration, opens a window onto a new pattern of reception for Appalachian-set fiction in its hour of formation. Almost 20 million whites migrated out of the South over the course of the twentieth century.[100] By the 1990s and early 2000s, as I argue in chapter 5, these out-migrants and their descendents would be responsible, in part, for the national popularity of nostalgic depictions of Appalachia. Best-selling novels like Jan Karon's Mitford series, Charles Frazier's *Cold Mountain*, Adriana Trigiani's Big Stone Gap trilogy, and Silas House's *Clay's Quilt* demonstrated the ongoing love affair of readers with rurality uncorrupted by the big city. Diasporic readers—scorned as a "cultural minority . . . of perceived hayseeds and yokels" and nurturing a sense of themselves as having been cast out of the Edenic essence of America—may have contributed to a notion of white innocence and victimhood for a new generation unable or unwilling to acknowledge white American nationalism and its corollary, the "white man's burden" of imperialism.[101]

Chapter 4

City to Country, circa 1967–1970

> We simply need that wild country available to us, even if we never do more than drive to its edge and look in. For it can be a means of reassuring ourselves of our sanity as creatures, a part of the geography of hope.
> —Wallace Stegner, "Wilderness Letter"

> Yes, I lied. But what has truth to do with me? I'm an artist. I *make* the truth.
> —James Dickey, in Henry Hart, *James Dickey: The World as a Lie*

In the twenty-first century, two pop culture touchstones continue to shape national perceptions of the Appalachian region perhaps more than any other fiction since John Fox's *The Trail of the Lonesome Pine* (1908). Catherine Marshall's *Christy* and James Dickey's *Deliverance*, novels published originally in 1967 and 1970, respectively, have had great staying power in the American imagination. *Deliverance*'s lasting influence came as a result, largely, of its 1972 film version (found regularly on cable television throughout the 1990s) and the haunting refrain of its signature music, "Dueling Banjoes." *Christy*, about a young girl who leaves her comfortable life in Asheville, North Carolina, to teach at a mission school in the East Tennessee mountains, has had a lower profile in the pop culture lexicon. Yet devoted intergenerational sharing and Christian audiences for the 1990s television series, made-for-television films, and young-adult fiction series based on *Christy*, plus mass-market reprints by Avon, have ensured that the story continues to affect popular understandings of the mountain South—particularly among white Christian women and girls.[1]

From World War I until the 1990s, Appalachian settings were largely absent from best-selling fiction. In chapter 3, I showed why Harriette

Arnow's best sellers were exceptions in the aftermath of World War II. In this chapter, I examine the reasons for the immense popularity of two divergent depictions of the region during the Vietnam era. Both *Christy* and *Deliverance* affirmed and compelled missionary and touristic perspectives, each of which relies upon an assumption of interchangeability among authentic rural "primitives" nationally and globally. They did so at a moment when anticonsumerist environmental and back-to-the-land movements fueled a romance with folkways centered on white rural communities. A 1972 ad suggests the contours of national interest in the region by describing the *New York Times* best seller *The Foxfire Book* as a "fascinating record of Appalachia's fast-vanishing folkways [that] covers everything from log cabin building to moonshining." This blurb, published by the Quality of Life Society division of the Book-of-the-Month Club, appeared alongside numerous other odes to wilderness and cautionary tales about modernity, including a modern edition of Thoreau's *In Wildness Is the Preservation of the World* (1962) and Rachel Carson's *Silent Spring* (1962).[2]

Christy and *Deliverance* are about as different as two novels could be. *Christy*, set in 1912, is ultimately pastoral (despite feuding violence and glimpses of wretched poverty), with a female missionary heroine. *Deliverance*, set in its contemporary readers' present day, is gothic, with a male rise-to-the-occasion hero. *Christy* fans were almost exclusively women and girls; most of *Deliverance*'s readers were men. *Christy* exalts heterosexual romance, *Deliverance* misogyny and homosocial bonding. *Christy* was most often read through the lens of popular religion; *Deliverance* was most often read by connoisseurs of literature and poetry. *Christy* is middlebrow to high middlebrow in literary status and ambition; *Deliverance* highbrow.

Yet fan mail indicates that both *Christy* and *Deliverance* performed for white high middlebrow readers the same functions that local-color fiction served for the Gilded Age and Neo–Gilded Age audiences that bookended the century: the production of region as authentic; the construction of identity and belonging via geographic affiliations; and the circulation of power across a variety of spaces and scales. It comes as little surprise that fan mail confirms scholars' suspicions that *Christy* and *Deliverance* each conceived of Appalachia as a distinctive world apart. And contemporary reviewers were alert to the third function in their commentaries on the missionary and imperialist thrusts of the novels (though none appear to have anticipated their seductive invitation to tourism). The most striking revelation in the fan mail, to my mind, is that these seemingly stereotypical representations of the region played such an important role in the generation or maintenance of regional identity among certain readers. (For more on my methodological choices and sources, see "Appendix: Methodological Essay.")

In appealing to readers' romance with authenticity, both novels banked on and contributed to readers' construction of Appalachia as a space exempt from market relations. As Marilyn Halter tells us, the "search for authenticity" stems from "nostalgia for an idealized . . . time when folk culture was supposedly untouched by the corruption . . . associated with commercial development."[3] As we will see, these novels' readers admired "getting back to [the] basics" and marveled at primitive ways of life that eschewed technology.[4] The novels evoked the promise of mountaineers as repositories of whites' supposed colorful collective past through their purported preservation of folklore, particularly music. Religious historian Mary Elisabeth Goin rightly (though incompletely) describes *Christy*'s appeal by noting that its representation of the supposedly "secluded Tennessee mountains of 1912, before world war or great depression touched twentieth century America, provided [readers] a quiet place in which to withdraw from modern pressures and unrest," a place "where God-fearing folk practiced self-reliance far from the institutional influence of either church or government."[5] *Deliverance* readers sought both titillation and reassurance from Dickey's premise that Appalachia permitted primitivism to endure in the modern world. Fans credited both authors with intimate knowledge of mountain people and with documentary accuracy in their representations—with only a rare complaint directed to Dickey. Readers' faith in Marshall's and Dickey's right relation to their settings—which both authors cannily claimed for the sake of marketing—was key to the novels' fabrication of authenticity.

Fans also found in both novels a means of constructing a sense of identity and belonging. As with all fiction, readers claimed status and belonging via pride in their own literary connoisseurship. Readers defined themselves against "hillbillies" or "mountaineers" by identifying with the protagonists, in each case an "outsider" who confronted mountain difference. At the same time, however, appreciation of mountain characters was crucial to readers' sense of affiliation with authentic place. Some readers found the novels a means to reclaiming their own mountain, southern, or rural roots, at times borrowing (or reviving their own previous) dialect to assert local knowledge. They sought rapport with authors whom they believed esteemed mountain distinctiveness and eccentricity as thoroughly as they did.

Fan mail suggests that both *Christy* and *Deliverance* contributed to the third function of regional fiction, the circulation of power across multiple geographic scales, by constructing a vision of the world that insisted upon shared responsibility for the well-being of primitive peoples among those who could recognize, appreciate, and guide them. At root an imperialist vision, it manifested itself in fans' expressions of desire for tourism, a call to mission, and pride in their ability to identify primitive rural types from within and beyond the southeastern Appalachian mountains. Often, recognition was accompanied by justifications for intervention. Mountain people appeared to demand of readers the same attitudes and actions as other supposedly uncivilized peoples the world over.

As in earlier stories by Mary Murfree, John Fox, and Harriette Arnow, Appalachia in *Christy* and *Deliverance* functions as a foil to "urbanity" and "civilization." Yet *Christy* and *Deliverance* fulfilled additional readerly needs and desires in a manner unique to each novel. *Christy* appealed to readers looking for security in an uncertain world.[6] In the face of the red scare, civil rights agitation, and the violence in Vietnam, Americans turned en masse to popular religion—not one particular theology, but a more comforting, more universal "religion-in-general."[7] Marshall speculated that *Christy*'s success might be attributed to Americans' sense of "feeling rudderless" as institutions "crumbl[ed] all around." She believed that Americans, "particularly after the violence in our country," sought a "return" to "basic human values."[8] Some readers found affirmation for their missionary outlook toward rural peoples, while for others, reading *Christy* compelled them to plan future vacations in the novel's East Tennessee setting in search of a lost American vitality and virtuousness. Both interpretations offered readers a return from city to countryside—the purported stronghold of basic human values.

Even as *Deliverance* bombards readers with its nightmare vision of the primitive, the power of Dickey's novel for many of his cosmopolitan fans lay precisely in its dangling before them a version of Appalachia calculated to fulfill their desires for a raw and pristine land peopled by white Americans uncorrupted by mass society. Fan mail shows that Dickey's most admiring readers were often either outdoor enthusiasts who saw in the region's mountains "a geography of hope" (to borrow from the Stegner epigraph above) or, even less predictably, out-migrants from the South whose homesickness was soothed by Dickey's depiction of Appalachian "grass-roots" people.[9] Southern elites and academics seeking national prominence in literary circles comprised another significant contingency of Dickey fans.

For many white Americans after John F. Kennedy's assassination, much seemed amiss in the world. In one woman's words, "We've had the Vietnam War, all the rioting. . . . Before then you were used to America winning everything, but now you sometimes think our day may be over."[10] The ability of *Deliverance*'s suburban-soft Ed to confront inexplicable brutality and overcome the enemy in the woods likely was a welcome relief for readers concerned about the threat posed by the primitive but wily Viet Cong. Perhaps it comforted white Americans to believe that if they steeled themselves, they could "man up" and prevail in the face of violence that they associated with racial Others—not only Vietnamese but blacks, with whom they associated rioting, a street crime epidemic, a skyrocketing homicide rate, and bombings by radical antiracist organizations.[11] White southerners furious over the civil rights movement but gung ho for corralling the threat of the Viet Cong may have identified with the hillbillies' attempts to discipline interlopers just as strongly as they did with the city protagonists' attempts to eradicate predatory hillbillies.[12]

Christy and *Deliverance* explicitly and implicitly share the laments of other midcentury novels which, Catherine Jurca observes, include "mass production, standardization, dullness, and conformity." Fan mail sent to Marshall and Dickey confirms that their critique of metropolitan and suburban culture was part of their novels' appeal. It also suggests that readers were beneficiaries of outward and upward mobility yet chose to view themselves, at least in part, as victims of what they saw as a "spiritually and culturally" deficient modern suburban life.[13]

Dickey and Marshall each felt, in Marshall's words, that "in writing the book" set in Appalachia, "I am, in a very real sense, coming home."[14] Their readers, often writing from metropolitan areas, similarly reported feeling like they were coming home or returning to ancestral roots by reading about the countryside. Perhaps the novels' imagined movement from city to country accounts for such disparate stories' ability to provoke such powerful reactions among readers with similar geographic anxieties and trajectories. A history of out-migration from the South, an uneasy sense of an increasingly mobile society, and a fear of moving away from the nation's simple "pioneer roots" all prompted readers to seek in the novels an imagined geography of refuge and return.

Christy

Christy's popularity at the time of its initial publication exceeds that of any other Appalachian-set novel after Fox's *Lonesome Pine*. There were three printings of the McGraw-Hill first edition, a Book Club version, and mass-market paperbacks from Avon in 1967, 1968, and 1969. The novel spent thirty-eight weeks on the *New York Times* hardback best-seller list, peaking at number two, and another thirty-six weeks on the paperback list. It was the fifth best-selling novel in all of 1967 and the ninth best-selling in 1968.[15] At least one devoted reader named her baby after the heroine.[16] Indeed, the novel may have played a part in the national popularity of the name between 1971 and 1981, when "Christy" appeared in the top one hundred names for girls in the United States, up from between two hundred and three hundred; it reached its zenith in 1975 as the fifty-third most popular name.[17] In 1970, *Life* magazine named *Christy* as one of the top five most influential books for youth seventeen to twenty-one years old. As late as 2006, *Christianity Today* ranked *Christy* as twenty-seventh among the top fifty "landmark" books that had most shaped the way evangelicals "think, talk, worship, witness, and live."[18]

It is difficult to overestimate the effect that *Christy* continues to have on perceptions of Appalachia today. This is partly due to the number of youthful readers the novel attracted; a fifteen-year-old who read the book in 1970 was in 2010 just fifty-four years old and, according to anecdotal accounts, eager to share her youthful favorite with her own daughters and granddaughters. The staying power of Marshall's mission novel is also due to well-organized support from Christian fans, who were largely responsible for securing television and film adaptations in the 1990s. Thanks to their loyalty, a reprint of *Christy* returned to best-seller lists in 1994 with the launch of the television series.[19]

Catherine Marshall (1914–1983) was born Sarah Catherine Wood to a Presbyterian minister father and a former missionary mother in Johnson City, not far from *Christy*'s more rural East Tennessee setting. She was raised in Mississippi and in Keyser, West Virginia, and attended Agnes Scott College in Atlanta, Georgia, where she met her first hus-

Advertisement for *Christy*, 1967.

band, the Scottish-born Peter Marshall.[20] Marshall began writing after her husband's death in 1949, partly out of economic necessity, and Peter's near-celebrity status as chaplain of the U.S. Senate helped ensure the success of her writing career. Marshall's first foray into publishing, a collection of her husband's sermons titled *A Man Called Peter* (1951), became a best seller. She then wrote five more Christian-themed nonfiction works. She married *Guideposts* editor Leonard LeSourd in 1959, and the two founded a Christian publishing company called Chosen Books.[21]

Despite the substantial popularity of Marshall's nonfiction, by 1978 about half of the books she had sold were copies of her first novel, *Christy*, based upon her mother's experiences.[22] The story's heroine, nineteen-year-old Christy Huddleston, is as a young woman called from her well-to-do Asheville upbringing to teach schoolchildren in the Great Smoky Mountains in 1912. She sets out by train and then, guided by the mail carrier, on foot to Cutter Gap, a fictionalized town based on Morgan Gap in Cocke County, Tennessee. There Christy works at a mission based on the onetime Ebenezer Mission. (Marshall changed its name because, as she put it, "I thought that the name 'Ebenezer' would be a little strong for most of my readers!")[23] When Christy's faith is tested by the challenges faced by her and her new mountain friends, she seeks wisdom from Alice Henderson, the Quaker who runs the mission. She learns the meaning of friendship from Fairlight Spencer, a young mountain mother. Christy guides her pupils as they navigate poverty, fatal medical superstitions, and the violent family feuds that break out over moonshining. The mission's minister, David Grantland, courts Christy but in the end is not a suitable match.[24] Christy falls instead for Dr. Neil MacNeill, the gruff local-boy-come-home who speaks (for some unexplained reason) with a Scottish brogue as he instructs Christy about the honorable cultural reasons behind the strange mountain ways she confronts.

Christy was not well received by reviewers. The *New York Times Book Review* denounced it as a "tract" rather than a novel, "long on heart, short on art." *Time* called the novel a "relentlessly uplifting honeypot."[25] Readers clearly found less fault. It appears that Marshall received between one hundred and two hundred fan letters about *Christy* per year for the first decade after its publication, and more than fifty letters annually from 1977 until her death in 1983. Most of these fan letters came from families of middle-class white-collar professionals with ambitions for status beyond their financial situations—including especially teachers, nurses, housewives, social workers, ministers' wives, and college students.[26] Readers skewed away from the usual concentration in the urban Northeast, with return addresses almost equally divided between Northeast (22 percent), Southeast (24 percent), Midwest (29 percent), and West (20 percent).[27] Marshall's *Christy* fans were almost exclusively women—comprising 90 percent of the letters I analyzed. In the first few years, fans were middle-aged and older, many of them familiar with Marshall through her Christian nonfiction. From the beginning, readers shared *Christy* with daughters and other young female relatives.[28] Girls quickly grew as a proportion of Marshall's readers, especially those ten to fourteen years old. Almost one in four correspondents were college age or younger. Over time, Marshall heard from young women who had first read the novel years ago and who continued to reread it loyally. Readers frequently opened their letters to Marshall with the statement "I have just finished [*Christy*] for the [sixth, tenth, etc.] time."[29]

When Marshall described *Christy*'s "chief points" to one young fan, she highlighted first its religious messages: "(1) Just social service work—bettering the material situation—does not change people. It takes, in addition, the love of God . . . (2) God does not love just the 'good' people, but all of us."[30] Overwhelmingly, Marshall's early readers responded warmly to these Christian themes and identified with Christy in her path to faith and self-realization. Marshall described *Christy*'s third "chief point" as: "(3) Let us be proud of our mountain folk and their great heritage."[31] My examination of the fan mail focused primarily upon those letters (approximately one in four) that mentioned this third theme: the people, places, or culture of the southern Appalachian mountains. Among fans who discussed the mountains or mountaineers, the two most frequent themes were a desire for more details about the characters (and the people on whom they were based) and a fascination with the region as a place and people apart. The next-largest clusters of readers included those whose responses I have grouped as "regional," "missionary," and "touristic" in affiliation. Although the letters to Marshall regarding the mountain characters and mountain setting of her story represent just a fraction of the *Christy* fan mail, they are our only clues regarding the impressions about the region that millions took away from a book that most readers initially embraced as the story of a young girl's spiritual journey and coming-of-age.

Marshall worked diligently to expand her audience beyond the loyal following for her Christian nonfiction works, and over time it paid off.

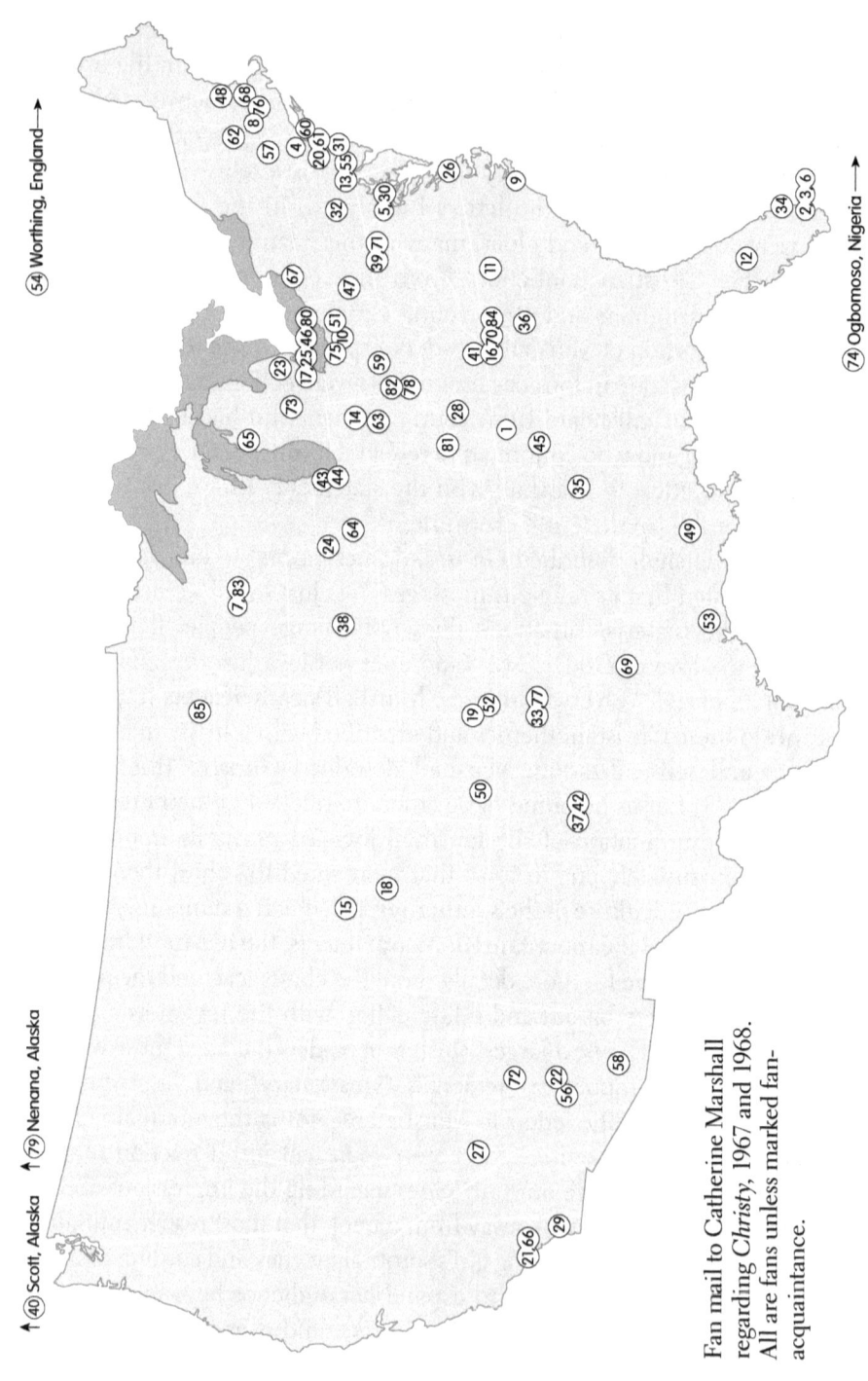

Fan mail to Catherine Marshall regarding *Christy*, 1967 and 1968. All are fans unless marked fan-acquaintance.

1. W. Don Rogers, Nashville, Tennessee. 2. Florence M. Sullivan, Boynton Beach, Florida. 3. Carolyn J. Wolf, Boynton Beach, Florida. 4. Marian Hittl, Pleasantville, New York. 5. C. Leslie Glenn, Washington, DC. 6. Mrs. E. R. Walker, Boynton Beach, Florida. 7. Mrs. Oscar E. Sanden, Minneapolis, Minnesota. 8. Emma Moody Powell, East Northfield, Massachusetts. 9. Alma B. Davis, Newport, North Carolina. 10. Miss Elizabeth Wood, Elyria, Ohio. 11. Mrs. William P. Gordon, Winston-Salem, North Carolina. 12. Mrs. W. J. Moss, Haines City, Florida. 13. Carl Tisall, Newtown Square, Pennsylvania. 14. Mrs. Keith E. Harris, Huntington, Indiana. 15. Mrs. Horace E. Moore, Jelm, Wyoming. 16. Max T. Harrison, Johnson City, Tennessee. 17. Harry D. Mills, Ann Arbor, Michigan. 18. J. H. Silversmith Jr., Denver, Colorado. 19. Margie Lacio, Wichita, Kansas. 20. Mrs. Earl A. Mosley, Tenafly, New Jersey. 21. Lowell and Betty Harvey, Long Beach, California. 22. Marlynn W. Barnes, Scottsdale, Arizona. 23. Rowena E. Ruggles, Lapeer, Michigan. 24. Mrs. James W. Clapp, Oxford Junction, Iowa. 25. D. C. Schubert, Detroit, Michigan. 26. George N. Nelson, Portsmouth, Virginia. 27. Lynette Presson, Las Vegas, Nevada. 28. Mrs. John Long, Rineyville, Kentucky. 29. C. Leslie Palmer, San Diego, California. 30. Frances Green, Washington, DC. 31. Louise Jost, Red Bank, New Jersey. 32. Loretta M. Olson, Liverpool, Pennsylvania. 33. E. E. Parks, Oklahoma City, Oklahoma. 34. Augustine Healy, Palm Beach, Florida. 35. Mrs. Dan O. Purgear, Pontotoc, Mississippi. 36. Lowell A. and Margaret Leonard, Hendersonville, North Carolina. 37. Jennie Lou Murphy, Lubbock, Texas. 38. Ruth M. Snyder, Perry, Iowa. 39. Bernice Idleman, fan-acquaintance, Mt. Lake Park, Maryland. 40. Waylon Sims, Scott, Alaska. 41. Anna Starkey, Pineville, Kentucky. 42. Jennie Lou Murphy, Lubbock, Texas. 43. Alane Repa, Norridge, Illinois. 44. Mildred Syversen, Matteson, Illinois. 45. Elmer M. White, Lawrenceburg, Tennessee. 46. Mrs. Stanley S. Kresge, fan-acquaintance, Detroit, Michigan. 47. Veronica E. Hale, fan-acquaintance, Zelienople, Pennsylvania. 48. C. Langdon Kenney, Pittsfield, New Hampshire. 49. Charlien Piper, Denham Springs, Louisiana. 50. Helen Wells, Sublette, Kansas. 51. Mildred W. Herbach, Aurora, Ohio. 52. Ann Sowden, Arkansas City, Kansas. 53. Carl D. Schubert, Nederland, Texas. 54. Ron Roper, Worthing, Sussex, England. 55. Anne Marshfield, Wallingford, Pennsylvania. 56. Wilma A. Phelps, Phoenix, Arizona. 57. Rose Damien, Round Top, New York. 58. Gracia Booth, Tucson, Arizona. 59. Lois J. Maroney, Galena, Ohio. 60. Harold S. Diehl, New York, New York. 61. Mrs. Herman A. Comfort, Dover, New Jersey. 62. Ruth M. E. Hennig, Wells, Vermont. 63. Bette McClintock, Anderson, Indiana. 64. Janet Irvin, Galesburg, Illinois. 65. Richard T. Jeffries, Manistee, Michigan. 66. Marjorie Laurane Hamilton, Whittier, California. 67. Gertrude R. Johnson, Jamestown, New York. 68. Mrs. Howard M. Stillman, Andover, Massachusetts. 69. Johnnie Sue True, Athens, Texas. 70. Annie H. Quekemeyer, Johnson City, Tennessee. 71. Gladys Harrison, McCoole, Maryland. 72. Ruth A. Grant, Flagstaff, Arizona. 73. Donald J. Thompson, Middleton, Michigan. 74. Betty Sledd, Ogbomoso, Nigeria. 75. Ruth Dodd, Lorain, Ohio. 76. Mrs. Robert F. Sweeney, Worcester, Massachusetts. 77. Curtis B. Day, Oklahoma City, Oklahoma. 78. Marlene C. Waggoner, Mount St. Joseph, Ohio. 79. Mrs. John A. Phillips, Nenana, Alaska. 80. Sue Olin, Birmingham, Michigan. 81. Sharon Eichele, Evansville, Indiana. 82. Ulanda Kiefer, Hamilton, Ohio. 83. Mrs. C. D. Holzinger, St. Paul, Minnesota. 84. Carl D. Cheek, Kingsport, Tennessee. 85. Mrs. Elmer Carlson, Sydney, North Dakota.

She had suggested to her editors that advertisements emphasize the book's "warm love story" rather than "toot anything religious," since that might "put off the new audience whom we hope to reach."[32] By the early to mid-1970s, more readers were drawn to the story itself, not merely its well-known Christian author. At least one reader viewed the mountaineers as more central to the story than its spiritual dimension: "To me this is the whole crux of your story—to know the mountain people. . . . Your story is no religious tract," wrote Mrs. Rubinstein in Illinois.[33] Signatures were increasingly preceded by "Sincerely yours" and "Love" rather than "God Bless You."

Christy's *Production of Place and Construction of Identity*

Christy, like other popular regional fiction, participated in the production and commodification of Appalachia through a romance of authenticity. For readers who focused upon mountain culture, the words that surfaced repeatedly included *folklore, folk songs, Elizabethan, customs, traditions, quaint, the old country, dialect, Scotland,* and *Highlanders*. Readers described the region's presumed distinctiveness as a matter of both geography (isolation) and chronology (behind the times). Both features, readers presumed, informed the racial and ethnic status of mountain people as Elizabethan, Ulster-Scot, Scottish, and/or "pioneer." "How 'advanced' are these people?" asked one reader. "Of course, the pride of their inheritance is still strong, but have they become 'modernized' to some extent?"[34] Others wanted to know how Marshall "managed to find traditions kept by the mountain people" and whether such people were "alive today in the Cutter Gap area."[35] Readers turned to Marshall for reassurance of mountaineers' British Isles origins, which *Christy* intimated through the Scottish American character Dr. MacNeill and through Marshall's use of the term *Highlander*. In reality, the most prominent European groups to settle the region were Germans, English, and Scots-Irish from Ulster (not the Scottish Highlands). Readers, however, found the misleading Scottish connection highly romantic. "What a beautiful land the Highlanders left!" enthused one fan. Ina Robison "had not known they were brot from Scotland and 'planted' in Appalachia."[36] A young folk singer writing an essay for her English class on folk songs begged Marshall to help her substantiate her "thesis that these hill people came originally from the British Isles."[37]

Christy wavers between delight in and dismay at mountain culture as it follows Christy's growing appreciation of supposedly "Elizabethan" customs and her confrontations with squalor. Alongside Christy's delighted discovery of music, there is her horror at the alcohol-ridden culture of running moonshine and the violence that it fuels. Alongside Christy's appreciation of Fairlight Spencer's love of nature, there is her sadness at Fairlight's longing for the sun, hidden too much of the day by the tall mountains overhead. On the one hand, Christy is charmed by the simplicity of the mountaineers. On the other, she is distressed by superstitions that hamper attempts to heal the sick, and on one occasion she is so stricken by the ugliness and foulness of a pupil's cabin that she vomits.

Readers were attuned to both aspects of mountain life, both of which underwrote their sense of it as an authentic and more enriching way of life. Fans found Cutter Gap "unscrubbed," "sordid," and full of violence, ignorance, and hardships; in equal measure they viewed the place as quaint and full of life.[38] For many readers, the lowliness of the mountain region in fact held the secret of its greatest potential. Their encomiums bordered on an offensive romanticization of extreme depravation. Although Ruth Burlison of Ohio found the situation of the mountain people "deplorable," she also enthused that "the people are so Simple and filled with love of life instead of material goods."[39] A couple in New Jersey felt that "even though physically they led a much more difficult life than we do, they had a faith that is lacking in modern life."[40]

Catherine Marshall was well aware of the tension between admiration and horror inherent in readers' imagination of the mountains as primordial in an era when technology and urbanity seemed to have attenuated humankind's relationships to nature and God. When one sixteen-year-old reader effused, "It's been the dream of my life to live in a world of *basics*. Hard physical work . . . log cabin-farm . . . not only a large garden but complete livestock, no electricity—just oil lamps," Marshall affirmed this response to her novel. In a reply that might just as easily have come from James Dickey, Marshall asked her secretary to tell Suzanne Hermanson "that I think her dream of getting back to basics is exactly right. This is what we shall eventually be facing all over the nation."[41]

Marshall was also a savvy self-promoter. She calculated her representation of Appalachia and her marketing strategy to negotiate prevalent assumptions about regional authenticity. In a typewritten memo, Marshall advised her editors, perhaps based on the many tourism brochures she had collected from Asheville, to "use 'Great Smoky Mountains'" in describing the novel's setting since the "word 'Appalachia,'" because of the War on Poverty, "immediately raises the picture in the public's mind of a negative, grubby kind of poverty, not attractive."[42] In replies to fan mail, Marshall insisted that the Tennessee/North Carolina border was more picturesque than the coal fields, and shrewdly provided the name "Christy Country" as an alternative to "Appalachia."[43] Although Marshall marketed her work as set in "the Smokies" as opposed to Appalachia, when fans expressed interest in "Appalachia," she readily asserted herself as an expert on the subject. She referred them to her sources on the region, including Horace Kephart's now infamous *Our Southern Highlanders* and her own list, "Suggested Books for Research on Folk Music of the Appalachians."[44]

Marshall not only represented herself as a scholar of Appalachia, but she also promoted herself as having an authentic relation to the story she told—having astutely perceived the importance of readers' trust in her "insider" status. Responding to a letter from Anna Mae Ogle of Sevierville, Tennessee, who graciously offered "to help you to meet some of our wonderful people," Marshall bristled. "I am a native of East Tennessee," she wrote. "All my father's folks are from that area. My mother is from western North Carolina. . . . And my [parents met at] . . . Ebenezer Mission. . . . Thus in writing the book . . . , I am, in a very real sense, coming home." She was ultimately forced to admit, however, that she needed Ogle's help to gather material for her story: "I do very much want to get into some of the homes way back in the mountains."[45]

Book jacket copy, the map inside the front and back cover, and especially the prologue assured readers that *Christy* was an authentic story about real-life places and events. Marshall's prologue promised that the story contained "true experiences" in order to establish her authority to "write about the mountains, my mountains. For these were the hills of home; I had been born among mountains like these."[46] Readers were convinced. They believed in the accuracy of the narrative and felt *Christy* was a reliable source of information regarding mountain "places and customs." Dianna McRoberts wrote, "Your book showed me how it used to be and, in some places, how it still is."[47] Carol Phillips's interest was piqued when, on "the day I started reading Christy, the National Geographic arrived with a picture essay on the Great Smokies," including "a haunting picture of . . . the dulcimers" and the places "where Christy and Fairlight might have wandered. It was a most satisfying coincidence to have the illustrations come with the book, so to speak." Several fans wrote to tell Marshall that her fictional novel was their first resource for their "study of the Appalachia Country."[48]

In addition to meeting readers' cravings for an authentic place and people, *Christy* fed their desire for identity and belonging. As we have seen, *Christy*'s presumed association with pioneer living offered some white readers a sense of national history and pride. Many more felt a personal affiliation with the novel's setting. A few of these overlapped with "missionary" and "touristic" readers, whom I discuss below as part of the circulation of power promoted by both *Christy* and *Deliverance*. Most fans with a geographic affiliation, however, simply and urgently wanted Marshall to know about their personal connections to the places featured in her novel, to link their identity to their sense that they belonged to a more authentic and grounded culture.

Readers for whom *Christy* was significant because of geographic affiliations fell loosely into three groups.[49] Some felt a connection by Scottish ancestry, including several who professed that they were descendants of the same "clan" in Scotland as Marshall's character Dr. MacNeill and wrote to compare notes on genealogy. Others, similar to the missionary and touristic readers discussed below, had had an encounter with the region during a brief residence there and shared Marshall's exoticization of it. They used the occasion of their fan mail to reminisce about the vividness of their years there but expressed little emotional attachment to the mountains. George Butz of Butz Lumber Company in Wilmington, Delaware, for example, had attended Biltmore Forest School in western North Carolina and regaled Marshall with a story about hiding out in the rhododendron bushes from a local man with a gun.[50]

Most readers with a geographic affiliation fell into a third group. They identified themselves or their families as being from the region and announced that *Christy* perfectly captured their beloved home in print or provided them a link to an ancestral homeland. Fan letters often originated from places that were destinations for out-migrants during the Southern Diaspora, the movement of millions of rural whites and African Americans northward, westward, and into southern cities. In every year between 1967 and 1982, Marshall received more letters from Ohio than any other state, primarily from the out-migrant destination cities of Cincinnati, Columbus, and Cleveland.[51] Whether they were still living in the mountains or were at a two-generation remove, the notion of heritage was key to this group's construction of a sense of belonging and identity.

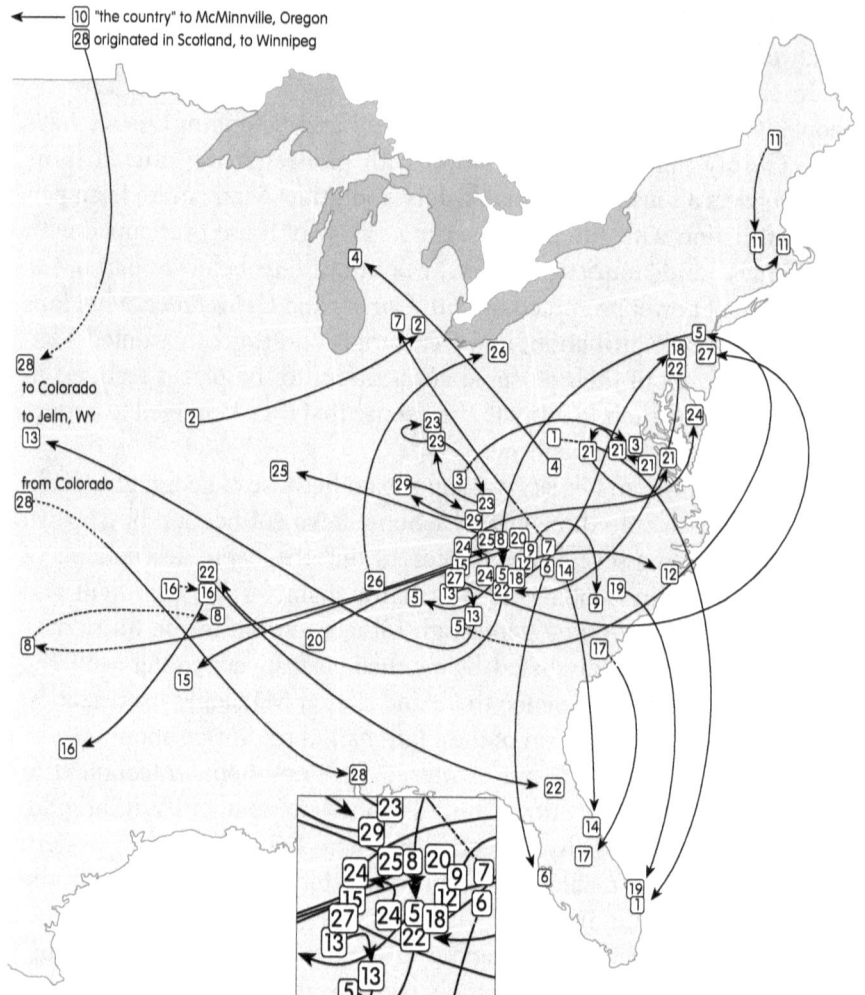

Fan mail to Catherine Marshall from migrant fans, 1967–1973. Both personal and family migrations are included, since *Christy* fans described their families' migration history as key to their sense of identity and displacement. Dotted line indicates that the precise location is not known.

1. Carolyn J. Wolf, West Virginia → Boynton Beach, Florida
2. Harry D. Mills, Kirksville, Missouri → Ann Arbor, Michigan
3. Frances Green, Kentucky → Washington, DC
4. Mrs. Richard T. Jeffries, Greenbrier County, West Virginia → Manistee, Michigan
5. Allen Joe Park, North Georgia? → Scotch Plains, New Jersey → Asheville, North Carolina → Signal Mountain, Tennessee
6. Louise Howard, western North Carolina → St. Petersburg, Florida
7. Richard Burnames, Blue Ridge → Albion, Michigan
8. Myra Reeves Hardin, Johnson City, Tennessee → southwest Oklahoma → Arkansas
9. Sheila Angel, Burnsville, North Carolina → Bennettsville, South Carolina
10. Jeanne Yohey, "in the country" → McMinnville, Oregon
11. Josephine Dobbyn, "small-town" Maine → Wakefield, Massachusetts → Chelsea, Massachusetts
12. Alma B. Davis, parents: Barnardsville, North Carolina → Newport, North Carolina
13. Mrs. Horace E. Moore, family "roots ... in the Smoky Mountain country (around Patty, Benton, and Ocoee)" → born North Georgia → Jelm, Wyoming
14. Judith P. Canant, "father's people were in North Carolina for generations" → Titusville, Florida ("Daddy came to Fla. as a child, and here we've been ever since.")
15. Cathey Poindexter, "grandfather, John Cathey, and his parents lived near Deep Creek and Indian Creek," Tennessee → Camden, Arkansas
16. Wilma Spencer Fonville, grandfather's ancestors from "the Appalachian section" of northern Arkansas → grandfather "reared in Northern Arkansas" → Fort Worth, Texas
17. Mrs. W. J. Moss, taught in cotton fields of South Carolina → Haines City, Florida
18. Carl Tisall, taught at Asheville Normal and Collegiate Institute, where he met wife, who hailed from nearby Marion, North Carolina → Newtown Square, Pennsylvania
19. Augustine Healy, Southern Pines, North Carolina → Palm Beach, Florida
20. Annie H. Quekemeyer, Mississippi → Johnson City, Tennessee
21. Mr. and Mrs. Russell Bargamin Jr., east coast of Virginia → boys' boarding school in Orange, Virginia, and girls' boarding school in Staunton, Virginia → Urbanna, Virginia
22. William A. Barnhill, photographer, Philadelphia → western North Carolina → Gamaliel, Arkansas → Gainesville, Florida
23. Olive M. Andrews, Cincinnati, Ohio → taught at Lotts Creek Community School, Knott County, Kentucky → Cincinnati → Englewood, Ohio (vacation home in Indian Lake, Florida)
24. George A. Butz Sr., graduated from Biltmore Forest School, North Carolina → Jellico Plains, Tennessee → Rehoboth Beach, Delaware
25. Mrs. Clen Lawson, "husband was born & raised near Sneedville Tenn." → Edwardsville, Illinois
26. Ruth M. Burlison, husband's family still live in Middle Tennessee → Brunswick, Ohio
27. Margaret Steward, college at Maryville, Tennessee → Piscataway, New Jersey
28. Catherine Riddell, the Riddells came from Scotland → Winnipeg, Manitoba, Canada → "one branch moved to Colorado, where I was born" → Mobile, Alabama
29. Joe and Elaine Armstrong, Louisville, Kentucky → taught in Harlan, Kentucky → Louisville, Kentucky

Despite the number of fans writing from out-migration destinations, just a small proportion talked about recent migrant experiences and those who did expressed little wistfulness for the mountains. The matter-of-fact tone of out-migrants who explained that they were "Kentuckian by birth" or "a native West Virginia hill girl" differed from that of the anguished readers who wrote to Arnow with poignant memories of home.[52] Seventy-six-year-old Harry Mills, a migrant from "a little farm community" in Missouri to Ann Arbor, Michigan, was a rare exception; he felt much of *Christy* "paralleled" his "life and experience" and that it captured "words and expressions . . . used by my 'kinfolks' when I was a youn[g]ster."[53] Out-migrants living in Washington, DC, Florida, or Michigan nonetheless relished seeing in print the places, "folklore," and "extraordinary mountain people" whom they proudly announced they knew firsthand.[54]

Unlike fans of Arnow, the Marshall fans who felt the greatest emotional urgency about the mountains were those who continued to make the mountains their home or those who traced family to the region in their grandparents' generation. Letters from readers who viewed Appalachia as home suggest that *Christy*, a novel rarely recognized for the identity affirmation with which readers generally credit Appalachian literature, in fact served this role for fans. Such readers included seventeen-year-old Vicki Hendrix in North Carolina, who was skeptical of the lengthy tome until she "realized you were describing my home." After reading *Christy*, her "love for the mountains, 'my mountains,' is growing deeper."[55] "Dear Frend," wrote Allen Joe Park of Signal Mountain, Tennessee, "Your book has all my kinfolks in it." Park explained that he knew it made "the 'feisty' sightseers mad" when he drove slowly, "but these are my Mountains."[56] Max Harrison of Johnson City, Tennessee, wrote to say that he and his coworkers at the Tennessee Department of Education "remember our fathers and grandparents telling about similar people and similar hardships." Though Harrison placed himself at a remove from "similar people," he ended his letter by thanking Marshall "for a beautiful story about my heritage."[57] Curiously, readers did not have to be from Appalachia to feel that *Christy* allowed them to visit their homes. They wrote movingly about their love for the rural places of their childhoods—the mountains in Washington State, the Oregon countryside, a farm in Ohio, and a small Maine town—with the assumption and hope that Marshall could understand the nature and depth of their attachments.[58]

Readers who viewed Appalachia as their ancestral homeland wrote perhaps the most passionate letters. In contrast to missives from genealogical researchers, sojourners, and out-migrants, ancestral fans offered emotionally laden testimonies as to their rightful belonging to the mountains and, perhaps more than any others, embraced a vision of so-called mountain folk as simple and content. Mrs. Horace Moore in Wyoming expressed pride that she was "a scant two generations away from the mountain folk you portrayed so accurately." Alma B. Davis in coastal North Carolina told Marshall that *Christy* was the "fulfillment of a dream for me—a book written with love and understanding of the mountain people" because the mountains were her mother's home. Judith Canant, whose "father's people were in North Carolina for generations," proclaimed that although she had been born in Florida, "a part of me belongs in these mountains— I hunger for them." Readers like these were keen to share with Marshall the fact that, in the words of Moore, their "family roots were deep in the Smoky Mountain country."[59]

Our surprise that *Christy*, with a reputation for stereotypical feuding and poverty-stricken mountaineers, could play such a key role in Appalachian identity politics might only be surpassed by our amazement that *Deliverance*'s depictions of the region's people as crude and violent did the same.

Deliverance

James Dickey's *Deliverance*, not as commercially successful as *Christy*, spent twenty-six weeks on the *New York Times* best-selling hardback list, and sixteen on that newspaper's paperback list (peaking at third on both). The novel was a selection of the Book-of-the-Month Club and the Literary Guild of America. Within two years it had achieved its eighth printing and sold almost 2 million copies.[60] Dickey's novel created for readers an Appalachia that served as the site of a collective "nightmare," to use a term adopted by several of Dickey's reviewers. The rape of city men by leering "hicks," central to the novel and iconic in its film version, became almost synonymous with popular conceptions of the mountain South.[61]

Deliverance's "nightmare" is best understood as a fantasy belonging to James Dickey III (1923–1997), a man reared in a wealthy neighborhood of Atlanta, Georgia, who feared and revered the mountainous North Georgia region that had loomed large in his childhood as a place apart.

Dickey's father, James II, was a lawyer who loved hunting and cockfighting; his North Georgia farm served as a refuge from his wife, her family inheritance, and the Buckhead mansion and servants that her wealth afforded them even in the depths of the Great Depression. Dickey, like his father, was uncomfortable with his mother's wealth. Ashamed of his family's profits from a patent medicine company that he believed preyed on the poor, and "fearing accusations of being a pampered and effeminate child," Dickey preferred to claim that he grew up in the mountains. He attributed his blustery aggressiveness to his "North Georgia folk heritage" and averred, "My people are all hillbillies. I'm only second-generation city." Though Dickey's ancestors had indeed lived in mountainous Fannin County, they were not the plain folk he made them out to be. He failed to acknowledge that they were slaveholders and among the largest landowners and wealthiest residents of the county.[62]

Dickey's romantic—and racist—vision of Appalachia as a place apart stayed with him his entire life. In 1963, he worked on a poem called "On Fannin County" in which he hoped to depict the area as Edenic: "industry moving out . . . land reverting . . . 'no niggers.'"[63] In 1980, Dickey sent a letter to Eliot Wigginton of *Foxfire* fame in which he confided, "I have a very real interest in the region, since my father's people came from there. . . . There is a certain yearning for place, for custom. . . . I not only admire greatly what you have done to make the uniqueness of 'the wilderness of heaven' known and appreciated by people who don't live there, but I feel that to some extent, by blood and natural affinity, I belong to the region, and thus to your cause." In 1981, Dickey wrote about North Georgia: "I love that area and hope to be buried there."[64]

Despite Dickey's felt identification with mountain people, his novel invites readers to identify with its protagonist, one of four businessmen from Atlanta, over and against the mountain people with whom the Atlantans have strained or violent encounters. This phenomenon arose partly from the fact that Dickey loosely based his novel on his own (less eventful) journeys on canoe trips in the summers of 1960 and 1961, accompanied by his advertising firm colleague Al Braselton and his tennis partner Lewis King.[65] Dickey's identification with both "hillbillies" and suburban Atlanta men provided a magnetizing tension in the novel.

The novel, unlike the film, opens in suburban Atlanta as the middle-aged businessmen plan a weekend canoe trip in the North Georgia mountains. The city men recognize that they "don't really know what we're getting into. There's not one of us knows a damned thing about the woods, or about rivers."[66] The novel, more so than the film, suggests that perhaps the travelers get a bit of what they deserve in so rashly venturing beyond their ken. Adman Ed Gentry, loosely based on Dickey, narrates the novel in the first person. It is through his eyes that readers meet the buff hunter Lewis King (memorably played by Burt Reynolds in the film version) and their city-soft companions, the overweight, "pink complexion[ed]" advertising salesman Bobby and the sensitive guitar-playing Drew (D, 5). The opening scenes of the novel introduce us to Ed's combination of skepticism and admiration for Lewis's machismo.

The remainder of the story is widely known from the film version. During the trip, two toothless armed mountain men in overalls take Bobby and Ed captive, and one rapes Bobby. Lewis appears and kills the hillbilly with a bow and arrow. Once the group is back on the river, the second hillbilly avenges his companion's death by murdering Drew (we think), capsizing the Atlantans' canoe. The virile Lewis is incapacitated and the blubbering Bobby is no help. The narrator, Ed, rises to the occasion. He scales a cliff and kills the enemy. He then coaches Lewis and Bobby on the story they must tell to avoid a trial that would be staged, the Atlantans presume, by relatives of the dead mountain men. Whereas the novel opens with Ed and Bobby's shared "understanding . . . that neither of us was to take Lewis too seriously" (D, 5), in the end it endorses Lewis's brute strength and glorifies Ed's manly capacity to live up to the sudden demands placed upon him.

Reviewers had their reservations. Benjamin DeMott was disappointed by the self-congratulatory and unreflective paean to hypermasculinity that ensues from Dickey's identification with Ed. He bemoaned *Deliverance*'s degeneration into "mindlessness," a western "played in canoes." Dickey, according to DeMott, appears "less troubled about being peddled as a white-hope poet-jock or faggot-fighter . . . than he might be." An otherwise rave review in the *Nation* echoed DeMott in this regard, calling the novel "muscle-bound." Christopher Ricks complained in the *New York Review of Books* that "*Deliverance* is too patently the concoction of a situation in which it will be morally permissible—nay, essential—to kill men with a bow and arrow. Such is clearly what the book wants to do from the outset, and the contrivance of such circumstances has its cold prurience."[67] As these objections to Dickey's "concoction" and "contrivance" suggest, critics found *Deliverance* more reverie than realism. "We don't believe a line of it," said the *Library Journal*, while the *New York Times Book Review* reported that readers are "not quite persuaded Dickey has told the truth."[68]

Deliverance's reviewers speculated that the novel's popularity might stem from the exhilarating escape it provided bored suburban readers from the monotony of mass society. A writer for the *New York Times* exclaimed, somewhat tongue-in-cheek, "Good God, I thought, cliff climbing must be the only primordial sensual-sexual experience left in an America gone plastic." DeMott noted that *Deliverance* allowed readers to "ris[e] out of tranced dailiness—habitual, half-lived life—into a more intense physicality." Less charitably, the London-based *New Statesman* observed that the novel offered relief from the "intense urban hideousness and the insipid suburbia in which the bulk of Mr. Dickey's readers live."[69]

Although many of Dickey's fans were familiar with the critical reception of *Deliverance*, their responses rarely followed the same lines of analysis.[70] Indeed, at least one Dickey proponent vigorously resisted DeMott's analysis with harsh ridicule and homophobia. Fred Exley, a regular Dickey correspondent, said he "really laughed at the asshole who reviewed the novel in *Saturday Review*, taking you to task . . . for flexing your muscles. He was obviously a cocksucker."[71] Overwhelmingly, fans saw the novel as an adventure tale and many wrote that they had been compelled to write immediately upon finishing the novel.

Nonetheless, fans' immense satisfaction with their vicarious experience of triumph confirms critics' suspicions about the novel's utility as a thrilling escape. From elementary school students to businessmen to housewives, readers reported experiencing the events of the novel "as if I had been in the canoe." Janet Kovach in New Jersey told Dickey, "I rode that river too," while James Isaacs wrote, "Thanks for the canoe trip. It was real." As admirer Joan Tuckerman Dick explained, "I've finished the book, but I'm still messing about in the river."[72] Readers found themselves wholly in sympathy with Ed and his transformation into manly hero. Sixteen-year-old Ellen Lane of South Carolina wrote, "When I finished *Deliverance* I put it down and wept" for "Ed the Reluctant Outdoorsman scaling the face of the cliff in the moonlight. . . . He was so real to me and I loved him so very much!"[73] Other readers, male and female alike, felt that they became Ed over the course of the novel. Catharine Meyer of *Harper's* magazine exulted, "I *made* it imaginatively and got my own kick out of doing it."[74]

For readers like these, the consequences of the novel for the national imagination of region were partially a function of readers' identification with Ed in opposition to a hillbilly threat. Yet despite their focus upon Ed's success—and thus their own success vicariously through him—the majority of readers rarely mentioned the novel's setting or the nature of Ed's challenge in the form of reprehensible mountaineers. We have to rely upon the small proportion of fans who mentioned mountaineers or the mountain setting to provide us with hints about the consequences of *Deliverance* for millions of readers' imagination of Appalachia.

Dickey's archive includes hundreds upon hundreds of glowing letters about *Deliverance* from friends, colleagues, and admirers, including 156 letters mailed in 1970 and 1971 alone. About 60 percent of *Deliverance* correspondence came from friends, fellow authors, associates, and literati who knew of Dickey through his poetry. About 40 percent I count as having been written by "fans," or unknown admirers who wrote unsolicited fan mail occasioned solely by their reaction to *Deliverance*. Of fans, two-thirds were male. Fan mail arrived from businessmen who fancied themselves sporting and from women of means. Almost all were adults, though Dickey received letters from boys as young as eleven.[75] Fans wrote from across the United States—approximately one-third from the Southeast, one-third the Northeast, and almost another one-third from the Midwest and West coast combined.[76]

According to Dickey's biographer, Dickey told "friends that he stayed away from his old canoeing haunts for fear of getting lynched" by angry locals.[77] For the most part, however, locally identified resistant readers did not leave their mark upon Dickey's correspondence, which is replete with appreciative fan mail. As we will see, just three correspondents outlined their grievances in letters to Dickey, presenting themselves as defenders of the mountain people and locales represented in Dickey's novel. With the exception of these few resistant readers, Dickey's fans comprised nationally identified cosmopolitan or touristic readers and southern-identified cosmopolitan readers—including out-migrants from the South, for whom Dickey's novel provided a glimpse of what they imagined as the simple people back home.

Neither reviewers nor readers, upon *Deliverance*'s publication or any time since, treated the novel as a work of regional fiction. Yet fan mail demonstrates that *Deliverance* produced Appalachia as a particular kind of place that appealed to his readers' romance with authenticity. It facili-

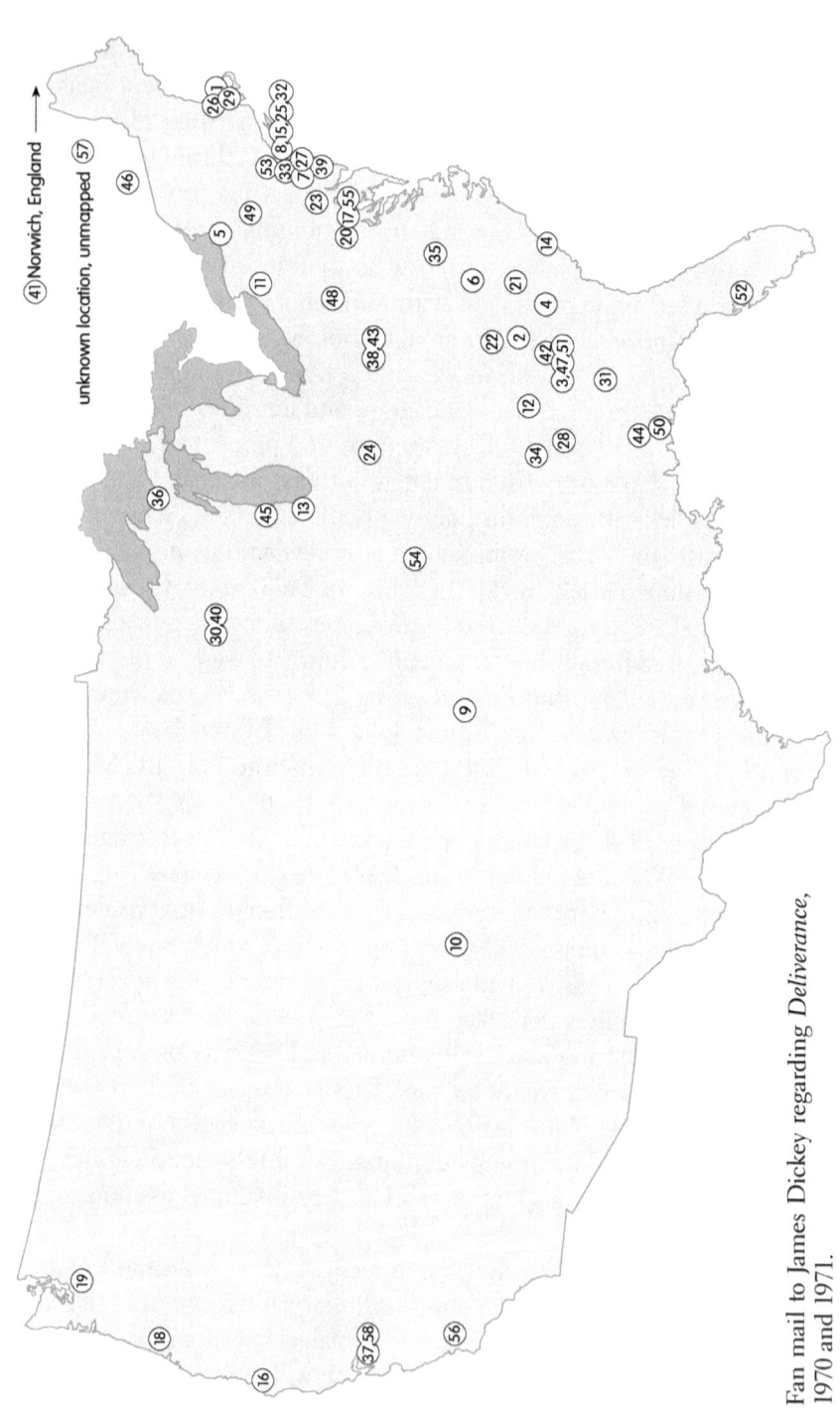

Fan mail to James Dickey regarding *Deliverance*, 1970 and 1971.

1. Rodger Kingston, Somerville, Massachusetts
2. Michael E. Ray, Greenville, South Carolina
3. Fred Lagerquist, Atlanta, Georgia
4. Donald Russell Jr., Columbia, South Carolina
5. Liliane Roberts, Rochester, New York
6. Charles W. Loftin, Jackson Hill, North Carolina
7. Robert M. Kearns, Flemington, New Jersey
8. Lawrence Lighter, Merrick, New York
9. Helena W. Anderson, Peru, Kansas
10. William Greer, Alamosa, Colorado
11. Charles R. Condon, Jamestown, New York
12. Robert Linn, Calhoun, Georgia
13. John H. Shinake, Chicago, Illinois
14. Le Nancie B. Downey, Charleston, South Carolina
15. Margaret Stenerson, Forest Hills, New York
16. James Vince, Fortuna, California
17. Paul Weiss Heffer, Washington, DC
18. Gordon Detzel, Eugene, Oregon
19. David Willson, Seattle, Washington
20. Susan Cryer, Rockville, Maryland
21. Ellen Lane, Rock Hill, South Carolina
22. G. Alex Bernhardt, Lenoir, North Carolina
23. John W. Freas, Haverton, Pennsylvania
24. Tim Alshouse, Indianapolis, Indiana
25. T. J. Koplik, Garden City, Long Island, New York
26. John Niles, Cambridge, Massachusetts
27. Janet R. Kovach, Edison, New Jersey
28. Anne Randolph, Birmingham, Alabama
29. Melvin B. Yoken, Dartmouth, Massachusetts
30. Barbara Mayor, Minneapolis, Minnesota
31. Abraham Baldwin, Tifton, Georgia
32. Jerome Stubenhaus, Mineola, New York
33. B. F. Driggers, Cranbury, New Jersey
34. Paul Neal, Athens, Alabama
35. W. H. Jefferson, Danville, Virginia
36. Blaine Betts, Marquette, Michigan
37. Marty Olmstead, San Francisco, California
38. David B. Buzzard, Columbus, Ohio
39. John H. Miller II, Rumson, New Jersey
40. John Berryman, Minneapolis, Minnesota
41. Cynthia Hack, Norwich, England
42. Coleman Barks, Athens, Georgia
43. Lynn Cansler, Columbus, Ohio
44. Richard Griffith, Andalusia, Alabama
45. Dewey Gill, New Berlin, Wisconsin
46. Susam Allnutt, Montreal, Quebec, Canada
47. Mary Margaret Oliver, Atlanta, Georgia
48. John Lawrence, Pennsylvania
49. Unknown name, Binghamton, New York
50. Eric Wallace, Pensacola, Florida
51. Michael Flynn, Atlanta, Georgia
52. Bill Penhallegon, Clearwater, Florida
53. Lynn Knight, Newburgh, New York
54. Madeline Negri, St. Louis, Missouri
55. Eugene Milligan, McLean, Virginia
56. James Isaacs, Hollywood, California
57. Richard J. Murphy Jr., unknown location
58. Unknown name, Oakland, California

tated readers' construction of identity and community by appealing to their geographic affiliations and through its simultaneous disdain and affection for the region of its setting. And *Deliverance* promoted the circulation of symbolic and financial power across the nation and the globe by enhancing the prestige of high middlebrow readers and training them to recognize Appalachian residents as one manifestation of primitives found the world over.

Deliverance's Production of Place and Construction of Identity

Deliverance manufactured a rural, premodern Appalachia set apart from consumer society and its purportedly banal suburban lifestyle that, despite the predatory nature of the mountain villains, somehow managed to activate readers' romance with authenticity. For some readers, unsurprisingly, *Deliverance*'s setting represented a nightmarish departure from the safe and suburban. Housewife Linda Rogers reported, "I find myself turning away from T.V. commercials with mountains or canoes in them."[78] Darlene LaPler insisted, "My white water trips will never be the same. . . . I'll be expecting to see two strangers standing with their guns pointed our direction."[79]

For a majority of fans, however, the wilderness setting held great appeal despite—or because of—its dangers. Dickey's mountain setting and mountain people promised the preservation of a supposedly authentic mode of life. While reviewers sometimes referred to the novel's villains generically as "hicks" or "rednecks," letters show that readers were pretty clear that they were "hillbillies," "hill folk," "mountaineers" or, as even an eleven-year-old could perceive, "mountain men."[80] Helena Anderson in Kansas wrote to say she could not stop thinking about *Deliverance*. "I am fascinated by the mountaineers, do they really exist in this modern world?" she asked.[81] Dick Stern at the University of Chicago enthused about Dickey's depiction of the "beauty, toughness and wildness of the place, its meanness, its fantastic power."[82] Multiple correspondents wrote affectionately about dulcimers, banjoes, and music associated with Appalachia and one presumed that Dickey would share his concern about preserving "folk archives."[83]

Dickey's Appalachian setting served as a welcome foil for the pitfalls of civilization and modernity. For Charles Loftin, *Deliverance* represented "man's attempt to reach back to the unspoiled past which he has left forever behind." Loftin identified Appalachia with the nation's pioneer roots by crediting it with enabling adventure "in an age which has [made] Daniel Boone almost . . . impossible."[84] Oddly enough, Michael Flynn of Atlanta declared that "your novel reminded us" that "we rarely know our neighbors and community activity is a thing of the past."[85] Readers thus endorsed Dickey's construction of Appalachia as a meaningful place outside commercialized mass society. More ominously, a couple of fans expounded doomsday prophecies for a society too far removed from the simple life. Dan Clark, for example, found *Deliverance* "right on target; the system is going to fail." The "inefficiency of our large institutions, particularly the city and large industry, is going to bring about a collapse."[86] Such anxieties were representative of those in the culture at large, as suggested by the 4 million copies sold of the 1972 book *The Limits to Growth*, which predicted destruction unless food and energy sources increased and population and industrialization decreased.[87]

Dan Clark's letter illuminates a gendered dimension of fans' construction of Authentic Appalachia when it boasts that he had "consistently refused to . . . get one of those soft middle class jobs . . . because I want to lose my domestication and learn to cut it in a scrambling world." As Clark's scorn for "soft" jobs indicates, *Deliverance* produced not only a premodern Appalachia but also a masculinized Appalachia that served as a virility test for men supposedly emasculated by wife-and-family-centered suburban lifestyles. One of Dickey's real-life canoeing buddies put it this way: "*Deliverance* was basically deliverance from women . . . [and] that GOD-DAMNED BIG MOTHER CITY, where the grass is cut, . . . women dominate . . . and children are underfoot." Another acquaintance of Dickey's unabashedly characterized the story as set in "that heaven" known as an "Eveless wilderness."[88]

Such characterizations of Appalachia might not be cause for concern if readers recognized them as fictional. Yet fan mail shows that many readers assumed that Dickey reproduced Appalachia "so real and true to life."[89] For one correspondent in New York who had "never been near the south," the novel "was an instructive trip." A man in Wisconsin wrote that he "had to keep from getting in the car . . . to search the woods somewhere, anywhere, for Ed." A fan of the film version wrote from Alexandria, Virginia, to demand, "You must tell me which of the characters around the gas station where the banjo was played were authentic hill people? . . . Were any of the scenes shot without the locals knowing they were on camera?"[90]

Moreover, readers were under the impression that Dickey was able to provide an accurate depiction in part because he had an authentic relationship to his story and his setting. Margaret Stenerson in New York assumed that "the terrain" of the novel must be familiar to Dickey, and mused that "possibly" he was "one of the characters represented," given his "precise and detailed knowledge of the locale" and its "people."[91] Dickey encouraged such perceptions, even asking his friends on whom his characters were based to say that the events of *Deliverance* had actually happened.[92]

These examples demonstrate that *Deliverance* satisfied readers' cravings for life outside mass commercial society by participating in regional fiction's production of authentic place. *Deliverance* fulfilled the second function of regional fiction by providing readers a sense of self and belonging. Fan mail shows that for many southerners and out-migrants from the South, being able to recognize hillbillies was a matter of pride. White southerners and out-migrants were far more likely to express indulgence toward hillbillies than horror. Certainly hillbillies served for them as a lower-class "Other" against whom they defined themselves. But as Ruth Frankenburg tells us, whites in search of belonging frequently turn to their region of origin as a source of meaning and identity. Dickey's characters allowed readers to appropriate "Appalachianness" while establishing themselves securely above it, thereby constructing an identity in contrast to what they saw as generic white Americanness—normative, cultureless, and empty.[93]

Of course, the fact that *Deliverance* was written by such a highly regarded writer also provided white southern readers an uncommon opportunity to feel proud of national literary attention to what they perceived to be "their" places and "their" people. Southern white readers were keen to capitalize on Dickey's national prominence and constructed their own sense of status and prestige based upon real and imagined ties to him through geographic affiliations. Promoting Dickey meant promoting South Carolina and Georgia. Articles in the *Columbia Record* and other South Carolina newspapers frequently featured Dickey's novel, and the film version of *Deliverance* was honored at the Atlanta film festival. Southern hopes for self-promotion were evident at the film's premiere in Atlanta. Dickey leaned over to say to Jimmy Carter, then the governor: "Ain't no junior league movie, is it, Governor?" "It's pretty rough," Carter agreed, "but it's good for Georgia." Carter paused. "It's good for Georgia. I hope."[94]

Rich's Department Store advertisement for *Deliverance*, 1970. Courtesy of Manuscript, Archives, and Rare Book Library, Emory University, Atlanta, GA.

Southern and southern-based fans saw Dickey's success as a poet and novelist as good for Appalachia and the South, or at least as good for their odds of making a connection with a talented and nationally renowned author. Fans saw in Dickey a compatriot and offered him invitation after invitation in the hopes that he might bestow status upon them through the mere sharing of his company. Professionals, businessmen, and even boarding-school students tried to lure Dickey with offers of sports tickets, hunting trips, canoe and rafting ventures, and their families' luxurious vacation homes in the mountains.[95]

Curiously, out-migrants from the South felt drawn to Dickey's rascally "grass-roots" southerners and avowed that his novel soothed a sense of homesickness. About 15 percent of Dickey's fans mentioned migration experiences. A graduate student at Ohio State in Columbus wrote to Dickey that he was reading *Deliverance* for the third time because, "being a 'hill' man myself (West Virginian), I am strongly attracted to your work."[96] An editor with the *St. Louis Post Dispatch* and "a self-proclaimed redneck from Valdosta, Georgia," wrote empathetically about Dickey's "desire to be buried on the west bank of the Chattooga River." The Right Reverend John E. Hines wrote from New York City to say that seeing "*Deliverance* on the screen . . . recreated for me years on that same river."[97] Migrant fans assumed, based on *Deliverance*, that Dickey could appreciate and ratify the rural upbringing that still formed an important piece of their identities. Thirty-year-old James Russell Burnham, writing from Illinois, sent a four-page handwritten epistle about his youth in Alabama. "After I moved north we lost touch," Burnham lamented, and "I haven't been back to AL since 1960."[98]

Some out-migrant fans explicitly mentioned dialect as an endearing attraction. Madeline Negri, born in Arkansas but living in St. Louis, wrote to say that "being a Southerner," she enjoyed the way Dickey shortened words "into 'our' own contractions. I'd never seen this in print and it brought back memories."[99] Well-educated southern and out-migrant readers sometimes mimed ungrammatical but lively dialect. Patrick Sky in Rhode Island asked Dickey to "write and tell me the latest in 'down home kuntry.'" Dr. Pat Ahrens of Columbia, South Carolina, invited Dickey: "If you ever feel like pickin' or talkin' some Bluegrass, give a holler."[100] In reviving or borrowing "southern" speech, these fans asserted their local knowledge and roots, perhaps seeking to link themselves to the "nongeneric" whiteness that Frankenburg identifies as a lingering need among those who feel themselves otherwise unmarked by class or race.

Carole Marsh demonstrates that a fan might bask in the fun of "slumming it" as a colorful southerner and yet nonetheless retain a sense of herself as above rural denizens. She opened her letter to Dickey playfully with "'That's a rit good piece,' as they would say in Oree," a town featured in *Deliverance*. A self-described "transplant" from Atlanta to Louisville, Kentucky, Marsh prided herself on "having traipsed through Rabun County a few times." She explained her frustrations in dealing with "semi-yankified" people whom she had to "educate" on "the backwoods": "I explained that after . . . you had banged and jounced down a four mile potholed gully . . . to a dead end you were most certainly 'fucked up'—not 'lost,' as they insisted." Even as she exclaimed, "Talk about homesick!" however, Marsh conveyed a sense of superiority and disdain toward rural places when she promised to write her own story, set in a Georgia town that "makes Oree look like a culture capital."[101]

For many of the readers I've discussed, reaching out to Dickey was about both feeling southern and feeling important. For others, Dickey's southernness was less a point of identification and more a geographic convenience for accessing a renowned author as a means to seek national prominence in literary circles. Foremost among fans gratified by Dickey's close proximity were academics. Dickey received more letters from academics than any other author of popular Appalachian-set fiction I examined—likely in part because he was one himself, having held academic positions in different parts of the country throughout his career, and because he regularly gave poetry readings on college campuses. Faculty members at universities within the Appalachian region were a substantial portion of these academic admirers. Not one used letter writing as a forum to take umbrage with Dickey's portrayal of mountain people or culture. Instead, Dickey received approving and at times fawning mail from professors, cultural events coordinators, librarians, and presidents at Young Harris College and North Georgia State (both in the Georgia mountains), East Tennessee State, Winthrop College in northwestern South Carolina, and Appalachian State, Western Carolina University, and UNC–Asheville in North Carolina. Founders of the *Appalachian Journal* at Appalachian State courted Dickey as an adviser in 1972, and the university awarded Dickey an honorary doctorate in 1984.[102]

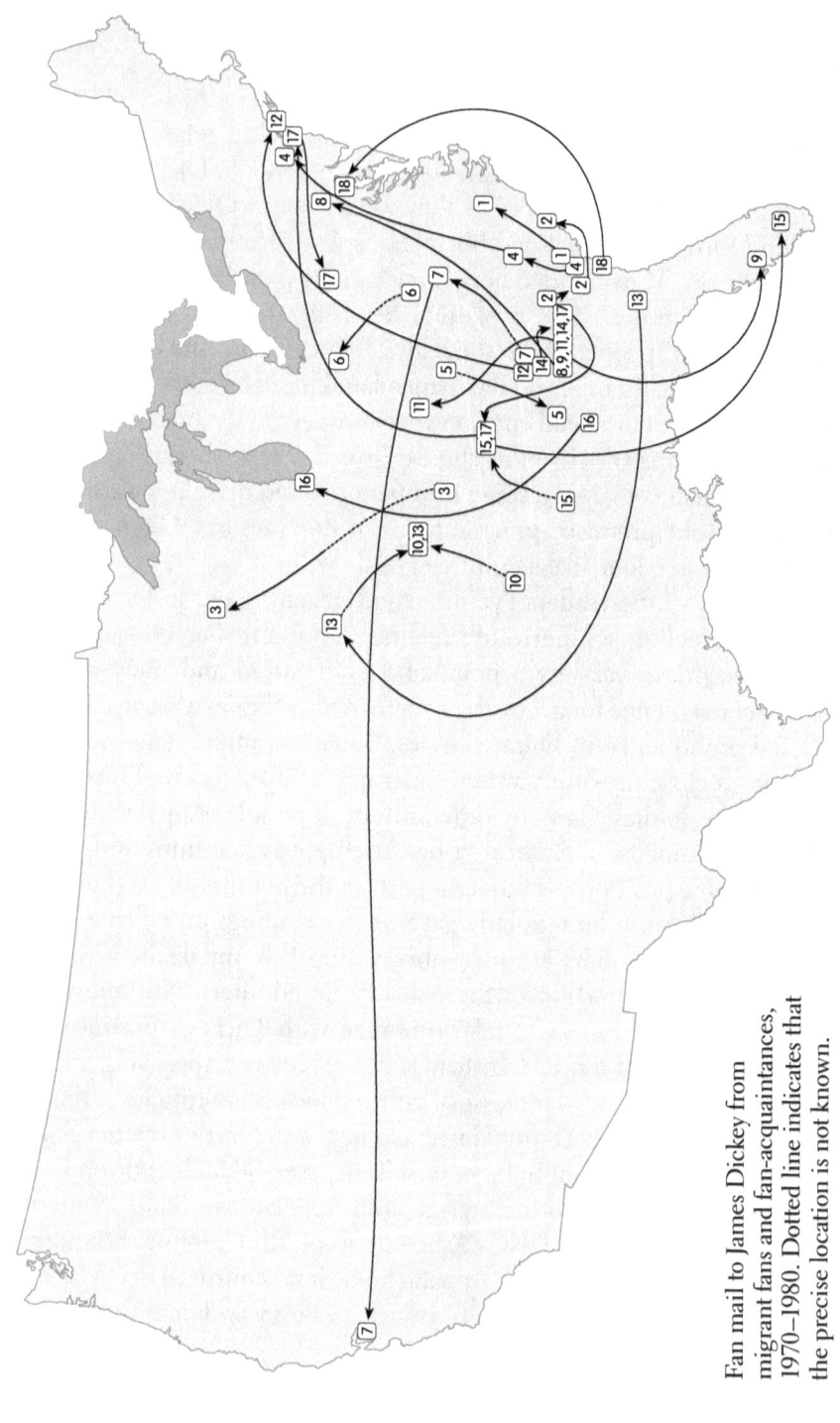

Fan mail to James Dickey from migrant fans and fan-acquaintances, 1970–1980. Dotted line indicates that the precise location is not known.

1. Charles W. Loftin, Colleton County, South Carolina → Jackson Hill, North Carolina
2. Le Nancie B. Downey, a plantation near Graves Mountain, South Carolina → Augusta, Georgia → Charleston, South Carolina
3. Barbara Mayor, southern Illinois → Minneapolis, Minnesota
4. B. F. Driggers, Berkeley County, South Carolina → Columbia, South Carolina → Cranbury, New Jersey
5. Paul Neal, Kentucky → Athens, Alabama
6. David B. Buzzard, West Virginia → Columbus, Ohio
7. Marty Olmstead, North Georgia → Hollins College, Roanoke, Virginia → San Francisco, California
8. Edwin Peeples, fan-acquaintance, Atlanta, Georgia → Phoenixville, Pennsylvania
9. Bill Penhallegon, Georgia Tech, Atlanta, Georgia → Clearwater, Florida
10. Madeline Negri, Arkansas → St. Louis, Missouri
11. Carole Spence Marsh, Atlanta, Georgia → Louisville, Kentucky
12. John E. Hines, fan-acquaintance, Chattooga, Georgia → New York, New York
13. Thomas B. Newsom, *Post-Dispatch*, Valdosta, Georgia → Iowa → St. Louis, Missouri
14. Lisa Price, fan-acquaintance, North Georgia College, Dahlonega, Georgia → Atlanta, Georgia
15. Charles Shores Jr., Mississippi → Vanderbilt University, Nashville, Tennessee → Ft. Lauderdale, Florida
16. James Russell, outside Birmingham, Alabama → Burnham, Illinois
17. Roy Blount Jr., *Sports Illustrated*, Decatur, Georgia → Vanderbilt University, Nashville, Tennessee → New York, New York → Pittsburgh, Pennsylvania
18. Raymond Lawing, Savannah, Georgia → Baltimore, Maryland

In fact, Dickey's perceptions of mountain people seemed to comport quite nicely with some of his academic fans' seeming lack of regard for the "locals." John Foster West at Appalachian State wrote after the film version's release to commend Dickey for "one bitch of a movie." "You have an eye for the decedant [decadent] mountaineer. That banjo picker looked like the product of a father-daughter relationship."[103] Some, like David McClellan at East Tennessee State, who was writing a novel about an "old Tennessee barroom brawler," learned directly from Dickey's writing workshops how to utilize "local color" for their own literary careers.[104] In some cases, the desire on the part of academics to ingratiate themselves with Dickey may indicate self-promotion and a sense of self-importance at the expense of real regional people—including their students. If any Appalachian-based academics took exception to Dickey's cavalier representation of mountain residents—and it is likely that they did, given the rise of Appalachian studies during this period—they utilized venues other than letter writing to express themselves.

Just two letter writers took issue with Dickey's depiction of mountaineers. Robert Linn of Calhoun, Georgia, "was much impressed" with *Deliverance*, given his interest "in literature, folk music, and the Appalachian wilderness country." He was puzzled, however, about Dickey's artistic reasons for "exaggerat[ing] to the point of distortion" the differences between "city" people and "mountain people," who come across as "almost symbolically evil."[105] Noel C. Dickey, a student at the University of South Carolina at Beaufort, was less willing to attribute Dickey's exaggerations to artistic license. After watching the film version of *Deliverance* three times, she "became obsessed with river, the theme music and the local color" so she took a "trip to the hills" for "the mountain people; to see them and talk with them." They "seemed hurt or disgusted by the roles of the villains." Noel shared their disgust. Whereas the movie gave her "the impression the people there were ugly, perverted, senseless," she found them "warm, eager, honest . . . , with an abundance of common sense." "In the movie the mountain people were the bad guys and the city slickers . . . were the good guys," she complained, "when in reality it's totally opposite. . . . It seems to me that in some way you must be responsible for this." Noel vowed, "I'm going to write a book about the type of people crazy enough to go out and try and beat a river like that," invoking what the novel version of *Deliverance* suggests at its opening may be its (later abandoned) intent.[106]

Tourism, Mission, and Imperialism in *Christy* and *Deliverance*

When *Christy* and *Deliverance* constructed authentic places peopled with coarse whites, they offered readers a destination for tourism, mission, and conquest. *Christy* fans responded eagerly to the novel's implicit invitations to become tourists or missionaries, while *Deliverance* invited both tourism and a harsher confrontation with primitive Others. Whether the novels invited a touristic, missionary, or "survive and conquer" lens for interpreting Appalachian settings and characters, they affirmed or ignited readers' willingness and ability to recognize primitives. *Christy* and *Deliverance* reminded readers of their so-called white man's burden in their supposed obligation to corral and care for nonwhite and not-quite-white peoples.

Because the Great Smokies were a popular tourist destination long before the publication of *Christy*, Marshall had a ready-made audience of readers for whom the scenes were familiar and appealing. Readers in New York, Texas, Indiana, and Ohio, to name a few, shared happy memories of time spent in the mountains—much like local-color readers in Murfree's and Fox's day. Wesley Applegate of Georgia, for example, explained that "when our sons and daughter were children, we visited the Great Smoky Mountains, 'a la tourists.'" He was sure that his "having been there, in those majestic hills, enabled me to 'live,' in spirit, the experience of Christy, and the mountain people of 'Cutter Gap.'"[107]

Some readers who had already visited the Great Smokies as well as readers who had not ever been there eagerly planned trips to visit the place where the real-life Christy had encountered the mountain people. Likely they were spurred in part by Marshall's prologue, which established that "the old mission house was still there" to be visited. Like Harriette Arnow before her, however, Marshall lamented the "changes" brought by two world wars. She bemoaned that war had "snatch[ed] away Cutter Gap men," some of whom returned with unfortunate evidence "of the world outside: brought-on clothes; canned food; soda pop; autos; battery radios over which blared hillbilly music and soap operas" (C, 1, 3). Despite the prologue's observation that the town was no longer pristinely rustic, readers eagerly sought it out. Judy Downing of Washington, for example, suddenly had "longings to go 'a travelin'" because *Christy* "left me with a consuming desire to see the Great Smokies, and some of their people."[108] Indeed, at least twenty-two fans were prompted by their love of *Christy* to undertake leisure travel to the mountains.

Some readers rekindled prior connections to the mountains by reading *Christy* and planning trips to the exact location where the novel was set. Margaret Steward, one of the New Jersey couple quoted earlier, recounted that she and her husband "both attended college at Maryville, Tennessee," about sixty miles west of *Christy's* setting. Steward reported that they had "fallen in love with the area and the people" and that "each of us separately and equally have . . . this compulsion to find this valley if at all possible." She hoped Marshall would give them directions.[109]

Like Steward, other fans wrote to ask Marshall about visiting the old mission.[110] Their requests indicate not only the novel's implicit local-color invitation to readers to become tourists but also point out the degree to which the prologue and maps fueled readers' desire to believe that the fictional story and setting were factual. Judith Canant wrote to ask after Cutter Gap's actual location: "I hope it isn't a secret—and most of all I hope that it is a real place."[111] When nineteen-year-old Diane Wells of Ohio wrote to ask for directions, she quoted Marshall's prologue to her and reported that she had "looked at all maps" but had been "unable to locate" Cutter Gap. Wells's faith in the authenticity of Marshall's story is further suggested by her query about the fictional characters Christy and Dr. MacNeill: "Are they able to have visitors?"[112]

In every case, Marshall wrote back obligingly with instructions that the would-be tourists look up Mary Ruble of Newport, Tennessee, who "can give you all the details about finding the spot."[113] The retired home economics teacher who helped Marshall research the novel must have stayed very busy; Marshall told her correspondents that because Ruble "has had so many requests," she had "virtually had to become a guide for this area."[114] Marshall apparently thought little of relying upon the unpaid labor of locals to promote fans' interest in her novel.[115]

Fans' stated plans to see the old mission house were not idle daydreams. What most tourists found when they completed their pilgrimages, however, was rarely akin to the uplifting experience they felt when reading the novel. Judy Brewer wrote from Knoxville after her trip to lament the condition of the roads: "At times we wondered if we would be able to get [our car] out of those hills." Her expectations about the residents were confirmed by her visit: "The people I talked to were exactly as you described them. . . . I was treated like an intruder, but I would not give up. Living conditions are still the *very* same; everyone has from 6–12 children, no improvement in living quarters, no plumbing or electricity. . . . I felt much sympathy for these people but my husband seems to think they're happy because it's the only way of li[f]e they know." Defeated by a mud hole, and with a "tired and hungry crew," Brewer threw in the towel without having quite made it to the mission, vowing to return again soon "much earlier in the day."[116] Judith Canant was also down in the mouth. "We ended up on foot & feeling 'spooky'" and so did not complete the journey, she reported. Canant found it "disappointing, as I had envisioned such a different scene."[117]

In addition to touristic desire, Marshall coached a missionary attitude among her middle- and upper-middle-class white readers. The mission impulse often began as readerly identification with the novel's young protagonist. "While reading 'Christy,' I become 'Christy,'" explained Koni Sowinski.[118] Reader after reader was inspired to help by reading Marshall's story. Sheldon D. Alquist Jr. of San Francisco told Marshall, "Long before I read Christy I felt that Appalachia was my call. Now I feel, that it is most definitely my challenge."[119] Many of these readers were teenagers or college students who, searching for their own path, found a potential outlet in Marshall's "Christy Country." Jeanne Yohey felt "that if I had the chance that Christy had my life would become important and full."[120] Deborah Butler wrote hopefully, "If Cutter Gap were still in need of teachers . . . I would go running to help."[121] Some admired Christy (or Marshall's mother) for her missionary impulse and felt guilt; they *should* share it but did not have the same passion.[122]

Christy drew upon, validated, and fueled 1960s and 1970s volunteerism akin to the settlement school movement on which it was based. Many readers had worked previously in North Carolina, Tennessee, or Kentucky, including some with the Christian-based Appalachia Service Project (ASP), and found affirmation for their work in Marshall's novel—as well as appreciation and explanation for what they saw as mountain peculiarities. Craig Wilcox found that *Christy*'s fictional depiction of life in 1912 "supplied the answers to many questions and mysteries" about the Appalachian people he had met through ASP.[123] Elizabeth Luca wrote from New Jersey, to tell Marshall that she had "worked in eastern Kentucky for a summer, your story evoked many wonderful memories for me. Upon completing your book, I wished I was back in the mountains where the true meaning of life and love has not been lost."[124] As Luca's comment suggests, readers seemed to romanticize primitive conditions as providing lessons that could give greater meaning to modern-day life.

In a few cases, reading *Christy* appeared to prompt a fuller apprecia-

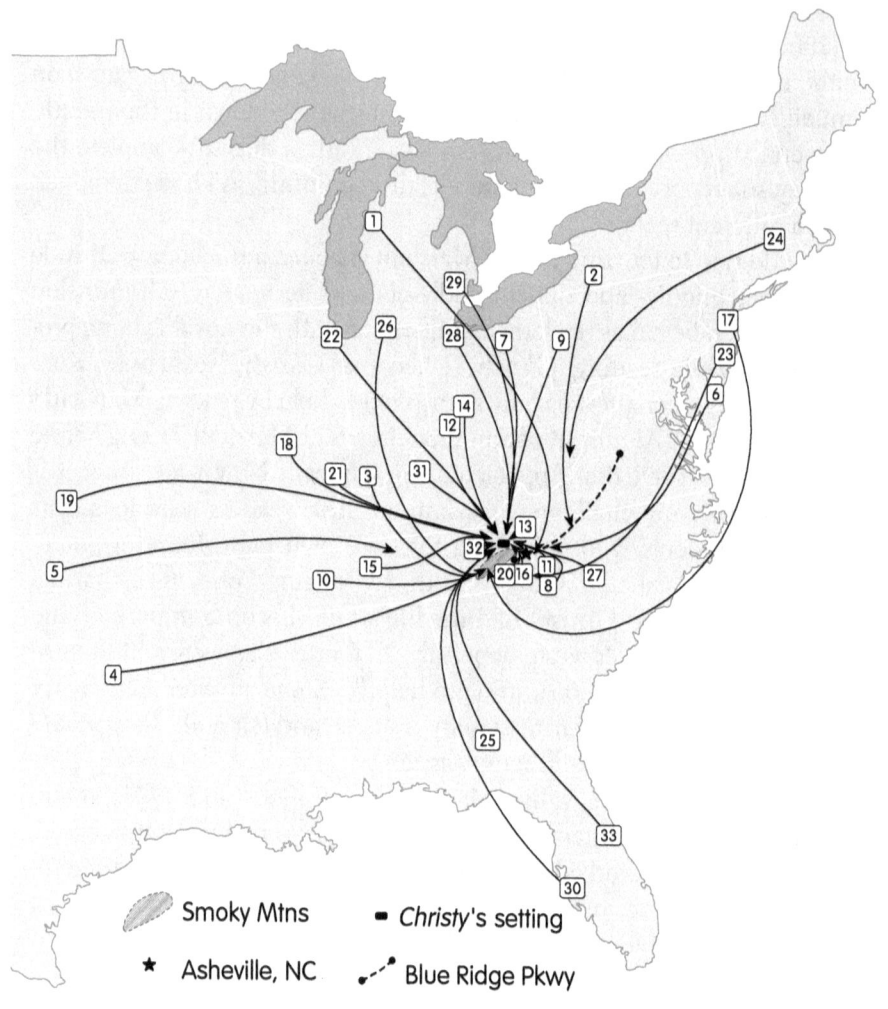

Fan mail from tourists to Catherine Marshall, 1967–1973.

Had visited prior to writing fan letter about *Christy*

1. Mrs. Richard T. Jeffries, Manistee, Michigan → Montreat, near Asheville, North Carolina
2. Gertrude R. Johnson, Jamestown, New York → Blue Ridge Pkwy
3. Sharon Eichele, Evansville, Indiana → Smoky Mtns
4. Mildred W. Spain, Paris, Texas → Smoky Mtns
5. Christi, Edmond, Oklahoma → Tennessee
6. George A. Butz Sr., Rehoboth Beach, Delaware → Mt. Pisgah, North Carolina
7. Ruth M. Burlison, Brunswick, Ohio → Smoky Mtns
8. E. B. Hallman, Spartanburg, South Carolina → *Christy*'s setting
9. Debby McGaffick, Beaver Falls, Pennsylvania → *Christy*'s setting
10. Mrs. John P. Donnel, Milan, Tennessee → Smoky Mtns

Planned to visit after reading *Christy*, including some who had previously visited the area

11. Lowell A. and Margaret Leonard, Hendersonville, North Carolina → *Christy*'s setting
12. Marlene G. Waggoner, Mount St. Joseph, Ohio → *Christy*'s setting
13. Carl D. Cheek, Kingsport, Tennessee → *Christy*'s setting
14. Olive M. Andrews, Englewood, Ohio → *Christy*'s setting
15. Herman S. Frey, author, Nashville and Murfreesboro, Tennessee → *Christy*'s setting
16. Vicki Hendrix, Candler, North Carolina → *Christy*'s setting
17. Margaret Steward, Piscataway, New Jersey → Smoky Mtns
18. Mrs. Clen Lawson, Edwardsville, Illinois → *Christy*'s setting
19. Cyd Drennen, Wichita, Kansas → *Christy*'s setting
20. Mrs. Jack W. Chapman, Canton, North Carolina → *Christy*'s setting
21. Barbara Spond, Mt. Carmel, Illinois → *Christy*'s setting
22. Wilma Brown, Steger, Illinois → *Christy*'s setting
23. Jane H. Celio, Rutherford, New Jersey → Balsam Grove, North Carolina
24. June Storie, Auburn, Massachusetts → Appalachia
25. Wesley D. Applegate, Camilla, Georgia → *Christy*'s setting
26. Janet Reynolds, Elkhart, Indiana → *Christy*'s setting
27. Jane Lineberger, Charlotte, North Carolina → *Christy*'s setting
28. Diane Wells, Napoleon, Ohio → *Christy*'s setting
29. Eleanor Kivela, Livonia, Michigan → *Christy*'s setting

Visited after reading *Christy*, including some who had previously visited the area

30. Louise Howard, St. Petersburg, Florida → *Christy*'s setting
31. Joe and Elaine Armstrong, Louisville, Kentucky → *Christy*'s setting and Harlan, Kentucky
32. Judy Brewer, Knoxville, Tennessee → *Christy*'s setting
33. Judith P. Canant, Titusville, Florida → *Christy*'s setting

tion for the social ills afflicting readers' contemporaries.[125] A ninth grader in New Mexico maintained, "I now understand the problem of poverty and education much more clearly. . . . I would like to learn a lot more about this."[126] A small number of readers proudly reported their charitable donations to the area, while for others the ideal of "mission" was less appropriate than that of secular activism or labor advocacy, with, for example, the United Mine Workers. Marshall commended one reader in Atlanta, "It is so great to know that somehow CHRISTY gave you that additional push that sent you into the work at the Fulton County Juvenile Court."[127] Just one fan's activism centered explicitly around contemporary coal issues. Anne Wallace of Frederick, Maryland, told Marshall that the girls on her mission trip "had all read 'Christy' and that is what" had "gotten us interested in Appalachia first." She wrote, "I have written several letters to senators and congressmen to get strip-mining abolished."[128]

Christy reflected, marshaled, and fed its era's widespread interest in evangelism, which escalated after 1966 when the Billy Graham Evangelistic Association sponsored the World Congress on Evangelism in Berlin. As the letter from Atlanta suggests, readers viewed efforts to uplift poor mountain whites as interchangeable with those to benefit "benighted" people of color elsewhere, including those on Native American reservations, in Africa, and in African American–dominated areas of the U.S. South.[129] Dee Ann Smith of New Jersey, for example, planned to attend college in North Dakota to give her "'Help-the-Indian-Reservation' idea a chance to grow."[130]

Readers found Marshall's mountaineers equivalent to many other kinds of "distinctive" folk, regardless of whether they were objects of missionary care per se. Penny Langston, "raised in large cities" but married to a "pastor at a small country church" in Arkansas, testified that "'Christy' has helped me to understand the people and their attitudes better."[131] Marshall's apparent love of mountain folk convinced readers that she would equally love to read or write about Swedes in Pennsylvania, local history in New Jersey, the coast of Maine, and a Sioux uprising in Minnesota. Like *Deliverance*, *Christy* benefited from and augmented readers' belief in equivalencies among rural or "ethnic" peoples everywhere.

Marshall took her readers' missionary impulses seriously. In reply to Susan Johnson of Miami, she wrote, "To answer your question about there being any places like Cutter Gap left in American today—yes, there are. You might contact any of the following mission-type schools," and listed the Martha Berry School in Rome, Georgia, the John C. Campbell folk school, and the Office of the Council of the Southern Mountains in Berea.[132] When Sheri Schumacher of California reported she'd like to help "the people in the Appalachia Mountains," Marshall responded encouragingly with a success story about New Jersey students inspired by *Christy* to run a vacation Bible school in the area. Schumacher, to her credit, wanted "to be sure I'm not just romanticizing the conditions of the people and their lives." Marshall assured her that the people of the Great Smokies have a "Scotch-Irish background . . . and working with the people is very worthwhile."[133] Marshall, perhaps inadvertently, reinforced readers' racist belief that mountaineers' British origins made them appropriate objects of their charity and uplift.

For some perturbed readers, the welcome message of mission at the center of *Christy* was undermined by the novel's ending. Marshall's efforts to establish the authenticity of *Christy* collided head-on with the fact that many readers were familiar with her life story through her nonfiction. She caused no end of trouble for herself when she took the creative liberty of making the novel's ending depart from her mother's real-life path. Christy realizes in the book's closing pages that she is in love with the doctor rather than the minister. Christy's abrupt change of heart and the novel's lack of denouement fueled the phenomenal amount of mail Marshall received, as readers wrote to her with innumerable questions about what they felt was an unfinished story. As one reader put it, Marshall had left her "standing in mid-air."[134] Marshall admitted that "in real life, my mother married the minister," but explained that, in her story, the minister was an unsuitable match for Christy because he had no "personal confrontation with Christ."[135]

Readers were perplexed and even agitated. In letter after letter they tried to reconcile what they knew about Marshall with the events of the novel. In asking these questions, readers collapsed the fictional story with the actual life of Marshall's mother. Susan Giboney's confusion is evident in her postscript: "P.s. In your book Christy, did your mother marry the doctor? How long did they stay with the mission? I assume then your father became a full-time preacher."[136] Marshall received so many letters containing long lists of questions about what "really" happened after the close of the novel that within the first two years she was forced to type up a standard Frequently Asked Questions form to include in her return correspondence.[137]

Reproachful readers recognized a contradiction between the stated commitments of selfless missionaries and the prologue's implication regarding the brevity of Marshall's mother's sojourn in the cove. Sandra van der Meulen of Ontario engaged in some extended mathematics, concluding that Christy "would almost have had to leave immediately" after the close of the book. "And that might mean," she extrapolated worriedly, "that none of Christy's ideas were fulfilled" or "that school did not even get started for another term."[138] To Joyce Godsey's mind, the virtuous Dr. MacNeill *"would not* leave his people." So if Christy married the doctor, Godsey persisted, "how is it that 'Christy' is returning to the Cove after forty-six years absence?"[139] Another reproachful fan put the question more bluntly: "If [Christy] was so committed to helping the people of Cutter Gap, why did she leave?"[140]

Christy continues to prompt tourism and mission in the region in the twenty-first century. ChristyFest, held annually at the edge of the Great Smoky Mountains in Townsend, Tennessee (two counties away from the original setting), provides fans with an opportunity to build community around a shared love for the novel and its setting—without the spookiness and mud holes encountered by Marshall's correspondents in the 1970s. Appalachia serves as the object of uplift for numerous organizations, many of which are willing to overlook similar wealth discrepancies and hardships in their own backyards.

The impetus for mission is less explicit in readers' responses to *Deliverance*, which sometimes prompted a darker attitude toward its primitives. Certainly Dickey's fans expressed an interest in tourism equal to that of *Christy* fans—surprisingly, given the hostile nature of the novel's mountain men. Many fans described their attempts to capture in their own outdoor hobbies the immediacy and refuge that the novel identified with Appalachia. A former student of Dickey wrote, "Though I carry no bow and there are no rednecks awaiting me at the top for me to stalk and kill, there is a quality of danger and desperation in rock climbing that makes me feel about as alive as anything I do."[141] These outdoor enthusiasts sought in their reading and hobbies "what Thoreau called the 'tonic of the wilderness,' something I have known in Wisconsin woods and waters."[142] Three coworkers at Merrill Lynch in Nashville sent a photo of their own wilderness adventure on which they cooked their "infamous 'Deliverance Chili.'"[143] These fans may have intended their stories to ingratiate them with a famous author; nonetheless, their belief in the invigorating power of the woods—in real life and in print—seems genuine.

Letters suggest that fans found Dickey's Appalachian mountain river interchangeable with places in Minnesota, Idaho, and Wisconsin, and presumed Dickey shared their love for such refuges for city-weary hearts and minds.[144] Darlene LaPler in California insisted that "anyone who can write about white water the way you can must love it as much as we do. Ours is the Rogue River in Oregon."[145] Most of these outdoor enthusiasts conveniently ignored, or perhaps were titillated by, the horrific consequences that the novel suggests may befall city people seeking excitement. Readers consistently embraced the very impulse that *Deliverance* suggests is foolhardy and even deadly.

Other white-water aficionados wrote to thank Dickey for introducing them to the Chattooga River. Indeed, readers' desire to repeat the thrill and heighten the sensation of Dickey's novel effectively turned North Georgia's rivers into a tourist destination. A white-water canoeist from the Upper Cuyahoga Association in Ohio wrote that he had read the book and seen the film and was inspired to "do a little white water kayaking" on the Chattooga River on his way home from a canoeing trip in the Okefenokee Swamp. "Thanks for turning me on to a new river that I hadn't heard about before," wrote Dean Norman. He might have been in for a disappointment, given his faith in the novel's reality. He told Dickey, "I can't wait to see that waterfall where the canoes were smashed up." Norman mused hopefully, "In an indirect way I'm sure your story will help us preserve the upper Cuyahoga—and other rivers—from dams such as the one that drowned the mythical Cahulawassee River."[146] Another river conservationist was not so sanguine about the effects of Norman and others being "turned on to" North Georgia rivers by Dickey's novel. Michael Ray at Furman University "commended" Dickey "for giving our beautiful Southern rivers a plug" but sternly warned him that the "repercussions of your novel," and especially of "filming on the Chattooga," might be "detrimental" to conservation efforts.[147]

In addition to inviting tourism, *Deliverance* also facilitated the circulation of power across scales by helping to construct a vision of the world that insisted upon a shared responsibility among those who could recognize and guide primitive peoples who might otherwise prove threatening. Two correspondents credited Dickey with training them how to detect "sinister" hillbillies. Tom Shapcott wrote from Australia to say, "From henceforth your vision colours my vision of that part of the world—I realized this when I saw the kids watching" a T.V. show and saw "sinister primitivism" lurking "behind the hillbilly antic[s]."[148] Bostonian Michael Blowen reported that his recent trip to the South "affirmed my initial reactions to . . . *Deliverance*." While he was eating at a North Georgia diner, "in came two men who fit your description of the hillbillies in *Deliverance*." One hillbilly's "innocent toothpick in his lips became horrifying" to Blowen, who insisted, incredibly, "The sensation of a brutal attack was omnipresent." Blowen "recalled the day when" Appalachia iconography would have gone "unnoticed by the sophisticated eye."[149] Dickey's novel trained the "sophisticated eye," and in doing so indoctrinated an entire generation of highbrow readers into the horror and romance of Appalachia.

Dickey's readers, like Marshall's, learned not only to recognize primitive types but to see them as interchangeable.[150] An author of a book set in the Yukon wrote, "From meeting some of your *Deliverance* people, I remember thinking that James Dickey was one person who would probably appreciate Yukoners."[151] A friend writing from France said he would "answer" Dickey "with an Irish equivalent. Your hillbillys are straight from rural Ulster."[152] These comments came from other authors, whose job it was to endow colorful locals with "universal appeal." But letters from fans like Helena Anderson in Kansas indicate that *Deliverance* also taught readers *without* authorial aspirations to see equivalencies among rural places. Anderson told Dickey, "We are supposed to have a certain type of mountaineer in the Ozark region, which is near to us." She regretted that they "put on a certain air to please the tourists in season, but in reality they exist about like everyone else in small villages." "*Your* kind," on the other hand, "are really out of this world, aren't they?" Anderson made explicit the links between missionary and imperialist stances toward so-called primitives when she wrote: "And to think of all the millions of dollars . . . sent to foreign lands to convert the primitives, while they are existing right here in the U.S."[153]

High middlebrow readers' prideful claims to recognize primitive backwardness in their own backyards may have translated into their readiness to endorse imperial ventures like the ongoing war in Vietnam. As *New Statesman* critic Anthony Thwaite noted with alarm, readers imagining unruly domestics could be convinced of the need to manage foreign primitives as well. Thwaite argues that the novel's "pernicious" James Bond–like "daydream" fails to acknowledge that "a real and bloody war is going on" in 1970. Even so, the novelistic "daydream" affects "the real world of real wildernesses and killings" in Vietnam, "dangerously" so.

According to Thwaite, the novel proposes that "southern hicks behave badly and inscrutably; so, by extension, do oriental gooks." When hicks and gooks behave badly they get what they deserve because a "resourceful city man—if pushed to an extreme situation—*can*, through sheer willpower, skill, and guts, deal with them." Thwaite argues that *Deliverance* is "an insidious invitation to believe that to be real and masculine," a man must achieve conquest over misbehaving others.[154]

Asserting equivalencies among supposedly undeveloped people and places was common in imperialist political rhetoric of the day. President Lyndon Johnson famously said that Vietnam was "just like the Alamo," while one humorist lampooned General Westmoreland's overconfidence about Vietnam by likening him to General Custer claiming to have the Sioux "on the run."[155] As these examples suggest, assumptions of interchangeability often relied upon presumptions of racial Otherness as well as primitivism. This is one reason that the city slickers' victory over *Deliverance*'s hillbillies may have reassured those southern white readers who were feeling anxious about repressing apparent insurgencies among African Americans and Asians alike. Oddly enough, however, some readers' surprising affection for Dickey's hillbilly characters—made visible by the fan mail—suggests a reversal of these racial assignations. Whites who cried foul at federal attempts to enforce civil rights for African Americans in the South may have found themselves simultaneously rooting for the simple put-upon white hicks defending their territory from intruders who, in this formulation, represent arrogant nigger lovers from the city with no regard for local custom.[156]

The consequences of fictional representation have never been more powerful for the imagination of mountainness—or perhaps even for southernness, ruralness, and "primitiveness" more generically—than in the case of *Deliverance*. Indeed, it would be difficult to overstate the thoroughness with which *Deliverance*, transformed by Dickey and director John Boorman into a film classic, has imbricated itself into Americans' understanding and worldview. From the ubiquitous rendition of the "Dueling Banjos" theme song to allude to danger from hicks to bumper stickers for tourists reading, "Paddle faster, I hear banjoes," the novel and film have created artifacts that many of us encounter on an almost weekly basis.

Even in the 2000s, readers report that *Deliverance* produces an authentic place by "mak[ing] us feel like we're alongside the group in their canoes" and by "accurately" representing "mountain people" as "toothless crackers and inbreds." The novel allows readers to establish self and Other through finding Ed "a wonderfully sympathetic everyman."[157] *Deliverance* continues to participate in the global circulation of power by training audiences into an imperial vision of the world. Jon Voigt, the actor who played Ed in the film version, recently illustrated critic Anthony Thwaite's worst fears about the way the story encourages imperialism. In 2007, Voigt told the *London Times* that *Deliverance* is about "what happens when a civilised man has to confront evil. That is what is going on today with the Islamic fanatics."[158] Like other Appalachian-set fiction, *Deliverance* allows audiences to negotiate issues of gender and sexuality, race and ethnicity, and nationality and imperialism by offering up poor whites whose cultural differences are in most cases less threatening than murderous African Americans and gooks.

Deliverance and *Christy* produced Appalachia as a rugged, primitive, white place that appealed to readers' romance with authentic rural southern culture. The novels facilitated readers' sense of belonging by appealing to their connections to southern places or their patronizing familiarity with so-called grassroots people. Finally, *Deliverance* and *Christy* promoted the circulation of power across the nation and the globe by enhancing the status of its high middlebrow readers and by training them to recognize Appalachia's hillbilly denizens as stand-ins for racial Others who call forth touristic, missionary, or imperialist responses. The continuing legacy of both *Christy* and *Deliverance* is the reinforcement of audiences' local-color strategies for imagining place, belonging, and empire via projections of Appalachia as both a romantic and nightmarish departure from the normative.

Chapter 5

A Sweet Land That Never Was, circa 1994–2001

> Appalachia is that longing in the heart to come home again.
> —Alice Faye Bragg, quoted in Douglas Reichert Powell, *Critical Regionalism*

> This is the reason for this journey into hyperreality, in search of instances where the American imagination demands the real thing and, to attain it, must fabricate the absolute fake.
> —Umberto Eco, *Travels in Hyperreality*

"When I attended a conference on Appalachia," wrote a customer on Amazon.com in 1999, "I asked the speaker, 'What is the definitive book about the Appalachians?' The answer was, 'Fair and Tender Ladies,' without hesitation. Now I have read all of Lee Smith's books." About ten years later, singer-songwriter Caroline Herring, upon returning home from the Mountain Heritage Literary Festival, posted a message for her festival audience to her online Facebook page: "Thanks for making me feel so incredibly welcome. Time for Appalachian Studies 101! What are the iconic books?" Her fans recommended a book on fiddles, the *Foxfire* folklore series, music by the likes of Hazel Dickens, a memoir, the Depression-era observations of *Cabins in the Laurel*, and Wilma Dykeman's 1955 book about the French Broad River. Mostly, however, they named novels. Three people recommended *Fair and Tender Ladies* or "anything by Lee Smith." Other recommendations included *Cold Mountain*, *Parchment of Leaves*, *River of Earth*, *Kinfolks*, *One Foot in Eden*, *Moon Women*, *Plant Life*, and *Clay's Quilt*. These novels, published between 1940 and 2003, are coming-home stories, coming-of-age stories, and romances with settings that range from the Civil War through the end of the twentieth century. It is not surprising that attendees of a literary festival would recommend literature as a way of learning about the world. Nonetheless, it is interesting to note that the "iconic books" for beginner-level instruction on Appalachia included no studies authored by professional historians, sociologists, anthropologists, folklorists, or Appalachian studies scholars.[1]

Regional fiction has a long history of serving as a primer on region. Since at least the local-color movement of the Gilded Age, its supposed ability to offer a window onto regional cultures has been one of its strongest selling points. Fiction of the 1880s and 1890s was judged not only according to its aesthetic value but also by its perceived scientific or ethnographic accuracy in documenting the cultural practices, dialects, and environments of purportedly peculiar people.[2] Michael Elliott notes the persistence of the belief that "literature has a unique ability to document the experience of cultural alterity . . . in a truthful and instructive manner." He points to the frequency with which college professors in the 1980s assigned literary works, particularly those by women of color, as a means of teaching about cultural differences in nonliterary disciplines from anthropology to political science to religion.[3]

Beginning in the 1980s, regional fiction has both regained the widespread affection of American readers and renewed its mission of documenting and explaining the distinctive cultures of rural places. I date this local-color revival to the 1985 publication of the best-selling *Lake Wobegon Days*, the first of Garrison Keillor's *A Prairie Home Companion* franchise.[4] Since then, we have seen an outpouring of regional fiction seemingly unmatched in numbers or in popularity after the Gilded Age.[5] When in 2004 *USA Today* featured the top one hundred best-selling books of the previous decade, regional fiction was well represented—including Charles Frazier's Appalachia-centered *Cold Mountain* (1997); *The Lovely Bones* (2002), set in "Fargo country"; the southern-set *The Secret Life of Bees* (2002) and *The Divine Secrets of the YA-YA Sisterhood* (1996); the New England tale *The Perfect Storm* (1997); the Northwest's *Snow Falling on Cedars* (1994); the Midwest's *The Bridges of Madison County* (1992); and the West's *The Horse Whisperer* (1995).[6] The fact that a film adaptation was made of each of these best-selling novels underscores the degree to which regionalized settings appealed to American audiences at the turn of the twenty-first century. Furthermore, the fact that the protagonists of the novels on the *USA Today* list are white, almost without exception, hints at the potential overlap between the popularity of regionalism and readers' investment in good white country folk.[7] Meanwhile, readers' belief that these best-selling novels teach us about cultural difference is documented by comments posted to the Web sites of online booksellers Amazon.com and BarnesandNoble.com. A glowing customer review of one of the "Appalachian Studies 101" novels, *Clay's Quilt*, declared approvingly, "Silas House perfectly captures the speech, spirit, and soul of rural Southeastern Kentucky." "I only hope," professed a customer reviewer of *Cold Mountain*, that the author "has more to tell about the history and people of a poor and poorly understood region."[8]

The similarities between the turns of the twentieth and twenty-first centuries extend beyond their respective local-color crazes. Both eras witnessed historically large gaps between rich and poor, decidedly high levels of unregulated corporate power, conspicuous degrees of consumption, marked influxes of immigration, and considerably expanded U.S. activities abroad. The parallels, in fact, led observers to designate the era from about 1985 to about 2008 the "Second Gilded Age" or the "Neo–Gilded Age."[9] In both the Gilded Age and the Neo–Gilded Age, high middlebrow readers expressed great concern about the perceived loss of local cultures—due to urbanization, industrialization, and homogenization in the late 1800s and due to globalization, mass culture, and geographic mobility in the late 1900s. Multiculturalist movements emerged in both eras, at least partly as a response to the same concerns about standardization and commercialization that stoked readers' interest in the promise of distinctive American cultures delivered by regional and ethnic fiction.[10]

Although I emphasize the similarities, there were important differences between the two eras. Perhaps the most important for understanding my argument here was the heightened mobility of readers during the Neo–Gilded Age. In chapter 3 we saw that the Southern Diaspora witnessed the migration of millions of rural whites and African Americans out of the South. Migration levels actually increased at the end of the twentieth century. In 1950, 27 percent of native-born Americans lived in a state other than their birth state; by 1990 this number had risen to 33 percent. Not only did the number of migrants increase, but Americans' sense of uprootedness accelerated. Commenting upon widespread sensations of displacement, isolation, and alienation, sociologist Manuel Castells argued that individuals at the end of the 1900s sought out connections and a "feeling of belonging" or "community." He found that individuals feeling threatened by the pace of change clung to notions of tradition, heritage, God, nation, family, and locality. In online customer reviews, readers conveyed their anxiety about loss of neighborliness and their desire for stable, secure places and knowable communities.[11]

As the list of USA Today best sellers suggests, the longing for roots that underwrote the local-color revival affected the imagined geography of the entire United States, from New England to the Southwest and from the Northwest to the South. But Appalachia had a special role to play in this resurgence among white readers, in part because of the legacy of white migration from the upland South during the Southern Diaspora. As we saw with *Christy* readers in chapter 4, second- and third-generation descendants of out-migrants endured longings for home and homeland as intensely as the migrants themselves. Out-migrants' descendants commonly evinced envy for the relationships to land, community, and family that they imagined their forebears experienced in their rural places of origin. They associated their families' departures from the upland South with what Raymond Williams called "lost identity, lost relations, and lost certainties."[12]

To paraphrase social theorists, identity is the new community.[13] The paramount question on readers' minds during the Neo–Gilded Age seemed to be, as the title of a review of a Silas House novel aptly put it, "Who are your people?"[14] Americans at the close of the twentieth century longed to "feel anchored to a secure, harmonious, and localized past," according to scholar Marilyn Halter. Here, too, Appalachia had a special role to play. Not only migrants and their descendants but millions of other high middlebrow readers turned to Appalachia as a source of distinctiveness. Because Appalachia was presumed to be inhabited by "nonstandard" whites due to differences in class, genetics, and culture, readers interpreted the region as "authentic but not threatening in [its] difference," in the words of Michael Elliott. As Halter observes, many upper-middle-class Americans participated in celebrations of ethnicity as part of their "search for recognizable or familiar points of reference in a cold, impersonal, and fragmented world." For white Americans who worried that "material abundance" promoted "spiritual impoverishment," Appalachianness purportedly offered "authentic" ethnic white culture preserved apart from consumer society.[15]

The publishing world took note of the region's marketability when readers bought more than 25 million books set in the region between 1998 and 2009. According to a publicist quoted on a publishing news blog, "Books based on life in small town southern Appalachia sell like hotcakes!" The blog cited an "industry spokesman" who observed, "I don't know of another region of the country that can tout such sales figures."[16] Writers, too, were quite savvy and articulate about these trends, much as they were during the original local-color era. In 2006, novelist Meredith Sue Willis noted that "unusual ethnic groups" were "viewed as a fad" by publishers in New York. Playwright Jo Carson explained, "We become more and more homogeneous and anybody who still has an identity, anyone who defines themselves in a regional way, is more fashionable." Lee Smith acknowledged that the "climate of multiculturalism has helped" regional fiction because "now people understand it's important to come from a place and know your people."[17]

In this chapter I examine the confluence of Neo–Gilded Age anxieties about culturelessness and the disappearance of authentic places, white Americans' desires for identity and belonging, and assumptions about the documentary accuracy of popular fictional representations of Appalachia. Fan mail, my primary resource for readers' responses in chapters 1 through 4, is not available in archival collections for the authors studied here. I therefore turn to "customer reviews" posted on the Web sites of Internet booksellers Amazon.com and BarnesandNoble.com in order to assess the appeal of Appalachian-set novels for their readers. In the face of what Lee Smith called a "veritable explosion of Appalachian writing" in this period, I selected just four best-selling novels for examination: Jan Karon's *At Home in Mitford* (1994), Charles Frazier's *Cold Mountain* (1997), Adriana Trigiani's *Big Stone Gap* (2000), and Silas House's *Clay's Quilt* (2001).[18] Though many other contemporary novels would also have suggested the contours of readers' investments in the idea of Appalachia, I was particularly interested in Appalachian-set books by unknown debut authors who met with commercial success and popular acclaim without the advantage of a loyal following (as that accumulated by veteran authors) or an Oprah Book Club endorsement (which guaranteed best-seller status in this period).[19] These four novels' publishers targeted them toward the "serious" reader by releasing them as handsomely designed "trade" paperbacks (rather than the chunky and less expensive "mass-market" paperbacks) and by promoting them through book club editions or Web-based reading guides.[20] I posit that the Appalachian settings of these four books played an important role in their touching a nerve with a broad swath of readers. (For more on my methodological choices and sources, see "Appendix: Methodological Essay.")

In an era of yearning for knowable communities of belonging, all four of these popular novels evoked ideals of home, hometown, home place, and homeland for their readers, though customer reviews show that readers made different meanings based upon their personal geographic histories and loyalties. A handful of commentators I label "jaded cosmopolitans" dismissed Appalachian-set books as boring and pointless. The two largest groups were "touristic cosmopolitans" and "nostalgic cosmopolitans." For touristic cosmopolitans, Appalachian settings represented "small-town America," the authentic roots of a wayward America—the nation's homeland and an ideal of home that touristic readers might access through reading or vacation travel. For nostalgic cosmopolitan readers, Appalachia represented lost community, ancestral home places, and in many cases, their own family's recent past. The third-largest group, "charmed Appalachians," consisted of both newcomers and longtime regional residents who felt themselves to be *in* but not *of* the region. They welcomed the national attention directed toward their home as augmenting their own status, and they interpreted the novels as sharing in their own delight in, and patronizing condescension toward, their mountain neighbors. Members of the fourth-largest group, "affirmed Appalachians," on the other hand, identified with the characters in the novels. They participated in the romantic construction of the region out of pride in their Appalachian hometowns and out of gratitude that the novels informed "outsiders" about a place they held dear. Finally, a small number of "offended Appalachians" expressed disappointment about what they perceived to be the novels' perpetuation of inaccuracies and stereotypes.

The pleasure that readers took in Appalachian difference often arose from an admirable commitment to cultural pluralism, and popular Neo–Gilded Age novels' tributes to small-town America certainly reject the usual prejudices against rural people and places.[21] Yet I also want to suggest that readers' uncritical embrace of Authentic Appalachia may also be cause for concern. The readers in the four largest groups (touristic, nostalgic, charmed, and affirmed) felt the novels authentically captured Appalachian people, places, and culture. When they learned about Appalachia via these popular novels, reviews suggest, they learned a fairly conventional version of the region as home to a colorful way of life that includes nonstandard speech, folk traditions, closeness to the land, and more authentic relationships between close-knit kin and neighbors. Popular novels, despite rejecting the devalorization of rural residents, may not offer up enough different stories about enough of the different kinds of people who make up Appalachian places to serve, on their own, as "Appalachian Studies 101."[22]

At Home in Mitford, Big Stone Gap, Clay's Quilt, and *Cold Mountain* make for an admittedly odd grouping. The first two novels emphasize quirky hometowns and were marketed with emphasis on their coziness and charm. Readers embraced them as "fun" and "recreational reading."[23] *At Home in Mitford* follows the life of an Episcopal priest named Father Tim, who falls in love with his new neighbor, Cynthia, a children's book illustrator, in a town modeled on Blowing Rock, North Carolina, where Jan Karon first published the novel's stories serially in the local newspaper. Lion Publishing, the evangelical Christian firm that released Karon's novel in 1994, described it as "set in Mitford, North Carolina, where life is peaceful and problems are overcome with prayer and some good cooking." Penguin later marketed *At Home in Mitford* as a "heartwarming book" that "introduces readers to a small, charming North Carolina town and its equally charming denizens."[24] Adriana Trigiani's *Big Stone Gap* also features a small mountain town, a "sleepy hamlet" in southwestern Virginia. Protagonist Ave Maria Mulligan, a thirty-something pharmacist "spinster," rejects a marriage proposal from a coal miner who has been dating the town's most eligible bachelorette, goes to Italy to meet her birth father for the first time, and finally falls in love with and marries the coal miner. Ballantine promoted the novel as "filled with big-time eccentrics and small-town shenanigans."[25]

The other two novels, *Clay's Quilt* and *Cold Mountain*, are darker, more violent, and more finely crafted. Their marketing emphasized the ideals of home and authenticity. Fans considered them self-consciously literary, praising them as "lyrical" and replete with "exquisite," "lush," beautiful writing.[26] *Clay's Quilt* is set in fictional Crow County, based in part on Leslie County in southeastern Kentucky. Its protagonist, Clay Sizemore, feels an emptiness in his routine and a yearning for something he cannot quite name. This free-floating yearning is satisfied by his falling in love with Alma and learning more about his mother's life and death. A reviewer for *Publishers Weekly* wrote, "A deep love for home suffuses this heartfelt, well-crafted debut novel set in the Kentucky hills."[27] The desire for home regularly appeared in the marketing for *Cold Mountain* as well. The copy on the book jacket described the novel as "the tale of Inman, a wounded Confederate soldier who walks away from the ravages of the Civil War and back home to Ada, his prewar sweetheart" and touted the book as "based on local history and family stories passed down" by the author's great-grandfather.

Although all four were popular and technically best sellers, the novels' reception differed greatly. The most popular, *Cold Mountain*, spent 94 weeks on the *New York Times* best-seller list and 82 weeks on the *Publishers Weekly* hardback and paperback lists. It appeared in *USA Today*'s list of the 150 top-selling books for 111 weeks between 1997 and 2004, reaching first place at its zenith.[28] *At Home in Mitford* appeared on the *New York Times* best-seller list for 8 weeks, on the *Publishers Weekly* list for 9, and among the 150 top-selling books for 151 weeks, reaching thirty-third at its zenith.[29] *Big Stone Gap* reached twenty-fifth on the *New York Times* list, made the *Publishers Weekly* paperback list for 14 weeks, and appeared in *USA Today*'s list for 26 weeks.[30] *Clay's Quilt* is an outlier in the sense that it reached just thirty-fifth place on the *New York Times* paperback best-seller list and did not appear on the *Publishers Weekly* or *USA Today* lists.[31] Arguably, each novel's popularity is also reflected to some extent in the number of reviews it garnered on Amazon.com. *Cold Mountain* attracted over fifteen hundred customer reviews, *Mitford* over four hundred, *Big Stone Gap* about two hundred, and *Clay's Quilt* just fifty-two.[32]

The novels' reception also differed in the degree to which readers recognized them as "Appalachian." Customer reviews commonly associated *Clay's Quilt* and *Big Stone Gap* with Appalachia but *Cold Mountain* and *At Home in Mitford* with "the South" more generically. Nonetheless, frequent references to the settings as mountainous (such as "my beloved Smokies," "Blue Ridge Mountains," and "mountain town") suggest that the novels contributed to the imagined geography of Appalachia even when that label was not prominent.[33] Certainly, each of the four novels relies upon, affirms, and contributes to familiar local-color themes. *Cold Mountain* includes a number of Appalachian icons, from fiddlers to corn whisky, from hog skinning to ballad singing, and barefooted and reclusive natives. *Clay's Quilt* reiterates major touchstones of Appalachian fiction, including coal mining (Clay's occupation), fiddling (Alma's calling), quilting, boozing, gambling, squirrel hunting, clogging, gospel singing, and Pentecostal religion. In *Mitford*, the mountain setting functions as an aesthetic feature more so than as a cultural or material landscape. The narrator introduces Mitford as sitting "snugly" in a "a hollow between the ridges" that rose "steeply on either side."³⁴ Nonetheless, the novel also includes references to customs like canning or drying apples often identified with mountain folklife. *Big Stone Gap* features coal miners, mining accidents, snake handlers, and a 'possum recipe. All four feature dialect in the dialogue.

Constructing Authentic Sense of Place

Fans' reception was strikingly similar for all four novels in at least one regard. Whether from the Appalachian region or not, readers assessed each according to whether it provided what they perceived to be a realistic portrayal of its setting. As Stephanie Foote and June Howard have argued, readers interpret regional fiction as an "authentic expression of the people depicted in it" or even as a manifestation of the region that emanates from it.³⁵ Readers' assumption of authenticity is so strong, in fact, that they sometimes demand that reality match the novel right down to the minutest of details. Jan Karon's orange marmalade cake was a figment of her imagination, but so many readers asked for the recipe that the author held a contest to create one.³⁶

Admirers' reviews praised Neo–Gilded Age Appalachian-set novels in vocabulary reminiscent of the praise heaped on local-color writers of the late 1800s. Charles Frazier "clearly paints word pictures," enthused one reader, while another praised "his accurate depiction [of] the Blue Ridge mountains." "Misty mountains and haunting music were all vividly brought to life" by Silas House. *Big Stone Gap* offers "detailed, vivid, realistic . . . sense of place" and "captures the essence of life" in the town.³⁷

Fans frequently evaluated the novels' capacity to provide vicarious experiences and journeys. For example, customers deemed *Cold Mountain* a success when it "grabbed and thrust me into the 1860s!" but deemed it a bust if "I was never quite there."³⁸ Typical accolades included the assertion that the fan could see, taste, feel, experience the place as if actually there. A *Cold Mountain* fan swore that it was "as if you were actually in Black Cove and [could] hear the fiddle playing."³⁹ A reader from Massachusetts wrote that *Clay's Quilt* "made the place so real that I feel as if I have not only been to Free Creek, Kentucky, but I have actually lived there, fallen asleep listening to its creek, smelled its coal smoke."⁴⁰ Sometimes authors were credited with having deliberately acquired meticulous knowledge of a place; Frazier, for example, was complimented for his "well-researched" novel. More often, the labor of research and writing, and the structural conditions for publishing and marketing, fell away. When readers emphasized novelists' narrative abilities, they sometimes suggested that authors were simply great untrained storytellers or that Appalachia itself was responsible for their talents because "the region produces brilliant storytellers."[41] Other reviewers implied that authors were craftspeople whose tools are not words at all, as the title of one reader's post suggests: "New author sews the fabric of Appalachian life."[42]

As was the case during the first local-color movement, readers expected authors to have an appropriate relation to the place depicted (being "from there") in order to represent it well. Professional reviewers emphasized Silas House's humble origins in Lily, Kentucky, in *USA Today*, *Booklist*, and southeastern newspapers, noting what they saw as an odd choice of residence for an aspiring writer and what they saw as a quirky and—because more proletarian than professional—authenticity-attesting occupation of postal worker.[43] Reviewers rarely noted, however, that House's perspective must have been shaped in part by the fact that his novel's setting was not Laurel County, where he was reared, but a fictionalized Leslie County, where he visited his grandparents during his childhood. *Cold Mountain*'s Charles Frazier, according to fans, "knows his terrain," "has deep roots in the territory that he describes," and "was inspired by [his] real life ancestors."[44] One reviewer insisted in all capital letters that Frazier "writes like a mountain man. It is in his soul—he can write no other way."[45] Fans did not know, or did not emphasize, that Frazier's years living in the Piedmont part of the state shaped his fictionalization of both the mountains and the Piedmont.[46] As for Harriette Arnow (see chapter 3), fans and reviewers rarely acknowledged the factors that enabled "authentic" authors to achieve "the necessary distance to write."[47]

A number of readers attested to Jan Karon's and Adriana Trigiani's firsthand knowledge of the places they represented even though their novels were considered "lighter" fare. Both writers grew up in or near the places that serve as their books' settings, adding to readers' sense of the authors' authenticity. For Trigiani fans, it was important that she represented "her own hometown"; one fan felt that the "lilt" of her accent on the audio version was perfect.[48] "Welcome to Mitford," wrote a Karon fan, "based on real-life Blowing Rock, North Carolina, where the author resides." "This isn't fiction, it's observation," wrote another *At Home in Mitford* reader.[49] Though readers were correct that the authors wrote from firsthand observation, the experience that these two authors knew best, and delivered most forcefully, was the fantasy fulfillment of cosmopolitans romanticizing small-town community. It seems more accurate to suggest that Karon (an award-winning advertising executive) and Trigiani (a writer and producer for television programs such as *The Cosby Show*)—like John Fox Jr. before them—did not so much capture Appalachian life as they captured and tapped into a widespread metropolitan malaise that they themselves likely experienced.[50]

In keeping with the pastoral's provision of an escape to a place of refreshment and transformation, these novels provided readers with a locale that harbors a distinct sense of place set apart from the so-called real world.[51] The towns of Big Stone Gap, Virginia; Mitford and Cold Mountain, North Carolina; and Free Creek, Kentucky, each represented a longed-for home and a haven largely buffered from the swirl of historical events ranging from the immigration of nonwhites to terrorism by virtue of their inhabiting, presumptively, another place and even another era. As a review for another book in the Mitford series professed, the town of Mitford "lies in a sweet land that never was, one that millions of us long for."[52] For cosmopolitans and proud readers from the region alike, the novels constructed and affirmed Appalachia as an authentic place with a discrete culture, breathtaking scenery, and people who live close to the land. *Clay's Quilt* "is about . . . love for the land," enthused a reader in Abingdon, Virginia.[53] Whatever dangers lurked, the novels' settings proffered readers loci for family, friendship, knowable communities, and a sense of belonging. With the possible exception of *At Home in Mitford*, wherein problems are slight (one reviewer scoffed at the presence of a token homeless man), the novels include troubling events—war, hunger, and death in *Cold Mountain,* violence in *Clay's Quilt*, mining accidents in *Big Stone Gap*. Nonetheless, readers largely idealized the Appalachian settings of all four novels. One reviewer of *Clay's Quilt* described its setting as "picturesque Appalachia," while another remarked, "I've always loved stories about folks living in the Appalachians—the lushness of the way it's described, the tight kinship, sense of family & the simple, honest way of living has always touched me. . . . I felt 'kin' to eveyone."[54]

Home and Community, Belonging and Identity

Readers' geographical affiliations affected the ways in which the novels provided them with a sense of belonging and vicarious community. Customer reviews demonstrate that some jaded cosmopolitans—those who pronounced the tediousness of the rural, regardless of their place of residence—had no use for small-town novels, which they roundly denounced as "slow-paced and boring." A critic in Philadelphia found *Big Stone Gap* "so boring and unoriginal," while a Florida reader labeled *Clay's Quilt* a "snore fest."[55] Representing the smallest number of reviewers, these readers picked up highly recommended mountain novels only to be astonished that anyone had found anything at all of worth in them. On the other hand, touristic cosmopolitans, nostalgic cosmopolitans, and even charmed Appalachians with a cosmopolitan outlook expressed a sometimes desperate craving for small communities, though on different, if overlapping, terms.

Touristic Cosmopolitans

For touristic cosmopolitans, the novels' representations of a pastoral homeland activated a desire to visit such a place, so different from one's actual home, through a virtual trip taken by reading or through an actual journey. Touristic cosmopolitans frequently emphasized small-town America as an ideal and sometimes purely mythical home. This was especially true for *At Home in Mitford,* which represented to readers a utopian small (southern) town. Yet each of the novels supplied for certain readers both a cozy virtual hometown and the mental escape and relaxation of a vacation without the time or expense involved in physical travel—though, as we shall see, some readers had also physically traveled to a novel's setting or intended to go there.

Touristic readers praised novels set in Appalachia for their "down-home" charm and for transporting the readers from "our too hurried world" to "somewhere that felt like home."[56] One customer review of *At Home in Mitford* exemplifies the reactions of touristic readers: "Welcome to Mitford, the kind of wonderful small town we all wish we lived in. . . . Once you visit Mitford . . . you will want to return soon."[57] Karon's town provided a "nice vacation from a stressed out world" full of "fax machines, beepers, the Bloomberg screen and Federal Express packages." "Really," one fan suggested, "when you need a break and can't spare the time for a week in Bermuda, a brief visit to Mitford will be just as good."[58] Although readers thought of Mitford as a typical southern mountain town and a well-lived-in "home," the town on which Mitford is based had been a tourist destination and a haven for vacation-home owners since the late nineteenth century.

Touristic cosmopolitans associated the Appalachia imagined in popular novels with nature, particularly in the case of *Cold Mountain* and *Clay's Quilt*. A once-professional reviewer wrote of *Clay's Quilt*, "The birds, the flowers, the trees . . . are extensions of the family and their love for each other."[59] "In these high, green hills, the air is pure," enthused an *At Home in Mitford* fan unfamiliar with air pollution in western North Carolina.[60] Perhaps partly due to the idea of a primeval place suggested by close links to nature, touristic readers also associated Appalachia with a desirable past. In the case of *Cold Mountain*, readers were drawn to a representation of America before the industrial revolution purportedly ruined the simple life, a time when life was slower and more primitive.[61] Reviewers expressed gratitude that *Mitford* presented them a "world from the 50's that slipped into the 90's."[62] One reader wrote that Mitford "makes one yearn for the more simple times when neighbors were neighborly and when people had morals and convictions. I felt as if I had actually visited Mitford and even moreso [found myself] wishing I could live there."[63] According to a professional reviewer, "Outside of the music the characters listen to, *Clay's Quilt* could take place in 1935 without changing a word."[64]

Appalachian-set novels implicitly criticized contemporary metropolitan culture, advocating life lived at a slower pace in contrast to readers' daily hustle and bustle. While any kind of fiction may serve a similar purpose, touristic cosmopolitans particularly relished Appalachian novels for allowing them to "savor" the "simple things," to "walk through life, not run," and to appreciate the quotidian.[65] *Big Stone Gap* offered a librarian in Seattle "escapism from the frenetic cosmo lifestyle."[66] Reading about Mitford "does not fail to ease my hectic bus ride," enthused one fan.[67]

While these customers emphasized reading Appalachian-set fiction as a virtual visit to a simpler time and place, reading also prompted a desire for actual vacations among touristic cosmopolitans eager to seek out the solace promised by the novels. *Mitford* fan Janet reported, "I've had a yearning to visit a small town in the mountains since I have started reading these books." A *Clay's Quilt* reviewer reported that if he had been able to identify the actual location of Free Creek, Kentucky, "I would have probably set out to tour this beautiful little town." *Cold Mountain* "made me long to see the mountains of North Carolina," wrote a fan.[68] Indeed, traveling to the setting of the novel was recommended by some reviewers as a means to better appreciate the fiction. Another *Cold Mountain*

"Experience the Real Cold Mountain." Tourism Web site for Asheville, North Carolina, 2010.

reviewer directed readers to a location he promised would "let you feel the experiences of Inman, Ruby, Ada and the mountain folk."[69]

Prior vacations sometimes prompted touristic cosmopolitans to relish regional novels, further suggesting the symbiotic relationship between tourism and regional fiction discussed in chapters 2 and 4. A woman from Florida who had traveled to the setting of the Mitford series wrote, "Visiting Blowing Rock many times, I found myself trying to figure out where I might find Father Tim."[70] A *Cold Mountain* fan wrote that he had vacationed in the Blue Ridge Mountains and Frazier's book "brings me back."[71]

Other touristic readers went further, contemplating moving to the settings permanently. The titles of *Mitford* reviews included "Please forward my mail to Mitford . . ." and "Call the Moving Company." "I want to move into the first vacant Mitford property," insisted the latter reviewer.[72] A reader in Virginia wrote, "This is the town where I want to retire" because "when one is sick, the town worries. On joyous occasions, the town celebrates."[73] Some readers had already made the move: "Mitford sounds so much like the small town on the Eastern Shore of Maryland where my husband and I chose to relocate. . . . We don't regret our decision to leave the big city behind—instead of traffic and congestion, we

"Find Your Way Home." Advertisement for the film adaptation of *Cold Mountain* as it appeared in the *New Yorker*, 22 and 29 December 2003.

now listen to geese honking in the winter and bullfrogs croaking on summer nights. Try it if you get the chance—you just might stay."[74]

The desire to move was prompted by Appalachian-set novels' enticing images of idyllic "smalltown USA" figured as home or potential home in comparison to the seemingly sterile landscapes and empty lifestyles of cities.[75] Mitford readers in particular "wish[ed] they could find a ['homey'] place just like that."[76] The small town's amenities and values included small-scale retail rather than chain corporations and abundantly observed religious faith: "We've all dreamed of it—life in a small town where . . .

the grocer knows everyone by name, where there's a church on every corner" as opposed to "cities or suburbs besieged by traffic, development, crime, and dysfunctional or anonymous neighbors."[77]

Perhaps most importantly, touristic readers credited Appalachian settings populated with simple whites as offering them a "safe, happy place." "The connectedness and roots in this town are strong," explained fans, and "the people 'take care of their own.'"[78] As one reader put it, "Mitford is the place where you would love to raise your children."[79] A reader from Columbia, South Carolina, noted that the novel spoke to "the need for a place where everyone helps one another, where the worst thing that happens doesn't spill blood, and life is predictable and reassuring and treasured and it's safe to go jogging at night."[80] Even the rough town of Cold Mountain, North Carolina, is depicted by the novel as "a good place to hide," a humble retreat from the materialism that Ada encountered in Charleston. The journey of Inman repeats this movement of escape from the corrupt, slave-owning lowland Old South toward the purportedly slaveless, "thinly settled" mountain homeland.[81] As one reviewer described it, "Inman is trying to escape to the lush, safety of the mountains."[82] Despite the violence of *Clay's Quilt*, a reviewer claimed that the novel "felt like a quilt! Every evening I curled up with this warm and comforting story."[83]

A handful of reviewers' extreme discomfort with the depiction of Mitford as both utopian and nearly all white points to the racial assumptions underlying other readers' imaginations of safe hometowns. One reader found the "village a bit too idyllic" and "a little too white bread."[84] Another sardonically noted that "everyone has blond hair and blue eyes."[85] "The picket-fence-perfection of the place defies belief," another reviewer complained, citing the lack of "black people in this Southern Eden." This incredulous reader observed, "There's only one—and she's a former domestic servant! . . . Kind of makes you wonder if the Klan didn't get to Mitford before Father Tim did."[86]

While idyllic small-town life was assumed to be utopian by touristic cosmopolitans, other readers—nostalgic cosmopolitans, charmed Appalachians, and affirmed Appalachians alike—professed as a matter of pride that it was still easy to find such places in the South. "Mitford is alive and well," they chided the unbelieving tourists—though they failed to address the racial dimensions of the naysayers' complaints.[87] Nostalgic readers also had a message for touristic readers regarding their longing for safety:

"You won't need to lock your doors here," promised a reader who had once lived in Big Stone Gap, "You will be safe."[88] Claiming to be insiders in the know, these three groups bolstered the notion that Appalachia embodied the ideals of small-town values, neighborliness, and peaceful homogeneity.

Touristic cosmopolitans believed that Appalachian-set novels offered not merely escape but also education, though it is not always clear exactly what readers thought they had learned. An Alabama reader had never "been to Kentucky" but felt that by reading *Clay's Quilt* she had "experienced the spirit of Appalachia."[89] Some readers may have welcomed the ways the novels served as a corrective to what they saw as their earlier unenlightened attitudes about mountain people. An appreciative reviewer from Aiken, South Carolina, for example, admitted about *Clay's Quilt*: "At first I shunned the Kentucky author figuring the story line to be something hum-drum or at the least a how to book on tipping cows."[90] At times the appeal was partly the way in which the novels presumptively taught touristic readers not so much about region as country: "Frazier's writing style and attention to detail paint a vivid picture of our nation's heritage," wrote one fan.[91]

Nostalgic Cosmopolitans

Like touristic readers, nostalgic cosmopolitans often lived in the city and could only imagine Appalachian settings as home. But this second-largest group differed from touristic readers because they identified themselves with the rural places featured in the novels, frequently announcing their own—or their parents' or grandparents'—rural origins. Nostalgic cosmopolitans discussed travel to these fictive places in terms of returning to a place they had known in their past or that their forebears had known. Appalachian settings prompted these white readers to talk of their "homesickness" for a bygone home place where the people and culture were distinctly different from mainstream America. They believed that wholesomeness and wholeness resided in rural mountain places. Reading for them was less a matter of accessing national heritage and more a matter of comprehending their own personal roots and heritage, though for some the two were related. Jayne in Washington, DC, wrote: "Having grown up in a small town not so far from the Blue Ridge [Mountains,] I never thought I'd miss it. Until *Big Stone Gap*. Trigiani's tapestry of characters will make any small town defacto reminisce fondly of the bizarre, conventional life we couldn't wait to leave. Bravo! A swift, heartwarming reminder. I'm going home."[92]

Despite the high numbers of African American out-migrants from the upland South during the Southern Diaspora of the mid-1900s, few seem to have joined the ranks of the nostalgic cosmopolitans. I have found no evidence of longing for Appalachian settings among out-migrants of color or their descendents. Admittedly, a reviewer's race might not be apparent, but online reviewing is a genre that seems to invite such self-identification (for example, "As a hillbilly, I . . ." or "As a non-American, I . . .").[93] I found no customer reviews that included comments such as "Although I am African American, I can identify with . . ." or "I liked this white-bread novel even though I am [African American, Latino, and so on]."

Additionally, I looked for African American fans of Appalachian-set fiction in the most likely place I could imagine, among members of the Eastern Kentucky Social Club (EKSC), a national organization of African American migrants who were reared in coal towns. EKSC members have ties to Appalachia and the means to buy or borrow books about the region. A survey of the reading histories of members who attended the reunion in 2003 found that few favored fiction set in Appalachia.[94] Three people asked for a copy of the questionnaire so that they could track down some of the books, but others insisted that they were more interested in local histories or in scholarly works by former Lynch, Kentucky, resident Bill Turner than in Appalachian-set novels. EKSC members embraced cosmopolitanism over nostalgia. One commented, "I don't like any place you can't fly into." Another explained his lack of interest in Appalachian books by saying, "See, I grew up there. What do I need to read about it for?"[95] Although they cherished relationships with people from their hometowns, they did not romanticize returning home.

Unlike African American members of EKSC, nostalgic cosmopolitan readers felt "homesick" for pastoral America. Out-migrant readers from this nostalgic group of readers strongly empathized with Inman's longing for his mountain home as he walks to Cold Mountain. A nostalgic Frazier fan wrote that the characters' "stories spoke to my heart. I was raised in the mountains of North Carolina. There is a feeling about living there that is hard to explain. Charles Frasier captures that."[96] "It's a love story, alrighty, but not between two people," wrote Keith. "The real object of Inman's desire, and the true source of Ada's strength" is "the mountain itself. Anyone . . . who never really left those mountains . . . can comprehend the depth of yearning."[97] Even more so than for touristic readers, for nostalgic cosmopolitans, reading about Appalachia involved returning to the past—often to one's childhood or the place where one grew up. A West Virginia reader described *At Home in Mitford* as "like a return to childhood when the days were simple and worries were few."[98] George in Tennessee called *Big Stone Gap* the "ticket for so many from small town America" to "experience our youth again, no matter w[h]ere we lived it out."[99]

Nostalgic out-migrants also included readers who had lived in Appalachia for just a short period of time, such as professionals who, like missionaries of old, did a "tour of duty" in the region. Indeed, short-term residents' perspectives on the region often exhibited the Othering typical of missionary attitudes. One physician recalled working in the Big Stone Gap emergency room: "I spent the better part of the '70s tending to many of the characters I have rediscovered in Adriana Trigiani's 'Big Stone Gap.'" The novel provides "new insight into the dreamlike world into which I was cast" as a "'feriner,' truly from another world."[100] A woman in Indiana attested that "time moves slower in North Carolina. I know. I lived there and walked the land."[101] These onetime residents offered firsthand testimony that the fictional representations of Appalachia's quaint eccentricity were accurate.

Nostalgic cosmopolitans, however, differed from touristic cosmopolitans in that, for most, reading regional fiction was a means of claiming geographic identity—an impulse they shared with self-identified rural affirmed Appalachian readers, as we will see. Susan in Seattle felt that, as "a southerner," she could recognize the characters in *Cold Mountain*: "I can put names and faces to each of the characters."[102] Even the fairy tale–like *At Home in Mitford* attracted nostalgic cosmopolitans, though usually these were from towns across the United States rather than Blowing Rock or the North Carolina mountains per se. The characters are "so real that they made my heart ache with pleasure for people I grew up knowing," wrote one.[103] Mitford took one reader "back to a forgotten time in my life in the small hometown I grew up in." She lamented that after "enrolling my daughter in a nearby university near Blowing Rock (alias Mitford)," she found it "hard to come back to life in" the coastal city of Wilmington.[104] These quotes point to the intense desire on the part of many white Americans to imagine the places of their childhood as protected from the evils and stresses of their adult lives and to ground their sense of selves in particular places. They also indicate that many readers assumed, thanks in part to popular fiction, that Appalachia had managed to preserve a sense of place and identity long lost in the rest of the nation.

Nostalgic cosmopolitans likely achieved higher salaries and educational attainment than affirmed Appalachians who did not ever leave the region, if one study of attendance at nine reunions in eastern Kentucky is any indication. Holly Barcus and Stanley Brunn distinguish between residents "rooted in place" by choice, lower-income residents with little choice but to move around in the region, and "mobile but attached" attendees who had "moved to take advantage of employment or education." This last group is akin to nostalgic cosmopolitans who have left the region but continue to feel strongly about it (though in the case of the mobile but attached residents, some had moved back home). They had "somewhat higher incomes, with a much larger proportion . . . earning more than seventy-five thousand dollars annually." They held "the most positive view of their home county" of any reunion attendees, describing it in terms of "family connectedness, safety, comfort, and peacefulness." Their "economic status and education . . . allow them freedom to migrate while maintaining strong place attachments."[105]

Susan Matt notes that contemporary Americans are generally resigned to Thomas Wolfe's dictum "You can't go home again," feeling "nostalgia" but not "melancholy." Instead, they "try to fashion a home . . . from the materials at hand," which is to say from "tokens of home and roots" available through consumer culture—not "mementos of their actual homes so much as items associated with the romantic image of home."[106] Like heritage festivals, popular fiction set in Appalachia "gained in popularity" due to its utility in assuaging what David Lowenthal describes as "isolation and dislocation of self from family . . . and even oneself from one's former selves." According to Matt, Americans accept "such re-created and reproduced objects" because, though commercialized, they "provide comfort and a connection to the past" alongside the acceptance that "one's true home" is "gone for good."[107]

Big Stone Gap attracted an especially high proportion of nostalgic out-migrants for whom geographic identity was foundational and self-defining and for whom the novel provided comfort. In fact, the critical Bo from Spokane may be right in his wry remark about the novel's appeal: "I guess you had to be there."[108] Lorene in North Carolina titled her review "Yes, You Can Go Home Again": "I grew up in this nice place" full of "quirky and lovable characters," she wrote, "and have all my life wished I could share it with the rest of the world. Now, Thanks to Adriana Trigiani, I can."[109] A "native" of Big Stone Gap who had moved "to the city" three years prior confessed, "I am so moved by this wonderful story that I am hopelessly homesick at the moment," while another reader who grew up there claimed to read the novel "every time I get homesick."[110]

As reviewers' references to "quirky" and "bizarre" characters suggest, some nostalgic readers distanced themselves from the distinctiveness that they cherished about their home place, despite the fact that these "quirky" and "lovely" characters seemed to play a significant role in ameliorating "homesickness."[111] Nostalgic out-migrants' sense of the Appalachian characters as "charming" and exotic allies them more to touristic readers than to affirmed Appalachians.[112] "I recognize so many of the characters presented here," claimed a woman from Kingsport, a small city near Big Stone Gap, who had moved to Atlanta; "Trigiani really captures the heart and soul of the people who populate the area"—people whom she really did not seem to count herself among.[113] Interestingly, while nostalgic cosmopolitans approved of depictions of mountain residents as a distinct population, they appreciated what they took to be the novels' refusal to make "the mountain folk" "out to be dumb hillbillies."[114] They therefore affirmed generalizations about Appalachians as different while insisting that those differences were positive, emphasizing "honor and chivalry" and charm.[115]

In this regard, best-selling fiction set in Appalachia seems to have operated for nostalgic readers in much the same way as paintings of mountain scenes. Kristin Kant, in her study of art sold in an Appalachian tourist town, found that "the paintings produced for [its] art market contain icons that portray Appalachia as a homogenous region of poor, white people frozen in the past. . . . Most of these icons, like a log cabin, are used to symbolize positive stereotypes." Most visitors buy paintings "because of the emotional reaction they experience towards the subject matter," which conventionally and iconically reminds them of "their grandparents' place." Kant observes that although they express "nostalgic reverence for the past," the tourists simultaneously insist on the distance between themselves and their grandparents. The artwork, like these best sellers, frequently "legitimates the social difference between those who are depicted, painted, and possessed and those who possess and paint. . . . In other words, this art provides a safe 'Other'—a hillbilly."[116]

Like Kant's tourists, nostalgic readers were thrilled to revisit or recon-

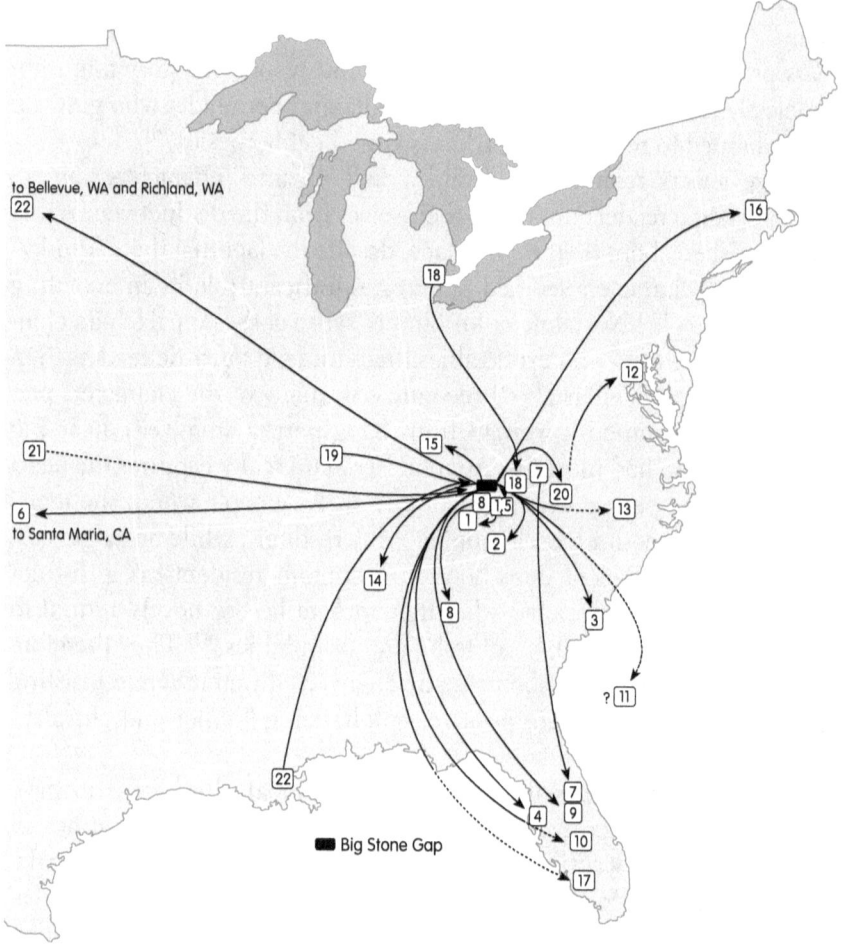

Big Stone Gap fans who mention migrations, 2000–2003. Dotted line indicates that the precise location is not known.

struct the places of their families' pasts as a way of maintaining a sense of identity, roots, and belonging. Although coal mining plays a relatively small role in the novel, a woman in California believed that Trigiani's novel taught her something about her father's years working underground in Big Stone Gap. Having a link to the mountains was important to this woman, who felt she "knew" "those people" even though she was not

Out-migrants
1. Johnson City, Tennessee → Talbott, Tennessee
2. BSG → Fletcher, North Carolina
3. BSG → Charleston, South Carolina
4. Wise County, Virginia → Port Richey, Florida
5. BSG → Johnson City, Tennessee
6. BSG → Santa Maria, California
7. Southwest Virginia → Apopka, Florida
8. Kingsport, Tennessee → Atlanta, Georgia
9. East Stone Gap, Virginia → Orlando, Florida
10. BSG → Florida
11. BSG → ?: "Having grown up in Big Stone Gap . . . I read the novel every time I get homesick."
12. "Not so far from the Blue Ridge" → Washington, DC

Descended from out-migrants
13. BSG → North Carolina: "My mom-in-law is from Big Stone Gap."
14. BSG → Madison, Alabama: "A Visit Home—My mother used to pack me up in the summer and send me to my grand parents in the Big Stone Gap area."
15. BSG → Lexington, Kentucky: "My father grew up in Big Stone Gap."
16. BSG → Boston, Massachusetts: "My mother's family is from near Big Stone Gap."
17. BSG → southwest Florida: "My mother's family has lived in or around Big Stone Gap for upward of 200 years, and . . . some of my fondest memories are of living . . . there during World War II and again briefly in the early fifties."

In-migrants
18. Detroit, Michigan → Abingdon, Virginia
19. Mt. Vernon, Indiana → BSG
20. ? → Wise County → Winston-Salem, North Carolina: spent "four very formative years in Wise Co."
21. Kansas → near BSG
22. New Orleans → BSG → Bellevue and Richland, Washington

---

one of them.[117] Appalachia lived on for her in a legendary, seminal role as home place and homeland.

Cold Mountain drew a surprising number of nostalgic cosmopolitans who thought the stories revealed to them something about their ancestors. Their comments emphasize the degree to which certain white Americans across the country like to trace their roots to Appalachia and reinforce the extent to which Appalachian-identified white readers welcomed the novel's seeming proclamation of Appalachians' innocence of the racist motivations for secession.[118] For the great-great-grandson of a Civil War deserter, reading Inman's story "brought me to peace with my own ancestry."[119] For several, *Cold Mountain* affirmed their belief that their ancestors "volunteered in a war that they didn't really understand" and that "mountain people were not fighting for slavery."[120]

Some white readers imagined their familial history—white, rural, and agrarian—as integrally related to or even essentially the same as national history. *Cold Mountain* "brought me face to face with history, both of the country, and my own family history," wrote one reviewer. "I still have memories of my grandmother wringing the necks of chickens, canning vegetables and killing hogs. . . . Ada could have been my great grandmother."[121] Another proclaimed, "Cold Mountain is full of my ancestors and your ancestors—their hardships, their determination, and their bond to the land."[122] Such comments indicate the extent to which white Americans to this day continue to imagine the "real" America as, at heart, simple white farmers just trying to get by—to the exclusion of other narratives about the racial diversity of the nation or the activities and ambitions of its economy domestically and internationally.

Charmed Appalachians

The third-largest group of readers, charmed Appalachians, resided within Appalachia—often in cities or large towns—and expressed delight in the national attention directed at places familiar to them. Some were newcomers, while others were longtime residents, but all were well-to-do readers whose own occupations did not fit their ideal of the charming Appalachian mountaineer. Nonetheless, like nonmetropolitan elites of Mary Murfree's day, these readers interpreted popular fiction set in the region as a sign of personal prominence. Charmed Appalachians rejoiced when best-selling novels put "our hometown on the map!"[123] They did not identify with/as locally colored characters. Instead, like touristic and nostalgic readers, they shared the novels' combined amusement and affection for the characters' eccentricities. They relied upon the same positive but patronizing adjectives ("delightful," "charming," and "oddball") used by publishers to sell books to metropolitan readers.[124]

Some charmed Appalachians fit sociologist Wendy Griswold's description of "cowbirds," cosmopolitan members of the reading class who move into a region and then set about familiarizing themselves with regional culture as a means of "nesting" and claiming belonging.[125] One reader who had "just moved to North Carolina" bought *At Home in Mitford* "with the hopes that I would learn more about my new home. I not only learned about my home, I learned about the beauty and wisdom that Jan Karon's characters possess . . . eccentric characters with passionate and shady backgrounds." Another in-migrant adopted regional slang in the title of her customer review of *Big Stone Gap*, "One of my all time favorites, y'all!" She bought the book "because I was moving from Kansas to the Appalachian mountain region very near Big Stone Gap and I thought I might be able to 'learn a thing or two.'" This instructive function of regional novels was also welcomed by charmed Appalachians interested in teaching others about their place. "I got this book [*Cold Mountain*] for my wife for Christmas because I wanted her to learn more about my native North Carolina," one man explained.[126]

Though recent in-migrants and others interested in "learning" about Appalachia may have contributed to the financial success of regional authors, in the end it is unclear what might be the value of discovering that local people are "eccentric," "passionate," and "shady." Scholars of reading continue to debate the extent to which novels help produce empathetic readers open to cultural differences. Elizabeth Long notes Martha Nussbaum's argument that "novels can be morally educative because they confront a reader with individual lives often quite different from the reader's own and demand an empathic yet reflective response to those lives." Long observes that book club discussions "can—but do not always—lead group members toward creative and expansive appraisals of social 'others.'"[127] Surely popular novels did help some readers learn about and appreciate the kinds of Appalachian people and places they featured, at times challenging dominant hierarchies that demean and mock lower-middle-class and working-class rural ways of life. On the other hand, the novels appeared to reinforce, even or especially among readers who lived in Appalachia, an essentialist view of quaint Appalachianness.

We can see this trend of celebrating quaint visions of Appalachia especially among charmed Appalachians who considered themselves *from* the area but not *of* it. These lifelong or longtime charmed residents comprised a greater proportion of charmed Appalachians than did the recently arrived cowbirds. Longtime charmed residents tended to have a romantic if condescending view of the supposedly simple mountain folk who surrounded them, and to endorse popular novels' perspectives on them. Curiously enough, James, who read *Cold Mountain* "at my home in the Blue Ridge Mountains," claimed regarding characters who were not only fictional but also meant to represent nineteenth-century Americans: "Living in these mountains I have met these people." James believed that "Ruby's father," the drunken ne'er-do-well, "lived up the road from our place." *Mitford* fans, too, avowed that Jan Karon's characters were real: "Being next door to Jan Karon's hometown, . . . I have met some of those people of the 'hollers.'"[128]

As we shall see, the smaller set of affirmed Appalachians frequently used "we" when referencing Appalachian characters, whereas charmed Appalachians are identifiable partly because they generally speak about Appalachians in terms of "they" and "them." Theresa, from the small city of London, Kentucky, about an hour west of the fictionalized setting of *Clay's Quilt*, felt like the characters "were people I saw and talked to everyday. . . . I am really proud to say this book captures the true essence of Kentucky, the family ties, the things they do." Other times, a reader might affect a "we" stance even when she clearly felt charmed rather than affirmed. Barbara, raised a "suburban Detroit girl," described herself as having lived "isolated in the mountains for 17 years" despite her own admission that Abingdon, Virginia, was "a fairly 'cultural' town." She found Trigiani's "affection for these people . . . most touching and it's how I've come to feel." She spoke patronizingly in favor of her adopted region when she informed other readers: "But that's the way we like it in Appalachia: Keep the 'happenings' to a minimum and just enjoy the beauty of the environment and the genuineness of the people. . . . We still wave at each other when we pass in our cars—whether BMW's or old pickup trucks."[129] Though Barbara is more likely to drive a BMW, she builds her identity partly through association with those old pickup trucks of "the people" who may find class differences not so unimportant as she does. If white middle classness is generic and empty, then charmed Appalachians can access meaning by loose association with less privileged "Appalachians" who supposedly exhibit a more colorful, cultureful way of life.

Big Stone Gap in particular drew charmed readers from nearby cities, including Kingsport, Roanoke, and Johnson City, who believed that Trigiani's quirky characters were faithful representations of mountain people. Angela in Johnson City wrote, "I know many mountain folk whose lives are exactly as she mentions." For a reader in Kingsport, Trigiani's novel "works well at depicting the folk of Appalachia!"[130] Despite their sometimes romantic or reductive notions about the way the novels introduced people of "the kind a person might actually encounter" in the area, charmed Appalachians insisted that the novelists' representations were not "exaggerated." One Johnson City reader was happy that *Big Stone Gap* "doesn't perpetuate the hillbilly stereotype." Barbara in Abingdon was happy Trigiani's novel "allowed one to view the people indigenous to this region as more than toothless illiterates." These readers were pleased to affirm positive descriptions of the region "where I am proud to live."[131] Charming "folk" in old pickup trucks helped them defend themselves against imagined or real put-downs about toothless illiterate hillbillies. Ultimately, charmed Appalachians seemed more concerned about promoting a favorable image of their homes than in addressing illiteracy or toothlessness.

Affirmed Appalachians

The fourth-largest group of readers, affirmed Appalachians, also looked to the novels as a resource for affirming their affection for the places of their lives but diverged from touristic, nostalgic, and charmed readers by identifying with popular novels' mountain characters. These self-identified rural readers might also be thought of as "proud country readers," since in some cases they were not from Appalachia per se. Unlike most cosmopolitan readers and charmed Appalachians, affirmed Appalachians did not accept metropolitan life as the norm from which rural residence was a substandard or quaint deviation. As Doug Reichert Powell observes, the "dominant and pervasive representational practices of mass media . . . focus attention away from" rural locales and rarely depict nonurban places "as vital spaces" of American life. Affirmed readers welcomed novels that, in Reichert Powell's phrasing, "communicated the idea that people like us . . . could make vital knowledge from local materials, could find something in the spaces at hand, seemingly so far from the cosmopolis, that was worth learning."[132] Unlike Reichert Powell, however, affirmed readers proudly pointed to fictional representations as completely true and flattering portrayals of their lives. They embraced generalizations about Appalachia that depict it as a privileged site of family and community and gratefully accepted the elements of the novels that construct Appalachian life as nonstandard or exotic. Just as important as the novels' affirmation of mountain life was the possibility that they might serve as educational tools for explaining mountain difference to the broader national audience that made them popular.[133]

Three of the four novels attracted affirmed Appalachians whose pride in place was bolstered by the books, with the seemingly mythical Mitford an apparent exception. A *Big Stone Gap* fan, "born and reared in this beautiful town," enjoyed seeing "the characters brought to life" because they helped prove that "we are not the people the world sees. We are normal small town people who work, live and respect Big Stone Gap and know our next door neighbors are there for us in times of need."[134] A Kentucky reader from Garner, near Hindman, felt that Silas House "captures a lot of Appalachian culture" in *Clay's Quilt*. "Anyone from the Eastern KY area can identify with one or more of his characters."[135] Rebecca from the western Kentucky town of Princeton read *Clay's Quilt* for a class at the University of Kentucky. "As a Kentucky girl" about Clay's age, she "could relate" to the book's depictions of "honky tonks [and] living next door to family members" and recommended it "to any one who wonders what growing up in Kentucky in my life time is really like."[136]

Affirmed Appalachians crowed over the success of *Cold Mountain* and proudly claimed affiliation with the setting. Brian, from "Horse Shoe in the NC mountains," exclaimed in all capital letters, "The places are real, I am from there!!"[137] But as it turns out, some of the proudest affirmed Appalachians were out-migrants to the suburban fringes of the region. One reviewer, who proclaimed, "It's a mountain thing—you wouldn't understand," wrote from just southeast of Charlotte. Cynthia, who "grew up almost within sight of Cold Mountain" but wrote from Bynum, just outside sprawling Chapel Hill, felt *Cold Mountain* "captured the culture lost—authentic and proud." Despite her lament that the culture was "lost," she endorsed "Inman's simplistic desire: if you get home to the mountains it will all be ok" and twice intoned: "It was my hills this fellow was writing about." Cynthia felt *Cold Mountain* avoided the pitfalls of previous representations of Appalachia. She also found in the novel ratification of her scorn for city folk, noting that Frazier captured a "scene I still see today . . . an educated, well-refined soul finding themselves facing life on the mountain—learning store-bought luxuries and book-learning do little to prepare one for the cold winds and hard winters."[138] She aligned herself with agrarian know-how above book learning and saw no conflict in doing so by writing an Internet review of a mass-produced store-bought literary artifact.

Quirky Charm

For all four groups of fans who posted positive reviews, touristic, nostalgic, charmed, and affirmed alike, eccentric characters who represent simple people were a crucial element of the novels' appeal. Unlike in stories published during the original Gilded Age, however, during the Neo–Gilded Age secondary characters served this function more so than protagonists. In local-color stories of the late 1800s, authors frequently employed frame narration wherein the dominant voice was a sophisticated visitor who introduced the reader to local cultures, often by presenting a native storyteller who then proceeded to tell the tales. The protagonists of contemporary Appalachian-set novels are sometimes geographical outsiders (*Cold Mountain*'s Ada is from Charleston; Father Tim moved to Mitford from Alabama) and sometimes not (such as Clay in *Clay's Quilt*). Ave Maria Mulligan, though born in Big Stone Gap, feels herself to be a black sheep because she's Italian and a spinster. But for the most part, the protagonists are "standard" Americans more than local caricatures (though Ave Maria's over-the-top name initially suggests otherwise). The protagonists provide universal elements with which the reader can identify (loss of mother, falling in love, feeling dissatisfied with life). It is largely through their eyes that the reader sees the local color—the mountain people who make up the "supporting cast," in the words of one reviewer, who noted that although the "leads aren't especially strong characters" in *Big Stone Gap*, "the supporting cast and setting is."[139]

Mitford's protagonists, for example, are white middle-class Americans whose education level, mobility, and ambitions readers shared, but the book is full of colorfully nonstandard small-town eccentrics. *Mitford* fans loved the "entertaining villagers" whom they found "so genuine, country-warm."[140] Most prominently "Appalachian" of these is a boy named Dooley ("barefoot, freckle-faced, . . . [and in] dirty overalls") whom Father Tim takes in as his ward (*AHM*, 95).[141] Readers of *Big Stone Gap* identified with Ave Maria and found her hometown chock-full of "wacky but loveable" characters, a "delightful assortment of small-town eccentrics."[142] *Clay's Quilt* featured "fascinating characters and their own little world."[143] These characters represent for readers the "real" Appalachia.

It did not escape readers' notice that *Cold Mountain* is peopled by conventionally craven poor white trash southerners, mountain laze-abouts of the Snuffy Smith variety. As Frazier describes them, "All they wished to do was hunt and eat and lay up all night drunk, making music" (*CM*, 287).

They are ignorant but noble, god-fearing, mountain people living off the land "pure and apart" from society (*CM*, 279). Diana described the characters as "American Appalacians—the hard working mountain dwellers and their steadfast beliefs and downright perserverance."[144] Readers unmoved by Ada and Inman fell in love with the goat woman, "Veasey, a misguided preacher" from the lowlands; the "country savant" Ruby, "a somewhat wild girl" whom readers felt "characterized the spirit of the mountain people, both then and now"; and Ruby's father, Stobrod.[145] The "fascinating," "colorful," and "quirky" characters along Inman's journey added zest to the story for Frazier's readers. Amy in Chicago "was haunted by the images of all these strange people lurking in the Blue Ridge Mountains."[146]

Dialect was a key feature in representing the characters' local color. In *Mitford*, the locals' speech is contrasted with the proper, almost stilted, speech (sprinkled with French) of the Episcopal rector, Father Tim. Locals speak instead in phonetically rendered mountain speech like that of diner owner Percy Mosely: "You mean th' one that's taken a likin' to you? . . . We never laid eyes on 'im 'til a week or two ago" (*AHM*, 15).[147] Silas House depicts dialect largely without phonetic representation, relying more on grammatical construction and vocabulary. For example, his protagonist Clay says, "You ain't read nothing since high school" and remarks that Alma is not "fixing to bear . . . a youngun."[148] Touristic, nostalgic, and charmed readers regularly praised the authors' ability to capture mountain speech. The "jargon" in *Cold Mountain* "caught the flavor of the mountain people so well," according to a man in Virginia.[149]

Offended Appalachians

A second set of self-identified rural readers, "offended Appalachians," comprised the smallest group of readers to commit their opinions to online reviews. Unlike affirmed Appalachians, offended readers expressed disappointment or indignation at finding their lives rendered in formulas that, they felt, helped justify others' false assumptions about Appalachian people. Like mountain residents in John Fox Jr.'s time, they found the representations of their homes stereotypical or simply ignorant. For example, a rural-identified reader of *Cold Mountain* titled his review "Don't read this book if you know anything about country life" and proceeded to outline in painstaking detail the missteps Frazier had made. A reviewer from the university town of Blacksburg, Virginia, in the Southwest Virginia mountains, complained: "We live in a small southern town and we are Episcopalians. I don't recognize either the atmosphere of the town of Mitford or the characteristics of the people."[150]

Clay's Quilt seemed to provoke particularly passionate complaints from offended Appalachians. A reviewer from London, Kentucky, who titled her review "My world," noted that the story was set "just a stone's throw from where I live." She felt that House rendered the characters and the story "a little 'more Appalachian' than southeastern Kentucky really is in modern times." House gave "readers who aren't familiar with Kentucky exactly what they expected—coal miners, bar fights, domestic violence, teenage marriages and people living in houses they built themselves. I wished it was clear that this is not an 'everyday' situation here in southeastern Kentucky." The reviewer acknowledged that coal, violence, and teen marriage were part of life but felt betrayed by what she saw as the suggestion that they were prevalent in, and unique to, her "world."[151]

Another Kentucky reviewer criticized what he called the theme of "celebrating one's heritage" in *Clay's Quilt* because he felt it "celebrates too many negative aspects of life in Kentucky's Eastern Appalachian Mountains." Clay, to his mind, "is an undereducated coal miner who drinks and does pot and spends his free time in bars," and "the other characters are equally undereducated, one a teenage mother." He continued, "It would be one thing to celebrate the families and communities if they were strong, but they are not. The Eastern Kentucky region is fraught with issues of poverty, under or no education, unemployment, drop outs, drug abuse, and a large amount of people on government assistance." He acknowledged that "other areas of America have the same issues" and praised House for addressing some key problems (such as absentee ownership and corporate power). Nonetheless, he wished "House's novels had explored these issues more instead of adopting the attitude of acceptance and celebration." He felt a heartwarming tale was not enough in the face of the challenges confronted by regional residents.[152]

It is intriguing that such criticism would be directed at House who, perhaps more than other popular novelists of his day, has engaged Appalachian issues politically as well as poetically. Particularly noteworthy is House's sustained and visible activism to raise awareness about, and fight the practice of, mountaintop-removal mining—a method of resource extraction destructive to both human and nonhuman communities. Perhaps in time, as readers become familiar with House's lobbying on this issue, it will inform the ways in which they read his stories.

* * *

Popular Appalachian fiction of the Neo–Gilded Age produced supposedly documentary and accurate portrayals of the region as a place full of authentic people living more authentic lives than the vast majority of the novels' readers. Most readers imagined Appalachia as populated by simple white Americans. In the words of one charmed Appalachian, the fiction "illuminat[es]" so-called "Appalachian values—home, music, the land and family."[153] Even for affirmed Appalachians, the value in the novels' Appalachian settings was their difference from "mainstream" culture, but difference along fairly predictable lines. As long as the novels seemed to cast that conventional difference in a favorable light, readers welcomed their emphasis on isolation, rurality, old-fashionedness, and poor or working-class characters. Readers—by and large members of the professional classes—embraced a notion of Appalachia as protected from the consumer capitalism that permeated their own lives. Alarmed by the seemingly endless processes of commodification around them, they wishfully projected onto Appalachia the notion of a more natural, less commodified, less materialistic place. Lamenting the anonymity, numbness, and pressures of life in the city, they hailed fictional refuges that presented more neighborly, more vibrant, and more tranquil places. Readers welcomed representations that turned a blind eye to labor conflict, the predations of the coal industry, the contingent laborers servicing the second-home and tourist industries, and the rise of new industries such as call centers and prisons—just to name a few of the features of Appalachia's industrial and postindustrial landscapes usually omitted from popular regional fiction.

Whereas John Fox Jr.'s 1908 *The Trail of the Lonesome Pine* represents mountain life as solitary, best-selling Neo–Gilded Age novels assign loneliness to the city (bastion of consumer capitalism) and attribute a sense of "community" to the (supposedly nonmaterialistic) mountains and the rural South. Recent popular regional fiction holds out the promise that Appalachia is still one place where neighborliness and family are valued. Neo–Gilded Age novels place kindred, home, community, and belonging above all. Readers of any fiction often demonstrate eagerness to belong to the world of the novel, and fans of Appalachian-set fiction talked with intensity about fictional characters as family and friends. *Clay's Quilt* left a reader from Minnesota with the welcome sensation that "I was part of the friendly, down-home Sizemore family."[154] A reader from Sugar Camp, Kentucky, wrote, "I loved [*Clay's Quilt*] because I felt as if I had met a new family and become life-long friends with them. They became very real to me, and I missed them once I finished the book."[155] This reaction was expressed even by fans who lived within the supposedly communal Appalachian region, but it was particularly strong among touristic and nostalgic cosmopolitans, as if the vicarious community provided by the novel were a lifeline. A negative review from a reader who thought the longing for camaraderie evident in others' customer reviews was a bit pathetic called *At Home in Mitford* "'Cheers' without the beer," referencing the 1980s television sitcom about a bar "where everybody knows your name."[156]

A majority of readers often treated the novels as unmediated missives sent by authentic residents. All the authors examined here grew up in or near the places that serve as their books' settings, lending to readers' sense of the stories' authenticity. In order to view Appalachian-set fiction as unmediated missives, however, consumers had to ignore the international publishing industry and book marketplaces that made their consumption of the rural possible. Readers purchased—and therefore helped produce—an Appalachia construed as a refuge from postmodern society. Readers with ties to Appalachia were central to the best sellers' success, critical to their perceived legitimacy, and therefore implicated in the continued circulation of romantic stereotypes about the region as home to a colorful way of life that includes nonstandard speech, folk traditions, closeness to the land, and more authentic relationships between close-knit neighbors. David Hsiung's observation for the Revolutionary antebellum eras holds true for the Second Gilded Age: cosmopolitan Appalachians actively contributed to the construction of regional distinctiveness.[157]

Appalachia has not ever been as isolated or lacking in industrial development as popular images purport. As Barcus and Brunn note, as of 2006 at least "60 percent of the region's population lives in a metropolitan area," and scholars "label much of the region as 'suburban.'"[158] By consuming best-selling local-color novels, readers may choose to ignore the processes of production (for example, mountaintop-removal coal mining) and consumption (for example, shopping at Wal-Mart) that take place within rural America in favor of celebrating Mitford's Main Street Grill or the "mom-and-pop" pharmacy depicted in *Big Stone Gap*.

It is easy to understand the resurgent appeal of fiction featuring local color at the turn of the twenty-first century. Zygmunt Bauman tells us that neither "identity" nor "community" is "available in our rapidly privatized and individualized, fast globalizing world, and for that reason each of the two can be safely, with no fear of practical test, imagined as a cosy shelter of security and confidence and for that reason hotly desired."[159] There is a risk, however, that readers have mistaken regional fiction, with its hotly desired fantasies of community, as documentary.

My concern is not with the accuracy or inaccuracy of any given novel, to paraphrase Doug Reichert Powell, but with the lack of a wide enough variety of stories to capture the complexity of Appalachian places and experiences. In order for a given text to be considered regional fiction at all, it is forced to embrace some particularly reductive assumptions about Appalachianness that make it difficult to see the internal variety and diversity of the region and the extent of its interconnectedness with national and global currents. Furthermore, as I explain in the conclusion, I fear that reductive versions of Appalachianness may be too readily harnessed for reactionary ends.[160]

Conclusion

The Production of Region and the Romance with Whiteness

> The idea of place, often described as a "sense" of place, is not so much sensory, as it is textual.... To know a place, to acquire that "sense" of place, is not to consume an experience, or witness a spectacle, or appreciate a landscape, but to participate, through consumption, through witness, through appreciation, in the ongoing creation of that place.
> —Douglas Reichert Powell, *Critical Regionalism*

> BRUCE: I know it sounds strange, but it's like Appalachia is home.
> KIRSTIN: It's like an inscape for us, a place to go, in our mind, to get away from it all.
> —Visitors to the Smithsonian Folklife Festival's 2003 "Appalachia: Heritage and Harmony" program

Each of the epigraphs above gestures toward distinct but overlapping sets of interests and concerns regarding the conclusions to be drawn from my examination of fans' responses to popular Appalachian-set fiction. Douglas Reichert Powell's quote speaks to the creation of place. In the first section below, "The Production of Regional Identity," I discuss the relationship between regional fiction and the construction of region and regionalism along lines that will be particularly useful, I hope, for those interested in literary regionalism. I claim that readers' responses demonstrate that a primary function of regional fiction has been to produce regional subjects.

My interview with Bruce and Kirstin (not their real names) speaks to the "love affair" some white Americans have with Appalachia in the twenty-first century.[1] We in Appalachian studies tend to focus our critiques on those who put down the region rather than those who celebrate it. In the second section, "Romancing Appalachia," I acknowledge the harm caused by denigration and scorn for the region and recognize the importance of examining the repercussions of negative stereotypes. I then suggest the urgency of critiquing the full range of popular representations of the region and express concern that, for some Americans, romance with Appalachia is a romance with simple authentic white folk that may, in some cases, reinforce racism, nationalism, and imperialism.

The Production of Regional Identity

The past decades have witnessed a brilliant flourishing of scholarship on the U.S. local-color movement of the late 1800s, much of which has shown us the ways in which the representation and consumption of regions has been in fact about imagining and producing the nation. Scholars have demonstrated the ways in which regional fiction served to "nationalize" readers after the Civil War—to teach readers to feel themselves participants in a nation that on the surface seemed a hodgepodge of regions that had just recently been at war with one another.

Tracking the reception geographies of popular Appalachian-set fiction has in some ways confirmed, if shifted, the emphasis of these earlier findings. Readers in Mary Noailles Murfree's and John Fox Jr.'s day included metropolitan elites fascinated by so-called backwater places. Chapters 1 and 2 demonstrate that imagining Appalachia had a salutary effect for readers who worried about the costs of American civilization in terms of masculinity; peace of mind; and attachments to land, nature, and place. White readers looked to Appalachia as a place that could be trusted to preserve what they saw as the nation's roots in Anglo agrarianism, especially in the face of immigration from southern and eastern Europe. Local elites, on the other hand, used regional fiction to project themselves into a highbrow literary community that they imagined as existing above and outside the region. They were more interested in self-promotion than in identifying with or advocating for regional residents fictionalized in local-color stories. Anecdotal evidence of reactions to Fox's works suggests that for some less privileged readers, however, caricatures of local life served to strengthen readers' resistance to national hierarchies based on locale, dialect, and class. It is also with Fox's readers that we first see evidence that regional fiction served to help articulate the emotional costs of upward mobility for white readers who imagined themselves as having moved up and out of distinctive, familial, vibrant, and backward home places. Reception geographies of Fox, in other words, signal the (perhaps emergent) role of regional fiction in generating regional identity.

It remains to be seen whether the popularity of southern mountain fiction from the 1910s through the 1940s (including popular novels by such authors as Thomas Wolfe, Elizabeth Madox Roberts, and Jesse Stuart) also contributed to the production of regional subjects. In the 1920s, the popularity of regional fiction was eclipsed by "revolt from the village" fiction that ridiculed small-town America. Yet as Amy Blair has shown, even fiction that mocked the nostalgia of regional writing was wrested to serve the purposes of local pride for readers unconvinced by hierarchies that set the metropolis at the pinnacle of civility and manners. Blair finds proud "provincials" misread Sinclair Lewis's *Main Street* as praiseful of small-town life rather than pejorative.[2] This sort of "populism" may have been touted by, and benefited, local elites more than the "salt-of-the-earth" characters they embraced—as was surely the case in the 2000s when George Bush Jr. and Alaskan governor Sarah Palin promoted "aw-shucks" images.

Chapter 3 explores how, in a period of relatively low productivity and popularity for regional fiction after World War II, Harriette Simpson Arnow's *Hunter's Horn* and *The Dollmaker* captured the attention of highbrow literati wistful for the nation's more agrarian past. Arnow's novels allowed cosmopolitan elites to "tsk-tsk" the tribulations of displaced farmers and enabled midwestern professionals to sympathize with, yet still lament the presence of, "hillbilly" migrants from the rural South. Fan mail demonstrates that Arnow's novels appealed powerfully to white readers who had themselves migrated out of Kentucky, who felt affirmed by Arnow's sympathetic representations of rural-at-heart people unkindly mocked and scorned. It is difficult to say what long-term political effects emerged from out-migrants' recognition/reconstruction of themselves via Arnow's fiction. They or their children may have later participated in Appalachian activism that challenged prejudice and discrimination in their adopted homes in Ohio, Michigan, Indiana, and Illinois.[3] Testimonials from fans of *Christy*, *Deliverance*, and popular novels published after 1985 suggest that the descendents of white out-migrants relied on fiction to construct Appalachian identities from outside the region.

In chapter 4 we saw that when Appalachia made the best-seller lists with *Christy* in 1967 and *Deliverance* in 1970, its image affirmed the touristic, missionary, and imperialist attitudes of many readers toward so-called primitive people. Both novels appealed to white readers outside the region who wished to claim affinity to it, thereby bolstering Appalachian and southern affiliations or identities that helped readers "ground" themselves despite highly mobile lives. Descendents of out-migrants from Appalachia were drawn to *Christy* as evidence of their humble but colorful heritage, while out-migrants from the broader South managed to find in Dickey's depraved hillbillies a comforting glimmer of home.

Not until the 1980s would regionalism resurge to the levels of production and consumption it had experienced during the local-color movement of the Gilded Age. In tandem with celebrations of multiculturalism and new ethnic identity politics that emerged among whites in the 1970s, literary regionalism flourished. Chapter 5 uses customer reviews to indicate that best-selling regional fiction served the needs of city-bound whites drawn to the pastoral and bolstered identity formation for white readers who feared generic whiteness or culturelessness. Readers with past or present affiliations with Appalachia turned to regional culture as a lifeline. They sometimes counted themselves as Appalachians; other times, they claimed authoritative knowledge of mountain people (classed and in some ways almost raced differently than themselves) as a means of asserting regional and cultural distinctiveness while maintaining a sense of themselves as normal mainstream Americans familiar with mountain ways but part of cosmopolitan highbrow culture.

In each era, thanks in large part to readers' faith in the authors as authentic representatives of the region, best-selling Appalachian-set fiction functioned to create Appalachia as a distinctive place apart from the mainstream United States; to offer readers much-desired senses of community and belonging; and to promote the interests of its readers in terms of status, pride in nation, and justification in managing "cultural" (racial, ethnic, and religious) difference domestically and internationally. These three functions served nationally oriented white elites and regionally oriented white readers (elite and not) equally, if differently. Readers' testimonies, alongside my mapping of mobile readers' geographic trajectories, indicate that—above all, perhaps—the role of regional fiction is to produce readers who learn to feel regionally. Readers' mobility in effect produced a market for regional fiction that in turn produced regional identity. Migration provoked among white Americans a sense of deep estrangement that they turned to fiction to ameliorate. Regional fiction speaks of regional pride and resistance to so-called progress. Its popularity speaks to the price of a hard-won, hard-felt cosmopolitanism that the fiction often suggests has been too costly.[4]

Other studies before this one have also noted regionalism's special function in identity formation. Wendy Griswold, for example, finds that regionalism nurtures "the wished-for identities of the reading class" who have the "resources . . . to put together their chosen cultural worlds" in order to provide "the pleasure of roots to the rootless."[5] Griswold's research highlights the importance of "cowbirds," or upper-middle-class newcomers to a region, in fostering regionalism, over and above that of what she terms "stayers" and "movers." As the preceding summary of my chapters' findings indicates, however, fan mail and customer reviews point to the equal or greater significance of stayers and movers. Longtime residents with cosmopolitan affiliations and movers of all kinds—out-migrants and internal migrants within the region as well as in-migrants, plus tourists and travelers for work, volunteerism, or schooling—played a critical role in sustaining regional generalizations and generating regional feeling. Little wonder that Appalachian regionalism has been so powerful, given the region's history of massive out-migration and its appeal as a destination for vacations and mission trips.

Another scholar who attends to the relationship between fiction and regional identity, Hsuan L. Hsu, argues against the widely held assumption that regional identity "expand[s] from" inside the region "outward into the nation." In other words, it's not merely a matter of isolated mountain people suddenly claiming pride in being Appalachian and setting out to inform the nation of their culture and identity. Instead, as Hsu points out, regionalism "originates in moments of prior, present, or imagined cosmopolitanism." But whereas for Hsu this means that regional identification "coalesces from the outside in," my examination of Appalachian-set best sellers leads me to describe the dynamic a bit differently.[6] Rather than starting outside, regional identity is generated by traffic between the outside and the inside. It's the result of a conversation between the outside and the inside among writers and readers with a cosmopolitan awareness but a familiarity with both the local and the global—with the especial assistance of readers who live within, or have at some point lived within, the region.

We can see from the responses of the Appalachian-set fiction fans examined in *Dear Appalachia* that scholars have been right to observe that regional fiction creates regions and regional identity. As Doug Reichert Powell puts it, "Acts of writing affect the meanings of places."[7] It is not that some regional authors capture the place better than others; they each create the place by writing about it, some more influentially so. Griswold rightly contends that "regional culture is peculiarly dependent on readers for its very existence." Readers "demand . . . place-specific mysteries, poetry, cookbooks, travel guides, magazines and local newspapers," and in doing so, they foster regional culture. "If no one read crime novels, there would still be crime," writes Griswold; "if there were no romance-novel fans, people would still discover love." But "turning space into place" requires words. "Take away readers, take away the apparatus of printing and distributing and reading about and writing about place, and regionalism atrophies."[8]

I think that this region-generating function of regional fiction is what Henry Shapiro must have had in mind when he noted that Americans during the Gilded Age accepted an "essentially literary vision of Appalachia as a discrete entity."[9] Shapiro also meant, I think, that it takes literature to make a region seem like "a discrete entity." Fiction makes a coherent whole out of an internally differentiated place or set of places. As Reichert Powell notes, the "depiction of communities [that lie] outside of the metropolitan center imagines them as altogether *too unified*, whether for good—nostalgia—or for ill—horror."[10]

Fiction's narrative power invests meaning in a swath of geographic territory that becomes important for readers in search of "culture" or "identity" as grounding in a postmodern world. Fiction's drive for coherence may obscure more than it reveals about variation within Appalachia. In my more optimistic moments, I think perhaps the continued popularity of regional fiction might prompt enough variations in the stories told to more fully capture regional heterogeneity. In my more pessimistic ones, I fear that the drive for coherence contributes to an essentialism that too readily works in the service of white American nativism, nationalism, and patronization of culturalized and racialized groups.[11]

Romancing Appalachia

Since the birth of Appalachian studies in the 1970s, scholars and other regional activists have decried negative stereotypes about the region and embraced the identity politics of regional pride. Stories that present the region in a glowing light serve as rebuttals to a devaluation of rural places and people that contributes to apathy or even antipathy toward some Appalachian residents' loss of land, landscape, and livelihood. An audience member at the 2010 Baltimore Radical Book Fair panel on mountaintop-removal mining, for example, asserted that coal field residents "hate us, they hate [President] Obama, they hate people from Baltimore, they hate black people, they hate Muslims. . . . You say there are people who care about what's happening but I see no evidence of that. Why are you there helping them? We should just say fuck 'em."[12] The geographic imagination of region may be socially constructed, but clearly its consequences are powerful and demand our attention and care.

Nevertheless, there is danger in countering assumptions that the region is "ignorant but simple" with the equally reductive notion that it is "beautiful but simple," to return to the dichotomy noted by Silas House. A few scholars have warned against celebratory fantasies that overgeneralize Appalachia as a pastoral region populated by self-sufficient yet communal people whose whiteness is presumed (though coded in words such as "simple," "American," and "pioneers").[13] They have made little headway. It's easy enough to understand why, given the preponderance of demeaning depictions of a region we hold dear. Nonetheless, we owe it to the region and to our organizing efforts to see Appalachia in a more complicated way, and to notice when celebrating it risks doing more harm than good. As Hsuan Hsu contends, "Artists and critics must find a way to care about both the distant and the local—to analyze regional communities without losing sight of the larger global community that requires and enables the production of regions." He recognizes the significant role that "the local may provide" for resistance and critique but argues that "anticapitalist struggles can only succeed by imagining and inhabiting larger terrains of sympathy, solidarity, and collaboration."[14]

Why Appalachia? Why Now?

Smithsonian Folklife Festival visitors Bruce and Kirstin, the Washington, DC–based couple quoted in the epigraph, help us see the link between festivalgoers, readers, tourists, and other consumers of Appalachian ethnicity, identity, and difference. The couple loves fiction about Appalachia; they cite in particular their admiration for Charles Frazier's 1997 best seller *Cold Mountain* and their excitement about having stayed in a room with a related theme at the Grove Park Inn in Asheville, North Carolina.

Their enthusiasm for western North Carolina led them to buy real estate for a vacation home in the hopes of one day becoming part of what they view as the tight-knit community in the area. They are fans of bluegrass music, which they describe as "white soul," making transparent their notion that racial or ethnic difference underwrites more authentic and vibrant cultural production as well as their belief that (white) Appalachians are somehow able to tap into that vibrancy more than other Americans. Though few Scots migrated directly to Appalachia, Bruce and Kirstin believe that they have a special connection to the region because Bruce has Scottish ancestors.

This couple's zeal for Appalachian music, tourism, "ethnicity," and literature has been matched by scores of white Americans since at least the 1870s. For over 150 years, the idea of folklife has served as "a response to, an instrument of, and a phenomenon of modernity," including as a site of resistance to a society in which all relations are increasingly commercialized.[15] Postmodern society has witnessed a further escalation in the desire for a folk ideal that stresses noncommercial human relationships and historical connection to land, place, and culture. As Manuel Castells argued in 1997, "We have experienced, in the last quarter of the century, the widespread surge of powerful expressions of collective identity that challenge globalization and cosmopolitanism on behalf of cultural singularity." Feeling uprooted, isolated, and alienated, individuals both seek connections (a "feeling of belonging" or a "community") and assert selfhood (by constructing an "identity" based upon an individual's selective emphasis of a particular cultural attribute). Feeling threatened by the pace of change, individuals furthermore cling to "tradition," a notion that can underwrite conservative ideals of, among others, gender and family.[16]

Increasingly since the 1970s, readers and nonreaders alike have turned to Appalachia in their quest for a sense of identity and belonging, and for authenticity and refuge from what they experience as an atomistic, impersonal, and market-driven society. White Americans at the turn of the twenty-first century, like their counterparts a century earlier, exhibited anxieties about race, immigration, and homogenization, as well as newly intensified concerns about identity, mass culture, rootlessness, and lack of "community."

Reading regional fiction was one venue through which white American readers attempted to work through such concerns. Best-selling novels responded to and affirmed the widespread belief that deep within the bounds of the United States people live in a region deprived of the benefits of metropolitan accoutrements but also blissfully indifferent to the dislocations and upheavals of postmodernity. For readers of best-selling fiction, Appalachia was an enchanting place apart, a world protected from the worst aspects of contemporary commercial and urban life.

Appalachian Whiteness: Pure, Innocent, Ethnic

In chapter 5 I observed that best-selling regional fiction circa 2004 featured white protagonists almost without exception. Appalachia's appeal as a world protected from commercial and urban life depends heavily on its association with whiteness. But the version of whiteness lauded by readers of Appalachian-set fiction is a complicated one rooted in long-standing nostalgia for Anglo-Saxon folk figured as simple and disadvantaged. The notions of simplicity and disadvantage are key because they allow for a threefold representation of Appalachians as (1) presumptively "pure" Anglo-Saxons *and* (2) racially innocent—which is to say, ignorant of slavery and racial violence—*and* (3) ethnic minorities. Appalachia becomes parallel to other minority groups and yet simultaneously represents the most quintessentially American culture possible.

There is a long history for each of these three features of Appalachian whiteness. First, from the moment the label "Appalachian America" was coined at the turn of the twentieth century, elite whites imagined Appalachia as a comforting reservoir of whites capable of replenishing an America experiencing the disconcerting upheavals of urbanization, industrialization, and mass immigration from eastern and southern Europe. Prominent men such as William Goodell Frost, president of Berea College in Kentucky, insisted that Appalachia was home to "the largest body of pure English folk" in America and the last bastion of Anglo-Saxonhood untainted by foreigners or slaves.[17]

Second, in addition to "pure," writers of the late 1800s portrayed white Appalachians, unlike white southerners, as "racially innocent"—as too self-reliant and hardworking to participate in slavery and therefore as pro-Union during the Civil War. Indeed, the mountains' supposed isolation from the Deep South kept mountaineers from having any contact with African Americans, or so observers believed, which meant they couldn't possibly feel racism or execute violence against blacks. In the end, northern white Americans' construction of Appalachians as racially innocent exhibited its own brand of racism by praising the fact that Appalachians' lack of exposure to "Negroes" protected them from picking up their purportedly bad habits.[18]

Third, representations of Appalachians as ethnically distinct date at least to the turn of the twentieth century, when some observers attempted to explain negative "mountaineer" characteristics like feuding through reference to Scottish ancestry. John Fox Jr.'s fiction evinced suspicions that mountain residents were, in the words of Darlene Wilson, "almost-white," including, I would argue, by his description in "A Mountain Europa" of mountaineers as "dun" colored and a "race of the soil."[19]

Fast-forward to the Second Gilded Age, circa 1985–2008. These three well-entrenched notions of Appalachian ethnicity (pure white, racially innocent, and not-quite-white) have if anything gained in strength. The flurry of popular regional fiction published in the 1990s and early 2000s permitted readers to envision Appalachia as embodying the (pure, white, pioneer) roots of "real American culture." Racial innocence is, as Barbara Ellen Smith argues, "a powerful myth" that persists to this day.[20] In fact, white Americans in the 1990s seemed to believe in a new variation of the "racial innocence" story that views mountain whites as incapable of being oppressors because they are themselves oppressed. Finally, Appalachia as ethnic was reaffirmed by best-selling novels that construct Appalachians as whites whose blandness is tempered by the wild masculine energies of Cherokee, Melungeon, Celtic, Scottish, or Scots-Irish blood. (Think, for example, of *Big Stone Gap* characters with Italian and Melungeon roots, or the more predictable Irish and Cherokee ethnicities as explanations of personal character in *Clay's Quilt*.) Keeping in mind this history of Appalachia as triply coded pure Anglo white, racially innocent, and not-quite-white in mind, let us now return to Bruce and Kirstin at the Smithsonian Folklife Festival and their love for *Cold Mountain*, white soul, and Scottishness.

"Appalachia: Heritage and Harmony" at the 2003 Smithsonian Folklife Festival

In the summer of 2003, I embarked on a different kind of reception study. Instead of examining fan mail or customer reviews, I conducted interviews and observed participants at the Smithsonian Folklife Festival's "Appalachia: Heritage and Harmony" program. There I saw evidence in audience reactions to Appalachia of what I later came to identify as the three major functions of popular regional fiction: producing authentic place, enabling a sense of identity and belonging, and maneuvering the flow of power. It's also where I became particularly attuned to the overlap, for some Americans, between romancing Appalachia and romancing whiteness. Though I discuss my Folklife Festival findings more thoroughly elsewhere, I hope that reviewing them here will make clear how I came to be concerned that celebrations of Appalachia grounded in notions of authenticity and heritage may in some instances unwittingly endorse racism, nationalism, and imperialism.[21]

For many visitors, the "Heritage and Harmony" program reaffirmed belief in Authentic Appalachia—a rural and static "cultural preserve" where people still live protected from commercial mass culture. Interviewees described Appalachian people as "good people, country folk"; "more folkish"; "hardworking" and "hardscrabble" "staunch pioneers." Festival visitors repeatedly spoke enviously not only of the region's authenticity but also of the "belonging" they assumed Appalachians felt. Bruce and Kirstin had recently bought land in western North Carolina. "We're outsiders," Bruce acknowledged. "I know that and I honor it, but it pisses me off, too." His wife added, "We hope to break in."

This simple, authentic culture of belonging, visitors believed, was a white folk culture. One visitor, for example, insisted that Appalachia signified "authentic traditional American culture." He called the region "not commercial . . . indigenous . . . undiluted." Visitors to the festival perceived Appalachia not only as "pure," "undiluted" Anglo-Saxon white, but also, simultaneously and paradoxically, as ethnically white. In part due to the simultaneous presence of a Scotland program, visitors often mistakenly described the region as "Scottish" or "Celtic." Such interpretations seemed to serve as reassurances that Appalachia offered something distinctive from a "generic" Americanness wherein "Americanness" was deemed synonymous with white middle or upper-middle classness.

In a few instances, visitors' expressions of enthusiasm for Appalachianess bordered on intolerance for difference and outright racism, as indicated by comments about the program on the African nation of Mali with which Appalachia (and Scotland) shared the spotlight. One visitor said of Appalachia: "That's America. Good down-home South, that's where it started. Downright American stuff. . . . We don't go in for that African stuff." When I asked whether she meant the Mali program and motioned toward that section of the festival, the woman replied, "Wherever it is. It's just noise." Another visitor waved toward the Mali program and said, "That down there we know nothing about. . . . We don't care for that down there. The singing sounded like a bunch of racket to me." When juxtaposed with these visitors' complaints about the inaccessibility of black African music, Bruce and Kirstin's love for Bluegrass music as "white soul" appears to confirm my sense that Appalachianness provides white Americans with a safe, intelligible Other, more vibrant than generic whiteness but seemingly less threatening or alien than people of color.

When visitors described the "point" of what they interpreted as a white folk program as "to see the development of the country" and "to be reeducated into our own roots, who we are, where we came from," they linked the region to the promotion of white American nationalism that claims U.S. culture is at root Anglo-Saxon (even "Elizabethan") culture. Visitors claimed present-day Appalachia as the embodiment not simply of "my roots" but the nation's roots: "*our* roots," "*our* heritage," and "real" American culture. As the embodiment of the nation's roots, furthermore, Appalachia represented for white visitors both "homeland" and "home." This figuration allowed visitors to entertain the wishful belief that the United States, at base, is wholly identified with an Appalachian hearth imagined as a simple place peopled by simple denizens.

Even before I began to map readers of Appalachian-set best sellers, my festival research suggested that the white Americans most drawn to Authentic Appalachia felt themselves one step removed from the region.[22] Visitors recounted family stories about their parents' or grandparents' migration from rural and often Appalachian places to the midsize cities where the visitors themselves grew up. Raised in cities such as Pittsburgh, Pennsylvania, or Lexington, Kentucky, these visitors later migrated to larger metropolitan areas. As it had for Harriette Arnow's migrant fans in chapter 3, the idea of simple, white Appalachia offered these visitors what Henry Shapiro calls the "peace . . . of going home"—"something one liked better to think about than to do."[23] For second- or third-generation metropolitan residents unwilling or unable to return to the idealized rural places of their parents' or grandparents' childhoods, the "Appalachia" at the festival served as a vicarious trip to the home place. Visitors to the festival seemed almost to think of people who lived in Appalachia as their own alter egos—their very best selves, their root selves—innocent, virtuous commoners from whom they have strayed but who, at base, they remain.[24]

Readers saw in Appalachia their familial histories and their own best simple selves. Image by Amanda Kubista.

Appalachian Ethnicity and Claims to Racial Victimization

In the wake of multiculturalism and cultural heritage revivals in the 1960s and 1970s, Appalachians' status in the national imagination as "not-quite-white" held certain advantages.[25] Claiming distant kinship to colorful Appalachians reassured white Americans of ethnic belonging unavailable to plain old whiteness, which they imagined as normal, bland, generic, empty, and unmoored.[26] The fact that Appalachia was supposedly "ethnic" promised a refuge from the sameness and sterility of what one journalist called "mallification" (perhaps now better termed big-boxification).[27] Ancestral Appalachianness therefore permitted participation in multiculturalism as a celebration of culture, downplaying race and structures of racial oppression and inequity.

Barbara Ellen Smith warns against "defenses of Appalachia that position the region and its people as the 'real' or truest Americans." When fans of Appalachia describe mountain whites as "hardworking," "country folk," and "American," Smith notes, they implicitly define them as deserving whites not only against elites but also against people of color: "For example, hillbillies are hard-working, unlike the pampered rich, but also unlike lazy welfare recipients; country folk, as opposed to rich city slickers, but also unlike those threatening denizens of the ghetto; and American, in contrast to globe-trotting CEOs, as well as those whose national/cultural origins are clearly 'not from here.'"[28]

Racial innocence and ethnic distinctiveness intertwine in regional fiction, whose popularity soared precisely in step with rhetoric that claimed some white Americans were "robbed" of American or Anglo "entitlements." Popular treatises like Jim Webb's *Born Fighting* assert that Scots-Irish Americans (commonly misunderstood as primarily Appalachian and southern) are oppressed by Anglo Americans, thus rendering complaints that are largely about class exploitation and class-based value systems in terms of ethnic discrimination. Historian Matthew Frye Jacobson cautions us to recognize that celebrations of white ethnicity can, in their extreme form, amount to a denial of white ethnic individuals' access to benefits based on race.[29]

Furthermore, there is a fallacious and dangerous tendency, familiar in Lost Cause rhetoric and reinforced by recent "explanations" of "southern culture" as unalloyed Celtic and Scots-Irish, to claim that Appalachian whites are the *most* victimized of Americans, "the last acceptable ethnic fools" in American popular culture.[30] In 2003, commentators angry over a proposed CBS "Beverly Hillbillies" reality television show repeated the allegation that hillbillies are the very last group Americans can ridicule with impunity. When defenders of the region employ the "language of racial justice" (by protesting against hillbillies' being "oppressed minorities"), Barbara Ellen Smith cautions us, their laments may "unintentionally resonate with neo-conservative and even white supremacist positions on racial victimization."[31]

The Dark Side of Community: Nationalism and Imperialism

Neo–Gilded Age regional fiction served to reassure readers of a soothingly safe ancestral home for the nation imagined as white community, particularly in novels like those by Adriana Trigiani and Jan Karon, which might best be described as community fantasy novels. Community fantasy novels satiated white longing for safety and belonging without acknowledging the active exclusion of other races required by such a selective white nationalism.[32]

As an astute *Newsweek* reporter warned in 2002, the compulsion for "home" and "community" can serve to endorse exclusionary practices. Zachary Karabell argued that "American culture" was "adrift," but would "soon discover a new Zeitgeist" in the energizing ideal of "community" underwritten by religion. Karabell noted that *At Home in Mitford* author Jan Karon had "sold more than 10 million copies of her novels, which weave a comforting picture of small-town life and religious values," and that Tim LaHaye's "Left Behind" novels provide "a darker take on similar themes" regarding the rewards due to a community of believers. Karon, according to Karabell, is "a writer who reflects contemporary culture more fully than almost any other living novelist" thanks to the "fantasy town" she offers needy readers.[33]

The danger, as Karabell observed, is that these community fantasy fictions not only sustain such romantic visions but that their popularity alerts corporations to the potential for profit in exclusionary constructed utopias. Karabell argues that the suburban development Celebration, Disney's reproduction of an idealized small-town, has "inspired similar communities across the country, many of which are surrounded by electric fences and guarded by private security firms." Karabell finds it disturbing that the number of people living in gated communities is over 10 million and "growing rapidly." Why? Because, he warns, "the yearning for connectedness has its Ozzie-and-Harriet side, but it also has a get-off-my-porch-or-I'll-shoot side." All this "talk of community" with its connotations of warm inclusion "may prove to be cover for something darker." Remember, Karabell cautions, "Those gated communities have walls and fences and armed guards."³⁴

Karabell is more accurate when he evokes fences and private security forces than shotguns, but he is helpful in thinking about the ways that calls for "community" can be covert demands for exclusion, whether what's excluded is local "riffraff" or would-be immigrants living outside the nation's borders. African Americans, Latino migrant workers, immigrants, Muslims, gays, and lesbians—almost completely absent from bestselling fictional portrayals of Appalachia—can be held at bay in the world of the novel if not in readers' daily lives. In an era of rising racially motivated anti-immigrant hysteria, and with a newfound enemy in the chimera of the Arab, representations of Appalachia may offer readers an imaginative space of whiteness and safety from global processes and conflicts.

When Appalachian distinctiveness was promoted because it supposedly represented the authentic rural roots of the nation, its promotion had a cost. Whatever delight readers took in best-selling novels' nonthreatening display of difference and authenticity, they simultaneously found reinforced their notion that virtue (family, home, faith, and true Americanness) resides primarily with simple, (mostly) white country folk. Class adds an important dimension here, with upper-middle-class white Americans turning to presumptively "salt-of-the-earth" humble Appalachians for colorful, lively, and foundational identity. Imagining a purportedly white, rural place as the "true" embodiment of America can fit too neatly with racist assumptions that the country fundamentally belongs to whites and that others are interlopers or visitors. As a consequence, such a romanticization can feed attitudes of xenophobia and nativism.

Celebrations of Appalachia, coded as an innocent ethnically white community, can in turn inform Americans' perceptions of U.S. imperialism. Readers' designation of white mountain folklife as the root of real America constructs Appalachia as home in contrast not only to heterogeneous domestic cities but also to sinister or invasive foreign places that seem to threaten home figured as the (innocent white) nation. Protecting "community" becomes a code for protectionism and a rationale for saber rattling in international affairs. Readers of fiction set in Appalachia sympathized with characters from a misunderstood region and themselves desired, like Cold Mountain residents, merely the "right to exist unmolested somewhere."³⁵ When acts are committed by an America that is imagined as populated, at root, by the simple white yeomen (racially innocent and multicultural but nonracial) of Appalachia, they may escape critique.³⁶ Such figurations suggest a disquieting willingness to romanticize and identify with a "victimized" Appalachia that shores up an aggressive American nationalism.

On the other hand, those quaint rural people, so the story goes, sometimes need a helping hand. Popular regional fiction's ethos toward group difference appears benign because, on its face, such fiction promotes tolerance for cultural pluralism by representing departures from "mainstream" metropolitan standards as virtues rather than embarrassments. While such appreciation is surely genuine, it may cultivate a sense of superiority and paternalism. Understandings of Appalachians as quaint, headstrong, but sometimes misdirected folk may invite fans to see themselves as benevolent aficionados and overseers of difference, not only domestically but also internationally. When paired with a romance of whiteness and American nationalism, this vision of responsibility for understanding and managing group difference can dovetail with U.S. imperialism. When Appalachian-set fiction approves the goodness of America as, at heart, simple white Appalachians just doing the best they can to get by, and flatters readers as knowledgeable people with only the best intentions for simple charming people everywhere (for they are, after all, themselves descendants of and at base simple folk), such fiction may rationalize self-serving interventions with claims to care for endearingly unsophisticated others.³⁷

The renewal of interest in local-color fiction during the Neo–Gilded Age was indicative of readers' impulses to "portray rural communities as simple and complete, structured by face-to-face (rather than market) transactions."³⁸ Yet ironically, readers' attempts to escape to rural worlds purportedly free of the materialism and stresses of consumer society necessarily entailed their participation in the commodification and consumption of those rural worlds via the publishing industry. In Marilyn Halter's phrasing, they were "shopping for identity" through the consumption of ethnicity.³⁹ According to Reichert Powell, "group affiliation" involves "a conscious, willful use of cultural commodities"—which, I would add, include books.⁴⁰

We would like to believe that our personal treasures—literature, folkways, Appalachia—are above commodification. Perhaps, though, we should be among the first to recognize when they are not. When best-selling fiction participated in the production of place, it did more than participate in the construction or invention of Appalachia as a certain kind of place. It also produced Appalachia as a commodity in the marketplace for literature—and, partly as a consequence, ultimately for tourism as well. Readers' search for a less commercialized way of life paradoxically enabled publishers to package Appalachia as a product liable to meet their desires. "Appalachia," when pitched in the right way to the right audiences, is a profitable commodity produced, marketed, sold, bought, and circulated like the best-selling novels that feature it.

The ideological ramifications of best-selling regional fiction have the potential to be either reactionary or progressive, or both. In Stephanie Foote's 2003 formulation, "Interest in regions and regional identity is on the rise. As in the nineteenth century, regions might be figured as the sites of nostalgia, as the sources of an imaginary wholeness and simplicity." On the other hand, she adds more optimistically, regions can be "imagined as a complex source of positive, rather than strictly nostalgic and conservative, resistance against the perceived anonymity of capitalism."[41] While we labor to make a dearly cherished Appalachia our resource for resistance, we are at our best when we simultaneously attend to the ways in which it might serve purposes antithetical to our own.

Appendix

Methodological Essay

"Reception geographies" methodologies might be considered analyses of what Raymond Williams called "writing in society," an apt label for a study that goes beyond examining the role of hypothetical or implied readers to study the interpretive tactics of actual readers.[1] Earlier reader-response theory included discussions of "postulated" or "ideal" readers of a text, a method that approaches formalist interpretation because it suggests that meaning is determined by the text and best interpreted by trained readers.[2] Reception geographies, on the other hand, recognize that texts mean different things for readers in different times and different social and geographic positions.

Reception geographies also part ways with reception theory, a body of scholarship spearheaded by Wolfgang Iser and Hans Robert Jauss in the late 1960s and 1970s. Jauss and Iser's distinctions between fiction that meets readers' expectations and fiction that forces readers' reevaluation of the world can too conveniently divide texts into those worthy or unworthy of scholarly consideration.[3] *Dear Appalachia* takes as its focus the relationship between each individual reader and each individual text, the consequences of that relationship for each reader, and the potential consequences of that relationship for regional residents and the politics of culture—regardless of the text's ability to challenge readerly expectations.

Though my approach adds a geographical lens, it most closely resembles that of new reception study scholars, particularly literary scholars interested in historical consequences. Barbara Ryan, Amy Blair, Paul Gutjahr, and Timothy Aubry employ qualitative analysis of fan mail (Ryan, Blair) or customer reviews (Gutjahr, Aubry) in order to examine the cultural work performed by particular fictional works for popular audiences.[4]

Below, I first explain the rationale for my selection of each work of fiction and the criteria I employed for assessing its popularity. In the second section, I describe the primary resources upon which I drew for my analysis of the reception of each popular Appalachian-set work. For additional discussion of my methodological choices, please see "On Methodologies and Anachronisms" in the introduction.

Evaluating Popularity and Selecting Texts

Chapter 1: 1878–1900

I begin my study during this most significant historical period, arguably, for the construction of the imagined geography of Appalachia, yet neither best-seller lists nor the concept "best seller" existed during the local-color literary movement. Mary Noailles Murfree was one of many popular authors of mountain fiction during this period. That *In the Tennessee Mountains* sold nine thousand copies in the first year alone was remarkable given editors' hesitance to publish story collections because of the low profits generally involved. By way of comparison, Sarah Orne Jewett's renowned *Deephaven* (1877) took nineteen years to go through twenty-three editions, while in just eight years *In the Tennessee Mountains* went through twenty-two (seventeen printed within the first two years).[5] Murfree is an especially helpful case study because of the volume of contemporary commentary regarding her identity due to her "revelation" that she was a woman after gaining celebrity under the pen name Charles Egbert Craddock.

Chapter 2: 1900–1919

The turn of the twentieth century witnessed the beginning of what Henry Holt referred to as "the mad quest of the golden seller."[6] The *Bookman*, founded in 1895, was the first periodical to regularly print monthly lists of the six best-selling books in sixteen to thirty metropolitan cities. Beginning in 1897, the *Bookman* compiled the city reports into one national list, "Best Selling Books." By 1902 the term *best seller* had gained widespread currency in the United States.[7] It is because John Fox Jr. published two best sellers within this first decade of "the mad quest" that, according to Alice Payne Hackett, his novels became "synonymous" with the newly coined phrase "best seller." Thanks largely to the popularity of Fox's 1903 *The Little Shepherd of Kingdom Come*, his 1908 *The Trail of the Lonesome Pine* garnered over sixty thousand advance orders and sold out its first edition in just a few months. *Lonesome Pine* was the third-best seller in 1908 and fifth-best seller in 1909. By 1967, it had sold over a million hardbound copies, making it the eleventh-best seller of all fictional books initially published between 1900 and 1909.[8] Not until the publication of *Christy* (1967) and *Deliverance* (1970) would the popularity and influence of *Lonesome Pine* be approached in Appalachian-set fiction.

Chapters 3 and 4: 1919–1990

Publishers Weekly and the *New York Times* publish "two of the most popular, widely disseminated, readily available and authoritative lists" of the twentieth century.[9] Keith Justice, author of *Bestseller Index: All Books, Publishers Weekly and the New York Times through 1990* (1998), dates the advent of modern-day best-seller lists to 1919, when *Publishers Weekly* introduced its monthly effort to tally national sales. The first *Publishers Weekly* list of ten "Best Selling Fiction" titles was based on sales reports from sixty-two booksellers (about one-third of which were from "the Eastern states" and about one-fifth from "the Southern states"). The precise number of booksellers and cities represented differed from month to month.[10] Justice's *Bestseller Index* covers the *New York Times Book Review*'s best-seller list from 1935, when it was first published as a monthly feature based upon sales figures from the distributor Baker & Taylor, to 1990. (Laura J. Miller, on the other hand, dates the *Times*' national list [versus individual city lists] to August 1942. The *Times* dropped its lists for most of 1940–1942; the revived list included reports from fourteen cities during the 1940s.)[11] Differences between the *New York Times* and *Publishers Weekly* lists are common, in part due to the fact that the former provides respondents a preconstructed list of titles while the latter does not. Furthermore, trade paperbacks may have trouble competing with mass-market paperbacks for placement on the *Times* list, which does not separate the two as does *Publishers Weekly*.[12]

The best-seller lists are the most useful documentation I have found for determining which books were popular with readers at the time of their release, although the vagaries of the lists are well known. Best-seller lists gauge which books sell relatively large numbers of copies through particular outlets over relatively short periods of time. They attempt to measure "fast sellers" in a given week or month, versus "steady sellers" over time. The number of copies a given title sold would give a better indication of longer-lasting popularity. (For example, Lee Smith's *Fair and Tender Ladies* or James Still's *River of Earth*, neither of which appeared on a best-seller list, may have sold more copies over time than Harriette Arnow's *Hunter's Horn*, which appeared on the *New York Times* best-seller list for five weeks.) But it is notoriously difficult to ascertain sales numbers. Although publishers track their own publications' sales figures, no accessible public record for copies printed or total copies sold existed until Nielsen Bookscan, available by monthly subscription, began its attempt to track point-of-sale statistics in January 2001.[13] An advantage of best-seller lists is that they indicate a given title's popularity relative to others published in the same year; the number of copies sold of a book in 1909 might mean something very different from the number of copies sold of a book released in 1999.

As sociologist Laura Miller notes, "The *New York Times* best-seller list is widely considered to be the preeminent gauge of what Americans are reading. Yet its methodology is highly problematic, and many people in the book industry assume that there are irregularities on the part of sources who report to the *Times*."[14] Furthermore, the number of books appearing on the lists varied, meaning that a book whose sales qualified it for the list in a given month in one year might not have made it to the list in a different month or year. *Publishers Weekly* included ten books when it published a monthly list, but once weekly lists began in 1942 anywhere from five to nine fiction best sellers appeared. The *New York Times* varied between listing ten and twenty-seven fiction best sellers.[15] According to the *Bestseller Index*, the *New York Times* added a paperback list in 1965, while the *Publishers Weekly*'s paperback list did not begin until 1976.[16] From 1967 to 1974, the *New York Times* only published the top five paperback titles, perhaps leading to an undercounting of the popularity of *Deliverance* and especially *Christy*, both released in mass-market paperbacks, compared to paperbacks released just a few years later, which may have appeared on the lists for many more months.[17] The *Times* altered its method of data collection in 1977 from phone calls to 250 stores to computerized tallying of questionnaires sent to 675 representatives of 1,400 stores, and by the 1990s the newspaper claimed to poll a mix of 4,000 chain and independent stores plus wholesalers—the inclusion of the latter creating potential issues such as double counting.[18] For fuller accounts of methodologies, idiosyncrasies, and manipulations of the lists, see overviews by Keith Justice and especially Laura Miller.[19]

In order to compile a list of potential Appalachian-set best sellers, I consulted scholarship about Appalachian literature as well as individual Appalachian literary scholars and booksellers. I consulted Cratis Williams's famous work, "The Southern Mountaineer in Fact and Fiction,"

Lorise Boger's bibliography *The Southern Mountaineer in Literature*, and the Berea College library's index "Mountain Fiction from Abernethy to Zugsmith."[20] I then tested my list of likely best sellers against Keith Justice's index as well as against *80 Years of Bestsellers: 1895–1975*, compiled by *Publishers Weekly* staffer Alice Payne Hackett and James Henry Burke.

The authors whose fan mail I chose to examine in chapters 3 and 4 published Appalachian-set novels that remained on the best-seller lists for months at a time. Harriette Arnow's *Hunter's Horn* made the *New York Times* best-seller list for 5 weeks, peaking at thirteenth. Her second novel, *The Dollmaker*, appeared for a total of 49 weeks on the *New York Times* and *Publishers Weekly* best-seller lists, reaching its zenith at number four on 27 June 1954.[21] James Dickey's *Deliverance* spent 70 weeks and Catherine Marshall's *Christy* spent 118 weeks on the *New York Times* and *Publishers Weekly* best-seller lists combined.[22]

Among those I was surprised not to find in Justice's index were Charles Neville Buck, author of *Call of the Cumberlands* (1913); Fielding Burke (pen name of Olive Tilford Dargan, author of proletarian fiction in the 1930s); Maristan Chapman; Billy Clark; Grace MacGowan Cooke; Albert Benjamin Cunningham, author of twenty-one novels and mysteries from 1918 to 1951; John Ehle; Lucy Furman; Janice Holt Giles; Alberta Pierson Hannum, author of *Roseanna McCoy* (1945); Harry Harrison Kroll; Alice MacGowan; Cormac McCarthy; Eliza C. Obenchain, author of *Aunt Jane of Kentucky* (1907); Elizabeth Madox Roberts; and Robert Weverka, author of *The Waltons* (1974).

A number of best-selling authors wrote mountain-themed novels that did not themselves make the best-seller lists, including Ben Lucien Burman; Betsy Byars, author of *Summer of the Swans* (1970); Christine Noble Govan; Joseph Hergesheimer, whose short story "Tol'able David" was made into a 1921 silent film infamous in Appalachian studies; Helen Topping Miller; Elizabeth Seifert, author of *Hillbilly Doctor* (1973); Thomas Stribling; and Robert Penn Warren. Thomas Wolfe had four best sellers, though his landmark *Look Homeward, Angel* (1929) was not among them.[23] Elizabeth Madox Roberts's historical novel *The Great Meadow* (1930), set in frontier Kentucky prior to the Revolutionary War, was on the *Publishers Weekly* list for eight weeks; *The Time of Man* (1926), set on a farm in central Kentucky, was a Book-of-the-Month Club selection but not a best seller.

Three authors who appear in Justice's index for the years 1919–1990 might have appeared in this book but do not. Davis Grubb's *A Dream of Kings* (1955), a Civil War love story set in what would become West Virginia, made the *New York Times* list for just one week. Jesse Stuart's *Taps for Private Tussie* (1943), a comedic interpretation of hardscrabble poverty set in Kentucky, was on the *New York Times* best-seller list for three weeks.[24] Gail Godwin's *A Mother and Two Daughters* (1982) and *A Southern Family* (1987), both set in her hometown of Asheville, North Carolina, were best sellers for fifty-two weeks and thirty-one weeks, respectively. Godwin is rarely considered an Appalachian author, yet her many popular books set in the region likely influenced the national geographic imagination.[25] Furthermore, future study of her fan mail may show that understanding Godwin's success is central to understanding a shift in this period from mass-market audiences to trade paperback and book club audiences for Appalachian characters and settings. Godwin herself benefited from this shift in the 1990s, when her Smoky Mountains–set novel *Evensong* (a sequel to *Father's Melancholy Daughter* [1991], set near Charlottesville, Virginia) was released as a Ballantine Reader's Circle edition.

Chapter 5: 1990–2003

No best-seller index comparable to Keith Justice's compilation for the years 1919–1990 yet exists for the post-1990 period, so in order to determine best-seller status for this period I consulted lists by *Publishers Weekly* and the *New York Times* via the Lexis Nexis Academic database. (See chapters 3 and 4, above, for discussion of the complexities of these two lists.) Additionally, I consulted *USA Today*, which began its list (believed to be heavily skewed toward chain bookstores) in 1993.[26]

For the period after 1990, I was particularly interested in novels written by little-known debut authors that nonetheless reached best-seller lists.[27] Nonetheless, space and time permitting, I might have included a number of additional best sellers for this period. Veterans of the best-seller lists include Barbara Kingsolver, whose *Prodigal Summer* (2000) spent forty-three weeks on the *USA Today* "Top 150 Best-Selling Books" list, with a peak position of nine, and David Baldacci, whose *Wish You Well* (2000) spent twenty-three weeks on the *USA Today* list, with a peak position of eleven. Homer Hickam's *Rocket Boys* (1998), later titled *October Sky* after its movie adaptation, spent twelve weeks on the *USA Today* list, with a zenith of thirty-seven. Four of Sharyn McCrumb's seven ballad novels (1990–2003) spent four to nine weeks on the *USA Today* list, with

The Rosewood Casket (1996) reaching the highest position (thirty-third) of the seven. *Gap Creek* (1999) by Robert Morgan and *Icy Sparks* (1998) by Gwyn Hyman Rubio were both Oprah Book Club selections; Morgan's novel spent thirty-one weeks on the *USA Today* list with a peak position of eight, while Rubio's spent twenty weeks with a height of four. Selection by Oprah's Book Club guaranteed these books best-seller status regardless of setting or appeal. (Every one of the forty-five books for adults selected by Winfrey during the years of her book club in its initial incarnation from September 1996 to April 2002 became a *USA Today* best-seller for at least eight months.)[28] Rubio fit the profile of a debut novelist who made the best-seller lists, but I was interested in constructions of Appalachia that were widely embraced by readers. As a high proportion of negative online customer reviews of Morgan's and Rubio's works demonstrates, best-seller status did not necessarily translate into favorable popular opinion.

Although it was not a criterion for their inclusion, all the texts examined in *Dear Appalachia* were in print in 2010, attesting to their continued circulation and lasting influence.

Evidence of Reception

Fan Mail

Modern use of the term *fan* dates to the late 1800s, when journalists used it to refer to baseball enthusiasts, and became widespread in the United States by the 1930s. It may derive from the term *the fancy*, used in the 1800s to describe a group of people who were "fanciers" of a given hobby. The term *fan mail* was first used in a 1924 *Motion Picture* magazine article, "The Business of Fan Mail."[29] Despite the fact that neither label, "fan" or "fan mail," was common until the 1930s, I use both terms throughout the book for ease of distinguishing between correspondents who wrote in response to a given text and those who had other reasons to write. When a citation designates a correspondent as a "fan," it indicates that the reader was a perfect stranger to the author prior to writing. (In the rare cases when correspondents questioned or criticized the author, I nonetheless label them "fans" to signal that they were strangers writing in response to a given text.) When letter writers had some prior connection to the author, I designate them as "fan-acquaintances" to indicate that they had met previously or had a professional relationship with the author (as reviewers, event organizers, and so on). In a few instances, I quote from admiring letters that I would not consider fan mail because the correspondent was well known to the author or had regular business dealings with him or her. I label such correspondents as "friend" or "colleague."

For the books examined in chapters 1 through 4, the authors' correspondence has been preserved in public archives. Fan mail provides rich evidence regarding contemporary assumptions about the nature of Appalachia, readers' investments in the authenticity of the author, and the readerly needs provoked and met by the literary marketplace. Especially when contrasted with professional print reviews, fan mail illuminates the ways in which readers' geographical histories and class affiliations shaped their readerly desires and literary interpretations. Of course, fan mail does not provide transparent evidence of the novel's appeal. As Amy Blair notes, because readers were often "conscious of the genre of fan mail," and their "letters are careful to situate themselves as somehow different from a perceived typical fan letter," we must acknowledge that "even the most self-revelatory fan letter was, at least partially, a performance of reader reception."[30]

In quoting fan mail sent to best-selling authors, I chose not to use pseudonyms for two reasons. First, the names and locations of the letter writers are often evocative of who they were and the contexts out of which they wrote. For example, knowing that a letter was written by Mrs. Hans Zinsser of New York—not Mrs. Delbert Moore, an out-migrant from rural Kentucky or Mrs. Johnnie Sue True from Texas—shapes the way I read the letter. I could resort to colorful naming practices and invent traditional surnames as replacements for Mrs. Hattie Abner and Ozro F. Grant, but my own inventions would pale by comparison.

Second, my investigation of these readers as historical figures is incomplete. Readers and audiences of my work to date have sometimes recognized fans' names and taught me more about Ellen Lane of South Carolina or other correspondents, information that gave insight into the reasons that that person might have found the best-selling novel appealing. If I had replaced real names with pseudonyms, I would not have discovered important details about readers' lives. For example, I did not recognize that fans John Wilson Townsend, William E. Connelley, Everett Webber, and Janisse (née Janeice) Ray were themselves published authors until late in the revision process, yet discovering who they were and what they published provided additional means to interpret their reactions. It matters that Arnow fan Gertrude Snodgrass may have been one of the cofounders of the Greater Chicago Food Depository in 1978, and that another Arnow fan, Irving Weissman, was a construction worker and former Communist. I anticipate learning even more as my suppositions reach, and are tested by, a larger audience. Indeed, I expect I may even hear from a few folks unhappy with me for sharing their youthful enthusiasms of forty or more years ago. I hope that the payoff will be worth it in the consequently clearer ideas about who was reading these novels, and why.

Customer Reviews

Perhaps the most unorthodox evidentiary sources I employ, customer reviews posted to the Internet, are also in some ways the most useful for reception geographies. Fan letters often provide long, detailed, rich accounts of readers' relationship to the texts from enthusiastic admirers moved so deeply and positively that they felt compelled to take the time to write and mail a letter. But thanks to reviews posted to booksellers' Web sites, for recent best sellers I can access far greater numbers of reader reactions that detail a broader range of enthusiasm and disappointment.

Customer reviews are different from fan mail in other respects as well. The stakes involved in the very public nature of publishing an online review, while not necessarily higher than those involved in writing to an admired literary figure, are nonetheless different. As opposed to more intimate epistles meant for an author's eyes only, Internet testimonials more often utilize a professional tone that mimics professional reviewers. Their publication implies different purposes than those motivating private letters, including at times a desire to establish a public reputation for oneself as a knowledgeable reader, or a desire to affect the purchases, reading selections, and opinions of other readers. Finally, compared to letters (or to recent case studies of reading groups based in one city or county, for that matter), Internet customer reviews provide information about geographic differentiation in the reception of novels—not only in reviewers' frequent references to the city and state from which they are writing (common on Amazon.com) but also in the conventionalized testimonies that they offer about the role of the novel in the trajectory of their own lives.

The legitimacy of customer reviews came under scrutiny after revelations that authors and their allies frequently post glowing reviews of their books—or blistering reviews of competitors' books—without revealing their identities.[31] In response, Amazon instituted a "Real Name™"

option for users that allows reviewers to claim credibility by backing their online name with a credit card or other identifying documentation. As fascinating as the review wars are, however, they have little bearing upon the validity of my research. Even bald-faced and "planted" promotions can be usefully studied for the rhetoric with which they praise a novel and describe its appeal. In other words, if authors commend their own work or a friend's on the grounds that the work allows them to vicariously experience the neighborliness of an Appalachian town, then their sense that this is what other readers desire is itself significant. Nonetheless, when possible I have attempted to identify published authors and note them as such, and have preferred to highlight examples from nonpublished authors. I have also noted in my citations when reviews were accompanied by the "Real Name" label. Yet in deference to legal concerns resulting from Amazon's aggressive claim to be copyright holder for reviews, I identify reviewers by first name and last initial only and/or, when available, by their screen name.

To all appearances, customer reviews provide a fairly representative sample of readers of Appalachian-set fiction, who, like all American fiction readers, tend to be female and upper middle class. The demographic of Internet users roughly parallels the demographic of middle-class and upper-middle-class readers at whom recent trade best sellers are aimed, so Web-based customer reviewers should be fairly representative of the novels' national audience in terms of class. On the other hand, white readers appear to comprise a higher proportion of online Appalachian fiction fans than of Internet users overall. In 2003, 65 percent of white Americans, 56 percent of black Americans, and 53 percent of Hispanic Americans were Internet users.[32] As far as I am able to determine from readers' own testimonies, which frequently incorporate discussion of identity politics, Appalachian fiction fans likely are more than 90 percent white.

Chapter 1: **In the Tennessee Mountains**

Mary Noailles Murfree, with the help of her sister Fanny, preserved a large body of correspondence from editors and fans. The collection is archived at the Manuscript, Archives, and Rare Book Library at Emory University. According to the finding aid, the collection includes 269 letters, most of which represent correspondence between Murfree and her publishers between 1877 and 1928. I read or skimmed all of the letters (folders 3–15) in order to identify twenty-one pieces of mail written by admirers who had no prior connection to Murfree. That these extant letters do not represent all the mail Murfree received is suggested by a fan's comment in 1922 that he first wrote Murfree in 1885; there is no record of the earlier letter.[33] I also examined correspondence between Theodore Roosevelt and Murfree housed at the Library of Congress.

I contrasted the image of Craddock/Murfree from the fan mail with print copy regarding the author, beginning with the *Boston Herald*'s account of her appearance in Boston. Reese M. Carleton's annotated bibliography provided an astonishingly detailed and thorough source that includes citations for collections of additional letters (largely *from* rather than *to* Murfree) and hundreds of reviews. I located additional reviews thanks to master's theses by Eva Malone Byrd and Eleanor B. Spence.[34] In total, I tracked down fifty reviews about *In the Tennessee Mountains* and Craddock's other mountain-set fiction, including *The Prophet of the Great Smoky Mountains*.

Chapter 2: The Trail of the Lonesome Pine

The largest collection of archival materials regarding John Fox Jr. is housed at the University of Kentucky's Special Collections and Digital Programs in Lexington. The Fox Family Papers include, among many other items, three boxes of correspondence. Eight scrapbooks, including one each devoted to Fox's best sellers *The Little Shepherd of Kingdom Come* (1903) and *The Trail of the Lonesome Pine* (1908), contain promotional materials, reviews, and letters. My analysis of Fox's attitudes about the southern mountains was partly informed by correspondence between Fox and famous politicians, authors, and artists. These included letters from Howard Taft and Theodore Roosevelt regarding *Lonesome Pine* and letters regarding *Little Shepherd* and other works from Charles Scribner, *Louisville Courier-Journal* editor Henry Watterson, Richard Harding Davis, Francis Hopkinson Smith, Robert Burns Wilson, the Roosevelt family, Owen Wister, Thomas Dixon, and James Lane Allen, among others.

My primary arguments center upon eleven fan letters from readers of *Little Shepherd*, fifteen from readers of *Lonesome Pine* (1908), and two regarding Fox's essay "On Horseback to Kingdom Come" (1910), which returns to the eastern Kentucky setting of *Little Shepherd*. These are archived in the scrapbooks and in box 3, Letters, 1899–1903; and box 4, Letters, 1904–1910, and Letters, 1911–1920. An earlier letter from J. F.

Bullitt in 1901 seems to have provided Fox material for *Lonesome Pine*. If Fox received multiple letters from the same fan or if a fan mentioned multiple books in one letter, I did not double count. The themes that emerged from these letters (migration, attachments to Kentucky or the region, the romantic imagination of unseen mountain places, and fans' requests for help with writing or publishing their own stories) enabled me to identify groups of readers.

The letters turned up no locally identified readers, whose presence I deduced from published anecdotes and from one scholarly article about locals' rebuttal to a Fox-influenced sociologist via their local newspaper.[35] Though some letter writers expressed nationally oriented sentiments, I primarily identified nationally oriented readers via seventy-eight reviews and fourteen articles published in 1908. I found the majority of these publications through archival research in the Fox Family Papers, particularly the scrapbooks. (These clippings sometimes omit the date or the name of the periodical and generally omit page numbers.) I located additional reviews and articles through secondary research thanks to *Book Review Digest*, the bibliography in Bill York's biography of Fox, and database searches of electronically available periodicals. I also found articles and booklets illustrative of Fox's enduring legacy in Kentucky at the John Fox Jr. Memorial Library, housed in Duncan's Tavern in Paris, Kentucky, and thanks to the gracious generosity of Fox's distant cousin Bettie J. Tuttle.

Chapter 3: Hunter's Horn *and* The Dollmaker

The Harriette Simpson Arnow Papers are housed with Special Collections and Digital Programs at the University of Kentucky Libraries in Lexington. In addition to correspondence between Arnow and her editors, the Correspondence Series includes thirty-eight fan letters written in response to *Hunter's Horn* and ninety letters that arrived after the release of *The Dollmaker*. In the *Hunter's Horn* number I include ten fan-acquaintances, whom I defined as readers with a business or personal connection to Arnow prior to writing (for example, reviewers; former teachers and professors; and friends of her sister Elizabeth, including one whose admiring letter was addressed to Elizabeth). Of the letters dated 1954 and after, thirty mention both *The Dollmaker* and *Hunter's Horn* (including one correspondent responding in 1954 to *The Dollmaker* and "all" of Arnow's books and one responding to her best sellers plus *Seedtime on the Cumberland* and *Flowering of the Cumberland*). Of the second set of letters, six were from fan-acquaintances. When fans wrote more than once I did not double count them.

It is unclear what percentage of Arnow's total fan mail these 128 extant letters represent. In a letter that Arnow wrote to her sister she suggests that an avalanche of mail began to arrive in the fall of 1954: "I am still answering letters. They will I suppose slack off one of these days, for Gertie [*The Dollmaker*] is slacking off the lists. Something happened back in October or September and everyone started to write."[36] Another possible indication that Arnow received more letters than she kept is that she once claimed that she received fewer fan letters from Kentucky than any other state.[37] She either misrepresented/misremembered reality or retained a wildly unrepresentative sample for her personal archive, since, as I note in chapter 3, one out of five of Arnow's fans had ties to Kentucky.

In addition to the fans with ties to Kentucky, another twelve letters mentioned current or past residence in Michigan. Only Fox had a higher percentage of fans with ties to his settings, 62.5 percent, with ten of sixteen authors of fan mail about *The Trail of the Lonesome Pine* having ties to Kentucky or mountainous portions of North Carolina, Virginia, or West Virginia. By contrast, just 15 percent of *Deliverance* readers were from Georgia and South Carolina, though if we include other states in which Dickey lived, such as Florida, California, and Wisconsin, the percentage of fans with ties to Dickey's residences rises to 31 percent.

In chapter 3 I observe, "Twenty percent or more of Arnow's admiring correspondents were rural-to-urban migrants." I derived this figure by noting that, of *Hunter's Horn* fans, five were Kentucky out-migrants, one fan moved from rural southern Illinois to Cleveland, and another moved from rural southwest Virginia to Wilmington, for a total of seven southern rural-to-urban out-migrants. Including a rural-to-urban migrant in England, eight of thirty-eight *Hunter's Horn* fan mail writers, or 20.5 percent, were rural-to-urban migrants. Of ninety *Dollmaker* fans, eighteen were themselves migrants—ten of whom felt Arnow's novel captured something they had experienced. In addition to out-migrant fans from Kentucky, three fans described other migration experiences in their letters (Indiana to Iowa, California to Colorado to Arizona, and New Mexico to Texas), for a total of 23 percent.

Chapter 4, Part I: **Christy**

Catherine Marshall's correspondence over the thirty-three years from the publication of her first book until her death, not including her business mail, fills thirty boxes at her alma mater, Agnes Scott College, in Atlanta, Georgia. It is my fortune that Marshall organized her mail according to topic rather than simply chronologically. Although Marshall had seven *New York Times* best sellers, she received more fan mail about *Christy* than any other title. The topic "Correspondence with Readers: *Christy*" fills three boxes (boxes 11–13), more than any of her other works, even though it represents fewer years (1967–1983) than five of her best sellers; only *Julie* (1984) was published later. By contrast, fan mail about the bestselling *A Man Called Peter* (1951) fits in one box; fan mail about *Beyond Ourselves* (1961), which was not a best seller, fills two boxes. Fan mail about her best seller *To Live Again* (1957) fills just one-third of a box.

The folders for the years 1967 and 1968 (box 11, folders 1 and 2) contain in each instance an original letter and Marshall's carbon-copied reply. There are 34 extant *Christy* fan letters and replies for 1967, the year of *Christy*'s release, and 49 letters and replies for 1968. Beginning in 1969, Marshall began to receive so much fan mail that she was unable to save it all. I counted 92 replies for the second half of the year alone, which suggests that she may have received as many as 184 letters; I counted 46 replies for a three-month period of the following year, which suggests that she may have received approximately 184 letters again in 1970. Unfortunately, only 10 percent to 20 percent of the original letters are attached to Marshall's replies from 1969 forward. I was unable to ascertain the criteria Marshall used to select which letters to retain despite the fact that, through 1970, Marshall's replies were so thorough and personal that they give a very good sense of the contents of the original. From extant originals, we can see that Marshall handwrote her response (or, in rare cases, noted "no answer") on each fan's letter, answering the fan's questions and directing her or him to resources. Marshall's secretary then included Marshall's notes in a typed reply and filed a carbon copy. The care Marshall took in responding to fans' comments and concerns in these early years often made it possible for me to deduce the topics covered in the original fan letter. After 1970, however, Marshall's more perfunctory replies contain little data about the unretained fan letters other than the fan's name and address.

Marshall explained her system in a letter to photographer William A. Barnhill: "Because of the tremendous volume of correspondence that crosses my desk, we have had to evolve a system whereby we make up an index card containing data on the writer of any particular letter, his address, and a brief synopsis of the contents—sometimes but one sentence or two—then file only the card. Otherwise we should have an office furnished only with filing cabinets! I shall, however, keep your letter of February 10 in a special file so that we can refer to it in the future. I fear the one of November 24 is long gone."[38]

By the ten-year anniversary of *Christy*'s publication, fan mail seems to have slackened somewhat, based on extant originals and replies. I counted 82 letters from 1977 and 69 from 1978. Marshall received at least 19 *Christy* letters in the second half of 1982 (June–December), just months before her passing. This final *Christy* folder (box 13, folder 5) contains many original letters, which suggests that those who organized Marshall's affairs after her death were not so quick to throw away fan mail as she was—or not as methodic, in any case.

In order to assess Marshall's copious fan mail, I first skimmed well over 500 extant letters and replies received from 1967 through 1973; at the ten-year anniversary of *Christy*'s publication in 1977; and in the nine months prior to Marshall's death in March 1983. When I found epistles regarding *Christy*'s mountain setting or characters, I took notes and/or photocopies for further analysis. In 1967 and 1968, about one-third of the letters mentioned the setting or the mountain characters. In 1969, 17 out of 65 letters (26 percent) in the January–April folder and 16 out of 92 (17 percent) in the May–December folder mentioned Appalachia. All told, the letters on which my arguments are based total 445: 3 in general correspondence; in *Christy* correspondence: 37 filed in 1967, 49 in 1968, 90 in 1969, 84 in 1970, 25 in 1971, 32 in 1972, 47 in 1973, 38 in 1977, 19 in 1982, and 1 in 1983; and 20 found in other folders (see below).

In addition to Marshall's *Christy* correspondence files, I examined her General Correspondence from Readers, where Marshall filed letters that referred to multiple books. In these twenty-six folders, a mere handful refer to *Christy* (see box 4, folder 3, Correspondence with Readers, 1962–1969). Marshall also kept nine boxes of files labeled Correspondence with Readers: Topical Files, which largely covered spiritual issues such as "Death," "Bereavement," and "Deliverance." My analysis includes the subject file "Appalachia," which contains just three replies to fan letters and a brochure about a children's home in Tennessee. Box 28, Correspondence with Readers: Would-be Writers, 1975–1983, includes nine folders containing letters that reference Marshall's nonfiction almost exclusively. Just eight letters from this box (all from folder 2, 1977) are included in my analysis. That I was able to get a sampling from this box is due to the generosity of Marianne Bradley, librarian at Agnes Scott College, who marked letters in this box for my attention.

Other archival sources include boxes 69–71, Christy Manuscripts: Research. I examined just one of them (box 70, Railroad–Women), which included a large number of tourist brochures about the "Southern Appalachian Mountains," the "Great Smoky Mountains," and "The Land of Sky" from Southern Railways, chambers of commerce, and tourist boards; a note from Marshall reminding herself about the "good chapter" on "Elizabethan Virtues" from *Land of Saddle Bags*; tracts on Scots-Irish ancestry in the mountains; comments from her informant Mary Ruble regarding the Craftsman's Fair in Gatlinburg; and a 1950s *Knoxville News-Sentinel* series on out-migration from Tennessee. My assessment of Marshall's imagined geography of Appalachia was informed by these materials, as well as by the books included in box 71, including John Campbell's *The Southern Highlander and His Homeland* (1921), Charles Dudley's *On Horseback: A Tour in Virginia, North Carolina, and Tennessee* (1888), and John Fox Jr.'s *A Knight of the Cumberland: Hell-fer-Sartain* (1906).

Chapter 4, Part II: Deliverance

The James Dickey Papers (ca. 1924–1997, bulk 1961–1997) are housed in the Manuscript, Archives, and Rare Book Library at Emory University in Atlanta, Georgia. Dickey's General Correspondence (Subseries 1.2) is filed separately from Family Correspondence. General Correspondence from the time between February 1970, when an excerpt of *Deliverance* was first published in the *Atlantic Monthly*, and Dickey's death in 1996 fills fifty-two boxes. The novel was released in March 1970.

From these boxes, I sought out letters that discussed Dickey's best-selling novel. I analyzed every extant *Deliverance* letter from February 1970 through 1971, totaling 156. I then examined letters that Dickey received in October 1972, shortly after the film version's release. *Deliverance* premiered in Los Angeles, New York, and Atlanta at the end of July and beginning of August 1972 and opened in South Carolina as late as December. I chose to examine October correspondence because it had by far the greatest volume of mail of all of 1972. (The disproportionate thickness of the October folder may be in part due to the fact that Dickey filed correspondence in the month he replied to letters, rather than the month he received them.) In order to get a sense of what proportion of fan mail over time continued to discuss *Deliverance*, I also examined all extant letters Dickey received in 1973, in April through October of 1980 (the ten-year anniversary of the novel's release), and in 1996 (the year of Dickey's death). In these later years, Dickey received increasing numbers of letters from fans who simply asked for an autograph or from students and would-be writers who hoped that Dickey would help with school papers or provide feedback on their writing. I also examined all undated correspondence (boxes 88–90) for *Deliverance* letters.

Most of Dickey's extant General Correspondence comprises letters from acquaintances: friends, business or literary associates, and regular correspondents who wrote for some reason other than *Deliverance*, though some of these mentioned *Deliverance* in the course of their epistolary exchanges. I labeled as "fan-acquaintance" correspondents who wrote because of *Deliverance* but who had some connection to Dickey prior to writing. Fan-acquaintances included, for example, correspondents who had met Dickey at an event, friends of friends, and people whom Dickey had sent a copy of the novel and who then wrote to thank him. I labeled as "fans" those correspondents with no prior connection to Dickey who wrote unsolicited fan letters motivated by *Deliverance* or by publicity surrounding it. I placed correspondents into one of the three categories largely based on context clues (for example, their form of address to Dickey as "Dear Jim" versus "Dear Mr. Dickey) but in some cases cross-checked names with the indexed list of Dickey's regular correspondents available at the archive. My arguments are based largely on eighty-five pieces of unsolicited fan mail from unknown admirers. (Forty of these are dated 1970, seventeen dated 1971, seven dated 1972, fifteen dated 1973, four dated 1980, and two dated 1996). I supplemented these arguments with data from *Deliverance* letters written by forty-two fan-acquaintances and seventy-nine acquaintances. The original envelopes plus typed copies of Dickey's replies usually accompanied the letters. These were often helpful in determining the name, address, and sometimes the occupations of his correspondents. I also drew upon Dickey's replies, where pertinent, to help me understand and characterize his construction of Appalachia.

In addition to correspondence, I examined materials from Series 6: Subject Files (box 232, Appalachia Books, *Appalachian Journal*, and Appalachian State University Commencement, 14 May 1994; and boxes 240–41, *Deliverance*); Series 8: Printed Material, including Subseries 8.1:

Promotional Material (boxes 286, OP 19, and OBV1); and Series 9: Clippings, Subseries 9.2: News Stories and Profiles (box 352), Subseries 9.3: Reviews (box 359), Subseries 9.4: Promotional Material (box 362), and Subseries 9.5: Other Miscellaneous Clippings (OP162, Miscellaneous Oversize Clippings). Of these, by far the most useful was Subseries 8.1, OBV1, a scrapbook containing a plethora of *Deliverance* review clippings. I augmented my archival research with additional reviews that I located using Web-based databases.

Chapter 5: **At Home in Mitford, Cold Mountain, Big Stone Gap, and Clay's Quilt**

When the total number of customer reviews for one of these four texts was relatively small, I examined all available customer reviews on Amazon.com and BarnesandNoble.com from the novel's publication through June 2010. This was possible for *Clay's Quilt* and *Big Stone Gap*. When the reviews numbered in the hundreds or the thousands, however, I began by examining all reviews on both bookseller sites posted during the first full year after the novel's publication. This was 10 July 1997–10 July 1998 for *Cold Mountain* and 16 June 1996–16 June 1997 for *At Home in Mitford* (though *Mitford* was initially published in 1994, there are no customer reviews available prior to 1996, by which time multiple editions were available, including from Penguin). To gain a sense of later reception patterns, I then read all reviews posted during the year 2003 (the congressionally designated "Year of Appalachia") on both sites. For all four novels, I identified patterns in readers' responses from these base sets. Once I established overarching themes, I sometimes drew from other years for the best examples of those themes for *Cold Mountain* and *At Home in Mitford*.

There are discrepancies between the versions of customer reviews available online at any given time. For example, between 2004 and 2010, some reviews disappeared and in some cases some information about the reviewer was removed. It is not uncommon for the dates of the reviews to have changed slightly. On Amazon, the dates are sometimes one day off (for example, the date in 2010 read 16 January 1997, but in 2004 it read 15 January 1997). On Barnes and Noble's Web site, I have found instances where the date shifted by four days. (A review titled *"Clay's Quilt"* was in 2004 dated 16 August 2002, but in 2010 dated 12 August 2002.) Because of the discrepancies and the possibility of ongoing revisions, I have relied on my earlier printouts from Amazon.com and BarnesandNoble.com (dated February 2004, in possession of the author) when constructing my citations. In 2004, Amazon listed anonymous posts as made by "A reader"; Barnes and Noble customers wishing for anonymity generally chose to identify themselves as "A reader" or "A reviewer." I have retained the label "A reader" for anonymous reviewers despite the fact that Amazon has now changed the designation to "A customer" and Barnes and Noble currently uses "Anonymous" in these instances. In some cases the reader has changed identifying information such as name or location at some point since 2004. Where I found discrepancies, I used the 2004 data.

Notes

Introduction

1. Silas House, "Love and Shame," http://silashouseblog.blogspot.com/2010/11/love-and-shame.html, 3 November 2010 (accessed 7 November 2010).

2. For horror movies, see *The Blair Witch Project* (1999), the *Wrong Turn* franchise (2003, 2007, 2009), *The Descent* (2005), *Masters of Horror: Incident on and off a Mountain Road* (2006), and *Timber Falls* (2008). For a discussion of the ways in which both positive and negative images of Appalachia historically center on notions of isolation and community, see David C. Hsiung, *Two Worlds in the Tennessee Mountains: Exploring the Origins of Appalachian Stereotypes* (Lexington: University Press of Kentucky, 1997), 1. On romantic notions of Appalachia, see Wilma Dunaway, who characterizes Americans' ongoing fascination with Appalachia as a "love affair" (*The First American Frontier* [Chapel Hill: University of North Carolina Press, 1996], 1). On the continuation of both romantic and negative images to the present day, see tourism researcher Matt Zuefle, who notes, "There are two archetypes of Appalachia: one is that of poverty and squalor, and the second is the romantic mountaineer living the simple life" (Ellen Gerl, "Destination: Appalachia? Study Examines Perceptions of Appalachia among Tourists," Ohio University press release, http://news.research.ohiou.edu/perspectives/archives/0301/anth_8.htm, sent to Appalnet listserv, appalnet@lsv.uky.edu, 31 March 2006. Copy in possession of the author).

3. I would like to thank Jennifer Meares for her help in formulating this point.

4. For an incisive argument about the "historical, political, and literary contexts for diverting attention to the hillbilly as a defense against criticism of America as an uncivilized nation," see Carol Mason, "The Hillbilly Defense: Culturally Mediating U.S. Terror at Home and Abroad," *NWSA Journal* 17, no. 3 (2005): 39.

5. Michael A. Elliott, *The Culture Concept: Writing and Difference in the Age of Realism* (Minneapolis: University of Minnesota Press, 2002), xxi.

6. Hsiung, *Two Worlds in the Tennessee Mountains*, 1.

7. "The process of reification, by which the perception of Appalachian otherness became transformed into a conception of Appalachia as a thing in itself, occurred within the context of the conventions of local-color writing, and in particular the claims of that genre to verisimilitude." Henry D. Shapiro, *Appalachia on Our Mind: The Southern Mountains and Mountaineers in the American Consciousness, 1870–1920* (Chapel Hill: University of North Carolina Press,

1978), 18–19. See also Shapiro's claim, 119, that William Goodell Frost, writing nonfiction during the same era, "did no less a work than the invention of Appalachia."

8. For "little corners," see ibid., xiii, 11. On the supposed supersession of local cultures "by a modern order," see Richard H. Brodhead, *Cultures of Letters: Scenes of Reading and Writing in Nineteenth-Century America* (Chicago: University of Chicago Press, 1994), 121. For the periodization of the local-color movement and its position vis-à-vis the larger literary movement of realism, see Nancy Glazener, *Reading for Realism: The History of a U.S. Literary Institution, 1850–1910* (Durham: Duke University Press, 1997); Amy Kaplan, *The Social Construction of American Realism* (Chicago: University of Chicago Press, 1992); and Stephanie Foote, *Regional Fictions: Culture and Identity in Nineteenth-Century American Literature* (Madison: University of Wisconsin Press, 2001). Foote, 58, rightly argues that the existence of regionalism is "predicated on the uneven development of capitalism," which allows wealth to accumulate in some places, often thanks to exploitation of the labor and natural resources of other places. This pattern of uneven economic development "produces" the "radically unbalanced cultural landscape" that makes regionalism possible.

9. Allen Batteau, *The Invention of Appalachia* (Tucson: University of Arizona Press, 1990). For the earliest use of the term *Appalachia* to refer to a region (as opposed to a mountain range), see William Goodell Frost, "Appalachian America," *Ladies Home Companion*, September 1896.

10. John Alexander Williams, *Appalachia: A History* (Chapel Hill: University of North Carolina Press, 2002), 13. Williams, 6–8, defines "core Appalachia" as consisting of the 164 counties that are included in all six of the major historical definitions of the region: those constructed by C. Willard Hayes and William G. Frost (1895), John C. Campbell (1921), the U.S. Department of Agriculture (1935), Thomas Ford (1962), the Appalachian Regional Commission (1965), and Karl B. Raitz and Richard Ulack (1984). See John Alexander Williams, "Counting Yesterday's People: Using Aggregate Data to Address the Problem of Appalachia's Boundaries," *Journal of Appalachian Studies* 2, no. 1 (1996): 3–27.

11. See, for example, Kristin Kant's discovery that paintings for sale in a mountain tourist destination during 2005 and 2006 "contain icons that portray Appalachia as a homogenous region of poor, white people frozen in the past." Kristin Mary Agnes Helen Kant, "Painting the Mountains: An Investigation of Tourist Art in North America" (PhD diss., University of Kentucky, 2009).

12. See T. J. Jackson Lears, *No Place of Grace: Antimodernism and the Transformation of American Culture, 1880–1920* (New York: Pantheon, 1981), 102, for "real life" quote.

13. According to Regina Bendix, the "crucial questions to be answered are not 'what is authenticity?' but 'who needs authenticity and why?' and 'how has authenticity been used?'" (*In Search of Authenticity: The Formation of Folklore Studies* [Madison: University of Wisconsin Press, 1997], 21). She argues that "the

continued craving for experiences of unmediated genuineness" is "a reaction to modernization's demythologization, detraditionalization, and disenchantment. . . . . Modernity's pace brought forth an anguish, occasioned by the oppositional desires for progress and nostalgia for what is left behind in the invariable transformations caused by progress" (10, 18). On authenticity, see also Michael Ann Williams, *Staging Tradition: John Lair and Sarah Gertrude Knott* (Urbana: University of Illinois Press, 2006).

14. Jeff Karem, *The Romance of Authenticity: The Cultural Politics of Regional and Ethnic Literatures* (Charlottesville: University of Virginia Press, 2004).

15. Foote, *Regional Fictions*, 3.

16. Richard Hofstadter, quoted in Dunaway, *The First American Frontier*, 2–3.

17. Brodhead, *Cultures of Letters*, 133. See Catherine Jurca, *White Diaspora: The Suburb and the Twentieth-Century American Novel* (Princeton: Princeton University Press, 2001), 6–8, 16.

18. According to Bendix, "Striving for selfhood is intertwined with the attempt to locate or articulate a more authentic existence" (*In Search of Authenticity*, 18).

19. Gunnar Almgren, quoted in Hsiung, *Two Worlds in the Tennessee Mountains*, 7. Hsiung notes that communities need not share the same geographic territory, yet readers exhibit an attachment to community in the sense that Gidean Sjoberg defines it, as "a collectivity of actors sharing in a limited territorial area as the base for carrying out the greatest share of their daily activities" (quoted in Hsiung, 6). Hsiung, 6, citing Ferdinand Tönnies, notes a romanticization with the *Gemeinschaft* (community or close personal ties associated with rural life), which is supposedly an earlier stage of society followed by *Gesellschaft* (which is "the mere co-existence of people independent of each other").

20. Amy L. Blair draws on Janice Radway and Pierre Bourdieu to show how, in different historical periods, including the 1920s, the literary establishment trained readers to distinguish between "commercial books" and "literary books" by associating the latter with what Radway calls "a more instrumental view that emphasized the benefits they conferred on the reader." Quoted in Blair, "Main Street Reading *Main Street*," in *New Directions in American Reception Study*, ed. Philip Goldstein and James L. Machor (New York: Oxford University Press, 2008): 141–42.

21. Brodhead, *Cultures of Letters*, 123–24.

22. On the concept of almost or not-quite-white, see Darlene Wilson, "The Felicitous Convergence of Mythmaking and Capital Accumulation: John Fox Jr. and the Formation of An(Other) Almost-White American Underclass," *Journal of Appalachian Studies* 1, no. 1 (1995): 13–14, 27–28, 34n15, 38n39; and Matt Wray, *Not Quite White: White Trash and the Boundaries of Whiteness* (Durham, NC: Duke University Press, 2006).

23. Shapiro, *Appalachia on Our Mind*, 19.

24. Recent studies indicate that southern out-migration, and the accompany-

ing sense of loss felt by whites, dates as far back as the First World War, rather than World War II as earlier historians suggested. See Chad Berry, *Southern Migrants, Northern Exiles* (Urbana: University of Illinois Press, 2000), 12.

25. Wendy Griswold, *Regionalism and the Reading Class* (Chicago: University of Chicago Press, 2008), 2.

26. Hsiung, *Two Worlds in the Tennessee Mountains*, xii, 8.

27. Hamlin Garland, *Crumbling Idols* (Cambridge, MA: Stone & Kimball, 1894), 64. Foote makes a similar point when she notes that a reviewer for the *Century* magazine praises local color for its "natural" voices, as if "local color is the authentic expression of the people depicted in it." *Regional Fictions*, 10.

28. Smith's comments were made at the Literary Festival at Emory and Henry College, Emory, Virginia, 22 September 2006. See "The Perils of Regionalism: Labels and their Limitations," *Iron Mountain Review* 23 (Spring 2007): 25.

29. According to Ross Posnock, intellectuals seek "solidarity with the marginal and disposessed" based on their belief that "the distance that constitutes intellectuals [can be] erased." *Color and Culture: Black Writers and the Making of the Modern Intellectual* (Cambridge, MA: Harvard University Press, 1998), 42. As Tom Lutz argues in *Cosmopolitan Vistas*, all literary authors, including those with regional loyalties, exhibit cosmopolitan commitments. Lutz, 28–29, draws on a 1914 story about a writer who goes to prison to write authentically about prisons but loses his sense of perspective to theorize that "if the writer lives the life he is writing about authentically enough, he ceases to be a writer. It is the writer's distance from his subject that allows him to write." Tom Lutz, *Cosmopolitan Vistas: American Regionalism and Literary Value* (Ithaca, NY: Cornell University Press, 2004).

30. Greeson observes that few southern writers have written about "the South" without having left it and "almost never do they write exclusively for a 'Southern' audience"; furthermore, southern writers usually publish and distribute their books through a press located outside the southeastern United States. ("The 'Mysteries and Miseries' of North Carolina: New York City, Urban Gothic Fiction, and *Incidents in the Life of a Slave Girl*," *American Literature: A Journal of Literary History, Criticism, and Bibliography* 73, no. 2 [2001], 284).

31. Jurca, *White Diaspora*, 15.

32. Blair, "Main Street Reading *Main Street*," 145.

33. Steven Mailloux, *Reception Histories: Rhetoric, Pragmatism, and American Cultural Politics* (Ithaca, NY: Cornell University Press, 1998); Brodhead, *Cultures of Letters*, 120; Janice Radway, "Interpretive Communities and Variable Literacies: The Functions of Romance Reading," *Daedalus* 113 (Summer 1984): 51, 53.

34. Foote, *Regional Fictions*, 4, 14; Stephanie Foote, "The Cultural Work of American Regionalism," in *A Companion to the Regional Literatures of America*, ed. Charles L. Crow (Malden, MA: Blackwell, 2003), 28.

35. The term *high middlebrow* is from Catherine A. Lutz and Jane L. Collins, *Reading National Geographic* (Chicago: University of Chicago Press, 1993), 7,

who derive it from the hierarchies constructed by Pierre Bourdieu's *Distinction: A Social Critique of the Judgment of Taste* (New York: Routledge, 1984); Lawrence Levine's *Highbrow/Lowbrow: The Emergence of Cultural Hierarchy* (Cambridge, MA: Harvard University Press, 1988); and Barbara Hernstein Smith's "Contingencies of Value," *Critical Inquiry* 10, no. 1 (1984).

36. Batteau, *The Invention of Appalachia*, 1.

37. I am grateful to Stephanie Foote for this formulation.

38. Brodhead, *Cultures of Letters*, 123.

39. Glazener, *Reading for Realism*, 202; Nancy Glazener, "Regional Accents: Populism, Feminism, and New England Women's Regionalism," *Arizona Quarterly* 52, no. 2 (1996): 33–53.

40. On the hegemonic nature of local-color texts, see Brodhead, *Cultures of Letters*. On the counterhegemonic nature of regional texts by insiders, see Judith Fetterley and Marjorie Pryse, *Writing out of Place: Regionalism, Women, and American Literary Culture* (Urbana: University of Illinois Press, 2002), 121; and Fetterley and Pryse, eds., *American Women Regionalists, 1850–1910: A Norton Anthology* (New York: Norton, 1992). Rather than distinguish between "local color" as mocking and "regionalism" as empowering the local, Tom Lutz uses the terms interchangeably but distinguishes between "literary" and "subliterary" varieties. (He argues that regionalism is literary when it has a "cosmopolitan ethic" that views the local from both an insider's perspective and from a worldly context.) Lutz notes that of course you can read literary local color as being either hegemonic or counterhegemonic because you can ignore exactly half of the textual evidence. *Cosmopolitan Vistas*, 27–28, 36.

41. Michael Berubé made similar points in his keynote address "What Happened to Cultural Studies?" (Reception Studies Society Conference, Purdue University, West Lafayette, Indiana, 11 September 2009). Berubé traces the first argument to communications scholars who, basing their arguments on political economy, suggest that popular representations are always owned by corporations and therefore are always hegemonic; he traces the second to media studies scholars who, drawing on cultural studies, argue that audiences are always active agents who always resist the messages delivered by mass media. Elizabeth Long articulates the cultural studies strain when she argues that "we not only are shaped by culture but also take it up and with it forge new meanings and new possibilities for our lives." *Book Clubs: Women and the Uses of Reading in Everyday Life* (Chicago: University of Chicago Press, 2003), 24.

42. Ward Clark, review of *The Trail of the Lonesome Pine*, by John Fox Jr., *Bookman*, December 1908; Dunaway, *The First American Frontier*, 3. See also Shapiro, *Appalachia on Our Mind*, xiii.

43. Emily Satterwhite, "Romancing Whiteness: Popular Appalachian Fiction and the Imperialist Imagination at the Turns of Two Centuries," in *At Home and Abroad: Historicizing Twentieth-Century Whiteness in Literature and Performance*, ed. La Vinia Delois Jennings (Knoxville: University of Tennessee Press,

2009), 97. See also Emily Satterwhite, "Imagining Home, Nation, World: Appalachia on the Mall," *Journal of American Folklore* 121, no. 479 (2008): 10–34.

44. Dunaway notes the importance of proximity in fueling infatuation during the colonial era. *First American Frontier*, 1.

45. According to Jennifer Greeson, fantasies of the South have, among other things, allowed readers to exercise "imaginative dominion" over a tropical "internal other." Her observation allowed me to see this at work for Appalachia as well. More frequently, however, fantasies of Appalachia figured it in terms of "home place" (from which readers have been displaced spatially) and "roots" (from which readers have been displaced by time and ancestral generations). Jennifer Rae Greeson, *Our South: Geographic Fantasy and the Rise of National Literature* (Cambridge, MA: Harvard University Press, 2010), 14, 3.

46. Raymond Williams, *The Country and the City* (New York: Oxford University Press, 1973), 282, 180.

47. Sarah Burns, *Pastoral Inventions: Rural Life in Nineteenth-Century American Art and Culture* (Philadelphia: Temple University Press, 1989), 237, 241, 225, 197, 224; Cratis Williams, "The Southern Mountaineer in Fact and Fiction," *Appalachian Journal* 3 (1975–76): 8–162. Late nineteenth-century literary representations of the mountain South drew from the travelogue tradition but were also greatly influenced by the dialect-peppered southwestern humor tales published in newspapers such as the *St. Louis Reveille* and the *New York Spirit of the Times*. See Shapiro, *Appalachia on Our Mind*, 18, xi. Journalist Ann Newport Royall is credited with discursively establishing differences between eastern and western Virginia as early as 1826. See Williams, *Appalachia*, 68. David Hunter Strother ("Porte Crayon") was one of the first authors to incorporate the travel sketch with a rudimentary plot and the southwestern humorist device of frame narration in his *Harper's* series, "A Winter in the South" (1857). See Talmage Apperson Stanley, "The Poco Field: Politics, Culture, and Place in Contemporary Appalachia" (PhD diss., Emory University, 1996), 26.

48. Shapiro, *Appalachia on Our Mind*, chapter 1. New copyright law in 1891 made reprinting British works prohibitively expensive, accelerating the trend toward publishing U.S. authors. Publisher Henry Holt describes this phenomenon in "The Commercialization of Literature," *Atlantic Monthly*, November 1905, 597. See also Foote: "The late nineteenth century saw an increase in the number of writers across the board—and also, because of the explosion of venues in which writers could publish their work, an increase in the number of writers who were professionalized—that is to say, who made a living from writing." "The Cultural World of American Regionalism," 35.

49. For example see Foote, *Regional Fictions*; and Brodhead, *Cultures of Letters*.

50. Brodhead, *Culture of Letters*, 120–21; Shapiro, *Appalachia on Our Mind*, 15. Foote also describes regional writing as "a form that works to preserve local customs, local accents, and local communities," a form that attempts to "protect . . . local identities by preserving them in literature" (*Regional Fictions*, 4).

51. Darlene Wilson, "A Judicious Combination of Incident and Psychology: John Fox Jr. and the Southern Mountaineer Motif," in *Confronting Appalachian Stereotypes: Back Talk from an American Region*, ed. Dwight B. Billings, Gurney Norman, and Katherine Ledford (Lexington: University Press of Kentucky, 1999), 98–118.

52. On weightlessness, see Lears, *No Place of Grace*; Foote, *Regional Fictions*, 14–15, 18, 35; Brodhead, *Cultures of Letters*, 205–6. Lucinda MacKethan, "Local Color," *Southern Spaces*, 29 February 2004, http://southernspaces.org/2004/local-color (accessed 6 May 2011). The cover image neatly captures the desire to see "something of themselves" among readers of twenty-first-century local color. While most Gilded Age local-color fiction may have catered to urban elite tastes at the expense of those without political and economic power, some early regional writing harnessed the genre to articulate warnings about the political consequences of uncritical regionalism. See Brodhead, *Cultures of Letters*, for the ways in which Charles Chesnutt's Uncle Julius stories perform a radical critique of cosmopolitan elites' condescension toward the "backward" local ways on which they are nonetheless psychically (and materially) dependent; and Foote, *Regional Fictions*, for the ways in which Hamlin Garland's fiction recognized rural-urban tensions in terms not only of cultural differences, but also of political and class differences created by uneven capitalist development (48).

53. Shapiro, *Appalachia on Our Mind*, 18. Shapiro, 310–16, includes a bibliography of essays, sketches, and stories published between 1850 and 1890. See Lorise C. Boger, *The Southern Mountaineer in Literature: An Annotated Bibliography* (Morgantown: West Virginia University Library, 1964), for additional publications not included in Shapiro. See also Donna Campbell on the beginnings of regionalism: "Realism and Regionalism," in *A Companion to the Regional Literatures of America*, ed. Charles L. Crow (Malden, MA: Blackwell, 2003), 95–100.

54. See, for example, Anthony Harkins's assessment that Murfree was "of greatest importance in terms of the nationalization of the Appalachian mountaineer image." *Hillbilly: A Cultural History of an American Icon* (New York: Oxford University Press, 2004), 30. Batteau observes that all later versions of Appalachia are based on Murfree's. *The Invention of Appalachia*, 40.

55. Boger, *The Southern Mountaineer in Literature*, vii.

56. Ibid., viii.

57. Alice Payne Hackett, *70 Years of Best Sellers, 1895–1965* (New York: Bowker, 1967), 99.

58. Dwight Billings, introduction to Billings, Norman, and Ledford, *Confronting Appalachian Stereotypes*, 14. Batteau calls Fox the "most popular writer of all times on Appalachian subjects" and argues that Fox and Berea College's William Frost were the "two central figures" for defining the region in the popular imagination from approximately 1889, when Frost became president of Berea College, to 1913, when Horace Kephart's nonfiction *Our Southern Highlanders*

reframed the popular landscape (*The Invention of Appalachia*, 57). Altina Waller similarly argues that "Fox, more than anyone else, shaped middle-class perceptions about southern Appalachians." "Feuding in Appalachia," in *Appalachia in the Making: The Mountain South in the Nineteenth Century*, ed. Mary Beth Pudup, Dwight B. Billings, and Altina Waller (Chapel Hill: University of North Carolina Press, 1995), 363.

    59. Harkins, *Hillbilly*, 220. J. W. Williamson also notes this shift to the urban in *Hillbillyland: What the Movies Did to the Mountains and What the Mountains Did to the Movies* (Chapel Hill: University of North Carolina Press, 1995), 182–83. Universalist sentiments generally won out over localist sensibilities in fiction published after 1910. Theorist David Harvey identifies the years 1910–1915 as a time of sharp divergence away from westerners' sense of "common places" like town, history, paternity, and morality (*The Condition of Postmodernity: An Enquiry into the Origins of Cultural Change* [Malden, MA: Blackwell, 1989], chapter 12). Lutz disagrees with critics and historians who see major differences before and after the First World War. He emphasizes similarities instead, pointing to the works of Willa Cather, the "revolt from the village" authors, the Southern Renaissance, and the Harlem Renaissance (*Cosmopolitan Vistas*, 99–100). The revolt from the village authors' aggressively nonsentimental portraits of small-town life may have been popular because they were read against the grain. As I discuss in the conclusion, recent scholarship on fan mail demonstrates that novels lambasting small-town life may have been misread by readers who failed to see, or refused to accept, the cynical views of authors. See Blair, "Main Street Reading *Main Street*." Carl Van Doren's list of "revolt from the village" authors includes Edgar Lee Masters, Sherwood Anderson, Sinclair Lewis, F. Scott Fitzgerald, and Dorothy Canfield. See *Contemporary American Novelists, 1900–1920* (New York: Macmillan, 1931), xi. For one theory of the cyclical nature of literary popularity, see Franco Moretti, *Graphs Maps Trees: Abstract Models for a Literary Theory* (New York: Verso, 2005), especially 20–21.

    60. According to Lutz, *Cosmopolitan Vistas*, 131, "Literary regionalism was given its first conscious statement in *The Midland* and the little magazines that followed it" in the 1910s.

    61. Boger, *The Southern Mountaineer in Literature*, viii; Keith L. Justice, *Bestseller Index: All Books*, Publishers Weekly *and the* New York Times *through 1990* (Jefferson, NC: McFarland, 1998). Robert Dorman speculates that "regionalism was itself revealed to be a symptom of the passing of the older America, which, after this brief renaissance, 'shrunk back to its own littleness in the modern world.'" Robert L. Dorman, *Revolt of the Provinces: The Regionalist Movement in America, 1920–1945* (Chapel Hill: University of North Carolina Press, 1993), xiv. See also Patrick Mazza's review of Dorman's book, "Uncovering the Hidden History of Regionalism: The American Regionalist Insurgency of the 1920s–40s," *Cascadia Planet*, 15 January 1997, http://www.tnews.com; and Lau-

ren Coates and Nihad M. Farooq, "Regionalism in the Era of the New Deal," in Crow, *A Companion to the Regional Literatures of America*, 74–91.

62. Jane S. Becker investigates the popularity of crafts in her incisive monograph, *Selling Tradition: Appalachia and the Construction of an American Folk, 1930–1940* (Chapel Hill: University of North Carolina Press, 1998).

63. Lutz, *Cosmopolitan Vistas*, 190.

64. Harkins, *Hillbilly*, 47, 3–11, 211–12. See also Richard A. Peterson, *Creating Country Music: Fabricating Authenticity* (Chicago: University of Chicago Press, 1997).

65. Mary Elisabeth Goin, "Catherine Marshall: Three Decades of Popular Religion," *Journal of Presbyterian History* 56, no. 3 (1978): 220; Henry Hart, *James Dickey: The World as a Lie* (New York: Picador, 2000), 455.

66. Edwin Peeples (fan-acquaintance, Phoenixville, Pennsylvania), 1 January 1971, folder 1, box 43, General Correspondence, James Dickey Papers, Manuscript Collection 745, Manuscript, Archives, and Rare Book Library, Emory University, Atlanta, GA.

67. A number of commentators, journalists, historians, and other academics have embraced this characterization of the turn of the twenty-first century as a Second or Neo–Gilded Age. See Michael McHugh, *The Second Gilded Age: The Great Reaction in the United States, 1973–2001* (Lanham, MD: University Press of America, 2006). Dean of Yale School of Management Jeffrey Garten warned that perceptions of unchecked corporate power might resurrect Gilded Age calls for government intervention ("Why Goliaths Need to Be Careful," *Financial Times*, 28 February 2005). William Gates Sr., father of Microsoft mogul Bill Gates, compared "the first Gilded Age" to the present moment, when, he argued, "the gap between the very rich and everyone else is once again at historic levels" (William H. Gates Sr. and Chuck Collins, "Tax the Rich?" *Sojourners*, January–February 2003, 36–39). Examples of more predictable liberal comments equating the present to the Gilded Age include media scholars Robert W. McChesney and John Nichols, "Media Democracy's Moment," *Nation*, 24 February 2003, 16; Ellen Goodman, "Taxing Our Children," *Boston Globe*, 13 March 2005, D11; "Bush's Gulf of Credibility," *Nation*, 17 February 2003, 4; Joan Walsh, "Plutocrats to the Rescue!" 15 February 2001, *Salon.com*, http://archive.salon.com/politics/feature/2001/02/15/buffett/ (accessed 12 April 2005); Juliet Schor, foreword to *Shifting Fortunes: The Perils of the Growing American Wealth Gap*, ed. Chuck Collins, Betsy Leonard-Wright, and Holly Sklar (Boston: United for a Fair Economy, 1999); E. J. Dionne Jr., "Revolution in Reverse: In Solidifying Its Power, the GOP Is Loosening Its Ethics," *Washington Post*, 19 November 2004, A29; and Bob Thompson, "Sharing the Wealth?" *Washington Post* magazine, 13 April 2003. Wall Street historian Steve Fraser reserves the term Gilded Age for the "socially negligent" Reagan era: quoted in Harold Evans, "Follow the Money," *New York Times*, 13 March 2005, a review of Fraser's *Every Man a Speculator: A History of Wall Street in American Life* (New York: Harper Collins, 2005).

68. Foote, *Regional Fictions*, 4.

69. In 2002, June Howard noted manifest similarities in contemporary and local-color-era fiction ("Toward an Understanding of 'Region' and 'Regionalism'" [paper delivered at the American Studies Association conference, Houston, 17 November 2002]). Tom Lutz also notes the resurgence of regionalism in the 1980s (*Cosmopolitan Vistas*, 190). Garrison Keillor's 1985 *Lake Wobegon* appeared for a total of 133 weeks on the *New York Times* and *Publishers Weekly* best-seller lists (Justice, *Bestseller Index*, 170).

70. Karem, *The Romance of Authenticity*, 213n1.

71. Dermot McEvoy and Daisy Maryles, "Everything All Over Again: Debut Novels Score Big in Trade; in Mass Market, It's Mostly Women's Fiction and, of Course, Dan Brown," *Publishers Weekly*, 28 March 2005.

72. See a feature article about *USA Today*'s first ten years of tracking best sellers, "Top 100: 10 Years' Best," *USA Today*, 11 March 2004, 7D.

73. Coordinated in conjunction with the United Nations' "International Year of the Mountain," the legislation instating a U.S. "Year of Appalachia" signaled the culmination of efforts to translate interest in the region into national recognition and legitimacy. This legislation echoed the 1998 passage of U.S. Congressional Resolution H.R. 214, which acknowledged Bristol, Tennessee/Virginia, and surrounding counties as "The Birthplace of Country Music"—a designation made in deference to the 1927 Bristol recording sessions that marked the early commercial popularity of rural southern music. The designated "year" straddled over two calendar years in order to encompass both the seventy-fifth anniversary of the Bristol Sessions in 2002 and the Smithsonian Folklife Festival's exhibit on Appalachia, which was delayed until the following year for pragmatic programming reasons. See Gary Robertson, "Twangs for the Memories . . . : Bristol Celebrates Sessions When Country Music Began," *Richmond Times-Dispatch*, 27 July 2002, Saturday city edition.

74. A reader (Napa, California), "Warm funny—perfect for reading in a big chair by the fire," review of *At Home in Mitford*, Amazon, 16 October 1996.

75. See Foote, *Regional Fictions*, for local color as site of negotiation rather than retreat.

1. Charm and Virility, circa 1884

An earlier version of this chapter appeared as "Reading Craddock, Reading Murfree: Local Color, Authenticity, and Geographies of Reception," *American Literature* 78, no. 1 (2006): 59–88. Reproduced by permission of Duke University Press.

1. "A Literary Surprise," *Boston Herald*, 5 March 1885, 4. In reality it was not Aldrich but Oliver Wendell Holmes who exclaimed, "Why, I expected to see a six-foot Tennessean, and in his place I am introduced to a young girl!" (Eva Malone Byrd, "The Life and Writings of Mary Noailles Murfree" [MA thesis,

University of Tennessee, 1937], 114; Eleanor B. Spence, "Collected Reminiscences of Mary N. Murfree" [MA thesis, George Peabody College for Teachers, 1928], 24).

2. "A Literary Surprise."

3. Ibid. The *Herald* reported that the "observing" Aldrich used "M. N. Murfree, Esq.," "taking it for granted that one who had so accurate a knowledge of legal methods as is shown in the stories must be a lawyer." This report is not born out by archival evidence.

4. Ibid.

5. Aldrich to Murfree, 18 September 1884, quoted in Edd Winfield Parks, *Charles Egbert Craddock (Mary Noailles Murfree)* (Chapel Hill: University of North Carolina Press, 1941), 117.

6. "A Literary Surprise."

7. Houghton, Mifflin & Co. to Murfree, 5 December 1883, Mary Noailles Murfree Papers, 1877–1928, Manuscript, Archives, and Rare Book Library, Emory University, Atlanta, GA. Further references to this collection will be cited as Murfree Papers.

8. Nancy Glazener discusses the pitfalls for a local-color writer in being classified as either an inartistic "native informant" or a more cosmopolitan but formula-dependent professional. See *Reading for Realism: The History of a U.S. Literary Institution, 1850–1910* (Durham, NC: Duke University Press, 1997), 199.

9. "Clever Miss Murfree," *Savannah News*, n.d., quoted in Mary Sue Mooney, "An Intimate Study of Mary Noailles Murfree, Charles Egbert Craddock" (MA thesis, George Peabody College for Teachers, 1928), 36; Byrd, "Life and Writings," 110.

10. On contemporary concerns, see, for example, Gail Bederman, *Manliness and Civilization: A Cultural History of Gender and Race in the United States, 1880–1917* (Chicago: University of Chicago Press, 1995); E. Anthony Rotundo, *American Manhood: Transformations in Masculinity from the Revolution to the Modern Era* (New York: Basic, 1993); T. J. Jackson Lears, *No Place of Grace: Antimodernism and the Transformation of American Culture, 1880–1920* (New York: Pantheon, 1981).

11. Richard H. Brodhead describes writer Constance Fenimore Woolson as a "person from 'nowhere'" (*Cultures of Letters: Scenes of Reading and Writing in Nineteenth-Century America* [Chicago: University of Chicago Press, 1994], 139). On postbellum consolidation, see Brodhead, *Cultures of Letters*, 132, 123; Robert H. Wiebe, *The Search for Order, 1877–1920* (New York: Hill & Wang, 1967); Alan Trachtenberg, *The Incorporation of America: Culture and Society in the Gilded Age* (New York: Hill & Wang, 1982).

12. See Judith Fetterley and Marjorie Pryse, eds., *American Women Regionalists, 1850–1910: A Norton Anthology* (New York: Norton, 1992); Fetterley and Pryse, *Writing out of Place: Regionalism, Women, and American Literary Culture* (Urbana: University of Illinois Press, 2002); Barbara C. Ewell and Pamela Glenn

Menke, eds., *Southern Local Color: Stories of Region, Race, and Gender* (Athens: University of Georgia Press, 2002), 100. Sherrie A. Inness and Diana Royer adapt theorist David Jordan's concept of a "decentred world-view" to discuss women's use of local color "to write subversively" in their introduction to *Breaking Boundaries: New Perspectives on Women's Regional Writing* (Iowa City: University of Iowa Press, 1997), 2, 5. Elizabeth Ammons and Valerie Rohy, in their introduction to *American Local Color Writing, 1880–1920* (New York: Penguin, 1998), propose Mary Louise Pratt's term *autoethnography* to refer to "instances in which colonized subjects undertake to represent themselves" (8) and state that "most" of the stories in their anthology (which includes Murfree's "Dancin' Party at Harrison's Cove") fit this description.

13. See Henry D. Shapiro, *Appalachia on Our Mind: The Southern Mountains and Mountaineers in the American Consciousness, 1870–1920* (Chapel Hill: University of North Carolina Press, 1978), 19–20; and Danny Miller, *Wingless Flights: Appalachian Women in Fiction* (Bowling Green, OH: Bowling Green State University Popular Press, 1996), 1–2.

14. See Jennifer A. Gehrman, "Mary Noailles Murfree," in *Nineteenth Century American Women Writers: A Bio-Bibliographical Sourcebook*, ed. Denise D. Knight (Westport, CT: Greenwood, 1997), 320; Ben Forkner and Patrick Samway, eds., *Stories of the Old South* (New York: Penguin, 1989), 99.

15. See Nancy Glazener, "Regional Accents: Populism, Feminism, and New England Women's Regionalism," *Arizona Quarterly* 52, no. 2 (1996): 33–53.

16. Susan Belasco, "The Cultural Work of National Magazines," in *A History of the Book in America: The Industrial Book, 1840–1880*, ed. Scott E. Casper, Jeffrey D. Groves, Stephen W. Nissenbaum, and Michael Winship (Chapel Hill: University of North Carolina Press, in association with the American Antiquarian Society, 2007), 3:269. Belasco, citing Sedgwick, notes that under Howells's leadership from 1866 to 1881, the *Atlantic*'s circulation declined from fifty thousand to twelve thousand. Brodhead, *Cultures of Letters*, 123; Glazener, *Reading for Realism*, 202. See also Glazener, "Regional Accents."

17. Postcard from "WMD" of Cambridge, Massachusetts, to Mr. F.J. Garrison at Houghton Mifflin, 12 May 1884, Murfree Papers, box 1, folder 3.

18. Regarding Aldrich's curiosity, Parks cites an exchange of letters dated 9 June and 8, 18, and 30 September 1884 (*Craddock*, 117). Murfree to Aldrich, 30 September 1884, quoted in Parks, *Craddock*, 119.

19. Richard Cary, *Mary N. Murfree* (New York: Twayne, 1967), 24. Byrd, "Life and Writings," 100–101; Parks, *Craddock*, 100, 122.

20. The account given here is taken from a statement written by Fanny Murfree for Mary Murfree's biographer (Parks, *Craddock*, 122–25). Fanny Murfree also gave interviews to master's students Mooney ("Intimate Study"); Byrd ("Life and Writings," 103–4); and Spence ("Collected Reminiscences"). Newspaper articles corroborate many of the events Fanny Murfree described.

21. Mary Noailles Murfree, *In the Tennessee Mountains*, ed. Nathalia Wright

(Knoxville: University of Tennessee Press, 1970), 157. Further references to *In the Tennessee Mountains* are to this edition and will be cited parenthetically in the text as *TM*.

22. "Literature/Recent Fiction," *Independent*, 12 June 1884, 727; "Clever Miss Murfree," quoted in Mooney, "Intimate Study," 36.

23. "A Literary Surprise"; review of *In the Tennessee Mountains*, by Mary Noailles Murfree, *Critic*, 16 August 1884, 75.

24. Parks, *Craddock*, 57–84. *Appleton's* accepted two mountain stories from "Charles Egbert Craddock" in 1876. "Taking the Blue Ribbon at the County Fair" appeared in *Appleton's Summer Book* in 1880. "The Panther of Jolton's Ridge" was passed along to *Christian Union*, which published the story in the 25 December 1885 issue.

25. Cary, *Mary N. Murfree*, 23; Parks, *Craddock*, 237–43. There has been some confusion about the extent of Murfree's firsthand observation of the Smoky Mountains to the east of Beersheba Springs, partly because few, if any, letters dating earlier than 1877 exist (Fanny Murfree reported that Mary Murfree's letters were burned by her request [Spence, "Collected Reminiscences," 5]). Murfree made at least one trip with her father, according to Fanny Murfree, sometime before 1871 (Spence, "Collected Reminiscences," 18) and "frequent summer trips . . . after 1871," according to Durwood Dunn, "Mary Noailles Murfree: A Reappraisal," *Appalachian Journal* 6 (1979): 198. During these trips Murfree may have lodged in private homes. Murfree made several trips to the Montvale Springs resort in the Smokies to escape St. Louis summers and seek out local-color material beginning in 1885 (when she may have also been fleeing new notoriety in St. Louis; see "Clever Miss Murfree," quoted in Byrd, "Life and Writings," 123). See Shapiro, *Appalachia on Our Mind*, 19; "Charles Egbert Craddock: A Five-Minute Chat about a Gifted Woman," *Macon (GA) Telegraph*, 15 November 1885; Dunn, "Mary Noailles Murfree," 198; Spence, "Collected Reminiscences," 40.

26. Parks, *Craddock*, 1–56.

27. Mooney, "An Intimate Study," 34; Byrd, "Life and Writings," 64.

28. "A Literary Surprise." Wright, introduction to Murfree, *In the Tennessee Mountains*, xiii; Bill Hardwig, introduction to *In the Tennessee Mountains*, by Mary Noailles Murfree (Knoxville: University of Tennessee Press, 2008), xi.

29. Bederman, *Manliness and Civilization*; Rotundo, *American Manhood*, 251. Horace Porter, "The Philosophy of Courage," *Century*, June 1888, 253.

30. "Not Namby-Pamby," review of *The Prophet of the Great Smoky Mountains*, by Mary Noailles Murfree, *New York Times*, 25 October 1885, 5. See also *Buyer*, April 1885, 73; *New York Times*, 15 June 1885, 3; *Cottage Hearth*, July 1885, 224; *Saturday Review*, 22 August 1885, 259; *Independent*, 27 August 1885, 3; *Book Buyer*, November 1885, 259; *New York Times*, 15 June 1885, 3; *Critic*, 14 November 1885, 239; and *New York Times*, 15 June 1885, 3. A lone critic persevered in describing Murfree's style as having a "distinctly feminine touch"

and a style "disfigured" by the "abuse of so-called word-painting" ("American Stories," *Saturday Review*, 7 November 1885, 615). Reese Carlton's meticulous bibliography directed me to the vast majority of the reviews cited in this chapter. See Carlton, "Mary Noailles Murfree (1850–1922): An Annotated Bibliography," *American Literary Realism, 1870–1910* 7 (1974): 293–378.

31. "The Magazines for April," *Critic*, 28 March 1885, 149.

32. William Perry Brown, "A Peculiar People," *Overland Monthly*, November 1888, 508.

33. Bederman, *Manliness and Civilization*, 22–23, 72, 186; Rotundo, *American Manhood*, 227; Thomas Wentworth Higginson, "Gymnastics," *Out-door Papers* (Boston: Lee & Shepard, 1886), 138.

34. Theodore Roosevelt, "The Strenuous Life," speech delivered on 10 April 1899 in Chicago, published in *The Strenuous Life: Essays and Addresses* (New York: Century, 1900).

35. Bederman, *Manliness and Civilization*, 184, 186–87, 192–93, 77–79, 172–73, 274n8. Bonnie James Shaker, in *Coloring Locals: Racial Formation in Kate Chopin's* Youth's Companion *Stories* (Ames: University of Iowa Press, 2003), xiii–xiv, characterizes *Youth's Companion* stories as "behavior manuals for a social order that was hierarchized with the 'whitest' people at the top and the 'blackest' at the bottom. Upper orders were responsible for those below; lower orders were to respect their superiors. . . . Hence, one of the primary legacies of [stories published in *Youth's Companion*] is the record they leave us of how people were taught to treat one another as a result of their distance from what the *Companion* normalized as a standard Wasp American identity."

36. For 1907–1908 correspondence between Roosevelt and Murfree, see Theodore Roosevelt Papers, Manuscript Division, Library of Congress, Washington, DC. Parks, *Craddock*, 221.

37. Ellery Sedgwick, *The Atlantic Monthly, 1857–1909: Yankee Humanism at High Tide and Ebb* (Amherst: University of Massachusetts Press, 1994), 162; Thomas Aldrich, "Unguarded Gates," *Atlantic Monthly*, July 1892, 57. Regarding Aldrich's membership in the Anti-immigration League, see Kenneth M. Price, "Charles Chesnutt, the *Atlantic Monthly*, and the Intersection of African American Fiction and Elite Culture," in *Periodical Literature in Nineteenth-Century America*, ed. Kenneth M. Price and Susan Belasco Smith (Charlottesville: University Press of Virginia, 1995), 261. "The Lady's Brilliant Line of Ancestry" is the subtitle of Robert Diable's article "The New Literary Star," *Boston Herald*, 27 March 1885, 3. Howells, on the other hand, is widely known for his anti-imperialist stance.

38. On the vitality of regions offered to local-color readers see Brodhead, "Reading of Regions," in *Cultures of Letters*. In 1894 literary critic Henry C. Vedder referred to Murfree as one of those "instances of sudden reputation won, and great gains made by men and women who were no more novelists than a negro kalsominer [whitewasher] is a painter." *American Writers of To-day* (New

York: Silver, Burdette, 1894), 175. Parks reports Howells's praise of Murfree's "Electioneerin' on Big Injun Mounting" in a letter dated 2 October 1879. Parks does not give the letter's archived location or quote it directly, but he says that Howells describes the story as having "a vigor and raciness of the soil" (*Craddock*, 97). Vedder also calls Murfree's fiction "racy of the soil" (*American Writers of To-day*, 186).

39. Of the five stories eschewing the tourist-observer framework, only "The 'Harnt' That Walks Chilhowie" and "Over on the t'Other Mounting" have been anthologized recently; see Fetterley and Pryse, *American Women Regionalists*; Forkner and Samway, *Stories of the Old South*; and *The Portable American Realism Reader*, ed. James Nagel and Thomas Quirk (New York: Penguin, 1997). Henry Shapiro, *Appalachia on Our Mind*, 19.

40. "New Publications/Not Namby-Pamby," *New York Times*, 25 October 1885, 5.

41. "Literary Bric-a-Brac," *New Orleans Times Democrat*, 15 March 1885.

42. From the *New York Christian Union*, quoted in a Houghton Mifflin advertising circular for *In the Tennessee Mountains*, Murfree Papers, box 1, folder 3.

43. Postcard from H. W. Pierson addressed to Charles Egbert Craddock, in care of Houghton Mifflin, dated 1 March 1884, postmarked 29 February 1884, Murfree Papers, box 1, folder 3. See *Oxford English Dictionary*, s.v. "Manner."

44. Lucy D. Laighton to Murfree, 20 April 1885, Murfree Papers, box 1, folder 5; William Glyndon to Murfree, 13 May 1886, Murfree Papers, box 1, folder 6; George K. Grant to Murfree, 17 July 1917, Murfree Papers, box 1, folder 15.

45. W. H. Peck to Murfree, 22 May 1884, Murfree Papers, box 1, folder 3. Peck's spelling of "Apalachian" reflects a common early variant. See, for example, George William Fitch, Alphonso J. Robinson, and Charles Carroll Morgan, *Outlines of Physical Geography* (n.p.: Sheldon, 1867); and Jedediah Hotchkiss "The Coal Fields of West Virginia and Virginia in the Great Ohio, or Trans-Apalachian, Coal Basin," *The Virginias: A Mining, Industrial and Scientific Journal* 1, no. 2 (1880): 18.

46. Sarah Orne Jewett to Murfree, 19 May 1884, Murfree Papers, box 1, folder 3; Celia Thaxter to Charles Egbert Craddock, 16 April 1885, Murfree Papers, box 1, folder 5. I am grateful to Chris Green for suggesting an alternate reading of Thaxter's interest in Craddock: that Craddock offered the nature writer an opportunity to encounter the natural world.

47. See Brodhead, *Cultures of Letters*, 121.

48. Byrd, "Life and Writings," 123–24.

49. Brodhead, *Cultures of Letters*, 119–24.

50. When Brodhead contends that "socially disparaged figures . . . [were] paradoxically advantaged" by elites' interest in their lives, he does not distinguish carefully enough between the conditions that turned some people's "folkways and speechways . . . into a valuable literary capital" for *others* versus the

extremely rare occasion when someone submersed in the "folkways and speechways" of a so-called cultural backwater could conceptualize and capitalize upon his or her own life as "valuable literary capital" and assert a "literary self." Ibid., 117–19.

51. See Byrd, "Life and Writings," 115–16, 119–20, 112.

52. According to an August 1882 article by Sylvester Baxter in *Century Illustrated*, escorting the Zuni visitors to the Atlantic Ocean was Cushing's only means, save marriage, of gaining "entrance into the Order of the Ka-ka" ("An Aboriginal Pilgrimage," 526). I am grateful to Michael Elliott for suggesting this parallel.

53. Ewell and Menke, *Southern Local Color*, 100, 254. "Decentred worldview" is from Inness and Royer, introduction to *Breaking Boundaries*, 2, 5, who adapt the concept from theorist David Jordan.

54. Fetterley and Pryse, introduction to *American Women Regionalists*, xviii, 255–56.

55. Rosemarie Garland Thomson labels this offensive trope "benevolent maternalism" because privileged caretaker characters are commonly female. *Extraordinary Bodies: Figuring Physical Disability in American Culture and Literature* (New York: Columbia University Press, 1997), 17.

56. John Stahl, *Growing with the West: The Story of a Busy, Quiet Life* (New York: Longmans, Green, 1930), 323–24.

57. Fetterley and Pryse, *Writing out of Place*, 148.

58. Lears, *No Place of Grace*.

2. Tonic and Rationale, circa 1908

Some of the ideas contained in this chapter initially appeared in "Romancing Whiteness: Popular Appalachian Fiction and the Imperialist Imagination at the Turns of Two Centuries," in *At Home and Abroad: Historicizing Twentieth-Century Whiteness in Literature and Performance*, ed. La Vinia Delois Jennings (Knoxville: University of Tennessee Press, 2009), 93–117.

1. Stonewall Jackson Female Institute was founded in 1868, renamed Stonewall Jackson College for Young Women in 1914, and closed in 1930. The only main building to survive a 1914 fire is now home to the Barter Theatre Stage II. Barter Theatre, "Barter Theatre . . . Buildings," http://www.bartertheatre.com/about/documents/HistoryofBuildings.pdf (accessed 6 January 2009). For more information, see Virginia Historical Highway Markers, Virginia Department of Historic Resources, http://www.dhr.virginia.gov/hiway_markers/marker.cfm?mid=2296 (accessed 6 January 2009).

2. Una M. Crawford (fan of *The Trail of the Lonesome Pine* [hereafter *TLP*], Stonewall Jackson College, Abingdon, Virginia) to John Fox Jr., 24 November 1917, box 4, Letters, 1911–1920, Fox Family Papers, Special Collections and Digital Programs, University of Kentucky Libraries, Lexington. Further references to this collection are cited as Fox Papers.

3. Fox's phrase "peculiar mountain-race" is from a letter from John Fox Jr. to Micajah Fible, 30 June 1887, quoted in Bill York, *John Fox, Jr., Appalachian Author* (Jefferson, NC: McFarland, 2003), 56. Darlene Wilson, 26, claims that from "1884 until 1895, John Fox was essentially a publicist for his brother and other entrepreneurs" and shows persuasively how Fox's novel participated in a racialization and colonization of mountain residents. "The Felicitous Convergence of Mythmaking and Capital Accumulation: John Fox Jr. and the Formation of An(Other) Almost-White American Underclass," *Journal of Appalachian Studies* 1, no. 1 (1995): 5–44. See also Wilson, "A Judicious Combination of Incident and Psychology: John Fox Jr. and the Southern Mountaineer Motif," in *Confronting Appalachian Stereotypes: Back Talk from an American Region*, ed. Dwight B. Billings, Gurney Norman, and Katherine Ledford (Lexington: University Press of Kentucky, 1999), 106. Allen Batteau argues that Fox was one of two individuals who redefined the region in the popular imagination between approximately 1889 and 1913 (*The Invention of Appalachia* [Tucson: University of Arizona Press, 1990]). Other scholars who criticize Fox include Cratis Williams, "The Southern Mountaineer in Fact and Fiction," *Appalachian Journal* 3 (1975–76): 8–162; Henry D. Shapiro, *Appalachia on Our Mind: The Southern Mountains and Mountaineers in the American Consciousness, 1870–1920* (Chapel Hill: University of North Carolina Press, 1978); and Rodger Cunningham, "Signs of Civilization: *The Trail of the Lonesome Pine* as Colonial Narrative," *Journal of the Appalachian Studies Association* 2 (1990): 21–46.

4. "Intimate knowledge" is from "Current Fiction," review of *TLP, Nation*, 12 November 1908, 466. Fox's promoters included his publisher, contemporary reviewers, and New South boosters, for whom Fox's repeated anthropological and biological explanations for backward mountain ways served to establish him as someone who wished to understand, excuse, and give credit to mountain people. Darlene Wilson summarizes some of these reactions in "A Judicious Combination," 110. A Harvard publication about its graduating class of 1883 reported that Fox had "portrayed the Kentucky mountaineer . . . graphically and truthfully" (66) and that he was a "potent influence for good in the lives of the mountain children whom he studied so sympathetically and loved so well" (118) (*Harvard College Class of 1883* [Cambridge, 1933]; copy in possession of the author, thanks to Fox's cousin Bettie J. Tuttle).

Fox's legacy as a sympathetic and reliable chronicler of the mountains persisted through much of the twentieth century and continues today, in some circles, in central Kentucky and southwest Virginia. An illustrated twelve-page hagiographic piece appeared in *Virginia Cavalcade* ("John Fox, Jr.," Spring 1972). Fox's brother-in-law, William Cabell Moore, gave a speech in 1957 before the Club of Colonial Dames in Washington, DC, in which he claimed, "It has been said" that Fox "was the best friend these people ever had." *John Fox, Jr., 1862–1919: An Address Delivered October 21, 1957, at the Club of Colonial Dames, Washington, D.C.* (Washington, DC, 1957). Moore's speech was reprinted in the *Kentucky Explorer*, January 1990, 8–14. (*Virginia Cavalcade* and *Kentucky Explorer* articles in possession of the author thanks to Tuttle.) Kentucky newspapers regularly published positive stories about Fox throughout the twentieth century. On 9 July 1957, *Louisville Courier Journal* writer Joe Creason called Fox "the best friend the Kentucky mountaineer ever had." In response to these glowing assessments, Appalachian scholar Don Askins subtitled his 1978 essay "With Friends Like That, Who Needs Enemies?" ("John Fox, Jr.: A Re-appraisal," in *Colonialism in Modern America: The Appalachian Case*, ed. Helen Lewis, Linda Johnson, and Donald Askins [Boone, NC: Appalachian Consortium, 1978]).

5. See Stuart M. Blumin, *The Emergence of the Middle Class: Social Experience in the American City, 1760–1900* (New York: Cambridge University Press, 1989).

6. According to Susan J. Matt, "In 1880, 71 percent of the population was rural; by 1930 only 43 percent was. Individuals who made the transition to urban life testified to the accompanying emotional strain. Buoyed by great expectations for their futures, they also experienced homesickness." "You Can't Go Home Again: Homesickness and Nostalgia in U.S. History," *Journal of American History* 92, no. 4 (2007): 490.

7. On the antimodernism of elites at the turn of the twentieth century, see T. J. Jackson Lears, *No Place of Grace: Antimodernism and the Transformation of American Culture, 1880–1920* (New York: Pantheon, 1981).

8. Darlene Wilson summarizes scholars' findings regarding the reasons for the popularity of Fox's fiction among middle-class white Americans in "A Judicious Combination," 100.

9. Literary scholar Nina Silber argues that, as northern whites increasingly began to accept southern whites' nostalgic portrayals of plantation life, the mountain-born "Little Shepherd's" simultaneous loyalty to the Union and affection for the South allowed white readers to have it both ways as well. "'What Does America Need So Much as Americans?': Race and Northern Reconciliation with Southern Appalachia, 1870–1900," in *Appalachians and Race: The Mountain South from Slavery to Segregation*, ed. John Inscoe (Lexington: University Press of Kentucky, 2001): 245–58.

10. Alice Payne Hackett, *70 Years of Best Sellers, 1895–1965* (New York: Bowker, 1967), 99. Whereas Mary Noailles Murfree's *In the Tennessee Mountains* (1884) had created a sensation two decades earlier by selling nine thousand copies in its first year, *The Trail of the Lonesome Pine* garnered over sixty thousand advance orders and sold out its first edition in just a few months. By some estimates, Fox earned at least $100,000 from the novel's print versions alone, including international sales. York, *John Fox, Jr.*, 176, 212. See also Hackett, *70 Years of Best Sellers*, 104.

11. Fox's novel *Heart of the Hills* was the fifth-best seller of 1913. *Erskine Dale: Pioneer*, completed by Fox's sister Elizabeth and published posthumously in 1920, appeared on the *Publishers Weekly* best-seller list for four weeks (Keith

L. Justice, *Bestseller Index: All Books, Publishers Weekly and the* New York Times *through 1990* [Jefferson, N.C.: McFarland, 1998], 116). Over the course of his career, Fox published in middlebrow to high middlebrow outlets including *Harper's, Century, Outing, Ladies' Home Journal, Scribner's,* and *Colliers.* Most of Fox's novels were serialized in *Harper's* or *Scribner's* magazines before book publication. For a chronology of Fox publications, see York, *John Fox, Jr.,* 277–80.

12. Charles Scribner III, who took the helm of the family's publishing company in 1932, claimed *Lonesome Pine* was probably the best-selling novel the firm ever had. "Charles Scribner Heads Book Firm," n.d., scrapbook number 8 on *The Trail of the Lonesome Pine* (hereinafter referred to as *TLP* scrapbook), 1, Fox Papers. By 1967, *Lonesome Pine* had sold over a million hardbound copies, making it the eleventh-best seller of all fictional books initially published between 1900 and 1909. Hackett, *70 Years of Best Sellers,* 24, 27, 34–35. On sales figures, see also Frank Luther Mott, *The Golden Multitudes: The Story of Best Sellers in the United States* (New York: Macmillan, 1947), 312; and Alice Payne Hackett and James Henry Burke, *80 Years of Best Sellers, 1895–1975* (New York: Bowker, 1977), 25.

On crossovers, see York, *John Fox, Jr.,* 245, 301n13; and Michael Bernier, "*The Trail of the Lonesome Pine* by John Fox, Jr.," in *20th-Century American Bestsellers,* http://www3.isrl.illinois.edu/~unsworth/courses/bestsellers/search.cgi?title=The+Trail+of+the+Lonesome+Pine (accessed 18 August 2010). Using Jerry Williamson's filmography, Darlene Wilson counts thirteen films inspired by Fox's fiction and notes that "one could easily argue that another fifty or more films were inspired by the recurrent themes popularized by Fox." "A Judicious Combination," 99; J. W. Williamson, "Southern Mountaineers Filmography," http://www.library.appstate.edu/appcoll/filmography.html (accessed 24 January 2005).

The ubiquity of the mountain feud story in the popular imagination by the time of the 1936 film is indicated in part by scriptwriter Grover Jones's defense in a copyright infringement suit brought by Fox's heirs. Jones planned to refute the charges simply by saying that he had not ever read Fox's book or seen the play ("Screen: Paramount Puts Color in an Old Blue Ridge Melodrama," *Time,* 29 February 1936, reproduced in *TLP* scrapbook, Fox Papers.)

According to Sharon Hatfield, national reporters' "almost incessant references" to Fox's novel during the murder trial of Edith Maxwell (accused of murdering her father in 1935) "would finally prompt one Wise County [Virginia] newspaper editor to quip that 'most of the news stories on the Maxwell case have been written in hotel rooms with a bottle of "corn" [liquor] in one hand and a copy of *The Trail of the Lonesome Pine* in the other'" (*Never Seen the Moon: The Trials of Edith Maxwell* [Urbana: University of Illinois Press, 2009], 44). Thanks to Dana Cochran for alerting me to this reference.

13. Henry Holt, "The Commercialization of Literature," *Atlantic Monthly,* November 1905, 599.

14. Lears, *No Place of Grace*, 32–47.

15. Wilson, "The Felicitous Convergence," 25–26. John Fox Jr., *The Trail of the Lonesome Pine* (New York: Scribner, 1908), 234. Further references to this novel are to this edition and will be referenced parenthetically in the text as *TLP*.

16. See Michael A. Elliott's reading of "Louisiana" in *The Culture Concept: Writing and Difference in the Age of Realism* (Minneapolis: University of Minnesota Press, 2002), 43–48. See also Leo Marx, *The Machine in the Garden: Technology and the Pastoral Ideal in America* (London: Oxford University Press, 1964).

17. "Mountain Romance by John Fox, Jr.: Charming Tale Told with Effect—Moonshiners and Feuds and a Bewitching Slip of a Cumberland Girl," review of *TLP*, *New York Times Saturday Review of Books*, 17 October 1908, 70.

18. The wording "development" in a land of "arrested civilisation" is from Ward Clark, "Mr. Fox's *The Trail of the Lonesome Pine*," *Bookman*, December 1908, 364. Review of *TLP*, *Washington, DC, Star*, 7 November 1908, *TLP* scrapbook, Fox Papers. The phrase "cultivated, educated, brave, resourceful" is from review of *TLP*, *New York Times* Holiday Book Number, 5 December 1908. The phrases "arous[es] . . . a mountain village" and "the type of American life" are from "A Strong, Human, American Love Story," *American Review of Reviews*, November 1908, 632.

19. "Appalachian Fiction," review of *TLP*, *Independent*, 12 November 1908, *TLP* scrapbook, Fox Papers. The phrase "semi-savage" is from the *Pittsburg Press*, 25 October 1908, *TLP* scrapbook, Fox Papers. The extent of readers' confusion over the racial status of mountaineers is captured by a 1925 article that described Fox's mountaineers as both members of a "tribe" and as "Anglo-Saxon": "Here in these hills, like a lost tribe, he found a remnant of the true Anglo-Saxon stock" which "preserv[ed]" ancient "customs." Bruce Crawford, "When John Fox Danced His Last Dance," *Literary Digest*, October 1925. Elsewhere, Crawford (editor of *Crawford's Weekly*, published from Norton in southwestern Virginia) challenged fantasy visions of Appalachia. See David E. Whisnant, *All That Is Native and Fine: The Politics of Culture in an American Region* (Chapel Hill: University of North Carolina Press, 1983), 197; Bruce Crawford, "The Coal Miner," in *Culture in the South*, ed. William Terry Couch (Chapel Hill: University of North Carolina Press, 1935). On "tribe," see Jane Hill, "Coming to Terms with the Appalachian 'Other' in the Novels of Gail Godwin," *Journal of Kentucky Studies* 11 (1995): 98–105.

20. Hartley Davis and Clifford Smyth, "Land of Feuds," *Munsey's*, November 1903, 172; "Appalachian Fiction," *Independent*, 12 November 1908, 1121; "Mountain Romance by John Fox, Jr.," 70.

21. "Tonic" is from *New York Churchman*, 14 November 1908; "fresh from the wilds" is from review of *TLP*, *Christian Endeavor World* (Boston), 12 November 1908; "breath of inspiration" and "modern men and women" are from *Portland Oregonian*, 15 November 1908, all in *TLP* scrapbook, Fox Papers.

22. Sinclair Lewis, "Modernity and the Mountains," *New York Times Saturday Review of Books*, 4 December 1908.

23. Agnes Reppelier, "A Sheaf of Autumn Fiction," *Outlook*, 28 November 1908, 701; review of *TLP*, *Booklist*, December 1908, 268.

24. Review of *TLP*, *Baltimore Sun*, 22 November 1908; review of *TLP*, *Christian Endeavor World*, 12 November 1908; both in *TLP* scrapbook, Fox Papers.

25. As Darlene Wilson observes, "At the core of Fox's lectures and stories was a calculated invitation for his audience to visit the strange world of the mountains, speculate in coal options and railroad expansion, harvest the timber, send relief packages and school books, mine the coal, enjoy the scenery and flora, even fish a little." She notes that an "expanding railway network meant that Big Stone Gap was but a weekend excursion from most Eastern cities." Wilson, "The Felicitous Convergence," 27, 26.

26. York, *John Fox, Jr.*, 298–99n9, 217, 233.

27. "A Strong, Human, American Love Story"; "Current Fiction."

28. "Personal and Press Notices," undated circular, Fox Papers.

29. In one review of Fox, for example, Williams Dean Howells praised Murfree by arguing, "It is high testimony to the truth of her art that one working in the same field confirms the impression of its reality by his later observation and report" (quoted in "Personal and Press Notices"). Clark, "Mr. Fox's *The Trail of the Lonesome Pine*." See also "A Strong, Human, American Love Story."

30. In December 1894, Fox reported to Thomas Nelson Page that he had "grown somewhat scientific and have a lecture on 'the Southern Mountaineer,' which I may deliver before the Anthropological Society of Philadelphia and at Harvard" (Fox to Page, 1 December 1894, quoted in Harriet Holman, ed., *John Fox and Tom Page as They Were: Letters, an Address, and an Essay* [Miami: Field Research Projects, 1970], 20). Fox's "scientific" speeches were later published in magazines ("The Southern Mountaineer" appeared in *Scribner's*) and the collected volume *Blue-grass and Rhododendron* (1901) (Wilson, "The Felicitous Convergence," 25). Helen Wheeler Bassett, secretary, International Folk Lore Association, to Fox, 13 August [no year], Fox Papers.

31. Wilson, "The Felicitous Convergence," 30; York, *John Fox, Jr.*, 2, 27.

32. John Fox Jr., "Personal Sketch by John Fox, Jr., 1908," in Elizabeth Fox Moore, ed., *John Fox, Jr.: Personal and Family Letters and Papers* (Lexington: University of Kentucky Library Associates, 1955), 1–9, reprinted as "A Sketch," in Harriet Holman, "John Fox, Jr.: Appraisal and Self-Appraisal," *Southern Literary Journal* 3, no. 2 (1971), 25.

33. Fox's first publications were two sentimental short stories, "The Betrothal Ring" in *Frank Leslie's Illustrated Weekly*, 22 August 1885, and "Deceiver's Ever" in *New York Life*, 21 November 1885, 81. See York, *John Fox, Jr.*, 277.

34. Fox, unpublished autobiographical sketch, Fox Papers.

35. James Lane Allen (Cincinnati, Ohio) to Fox, 26 January 1894, *TLP* scrapbook, Fox Papers.

36. Fox, "A Story of Some Stories," unpublished manuscript, Fox Papers, quoted in York, *John Fox, Jr.*, 5. Fox, "Personal Sketch by John Fox, Jr., 1908."

37. "Appalachian Fiction," *Independent*, 12 November 1908; review of *TLP*, *Baltimore Sun*, 22 November 1908, *TLP* scrapbook, Fox Papers.

38. Review of *TLP*, *Congregationalist*, 21 November 1908, *TLP* scrapbook, Fox Papers.

39. The phrase "of the soil" is from "Mountain Romance by John Fox, Jr.," 78; "tale is American" is from review of *TLP*, *Congregationalist*; "intensely national note" is from "A Strong, Human, American Love Story."

40. The phrase "half-civilized" is from review of *TLP*, *Detroit Tribune*, ca. October–November 1908; "race and a type" and "remnant" are from review of *TLP*, *Richmond Dispatch*, 8 November 1908; both in *TLP* scrapbook, Fox Papers.

41. See Whisnant, *All That Is Native and Fine*.

42. Review of *TLP*, *St. Paul Dispatch*, 22 November 1908, *TLP* scrapbook, Fox Papers. As Jennifer Greeson has observed, Americans after the Civil War described and governed the South as a subordinated territory, thereby learning to imagine the nation as an imperial power on par with European colonial giants (*Our South: Geographic Fantasy and the Rise of National Literature* [Cambridge, MA: Harvard University Press, 2010], 14–15, 4).

43. Sam Budd mimes the sentiments professed by Joshua F. Bullitt in a letter thanking Fox for dedicating his book to Bullitt as one of the "first three captains of the guard." J. F. Bullitt (fan of *Blue-grass and Rhododendron*, Bullitt & Kelly, Attorneys at Law, Big Stone Gap, Virginia) to Fox, 8 October 1901, Fox Papers. Fox, "The Southern Mountaineer," *Blue-grass and Rhododendron: Out-doors in Old Kentucky* (Scribner 1901), 8. This same language appears in Fox's "scientific" speeches.

44. "Comment on Current Books," *Outlook*, 17 October 1908, 361.

45. "A Talk with John Fox, Jr., Author and Correspondent," *Milwaukee Sentinel*, 10 December 1900, 3. Fox had personally hoped to participate in imperial ventures and was disappointed he could not join his pen pal Roosevelt and his Rough Riders to wrest control of Cuba from Spain in 1898. Darlene Wilson makes a case for the imperialist nature of Fox's fiction in "The Felicitous Convergence." She notes that members of the Guard in attendance at the hanging of the notorious Talt Hall were photographed and sketched for national periodicals wearing "'uniforms' modeled after those of British military officers in India" (20). She also points to Fox's portrayal of mountain people as childlike as an instance of what Jerry Phillips describes as imperialism's "ideology of instruction" in which the "Other" is described as "savage," "infantile," "untutored," "backward," "undeveloped," and in need of "uplift." Wilson, "The Felicitous Convergence," 29–30, about Phillips, "Educating the Savages: Melville, Bloom and the Rhetoric of Imperialist Instruction," in *Recasting the World: Writing after Colonialism*, ed. Jonathan White (Baltimore: Johns Hopkins University

Press), 1994. See Emily Satterwhite, "Romancing Whiteness: Popular Appalachian Fiction and the Imperialist Imagination at the Turns of Two Centuries," in *At Home and Abroad: Historicizing Twentieth-Century Whiteness in Literature and Performance*, ed. La Vinia Delois Jennings (Knoxville: University of Tennessee Press, 2009), 102.

46. Agnes Reppelier, "A Sheaf of Autumn Fiction," *Outlook*, 28 November 1908, 701.

47. Frederic Remington (Endion, New Rochelle, New York) to Fox, n.d., box 4, Undated and Fragments, Fox Papers.

48. Arthur Wm. Barber (fan of *LSKC*, New York, New York) to Fox, 10 August 1910, box 4, Letters 1911–1920, Fox Papers; "Prizes Won at Cornell," *New York Times*, 21 June 1895.

49. Henry S. Whitehead (fan of *TLP*, assistant editor, *Port Chester Record*, New York) to Fox, 31 December 1908, *TLP* scrapbook, Fox Papers.

50. See Wilson, "A Judicious Combination," 117; and Wilson, foreword to *Heart of the Hills*, by John Fox Jr. (Lexington: University Press of Kentucky, 1996), viii.

51. A rare example of locally oriented readers committing their reactions to print (though not via letter writing) is a 1913 exchange in the *Madison County (NC) News Record* regarding an article published in a Missouri newspaper by a well-known rural-life expert after his brief visit to North Carolina. Madison County residents objected to Harold W. Foght's characterizations of the people and places he encountered on his trip, for which he relied heavily on Fox's *The Trail of the Lonesome Pine*. See Katie Algeo, "Locals on Local Color: Imagining Identity in Appalachia," *Southern Cultures* 4, no. 4 (2003), 27–54.

52. A published version of Tom Wallace's speech, given at the 24 October 1950 dedication of the John Fox, Jr. Library, is included in the John Fox Jr. scrapbook, John Fox Jr. Memorial Library, Duncan's Tavern, Paris, KY, but does not include original publication information. The clipping's headline, "9 Times," may be the title of the publication in which it appeared. Two visitors to Big Stone Gap, on the other hand, claimed that locals were not insulted by Fox. University of Kentucky history professor Thomas D. Clark asserted in 1934 that Fox had read his fiction aloud to "mountaineer friends" near Big Stone Gap "without offending," either because he read "so naturally that they took it as such" or because "they believed that the fellow quoted was on up the hollow" ("John Fox, Jr.," no. 1 of 2, radio address, WHAS, 28 November 1934, transcript housed at Duncan's Tavern and reprinted in *Paris Kentuckian-Citizen*, 16 January 1935). Similarly, EVB von Brandenburg, a visitor on business from New York, wrote in a note to Fox, "Imagine my delight when person after person in answer to questions has told me this day, that though you have written about these people, wrung narratives from them and their lives that they love you for the way you have done it in truth and with understanding sympathy" (von Brandenburg to

Fox, n.d., "Monday Evening 8:30," on letterhead from Monte Vista Hotel, Big Stone Gap, Fox Papers).

53. Horace Kephart, *Our Southern Highlanders: A Narrative of Adventure in the Southern Appalachians and a Study of Life among the Mountaineers* (Knoxville: University of Tennessee Press, 1913), 350.

54. Wilson, "The Felicitous Convergence," 24. Wilson draws from a review found in scrapbook no. 1, Fox Papers. William Frost recounts the event as evidence of mountaineers' ignorance of belles lettres in "Our Contemporary Ancestors in the Southern Mountains," *Atlantic Monthly*, March 1899, 316.

55. Fox, "On Horseback to Kingdom Come," *Scribner's*, August 1910, 177, 184. Fox, 177–78, wrote that the verdict "You are all right" was "cheering news, for it had not been always like this in the olden days. I recalled having no little trouble over my first book about the mountaineers, of just escaping a 'rough house' at the hands of some students of a mountain college, and of being often charged by educated mountaineers that I had not done them justice, and by 'furriners' [nonmountaineers] of having given the mountaineers credit for more than was their due." According to Wilson, Fox's fear of recrimination forced him to avoid eastern Kentucky and parts of southwestern Virginia between 1885 and 1910 and to use caution, even after that time, about revealing his identity when in the mountains. "A Judicious Combination," 118; "The Felicitous Convergence," 30.

56. Fox, "On the Trail of the Lonesome Pine," *Scribner's*, October 1910, 428. The girl's savvy regarding local-color depictions is further evidenced by her reassurance to her father that his ragged breeches and unkempt appearance were "just the way they want you" in a photograph taken by the artist accompanying Fox (429). Fox similarly describes discovering a girl just like the *Little Shepherd* character Melissa in his essay "On Horseback to Kingdom Come," *Scribner's*, August 1910, 182–83.

57. Fox, "On the Trail of the Lonesome Pine, " 428.

58. Fox, "Personal Sketch," 9. Also, for example, Fox autographed the back of an L&N train schedule for a mountain resident with "John Fox Jr. 1903—*Guilty of 'Hell-fer'Sartin'* [sic] and other stories of home-life in the South." Reported by Wilson, who now owns the autograph, in "A Judicious Combination," 118.

59. See Wilson's argument regarding the "utility" (100) of Fox's fiction for middle-class Kentuckians in "A Judicious Combination."

60. B. A. Logan (fan of *TLP*, principal, Shelby Graded School, Shelbyville, Kentucky) to Fox, 6 April 1909, *TLP* scrapbook, Fox Papers. Francis W. H. Clay (fan of *LSKC*, grandson of Cassius M. Clay, "formerly of Whitehall, Kentucky," Pittsburgh, Pennsylvania) to Fox, 26 February 1904, retyped, box 4, Letters, 1904–1910, Fox Papers.

61. No name (fan of *Little Shepherd of Kingdom Come*) to Fox, August 1903, retyped, box 3, Letters, 1899–1903, Fox Papers.

62. Mrs. Jackson Hendrick (fan of *TLP*, Hendrick, Abberley & Hendrick let-

terhead, New York, New York) to Fox, 17 October 1908, *TLP* scrapbook, Fox Papers.

63. James Beauchamp ("Champ") Clark, Speaker of the House of Representatives, wrote that he read Fox's *Little Shepherd of Kingdom Come* due to a familiarity with Kentucky University. He "sat up all night to read it" and pronounced it "the best novel written in the United States within the last 25 years" and "one of the very few books that give the border state soldiers anything like a fair deal." Champ Clark (fan of *LSKC*, The Speaker's Rooms, House of Representatives letterhead, Washington, DC) to Fox, 6 May 1918, box 4, Letters, 1911–1920, Fox Papers.

64. Rev. R. W. Cleland (fan of *LSKC*, Long Beach, California) to Fox, September 1903, retyped, box 3, Letters, 1899–1903, Fox Papers.

65. York, *John Fox, Jr.*, 183. Currie Duke Mathews (fan-acquaintance, Lenox, Massachusetts) to Fox, 16 October 1903, box 3, Letters, 1899–1903, Fox Papers.

66. The United States instituted public education in 1870. The state of Virginia instituted compulsory education, for several months per year, in 1908 (Katrina M. Powell, *The Anguish of Displacement: The Politics of Literacy in the Letters of Mountain Families in Shenandoah National Park* [Charlottesville: University of Virginia Press, 2007], 22).

67. For examination of a slightly earlier manifestation of these anxieties and ambitions, see Brian Luskey, *On the Make: Clerks and the Quest for Capital in Nineteenth-Century America* (New York: New York University Press, 2010).

68. Una M. Crawford (fan of *TLP*, Stonewall Jackson College, Abingdon, Virginia) to Fox, 24 November 1917, box 4, Letters, 1911–1920, Fox Papers.

69. William E. [Elsey] Connelley (fan of *TLP*, Topeka, Kansas) to Fox, 28 March 1912, *TLP* scrapbook, Fox Papers. For more on Connelley, see John Wilson Townsend's hagiographic "William E. Connelley," *Kentucky in American Letters, 1784–1912* (Cedar Rapids, IA: Torch, 1913), 2:63–65. According to Townsend, Fox "sat at the feet of the historian [Connelley] and learned of his people"—though the date of Connelley's letter of introduction suggests that if this scenario occurred, it occurred years after Fox published his first two best sellers (64).

70. Connelley hints at the exclusionary racial dimensions of his regional pride when he mentions bragging to a friend that he had "secured the votes of fifteen hundred negroes," something "only a mountaineer could have done." William E. [Elsey] Connelley (fan of *TLP*, Topeka, Kansas) to Fox, 28 March 1912, *TLP* scrapbook, Fox Papers.

71. Rita Parker (fan of *TLP*, Mobile, Alabama) to Fox, 21 February 1908, *TLP* scrapbook, Fox Papers. Parker included a poem she wrote about a pine tree.

72. Kent Brooklyn Stiles (fan of *The Little Shepherd of Kingdom Come*, seventeen years old, Brooklyn) to Fox, 8 September 1904, box 4, Letters, 1904–1910, Fox Papers. Subsequent references to *The Little Shepherd of Kingdom Come* will be abbreviated as *LSKC*.

73. Fred Brewster (fan of *TLP*, West Hartlepool, England) to Fox, 27 February 1908, *TLP* scrapbook, Fox Papers.

74. Signature illegible (fan of *TLP*, Eldora, Iowa) to Fox, 17 January 1911, box 4, Letters, 1911–1920, Fox Papers.

75. W. P. Matheney (fan of *TLP* and *A Knight of the Cumberland* [1906]) to Fox, 6 March 1911, *TLP* scrapbook, Fox Papers.

76. Francis W. H. Clay (fan of *LSKC*, Pittsburgh, Pennsylvania) to Fox, 26 February 1904, retyped, box 4, Letters, 1904–1910, Fox Papers.

77. Louis Nesom (fan, Los Angeles, California), 1 November 1910, box 4, Letters, 1904–1910, Fox Papers.

78. S. S. Burch (fan of "your several books," VP and secretary, Brand Shoe Company, Inc., Roanoke, Virginia) to Fox, 8 October 1910, box 4, Letters, 1911–1920, Fox Papers.

79. W. H. Witten (fan of *TLP*, St. Albans, West Virginia) to Fox, 18 March 1919, box 4, Letters, 1911–1920, Fox Papers. The phrase "rough, wild lands" is from review of *TLP*, *Boston Herald*, 17 October 1908; "Life is lived there, not evaded" is from review of *TLP*, *St. Paul Dispatch*, 22 November 1908, both in *TLP* scrapbook, Fox Papers. E. D. Bostick, "representing M. Cohen Son & Co, converters, jobbers, mill agents white goods, dry goods and notions, Richmond Va," hoped to "place . . . in the hands of someone who has the ability to handle them" some "facts and legends that have come down traditionally from my ancestors" regarding Indians, planters, the "faithfull Negro," and lower-class whites similar to Fox's *Little Shepherd* characters and those of "Thomas Dixons 'Clansman.'" Bostick, like Witten, had extensive migratory experiences, which were underscored by his revisions to his letterhead. A location printed after Richmond on the letterhead, "Camden, S.C.," was crossed out and replaced with a handwritten "Atlanta, Ga." Below the dateline, Bostick noted that he wrote from New York City. In keeping with his proposed storyline, his primary geographic identification was with "the Savannah River Valley." E. D. Bostick (fan of "On Horseback," Atlanta, Georgia) to Fox, 4 August 1910, box 4, Letters, 1911–1920, Fox Papers.

80. Richard H. Brodhead, *Cultures of Letters: Scenes of Reading and Writing in Nineteenth-Century America* (Chicago: University of Chicago Press, 1994), 120.

81. Fox, "On Horseback to Kingdom Come," 175.

82. S. B. Chapman (fan of "On Horseback," Kanawha Hardwood Company letterhead, Andrews, North Carolina) to Fox, 4 August 1910, box 4, Letters, 1911–1920, Fox Papers. Chapman addressed his letter "Dear John." From this and other context clues, it appears that Chapman and Fox were friends.

83. Remarks of Mrs. Stephen T. Davis, state historian, at the dedication of the John Fox Jr. Memorial Library, Fox scrapbook, John Fox Jr. Memorial Library.

84. Hatfield, *Never Seen the Moon*, 44–45.

85. Catherine Jurca, *White Diaspora: The Suburb and the Twentieth-Century*

American Novel (Princeton: Princeton University Press, 2001), 5, 6, 8; Barbara Sicherman, "Reading and Middle-Class Identity in Victorian America: Cultural Consumption, Conspicuous and Otherwise," in *Reading Acts: U.S. Readers' Interactions with Literature, 1800–1950*, ed. Barbara Ryan and Amy M. Thomas (Knoxville: University of Tennessee Press, 2002), 137–55.

86. Fox Sr. built a private school for locals and boarders behind his home on the Paris-Winchester road in Bourbon County. The family was committed to the trappings of refinement (Fox's father bought a piano for him when he was six years old), but the Foxes often had to perform odd jobs such as selling grass seed in Lexington in order to make ends meet. Biographical information about Fox's childhood is taken from chapter 2 of York's biography, *John Fox, Jr.* According to York, none of the Foxes' neighbors had more material goods, "and many had less." Fox's piano is mentioned in a brochure, *John Fox, Jr.*, written in 1995 by his distant cousin Bettie J. Tuttle of Lexington, Kentucky, and distributed by the Daughters of the American Revolution branch in Paris, Kentucky (copy in possession of the author thanks to Tuttle).

87. On financial straits and the Garth Fund for Poor Boys, see York, *John Fox, Jr.*, 29; Wilson, "The Felicitous Convergence," 10. On feeling homesick in Cambridge: shortly after the holidays in 1882, Micajah Fible of Louisville wrote home to his sister that "all the Kentucky boys—Berryman, Drane, Fox & Davis are here, & Christmas is by no means not lively," Betty Fible Martin, *John Fox Letters: 1883–1889*, Barrett Collection, University of Virginia, quoted in York, *John Fox, Jr.*, 30. In 1881, Fox wrote to his mother "I shall be very glad to get some of your fried-chicken for I haven't had any since I left Ky. People don't live here as well as we do in Kentucky" (24 April 1881, Fox Papers). "Cleanse him of the city" is York's paraphrase of a letter from Fox to his mother, 5 June 1884, in *John Fox, Jr.*, 45. In another letter home, Fox claimed that he did not "think much of these fashionable people" he met through his classmates yet he was often frustrated that financial straits kept him from parties, society circles, and career opportunities (Fox to his mother, 23 November 1883, Fox Papers, quoted in York, *John Fox, Jr.*, 42). Fox took a banjo with him to Harvard, and reports of his time on the lecture circuit suggest he knew how to play the instrument. He sold it to fund his time in Cambridge. After Fox's college graduation and before his widening circle of contacts allowed him to accept invitations from other writers and artists in cities around the country, his ability to move back and forth between rural Kentucky and New York City depended largely upon the open arms of his parents in Bourbon County and of his older half brother Sidney, a physician in New York.

88. York, *John Fox, Jr.*, 41; James Fox to Fox, 29 July 1883, Fox Papers, quoted in York, *John Fox, Jr.*, 39; Fox to Micajah Fible, 13 May 1887, collected in Martin, *John Fox Letters*, 89, quoted in York, *John Fox, Jr.*, 55.

89. See Matt, "You Can't Go Home Again."

3. Country to City, circa 1949–1954

1. Barbara L. Baer, "Harriette Arnow's Chronicles of Destruction," in *Harriette Simpson Arnow: Critical Essays on Her Work*, ed. Haeja K. Chung (East Lansing: Michigan State University Press, 1995), 53, reprinted from *Nation*, 31 January 1976, 117–20; "Introduction to *Mountain Path*, First Appalachian Heritage Edition," 1963, reprinted in Chung, *Harriette Simpson Arnow*, 247.

For more on out-migration from Appalachia, see Phillip J. Obermiller, "Migration," in *High Mountains Rising: Appalachia in Time and Place*, ed. Richard Straw and H. Tyler Blethen (Urbana: University of Illinois Press, 2004), 88–100; Phillip J. Obermiller and Ray Rappold, "Bury Me Not in a Sidewalk: The Appalachian Way of Death in the Cities," *Now and Then: The Appalachian Magazine*, Summer 1990, 28–29; Kathryn M. Borman and Phillip J. Obermiller, eds., *From Mountain to Metropolis: Appalachian Migrants in American Cities* (Westport, CT: Bergin & Garvey, 1994); Roger Guy, "A Common Ground: Urban Adaptation and Appalachian Unity," in *Appalachian Odyssey: Historical Perspectives on the Great Migration*, ed. Phillip J. Obermiller, Thomas E. Wagner, E. Bruce Tucker (Westport, CT: Praeger, 2000), 49–66.

2. Eve Silberman, "Harriette Arnow: Ann Arbor's Most Acclaimed Novelist, Author of *The Dollmaker*, Shuns the Literary Scene," *Ann Arbor Observer*, 3 March 1980, quoted in Ballard, "Harriette Simpson Arnow's Life as a Writer," 22–23. Covici-Friede, the publisher that released *Mountain Path* in 1936, went bankrupt in 1938. See Chris Green, *The Social Life of Poetry: Appalachia, Race, and Radical Modernism* (New York: Palgrave Macmillan, 2009), 197. By the time Arnow's readers met her hill-country characters in Detroit, Arnow's first novel was out of print and virtually impossible to locate. Correspondent after correspondent attested that they had read *Hunter's Horn* after falling in love with *The Dollmaker* but could not locate *Mountain Path*, and begged Arnow to lend or sell them a copy. See Correspondence Series, Harriette Simpson Arnow Papers, Special Collections and Digital Programs, University of Kentucky Libraries, Lexington, hereinafter cited as Arnow Papers. All correspondence cited below is from this collection.

3. The greater success of the second and third novels might also be attributed to the greater marketing reach of Macmillan versus that of Arnow's first publisher, Covici-Friede.

4. Joyce Carol Oates, "On Harriette Arnow's *The Dollmaker*," in Danny Miller, Sharon Hatfield, and Gurney Norman, *An American Vein: Critical Readings in Appalachian Literature* (Athens: Ohio University Press, 2005), 59. Unlike John Fox, Catherine Marshall, and James Dickey, Arnow did not reach the top ten best sellers of the year list with either of her books. See Alice Payne Hackett and James Henry Burke, *80 Years of Best Sellers, 1895–1975* (New York: Bowker, 1977).

5. *Hunter's Horn* was named one of the year's ten best novels by the *New*

York Times Book Review; the *Saturday Review*'s "national critics' poll voted it best novel of the year." Sandra L. Ballard, "Harriette Simpson Arnow's Life as a Writer," in Chung, *Harriette Simpson Arnow*, 26. *Hunter's Horn* was so well received that observers widely believed that Arnow would win the Pulitzer Prize for Literature in 1949. See Orville Prescott, "Books of the Times," *New York Times*, 6 July 1949, 25. *The Dollmaker* revived rumors that Arnow would win the Pulitzer. See Paul Jordan-Smith, "Recent Polls Indicate '*Dollmaker*' Merits Pulitzer Prize Judges' Consideration," Books and Authors, *Los Angeles Times*, 11 June 1954, D6. *The Dollmaker* was a runner-up for the National Book Award (William Faulkner won for *A Fable*) and the *Saturday Review*'s critics' poll named it the best novel of the year. See Ballard, "Harriette Simpson Arnow's Life as a Writer," 26.

6. As Chad Berry has noted, no move was ever "permanent." By the 1960s, the population of the Tennessee Valley region increased significantly, though cities grew more than rural areas (207–8). Relatively close proximity allowed for a great deal of shuttling between the Midwest and places of origin (212); visits of several months were not uncommon (124). Even out-migrants who spent their entire careers in the Midwest often moved again upon retirement, including sometimes back home to care for aging parents (208). *Southern Migrants, Northern Exiles* (Urbana: University of Illinois Press, 2000).

7. Gunnar Almgren, "Community," 244n17, in *Encyclopedia of Sociology*, ed. Edgar F. Borgatta and Rhonda J. V. Montgomery (New York: Macmillan, 2000), 362–69, quoted in David C. Hsiung, *Two Worlds in the Tennessee Mountains: Exploring the Origins of Appalachian Stereotypes* (Lexington: University Press of Kentucky, 1997), 7.

8. Glenda Hobbs, "Harriette Simpson Arnow," in *Dictionary of Literary Biography: American Novelists since World War II*, second series, vol. 6, ed. James E. Kibler Jr. (Detroit: Gale, 1980), 3–8. Sandra Ballard and Haeja Chung credit Arnow with having "developed empathy with the poor" from a very young age. Introduction to *The Collected Short Stories of Harriette Simpson Arnow*, ed. Sandra L. Ballard and Haeja K. Chung (East Lansing: Michigan State University Press, 2005), ix.

9. For a discussion of the elision of biographical details in order to ensure the perception of fiction's authenticity, see Jennifer Rae Greeson, "The 'Mysteries and Miseries' of North Carolina: New York City, Urban Gothic Fiction, and *Incidents in the Life of a Slave Girl*," *American Literature: A Journal of Literary History, Criticism, and Bibliography* 73, no. 2 (2001): 277–309.

10. In this regard, Arnow's fiction served a function filled in an earlier era by radio. The National Barn Dance on WLS in Chicago in the 1920s "became a palliative, profitable, and alternative salve countering" the urban diversity represented on other stations. Chad Berry, "Introduction: Assessing the National Barn Dance," in *The Hayloft Gang: The Story of the National Barn Dance*, ed. Chad Berry (Urbana: University of Illinois Press, 2008), 5. WLS appealed to those who

"feared the loss of connectedness" (10, referencing Paul L. Tyler's chapter, "The Rise of Rural Rhythm," 19–71). In the 1930s, the country's search for the authentic centered in part on crafts from the South. See Jane S. Becker, *Selling Tradition: Appalachia and the Construction of an American Folk, 1930–1940* (Chapel Hill: University of North Carolina Press, 1998).

11. Irving and Freda Weissman (fans of *The Dollmaker*, New York, New York) to Arnow, 12 November 1962; Helen (Mrs. Ira) Wolfert (fan of *The Dollmaker* and *Hunter's Horn*, Lake Hill, Ulster County, New York) to Arnow, 7 August 1954; Mrs. Hans Zinsser (fan of *Hunter's Horn*, New York, New York) to Arnow, 27 October 1949. Subsequent references to *The Dollmaker* will be abbreviated as *D. Hunter's Horn* will be abbreviated as *HH*.

12. Music was another significant outlet for out-migrants' desire to reflect upon rural pasts. See Berry, introduction to *The Hayloft Gang*; and Berry, *Southern Migrants*, 155–66.

13. James N. Gregory, *The Southern Diaspora: How the Great Migrations of Black and White Southerners Transformed America* (Chapel Hill: University of North Carolina Press, 2005), 11, 14–15.

14. Berry, *Southern Migrants*, 62, 84–86.

15. Wayne W. Daniel, "Music of the Postwar Era," in Berry, *The Hayloft Gang*, 72; Michael T. Bertrand, "Race and Rural Identity," in Berry, *The Hayloft Gang*, 130–52.

16. Jesse Stuart's 1943 *Taps for Private Tussie*, which made the *New York Times* best-seller list for just 3 weeks, is the only exception. The popularity of Betty MacDonald's *The Egg and I* (1947), about her move to a farm in Washington State, also points to metropolitan desires regarding the rural during this period; it appeared on the best-seller lists for a total of 187 weeks. Keith L. Justice, *Bestseller Index: All Books, Publishers Weekly and the* New York Times *through 1990* (Jefferson, NC: McFarland, 1998), 202.

17. Marcella Ahal (friend) to Arnow, 28 June 1954.

18. George H. Latham (fan of *HH*, Wilmington, Delaware) to Arnow, 10 January 1950.

19. Mrs. Delbert Moore (fan of *D*, Blanchester, Ohio) to Arnow, 26 and 30 November 1954. Berry finds that out-migrants were divided on the question of burial in the North or South. Some chose to be buried in the North near their children while others were "quite adamant about being interred" in a favored place back home (*Southern Migrants*, 211). See Dot Jackson, "The Ideal Home: Return from Flatland Exile," *Now and Then: The Appalachian Magazine*, Spring 1988, 5–6; "The Green Hills of Home Far Away," *Now and Then: The Appalachian Magazine*, Spring 1990, 5–7; and especially Obermiller and Rappold, "Bury Me Not in a Sidewalk," 28–29.

20. R. L. Cassell (fan of *D* and *HH*, Cadiz, Ohio) to Arnow, 25 October 1954.

21. Berry, *Southern Migrants*, suggests that perhaps chronology may provide a clue to class, given that migrants in the earlier decades of the twen-

tieth century seem to him to have been better educated than midcentury migrants.

22. Undated letter from Arnow to her editor Granville Hicks, quoted in Sandra L. Ballard, introduction to *Hunter's Horn*, by Harriette Simpson Arnow (East Lansing: Michigan State University Press, 1997), v–xv. Ballard speculates that the letter was written in July or August 1949 (xi). AAA refers to the Agricultural Adjustment Act; the agricultural extension service agent who serves as a resource to Nunn Ballew is similar to a present-day county extension agent.

23. Harriette Simpson Arnow, *Hunter's Horn* (East Lansing: Michigan State University Press, 1997), 263. Further references to this novel are to this edition and are cited parenthetically in the text as *HH*.

24. Haeja K. Chung, "Fictional Characters Come to Life: An Interview," in Chung, *Harriette Simpson Arnow*, 278.

25. Other characters' gains from city employment complicate this picture further. The no-good Willie Cooksey returns from work in the Midwest with a "big range cookstove." Granted, Arnow makes tragicomic the Cookseys' attempt to haul in the appliance: "Willie nearly killed his mule and then he almost killed himself and all his family" installing the monstrous stove (*HH*, 241–42). But Lureenie's inability to cook for her children because she is too weak to collect firewood makes it impossible to completely dismiss the Cookseys' new advantage.

26. Though Arnow genders "love of land" as feminine through Gertie, Berry finds that "many of the men interviewed were much more homesick than women" because "urban areas often made life easier and more pleasant for women" (*Southern Migrants*, 147; see also Berry's interview with Hollye War, 121).

27. The "grim side of life on Little Smokey Creek is always present" in *Hunter's Horn* (Orville Prescott, "Books of the Times," *New York Times*, 31 May 1949, 25, Arnow Papers). *The Dollmaker* "is grim enough, it must be admitted, but it is not a bleakly depressing book" (Orville Prescott, "Books of the Times," *New York Times*, 20 April 1954, 27, Arnow Papers).

28. Prescott, "Books of the Times," 31 May 1949; Sterling North, "A Classic of the Kentucky Hills," review of *Hunter's Horn*, *New York Post*, 31 May 1949, Arnow Papers. The *New York Post* reviewer went so far as to claim that *Hunter's Horn* "is a quiet reproof to those of us who have overemphasized the echoes of Elizabethan phraseology and balladry among the English and Scotch-Irish mountaineers," suggesting that Arnow's novel had a far different effect than best sellers before it. Prescott insisted that the "regional setting is secondary" in *Hunter's Horn*, and "not caricatured . . . not sentimentalized."

29. Reviewers' quotes are taken from the following: "hunting companions," Prescott, "Books of the Times," 31 May 1949; "molasses making," A. J. Beeler, "Fox Hunt in Kentucky," *Louisville Courier-Journal*, 5 June 1949; "Bible-quoting," North, "A Classic of the Kentucky Hills"; "mountain men," "canned stuff," and "bastard," Florence Haxton Bullock, "Kentucky Hill Folk, Vividly Seen," *New York Herald Tribune*, 5 June 1949, all in Arnow Papers.

30. Only two critics mentioned that *Hunter's Horn* takes place in the years immediately preceding Pearl Harbor, as a Macmillan press release explained (Jane Voiles, "A Bookman's Notebook/Novel of Kentucky," review of *Hunter's Horn*, *L.A. Times*, 7 June 1949, A5; John Cournos, review of *Hunter's Horn*, *New York* [*Sun?*], 31 May 1949). Book reviews of *Hunter's Horn*, Arnow Papers. Only three mentioned industrial activities in Kentucky: Bullock, "Kentucky Hill Folk, Vividly Seen"; Paul Jordan-Smith, "Kentucky Lore Told in Bitter Farm Tale: Story of Family Bedeviled by Fox Related with Zest, Humor, Pathos," review of *HH*, *L.A. Times*, 29 May 1949; and Prescott, "Books of the Times," 20 April 1954, 27. Bullock in the *Herald Tribune* alone noted the significance of modern arrivals that concerned Arnow, including "the AAA and the county agent," and the gravel road that "links the Ballew farm with the outside world and sends a school bus past the house."

31. The one exception is from one of Arnow's former professors; by way of praise for *Hunter's Horn* he enthused, "One sees the house, ugly, bare, very clean." William J. Hutchins (fan-acquaintance, St. Louis, Ohio) to Arnow, 27 June 1949.

32. Mrs. Hattie Abner (fan of *D* and *HH*, Tapcheedah, Wisconsin) to Arnow, 1 July 1954; Mrs. Jessie M. Reaves (fan of *D* and *HH*, Oberlin, Ohio) to Arnow, 26 December 1955. Out-migrant Mrs. Clyde Burnette praised the novel for "pictur[ing] the hill people as decent and God Fearing where some authors, Jesse Stuart, for one, picture them as trash." Mrs. Clyde Burnette (fan of *HH*, thirty-nine years old, Monticello, Kentucky, and Peoria, Illinois) to Arnow, 10 May 1954.

33. Mrs. Clyde Burnette (fan of *HH*, thirty-nine years old, Monticello, Kentucky, and Peoria, Illinois) to Arnow, 10 May 1954.

34. Helen Wolfert (fan of *HH*, Lake Hill, Ulster County, New York) to Arnow, 7 August 1950; Leah Jones (fan of *HH*, Lebanon, Ohio) to Arnow, 15 January 1950. See also Jennie Broujos (fan of *HH*, Wilmington, Delaware) to Arnow, 30 November 1949.

35. Danny L. Miller, "Harriette Simpson Arnow and Harold Arnow in Cincinnati: 1934–1939," in Chung, *Harriette Simpson Arnow*, 39; Ballard, "Harriette Simpson Arnow's Life as a Writer," 24–29. For biographical information, see also Ballard and Chung, introduction to *The Collected Short Stories of Harriette Simpson Arnow*, vii–xvii. Arnow's works of nonfiction are *Seedtime on the Cumberland* (1960) and *Flowering of the Cumberland* (1963). Her other works include two novels, *The Weedkiller's Daughter* (1970), set in suburban Michigan, and *The Kentucky Trace* (1974), as well as the autobiographical *Old Burnside* (1977). The 1983 awards included the Milner Award and Berea College's Outstanding Alumni Award.

36. Macmillan Co., "Advance News of Books," 18 April 1949, 1; Macmillan Co., biography of Arnow, n.d., both in Arnow Papers. Macmillan provided no information about Arnow other than that she was the author of *Hunter's Horn*

with its description of *The Dollmaker* in either its Spring 1954 *New Books* catalogue, 9, or its *Macmillan Library News*, April 1954, 1. Archived advertisements offered no additional biographical information. All in Arnow Papers.

37. The phrase "recorded with authentic skill" is from John Cournos, "Book Reviews," review of *HH*, *New York Sun*, 31 May 1949; "earthy reporting" and "Having lived all her life" are from North, "A Classic of the Kentucky Hills"; "familiarity" is from Beeler, "Fox Hunt in Kentucky"; "close observation" is from Bullock, "Kentucky Hill Folk, Vividly Seen."

38. At least one professional reviewer, however, attempted to navigate between documentary accuracy and the creativity required for great literature. The *New York Herald Tribune* critic takes great pains to assert that "*The Dollmaker* could only have been written out of intimate knowledge" and mentions Arnow's farm "in the Cumberland National Forest" but he also notes that "only an extraordinary talent . . . can explain the novel which she fashioned in part from her experience." Coleman Rosenberger, "A Novel of Extraordinary Power, One That Will Be Long Remembered," *New York Herald Tribune*, 25 April 1954, Arnow Papers.

39. Harnett T. Kane, "The Transplanted Folk," *New York Times*, 25 April 1954, BR4; Harrison Smith, "Lead Review of the Week," Book Service for Newspapers, 24 April 1954, Arnow Papers.

40. Harriette Simpson Arnow, introduction to reprint of *Mountain Path* (Berea, KY: Council of the Southern Mountains, 1963), v.

41. These biographical details are available in Ballard, "Harriette Simpson Arnow's Life as a Writer," 16–17, based on Arnow's autobiography, *Old Burnside* (Lexington: University Press of Kentucky, 1977), 29, 118, 121.

42. Miller, "Harriette Simpson Arnow and Harold Arnow," 38.

43. Helen Wolfert (fan of *HH*, Lake Hill, Ulster County, New York) to Arnow, 7 August 1949; Claudine Lewis (fan of *D* and *HH*, Mayfield, Kentucky, on the letterhead of U.S. House of Representatives, Noble J. Gregory) to Arnow, 7 May 1954. See also Mrs. Katherine Wolbarst (fan of *D*, Lake Como, Pennsylvania, and Park Avenue, New York, New York) to Arnow, 10 August 1954, who wrote: "I cannot believe this work is a novel. You must have *known* these people."

44. Baer, "Harriette Arnow's Chronicles of Destruction," 58; Chung, "Fictional Characters," 273, 278, 270. Hicks, the son of a foundry manager and a prominent Marxist literary critic, had his own reasons to want to see the author as a working-class hero like Gertie given his concern with the dislocations of industrialism, his faith in small towns, and his agreement with Karl Marx that literature had failed to grapple with capitalism effectively due to the fact that most writers were members of the bourgeoisie (Steven Rosendale, "Granville Hicks," in *Twentieth-Century American Cultural Theorists*, ed. Paul Hansom, *Dictionary of Literary Biography*, vol. 246 [Detroit: Gale, 2001]). Hicks hoped to "renew a more purely proletarian writing" (Green, *The Social Life of Poetry*, 169).

45. Jeff Karem notes that "demands for authenticity all too often confine marginal authors and their texts to narrowly representative positions, circumscribing both what they are able to produce and to publish and how their works are received." *The Romance of Authenticity: The Cultural Politics of Regional and Ethnic Literatures* (Charlottesville: University of Virginia Press, 2004), 15.

46. Migration was segregated. Some cities, like Akron in the 1920s, received very few African Americans from the South. Others, like Youngstown, Gary, and Cleveland, received a relatively low proportion of white immigrants. The relatively high proportion of white instead of black migrants to Detroit allows for this imagination of migration as a white phenomenon. Berry, *Southern Migrants*, 34. On the relation between pastoral and urban local color, see Stephanie Foote, *Regional Fictions: Culture and Identity in Nineteenth-Century American Literature* (Madison: University of Wisconsin Press, 2001), 123–24.

47. See Bertrand, "Race and Rural Identity," 130–52, for his discussion of the construction of whiteness via popular representations of put-upon rural people. See also Thomas J. Sugrue, *The Origins of the Urban Crisis: Race and Inequality in Postwar Detroit* (Princeton: Princeton University Press, 1996), on the fluid racial order after World War II. On the prevalence of disdain for the suburbs, see Catherine Jurca, *White Diaspora: The Suburb and the Twentieth-Century American Novel* (Princeton: Princeton University Press, 2001); and Amy L. Blair, "Main Street Reading *Main Street*," in *New Directions in American Reception Study*, ed. Philip Goldstein and James L. Machor (New York: Oxford University Press, 2008), 139–58. The tensions among hillbillies, Poles, and Irish Catholics in *The Dollmaker* may have seemed reassuringly quaint compared to the racial strife that reared its head in Detroit and other urban centers after the war.

48. John Cournos, "Book Reviews," review of *HH*, *New York Sun*, 31 May 1949, Arnow Papers. See also Smith, "Lead Review of the Week."

49. Smith, "Lead Review of the Week." See also Gertie "finds life away from the earth almost impossible" despite her poverty ("The Dollmaker," *Chicago Daily Tribune*, 18 April 1954, D3); Kentucky represents a "life of sure values" and for Gertie "the land holds the promise of security and fulfillment, a good life" (Rosenberger, "A Novel of Extraordinary Power, One That Will Be Long Remembered").

50. Frustrated by the dialect and bored by the "long, diffuse, monotonous" story, reviewers in the *Times* (London), the *Daily Worker* (London), and the *Manchester Evening News* were far less taken than American reviewers with ugly, brawny Gertie and what they saw as her coarse countryness. Margaret Lane, "Happy Marriage," *Sunday Times* (London), 10 July 1955; Judy Martin, "Soothing Medicine—for the Conscience," *Daily Worker* (London), 4 August 1955; "The Dollmaker," *Manchester Evening News*, 6 August 1955, all in Arnow Papers.

51. Macmillan Co., "Advance News of Books." Prescott, "Books of the Times."

52. Books like *The Lonely Crowd* (1950) argued that suburbanization promoted conformity yet subverted true companionship.

53. Historically, the United States is among the most mobile nations in the world. Increased homeownership may have reduced mobility for some following WWII, but nonetheless 20 percent of Americans moved every year from the 1940s to the 1970s. James T. Patterson, *Grand Expectations: The United States, 1945–1974* (New York: Oxford University Press, 1996), 66.

54. Martha (Mrs. E. L.) Henes, (fan of *D*, Wellington, Ohio) to Arnow, 26 October 1954.

55. Alice (Mrs. H. W.) Lloyd (fan of *D* and *HH*, Dedham, Massachusetts) to Arnow, 6 January 1956. Lloyd acknowledged a connection to Alice Lloyd College: "For over twenty years it has been my privilege to lend a small helping hand to a namesake of mine, one Alice Lloyd of Caney Creek, Pippa Passes, KY."

56. Gertrude (Mrs. J. T.) Snodgrass (fan of *D*, Elgin, Illinois) to Arnow, 21 February 1954.

57. L. Ramsay (fan of *HH*, Burnt Hills, New York) to Arnow, 12 December 1949.

58. Mr. W. W. Duck (fan of *HH*, Sheffield, England) to Arnow, 10 March 1951; Mrs. Hans Zinsser (fan of *HH*, New York City, New York) to Arnow, 27 October 1949.

59. Ferne Denney (fan-acquaintance of *D*, Berea, Kentucky) to Arnow, 3 February 1955. This may be the same Ferne Denney who later became Dr. Ferne Denney Garret, chairperson of the antipoverty organization Christian Women's Job Corp of Lee County, Alabama, and director of the 21st Century Leadership Academy for the improvement of schools at Auburn University. Ozro F. Grant (fan of *D*, Tulare, California) to Arnow, 6 November 1954.

60. Mrs. Fowler Curtis (fan of *D* and *HH*, forty-five years old, Rosiclare, Illinois) to Arnow, 3 August 1954. Rana Vaught provides another example of being from the mountains but not feeling of the same class background as mountain characters: "I was born in the Ky mountains and love them very much. . . . I know quite a bit about the Cumberland Mt. Country tho we were not as poor as some people were in the real hill country." Mrs. Rana Vaught (fan of *D*/all, Cincinnati, Ohio) to Arnow, 10 October 1954.

61. Frank Hines belongs to this group, partly rooting for rural people, whom he understood from firsthand experience, and partly casting a sociological eye upon them. Raised in southern Illinois, Hines remembered fondly rural people's "pride in themselves for what they like and believe important." Hines contrasted rural pride to the pride that "people who live in the big cities" have "because their parents and bosses have demonstrated [the city's] rightness." Frank Hines (fan, Hawken School, Cleveland, Ohio,) to Arnow, 27 March 1950.

62. Mrs. Charles S. Stowell (fan of *HH*, Seattle, Washington) to Arnow, 24 July 1961.

63. Susan J. Matt, "You Can't Go Home Again: Homesickness and Nostalgia in U.S. History," *Journal of American History* 92, no. 4 (2007): 497, 494.

64. Minnie (Mrs. Herbert H.) Holt (fan of *D* and *HH*, Lee's Summit, Mis-

souri) to Arnow, 5 February 1955; Irene Watt (fan of *D*, Ypsilanti, Michigan) to Arnow, 8 December 1962; R. L. Cassell (fan of *D* and *HH*, Cadiz, Ohio) to Arnow, 25 October 1954.

65. See Bertrand, "Race and Rural Identity," 137, for his discussion of letters to radio station WLS that use the opportunity to regale presumed readers with stories of rural home places and ways. See Matt on Americans' use of consumer objects to assuage the pangs of displacement after World War II: "Acting on feelings of nostalgia, they try to fashion a home in a new location and a new era from the materials at hand." "You Can't Go Home Again," 497.

66. Mildred Schulze (fan of *HH*, Detroit, Michigan) to Arnow, 23 December 1949.

67. John Wilson Townsend (fan of *Mountain Path* and *HH*, Lexington, Kentucky) to Arnow, 22 October 1949. Townsend, author of *Kentucky in American Letters* (1913), among other volumes featuring prominent figures in Kentucky, had an investment in Kentucky authors as a means for promoting his home state. The son of a lawyer and journalist, Townsend graduated from Kentucky University, where he met his longtime friend James Lane Allen. Townsend was also friends with John Fox Jr. He worked as assistant librarian for the Lexington Public Library and for the *Lexington Herald*. See Dorothy Edwards Townsend, *Kentucky's Boswell: A Tribute to John Wilson Townsend, Kentucky Author and Historian, Nov. 2, 1885–Jan. 12, 1968* (Lexington, 1968). Another expression of pride came from Lena Voiers, former teacher of author Jesse Stuart: "I am proud of both you and Jesse Stuart as Kentucky writers." Lena Wells (Mrs. William) Voiers (fan of *HH*, Vanceburg, Kentucky) to Arnow, 25 February 1951.

68. Helen C. Little (fan-acquaintance of *HH*, Cincinnati, Ohio) to Miss Elizabeth Simpson, 7 September 1949. Little represented the Cincinnati chapter of the Special Libraries Association at the National Membership Committee, 1944–1945. See "War Projects," Special Libraries Association Cincinnati Chapter, http://units.sla.org/chapter/ccin/history/chapter-history3.asp (accessed 19 August 2010).

69. Elisabeth (Mrs. F. C.) Ewen (Arnow's former teacher, fan of *HH*, Morehead, Kentucky) to Arnow, 13 June 1949; Katherine (Mrs. C. S.) Green (fan of *D* and *HH*, Midland, Texas), 7 June 1954.

70. Mrs. Clyde Burnette (fan of *HH*, thirty-nine years old, reared in Monticello, Kentucky) to Arnow, 10 May 1954.

71. Elizabeth (Mrs. Raymond) Neff (fan of *D*, Telford, Pennsylvania) to Arnow, 6 November 1955.

72. Irving and Freda Weissman (fans of *D*, New York City, New York) to Arnow, 12 November 1963; "Guide to the Irving Weissman Papers," Tamiment Library and Wagner Labor Archives, New York University, http://dlib.nyu.edu/findingaids/html/tamwag/weissman.html (accessed 19 August 2010). See also: "Perhaps the fact that my husband was a factory superintendent and that I was

familiar for many years with the suffering of workers who, to his great grief, were underpaid and overworked" was the reason that "I seemed to be reliving the suffering of Gertie and her family" when reading *The Dollmaker*. Blanche (Mrs. M.) Balfour (fan of *D*, Sewaren, New Jersey) to Arnow, 11 November 1954.

73. Miss Mary Jane White (fan of *HH*, principal, Raschig School, Cincinnati, Ohio) to Arnow, 10 March 1949.

74. Mildred Schulze (fan of *HH*, Elmwood, Cincinnati, Ohio) to Arnow, 23 December 1949.

75. Gertrude Snodgrass may be the same credited with cofounding the Greater Chicago Food Depository in 1978. See "History of the Greater Chicago Food Depository," Greater Chicago Food Depository, http://www.chicagosfoodbank.org/site/PageServer?pagename=abt_whoweare_history (accessed 19 August 2010). Gertrude (Mrs. J. T.) Snodgrass (fan of *D*, Elgin, Illinois) to Arnow, 21 February 1954.

76. Lauren Berlant, "Introduction: Compassion (and Withholding)," in *Compassion: The Culture and Politics of an Emotion*, ed. Lauren Berlant (New York: Routledge, 2004), 5, 7, 9, 10. For a counter perspective, see Kimberly Chabot Davis, "White Book Clubs and African American Literature: The Promise and Limitation of Cross-Racial Empathy," *Literature Interpretation Theory* 19, no. 2 (2008): 155–86.

77. Phyllis McKishnie Kribs (fan of *HH*, Toronto, Ontario, Canada) to Arnow, 13 July 1949. Kribs told Arnow that she was "the daughter of one of Canada's most loved writers," Archie P. McKishnie, who "wrote of the early settlers here in his Ontario as you write of those hill people."

78. Mrs. Everdean Johnson (fan of *HH*, Trenton, Michigan) to Arnow, 31 July 1949. Johnson's stories were published as a pamphlet by the Women's Board of Domestic Missions. See also: "I am a Kentuckian and have a deep appreciation of the hills and its people. Last fall I published a small volume of Ky. folk-lore poetry entitled 'Trammel Fork Creek,' my section of the state." Dolly Gilmore Barmann (fan of *HH* and looking for *Mountain Path*) to Arnow, 8 June 1953.

79. Mariane L. Williams (fan of *D* and *HH*, Calgary, Alberta, Canada) to Arnow, 9 July 1954.

80. Joyce Spragins wrote wistfully, "But what about Gertie? Don't you ever wonder about her? . . . Anyway I like to think she found a way to return home. Maybe she did!" Joyce Spragins (fan of *D*) to Arnow, 31 October [no year]. A librarian in a "little village in the hills of western N.Y." insisted that Gertie "deserves a break" and wished "that Gertie may get back into her own environment again and forget her unhappy days living in the war housing project." Mrs. Elizabeth Van Lise (fan of *D*, Cowlesville, New York) to Arnow, 1 February 1955.

81. Katherine (Mrs. C. S.) Green (fan of *D* and *HH*, Midland, Texas) to Arnow, 7 June 1954.

82. Stephen W. Harvey (fan of *D*, seventeen years old, Seattle, Washington) to Arnow, 17 February 1958.

83. Mrs. Delbert Moore (fan of *D*, Blanchester, Ohio) to Arnow, 26 November 1954. This may be the mother of the Delbert Moore who was a salesman for Nationwide Insurance in 1976; see *Cincinnati* magazine, May 1976, 5.

84. Arnow "keeps her folk faith" (W.D.P., 6 November 1954, Arnow Papers); *The Dollmaker* is a "folk tale" (*Chicago Daily Tribune*, 18 April 1954, C2); and Harnette T. Kane, "The Transplanted Folk," *New York Times*, 25 April 1954, BR4.

85. Paul Jordan-Smith, "Mountain Mother Is Inspiration Even out of Element in City: Creature of Fresh Air, Freedom and Good Food Survives Toxic Urbanity," *Los Angeles Times*, 18 April 1954, D6; Fanny Butcher, "'Dollmaker' a Novel of Terrific Reality," *Chicago Daily Tribune*, 18 April 1954, D3.

86. *Saturday Review Syndicate*, 30 October 1954, Arnow Papers; W.D.P., 6 November 1954, Arnow Papers; A. J. Beeler, "A Pathetic Life Well Portrayed," *Courier Journal*, 25 April 1954, Arnow Papers; Hanna, "A Powerful Story of a Kentucky Woman"; Victor P. Hass, "The Novels," *Chicago Daily Tribune*, 5 December 1954, B14.

87. Alma Weber (fan-acquaintance of *HH*, Blue Ash, Ohio) to Arnow, 2 August 1949; R. L. Cassell (fan of *D* and *HH*, Cadiz, Ohio) to Arnow, 25 October 1954; Claudine Lewis (fan of *D* and *HH*, Mayfield, Kentucky, on the letterhead of U.S. House of Representatives, Noble J. Gregory) to Arnow, 7 May 1954.

88. Sidney Ernestine (Mrs. Herbert) Warfel (fan of *D* and *HH*, Plainfield, Illinois) to Arnow, 5 November 1954. Warfel may be the same Sidney Ernestine Warfel who graduated Butler University in 1911. See *Butler Alumnal Quarterly*, April 1913, 152, http://www.archive.org/stream/butleralumnalqua21913butl/butleralumnalqua21913butl_djvu.txt (accessed 19 August 2010).

89. Ozro Grant, *Bad 'un* (New York: Ace, 1954). Grant was given sole credit for authorship, but in his letter to Arnow he says, "We had a novel published in March . . . and although it sold 130,000 copies we received not one single solitary letter about it either good or bad." Ozro F. Grant (fan of *D*, Tulare, California) to Arnow, 5 November 1954.

90. Edna Candy (fan of *D*, no place given, probably California) to Arnow, 5 February 1957; Chung, "Fictional Characters," 273.

91. Berry, *Southern Migrants*, 6, 91. Though Berry's earlier work suggested that out-migrants had better economic situations than they had left at home, a recent article suggests that some out-migrants experienced socioeconomic disadvantages compared to other native-born whites for generations after the move. Compared to other native-born whites in the Midwest, midwestern whites who self-reported as "Appalachian" (mostly men) in the 2000 census experienced double the unemployment rate and made an average of $7,000 less ($33,000 versus $40,000). Just 30 percent of self-reported Appalachians held professional clerical jobs (versus 50 percent), just 31 percent had any college education (versus 53 percent), and 14 percent were living in poverty (versus 8 percent.). The socioeconomic differences between self-reported Appalachians and all native-

born whites were exacerbated in the Midwest compared to the national averages (J. Trent Alexander and Chad Berry, "Who Is Appalachian? Self-Reported Appalachian Ancestry in the 2000 Census," *Appalachian Journal* 38, no. 1 [2010]: 52). It is difficult to say whether these particular self-reported Appalachians were financially better off than they would have been had their ancestors not migrated.

92. Berry, *Southern Migrants*, 211.

93. Ibid., 7, 8.

94. Miller, "Harriette Simpson Arnow and Harold Arnow," 35; Baer, "Harriette Arnow's Chronicles of Destruction," 56. Arnow observed to a reporter: "I had more time when we lived in Detroit than I had in Kentucky, and more in Kentucky than" in Ann Arbor. "I was just going good on Gertie [*The Dollmaker*]," she explained, "when we moved to the country. Between painting the living room, landscaping the lawn, etc., etc., I had to leave her for months." Lois Decker O'Neill, "Looks at Books," *Louisville Courier Journal*, 25 April 1954, Arnow Papers.

95. Berry, *Southern Migrants*, 130. See note 91 for a qualification.

96. Jurca, *White Diaspora*, 4, 137, 18–19.

97. Henry D. Shapiro, *Appalachia on Our Mind: The Southern Mountains and Mountaineers in the American Consciousness, 1870–1920* (Chapel Hill: University of North Carolina Press, 1978), 261.

98. Lisa Krissoff Boehm, "Chicago as Forgotten Country Music Mecca," in Berry, *The Hayloft Gang*, 107.

99. John Kenneth Galbraith, *The Affluent Society* (Boston: Houghton Mifflin, 1958). See Anthony Harkins, *Hillbilly: A Cultural History of an American Icon* (New York: Oxford University Press, 2004), on the idea that the hillbilly represents, in Berry's words, "rootedness, identity, and distinctiveness from the metropolis's masses." Berry, introduction to Berry, *The Hayloft Gang*, 7.

100. Gregory, *Southern Diaspora*, 14.

101. Bertrand, "Race and Rural Identity," 132.

4. City to Country, circa 1967–1970

1. *Christy, the Movie: Return to Cutter Gap* (2000). *Christy, Choices of the Heart*, parts 1 and 2 (May 2001) originally aired on Pax TV. In 2007, my white Christian female college students reported having read the novel on the recommendation of their mothers.

2. "Announcing the New Quality of Life Society," *New York Times*, 5 March 1972, BR25; Doubleday, "The Foxfire Book," *New York Times*, 9 April 1972; "Paperbacks: Current Best Sellers," *New York Times*, 9 July 1972, BR31. *Future Shock*, in which the "too-fast rate of technological change is the villain," shared the top five in July 1972. *The Foxfire Book* appeared on the list again 13 August and 10 September 1972, and was offered through the regular Book-of-the-Month

Club selection as well as the "Quality of Life Society" division. See also Nelson Bryant, "How to Make Quilts and Slaughter Hogs," *New York Times*, 19 March 1972, BR20; and "Education: Spreading Foxfire," *Time*, 14 August 1972.

3. Marilyn Halter, *Shopping for Identity: The Marketing of Ethnicity* (New York: Schocken, 2000), 17.

4. Suzanne Hermanson (sixteen years old, fan, Sanborn, New York) to Marshall, 4 November 1970, folder 6, box 11, Catherine Marshall Collection, Agnes Scott College, Atlanta, GA. Further references to this collection will be abbreviated as Marshall Papers.

5. Mary Elisabeth Goin, "Catherine Marshall: Three Decades of Popular Religion," *Journal of Presbyterian History* 56, no. 3 (1978): 228.

6. Ibid., 229. As Goin observes, this was the era when Americans added "under God" to their Pledge of Allegiance. Scholar June Zaragoza emphasizes Marshall's decidedly apolitical take on mountain life in the early twentieth century. The novel's primary message is that love is "the basis for everything." One surrenders to God and then the "answers are revealed for all of life's difficult choices" ("To Edify or Entertain: The Fiction of Catherine Marshall," *Christianity and the Arts* 3, no. 3 [1996]: 11). Marshall introduced to readers the evangelical tradition of "rescuers" who promote the need for an "individual response to Jesus rather than . . . social action." Goin clearly finds Marshall's version of religion as individual inspiration lacking compared to that of her husband, Peter, which called "for Christian witness against racism and corruption" ("Catherine Marshall," 233).

7. Goin, "Catherine Marshall," 220–21.

8. Quoted in Clarence Petersen, *Book World*, 13 October 1968.

9. Edwin Peeples (fan-acquaintance, Phoenixville, Pennsylvania), 1 January 1971, box 43, folder 1, General Correspondence, James Dickey Papers, Manuscript Collection 745, Manuscript, Archives, and Rare Book Library, Emory University, Atlanta, GA. Further references to this collection will be abbreviated as Dickey Papers.

10. Quoted in James T. Patterson, *Grand Expectations: The United States, 1945–1974* (New York: Oxford University Press, 1996), 782–83.

11. Ibid., 665.

12. I am grateful to Barbara Ellen Smith for her assistance in formulating the idea of the dual nature of white southerners' potential identifications in *Deliverance*.

13. Catherine Jurca, *White Diaspora: The Suburb and the Twentieth-Century American Novel* (Princeton, NJ: Princeton University Press, 2001), 6–8, 16.

14. Catherine Marshall to Mrs. H. T. Ogle (fan, Sevierville, Tennessee), 7 April 1959, folder 7, box 34, Marshall Papers.

15. *Christy* also made the *Publishers Weekly* paperback list for 44 weeks, including number one for twelve, for a total of 118 weeks on the lists. Keith L. Justice, *Bestseller Index: All Books*, Publishers Weekly *and the* New York Times *through 1990* (Jefferson, NC: McFarland, 1998), 212. *Christy* sold 7,944,614 cop-

ies by 1978 (Goin, "Catherine Marshall," 220). According to Marshall, by 1978 *Christy* had eighteen printings in hardcover and sixty-six printings in paperback (Marshall to Mr. John Wright, chairman, United Media Finance Limited, London, England, 3 September 1982, folder 5, box 34, Marshall Papers).

16. Mrs. Mary Kellet (fan) to Marshall, 30 April 1973 (filed with Marshall to Mrs. Mary Kellett, 8 May 1973, folder 2, box 12, Marshall Papers).

17. Social Security Association, http://www.ssa.gov/cgi-bin/babyname.cgi (accessed 9 June 2008). By 2004, the name Christy had declined in popularity so much that it had dropped out of the top one thousand names. Fans often misspelled the book's title as "Christie." This name, too, rose in popularity from the four hundreds to ninety-sixth at the height of its popularity in 1975.

18. "A New Youth Poll," *Life*, 8 January 1970, 22, 30; *Christianity Today*, October 2006, 51–55.

19. "*USA Today* Best-Selling Books," *USA Today*, 14 April 1994, 4D. *Christy* reached number fifteen. *USA Today*'s list was based on three thousand large bookstores, including Barnes and Noble, Books-a-Million, and Borders Books and Music.

20. They married in 1936. Elise Chase, "Peter and Catherine Marshall," in *Twentieth Century Shapers of American Popular Religion* (New York: Greenwood, 1989), 283.

21. In 1980, the couple established a prayer ministry named "the Intercessors." Ibid., 286. Marshall's other works include *Mr. Jones, Meet the Master* (1949) and *To Live Again* (1957).

22. Goin, "Catherine Marshall," 219. Whereas *Christy* sold almost 4 million copies by 1975, *A Man Called Peter* had sold almost 1 million. Alice Payne Hackett and James Henry Burke, *80 Years of Best Sellers, 1895–1975* (New York: Bowker, 1977), 12, 28. Marshall's *A Man Called Peter, The Prayers of Peter Marshall* (which she edited), and *To Live Again* were each top ten nonfiction best sellers in 1953 and 1955, 1954, and 1957, respectively. Hackett and Burke, *80 Years*, 160, 163, 166, 171. Marshall's second novel, *Julie* (1984), was a best seller for a total of sixteen weeks on the *New York Times* and *Publishers Weekly* lists. Justice, *Bestseller Index*, 212.

23. Marshall to Mr. Augustine Healy (fan, Palm Beach, Florida), 15 December 1967, folder 1, box 11, Marshall Papers.

24. As Marshall explained to a fan, she created the character David "to dramatize my deep conviction that when our" seminaries "graduate men who have had no personal confrontation with Christ, [and] whose belief is predicated only on church structure and organization, along with so-called social service and community work—this is not enough." Marshall to Mr. W. Don Rogers (fan, Sunday School Board of the Baptist Convention, Nashville, Tennessee), 28 June 28 1967, folder 1, box 11, Marshall Papers.

25. Adele Silver, "Doing Good," *New York Times Book Review*, 22 October 1967, sec. 7, 70; "*Christy*," *Time*, 13 October 1967, 117, 119.

26. Later letters exhibit much less polished writing, in part because they were written by young people, but also because farm wives and country ministers' wives may have had less formal education than Marshall's original Episcopalian audiences. There were exceptions to the largely middle-class status of Marshall's fans. Upper-class fans included a doctor's wife and a member of a pharmaceutical dynasty. Working-class backgrounds were evidenced in letters from military personnel, working women, and farmers' wives. An Iowa woman "read the book in between jumps—hauling in corn. . . . The book rode the tractor with me every spare moment." (Mrs. James W. Clapp (fan, Oxford Junction, Iowa) to Marshall, 20 November 1967, folder 1, box 11, Marshall Papers. Filed with Marshall to Mrs. James W. Clapp, 30 November 1967, folder 1, box 11, Marshall Papers.)

27. These figures are based on all the letters I read, an unrepresentative sample of 452 letters that indicated the locations from which they were sent. Mapped locations for 1967–1968 fans and fan-acquaintances give a similar distribution, though readership apparently was initially slightly more skewed toward the Midwest: 24 percent from the Northeast, 20 percent Southeast, 35 percent Midwest, 16 percent West. See map on page 140.

28. Johnnie Sue True called the novel "inspiring" reading for "both my teenage daughter and me." Johnnie Sue (Mrs. Ted W.) True (fan, Athens, Texas) to Marshall, 21 April 1968, folder 2, box 11, Marshall Papers. Mrs. Schubert wrote that her "two daughters, 13 and 15, also love good books and will enjoy yours as much as I have." Mrs. Carl D. Schubert (fan, Nederland, Texas) to Marshall, 14 February 1968, folder 2, box 11, Marshall Papers.

29. In 1977, Rosanne Guarrarra, writing from Brooklyn, explained, "I've read [*Christy*] every year since 1974 . . . I'm just the age now Christy was when she went off to the mountains (19)" and have "always identified with her." Ms. Rosanne Guarrarra (fan, Brooklyn, New York) to Marshall, 2 November 1977, folder 7, box 12, Marshall Papers.

30. Marshall to Miss Ruby Misner (fan, Kent, Iowa), 19 March 1969, folder 3, box 11, Marshall Papers.

31. Ibid.

32. Catherine Marshall to Frank Taylor, William Goyen, Joseph Allen, and Sonia Levinthal, "Memo on *Christy* Advertising," 25 July 1967, folder 5, box 39, Marshall Papers.

33. E. (Mrs. Herbert) Rubinstein (fan, Oak Park, Illinois) to Marshall, 5 February 1969, folder 3, box 11, Marshall Papers.

34. Joyce Suckow (fan, Hull, Iowa, and social work major at Augustana College in Sioux Falls, South Dakota) to Marshall, 18 August 1971, folder 7, box 11, Marshall Papers. An eighth-grade reader wrote how much she loved books about "the pioneer times," which *Christy* appeared to represent despite its setting in the year 1912. Cindy Weinberg (fan, Arlington Heights, Illinois) to Marshall, 13 September 1972, folder 1, box 12, Marshall Papers. Another reader told Marshall that the novel "had the spirit of a frontier community." Joyce Koncos (fan, North

Riverside, Illinois) to Marshall, 10 December 1973, folder 2, box 12, Marshall Papers.

35. Marshall to Miss Mary Davis (fan, Oak Harbor, Washington), 16 April 1970, folder 5, box 11, Marshall Papers; Laura Duey (fan, thirteen years old, Miami, Florida) to Marshall, 28 August 1971, folder 7, box 11, Marshall Papers.

36. Mrs. Ina M. Robison (fan, St. Helena, California) to Marshall, 11 June 1973, folder 2, box 12, Marshall Papers.

37. Miss Mary Lea (fan, eighteen years old [?], Leaside, Toronto, Ontario, Canada), to Marshall, 15 April 1971, folder 7, box 11, Marshall Papers. Marshall responded by asserting that there was "no question" about the hill peoples' origins in the British Isles. Marshall to Miss Mary Lea (fan, eighteen years old [?], Leaside, Toronto, Ontario, Canada), 27 April 1971, folder 7, box 11, Marshall Papers. Another fan asked for help finding fiddle tunes. Miss Charlene A. Markey (fan, Glendale, California) to Marshall, 22 April 1972, folder 1, box 12, Marshall Papers.

38. Miss Dee Ann (Dede) Smith (fan, Montville, New Jersey) to Marshall, Summer 1969, folder 4, box 11, Marshall Papers. See also "I truly felt and senced all the hardships, hallarities, joys, and sorrows of those mountain folk." Miss Dee Ann (Dede) Smith (fan, Montville, New Jersey) to Marshall, Summer 1969, folder 4, box 11, Marshall Papers. Some readers, however, emphasized one aspect over the other. A fan who noticed only the cheery aspects of mountain life might mention wanting to join in on the "jambourees," while others emphasized concern over having such a "needy, benighted area as Apalachia right within our own borders." Barbara Angus (fan, sixteen years old, Windsor, Ontario, Canada), 20 June 1973, folder 2, box 12, Marshall Papers. Mrs. Ina M. Robison (fan, St. Helena, California) to Marshall, 18 July 1973 (filed with Marshall to Mrs. Ina M. Robison, 26 June 1973, folder 2, box 12, Marshall Papers).

39. Mrs. Ruth M. Burlison (fan, Brunswick, Ohio) to Marshall, 24 October 1972, folder 1, box 12, Marshall Papers.

40. Margaret (Mrs. Dennis) Steward (fan, Piscataway, New Jersey) to Marshall, 27 August 1973, folder 2, box 12, Marshall Papers. Similarly, Elizabeth Luca felt that "the true meaning of life and love has not been lost" in the mountains. Elizabeth (Mrs. Peter W.) Luca (fan, Montvale, New Jersey) to Marshall, 20 August 1969, folder 4, box 11, Marshall Papers. The way in which readers couched their praise of the mountains was reminiscent of popular language in circulation at this time, thanks in part to Henry Caudill's *Night Comes to the Cumberlands* (1963) and the discussion of the needs of African American families in the Moynihan Report (1965). *Christy* may have in turn ratified ideas popularized by the best-selling *Yesterday's People* (1972), used for decades by missionaries to understand the so-called culture of poverty in the region.

41. Miss Suzanne Hermanson (fan, sixteen years old, Sanborn, New York) to Marshall, 4 November 1970, folder 6, box 11, Marshall Papers; Marshall to Miss Suzanne Hermanson, 23 December 1970, folder 6, box 11, Marshall Papers.

The sentiment that simplicity and even scarcity were highly valued and admired virtues was sometimes expressed in terms of readers' affection for the character of Fairlight Spencer, Christy Huddleston's beloved mountain friend. Fairlight appeared to fans as "a princess in homespun" who "teaches us to see beauty in everyday things." Readers were enchanted by the "emergence of a strong beautiful character out of degrading surroundings." Anne Marshfield (fan, Wallingford, Pennsylvania) to Marshall, 15 February 1968, folder 2, box 11, Marshall Papers; Carol (Mrs. John A.) Phillips (fan, St. Mark's Mission, Nenana, Alaska) to Marshall, 16 October 1968, folder 2, box 11, Marshall Papers.

42. Marshall to Taylor, Goyen, Allen, and Levinthal, "Memo on *Christy* Advertising."

43. "Christy Country" as a designation not only removes the region from the "grubbiness" of Appalachia but also simultaneously suggests its kinship with the wholeness and purity of "God's Country" and the noble savages of "Indian Country." On several occasions Marshall corrected fans on their images of Appalachia, including: "Let me point out that the Great Smokies—'Christy Country'—are really quite different from other areas of the Appalachians, such as the coal mining regions of West Virginia." Marshall to Miss Laura Nelson (fan, Andover, Ohio), 7 April 1970, folder 5, box 11, Marshall Papers. See also: "There is a vast difference between Appalachia as we are seeing it spread across our magazines and newspapers as largely the coal mining regions in West Virginia, Kentucky, etc. and the Great Smoky Mountain portion of Appalachia about which I was writing in *Christy*." Marshall to Miss Sheri Schumacher (fan, Lemon Grove, California), 16 April 1971, folder 7, box 11, Marshall Papers.

44. Marshall assured fans of her extensive research. See Marshall to Miss Mary Davis (fan, Oak Harbor, Washington), 16 April 1970, folder 5, box 11, Marshall Papers; Marshall to Miss Debbie Keller (fan, ninth grader, Sandia Base, New Mexico), 1 May 1969, folder 4, box 11, Marshall Papers; Marshall to Miss Mary Lea (fan, eighteen years old, Leaside, Toronto, Ontario, Canada), 27 April 1971, folder 7, box 11, Marshall Papers. The bibliography included T. F. Henderson's *Minstrelsy of the Scottish Border* (1932) and works by ballad collector Cecil Sharp.

45. Anna Mae Ogle (acquaintance, Sevierville, Tennessee) to Marshall, 10 May 1959, folder 7, box 34, Marshall Papers. Marshall apparently also needed others' words to help her reconstruct an "accurate" depiction of mountaineer language. Her archives include a letter written by a girl living at the Smoky Mountain Academy boarding school in Sevierville, Tennessee. Although the letter is not addressed to Marshall but to "Dear Lois & all," Marshall evidently borrowed from it, circling words and turns of phrase (such as "he knowed you") that she might find useful.

46. Catherine Marshall, *Christy* (New York: Avon, 1996), 5. Further references to *Christy* are to this edition and are cited parenthetically in the text as C.

47. Dianna McRoberts (fan, Paramount, California) to Marshall, 10 April 1973, folder 2, box 12, Marshall Papers. Readers saw Marshall not so much as a

fiction author than as someone who deserved thanks for "writing up" a preexisting story. Miss Louise Howard (fan, St. Petersburg, Florida) to Marshall, 31 October 1969, folder 4, box 11, Marshall Papers. Mildred Spain's letter noted that the "front flap" claimed that "the author goes back to the roots of her life, since she and her parents were born in Appalachia. With authentic background, meticulously researched, this book was nine years in the making." When Spain asked her to elaborate upon "those 'roots,'" Marshall readily provided details. Miss Mildred W. Spain (fan, Paris, Texas) to Marshall, 17 May 1969, and Marshall to Spain, 27 May 1969, both in folder 4, box 11, Marshall Papers. To another reader Marshall explained, "I was born in the mountains, but not in Cutter Gap." Marshall to Miss Anne Gulliford (fan, British Columbia, Canada), 16 January 1969, folder 3, box 11, Marshall Papers.

48. Carol (Mrs. John A.) Phillips (fan, St. Mark's Mission, Nenana, Alaska) to Marshall, 16 October 1968, folder 2, box 11, Marshall Papers; Mrs. Jane H. Celio (fan, Rutherford, New Jersey) to Marshall, 25 October 1972, folder 1, box 12, Marshall Papers.

49. Analysis based on ten fan letters about Scottish connections, six about youthful encounters, and thirty from readers who were "from there" (fifteen), whose families were from there (five), who felt they were from somewhere just like it (five), who married people from there (three), or who lived there at the time of writing (two).

50. Mr. George A. Butz Sr. (fan, Rehoboth Beach, Delaware) to Marshall, 24 August 1970, folder 6, box 11, Marshall Papers.

51. Only rarely did letters arrive from Appalachian southeastern Ohio. Between 1967 and 1970, a disproportionate number arrived from Michigan, especially the Detroit area.

52. Mrs. Frances Green (fan, Washington, District of Columbia) to Marshall, 1 December 1967, folder 1, box 11, Marshall Papers; Carolyn J. Wolf (fan, Delray Beach Library, Boynton Beach, Florida) to Marshall, 21 September 1967, folder 1, box 11, Marshall Papers.

53. Mr. Harry D. Mills (fan, seventy-six years old, Ann Arbor, Michigan) to Marshall, 8 November 1967, folder 1, box 11, Marshall Papers. Myra Reeves Hardin, raised in Johnson City, confided to Marshall, "I am probably about the age of your mother and so I know all about the mudholes." Hardin lamented that the mud holes were probably gone, now that her hometown had "grown into just another strange city." She reminisced about her "beloved East Tenn. Nothing can quite take the place of the old home town." Myra Reeves (Mrs. J. M.) Hardin (fan, Arkansas) to Marshall, 29 October 1972, folder 1, box 12, Marshall Papers.

54. Mrs. Frances Green (fan, Washington, District of Columbia) to Marshall, 1 December 1967, folder 1, box 11, Marshall Papers.

55. Miss Vicki Hendrix (fan, seventeen years old, Candler, North Carolina) to Marshall, 8 September 1971, folder 7, box 11, Marshall Papers (first read *Christy* three years earlier at age fourteen). Thirteen-year-old Sheila wrote that

she was originally from "a small town" outside Asheville. Perhaps because she had moved away, she was aware even before reading the novel that "I love the mountains just as much as Christy did." Sheila Angel (fan, thirteen years old, Bennettsville, South Carolina) to Marshall, 4 July 1973, folder 2, box 12, Marshall Papers.

56. Mr. Allen Joe Park (fan, Signal Mountain, Tennessee) to Marshall, 9 October 1969, folder 4, box 11, Marshall Papers.

57. Mr. Max T. Harrison (fan, Tennessee Department of Education letterhead, Johnson City, Tennessee) to Marshall, 8 November 1967, folder 1, box 11, Marshall Papers.

58. Judy Downing (fan, Valley, Washington) to Marshall, 1 February 1969, folder 3, box 11, Marshall Papers; Miss Jeanna Yohey (fan, twenty years old, McMinnville, Oregon) to Marshall, 16 November 1968, folder 3, box 11, Marshall Papers; Miss Ramona Rhodus (fan, sixteen years old, Camden, Ohio) to Marshall, 13 May 1973, folder 2, box 12, Marshall Papers; Josephine (Mrs. Charles) Dobbyn (fan, seventy-four years old, Chelsea, Massachusetts) to Marshall, 24 August 1972, folder 1, box 12, Marshall Papers.

59. Mrs. Horace E. Moore (fan, Jelm, Wyoming) to Marshall, 3 November 1967, folder 1, box 11, Marshall Papers. Moore listed as a badge of honor the "mountain" names her grandmother gave her children, including Ovel, Artle, and Exie. Mrs. Alma B. Davis (fan, Newport, North Carolina) to Marshall, 22 October 1967, folder 1, box 11, Marshall Papers; Judith P. (Mrs. A. E.) Canant Jr. (fan, Titusville, Florida) to Marshall, 20 July 1972, folder 1, box 12, Marshall Papers.

60. *Deliverance* also spent 28 weeks on the *Publishers Weekly* list (with a peak of second place) for a total of 70 weeks on the best-seller lists (versus 118 for *Christy*). Justice, *Bestseller Index*, 93–94; Henry Hart, *James Dickey: The World as a Lie* (New York: Picador, 2000), 455. By 1975, *Deliverance* had sold 2,201,244 copies (Hackett and Burke, *80 Years*, 18).

61. "Nightmare" is from William McPherson, "Most Serious Kind of Game," review of *Deliverance*, *Washington Post*, 21 March 1970; and Richard Schickel, "Books in Brief," review of *Deliverance*, *Harper's*, April 1970, 106–7. "Hicks" is from Anthony Thwaite, "Out of Bondage," review of *Deliverance*, *New Statesman*, 11 September 1970, 310–11.

62. Hart, *James Dickey*, 6–7, 11, 13, 14, 16.

63. Ibid., 326.

64. Dickey to Janeice Ray (fan-acquaintance, Dahlonega, Georgia), 16 November 1981, folder 1, box 240, Subject Files, Dickey Papers. "Wilderness of Heaven" was the planned title of a coffee-table book about Appalachia (never published) that Dickey was working on at the time. Dickey to Eliot Wigginton, 25 November 1980, box 90, folder 4, Dickey Papers. Dickey to Janeice Ray (fan-acquaintance, Dahlonega, Georgia), 16 November 1981, box 240, folder 1, Subject Files, Dickey Papers. Ray authored *Ecology of a Cracker Childhood* (1999) under the name Janisse.

65. Hart, *James Dickey*, 247.

66. James Dickey, *Deliverance* (Boston: Houghton Mifflin, 1970), 7. Further references to this novel are to this edition and are noted parenthetically in the text as *D*.

67. Benjamin DeMott, review of *Deliverance*, *Saturday Review of Books*, 28 March 1970, 25–26, 38; Calvin Bedient, "Gold-Glowing Mote," review of *Deliverance*, *Nation*, 6 April 1970; Christopher Ricks, "Man Hunt," *New York Review of Books*, 23 April 1970.

68. Walter Clemons, "James Dickey, Novelist," *New York Times Book Review*, 22 March 1970, 298; John Alfred Avant, review of *Deliverance*, *Library Journal Book Review*, 1970, 714–15.

69. Patti Hagan, "The Erotic Mountains? One Woman Finds Joy in a Flower Guide," *New York Times*, 18 February 1973, 491; DeMott, review of *Deliverance*; Thwaite, "Out of Bondage," 310–11.

70. Dickey's correspondents had read *about* the novel, oftentimes even prior to or instead of reading the novel itself. Their level of familiarity with meta-conversations about the novel was extremely high, especially compared with readers of *Christy*. Many commented on the publicity for the novel or wrote because they had read a review, seen an ad, or heard Dickey on a TV or radio program. While Marshall received an exponentially higher volume of fan mail, her readers mentioned only reading the novel—never reading *about* the novel.

71. Frederick E. Exley (friend/colleague and novelist, Antwerp, New York) to Dickey, 6 April 1970, folder 1, box 40, General Correspondence, Dickey Papers.

72. Marty Olmstead (fan, San Francisco, California) to Dickey, 11 November 1970, folder 10, box 42; Mrs. Janet R. Kovach (fan, Edison, New Jersey) to Dickey, 14 July 1970, folder 7, box 41; James Isaacs (fan, Hollywood, California) to Dickey, 26 July 1971, folder 8, box 43; Joan Tuckerman Dick (fan-acquaintance, Berkeley, California) to Dickey, 2 April 1970, folder 1, box 40, all in General Correspondence, Dickey Papers. Readers' sense of vicarious experience was widespread, with at least an additional sixteen comments that indicated readers felt they had gone "along for the ride." Linda Rogers (fan) to Dickey, 31 August 1973, folder 9, box 46, General Correspondence, Dickey Papers.

73. Ellen Lane (fan, sixteen years old, Rock Hill, South Carolina) to Dickey, 20 June 1970, folder 4, box 41, General Correspondence, Dickey Papers.

74. Catharine Meyer (*Harper's*, New York, New York) to Dickey, 29 March 1970, folder 9, box 39, General Correspondence, Dickey Papers. As comments from female readers indicate, identification with Ed was not limited to the reader who cared to think of himself as a man's man. Dickey told female fans that his publisher had not expected women to read *Deliverance* and repeated the explanation provided to him by "a tough little lady book seller in New York," that "women want to know what men do and what happens to them when they go off by themselves." What Dickey failed to notice, however, was that almost all the women fans to whom he replied claimed to have experienced the novel from

the perspective of the protagonist, Ed Gentry—not that of Ed's wife left back in Atlanta with their son. See also: "I am climbing up that cliff with Ed every inch of the way!" Jane Gabrio (fan, La Jolla, California) to Dickey, 9 April 1980, folder 1, box 55, General Correspondence, Dickey Papers.

75. Gender estimates are based on letters from 1970 to 1973.

76. Geographic estimates are based on 1970–1971 letters only.

77. Hart, *James Dickey*, 452.

78. Mrs. Linda Rogers (fan) to Dickey, 31 August 1973, folder 13, box 47, General Correspondence, Dickey Papers.

79. Darlene LaPler (fan, Crow's Landing, California) to Dickey, ca. October 1972, folder 6, box 45, General Correspondence, Dickey Papers. Susann Allnutt of Montreal, a longtime fan of Dickey's poetry, told the author that *Deliverance* "left me with a fever and shaking." She described a disturbing camping trip she had taken with four friends when she was sixteen. "Two hunters, drunk and armed with rifles and a high power flashlight, besieged us the night long; we barricaded the doors." She concluded, "We all have our forest fears and they are not ungrounded—what demons occupy the unknown places." Susann Allnutt (fan, Montreal, Quebec, Canada) to Dickey, 24 March 1971, folder 3, box 43, General Correspondence, Dickey Papers.

80. See J. Watson Smoot Jr. (fan-acquaintance, Tarboro, North Carolina) to Dickey, 22 May 1970, folder 13, box 40, General Correspondence, Dickey Papers; John Niles Jr. (fan, Cambridge, Massachusetts) to Dickey, 6 June 1970, folder 3, box 41, General Correspondence, Dickey Papers; William R. Higgins (fan-acquaintance, Sylva, North Carolina) to Dickey, 30 April 1970, folder 7, box 40, General Correspondence, Dickey Papers; Mrs. Janet R. Kovach (fan, Edison, New Jersey) to Dickey, 14 July 1970, folder 7, box 41, General Correspondence, Dickey Papers; Stephen Goldberg (fan, Long Island, New York) to Dickey, 1 November 1973, folder 1, box 47, General Correspondence, Dickey Papers.

81. Helena Anderson (fan, Peru, Kansas) to Dickey, ca. May 1970, folder 10, box 40, General Correspondence, Dickey Papers.

82. Dick Stern (Department of English, University of Chicago, Chicago, Illinois) to Dickey, 7 April 1970, folder 1, box 40, General Correspondence, Dickey Papers.

83. "About the funds required for the preservation of the folk archives up there, I can't help you." Dickey to Rev. John S. Ullman (fan-acquaintance, St. John's Universal Life Church, Seattle, Washington), 19 June 1970, folder 4, box 41, General Correspondence, Dickey Papers.

84. Charles W. Loftin (fan, Jackson Hill, North Carolina) to Dickey, 28 April 1970, folder 7, box 40, General Correspondence, Dickey Papers.

85. Michael Flynn (fan, Atlanta, Georgia) to Dickey, ca. August 1971, folder 9, box 43, General Correspondence, Dickey Papers. Jon Voigt observed that the movie *Deliverance* was about the "emotional voyeurism" that exists "because we're cutting away something that is necessary" and about the problem of "our

civilization in our cities, the urban life." "Hollywood or Vietnam—It's All One to Jon," *Los Angeles Times*, 22 October 1972, M1.

86. Dan Clark (fan, Jacksonville, Illinois) to Dickey, n.d., folder 5, box 88, General Correspondence, Dickey Papers.

87. Patterson, *Grand Expectations*, 727.

88. Ibid.; Hart, *James Dickey*, 253; Al Poulin (fan-acquaintance, Bidford, Maine) to Dickey, 1975, folder 5, box 88, General Correspondence, Dickey Papers.

89. Margaret Stenerson (fan, Forest Hill, New York) to Dickey, 17 July 1970, folder 8, box 41, General Correspondence, Dickey Papers.

90. Peter F. Neumeyer (fan-acquaintance, Stony Brook, New York) to Dickey, 8 May 1970, folder 9, box 40, General Correspondence, Dickey Papers; Dewey Gill (fan, New Berlin, Wisconsin) to Dickey, 20 January 1971, folder 1, box 43, General Correspondence, Dickey Papers; Terry (Hunt America Time, Alexandria, Virginia) to Dickey, 24 February 1973, folder 3, box 46, General Correspondence, Dickey Papers.

91. Margaret Stenerson (fan, Forest Hill, New York) to Dickey, 17 July 1970, folder 8, box 41, General Correspondence, Dickey Papers.

92. Hart, *James Dickey*, 443–44.

93. Ruth Frankenburg, *White Women, Race Matters: The Social Construction of Whiteness* (Minneapolis: University of Minnesota Press, 1993), 205, 192.

94. Hart, *James Dickey*, 511.

95. See a letter from the humorist Roy Blount Jr. While a staff writer for *Sports Illustrated* (1960–1975), Blount tried to establish a connection with Dickey by mentioning that he was "a Vanderbilt grad, a native of Decatur, Ga., a sometimes frequenter of the North Georgia mountains" before offering to introduce Dickey to "some of the Steelers." Roy Blount Jr. (fan, Pittsburgh, Pennsylvania) to Dickey, 1970, folder 2, box 90, General Correspondence, Dickey Papers. See also an invitation for a weekend in the mountains (Alex Bernhardt [fan, Bernhardt Furniture, Lenoir, North Carolina] to Dickey, 14 August 1970, folder 11, box 41) and a hunting trip (Jonathan Winthrop [fan, senior at Saint Mark's School, Southborough, Massachusetts], 10 October 1970, folder 7, box 42), both in General Correspondence, Dickey Papers.

96. David B. Buzzard (fan, Columbus, Ohio) to Dickey, 9 November 1970, folder 9, box 42, General Correspondence, Dickey Papers.

97. Thomas B. Newsom (fan, editor, *St. Louis Post Dispatch*, Sunday Pictures magazine, St. Louis, Missouri) to Dickey, 18 October 1973, folder 11, box 46, General Correspondence, Dickey Papers. Right Rev. John E. Hines (fan, presiding bishop, Episcopal Church, New York, New York) to Dickey, 16 March 1973, folder 4, box 46, General Correspondence, Dickey Papers.

98. James Russell Burnham (fan, Illinois) to Dickey, n.d., folder 4, box 88, General Correspondence, Dickey Papers.

99. Madeline Negri (fan, St. Louis, Missouri) to Dickey, July 1971, folder 8, box 43, General Correspondence, Dickey Papers.

100. Dr. Pat J. and Mrs. Leslie H. Ahrens (fan-acquaintances, Columbia, South Carolina) to Dickey, 11 January 1973, folder 1, box 46, General Correspondence, Dickey Papers; Patrick Sky (fan-acquaintance, Rhode Island), n.d. [circa March 1971], folder 1, box 41.

101. Carole Spence Marsh (fan, Louisville, Kentucky) to Dickey, 16 January 1973, folder 1, box 46, General Correspondence, Dickey Papers.

102. Douglas Reid Sasser (president, Young Harris College, Young Harris, Georgia) to Dickey, 8 April 1970, folder 2, box 40; William R. Higgins (fan-acquaintance, Western Carolina State University, Cullowhee, North Carolina) to Dickey, 30 April 1970, folder 70, box 40; Tom Liner (fan, Abraham Baldwin Agricultural College, Tifton, Georgia) to Dickey, 13 August 1971, folder 9, box 43; Dean Cadle (assistant librarian, UNC–Asheville) to Dickey, 29 December 1970, folder 11, box 42; Dickey to Mr. Bill Dunlop (art department, Appalachian State University, Boone, North Carolina), 26 March 1973, folder 5, box 46; Dickey to Francis T. Borkowski (chancellor, Appalachian State University, Boone, North Carolina), 6 August 1994, folder 1, box 85; Janeice Ray (fan-acquaintance, Cultural Affairs, College Union Governing Board, North Georgia College, Dahlonega, Georgia) to Dickey, 22 January 1982, folder 7, box 62; John M. Carter (fan-acquaintance, librarian, Winthrop College, Rock Hill, South Carolina) to Dickey, 27 March 1973, folder 5, box 46; Rodger Butler (Johnson City, Tennessee) to Dickey, n.d., folder 9, box 88. Butler invited Dickey to lecture at East Tennessee State University, offering as enticement: "We're right next door to the Appalachian Mountains (Buffalo Mountain)." Jerry Williamson (Appalachian State University, Boone, North Carolina) to Dickey, 2 May 1972, folder 2, box 45. All the above are filed in General Correspondence, Dickey Papers. Dickey's honorary Doctor of Humane Letters from Appalachian State University, 1984, is housed in box 407, folder 7, Series 14: Honors and Awards, Dickey Papers.

103. John Foster West (Boone, North Carolina) to Dickey, 2 March 1973, folder 4, box 46, General Correspondence, Dickey Papers. West was born in the mountains, in Wilkes County, North Carolina, and received an undergraduate degree from Mars Hill College outside of Asheville. See North Carolina Arts Council, "Remember John Foster West," http://ncarts.org/freeform_scrn_template.cfm?ffscrn_id=470 (accessed 3 March 2010).

104. David McClellan (Department of English, East Tennessee State University) to Dickey, 4 September 1970, folder 5, box 42, General Correspondence, Dickey Papers. McClellan wanted Dickey to know that he had been an undergraduate in the mountains at Emory and Henry College in Southwest Virginia.

105. Robert Linn (fan, Calhoun, Georgia) to Dickey, 24 May 1970, folder 13, box 41, Dickey Papers.

106. Noel C. Dickey (fan, Beaufort, South Carolina) to Dickey, 28 August 1973, folder 9, box 46, Dickey Papers.

107. Mr. Wesley D. Applegate (fan, Camilla, Georgia) to Marshall, 16 March

1970, folder 5, box 11, Marshall Papers. A woman in Jamestown, New York, waxed poetic about a past trip to the Blue Ridge Parkway, and a woman in Indiana wrote of her "love of the Great Smokies and nature in general." Miss Gertrude R. Johnson (fan, Zion Covenant Church, Jamestown, New York) to Marshall, 18 April 1968, folder 2, box 11, Marshall Papers; Miss Sharon Eichele (fan, Evansville, Indiana) to Marshall, 21 October 1968, folder 2, box 11, Marshall Papers.

108. Judy Downing (fan, Valley, Washington) to Marshall, 1 February 1969, folder 3, box 11, Marshall Papers.

109. Margaret (Mrs. Dennis) Steward (fan, Piscataway, New Jersey) to Dickey, 27 August 1973, folder 2, box 12, Marshall Papers.

110. Herman S. Frey (fan, Democratic candidate for U.S. senator, Nashville, Tennessee), to Marshall, 7 September 1970, folder 6, box 11, Marshall Papers. See also: "Could you give me any directions as to how I could visit the cove?" Miss Vicki Hendrix (fan, seventeen years old, Candler, North Carolina) to Marshall, 8 September 1971, folder 7, box 11, Marshall Papers.

111. Judith P. (Mrs. A. E.) Canant Jr. (fan, Titusville, Florida) to Marshall, 20 July 1972, folder 1, box 12, Marshall Papers.

112. Miss Diane Wells (fan, nineteen years old, Napoleon, Ohio) to Marshall, 21 February 1971, folder 7, box 11, Marshall Papers.

113. Marshall to Mrs. Jack W. Chapman (fan, Canton, North Carolina), 15 January 1969, folder 3, box 11, Marshall Papers.

114. Marshall to Miss Diane Wells (fan, Napoleon, Ohio), 2 April 1971, folder 7, box 11, Marshall Papers; Marshall to Mrs. John T. R. (Olive M.) Andrews (fan, Englewood, Ohio), 5 June 1970, folder 6, box 11, Marshall Papers.

115. For an account of Myers's life, see Barbara League, *Letters to Lori: The Family History and Stories of Opal Corn Myers* (Elsmere, KY, 2007), available at http://www.letterstolori.org/ (accessed 22 November 2010). Marshall also suggested that readers contact "Mrs. Opal Myers," who, though "not a well-educated woman, . . . is very much in touch with the local situation at the grass roots level." Marshall to Miss Sheri Schumacher (fan, Lemon Grove, California), 16 April 1971, folder 7, box 11, Marshall Papers.

116. Judy (Mrs. Robert L.) Brewer (fan, Knoxville, Tennessee) to Marshall, 8 July 1972, folder 1, box 12, Marshall Papers.

117. Judith P. (Mrs. A. E.) Canant Jr. (fan, Titusville, Florida) to Marshall, 4 November 1975 (filed with Canant to Marshall, 20 July 1972, folder 1, box 12, Marshall Papers).

118. Mrs. Koni Sowinski (fan) to Marshall, 20 October 1973, folder 2, box 12, Marshall Papers. For Mary King, at college in Indiana, "it was difficult to tell whether I was myself, or Christy." Miss Mary King (fan, Huntington College, Huntington, Indiana) to Marshall, 27 October 1972, folder 1, box 12, Marshall Papers.

119. Mr. Sheldon D. Alquist Jr. (fan, San Francisco, California) to Marshall, 27 January 1970, folder 5, box 11, Marshall Papers.

120. Miss Jeanne Yohey (fan, twenty years old, McMinnville, Oregon) to Marshall, 16 November 1968, folder 3, box 11, Marshall Papers.

121. Miss Deborah Butler (fan, sixteen years old) to Marshall, n.d. (filed under Marshall to Butler, 2 April 1969, folder 2, box 11, Marshall Papers).

122. Sixteen-year-old Barbara wrote, "I'm glad this world has people like" your mother and "I wish I could be like her." Barbara Angus (fan, sixteen years old, Windsor, Ontario, Canada) to Marshall, 20 June 1973, folder 2, box 12, Marshall Papers.

123. Wilcox reported that teens on his trip read *Christy* upon their return home from Barbourville, Kentucky. Mr. Craig J. Wilcox (fan) to Marshall, 30 September 1972, folder 1, box 12, Marshall Papers. Anna Starkey "relived many of my own experiences" at a mission school in Pineville, Kentucky, in 1944. Miss Anna Starkey (fan, Pineville, Kentucky) to Marshall, 14 January 1968, folder 2, box 11, Marshall Papers.

124. Elizabeth (Mrs. Peter W.) Luca (fan, Montvale, New Jersey) to Marshall, 20 August 1969, folder 4, box 11, Marshall Papers.

125. Other missionary fans included Susan Giboney, who had "spent 3 years on the mission field in Japan," and a former missionary to Nigeria. Susan (Mrs. Terry T.) Giboney (fan, La Habra, California) to Marshall, 26 November 1969, folder 4, box 4; no name (Ogbomosho, Nigeria) to Marshall, 3 June 1968, folder 8, box 29, both in Marshall Papers.

126. Miss Debbie Keller (fan, ninth grade, Sandia Base, New Mexico) to Marshall, 7 March 1969, folder 4, box 11, Marshall Papers.

127. Marshall to Miss Nancy Barnes (fan, Atlanta, Georgia), 20 January 1969, folder 3, box 11, Marshall Papers.

128. Miss Anne Wallace (fan, Frederick, Maryland) to Marshall, 17 July 1972, folder 1, box 12, Marshall Papers. Ina Robison, a missionary for decades in Africa and Europe, "couldn't imagine such a needy, benighted area as Apalachia right within our own borders." Mrs. Ina M. Robison (fan, St. Helena, California) to Marshall, 18 July 1973, filed under her original letter of 11 July 1973, folder 2, box 12, Marshall Papers.

129. The term *mountain whites* had largely fallen out of popular usage by the 1960s, but it is appropriate in this context given that it was coined in the 1880s by missionaries working in the mountains.

130. Miss Dee Ann ("Dede") Smith (fan, Montville, New Jersey) to Marshall, n.d. (filed with Marshall to Smith, 9 September 1969), folder 4, box 11, Marshall Papers.

131. Mrs. Penny Langston (fan, Prescott, Arkansas) to Marshall, 16 May 1969, folder 4, box 11, Marshall Papers.

132. Marshall to Miss Susan Johnson (fan, Miami, Florida), 30 January 1970, folder 5, box 11, Marshall Papers. Marshall often mailed copies of *Mountain Life and Work* to such fans. See Marshall to Miss Laura Nelson (fan, Andover, Ohio), 7 April 1970, folder 5, box 11, Marshall Papers.

133. Miss Sheri Schumacher (fan, Lemon Grove, California) to Marshall, 30 March 1971; Marshall to Miss Sheri Schumacher (fan, Lemon Grove, California), 16 April 1971, both in folder 7, box 11, Marshall Papers.

134. Marshall to Miss Cyd Drennen (fan, Wichita, Kansas), 20 January 1969, folder 3, box 11, Marshall Papers. Marshall quotes Drennen's letter (not extant) in her reply.

135. Marshall to Miss Sharon Eichele (fan, Evansville, Indiana), 31 October 1968, folder 2, box 11, Marshall Papers. Marshall to Mr. W. Don Rogers (fan, Sunday School Board of the Baptist Convention, Nashville, Tennessee), 28 June 1967, folder 1, box 11, Marshall Papers. "Your aunt is correct, [David is modeled on my father.] My problem was that I had sort of written myself into a corner by characterizing David exactly as I did." Marshall to Mrs. R. L. Zavasky (fan, Newport News, Virginia) to Marshall, 3 March 1969, folder 3, box 11, Marshall Papers. In other letters, Marshall gives additional explanations for deviating from her mother's biography. In one instance, she claimed she did it "in order to provide a dramatic conclusion." Marshall to Miss Mildred W. Spain (fan, Paris, Texas), 27 May 1969, folder 4, box 11, Marshall Papers. Curiously, Marshall once told a reader she would not be wrong to see Dr. MacNeill as "the Peter Marshall type of man—if you have ever seen a picture of Peter Marshall." This suggests that Marshall rewrote her mother's story to have her mother's character marry Marshall's husband rather than Marshall's father. Marshall to Miss Susan Sunseri (fan, San Jose, California), 21 January 1969, folder 3, box 11, Marshall Papers.

136. Of all readers who discussed characters or places, most wanted to know if the "real-life Christy" married the doctor and, if so, what happened to the minister. Marshall to Billy Click Jr. (fan, Shelby, North Carolina), 12 December 1978, folder 1, box 13, Marshall Papers. Marshall quotes Click's letter (which is not extant) in her reply. Susan (Mrs. Terry T.) Giboney (fan, La Habra, California) to Marshall, 26 November 1969, folder 4, box 4, Marshall Papers.

137. In 1971, a nineteen-year-old woman in Ohio wrote perhaps the most outrageously long list of questions of the many Marshall received. Diane Wells had typed forty-five questions, a sampling of which conveys the intense interest readers had in the details surrounding the novel and their confusion about the relationship between the author and the characters: "3. Were you born in the cove? 4. When did you leave the cove? 5. Who took over doctoring the people? . . . 45. Did Dr. MacNeill and Christy ever have a big wedding?" Miss Diane Wells (fan, Napoleon, Ohio) to Marshall, 21 February 1971, folder 7, box 11, Marshall Papers. Marshall told Miss Wells that although she had "received many letters with questions, I believe that you get the prize for the most!" Marshall to Miss Diane Wells (fan, Napoleon, Ohio), 2 April 1971, folder 7, box 11, Marshall Papers.

138. Sandra van der Meulen tried to rationalize this outcome by suggesting the doctor's need to conduct research elsewhere, but wondered that he and

Christy would not have visited often. Mrs. Sandra J. van der Meulen (fan, Waterloo, Ontario, Canada) to Marshall, 22 August 1973, folder 2, box 12, Marshall Papers.

139. Joyce (Mrs. H. C.) Godsey (fan, Houston, Texas) to Marshall, n.d. (filed with Marshall to Godsey, 24 January 1969, folder 3, box 11, Marshall Papers).

140. Mrs. Elisa T. Sywulka (fan, Syracuse, New York) to Marshall, 28 November 1969, folder 4, box 11, Marshall Papers. Marshall replied to Sywulka that her parents "felt called to work in a country parish in Greenville, Tennessee." Marshall to Mrs. Elisa T. Sywulka (fan, Syracuse, New York), 8 December 1969, folder 4, box 11, Marshall Papers.

141. Jim Peterson (fan-acquaintance, Billings, Montana) to Dickey, ca. May 1990, folder 5, box 89, General Correspondence, Dickey Papers.

142. Don Markos (fan-acquaintance, California State University, East Bay, Castro Valley, California) to Dickey, 4 August 1971, folder 9, box 43, General Correspondence, Dickey Papers.

143. Andy Valentine (fan, Nashville, Tennessee) to Dickey, n.d., folder 1, box 89, General Correspondence, Dickey Papers.

144. Another couple reported that they "spend as much time as we possibly can out of doors" on the Mississippi River. H. R. "Rod" Hurd (fan-acquaintance, President, KWNO, Winona, Minnesota) to Dickey, 22 May 1970, folder 13, box 40, General Correspondence, Dickey Papers. Barbara Mayor in Minneapolis wrote, "My husband & I are canoe enthusiasts in love with the St. Croix river. You should try it." Barbara Mayor (fan, Minneapolis, Minnesota) to Dickey, 9 September 1970, folder 5, box 42, General Correspondence, Dickey Papers.

145. Darlene LaPler (fan, Crow's Landing, California) to Dickey, ca. October 1972, folder 6, box 45, General Correspondence, Dickey Papers.

146. Dean Norman (fan, Upper Cuyahoga Association, Ohio) to Dickey, 30 October 1972, folder 11, box 46, General Correspondence, Dickey Papers.

147. Michael E. Ray (fan, Furman University, Greenville, South Carolina) to Dickey, 19 March 1970, folder 7, box 39, General Correspondence, Dickey Papers.

148. Tom Shapcott (fan-acquaintance, Shapcott Public Accountants, Ipswich, Queensland, Australia,) to Dickey, 2 April 1971, folder 1, box 41, General Correspondence, Dickey Papers.

149. Michael Blowen (fan-acquaintance, Brookline, Massachusetts) to Dickey, 2 July 1971, folder 8, box 43, General Correspondence, Dickey Papers.

150. One friend of Dickey told him that "touches of what Wyeth has done for Maine were in your Georgia." Peter F. Neumeyer (fan-acquaintance, Stony Brook, New York) to Dickey, 8 May 1970, folder 9, box 40, General Correspondence, Dickey Papers.

151. Jack Hope (fan-acquaintance, New York, New York) to Dickey, 10 October 1980, folder 4, box 56, General Correspondence, Dickey Papers. An author of a book "set among the Acadian people" but with "universal appeal" asked

Dickey to provide a blurb. Chris Segure (fan-acquaintance, Abbeville, Louisiana) to Dickey, n.d., folder 9, box 88, General Correspondence, Dickey Papers.

152. John Montague (friend, Paris, France) to Dickey, 10 June 1971, folder 7, box 43, General Correspondence, Dickey Papers. Another described his writing retreat by saying "Cornwall is the English Ozarks." Harry Minetree (friend, Bodmin, England) to Dickey, 15 April 1970, folder 5, box 40, General Correspondence, Dickey Papers.

153. Helena Anderson (fan, Peru, Kansas) to Dickey, 11 May 1970, folder 10, box 40, General Correspondence, Dickey Papers.

154. Thwaite, "Out of Bondage," 310–11.

155. Patterson, *Grand Expectations*, 593, 681.

156. We know of several racial equivalencies or reversals that informed Dickey's novel. First, *Heart of Darkness* influenced *Deliverance* more than any other literature (Hart, *James Dickey*, 449). Second, the hillbillies in *Deliverance* were inspired in part by a story about a black man from Atlanta who was killed after his move to North Georgia. On one of Dickey's canoeing trips with Lewis King and Al Braselton, King had ventured off on his own when, according to Hart, he aroused the suspicions of Ira Gentry and his son, Lucas. The Gentrys, according to the Atlantans, thought King was from the Revenue Service and waited with King for Dickey and Braselton to arrive by canoe to confirm King's assertion to the contrary (250). The Gentrys' curious appearance, in Dickey's eyes (overalls, rotten teeth, accompanied by rifle and dog), and Dickey's anxiety about their reaction to the trio, spurred his depiction of mountain residents (251). According to Hart, "Ira asked, 'Where y'all boys from?' They replied, 'Atlanta,' so Ira shot back: 'She-ut, we kill people like you up here.' He chortled to indicate that he was only half-serious, but his comment frightened Dickey." Ira told them a story about a "nigger" who moved there from Atlanta. The man "just started acting up and we just had to get the sheriff to kill him" (251). Hart wonders in his biography "why . . . Dickey turn[ed] a North Georgia sheriff's murder of a black man from Atlanta into a redneck's rape of a white man from Atlanta" (254). It is also curious that Dickey used the Gentrys' name for his city protagonist.

157. K. A. G. (Chicago), "Stark, Gripping, Tale," 20 January 2007, review of *Deliverance*, Amazon.com (accessed 15 March 2007); T. L. "Jr.," (Midwest), "They Don't Make Them Like This Anymore," 26 June 2006, review of *Deliverance*, Amazon.com (accessed 15 March 2007).

158. Ed Potton, "Southern Discomfort," *Times* (London), 22 September 2007, Features, 6.

5. A Sweet Land That Never Was, circa 1994–2001

Some of the ideas contained in this chapter initially appeared in "Romancing Whiteness: Popular Appalachian Fiction and the Imperialist Imagination at the Turns of Two Centuries," in *At Home and Abroad: Historicizing Twentieth-*

Century Whiteness in Literature and Performance, ed. La Vinia Delois Jennings (Knoxville: University of Tennessee Press, 2009), 93–117; and "Objecting to Insider/Outsider Politics and the Uncritical Celebration of Appalachia," *Appalachian Journal* 38, no. 1 (2010): 68–73.

1. A reader, "As real as a character can be—Miss Ivy Rowe," review of *Fair and Tender Ladies*, Amazon, 29 May 1999; Caroline Herring, Facebook fan site, http://www.facebook.com/pages/Caroline-Herring/71530870168?ref=ts, 13 June 2010 (accessed 16 June 2010).

2. Though local color has traditionally been understood as a representation of rural peoples, Stephanie Foote has shown how its strategies were applied also to urban settings. Foote, *Regional Fictions: Culture and Identity in Nineteenth-Century American Literature* (Madison: University of Wisconsin Press, 2001), 124–25.

3. For more on the relationship between literature and ethnography during the Gilded Age, see Michael A. Elliott, *The Culture Concept: Writing and Difference in the Age of Realism* (Minneapolis: University of Minnesota Press, 2002). Quote is from xxv. Henry D. Shapiro notes that the "claims of [local-color writing] to verisimilitude were key to the process by which the concept of Appalachia was generated" (*Appalachia on Our Mind: The Southern Mountains and Mountaineers in the American Consciousness, 1870–1920* [Chapel Hill: University of North Carolina Press, 1978], 18–19). Tom Lutz observes that reviewers called local-color writer Hamlin Garland a "historian" in 1904; Sarah Orne Jewett a "social historian" in 1886; and George Washington Cable a writer of "romance and sociology." Lutz says the critics' claims were exaggerated but were intended to suggest that literature stood above, and encompassed, the sciences (*Cosmopolitan Vistas: American Regionalism and Literary Value* [Ithaca, NY: Cornell University Press, 2004], 35). Reviews of *In the Tennessee Mountains* tended to emphasize the poetry, descriptiveness, and artistry of Craddock's writing (see Oscar Fay Adams, "The Prose of Mr. Craddock," *Literary World*, 4 October 1884, 330) more than they credited "him" with scientific accuracy, but several mentioned realism, particularly in regard to "his" rendering of the mountain *"patois"* (review of *In the Tennessee Mountains*, *Dial*, June 1884, 43). One reviewer credited Craddock with being a "keen observer" who "made his studies at first hand" and whose book provided a "transcript of peculiar scenery" (review of *In the Tennessee Mountains*, *Literary World*, 31 May 1884, 179). A review of Fox's *The Trail of the Lonesome Pine* in the *Baltimore Sun* called it "a study of anthropology." (*Baltimore Sun*, 22 November 1908, *Trail of the Lonesome Pine* scrapbook, Fox Family Papers, Special Collections and Digital Programs, University of Kentucky Libraries, Lexington).

4. By 2002, scholars of late-nineteenth-century regional literature like June Howard had begun to note manifest similarities in contemporary and local-color-era fiction (June Howard, "Toward an Understanding of 'Region' and 'Regionalism'" [paper delivered at the American Studies Association, Houston,

17 November 2002]. Notes in possession of the author). During the early 2000s, bookseller Barnes and Noble placed such works within the browsing category of "Settings and Atmosphere," from which one could then select "Rural Settings" or "Small Towns" (BarnesandNoble.com, http://search.barnesandnoble.com/booksearch/results.asp?CAT=73userid=2VXCEW10 [accessed 27 February 2004]). Garrison Keillor's *Lake Wobegon Days* spent six weeks at the top of the *New York Times* best-seller list in 1985 and remained in the top ten for forty-eight weeks; his *Leaving Home* was the eighteenth best-selling fiction book of the 1980s (John Bear, *The #1 New York Times Bestseller: Intriguing Facts about the 484 Books That Have Been #1 New York Times Bestsellers since the First List in 1942* [Berkeley: Ten Speed, 1992], 194–95).

5. The market expansion of trade paperback fiction beginning in the mid-1980s opened up a new venue for regional writing by marketable newcomers. Prior to this time, best-selling fiction was released in mass-market paperbacks and was usually written by well-established veteran best-selling authors. But by the 1990s, publishers expanded the number of novels released in a "trade" paperback format. (Trade paperbacks are taller, thinner, and pricier books, costing around $14 in 2003 versus $8 for mass-market paperbacks. They are ornamented with more handsomely designed cover artwork targeted toward literary-minded readers.) By 2004, trade paperback sales had surged, likely due in large part to the success of Oprah Winfrey's and other book clubs. In a striking break with the convention of reserving the trade format for nonfiction, in 2004 more than half of the trade paperbacks that sold over one hundred thousand copies were novels. Trade fiction featured large numbers of first novels by unknown authors—unheard of when the mass-market format, with its low profit margin, dominated the fiction market (Dermot McEvoy and Daisy Maryles, "Playing the Numbers: More Trade Fiction, but the Top Seller Is a Cookbook; in Mass, Veterans Dominate," *Publishers Weekly*, 24 March 2003; Dermot McEvoy and Daisy Maryles, "Numbers Up: Fiction Dominates; Make Way for Veterans, Movie Tie-ins and More Novels in All Editions," *Publishers Weekly*, 22 March 2004; Dermot McEvoy and Daisy Maryles, "Everything All over Again: Debut Novels Score Big in Trade; in Mass Market, It's Mostly Women's Fiction and, of Course, Dan Brown," *Publishers Weekly*, 28 March 2005). The meteoric rise of trade paperbacks occurred simultaneously with the "almost explosive growth in the number of women participating in informal reading groups since the 1980s." More research is needed to understand whether the geographical distribution of book clubs promoted the popularity of regional writing in particular. See Elizabeth Long, *Book Clubs: Women and the Uses of Reading in Everyday Life* (Chicago: University of Chicago Press, 2003), 19.

6. "Top 100: 10 Years' Best," *USA Today*, 11 March 2004, 7D. Additional harbingers of the rising popularity of regional settings include *Cold Sassy Tree*, set in small-town Georgia, which received national acclaim in 1984; Carolyn Chute's chronicle of working-class and impoverished New Englanders, *The*

Beans of Egypt, Maine, which was a surprise *New York Times* best seller in 1985; Fanny Flagg's *Fried Green Tomatoes at the Whistle Stop Café* (1992); and Annie Proulx's *Shipping News* (1994). Louis L'Amour's westerns were among the top fifteen national best sellers in 1983 and in 1985 through 1988 (John Unsworth, "20th Century Bestsellers," http://www3.isrl.illinois.edu/~unsworth/courses/bestsellers/best80.cgi [accessed 11 January 2010]).

7. Perhaps the Japanese protagonist in *Memoirs of a Geisha* is one such exception. None appear to be African American. The race of Dinah from the book of Genesis (*The Red Tent*) and the main character of *Green Eggs and Ham* are up for debate.

8. Julia W. (Knoxville, Tennessee), "Real Appalachian Fiction," review of *Clay's Quilt*, Amazon, 28 March 2001; A reader, "Interesting but uneven first novel," review of *Cold Mountain*, Amazon, 10 December 1997. *Clay's Quilt* will hereafter be designated as *CQ*; *Cold Mountain* as *CM*.

9. See the introduction for a fuller discussion of this period.

10. On the popularity of ethnic fiction and its relation to regional fiction, see Jeff Karem, *The Romance of Authenticity: The Cultural Politics of Regional and Ethnic Literatures* (Charlottesville: University of Virginia Press, 2004). The Ethnic Heritage Act of 1974 and the American Folklife Preservation Act of 1976 were harbingers of the multiculturalism movement that surged in the 1970s through at least the end of the century.

11. Migration figures are from Wendy Griswold, *Regionalism and the Reading Class* (Chicago: University of Chicago Press, 2008), 71n2, based on the U.S. Census; Manuel Castells, *The Information Age—Economy, Society, and Culture*, vol. 2, *The Power of Identity* (Malden, MA: Blackwell, 1997), 2, 6, 7, 60–61, 67. "Knowable communities" is Raymond Williams's term, *The Country and the City* (New York: Oxford University Press, 1973), 165.

12. Williams, *The Country and the City*, 138–39.

13. Jock Young sums up Eric Hobsbawm's observations when he writes, "Just as community collapses, identity is invented." Quoted in Zygmunt Bauman, *Community: Seeking Safety in an Insecure World* (Malden, MA: Polity, 2001), 15.

14. A reader, "Who are your people," review of *Parchment of Leaves*, Amazon, 8 November 2002.

15. Marilyn Halter, *Shopping for Identity: The Marketing of Ethnicity* (New York: Schocken, 2000), 12; Elliott, *The Culture Concept*, xxi. For more on the white ethnic identity revival, see Matthew Frye Jacobson, "Ethnic Revival and the Denial of White Privilege," in *Whiteness of a Different Color: European Immigrants and the Alchemy of Race* (Cambridge, MA: Harvard University Press, 1998), 274–282, and *Roots Too: White Ethnic Revival in Post–Civil Rights America* (Cambridge, MA: Harvard University Press, 2006). For an example of Scots-Irish identity politics, see James Webb, *Born Fighting: How the Scots-Irish Shaped America* (New York: Broadway, 2004). For a discussion of the potential dangers of Appalachian ethnic identity politics, see the conclusion to this book.

16. Brian Scott, "America Loves 'Southern Appalachian' Fiction," Book Publishing News Blog, 18 January 2009, http://bookpublishingnews.blogspot.com/ (accessed 14 March 2011).

17. Authors' comments were made at the Literary Festival, Emory and Henry College, Emory, Virginia, 21 and 22 September 2006. Notes in possession of the author.

18. Lee Smith, "Mountain Music's Moment in the Sun," *Washington Post*, 12 August 2001, G01. Smith also cited NASCAR auto racing and the 2000 film *O Brother, Where Art Thou?* as part of what she called "the Appalachianization of mainstream America." She named as part of the "veritable explosion of Appalachian writing" Charles Frazier's *Cold Mountain* (1997), Barbara Kingsolver's *Prodigal Summer* (2001), Sharyn McCrumb's ballad novels, Homer Hickam's *Rocket Boys* (and the movie version of the book, *October Sky*), and two Oprah Book Club selections, Robert Morgan's *Gap Creek* (1999) and Gwyn Hyman Rubio's *Icy Sparks* (2001). The flurry of Appalachian-set writing during the Second Gilded Age also included the Christian-themed frontier series Spirit of Appalachia (beginning in 1997), children's books, memoirs, and popular nonfiction releases such as Bill Bryson's *A Walk in the Woods* (1997) and Noah Adams's *Far Appalachia* (2001).

19. Richard J. Butler, Benjamin W. Cowan, and Sebastian Nilsson, "From Obscurity to Bestseller: Examining the Impact of Oprah's Book Club Selections," *Publishing Research Quarterly* 20, no. 4 (2005): 23–34; McEvoy and Maryles, "Playing the Numbers"; McEvoy and Maryles, "Numbers Up."

20. See note 4 for a discussion of the rise of trade paperback novels. The 1994 release of *Mitford* had a small distribution through its Christian publisher, Lion. It was republished in 1996 by publishing giant Penguin. *Clay's Quilt* was initially published in March 2001 by the independent press Algonquin Books of Chapel Hill; in 2002 Ballantine, a division of Random House, released a trade paperback edition. *Cold Mountain* was initially published by the independent Grove/Atlantic before rights were acquired by Vintage, a division of Random House. Only *Big Stone Gap*, perhaps due to the author's connections thanks to her time writing for the *Cosby Show*, debuted with a major conglomerate (Random House/Ballantine). Editions of *Clay's Quilt* and *Big Stone Gap* include reading guides in the back matter of the novels. For online reading guides, see *At Home in Mitford*, http://www.penguinputnam.com/static/rguides/us/mitford_years_series.html, and *Cold Mountain*, http://www.randomhouse.com/catalog/display.pperl?isbn=9780375700750&view=rg (accessed 18 June 2010).

21. On celebrations of small-town America, see Frederic Jameson, "Nostalgia for the Present," in *Postmodernism; or, The Cultural Logic of Late Capitalism* (Durham: Duke University Press, 1991), 279–96.

22. As Doug Reichert Powell explains, a "complete understanding of place is derived not by surveying the relative accuracy of any one text." Rather, "varied

and competing representations" create "a dynamic and evolving mosaic." Douglas Reichert Powell, *Critical Regionalism: Connecting Politics and Culture in the American Landscape* (Chapel Hill: University of North Carolina Press, 2007), 171. My contention is that in best-selling fiction, characters who contest conventional good-hearted white Appalachian residents (for example, Lusa, a woman of Polish Jewish and Palestinian descent who marries into a white mountain family in Barbara Kingsolver's *A Prodigal Summer*) are the exceptions that prove the rule.

23. Kelly R. (South Dakota), "lovely read," review of *Big Stone Gap*, Amazon, 25 July 2000; L. C. (Gloversville, New York), "Spend Some Time in Big Stone Gap," review of *Big Stone Gap*, Amazon, 4 August 2000. *Big Stone Gap* will hereafter be designated as *BSG*.

24. Lion Publishing is based in Elgin, Illinois. Publication history available on Worldcat database, http://io.gsu.edu/cgi-bin/homepage.cgi?style=&_id=aa8cd646-1151672535-1755&_cc=1 (accessed 15 November 2004). Barnes and Noble, "Annotation," *At Home in Mitford*, http://hpsearch.barnesandnoble.com/At-Home-in-Mitford/Jan-Karon/e/9780140254488/?itm=9—TABS (accessed 10 November 2004).

25. Laurel-Rain S. ("Rain") [real name] (Fresno, California), "Destiny Takes a U-turn," review of *BSG*, Amazon, 6 March 2010; Barnes and Noble, "From the publisher," *Big Stone Gap*, http://search.barnesandnoble.com/Big-Stone-Gap/Adriana-Trigiani/e/9780345438324#TABS (accessed 10 November 2010).

26. For "lyrical," see A reader, "*Clay's Quilt* sings!" review of *CQ*, Amazon, 17 April 2001; S. L. ("Shannon") (Birmingham, Alabama), "Long live House!" review of *CQ*, 20 May 2006; A reader, "Lyrical and literate," review of *CM*, Amazon, 26 August 1997. For "exquisite," see Elizabeth M. (Arlington, Virginia), "Best Book I've read this year, except for *A Fine Balance*," review of *CM*, Amazon, 16 October 1997. For "lush," see A reader (Bascom, Florida), "One of the best books I've ever read," review of *CM*, Amazon, 20 September 2003.

27. "From Publishers Weekly," 2001, *Clay's Quilt*, Amazon, http://www.amazon.com/Clays-Quilt-Ballantine-Readers-Circle/dp/0345450698 (accessed 10 November 2010).

28. "Best Selling Books Database," *USA Today*, http://content.usatoday.com/life/books/booksdatabase/default.aspx (accessed 28 May 2010). *Cold Mountain* was the second-best-selling fiction book for all of 1997, according to "Bestseller Lists, 1900–1995" [based on *Publishers Weekly*], Calder Books, http://www.calderbooks.com/bestintro.html (accessed 16 June 2010). On *Publishers Weekly* figures, see "Paperback Bestsellers," 31 August 1998 through 13 February 1999, and "Hardcover Bestsellers," 30 June 1997 through 24 August 1998. On *New York Times* figures, see "Best Sellers," 13 July 1997 through 6 September 1998, and "Paperback Best Sellers," 6 September 1998 through 6 February 2000, and 21 November 2003 through 7 March 2004.

29. "Paperback Best Sellers," *New York Times*, 17 August–5 October 1997; "Best Selling Books Database," *USA Today*, http://content.usatoday.com/life/

books/booksdatabase/default.aspx (accessed 28 May 2010). All of Karon's books have made the *USA Today* top 150 list.

30. *Big Stone Gap* also reached twelfth on the *New York Times* "Best Sellers Plus" independent store list and fourteenth on the chain store list. (For an account of the creation of the separate independent/chain stores best-seller lists, see Laura J. Miller, "The Best-Seller List as Marketing Tool and Historical Fiction," *Book History* 3 [2000]: 298.) "Paperback Bestsellers," *Publishers Weekly*, 13 August 2001, 322; "Best Selling Books Database," *USA Today*, http://content.usatoday.com/life/books/booksdatabase/default.aspx (accessed 28 May 2010); "Best Sellers Plus," *New York Times*, 8 July 2001, http://www.nytimes.com/books/01/07/08/bsp/bestpaperfiction.html and http://www.nytimes.com/books/01/07/08/bsp/paperfictioncompare.html; "Best Sellers Plus," *New York Times*, 15 July 2001, http://www.nytimes.com/books/01/07/08/bsp/bestpaperfiction.html (all accessed 13 October 2010).

31. *Clay's Quilt* "was tracked on the *New York Times* best-seller list at 35, but only the top 25 best-selling books are listed as best sellers" (Alicia Carmichael, "Family Is Background for Author's Book," *Bowling Green [KY] Daily News*, 4 March 2002, 1A, http://news.google.com/newspapers?nid=1696&dat=20020304&id=D_ceAAAAIBAJ&sjid=LZgEAAAAIBAJ&pg=2379,409159 [accessed 16 April 2010]).

32. As of 18 June 2010. For the sake of comparison, *The Da Vinci Code* (2003) had about 4,000 customer reviews and *Harry Potter and the Sorcerer's Stone* (1998) had over 5,500. A longer time since publication does not necessarily correlate to a higher number of reviews. BarnesandNoble.com reviews represent just a fraction of the overall reviews available, with approximately 150 reviews of *Cold Mountain* and just 10 of *Clay's Quilt*.

33. For *Cold Mountain*, see drebbles (Arlington, Massachusetts), "Ultimately Left Me Cold," review of *CM*, Amazon, 15 November 2008; S. S. ("Media Maven") (Mason, Ohio), "Book and Film—No Better, No Worse, All Good," review of *CM*, Amazon, 26 June 2008; Sandy N. (California), "Marvelous Historical Romance," review of *CM*, Amazon, 13 January 2008. For customer reviews of *At Home in Mitford* that recognize Mitford as a "mountain town," see A reader, "A very light-hearted, entertaining look at a small town," review of *At Home in Mitford*, Amazon, 21 December 1998; A reader, "This book is like a breath of fresh air," review of *At Home in Mitford*, Amazon, 27 September 1996. *At Home in Mitford* will hereafter be designated as *AHM*.

34. Jan Karon, *At Home in Mitford* (New York: Penguin, 1996), 16. Further references to this novel are to this edition and are noted parenthetically in the text as *AHM*.

35. Foote, *Regional Fictions*, 10; June Howard, "Unraveling Regions, Unsettling Periods: Sarah Orne Jewett and American Literary History," *American Literature: A Journal of Literary History, Criticism, and Bibliography* 68, no. 2 (1996): 367.

36. Mary Susan Herczog, "Love of a Good Book Makes Life Imitate Art; Clubs: Jan Karon's 'The Mitford Years' Series Has Readers Dressing Up and Eating Just Like the Novels' Characters," *Los Angeles Times*, 6 July 1997, 1; Jan Karon and Martha McIntosh, *Jan Karon's Mitford Cookbook and Kitchen Reader* (New York: Viking, 2004).

37. For similar claims about Gilded Age authors' accuracy, see note 3. A reader, "Required reading for American History and/or social sciences," review of *CM*, Amazon, 20 August 1997; shidal (Texas), "Frazier Captures the Heart of a Man and a Woman," review of *CM*, Amazon, 25 November 1997; J. F. (Calgary, Alberta, Canada), "A fine debut novel," review of *CQ*, Amazon, 24 March 2003; Anna M. A. [real name] ("Teacher and Reader") (Talbott, Tennessee), "One of the best ever," review of *BSG*, Amazon, 22 August 2003; Frank E. C. (Florida), "Real People Living the Good Life," review of *BSG*, Amazon, 6 April 2000.

38. John P. (Plano, Texas), "Grabbed and thrust me into the 1860s!" review of *CM*, Amazon, 7 December1997; A reader, "Good Nature, Average People, No Issues," review of *CM*, Amazon, 6 December 1997.

39. jimds (Lakeland, Florida), "The most consuming novel I have read in years," review of *CM*, Amazon, 29 December 1997.

40. A reader, "*Clay's Quilt*," review of *CQ*, Barnes and Noble, 16 August 2002. The flip side was that if readers determined a fiction author did not reproduce the details precisely as in real life, the author was condemned for not getting it right. Locals in particular felt it "a slight" when, for example, *Big Stone Gap* placed television affiliate WCYB in Kingsport. Amy G. ("Amycougar") [real name] (Bluff City, Tennessee), "An okay read," review of *BSG*, Amazon, 5 May 2000. "We called it 'Big Stone,' not 'the Gap,' as the book terms it," huffed another reviewer. A reader (southwest Florida), "How did this book get published?" review of *BSG*, Amazon, 19 June 2000.

41. A reader (Tennessee), "Compelling Read," review of *CQ*, Amazon, 30 March 2002.

42. Christine G. (Shenandoah, Pennsylvania), "New author sews the fabric of Appalachian life," review of *CQ*, 27 June 2001. See also A reader, "The fabric of life, stitched with style," review of *CQ*, Barnes and Noble, 27 June 2001.

43. See Bob Minzesheimer's characterization of House as "mail carrier by day, novelist by night" ("House Letter-Perfect with His First Novel," *USA Today*, 19 April 2001, 5D); Scott Eyman opens his article with "Silas House is a rural mailman by trade, a writer by birth" ("Mountain-Style Survival," *Palm Beach Post*, 5 August 2001); see also Michele Leber, "*Clay's Quilt*," *Booklist*, 1 March 2001, 1226. An Associated Press article observes that House is a "mountain mail carrier and author" whose voice is "true to his homeland," and that his "home and heart are in the hills and hollows of Lily, population 800" (Karen Meiman, "Author Dispels Appalachian Stereotypes in Book," *Covington Kentucky Post*, 3 December 2001). A Knoxville-based author's customer review dubbed *Clay's*

Quilt "real Appalachian fiction," in contrast to the "so-called Appalachian fiction [that] reads as though the author became acquainted with the region by quickly driving through it on Interstate 75." Julia W. (Knoxville, Tennessee), "Real Appalachian Fiction," review of *CQ*, Amazon, 28 March 2001.

44. "Knows his terrain" is from A reader, "a perfectly realized vision of love and war," review of *CM*, Amazon, 1 July 1997; "has deep roots" is from A reader, "A Magnificent, Gripping Story Better Heard Than Read," review of *CM*, Barnes and Noble, 10 December 1999; "was inspired by [his] real life ancestors" is from Rosemarie M. ("rosemarie") [real name] (San Francisco Bay Area), "Cold Mountain," review of *CM*, Amazon, 2 May 2000.

45. A reader, "*Cold Mountain* Is a Testimony to North Carolina Determination," review of *CM*, Amazon, 2 October 1997. For a review that combines an argument that Frazier is cosmopolitan with great knowledge of literature plus has the accoutrements of authenticity (for example, tintypes and guns), see Talton W. (Amish Country, Ohio, USA), "Golden fodder . . . ," review of *CM*, Amazon, 16 June 1998.

46. I would like to thank Katherine Ledford for suggesting this point.

47. "Necessary distance to write," also quoted in the introduction to this book, is from Lee Smith's comments at the Literary Festival at Emory and Henry College, Emory, Virginia, 22 September 2006. Notes in possession of the author.

48. K. V. ("Kmarie") [real name] (Appalachian Mountains, Southwest Virginia), "One of my all time favorites, y'all!" review of *BSG*, Amazon, 23 August 2003; Denise B. ("Kelsana") (California Redwoods), "Small town America at it's best," review of *BSG*, Amazon, 1 September 2001. On the other hand, one Trigiani detractor surmised that her book was so successful because she "made so many contacts when she worked in Hollywood." A reader, "Entertainment industry hype?" review of *BSG*, Amazon, 21 June 2000.

49. Parchment Girl, "Ideal Summer Read," review of *AHM*, Amazon, 20 August 2009. A reader, "Discover an attitude that could change your life," review of *AHM*, Amazon, 16 October 1998.

50. Jan Karon, née Janice Meredith Wilson, was born in piedmont Lenoir, North Carolina, in 1937, and retired to the mountain tourist town of Blowing Rock, North Carolina. "Meet the Writers: Jan Karon," http://www.barnesandnoble.com (accessed 27 February 2004). Karon experienced something like John Fox Jr.'s ambivalence about her childhood home. She reported on her *Mitford* Web site, "As a young girl I couldn't wait to get off that farm, to go to Hollywood or New York. But living in those confined, bucolic circumstances was one of the best things that ever happened to me. . . . On the farm there is time to muse and dream."

51. See Griswold, *Regionalism and the Reading Class*, 26–29, for a useful gloss on the history and theory of the pastoral.

52. Review of *In This Mountain, Audiophile*, October–November 2002, http://www.audiofilemagazine.com/dbsearch/showreview.cfm?Num=11004 (accessed 10 September 2010).

53. Avudreedr (Abingdon, Virginia), "A Wonderful Book," review of *CQ*, Amazon, 19 March 2001.

54. Christine G. (Shenandoah, Pennsylvania), "New author sews the fabric of Appalachian life," review of *CQ*, Amazon, 27 June 2001; T. K. (Canton, Ohio), "Heart-warming & well told story . . . ," review of *CQ*, Amazon, 28 November 2005.

55. A reader, "Slow-paced and boring," review of *AHM*, Amazon, 15 December 1998; Pat K. (Philadelphia), "The Same Old Thing," review of *BSG*, Amazon, 25 May 2000; BarbaraBee (Florida), "Snore fest," review of *CQ*, Amazon, 22 February 2011. A critical reviewer asked of *Cold Mountain*, "Why is this book so boring?" A reader, "why?" review of *CM*, Amazon, 30 December 2003. See also *At Home in Mitford* is "like candy, empty sugar, no value. . . . [It is] escapist nonsense. . . . This author can only appeal to those of little faith who cannot accept and live in the world given us by the creator but instead want to live in a sappy dream." A reader (Beaver Dam, Wisconsin), "We all agree this book is complete schlock," review of *AHM*, Amazon, 7 February 1999.

56. "Down-home" is from K. D. ("kclynnd") (Minnesota), "Wonderful Story!" review of *CQ*, Amazon, 9 February 2004; "our too hurried world" is from A reader, "Warm funny—perfect for reading in a big chair by the fire," review of *AHM*, Amazon, 16 October 1996; "somewhere that felt like home" is from Dawn K. (Lima, Ohio), "Spend time w/Ave Maria &friends, feel at home in BSG," review of *BSG*, Amazon, 1 August 2002.

57. A reader (Napa, California), "Warm funny—perfect for reading in a big chair by the fire," review of *AHM*, Amazon, 16 October 1996.

58. A reader, "A easy gentle read—nice vacation from a stressed out world," review of *AHM*, Amazon, 3 June 1998; A reader, "A Comfortable Read," review of *AHM*, Amazon, 9 July 1999. See also: "I work in a very high pressure corporate job and find the quirky, imperfect, loveable characters an appealing reminder that there is another way to live. . . . Come to Mitford and remember that there are good people in the world." A reader, "I'd like to escape my corporate world to live in Mitford," review of *AHM*, Amazon, 12 July 1999.

59. Jana Riess of *The Review Revolution*, janariess.typepad.com (Cincinnati, Ohio), "A Welcome New Voice in Southern Fiction," review of *CQ*, Amazon, 26 March 2006.

60. parchment girl, "Ideal Summer Read," review of *AHM*, Amazon, 20 August 2009; Ashley DeVino, "The Effect of Air Pollution in Western North Carolina," 6 October 2010, Associated Content, http://www.associatedcontent.com/article/5842258/the_effect_of_air_pollution_in_western.html (accessed 29 December 2010). Some readers felt that reading about Appalachia brought them in closer contact with the natural world; see: "I love hiking and being in the mountains." E. L. H. [real name] (Laurel, Maryland), "An outstanding effort!" review of *CQ*, Amazon, 7 January 1998.

61. jshonebarger (Hope Mills, North Carolina), "Excellent Historical Novel," review of *CM*, Amazon, 3 March 2001.

62. A reader, "A easy gentle read—nice vacation from a stressed out world," review of *AHM*, Amazon, 3 June 1998.
63. A reader, "A heartwarming story that leaves you wanting more!" review of *AHM*, Amazon, 2 August 1999. Similarly, *Big Stone Gap* "makes you yearn for the traditional values of yester year." Frank E. C. (Florida), "Real People Living The Good Life," review of *BSG*, Amazon, 6 April 2000.
64. Eyman, "Mountain-Style Survival." Curiously, this same reviewer perceived the characters in *Clay's Quilt* as "largely non-verbal."
65. "Savor" is from blakel (Fairmont, West Virginia), "Slow your 20th century pace for this one!" review of *CM*, Amazon, 25 November 1997; "simple things" is from Susan E. A. [real name] (Williamstown, New Jersey), "*Cold Mountain*," review of *CM*, Amazon, 19 February 2003; "walk not run" is from Clint D. H. (Dallas, Texas), "*Cold Mountain* is for the walkers of life," review of *CM*, Amazon, 14 December 1997.
66. lavedaal (Seattle, Washington), "Escapism from the frenetic cosmo lifestyle," review of *BSG*, Amazon, 24 March 2001.
67. A reader, "her books take you away from hectic reality and show love," review of *AHM*, Amazon, 7 December 1997. In the face of a landslide of criticism that *Cold Mountain* was miserably paced and boring, fans retorted that "too many readers of today have the movie mentality . . . [of] give it to me and give it to me now. " A reader, "Frazier is no Cormac McCarthy *Thank Goodness!*" review of *CM*, Amazon, 16 December 1997. See also: "This isn't . . . told quickly and efficiently. It's . . . for . . . the . . . reader who has the patience . . . to regain that 'old consciousness' that we rarely find." A reader (Bascom, Florida), "One of the best books I've ever read," review of *CM*, Amazon, 20 September 2003. "They God, chew that fatback," expostulated a reviewer who praised the plodding beauty of the novel. mrnrpr (Boston, Massachusetts), "They God, chew that fatback," review of *CM*, Amazon, 12 November 1997.
68. "janet from a small Carolina town," review of *AHM*, Amazon, 23 November 1999; hankoverdrive, "Best Surprise of Last Year," review of *CQ*, Amazon, 4 January 2002; A reader, "A Modern Classic," review of *CM*, Amazon, 28 July 2001.
69. A reader, "Where to see Cold Mountain," review of *CM*, Amazon, 9 December 1997.
70. peoplemove (Melbourne, Florida), "Longing for days gone by," review of *AHM*, Amazon, 5 February 1998. See also: "recently visited Blowing Rock, NC," A reader, "Where's the TV series for Jan Karon's books?" review of *AHM*, Amazon, 25 July 1997.
71. A reader, "Required reading for American History and/or social sciences," review of *CM*, Amazon, 20 August 1997. See also: "I was fortunate enough to read this wonderful book while I was vacationing in Asheville, North Carolina, not far, apparently, from where the novel takes place." A reader, "A great read!" review of *CM*, Amazon, 20 August 1999. A *Clay's Quilt* reviewer from New

Hampshire with a home in Florida wrote, "Next time I go through Cumberland Gap, Clay, Alma, Dreama, Cake and all the rest will be with me, for sure!" jladdwallace (Florida and New Hampshire), "Praise From the White Mountains of NH," review of *CQ*, Amazon, 16 March 2005.

72. A reader, "Please forward my mail to Mitford . . . ," review of *AHM*, Amazon, 9 September 1999; A reader, "Call the Moving Company," review of *AHM*, Barnes and Noble, 16 February 2000. See also: "This book is homey, calming and charming; it makes me want to move to Mitford!" A reader, "Simply the best book I have ever read!" review of *AHM*, Amazon, 14 June 1999.

73. A reader (Virginia), review of *AHM*, Amazon, 17 December 1998.

74. A reader, "Sounds Almost Like Home," review of *AHM*, Barnes and Noble, 9 May 2002.

75. Janey D. (West Virginia), "Better than Calgon, taking me away to small-town USA," review of *AHM*, Amazon, 6 July 1998.

76. A reader, "Home away from home," review of *AHM*, Barnes and Noble, 18 September 2000.

77. parchment girl, "Ideal Summer Read," review of *AHM*, Amazon, 20 August 2009; Julie C. (Orlando, Florida), review of *AHM*, Amazon, 23 November 1999.

78. A reader, "Speaks to the Heart," review of *AHM* on audiocassette, Barnes and Noble, 7 August 2000; huxley_b2 (Mesa, Arizona), "A terrific edition to any library," review of *AHM*, Amazon, 31 August 2000.

79. A reader, "How I wish I lived in Mitford . . . ," review of *AHM*, Amazon, 16 November 1998.

80. iloveprovence (Columbia, South Carolina), "Jan Karon introduces readers to her mountain village!" review of *AHM*, Amazon, 23 August 2000. Mitford represented for readers "the small-town America that our society longs for" in an "age when guns and violence in the schools is commonplace." Thomas C. N. ("Music Teacher") (Ebensburg, Pennsylvania), "Love Grows Here!" review of *AHM*, Amazon, 1 September 2000.

81. Charles Frazier, *Cold Mountain* (New York: Vintage, 1998), 36, 261. Further references to this novel are to this edition and are noted parenthetically in the text as *CM*.

82. Stacey M. J. [real name] (Conway, Arkansas), "The Odyssey of a Confederate soldier and his Penelope," review of *CM*, Amazon, 3 July 2003.

83. Deanie N. (Tennessee), "Very pleasant read," review of *CQ*, Amazon, 20 January 2006.

84. Marna ("Writing Professional"), "A Big Disappointment," review of *AHM*, Amazon, 5 January 1998.

85. A reader, "A book of Faith, in a town, and a time which is pure fiction," review of *AHM* on audiocassette, Amazon, 18 February 1999.

86. A reader, "Molasses for the Masses," review of *AHM*, Amazon, 18 April 2000.

87. A reader, "warm and fuzzies," review of *AHM*, Amazon, 11 January 1998. "For all those who indicated this is unrealistic you obviously don't live in the South," huffed one. "There are those of us who still value honesty, integrity, faithfulness and love for God and community." A reader (Franklin, Tennessee), "Sweet and charming story," review of *AHM*, Amazon, 11 May 1998. A reader living in Kentucky's largest city, Louisville, but "who grew up in a rural town of 6,000 people," said testily, "I would suggest to those of you who think life in Mitford is pure fiction that you pack your bags and drive around the back roads of this country." A reader (Louisville, Kentucky), "My thanks to Jan Karon for her wonderful book," review of *AHM*, Amazon, 19 February 1999.

88. Lorene ("Reader in NC") (Fletcher, North Carolina), "Yes, You Can Go Home Again," review of *BSG*, Amazon, 3 July 2003.

89. S. L. ("Shannon") (Birmingham, Alabama), "Long live House!" review of *CQ*, Amazon, 21 May 2006.

90. K. D. A. [real name] (Aiken, South Carolina), "Couldn't put it down; and I hate to read!!!!" review of *CQ*, Amazon, 23 February 2006.

91. A reader, "Soul-stirring, primal and dark—outstanding," review of *CM*, Amazon, 4 January 1998.

92. Jayne T. (Alexandria, Virginia), "Big Stone Gap is no Small Time Sensation," review of *BSG*, Amazon, 5 April 2000.

93. A reader, "make room for Charles Frazier," review of *CM*, Amazon, 16 July 1997; A reader, "Diminishing returns," review of *CM*, Amazon, 24 February 1999.

94. Of over four hundred Eastern Kentucky Social Club (EKSC) members registered at the 2003 reunion in Atlanta, I collected questionnaires from thirty-nine. Of that thirty-nine, thirteen were male and twenty-six female. Only three respondents were under thirty years old, and the vast majority were over fifty, with over half of the respondents reporting that they have attended the reunion for more than thirty years. Thirty out of thirty-nine reported that their fathers were coal miners, and thirty out of thirty-nine were raised in Lynch, Benham, Jenkins, or Harlan, in Harlan County, Kentucky. Most of those thirty left Harlan County when they were eighteen years old, with a number of them leaving sooner (as young as ten) and a few leaving in their twenties (and as late as forty years old). Few EKSC members living outside Kentucky reported ever "getting back to" Harlan County. The concept "Appalachia" held little appeal for EKSC members, with only eight of thirty-nine survey respondents claiming an Appalachian identity.

Just three members accounted for one-third of all forty-six Appalachia-related books or movies read or viewed by participating EKSC members. *Deliverance* (eleven viewers), Henry Louis Gates Jr.'s *Colored People* (1994) (ten readers), and *O Brother, Where Art Thou?* (2000) (seven viewers) were by far the most read or viewed. Only four participants had read the 1991 children's book *Willie Pearl*, about an African American girl in Harlan County, which was written by a former resident. The author, Michelle Green, had promoted her book at the California reunion (EKSC member comment, personal conversation, 2 August 2003).

EKSC, founded in 1970, holds reunions in the new hometowns of its scattered members. Its eleven chapters are located across the United States, including Cleveland, Detroit, California, and Indianapolis. The Atlanta chapter organized in 1990 under the name Southeastern Kentucky Heritage Association in an effort to present itself as a professional and civic organization rather than a social club. I offer my sincere thanks to the Atlanta chapter leadership for granting me permission to conduct research at the 2003 reunion. For more about the organization, see Thomas E. Wagner and Philip J. Obermiller, *African American Miners and Migrants: The Eastern Kentucky Social Club* (Champaign: University of Illinois Press, 2004).

95. Freida Hopkins Outlaw, personal conversation, EKSC reunion, Atlanta, GA, 1 August 2003; unidentified man, personal conversation, EKSC reunion, Atlanta, GA, 1 August 2003. Notes in possession of the author.

96. A reader, "Delightful story that you will want to share with others," review of *CM*, Amazon, 27 July 1997. See also: "For any person who has worked or lived in the Appalachian mountains, this superb novel will remind you again of the unique character and honest pride of the people." carl.s. (Tennessee), "Poetry on every page," review of *CM*, Amazon, 11 July 1999.

97. Keith E. (Victoria, British Columbia, Canada), "It's a love story, alrighty, but not between two people," review of *CM*, Amazon, 7 January 1998.

98. Elizabeth M. [real name] (Clarksburg, West Virginia), "How Does One Top This Read . . . Now, there's the Rub!!" review of *AHM*, Amazon, 11 April 2001.

99. George S. (Church Hill, Tennessee), "Who says there is no such thing as a 'time machine'!" review of *BSG*, Amazon, 15 April 2000. See also Bette M. N. in Lexington, North Carolina, who recommended *Big Stone Gap* for "any woman who remembers what it was like to be single in a small Southern town in the 70s" because it "is a story about . . . the kind of fundamental goodness that many of us attach, correctly or incorrectly, to the small towns of our youth but find so rarely in the Information Age." Bette M. N. (Lexington, North Carolina), "Gender, Generations, and Grace in the Gap," review of *BSG*, Amazon, 6 August 2000.

100. L. B. S. R. [real name] (Bellevue and Richland, Washington), "Taste of Appalachia served on a platter of family intrigue," review of *BSG*, Amazon, 10 April 2000.

101. Gloria E. S. (Middlebury, Indiana), "The North Carolina Test of Time," review of *CM*, Amazon, 10 June 1998.

102. Susan P. (Seattle, Washington), "A gloriously told chapter of a southern family history," review of *CM*, Amazon, 30 November 1997.

103. A reader, "a joyfilled refreshing look at God 'at work,'" review of *AHM*, Amazon, 30 September 1998.

104. A reader (Wilmington, North Carolina), "I was totally captivated by this lovely book," review of *AHM*, Amazon, 16 March 1999. See also: "Reading this delightful story and getting to know the inhabitants of Mitford during a tumultuous time in my life has given me some peace. I grew up in a small town and this story has brought to mind many memories of that time. I'm considering moving back to my hometown after living away for nearly 30 years. I want to live the simple, meaningful life found in places like 'Mitford.'" A reader, "I didn't want to leave this wonderful town," review of *AHM*, Amazon, 7 July 1999.

105. Holly R. Barcus and Stanley D. Brunn, "Towards a Typology of Mobility and Place Attachment," *Journal of Appalachian Studies* 15, nos. 1–2 (2009): 39, 42–44.

106. Peter Fritsche, quoted in Susan J. Matt, "You Can't Go Home Again: Homesickness and Nostalgia in U.S. History," *Journal of American History* 92, no. 4 (2007): 497.

107. David Lowenthal, quoted in ibid.

108. Bo C. (Spokane, Washington), "No Literary Masterpiece Here," review of *BSG*, Amazon, 22 April 2000.

109. Lorene ("Reader in NC") (North Carolina), "Yes, You Can Go Home Again," review of *BSG*, Amazon, 3 July 2003.

110. Janet C. (Port Richey, Florida), "Thank You, Adriana, for the Memories of Home," review of *BSG*, Amazon, 6 January 2002. Sue V., "Sensational Small-town Novel," review of *BSG*, Barnes and Noble, 24 September 2003. For a reader in Alabama who had spent summers with his grandparents in "the Big Stone Gap area," the novel was "a visit home." James W. (Madison, Alabama), "A Visit Home," review of *BSG*, Amazon, 27 August 2000.

111. janett (Nashville, Tennessee), "Soothing after a daily dose of reality," review of *AHM*, Amazon, 28 February 1998.

112. lla (Atlanta, Georgia), "I found this to be extraordinarily charming . . . ," review of *BSG*, Amazon, 22 June 2000.

113. Ibid.

114. A reader (Lexington, Kentucky), "Daughter of Big Stone Gap native loved it," review of *BSG*, Amazon, 6 August 2000.

115. Frank E. C. (Florida), "Real People Living The Good Life," review of *BSG*, Amazon, 6 April 2000.

116. Kristin Mary Agnes Helen Kant, "Painting the Mountains: An Investigation of Tourist Art in North America" (PhD diss., University of Kentucky, 2009), 164, 166–67.

117. A reader (Santa Maria, California), "My trip to Bountiful . . . ," review of *BSG*, Amazon, 25 January 2001. Another "Daughter of a Big Stone Gap native," living in Lexington, Kentucky, also found the novel a means of becoming closer to her father: "Now I want to ask him more about those places and revisit them!" Beth R. T. (Lexington, Kentucky), "Daughter of Big Stone Gap native loved it," review of *BSG*, Amazon, 6 August 2000.

118. See J. Trent Alexander and Chad Berry, "Who Is Appalachian? Self-Reported Appalachian Ancestry in the 2000 Census," *Appalachian Journal* 38, no. 1 (2010): 46–54.

119. A reader, "Relative Redemption of my own," review of *CM*, Amazon, 30 December 1997. See also: "Charles Frazier describes the Appalachian region in much the same way as I have always viewed it. My ancestors also came from this area and served on both sides of the Civil War, and his story could have been theirs. I longed for such a story to be told," pgh2 (Knoxville, Tennessee), "the most beautifully written book I've ever read," review of *CM*, Amazon, 11 August 1998.

120. K. B. [real name] ("Doctor teacher") (North Carolina), "Riveting, poetic, destined to be a classic," review of *CM*, Amazon, 9 March 1999.

121. mcgo (Arlington, Virginia), "Best Book I've read this year, except for *A Fine Balance*," review of *CM*, Amazon, 16 October 1997.

122. A reader, "*Cold Mountain* Is a Testimony to North Carolina Determination," review of *CM*, Amazon, 2 October 1997.

123. Martha M. [real name] (Johnson City, Tennessee), "I Grew Up With the Author," review of *BSG*, Amazon, 27 September 2001.

124. A reader, "Big Stone Gap," review of *BSG*, Amazon, 17 October 2002; carmenmiranda, "This book is a jewel," review of *BSG*, Amazon, 6 July 2004.

125. Griswold, *Regionalism and the Reading Class*, 2.

126. A reader, "What a Breath of Fresh Air!" review of *AHM*, Amazon, 27 June 1997; Kmarie [real name] (Appalachian Mountains, Southwest Virginia), "One of my all time favorites, y'all!" review of *BSG*, Amazon, 23 August 2003; A reader, "They God! What a book!" review of *CM*, Amazon, 11 December 1999.

127. Long, *Book Clubs*, xviii, 72–78.

128. James O. P. (Winchester, Virginia), "Write your name and address in this one . . . ," review of *CM*, Amazon, 2 September 1997; A reader, "A very light-hearted, entertaining look at a small town," review of *AHM*, Amazon, 21 December 1998.

129. Theresa (London, Kentucky), "What Appalacia truly is like," review of *CQ*, Amazon, 24 March 2001; Barbara G. (Abingdon, Virginia), "Elizabeth Taylor *really did* choke on a chicken bone!" review of *BSG*, Amazon, 27 July 2000.

130. Angela B. (Johnson City, Tennessee), "This hits close to home . . . ," review of *BSG*, Amazon, 7 June 2000; A reader (Kingsport, Tennessee), "a book that works well at depicting the folk of appalachia!" review of *BSG*, Amazon, 21 May 2001. This reviewer did note that other members of her reading group from northeastern Tennessee and southwestern Virginia found Trigiani's "writing style overly sentimentalized."

131. "The kind a person might actually encounter" is from Judy O. H. (Maryville, Tennessee), "Good Book to Curl Up With," review of *BSG*, Amazon, 4 July 2000; "exaggerated" is from Elizabeth W. [real name] (Delano, Tennessee), "Big Stone Gap really exists!" review of *BSG*, Amazon, 11 July 2000;

"Doesn't perpetuate the hillbilly stereotype" is from Anna M. A. [real name] ("Teacher and Reader") (Talbott, Tennessee), "One of the best ever," review of *BSG*, Amazon, 22 August 2003; "A fairly 'cultural' town" is from Barbara G. (Abingdon, Virginia), "Elizabeth Taylor *really did* choke on a chicken bone!" review of *BSG*, Amazon, 27 July 2000; "where I am proud to live" is from sherchez (Roanoke, Virginia), "Mountain Magic," review of *BSG*, Amazon, 3 June 2001.

132. Reichert Powell, *Critical Regionalism*, 99, 105, 101.

133. Responding to popular novels through online reviews also provided affirmed Appalachians an international space for the assertion of local ways of knowing and saying, as when a young reader in Stanford, Kentucky, employed mountain phrasing in her observation that the character Alma "doesn't care to be different" (meaning that Alma doesn't mind being different from other people). It's possible the reviewer's usage of "care *to*" indicates a self-conscious embrace of mountain language (morgaan l. [Stanford, Kentucky], "Perfectly Stiched," review of *CQ*, Amazon, 28 August 2003). It seems more likely, however, that her usage is unself-conscious, and that she fails to understand that others may misinterpret the phrase. See also one reviewer's description of the epistolary novel *Fair and Tender Ladies*: "The 'letters' are wrote in everyday 'Dixie' language." Barbara ("Queen of her castle *and* her home library") ("beautiful" Charleston, South Carolina), "One of the best books I've read," review of *Fair and Tender Ladies*, Amazon, 30 September 2000.

134. A reader, "BSG, You Go Girl . . . We Southern Women Can Be Intelligent," review of *BSG*, Amazon, 6 September 2001.

135. shawana s. (Garner, Kentucky), "Wonderful Appalacian Based Book," review of *CQ*, Amazon, 1 December 2003.

136. Rebecca J. (Princeton, Kentucky), "beauiful and heart-warming," review of *CQ*, Amazon, 7 February 2005.

137. Brian (Horse Shoe in the North Carolina mountains), "The Places Are Real, I Am from There!!" review of *CM*, Amazon, 13 December 1999.

138. JStegFam (Monroe, North Carolina), "It's a mountain thing, you wouldn't understand," review of *CM*, Amazon, 8 November 1997; Cynthia R. [real name] (Bynum, North Carolina), "In sight of Cold Mountain," review of *CM*, Amazon, 8 October 2000. "Being a person that loves the mountains and desires a simpler life," wrote a Florida reviewer of *Cold Mountain*, "I found myself identifying with Inman from the very beginning." John P. D. ("Author of Historical Fiction Novel Until My Last Breath") (Jacksonville, Florida), "A Wonderful Novel," review of *CM*, Amazon, 3 September 2006.

139. Herbert H. N. (College Station, Connecticut), "Ordinary plot and characters in above average setting," review of *BGS*, Amazon, 15 January 2003.

140. "Entertaining villagers" is from A reader, "This book is like a breath of fresh air," review of *AHM*, Amazon, 27 September 1996; "Quirky familiar characters" is from Sody C. (Oklahoma City, Oklahoma), "A lovely, relaxing read

with quirky familiar characters," review of *AHM*, Amazon, 24 September 1997; "country-warm" is from A reader, "Delightful! A breeze-read; thoroughly engaging, enjoyable," review of *AHM*, Amazon, 27 September 1996.

141. Even Dooley's name has an "aw-shucks" country quality about it, and was perhaps inspired by western North Carolina legend Tom Dooley, made famous by the Kingston Trio's hit pop song.

142. Melissa G. (Granbury, Texas), review of *BSG*, Amazon, 2 May 2000; Sharon G. C. (Wichita Falls, Texas), review of *BSG*, Amazon, 26 April 2000; Susan R. (Dyersburg, Tennessee), "Charming, but predictable," review of *BSG*, Amazon, 15 June 2000; Lena R. (Derby, Virginia [Coal Mine Collery near Appalachia, Va]), "disappointed," review of *BSG*, Amazon, 7 May 2000.

143. Bashir H. A. [real name], "Like a Quilt!" review of *CQ*, Amazon, 19 April 2001.

144. In an explicit reference to a Gilded Age–era African American local-color character, she continued: "Each chapter brings to life new characters in an Uncle Remus–like simplicity—mundane everyday life raised to [a] new level of importance." Diana F. V. B. (Kenner, Louisiana), "Grows On You—Lovely and Lyrical," review of *CM*, Amazon, 16 December 2003.

145. A reader, "Cold Mountain is one of the best books I have yet read," review of *CM*, Amazon, 29 June 1997; A reader, "People! The Emperor has no clothes!" review of *CM*, Amazon, 24 November 1997; K. B. [real name] ("Doctor teacher") (North Carolina), "Riveting, poetic, destined to be a classic," review of *CM*, Amazon, 9 March 1999.

146. For "fascinating," see A reader, "Tremendously valueable as entertainment and enlightenment," review of *CM*, Amazon, 18 December 1998; and DCgal62 ("What's not to love?") (Washington, District of Columbia), "Read this book during the Hurricane," review of *CM*, Amazon, 9 January 2004. For "colorful," see Thomas B. (Houston, Texas), "The best war-related novel I have read in years," review of *CM*, Amazon, 2 December 1997; and A reader, "colorful characters," review of *AHM*, Amazon, 31 August 1998. For "quirky," see torim (Philadelphia, Pennsylvania), "Still can't decide!" review of *CM*, Amazon, 3 March 1998, and A reader, "Over Rated," review of *CM*, Amazon, 7 July 2001. Amy V. (Chicago, Illinois), "one of the best," review of *CM*, Amazon, 14 March 2002. See also: "Far more interesting than the leads . . . were the incidental characters—Sara, the young pioneer mother . . . the old goat woman, or Stobrod the fiddler." Angela M. (Hollywood, Florida), "Lovely but overpraised," review of *CM*, Amazon, 16 September 2003.

147. Malapropisms are the source of humor for Father Tim and for readers, as are names like Mule Skinner (the real estate agent) and quaint expressions like "Boys howdy, this cofee'll curl your hair" (*AHM*, 32).

148. Silas House, *Clay's Quilt* (Chapel Hill: Algonquin, 2001; repr., New York: Ballantine, 2002), 106, 103.

149. James O. P. (Winchester, Virginia), "Write your name and address in this one . . . ," review of *CM*, Amazon, 2 September 1997.

150. Janet P. (Flemington, New Jersey), "Don't read this book if you know anything about country life," review of *CM*, Amazon, 18 January 2004; A reader (Blacksburg, Virginia), "Boring!" review of *AHM*, Amazon, 31 May 1999.

151. A reader (London, Kentucky), "My world," review of *CQ*, Amazon, 23 August 2003.

152. J. M. (Kentucky), "Truth and honesty???" review of *CQ*, Amazon, 1 October 2006.

153. A reader (Tennessee), "Compelling Read," review of *CQ*, Amazon, 30 March 2002.

154. A reader (Minnesota), review of *CQ*, Amazon, 9 February 2004.

155. esloaney (Sugar Camp, Kentucky), "My Favorite Book," review of *CQ*, Amazon, 28 October 2001. See also: "This remarkable book by Silas House made me *feel* the Kentucky hills, smell the air, become part of the family." jladdwallace (Florida and New Hampshire), "Praise From the White Mountains of NH," review of *CQ*, Amazon, 16 March 2005.

156. A reader, "Don't waste your money," review of *AHM*, Amazon, 7 September 1999.

157. David C. Hsiung, *Two Worlds in the Tennessee Mountains: Exploring the Origins of Appalachian Stereotypes* (Lexington: University Press of Kentucky, 1997), xii, 8.

158. K. M. Pollard, quoted in Barcus and Brunn, "Towards a Typology of Mobility and Place Attachment," 29, and M. E. Maloney and Phillip J. Obermiller, quoted in ibid., 30. See also Emily Satterwhite, "Seeing Appalachian Cities," in *Appalachia: Social Context Past and Present*, ed. Phillip Obermiller and Michael Maloney (Dubuque, IA: Kendall/Hunt, 2002); and work by John Inscoe, Wilma Dunaway, Ron Lewis, Ron Eller, Altina Waller, Dwight Billings, and Kathleen Blee.

159. Bauman, *Community*, 15–16.

160. Some reactions to Sharyn McCrumb's popular ballad novels (some of which are best sellers) exhibit greater awareness of (and possibly inclination toward) progressive political action. See: "This book is a warning to treasure the wild spaces," from turtlechick (Shawsville, Virginia), "*She Walks* is wonderful!!" review of *She Walks These Hills*, by Sharyn McCrumb, Amazon, 12 May 2003; "This is a book that depicts the way small family farms are disappearing throughout North America," from romonko [real name] (Alberta, Canada), "Not big on suspense," review of *The Rosewood Casket*, by Sharyn McCrumb, Amazon, 8 December 2008.

Conclusion

Portions of this conclusion initially appeared in "'That's What They're All Singing About': Appalachian Heritage, Celtic Pride, and American Nationalism at the 2003 Smithsonian Folklife Festival," *Appalachian Journal* 32, no. 3 (2005):

302–38; "Imagining Home, Nation, World: Appalachia on the Mall," *Journal of American Folklore* 121, no. 479 (2008): 10–34; "Romancing Whiteness: Popular Appalachian Fiction and the Imperialist Imagination at the Turns of Two Centuries," in *At Home and Abroad: Historicizing Twentieth-Century Whiteness in Literature and Performance*, ed. La Vinia Delois Jennings (Knoxville: University of Tennessee Press, 2009), 93–117; and "Objecting to Insider/Outsider Politics and the Uncritical Celebration of Appalachia," *Appalachian Journal* 38, no. 1 (2010): 68–73.

1. Wilma A. Dunaway, *The First American Frontier: Transition to Capitalism in Southern Appalachia, 1700–1860* (Chapel Hill: University of North Carolina Press, 1996), 1. Whereas I have chosen to use the real names found in decades-old fan mail, when I conducted face-to-face interviews in 2003 I offered participants anonymity. Bruce and Kirstin are pseudonyms.

2. Amy L. Blair, "Main Street Reading *Main Street*," in *New Directions in American Reception Study*, ed. Philip Goldstein and James L. Machor (New York: Oxford University Press, 2008): 139–58.

3. Such activism may at times have generated tensions among neighboring African Americans. Barbara Ellen Smith and Stephen Fisher, "Conclusion: Transformations in Place," in Fisher and Smith, eds., *Transforming Places: Lessons from Appalachia* (Champaign: University of Illinois Press, 2012).

4. I am grateful for Stephanie Foote's assistance with the articulation of these ideas.

5. Wendy Griswold, *Regionalism and the Reading Class* (Chicago: University of Chicago Press, 2008), 173–74.

6. Hsuan L. Hsu, "Literature and Regional Production," *American Literary History* 17, no. 1 (2005): 62.

7. Douglas Reichert Powell, *Critical Regionalism: Connecting Politics and Culture in the American Landscape* (Chapel Hill: University of North Carolina Press, 2007), 35.

8. Griswold, *Regionalism and the Reading Class*, 9–10, 36.

9. Henry D. Shapiro, *Appalachia on Our Mind: The Southern Mountains and Mountaineers in the American Consciousness, 1870–1920* (Chapel Hill: University of North Carolina Press, 1978), 57.

10. Reichert Powell, *Critical Regionalism*, 105; emphasis added.

11. "Culturalization" of differences is from Stephanie Foote, "The Cultural Work of American Regionalism, in *A Companion to the Regional Literatures of America*, ed. Charles L. Crow (Malden, MA: Blackwell, 2003), 28, 39.

12. Zada Mae, "No, I Don't Find Your Hillbilly Jokes Funny: Cultural Stereotyping and the Destruction of Appalachia," 3 November 2010, http://seamsandstory.wordpress.com/2010/11/03/no-i-dont-find-your-hillbilly-jokes-funny-cultural-stereotyping-the-destruction-of-appalachia/ (accessed 7 November 2010). Zada Mae is the nom de plume for the online blog *The Seams and the Story*.

13. See, for example, Dunaway, *The First American Frontier*, 1–3; Barbara Ellen Smith, "De-gradations of Whiteness: Appalachia and the Complexities of Race," *Journal of Appalachian Studies* 10, nos. 1–2 (2004): 47–49.

14. Hsu, "Literature and Regional Production," 55.

15. Robert Cantwell, *Ethnomimesis: Folklife and the Representation of Culture* (Chapel Hill: University of North Carolina Press, 1993), xv, 218. According to Regina Bendix, "The notion of national uniqueness harbors a conservative ethos of the past. Because of the insistence on national purity or authenticity inherent in the idea of a unique nation, the notion of authenticity ultimately undermines the liberating and humanitarian tendencies from which it grew." *In Search of Authenticity: The Formation of Folklore Studies* (Madison: University of Wisconsin Press, 1997), 8.

16. Manuel Castells, *The Information Age—Economy, Society, and Culture*, vol. 2, *The Power of Identity* (Malden, MA: Blackwell, 1997), 2, 6, 7, 60–61, 67.

17. See David E. Whisnant, *All That Is Native and Fine: The Politics of Culture in an American Region* (Chapel Hill: University of North Carolina Press, 1983), 13; William Goodell Frost, "Appalachian America," *Ladies Home Companion*, September 1896, 3–4, 21; and appended articles in the same issue by N. S. Shaler (the Harvard professor quoted here; "Needs of the Mountain People") and the Reverend A. D. Mayo (who refers to Appalachians as being of "good British stock"; "The New Crisis at the South"). Henry Shapiro observes that identifying mountaineers as American "folk" during the early twentieth century construed them as foundational for American nationhood, "place[d] them at the very center of American civilization," and gave them a "symbolic function" in grounding a seemingly fragmented society in "Merrie Olde England." Shapiro, *Appalachia on Our Mind*, 259, 247.

18. Nina Silber, "'What Does America Need So Much as Americans?': Race and Northern Reconciliation with Southern Appalachia, 1870–1900," in *Appalachians and Race: The Mountain South from Slavery to Segregation*, ed. John Inscoe (Lexington: University Press of Kentucky, 2001), 245–58; William Goodell Frost, "Our Contemporary Ancestors in the Southern Mountains," *Atlantic Monthly*, March 1899, 313, 312, 316.

19. Darlene Wilson discovered that Fox depicted June as Melungeon (triracial) in early drafts. Darlene Wilson, "The Felicitous Convergence of Mythmaking and Capital Accumulation: John Fox Jr. and the Formation of An(Other) Almost-White American Underclass," *Journal of Appalachian Studies* 1, no. 1 (1995): 13–14, 27–28, 34n15, 38n39. John Fox Jr., *A Mountain Europa; A Cumberland Vendetta; The Last Stetson* (New York: Scribner's, 1912), 23.

20. Smith, "De-gradations of Whiteness," 42.

21. For a complete discussion of my methodology and findings, see Satterwhite, "'That's What They're All Singing About.'" The dates of the 2003 festival were 26–29 June and 2–6 July.

22. Of the sixty-four interviewees who gave their hometowns, only two were

raised in southern Appalachia. Yet 44 percent were raised in an Appalachian state (according to the Appalachian Regional Commission's expansive definition). For a discussion of Appalachian identity as an out-migrant and out-migrant descendent identity, see J. Trent Alexander and Chad Berry, "Who Is Appalachian? Self-Reported Appalachian Ancestry in the 2000 Census," *Appalachian Journal* 38, no. 1 (2010): 46–54.

23. Shapiro, *Appalachia on Our Mind*, 261.

24. For a literary acknowledgment of the notion that "the Appalachian 'other' when examined closely is really a rawer, more primitive version of self," see Jane Hill's discussion of Gail Godwin. I am arguing that, like Godwin's citified characters, most readers of popular Appalachian-set fiction feel themselves to "bend down, in effect, when they embrace" Appalachian characters who represent their root selves. "Coming to Terms with the Appalachian 'Other' in the Novels of Gail Godwin," *Journal of Kentucky Studies* 11 (1995): 102.

25. Matt Wray, *Not Quite White: White Trash and the Boundaries of Whiteness* (Durham, NC: Duke University Press, 2006).

26. For white Americans' anxieties regarding "generic" whiteness, see Ruth Frankenburg, *White Women, Race Matters: The Social Construction of Whiteness* (Minneapolis: University of Minnesota Press, 1993); Patricia Yaeger, *Dirt and Desire: Southern Women's Writing, 1930–1990* (Chicago: University of Chicago Press, 2000); and Toni Morrison, *Playing in the Dark: Whiteness and the Literary Imagination* (Cambridge, MA: Harvard University Press, 1992). Vincent J. Cheng discusses "anxiety over authentic cultural identity" and "seemingly vacated identities" in *Inauthentic: The Anxiety over Culture and Identity* (New Brunswick, NJ: Rutgers University Press, 2004), 3.

27. "Mallification" is from an article about a Mitford series promotional event (Mary Susan Herczog, "Love of a Good Book Makes Life Imitate Art," *Los Angeles Times*, 6 July 1997, 1).

28. Smith, "De-gradations of Whiteness," 47–49.

29. James Webb, *Born Fighting: How the Scots-Irish Shaped America* (New York: Broadway, 2004). See also Bethany Bultman's paean to Celtic America, *Redneck Heaven: A Portrait of a Vanishing Culture* (New York: Bantam, 1996). Matthew Frye Jacobson, *Whiteness of a Different Color: European Immigrants and the Alchemy of Race* (Cambridge, MA: Harvard University Press, 1998), 276. In his research on Polish, Italian, Greek, and Slavic American ethnic revivalism in the 1970s urban Northeast, Jacobson found that white ethnics who "vaguely articulated class-based grievances" contended that if they didn't *feel* empowered by their "whiteness," then they received none of the privileges of being white. See also Michael Novak, *The Rise of the Unmeltable Ethnics: Politics and Culture in the Seventies* (New York: Macmillan, 1972). For another interpretation, see John Hartigan, *Odd Tribes: Toward a Cultural Analysis of White People* (Durham, NC: Duke University Press, 2005).

30. John Shelton Reed, *Southern Folk, Plain and Fancy* (Athens: University

of Georgia Press, 1986), 43. Reed also states that "rednecks seem to be the last remaining identifiably ethnic villains." International newspapers like the *London Times* have repeated the claim that Appalachians are the last ethnic group that can be ridiculed with impunity in the United States. Ben Macintyre, "Who'd Have Thought It? There's a Redneck Revolution Taking Shape in Them Thar' Hills," *Times* (London), 4 October 2008, Overseas News, 43.

31. As Smith notes, in 1971 James Branscome claimed that the television series *The Beverly Hillbillies, Green Acres,* and *Hee-Haw* represented "the most intensive effort ever exerted by a nation to belittle, demean, and otherwise destroy a minority people within its boundaries." Smith, "De-gradations of Whiteness," 48. On white Appalachian claims to victimization, see also Carol Mason, *Reading Appalachia from Left to Right: Conservatives and the 1974 Kanawha County Textbook Controversy* (Ithaca, NY: Cornell University Press, 2009).

32. For more on white American nationalism, see Nikol Alexander-Floyd, *Gender, Race and Nationalism in Contemporary Black Politics* (New York: Palgrave Macmillan, 2007).

33. Zachary Karabell, "What's in After Greed? A Post-bubble Focus on Community Is Becoming Visible in a Thousand Small Ways, Not All of Them Comforting," *Newsweek*, international ed., 16 September 2002, 70. For a discussion of the tension between freedom and security in idealizations of community, see also Zygmunt Bauman, *Community: Seeking Safety in an Insecure World* (Malden, MA: Polity, 2001), 4, 12, 14, 17–18.

34. Karabell, "What's in After Greed?"

35. Charles Frazier, *Cold Mountain* (New York: Vintage, 1998), 85; Satterwhite, "Romancing Whiteness."

36. I am grateful to Barbara Ellen Smith for her help in articulating these points.

37. Jennifer Rae Greeson argues that literary representations of the Reconstruction South trained audiences to cope imaginatively with U.S. relations to imperial subjects. See Greeson, "The Figure of the South and the Imagination of Nation in the United States" (PhD diss., Yale University, 2001); Greeson, *Our South: Geographic Fantasy and the Rise of National Literature* (Cambridge, MA: Harvard University Press, 2010). See also Matthew Frye Jacobson, *Barbarian Virtues: The United States Encounters Foreign Peoples at Home and Abroad* (New York: Hill & Wang, 2000).

38. Stephanie Foote, *Regional Fictions: Culture and Identity in Nineteenth-Century American Literature* (Madison: University of Wisconsin Press, 2001), 15.

39. Marilyn Halter, *Shopping for Identity: The Marketing of Ethnicity* (New York: Schocken, 2000).

40. Reichert Powell, *Critical Regionalism*, 40.

41. Foote, "The Cultural Work of American Regionalism," 40.

Appendix

1. Raymond Williams, *Writing in Society* (London: Verso, 1983).

2. A number of scholars have examined hypothetical readers. In addition to Ralph Waldo Emerson's "creative reader," critics have identified the narratee (the reader addressed by the narrator, whom Gerald Prince argues is better understood as another character), the implied reader (expected and controlled by the text, according to Wolfgang Iser), and the model reader (a reader whose shared codes are assumed by the author, according to Umberto Eco). Criticism employing the concept of an "ideal" reader may construe him or her as a universal figure or may assume that each text has its own optimal reader. Similarly, critics of the "interpretive communities" framework advanced by Stanley Fish claim that his theory suggests a reader is confined to interpretations that are intended by the author and that the reader is trained to make. See Elizabeth Freund, *The Return of the Reader: Reader-Response Criticism* (New York: Methuen, 1987), 7, 107–8; Stanley Fish, *Is There a Text in This Class? The Authority of Interpretive Community* (Cambridge, MA: Harvard University Press, 1980).

3. Wolfgang Iser, "Indeterminacy and the Reader's Response in Prose Fiction," in *Aspects of Narrative*, ed. J. Hillis Miller (New York: Columbia University Press, 1971), 4–12; Hans Robert Jauss, *Toward an Aesthetic of Reception* (Minneapolis: University of Minnesota Press, 1981). Critics of Iser and Jauss, like those of Fish, argue that their imagined reader is too universalized, without recognition of individual, racial, gendered, and classed experiences. See Rona Kaufman, "'That, My Dear, Is Called Reading': Oprah's Book Club and the Construction of a Readership," in *Reading Sites: Social Difference and Reader Response*, ed. Patrocinio P. Schweickart and Elizabeth A. Flynn (New York: Modern Language Association, 2004), 251.

4. See Philip Goldstein and James L. Machor, eds., *New Directions in American Reception Study* (New York: Oxford University Press, 2008). For a critique of this text-centered approach, see Janice Radway's contribution to this collection, "What's the Matter with Reception Study? Some Thoughts on the Disciplinary Origins, Conceptual Constraints, and Persistent Viability of a Paradigm," 327–51.

5. Richard H. Brodhead, *Cultures of Letters: Scenes of Reading and Writing in Nineteenth-Century America* (Chicago: University of Chicago Press, 1994), 153; Nathalia Wright, introduction to *In the Tennessee Mountains*, by Mary Noailles Murfree (Knoxville: University of Tennessee Press, 1970), xiii.

6. Henry Holt, "The Commercialization of Literature," *Atlantic Monthly*, November 1905, 577–600.

7. Alice Payne Hackett, *70 Years of Best Sellers, 1895–1965* (New York: Bowker, 1967), 2; Frank Luther Mott, *The Golden Multitudes: The Story of Best Sellers in the United States* (New York: Macmillan, 1947), 204–6. See also Laura

J. Miller, "The Best-Seller List as Marketing Tool and Historical Fiction," *Book History* 3 (2000): 289.

8. Bill York, *John Fox, Jr., Appalachian Author* (Jefferson, NC: McFarland, 2003), 176. Hackett, *70 Years of Best Sellers*, 24, 27, 34–35, 99, 104.

9. Keith L. Justice, *Bestseller Index: All Books, Publishers Weekly and the New York Times through 1990* (Jefferson, NC: McFarland, 1998), 1.

10. From 1911 to 1919, *Publishers Weekly* had published various best-seller lists produced by, or based on, other publications. Mott, *Golden Multitudes*, 205; Justice, *Bestseller Index*, 4.

11. The *New York Times*' first published list in 1931 noted the five best sellers for New York City. Over the following months and years, the *Times* expanded its lists based on sales information from "major bookstores, department stores, and wholesalers" for multiple cities (Miller, "The Best-Seller List," 290). Justice, *Bestseller Index*, 7.

12. Miller, "The Best-Seller List," 292.

13. Nielsen, http://en-us.nielsen.com/content/nielsen/en_us/insights/rankings/books.html (accessed 11 October 2010). According to the Web site, Nielsen Bookscan does not include sales from Wal-Mart and Sam's Club, or to libraries.

14. Miller, "The Best-Seller List," 287.

15. Justice, *Bestseller Index*, 6–8.

16. Ibid., 3. Miller, citing Kenneth C. Davis, *Two-Bit Culture* (1984), contradicts Justice when she states that the *New York Times* "featured a list of best-selling paperbacks for the first time in 1962" but "expanded its regular weekly lists to include paperbacks only in 1976" ("The Best-Seller List," 293).

17. Justice, *Bestseller Index*, 9.

18. Miller, "The Best-Seller List," 291.

19. Justice, *Bestseller Index*, 1–3; Miller, "The Best-Seller List," 289–300.

20. Cratis Williams, "The Southern Mountaineer in Fact and Fiction," *Appalachian Journal* 3 (1975–76): 8–162; Lorise C. Boger, *The Southern Mountaineer in Literature: An Annotated Bibliography* (Morgantown: West Virginia University Library, 1964); "Mountain Fiction from Abernethy to Zugsmith . . . from 1832 to 1985: 1,517 Works of Fiction by Southern Appalachian Authors, or with Southern Appalachian Settings" (Hutchins Library, Berea College, Berea, KY, 1985).

21. *Hunter's Horn* peaked during the week of 14 August 1949. Justice, *Bestseller Index*, 26. In 1949, the list was based on thirty-four cities ("The Best Sellers," *New York Times*, 26 June 1949, BR8). *The Dollmaker* appeared from 16 May to 21 November 1954, and then reappeared three times between 5 December 1954 and 9 January 1955. The 1954 lists were based on thirty-six cities ("Best Seller List," *New York Times*, 16 May 1954, BR8).

22. Justice, *Bestseller Index*, 93–94, 212.

23. *Look Homeward* was, however, a surprise hit, according to an advertisement Scribner placed in the *New York Times*: "Within ten days a first printing

twice as large as that of the average first novel was completely exhausted and a second was necessary" (12 January 1930, 71). *Of Time and the River* (1935), in which Eugene Gant leaves Asheville for Harvard, New York, and Europe was on the *Publishers Weekly* list for twenty-eight weeks. *You Can't Go Home Again* (1940) was on the *Publishers Weekly* list for twelve weeks. *The Web and the Rock* (1939) made the *Publishers Weekly* and *New York Times* lists for a total of twenty weeks. *The Hills Beyond* (1941) appeared on the *Publishers Weekly* list for four weeks (Justice, *Bestseller Index*, 333). Wolfe's correspondence is housed at the University of North Carolina.

24. Stuart's correspondence is housed at the University of Louisville.

25. For a rare and insightful treatment of Godwin's treatment of Appalachia, see Jane Hill, "Coming to Terms with the Appalachian 'Other' in the Novels of Gail Godwin," *Journal of Kentucky Studies* 11 (1995): 98–105. Justice, *Bestseller Index*, 333, 136, 297, 258, 128. The southern elite in Godwin's Asheville of *A Southern Family* begrudgingly acknowledge the "acceptability" of middle-class Jewish and even African American neighbors, who (because they are immaculate gardeners) assimilate nicely into the 1980s suburban world of the bluebloods. The novel's mountain white "tribe" (*A Southern Family* [New York: Morrow, 1987], 306), however, lives in a "a god-awful place worse than Dogpatch where [they] have camped out in squalor for ten generations" (280), a debris-littered holler that serves as "tangible evidence of a cluster of attitudes that, if shared by enough people, could bring down civilization" (374). Hill provides a counter-reading to this scene. Godwin's correspondence is housed at the University of North Carolina.

26. Miller, "The Best-Seller List," 292. See "Best Selling Books Database," *USA Today*, http://content.usatoday.com/life/books/booksdatabase/default.aspx (accessed 28 May 2010).

27. It is industry commonplace that best-selling authors publish best sellers. For discussion of the ways in which movies, Oprah's Book Club, and authors' veteran status contributed to creating best sellers in the United States, see Dermot McEvoy and Daisy Maryles, "The Paperback Game; Movies, Oprah and Current Events Influence the Lists; Fiction Veterans Ride High," *Publishers Weekly*, 18 March 2002. In her study of the British publishing industry, Claire Squires notes industry insiders attest that known authors are one of the most persuasive means of encouraging a consumer to buy a book (*Marketing Literature: The Making of Contemporary Writing in Britain* [New York: Palgrave Macmillan, 2007], 87).

28. See Richard J. Butler, Benjamin W. Cowan, and Sebastian Nilsson, "From Obscurity to Bestseller: Examining the Impact of Oprah's Book Club Selections," *Publishing Research Quarterly* 20, no. 4 (2005): 23–34. According to Beth Driscoll, selection by Oprah "generates sales of 500,000 to one million copies, whereas most literary titles in the United States struggle to reach 30,000 sales." "How Oprah's Book Club Reinvented the Woman Reader," *Popular Nar-*

rative Media 1, no. 2 (2008): 144. On the role of Oprah and film adaptations in creating best sellers, see also Bob Minzesheimer, "10 Years of Best Sellers: How the Landscape Has Changed," *USA Today*, 11 March 2004, cover story.

29. *Oxford English Dictionary*, s.v. "Fan," http://dictionary.oed.com/cgi/entry/50082087/50082087se4?single=1&query_type=word&queryword=fan+mail&first=1&max_to_show=10&hilite=50082087se4 (accessed 18 August 2010); Daniel Cavicchi, *Tramps Like Us: Music and Meaning among Springsteen Fans* (New York: Oxford University Press, 1998), 38–39. On "the fancy" and "fanciers," Cavicchi quotes etymologist Robert Barnhart.

30. Amy L. Blair, "Main Street Reading *Main Street*," in *New Directions in American Reception Study*, ed. Philip Goldstein and James L. Machor (New York: Oxford University Press, 2008), 145. Models for analysis of fan mail include articles by Barbara Ryan and Amy Blair. Barbara Ryan accesses fan mail through thirty-seven letters written to Gene Stratton-Porter, author of *Freckles* (1904) and *A Girl of the Limberlost* (1909). The letters were solicited by the author herself in response to a poor reception by critics and published in a memoir by her daughter. See Ryan, "'A Real Basis from Which to Judge': Fan Mail to Gene Stratton Porter," in *Reading Acts: U.S. Readers' Interactions with Literature, 1800–1950*, ed. Barbara Ryan and Amy M. Thomas (Knoxville: University of Tennessee Press, 2002), 161–78, and "'Wherever I Am Living': The 'Lady of the Limberlost' Resituates," in *Breaking Boundaries: New Perspectives on Women's Regional Writing*, ed. Sherrie A. Inness and Diana Royer (Iowa City: University of Iowa Press, 1997), 162–79. Blair's work on Sinclair Lewis's *Main Street* examines eighty-two letters, twenty-six of which she examined more closely as "substantial letters from relative strangers that discuss *Main Street* at some length"; she carefully distinguishes between letters that were received in the years immediately following the novel's initial release and those that discuss the novel "retrospectively." See also Blair's "Misreading *The House of Mirth*," *American Literature* 76, no. 1 (2004): 149–75.

31. See, for example, Amy Harmon, "Amazon Glitch Unmasks War of Reviewers," *New York Times*, 14 February 2004.

32. Pew Internet and American Life Project, "Usage Over Time," http://www.pewinternet.org/Static-Pages/Trend-Data/Usage-Over-Time.aspx, n.d. (accessed 22 September 2004). Data is from surveys conducted in 2002.

33. Andrew Stevenson to Murfree, 6 January 1922, Mary Noailles Murfree Papers, 1877–1928, Manuscript, Archives, and Rare Book Library, Emory University, Atlanta, GA.

34. Reese M. Carleton, "Mary Noailles Murfree (1850–1922): An Annotated Bibliography," *American Literary Realism, 1870–1910* 7 (1974): 293–378; Eva Malone Byrd, "The Life and Writings of Mary Noailles Murfree" (MA thesis, University of Tennessee, 1937); Eleanor B. Spence, "Collected Reminiscences of Mary N. Murfree" (MA thesis, George Peabody School for Teachers, 1928).

35. Katie Algeo, "Locals on Local Color: Imagining Identity in Appalachia," *Southern Cultures* 4, no. 4 (2003): 27–54.

36. Arnow to "Elizabeth," likely her sister Elizabeth Whiting, undated but filed between letters dated 30 November and 3 December 1954, Harriette Simpson Arnow Papers, Special Collections and Digital Programs, University of Kentucky Libraries, Lexington.

37. Sandra L. Ballard, "Harriette Simpson Arnow's Life as a Writer," in *Harriette Simpson Arnow: Critical Essays on Her Work*, ed. Haeja K. Chung (East Lansing: Michigan State University Press, 1995), 28.

38. Marshall to William A. Barnhill, 17 February 1970, Catherine Marshall Collection, box 11, folder 5, Agnes Scott College, Atlanta, GA. Based on the finding aid and librarian Marianne Bradley's observations, it does not appear that the index card system Marshall described was preserved for prosperity.

Selected Bibliography

Manuscript Collections

Harriette Simpson Arnow Papers. Special Collections and Digital Programs, University of Kentucky Libraries, Lexington.
James Dickey Papers, ca. 1924–1997. Manuscript, Archives, and Rare Book Library, Emory University, Atlanta, GA.
John Fox Jr. Memorial Library. Duncan's Tavern (headquarters of the Daughters of the American Revolution), Paris, KY.
John Fox Jr. Vertical Files Collection. Southern Appalachian Archives, Biography, Kentucky Authors, Hutchins Library, Special Archives and Collections, Berea College, Berea, KY.
Fox Family Papers. Special Collections and Digital Programs, University of Kentucky Libraries, Lexington.
Catherine Marshall Collection. Agnes Scott College, Atlanta, GA.
Mary Noailles Murfree Papers, 1877–1928. Manuscript, Archives, and Rare Book Library, Emory University, Atlanta, GA.

Fiction

Adams, Sheila Kay. *Come Go with Me: Stories*. Chapel Hill: University of North Carolina Press, 1995.
———. *My Old True Love*. Chapel Hill: Algonquin, 2004.
Aldrich, Thomas Bailey. *The Story of a Bad Boy*. Boston: Houghton, 1869.
———. "Unguarded Gates." *Atlantic Monthly*, July 1892, 57.
Arnow, Harriette Simpson. *The Dollmaker*. New York: Macmillan, 1954.
———. *Hunter's Horn*. New York: Macmillan, 1949. Reprint, East Lansing: Michigan State University Press, 1997.
———. *Mountain Path*. New York: Covici-Friede, 1936. Reprint, Berea, KY: Council of the Southern Mountains, 1963.
Baldacci, David. *Wish You Well*. New York: Warner, 2000.
Brown, William Perry. "A Peculiar People." *Overland Monthly*, November 1888, 505–8.
Caldwell, Erskine. *Tobacco Road*. New York: Grosset & Dunlap, 1932.
Chesnutt, Charles. *The Conjure Woman*. Boston: Houghton Mifflin, 1899.
Chute, Carolyn. *The Beans of Egypt, Maine*. New York: Ticknor & Fields, 1985.
Cooke, Grace MacGowan. *The Power and the Glory*. New York: Doubleday, 1910.

Crews, Harry. *A Childhood: The Biography of a Place*. New York: Harper & Row, 1978.
Davis, Rebecca Harding. *Life in the Iron Mills, and Other Stories*. Boston: Ticknor & Fields, 1861.
———. "The Yares of Black Mountain." *Lippincott's*, July 1875, 35–47.
Dickey, James. *Deliverance*. Boston: Houghton Mifflin, 1970.
Fox, John, Jr. "Betrothal Ring." *Frank Leslie's Illustrated Weekly*, 22 August 1885, 6.
———. *Blue-grass and Rhododendron: Out-doors in Old Kentucky*. New York: Scribner, 1901.
———. "Deceiver's Ever." *New York Life*, 21 November 1885.
———. *Heart of the Hills*. New York: Scribner, 1913.
———. *The Little Shepherd of Kingdom Come*. New York: Scribner, 1903.
———. *A Mountain Europa; A Cumberland Vendetta; The Last Stetson*. New York: Scribner, 1912.
———. *The Trail of the Lonesome Pine*. New York: Scribner, 1908.
———. "The Wanderers." Special Collections and Digital Programs, University of Kentucky Libraries, Lexington.
Frazier, Charles. *Cold Mountain*. New York: Grove, 1997. Reprint, New York: Vintage, 1998.
Freeman, Mary Wilkins. *A New-England Nun, and Other Stories*. New York: Penguin, 2000.
Garland, Hamlin. *Main Travelled Roads: Six Mississippi Valley Stories*. Boston: Arena, 1891.
Giardina, Denise. *Storming Heaven*. New York: Norton, 1987.
Giovanni, Nikki. "Knoxville, Tennessee." *Now and Then: The Appalachian Magazine*, Summer 1987, 11.
Godwin, Gail. *Evensong*. New York: Ballantine, 1999.
———. *Father Melancholy's Daughter*. New York: Morrow, 1991.
———. *A Mother and Two Daughters*. New York: Viking, 1982.
———. *A Southern Family*. New York: Morrow, 1987.
Green, Michelle Y. *Willie Pearl*. William Ruth, 1990.
Harte, Bret. *The Luck of the Roaring Camp*. Boston: Fields, Osgood, 1870.
Hickam, Homer. *Rocket Boys: A Memoir*. New York: Delacourte, 1998.
Hoffman, William. *Blood and Guile*. New York: HarperCollins, 2000.
House, Silas. *Clay's Quilt*. Chapel Hill: Algonquin, 2001. Reprint, New York: Ballantine, 2002.
———. *Coal Tattoo*. Chapel Hill: Algonquin, 2004.
———. *A Parchment of Leaves*. Chapel Hill: Algonquin, 2002.
Jacobs, Harriet. *Incidents in the Life of a Slave Girl: Written by Herself*. Boston: Published for the author, 1861.
Jewett, Sarah Orne. *The Country of the Pointed Firs*. Boston: Houghton Mifflin, 1896.

Judd, Kirk. "Visitin' Charleston." *Now and Then: The Appalachian Magazine*, Summer 1990, 17.
Junger, Sebastian. *The Perfect Storm: A True Story of Men against the Sea*. New York: Norton, 1997.
Karon, Jan. *At Home in Mitford*. Elgin, IL: Lion, 1994. Reprint, New York: Penguin, 1996.
———. *A Common Life: The Wedding Story*. New York: Viking, 2001.
———. *In This Mountain*. New York: Viking, 2002.
———. *Light from Heaven*. New York: Viking, 2005.
———. *A Light in the Window*. Elgin, IL: Lion, 1995.
———. *A New Song*. New York: Penguin, 1999.
———. *Out to Canaan*. New York: Viking, 1997.
———. *Shepherds Abiding: A Mitford Christmas Story*. New York: Viking, 2003.
———. *These High, Green Hills*. New York: Viking, 1996.
Kidd, Sue Monk. *The Secret Life of Bees*. New York: Viking, 2002.
Kingsolver, Barbara. *Prodigal Summer: A Novel*. New York: Harper Perennial, 2001.
MacGowan, Alice. *Judith of the Cumberlands*. New York: Putnam, 1908.
Majors, Inman. *Swimming in the Sky*. Dallas: Southern Methodist University Press, 2000.
Marshall, Catherine. *Christy*. New York: McGraw-Hill, 1967. Reprint, New York: Avon, 1996.
Maynard, Lee. *Crum*. New York: Washington Square, 1988.
McCrumb, Sharyn. *The Ballad of Frankie Silver*. New York: Dutton, 1998.
———. *The Devil amongst the Lawyers*. New York: Thomas Dunne, 2010.
———. *The Hangman's Beautiful Daughter*. New York: Scribner, 1992.
———. *If Ever I Return, Pretty Peggy-O*. New York: Scribner, 1990.
———. *The Rosewood Casket*. New York: Dutton, 1996.
———. *She Walks These Hills*. New York: Scribner, 1994.
———. *The Songcatcher: A Ballad Novel*. New York: Dutton, 2001.
Morgan, Robert. *Gap Creek*. New York: Simon & Schuster, 1999.
Murfree, Mary Noailles [R. Emmet Dembry, pseud.]. "Flirts and Their Ways." *Lippincott's*, May 1874, 629–35.
——— [Charles Egbert Craddock, pseud.]. *In the Tennessee Mountains*. Boston: Houghton, 1884. Reprint, edited by Nathalia Wright. Knoxville: University of Tennessee Press, 1970.
——— [R. Emmet Dembry, pseud.]. "My Daughter's Admirers." *Lippincott's*, July 1875, 117–23.
——— [Charles Egbert Craddock, pseud.]. "Taking the Blue Ribbon at the County Fair." *Appleton's Summer Book* (1880): 124–33.
Norman, Gurney. *Kinfolks*. New York: Dial, 1977.
Offutt, Chris. *Kentucky Straight: Stories*. New York: Vintage, 1992.

Proulx, Annie. *The Shipping News*. New York: Scribner, 1993.
Ross, Ann B. *Miss Julia Speaks Her Mind*. New York: William Morrow, 1999.
Rubio, Gwyn Hyman. *Icy Sparks*. New York: Penguin, 1998.
Russo, Richard. *Empire Falls*. New York: Knopf, 2001.
Schenkkan, Robert. *The Kentucky Cycle*. New York: Plume, 1993.
Secreast, Donald. *White Trash, Red Velvet*. New York: HarperCollins, 1993.
Sheppard, Muriel Earley. *Cabins in the Laurel*. Chapel Hill: University of North Carolina Press, 1935.
Smith, Lee. *Fair and Tender Ladies*. New York: Ballantine, 1989.
——. *The Last Girls*. Chapel Hill: Algonquin, 2002.
——. *Oral History*. New York: Putnam, 1983.
Stegner, Wallace. *Angle of Repose*. Garden City, NY: Doubleday, 1971.
Still, James. *River of Earth*. New York: Viking, 1940.
Trigiani, Adriana. *Big Cherry Holler*. New York: Random House, 2001.
——. *Big Stone Gap*. New York: Random House, 2000.
——. *Milk Glass Moon: A Big Stone Gap Novel*. New York: Random House, 2002.
Whitehead, Colson. *John Henry Days*. New York: Doubleday, 2001.
Wilkinson, Alec. *Moonshine: A Life in Pursuit of White Liquor*. New York: Knopf, 1985.
Wolfe, Thomas. *Look Homeward, Angel: A Story of the Buried Life*. New York: Scribner, 1929.
Wright, Harold Bell. *Shepherd of the Hills*. New York: A. L. Burt, 1907.
Wright, Richard. *Black Boy (American Hunger)*. New York: Viking, 1945.

Books, Articles, and Other Materials

Adams, Noah. *Far Appalachia: Following the New River North*. New York: Delacorte, 2001.
Agee, James, and Walker Evans. *Let Us Now Praise Famous Men*. Boston: Houghton, 1939.
"Albion's Seed: Four British Folkways in America—A Symposium." *William and Mary Quarterly* 48, no. 2 (1991): 223–59.
Alexander, J. Trent, and Chad Berry, "Who Is Appalachian? Self-Reported Appalachian Ancestry in the 2000 Census." *Appalachian Journal* 38, no. 1 (2010): 46–54.
Algeo, Katie. "Locals on Local Color: Imagining Identity in Appalachia." *Southern Cultures* 4, no. 4 (2003): 27–54.
Allen, Barbara, and Thomas J. Schelereth. *Sense of Place: American Regional Culture*. Lexington: University Press of Kentucky, 1992.
Allen, James Lane. *The Blue-grass Region of Kentucky, and Other Kentucky Articles*. New York: Harper, 1899.
——. "Through Cumberland Gap on Horseback." *Harper's*, June 1886, 23.

Ammons, Elizabeth, and Valerie Rohy, eds. *American Local Color Writing, 1880–1920*. New York: Penguin, 1998.
Anderson, Benedict. *Imagined Communities: Reflections on the Origin and Spread of Nationalism*. New York: Verso, 1991.
Askins, Don. "John Fox, Jr.: A Re-appraisal; or, With Friends Like That, Who Needs Enemies?" In *Colonialism in Modern America: The Appalachian Case*, edited by Helen Lewis, Linda Johnson, and Donald Askins, 251–57. Boone, NC: Appalachian Consortium, 1978.
"Assessing Appalachian Studies." Special issue, *Appalachian Journal* 9, nos. 2–3 (1982).
Aubry, Timothy. "Afghanistan Meets the Amazon: Reading *The Kite Runner* in America." *PMLA: Publications of the Modern Language Association of America* 124, no. 1 (2009): 25–43, 351.
———. "Beware the Furrow of the Middlebrow: Searching for Paradise on the *Oprah Winfrey Show*." *MFS: Modern Fiction Studies* 52, no. 2 (2006): 350–73.
———. "Erica Jong's Textual Bulimia: *Fear of Flying* and the Politics of Middlebrow Consumption." *Journal of Popular Culture* 42, no. 3 (2009): 419–41.
———. "John Cheever and the Management of Middlebrow Misery." *Iowa Journal of Cultural Studies* 3 (Fall 2003): 64–83.
———. "Literature as Self-Help: Postwar U.S. Fiction and the Middle-Class Hunger for Trouble." PhD diss., Princeton University, 2003.
"Authors Nix the Hillbilly Campaign." Press release e-mailed to H-Appalachia list-serv, 29 May 2003. http://www.h-net.org/~appalach/ (accessed 22 January 2005).
Ayers, Edward, Patricia Nelson Limerick, Stephen Nissenbaum, and Peter S. Onuf, eds. *All over the Map: Rethinking American Regions*. Baltimore: Johns Hopkins University Press, 1996.
Ballard, Sandra L., and Haeja K. Chung. Introduction to *The Collected Short Stories of Harriette Simpson Arnow*, edited by Sandra L. Ballard and Haeja K. Chung, vii–xvii. East Lansing: Michigan State University Press, 2005.
Baltzell, E. Digby. *The Protestant Establishment: Aristocracy & Caste in America*. New York: Random House, 1964.
Banker, Mark T. *Appalachians All: East Tennesseans and the Elusive History of an American Region*. Knoxville: University of Tennessee Press, 2010.
Barcus, Holly R., and Stanley D. Brunn. "Towards a Typology of Mobility and Place Attachment." *Journal of Appalachian Studies* 15, nos. 1–2 (2009): 26–48.
Batteau, Allen. *The Invention of Appalachia*. Tucson: University of Arizona Press, 1990.
Bauman, Richard, Patricia Sawin, and Inta Gale Carpenter. *Reflections on the Folklife Festival: An Ethnography of Participant Experience*. Bloomington: Folklore Institute of Indiana University, 1992.

Bauman, Zygmunt. *Community: Seeking Safety in an Insecure World.* Malden, MA: Polity, 2001.
Bear, John. *The #1 New York Times Bestseller: Intriguing Facts about the 484 Books That Have Been #1 New York Times Bestsellers since the First List in 1942.* Berkeley: Ten Speed, 1992.
Becker, Jane S. *Selling Tradition: Appalachia and the Construction of an American Folk, 1930–1940.* Chapel Hill: University of North Carolina Press, 1998.
Bederman, Gail. *Manliness and Civilization: A Cultural History of Gender and Race in the United States, 1880–1917.* Chicago: University of Chicago Press, 1995.
Bell, Michael Davitt. *The Problem of American Realism: Studies in the Cultural History of a Literary Idea.* Chicago: University of Chicago Press, 1993.
Bendix, Regina. *In Search of Authenticity: The Formation of Folklore Studies.* Madison: University of Wisconsin Press, 1997.
Bennet, Tony. "Texts, Readers, Reading Formations." *Literature and History* 9, no. 2 (1983): 214–27.
Bergeron, Jill. *Jill Bergeron Returns to Direct Trail of the Lonesome Pine.* The Commonwealth of Virginia's Official Outdoor Drama, "The Trail of the Lonesome Pine," 2004 program.
Berlant, Lauren. "Introduction: Compassion (and Withholding)." In *Compassion: The Culture and Politics of an Emotion*, edited by Lauren Berlant, 1–13. New York: Routledge, 2004.
Berry, Chad. *Southern Migrants, Northern Exiles.* Urbana: University of Illinois Press, 2000.
Berry, Wendell. *A Continuous Harmony: Essays Cultural and Agricultural.* New York: Harcourt Brace Jovanovich, 1972.
Bhaba, Homi K. *The Location of Culture.* New York: Routledge, 2004.
Biggers, Jeff. "His Side of the Mountains: The Enduring Legacy of Southern Poet James Still; An Interview with Ted Olson." *Bloomsbury Review*, July–August 2002, 17–18.
Billings, Dwight B., Gurney Norman, and Katherine Ledford, eds. *Confronting Appalachian Stereotypes: Back Talk from an American Region.* Lexington: University Press of Kentucky, 1999.
Blair, Amy L. "Main Street Reading *Main Street.*" In *New Directions in American Reception Study*, edited by Philip Goldstein and James L. Machor, 139–58. New York: Oxford University Press, 2008.
———. "Misreading *The House of Mirth.*" *American Literature: A Journal of Literary History, Criticism, and Bibliography* 76, no. 1 (2004): 149–75.
Blethen, H. Tyler, and Curtis W. Wood Jr. *From Ulster to Carolina: The Migration of the Scotch-Irish to Southwestern North Carolina.* Raleigh: NC Division of Archives and History, 1998.
———, eds. *Ulster and North America: Transatlantic Perspectives on the Scotch-Irish.* Tuscaloosa: University of Alabama Press, 1997.

Boger, Lorise C. *The Southern Mountaineer in Literature: An Annotated Bibliography*. Morgantown: West Virginia University Library, 1964.

Borman, Kathryn M., and Phillip J. Obermiller, eds. *From Mountain to Metropolis: Appalachian Migrants in American Cities*. Westport, CT: Bergin & Garvey, 1994.

Bourdieu, Pierre. *Acts of Resistance against the Tyranny of the Market*. New York: New Press, 1998.

——. *Distinction: A Social Critique of the Judgment of Taste*. New York: Routledge, 1984.

——. *The Field of Cultural Production: Essays on Art and Literature*. New York: Columbia University Press, 1993.

——. *An Invitation to Reflexive Sociology*. Chicago: University of Chicago Press, 1992.

Bradshaw, Michael. *Regions and Regionalism in the United States*. Jackson: University Press of Mississippi, 1988.

Brimelow, Peter. *Alien Nation: Common Sense about America's Immigration Disaster*. New York: Random House, 1995.

Brinkmeyer, Robert H., Jr. *Remapping Southern Literature: Contemporary Southern Writers and the West*. Athens: University of Georgia Press, 2000.

Brodhead, Richard H. *Cultures of Letters: Scenes of Reading and Writing in Nineteenth-Century America*. Chicago: University of Chicago Press, 1994.

——. "Regionalism and the Upper Class." In *Rethinking Class: Literary Studies and Social Formations*, edited by Wai Chee Dimock and Michael T. Gilmore, 150–74. New York: Columbia University Press, 1994.

Bronner, Simon J. "In Search of American Tradition." In *Folk Nation: Folklore in the Creation of American Tradition*, edited by Simon Bronner, 3–70. Wilmington, DE: Scholarly Resources, 2002.

Brosi, George. "Appalachian Literature." In *The Companion to Southern Literature*, edited by Joseph M. Flora and Lucinda H. Mackethan, 43–48. Baton Rouge: Louisiana State University Press, 2002.

Brown, Dona. *Inventing New England: Regional Tourism in the Nineteenth Century*. Washington, DC: Smithsonian Institution Press, 1995.

Brubaker, Rogers, and Frederick Cooper. "Beyond 'Identity.'" *Theory and Society* 29 (2000): 1–47.

Bryson, Bill. *A Walk in the Woods: Rediscovering America on the Appalachian Trail*. New York: Broadway, 1998.

Bultman, Bethany. *Redneck Heaven: A Portrait of a Vanishing Culture*. New York: Bantam, 1996.

Burnham, Mary, and Bill Burnham. *Rediscovering America: Exploring the Small Towns of Virginia and Maryland*. Edison, NJ: Hunter, 2002.

Burns, Sarah. *Pastoral Inventions: Rural Life in Nineteenth-Century American Art and Culture*. Philadelphia: Temple University Press, 1989.

Butler, Richard J., Benjamin W. Cowan, and Sebastian Nilsson. "From Obscu-

rity to Bestseller: Examining the Impact of Oprah's Book Club Selections." *Publishing Research Quarterly* 20, no. 4 (2005): 23–34.
Byrd, Eva Malone. "The Life and Writings of Mary Noailles Murfree." MA thesis, University of Tennessee, 1937.
Camp, Charles, and Timothy Lloyd. "Six Reasons Not to Produce Folklife Festivals." *Kentucky Folklore Record* 26, nos. 1–2 (1980): 67–74.
Campbell, Donna. "Realism and Regionalism." In *A Companion to the Regional Literatures of America*, edited by Charles L. Crow, 92–110. Malden, MA: Blackwell, 2003.
Campbell, John C. *The Southern Highlander and His Homeland.* New York: Russell Sage Foundation, 1921.
Campbell, Roberta. "Appalachian Experience and Appalachian Self-Concept: Toward a Critical Theory of Regional Identity." PhD diss., University of Kentucky, 1994.
Cantwell, Robert. "Conjuring Culture: Ideology and Magic in the Festival of American Folklife." *Journal of American Folklore* 104, no. 412 (1991): 148–63.
———. *Ethnomimesis: Folklife and the Representation of Culture.* Chapel Hill: University of North Carolina Press, 1993.
———. *When We Were Good: The Folk Revival.* Cambridge, MA: Harvard University Press, 1996.
Carleton, Reese M. "Mary Noailles Murfree (1850–1922): An Annotated Bibliography." *American Literary Realism, 1870–1910* 7 (1974): 293–378.
Cary, Richard. *Mary N. Murfree.* New York: Twayne, 1967.
Casper, Scott E. "Antebellum Reading Prescribed and Described." In *Perspectives on American Book History*, edited by Scott E. Casper, Joanne D. Chaison, and Jeffrey D. Groves, 135–64. Amherst: University of Massachusetts Press, 2002.
Castells, Manuel. *The Information Age—Economy, Society, and Culture.* Vol. 2, *The Power of Identity.* Malden, MA: Blackwell, 1997.
Caudill, Harry. *Night Comes to the Cumberlands.* Boston: Little, Brown, 1963.
———. *Theirs Be the Power: The Moguls of Eastern Kentucky.* Champaign: University of Illinois Press, 1983.
Cavicchi, Daniel. *Tramps Like Us: Music and Meaning among Springsteen Fans.* New York: Oxford University Press, 1998.
Chase, Elise. "Peter and Catherine Marshall." In *Twentieth Century Shapers of American Popular Religion*, ed. Charles H. Lippy, 283–86. New York: Greenwood, 1989.
Chepesiuk, Ron. *The Scotch-Irish: From the North of Ireland to the Making of America.* Jefferson, NC: McFarland, 2000.
Chung, Haeja K., ed. *Harriette Simpson Arnow: Critical Essays on Her Work.* East Lansing: Michigan State University Press, 1995.
Clark, Thomas D. "John Fox, Jr." No. 1 of 2, radio address, WHAS, 28 Novem-

ber 1934. Transcript housed at Duncan's Tavern, Paris, KY, and reprinted in *Paris Kentuckian-Citizen*, 16 January 1935.
Comer, Krista. *Landscapes of the New West: Gender and Geography in Contemporary Women's Writing*. Chapel Hill: University of North Carolina Press, 1999.
Conway, Cecelia. *African Banjo Echoes in Appalachia*. Chapel Hill: University of North Carolina Press, 1997.
Coser, Lewis A., Charles Kadushin, and Walter W. Powell. *Books: The Culture and Commerce of Publishing*. New York: Basic, 1982.
Couto, Richard. *An American Challenge: A Report on Economic Trends and Social Issues in Appalachia*. Dubuque, IA: Kendall/Hunt, 1994.
———. "The Spatial Distribution of Wealth and Poverty in Appalachia." *Journal of Appalachian Studies* 1, no. 1 (1995): 99–120.
Crow, Charles L., ed. *A Companion to the Regional Literatures of America*. Malden, MA: Blackwell, 2003.
"Culture Wars: David Hackett Fischer's *Albion's Seed*." *Appalachian Journal* 19, no. 2 (1992): 161–200.
Cunningham, Rodger. *Apples on the Flood: Minority Discourse and Appalachia*. Knoxville: University of Tennessee Press, 1987.
———. "Signs of Civilization: *The Trail of the Lonesome Pine* as Colonial Narrative." *Journal of the Appalachian Studies Association* 2 (1990): 21–46.
Davidson, Cathy. *Revolution and the Word: The Rise of the Novel in America*. New York: Oxford University Press, 1984.
Davis, Kimberly Chabot. "White Book Clubs and African American Literature: The Promise and Limitation of Cross-Racial Empathy." *Literature Interpretation Theory* 19, no. 2 (2008): 155–86.
Desan, Philippe, Priscilla Parkhurst Ferguson, and Wendy Griswold. *Literature and Social Practice*. Chicago: University of Chicago Press, 1988.
Dewey, John. "Americanism and Localism." In *John Dewey, Reconstruction in Philosophy and Essays, 1920: The Middle Works of John Dewey*, edited by Jo Ann Boydston, 12:12–16. Carbondale: Southern Illinois University Press, 1988.
Dimock, Wai Chee, and Michael T. Gilmore, eds. *Rethinking Class: Literary Studies and Social Formations*. New York: Columbia University Press, 1994.
Douglas, Ann. *The Feminization of American Culture, 1820–1875*. New York: Farrar, Straus & Giroux, 1998.
Driscoll, Beth. "How Oprah's Book Club Reinvented the Woman Reader." *Popular Narrative Media* 1, no. 2 (2008): 139–50.
Dunaway, Wilma A. *The First American Frontier: Transition to Capitalism in Southern Appalachia, 1700–1860*. Chapel Hill: University of North Carolina Press, 1996.
———. *Slavery in the American Mountain South*. New York: Cambridge University Press, 2003.

Dunn, Durwood. "Mary Noailles Murfree: A Reappraisal." *Appalachian Journal* 6 (1979): 197–204.
DuPlessis, Rachel Blau. *Writing beyond the Ending: Narrative Strategies of Twentieth-Century Women Writers*. Bloomington: Indiana University Press, 1985.
Eagleton, Terry. *Raymond Williams: Critical Perspectives*. Boston: Northeastern University Press, 1989.
Eller, Ronald D. *Miners, Millhands, and Mountaineers: Industrialization of the Appalachian South, 1880–1930*. Knoxville: University of Tennessee Press, 1982.
Elliott, Michael A. *The Culture Concept: Writing and Difference in the Age of Realism*. Minneapolis: University of Minnesota Press, 2002.
Engelhardt, Elizabeth Sanders Delwiche. *The Tangled Roots of Feminism, Environmentalism, and Appalachian Literature*. Athens: Ohio University Press, 2003.
Ewell, Barbara C. "Changing Places: Women, the Old South; or, What Happens When Local Color Becomes Regionalism." *Amerikastudien* 42, no. 2 (1997): 159–79.
Ewell, Barbara C., and Pamela Glenn Menke, eds. *Southern Local Color: Stories of Region, Race, and Gender*. Athens: University of Georgia Press, 2002.
Falk, John H., and Lynn D. Dierking. *Learning from Museums: Visitor Experiences and the Making of Meaning*. Walnut Creek, CA: AltaMira, 2000.
Fetterley, Judith, and Marjorie Pryse, eds. *American Women Regionalists, 1850–1910: A Norton Anthology*. New York: Norton, 1992.
———. *Writing out of Place: Regionalism, Women, and American Literary Culture*. Urbana: University of Illinois Press, 2002.
Fields, Barbara. "Ideology and Race in American History." In *Region, Race, and Reconstruction: Essays in Honor of C. Vann Woodward*, edited by Morgan Kousser and James M. McPherson, 143–77. New York: Oxford University Press, 1982.
Filene, Benjamin. *Romancing the Folk: Public Memory and American Roots Music*. Chapel Hill: University of North Carolina Press, 2000.
Fischer, David Hackett. *Albion's Seed: Four British Folkways in America*. New York: Oxford University Press, 1989.
Fish, Stanley. *Is There a Text in This Class? The Authority of Interpretive Community*. Cambridge, MA: Harvard University Press, 1980.
Fisher, Stephen L., ed. *Fighting Back in Appalachia: Traditions of Resistance and Change*. Philadelphia: Temple University Press, 1993.
Foote, Stephanie. "The Cultural Work of American Regionalism." In *A Companion to the Regional Literatures of America*, edited by Charles L. Crow, 25–41. Malden, MA: Blackwell, 2003.
———. "'I Feared to Find Myself a Foreigner': Revisiting Regionalism in Sarah Orne Jewett's *The Country of the Pointed Firs*." *Arizona Quarterly* 52, no. 2 (1996): 37–61.

———. *Regional Fictions: Culture and Identity in Nineteenth-Century American Literature.* Madison: University of Wisconsin Press, 2001.

———. "The Value of Regional Identity: Labor, Representation, and Authorship in Hamlin Garland." *Studies in American Fiction* 27, no. 2 (1999): 159–82.

Foster, Stephen William. *The Past Is Another Country: Representation, Historical Consciousness, and Resistance in the Blue Ridge.* Berkeley: University of California Press, 1988.

Fox, John, Jr. "On Horseback to Kingdom Come." *Scribner's*, August 1910, 175–86.

———. "On the Trail of the Lonesome Pine." *Scribner's*, October 1910, 417–28.

———. "Personal Sketch," 1908. In Harriet Holman, "John Fox, Jr.: Appraisal and Self-Appraisal." *Southern Literary Journal* 3, no. 2 (1971): 27–34.

Frankenburg, Ruth. *White Women, Race Matters: The Social Construction of Whiteness.* Minneapolis: University of Minnesota Press, 1993.

Freund, Elizabeth. *The Return of the Reader: Reader-Response Criticism.* New York: Methuen, 1987.

Frost, William Goodell. "Appalachian America." *Ladies Home Companion*, September 1896, 3–4, 21.

———. "Our Contemporary Ancestors in the Southern Mountains." *Atlantic Monthly*, March 1899, 311–19.

Galbraith, John Kenneth. *The Affluent Society.* Boston: Houghton Mifflin, 1958.

Garland, Hamlin. *Crumbling Idols.* Cambridge, MA: Stone & Kimball, 1894.

Gates, Henry Louis. *Colored People: A Memoir.* New York: Knopf, 1994.

Gaventa, John. "Appalachian Studies from and for Social Change." *Appalachian Journal* 5, no. 1 (1977): 23–30.

———. *Power and Powerlessness: Quiescence and Rebellion in an Appalachian Valley.* Urbana: University of Illinois Press, 1980.

Gilmore, Peter. "Gaelic, Celtic Identity, and the Scots-Irish." *Naidheachd* (Autumn 1994): 26–41.

Glazener, Nancy. *Reading for Realism: The History of a U.S. Literary Institution, 1850–1910.* Durham, NC: Duke University Press, 1997.

———. "Regional Accents: Populism, Feminism, and New England Women's Regionalism." *Arizona Quarterly* 52, no. 2 (1996): 33–53.

Goffman, Erving. *Stigma: Notes on the Management of Spoiled Identity.* New York: Simon & Schuster, 1963.

Goin, Mary Elisabeth. "Catherine Marshall: Three Decades of Popular Religion." *Journal of Presbyterian History* 56, no. 3 (1978): 228.

Goldfarb, Michael. "A Southern State of Mind." Radio program produced by Inside Out Documentaries of WBUR Boston. Aired 2 November 2004. http://www.insideout.org/documentaries/southernstate/ (accessed 7 November 2004).

Goldfield, David R. *Cottonfields and Skyscrapers: Southern City and Region, 1607–1980.* Baton Rouge: Louisiana State University Press, 1982.

Goldstein, Philip, and James L. Machor, eds. *New Directions in American Reception Study.* New York: Oxford University Press, 2008.
Gramsci, Antonio. *Selections from the Prison Notebooks.* New York: International, 1971.
Grantham, Dewey W. *The Regional Imagination: The South and Recent American History.* Nashville: Vanderbilt University Press, 1979.
Gray, Richard. *Writing the South: Ideas of an American Region.* New York: Cambridge University Press, 1989.
Green, Chris. *The Social Life of Poetry: Appalachia, Race, and Radical Modernism.* New York: Palgrave Macmillan, 2009.
Green, Harold Everett. *Towering Pines: The Life of John Fox, Jr.* Boston: Meador, 1943.
"The Green Hills of Home Far Away." *Now and Then: The Appalachian Magazine,* Spring 1990, 5–7.
Greenslet, Ferris. *The Life of Thomas Bailey Aldrich.* Boston: Houghton, 1908.
Greeson, Jennifer Rae. "The Figure of the South and the Imagination of Nation in the United States." PhD diss., Yale University, 2001.
———. "The 'Mysteries and Miseries' of North Carolina: New York City, Urban Gothic Fiction, and *Incidents in the Life of a Slave Girl.*" *American Literature: A Journal of Literary History, Criticism, and Bibliography* 73, no. 2 (2001): 277–309.
———. *Our South: Geographic Fantasy and the Rise of National Literature.* Cambridge, MA: Harvard University Press, 2010.
Griffin, Larry J. "Whiteness and Southern Identity in the Mountain and Lowland South." *Journal of Appalachian Studies* 10, nos. 1–2 (Spring–Fall 2004): 7–37.
Griswold, Wendy. *Regionalism and the Reading Class.* Chicago: University of Chicago Press, 2008.
"A Guide to Appalachian Studies." Special issue, *Appalachian Journal* 5, no. 1 (1977).
Gutjahr, Paul C. "No Longer Left Behind: Amazon.com, Reader-Response, and the Changing Fortunes of the Christian Novel in America." *Book History* 5 (2002): 209–36.
Guy, Roger. "A Common Ground: Urban Adaptation and Appalachian Unity." In *Appalachian Odyssey: Historical Perspectives on the Great Migration,* edited by Phillip J. Obermiller, Thomas E. Wagner, and E. Bruce Tucker, 49–66. Westport, CT: Praeger, 2000.
Hackett, Alice Payne. *70 Years of Best Sellers, 1895–1965.* New York: Bowker, 1967.
Hackett, Alice Payne, and James Henry Burke. *80 Years of Best Sellers, 1895–1975.* New York: Bowker, 1977.
Hahn, Steven, and Jonathan Prude, eds. *The Countryside in the Age of Capitalist Transformation: Essays in the Social History of Rural America.* Chapel Hill: University of North Carolina Press, 1985.

Halter, Marilyn. *Shopping for Identity: The Marketing of Ethnicity*. New York: Schocken, 2000.
Hanna, Stephen P. "Appalshop Films." *Appalachian Journal* 25, no. 4 (1998): 380–410.
Hardwig, Bill. Introduction to *In the Tennessee Mountains*, by Mary Noailles Murfree, xi–xl. Knoxville: University of Tennessee Press, 2008.
Harkins, Anthony. *Hillbilly: A Cultural History of an American Icon*. New York: Oxford University Press, 2004.
Harrington, Michael. *The Other America: Poverty in the United States*. 1962. Reprint, New York: Collier, Macmillan, 1994.
Harris, Isabella D. "Charles Egbert Craddock as an Interpreter of Mountain Life." MA thesis, Duke University, 1933.
Hart, Henry. *James Dickey: The World as a Lie*. New York: Picador, 2000.
Harvard College. *Harvard Class of 1883: Fiftieth Anniversary*. Cambridge, MA: Murray, 1933.
Harvey, David. *The Condition of Postmodernity: An Enquiry into the Origins of Cultural Change*. Malden, MA: Blackwell, 1989.
———. *Justice, Nature, and the Geography of Difference*. Malden, MA: Blackwell, 1996.
Hayden, Dolores. *The Power of Place: Urban Landscapes as Public History*. Cambridge, MA: MIT Press, 1995.
Healy, David. *U.S. Expansionism: The Imperialist Urge in the 1890s*. Madison: University of Wisconsin Press, 1970.
Higham, John. *Strangers in the Land: Patterns of American Nativism, 1860–1925*. New York: Athenaeum, 1974.
Hill, Jane. "Coming to Terms with the Appalachian 'Other' in the Novels of Gail Godwin." *Journal of Kentucky Studies* 11 (1995): 98–105.
———. *Gail Godwin*. New York: Twayne, 1992.
Hinckley, Karen, and Barbara Hinckley. *American Best Sellers: A Reader's Guide to Popular Fiction*. Bloomington: Indiana University Press, 1989.
Hobsbawm, Eric, and Terence Ranger, eds. *The Invention of Tradition*. New York: Cambridge University Press, 1992.
Hochman, Barbara. *Getting at the Author: Reimagining Books and Reading in the Age of American Realism*. Amherst: University of Massachusetts Press, 2001.
Holman, Harriet, ed. *John Fox and Tom Page as They Were: Letters, an Address, and an Essay*. Miami: Field Research Projects, 1970.
———. "John Fox, Jr.: Appraisal and Self-Appraisal." *Southern Literary Journal* 3, no. 2 (1971): 18–38.
Howard, June, ed. *New Essays on* The Country of the Pointed Firs. Cambridge: Cambridge University Press, 1994.
———. "Unraveling Regions, Unsettling Periods: Sarah Orne Jewett and American Literary History." *American Literature: A Journal of Literary History, Criticism, and Bibliography* 68, no. 2 (1996): 365–84.

Hsiung, David C. *Two Worlds in the Tennessee Mountains: Exploring the Origins of Appalachian Stereotypes.* Lexington: University Press of Kentucky, 1997.
Hsu, Hsuan L. "Literature and Regional Production." *American Literary History* 17, no. 1 (2005): 36–69.
Inness, Sherrie A., and Diana Royer, eds. *Breaking Boundaries: New Perspectives on Women's Regional Writing.* Iowa City: University of Iowa Press, 1997.
Inscoe, John. *Appalachians and Race: The Mountain South from Slavery to Segregation.* Lexington: University Press of Kentucky, 2001.
Iser, Wolfgang. "Indeterminacy and the Reader's Response in Prose Fiction." In *Aspects of Narrative,* edited by J. Hillis Miller, 1–45. New York: Columbia University Press, 1971.
———. *Prospecting: From Reader Response to Literary Anthropology.* Baltimore: Johns Hopkins University Press, 1989.
Jackson, Dot. "The Ideal Home: Return from Flatland Exile." *Now and Then: The Appalachian Magazine,* Spring 1988, 5–6.
Jacobson, Matthew Frye. *Roots Too: White Ethnic Revival in Post–Civil Rights America.* Cambridge, MA: Harvard University Press, 2006.
———. *Whiteness of a Different Color: European Immigrants and the Alchemy of Race.* Cambridge, MA: Harvard University Press, 1998.
Jameson, Frederic. *The Political Unconscious: Narrative as a Socially Symbolic Act.* Ithaca, NY: Cornell University Press, 1982.
———. *Postmodernism; or, The Cultural Logic of Late Capitalism.* Durham, NC: Duke University Press, 1991.
Jauss, Hans Robert. *Toward an Aesthetic of Reception.* Minneapolis: University of Minnesota Press, 1981.
Joseph, Philip. "Landed and Literary: Hamlin Garland, Sarah Orne Jewett, and the Production of Regional Literatures." *Studies in American Fiction* 26, no. 2 (1998): 147–70.
Jurca, Catherine. *White Diaspora: The Suburb and the Twentieth-Century American Novel.* Princeton: Princeton University Press, 2001.
Justice, Keith L. *Bestseller Index: All Books,* Publishers Weekly *and the* New York Times *through 1990.* Jefferson, NC: McFarland, 1998.
Kant, Kristin Mary Agnes Helen. "Painting the Mountains: An Investigation of Tourist Art in North America." PhD diss. University of Kentucky, 2009.
Kaplan, Amy. "Nation, Region, and Empire." In *Columbia History of the American Novel,* edited by Emory Elliott and Cathy Davidson, 240–66. New York: Columbia University Press, 1991,
———. "Romancing the Empire: The Embodiment of American Masculinity in the Popular Historical Novel of the 1890s." *American Literary History* 2, no. 4 (1990): 659–90.
———. *The Social Construction of American Realism.* Chicago: University of Chicago Press, 1992.

Kaplan, Amy, and Donald Pease, eds. *Cultures of United States Imperialism.* Durham, NC: Duke University Press, 1993.
Karem, Jeff. *The Romance of Authenticity: The Cultural Politics of Regional and Ethnic Literatures.* Charlottesville: University of Virginia Press, 2004.
Karp, Ivan, and Steven Levine, eds. *Exhibiting Cultures: The Poetics and Politics of Museum Display.* Washington, DC: Smithsonian Institution Press, 1991.
Kaufman, Rona. "'That, My Dear, Is Called Reading': Oprah's Book Club and the Construction of a Readership." In *Reading Sites: Social Difference and Reader Response,* edited by Patrocinio P. Schweickart and Elizabeth A. Flynn, 221–55. New York: Modern Language Association, 2004.
Kephart, Horace. *Our Southern Highlanders: A Narrative of Adventure in the Southern Appalachians and a Study of Life among the Mountaineers.* Knoxville: University of Tennessee Press, 1913.
Kiberd, Declan. "Imagining Irish Studies." In *Inventing Ireland,* 641–54. Cambridge, MA: Harvard University Press, 1995.
Kirby, Jack Temple. *Media-made Dixie: The South in the American Imagination.* Athens: University of Georgia Press, 1986.
Kirshenblatt-Gimblett, Barbara. *Destination Culture: Tourism, Museums, and Heritage.* Berkeley: University of California Press, ca. 1998.
Kracauer, Siegfried. *The Mass Ornament.* Cambridge, MA: Harvard University Press, 1995.
Kratz, Corinne A. *The Ones That Are Wanted: Communication and the Politics of Representation in a Photographic Exhibition.* Berkeley: University of California Press, 2002.
Kreyling, Michael. *Inventing Southern Literature.* Jackson: University Press of Mississippi, 1998.
Ladd, Barbara. "Dismantling the Monolith: Southern Places—Past, Present, and Future." *Critical Survey* 12, no. 1 (2000): 28–42.
———. *Nationalism and the Color Line in George Washington Cable, Mark Twain, and William Faulkner.* Baton Rouge: Louisiana State University Press, 1996.
Lang, Amy Schrager. *The Syntax of Class: Writing Inequality in Nineteenth-Century America.* Princeton: Princeton University Press, 2003.
Lears, T. J. Jackson. *No Place of Grace: Antimodernism and the Transformation of American Culture, 1880–1920.* New York: Pantheon, 1981.
Lefebvre, Henri. *The Production of Space.* Translated by Donald Nicholson-Smith. Cambridge, MA: Blackwell, 1991.
Levine, Lawrence. *Black Culture and Black Consciousness: Afro-American Folk Thought from Slavery to Freedom.* New York: Oxford University Press, 1977.
———. *Highbrow/Lowbrow: The Emergence of Cultural Hierarchy.* Cambridge, MA: Harvard University Press, 1988.
Limerick, Patricia Nelson. *The Legacy of Conquest: The Unbroken Past of the American West.* New York: Norton, 1987.

Long, Elizabeth. *Book Clubs: Women and the Uses of Reading in Everyday Life*. Chicago: University of Chicago Press, 2003.
Lott, Eric. *Love and Theft: Blackface Minstrelsy and the American Working Class*. New York: Oxford University Press, 1993.
Luskey, Brian. *On the Make: Clerks and the Quest for Capital in Nineteenth-Century America*. New York: New York University Press, 2010.
Lutz, Catherine A., and Jane L. Collins. *Reading National Geographic*. Chicago: University of Chicago Press, 1993.
Lutz, Tom. *Cosmopolitan Vistas: American Regionalism and Literary Value*. Ithaca, NY: Cornell University Press, 2004.
MacCannell, Dean. *The Tourist: A New Theory of the Leisure Class*. Berkeley: University of California Press, 1999.
Machor, James L., and Philip Goldstein, eds. *Reception Study: From Literary Theory to Cultural Studies*. New York: Routledge, 2001.
Mailloux, Steven. *Reception Histories: Rhetoric, Pragmatism, and American Cultural Politics*. Ithaca, NY: Cornell University Press, 1998.
Marx, Leo. *The Machine in the Garden: Technology and the Pastoral Ideal in America*. New York: Oxford University Press, 1964.
Mason, Carol. "The Hillbilly Defense: Culturally Mediating U.S. Terror at Home and Abroad." *NWSA Journal* 17, no. 3 (2005): 39–63.
———. *Reading Appalachia from Left to Right: Conservatives and the 1974 Kanawha County Textbook Controversy*. Ithaca, NY: Cornell University Press, 2009.
Massey, Doreen B. *Space, Place, Gender*. Minneapolis: University of Minnesota Press, 1994.
———. *Spatial Divisions of Labor: Social Structures and the Geography of Production*. Basingstoke: Macmillan, 1995.
Matt, Susan J. "You Can't Go Home Again: Homesickness and Nostalgia in U.S. History." *Journal of American History* 92, no. 4 (2007): 469–97.
McKee, Matthew. "'A Peculiar and Royal Race': Creating a Scotch-Irish Identity, 1889–1901." In *Atlantic Crossroads: Historical Connections between Scotland, Ulster, and North America*, edited by Patrick Fitzgerald and Steve Ickringill, 67–83. Newtownards, Northern Ireland: Colourpoint, 2001.
McPherson, Tara. *Reconstructing Dixie: Race, Gender, and Nostalgia in the Imagined South*. Durham, NC: Duke University Press, 2003.
Meinig, David. *The Shaping of America: A Geographical Perspective on 500 Years of History*. Vol. 2. New Haven: Yale University Press, 1988.
Michaels, Walter Benn. "Anti-imperial Americanism." In *Cultures of United States Imperialism*, edited by Amy Kaplan and Donald Pease, 365–91. Durham, NC: Duke University Press, 1993.
———. "Race into Culture: A Critical Genealogy of Cultural Identity." In *Identities*, edited by Anthony Appiah and Henry Louis Gates Jr., 32–62. Chicago: University of Chicago Press, 1995.

Miles, Emma Bell. *The Spirit of the Mountains*. New York: J. Pott, 1905. Reprint, Knoxville: University of Tennessee Press, 1975.
Miller, Danny. *Wingless Flights: Appalachian Women in Fiction*. Bowling Green, OH: Bowling Green State University Popular Press, 1996.
Miller, Laura J. "The Best-Seller List as Marketing Tool and Historical Fiction." *Book History* 3 (2000): 286–304.
Mitchell, Robert D., ed. *Appalachian Frontiers: Settlement, Society, and Development in the Preindustrial Era*. Lexington: University Press of Kentucky, 1991.
Mooney, Mary Sue. "An Intimate Study of Mary Noailles Murfree, Charles Egbert Craddock." MA thesis, George Peabody College for Teachers, 1928.
Moore, Elizabeth Fox, ed. *John Fox, Jr.: Personal and Family Letters and Papers*. Lexington, Kentucky: University of Kentucky Library Associates, 1955.
Moore, William Cabell. *John Fox, Jr., 1862–1919: An Address Delivered October 21, 1957, at the Club of Colonial Dames, Washington, D.C.* Washington, DC, 1957.
Moretti, Franco. *Graphs Maps Trees: Abstract Models for a Literary Theory*. New York: Verso, 2005.
Morgan, Stacy I. "Migration, Material Culture, and Identity in William Attaway's *Blood on the Forge* and Harriette Arnow's *The Dollmaker*." *College English* 63, no. 6 (2001): 712–40.
Morrison, Toni. *Playing in the Dark: Whiteness and the Literary Imagination*. Cambridge, MA: Harvard University Press, 1992.
Mott, Frank Luther. *The Golden Multitudes: The Story of Best Sellers in the United States*. New York: Macmillan, 1947.
"Mountain Fiction from Abernethy to Zugsmith . . . from 1832 to 1985: 1,517 Works of Fiction by Southern Appalachian Authors, or with Southern Appalachian Settings." Hutchins Library, Berea College, Berea, KY, 1985.
Mumford, Lewis. *The Culture of Cities*. New York: Harcourt, Brace, 1938.
Myadze, Theresa. "Rethinking Urban Appalachian Ethnicity." *Journal of Appalachian Studies* 3, no. 2 (1997): 243–52.
Nezar, AlSayyad, ed. *Consuming Tradition, Manufacturing Heritage: Global Norms and Urban Forms in the Age of Tourism*. New York: Routledge, 2001.
Novak, Michael. *The Rise of the Unmeltable Ethnics: Politics and Culture in the Seventies*. New York: Macmillan, 1972.
Obermiller, Phillip J., and William W. Philliber, eds. *Too Few Tomorrows: Urban Appalachians in the 1980s*. Boone, NC: Appalachian Consortium, 1987.
Obermiller, Phillip J., and Ray Rappold. "Bury Me Not in a Sidewalk: The Appalachian Way of Death in the Cities." *Now and Then: The Appalachian Magazine*, Summer 1990, 28–29.
O'Brien, John. *At Home in the Heart of Appalachia*. New York: Knopf, 2001.
Ohmann, Richard. *Selling Culture: Magazines, Markets, and Class at the Turn of the Century*. New York: University Press of New England, 1996.
Parks, Edd Winfield. *Charles Egbert Craddock (Mary Noailles Murfree)*. Chapel Hill: University of North Carolina Press, 1941.

Patterson, James T. *Grand Expectations: The United States, 1945–1974*. New York: Oxford University Press, 1996.
Peterson, Richard A. *Creating Country Music: Fabricating Authenticity*. Chicago: University of Chicago Press, 1997.
Posnock, Ross. *Color and Culture: Black Writers and the Making of the Modern Intellectual*. Cambridge, MA: Harvard University Press, 1998.
Powell, Katrina M. *The Anguish of Displacement: The Politics of Literacy in the Letters of Mountain Families in Shenandoah National Park*. Charlottesville: University of Virginia Press, 2007.
Price, Kenneth M., and Susan Belasco Smith, eds. *Periodical Literature in Nineteenth-Century America*. Charlottesville: University Press of Virginia, 1995.
Pryse, Marjorie. "Exploring Contact: Regionalism and the 'Outsider' Standpoint in Mary Noailles Murfree's Appalachia." *Legacy* 17, no. 2 (2000): 199–212.
Puckett, Anita. "Identity, Hybridity, and Linguistic Ideologies of Racial Language in the Upper South." In *Linguistic Diversity in the South: Changing Codes, Practices, and Ideology*, edited by Margaret Bender, 120–37. Southern Anthropological Society Proceedings 37. Athens: University of Georgia Press, 2004.
———. "The 'Value' of Dialect as Object: The Case of Appalachian English." *Pragmatics: Quarterly Publication of the International Pragmatics Association* 13, nos. 3–4 (2003): 539–49.
Pudup, Mary Beth. "The Boundaries of Class in Preindustrial Appalachia." *Journal of Historical Geography* 15 (1989): 139–62.
Pudup, Mary Beth, Dwight B. Billings, and Altina Waller, eds. *Appalachia in the Making: The Mountain South in the Nineteenth Century*. Chapel Hill: University of North Carolina Press, 1995.
Radway, Janice. *A Feeling for Books: The Book-of-the-Month Club, Literary Taste, and Middle-Class Desire*. Chapel Hill: University of North Carolina Press, 1997.
———. "Interpretive Communities and Variable Literacies: The Functions of Romance Reading." *Daedalus* 113, no. 3 (1984): 49–73.
———. *Reading the Romance: Women, Patriarchy, and Popular Literature*. Chapel Hill: University of North Carolina Press, 1984.
———. "What's the Matter with Reception Study? Some Thoughts on the Disciplinary Origins, Conceptual Constraints, and Persistent Viability of a Paradigm." In *New Directions in American Reception Study*, edited by Philip Goldstein and James L. Machor, 327–51. New York: Oxford University Press, 2008.
"Rave Reviews: Bestselling Fiction in America." Curated by Lynda Fuller Clendenning and John Unsworth. 16 December 2009. http://www2.lib.virginia.edu/exhibits/rave_reviews/introduction.html (accessed 13 October 2010).
Reichert Powell, Douglas. *Critical Regionalism: Connecting Politics and Culture in the American Landscape*. Chapel Hill: University of North Carolina Press, 2007.

Roberts, Mark A. "The Performing Hillbilly: Redeeming Acts of a Regional Stereotype." *Appalachian Journal* 38, no. 1 (2010): 78–90.
Roediger, David R. *The Wages of Whiteness: Race and the Making of the American Working Class*. New York: Verso, 1991.
Romero, Laura. *Homefronts*. Durham, NC: Duke University Press, 1997.
Rotundo, E. Anthony. *American Manhood: Transformations in Masculinity from the Revolution to the Modern Era*. New York: Basic, 1993.
Ryan, Barbara. "'A Real Basis from Which to Judge': Fan Mail to Gene Stratton Porter." In *Reading Acts: U.S. Readers' Interactions with Literature, 1800–1950*, edited by Barbara Ryan and Amy M. Thomas, 161–78. Knoxville: University of Tennessee Press, 2002.
———. "'Wherever I Am Living': The 'Lady of the Limberlost' Resituates." In *Breaking Boundaries: New Perspectives on Women's Regional Writing*, edited by Sherrie A. Inness and Diana Royer, 162–79. Iowa City: University of Iowa Press, 1997.
Ryan, Barbara, and Amy M. Thomas, eds. *Reading Acts: U.S. Readers' Interactions with Literature, 1800–1950*. Knoxville: University of Tennessee Press, 2002.
Said, Edward W. *Orientalism*. New York: Vintage, 1979.
Sanchez, George J. "Face the Nation: Race, Immigration, and the Rise of Nativism in Late Twentieth Century America." *International Migration Review* 31, no. 4 (1997): 1009–30.
Satterwhite, Emily. "Imagining Home, Nation, World: Appalachia on the Mall." *Journal of American Folklore* 121, no. 479 (2008): 10–34.
———. "Objecting to Insider/Outsider Politics and the Uncritical Celebration of Appalachia." *Appalachian Journal* 38, no. 1 (2010): 68–73.
———. "Reading Craddock, Reading Murfree: Local Color, Authenticity, and Geographies of Reception." *American Literature: A Journal of Literary History, Criticism, and Bibliography* 78, no. 1 (2006): 59–88.
———. "Romancing Whiteness: Popular Appalachian Fiction and the Imperialist Imagination at the Turns of Two Centuries." In *At Home and Abroad: Historicizing Twentieth-Century Whiteness in Literature and Performance*, edited by La Vinia Delois Jennings, 93–117. Knoxville: University of Tennessee Press, 2009.
———. "Seeing Appalachian Cities." In *Appalachia: Social Context Past and Present*, edited by Phillip Obermiller and Michael Maloney, 104–7. Dubuque, IA: Kendall/Hunt, 2002.
———. "Seeing Appalachian Cities." *Southern Changes* 21, no. 2 (1999): 20–22.
———. "'That's What They're All Singing About': Appalachian Heritage, Celtic Pride, and American Nationalism at the 2003 Smithsonian Folklife Festival." *Appalachian Journal* 32, no. 3 (2005): 302–38.
Schiffrin, André. *The Business of Books: How International Conglomerates Took over Publishing and Changed the Way We Read*. New York: Verso, 2000.

Schivelbusch, Wolfgang. *The Culture of Defeat: On National Trauma, Mourning, and Recovery*. New York: Metropolitan, 2003.
Schweickart, Patrocinio P., and Elizabeth A. Flynn. *Reading Sites: Social Difference and Reader Response*. New York: Modern Language Association, 2004.
Shaker, Bonnie James. *Coloring Locals: Racial Formation in Kate Chopin's Youth's Companion Stories*. Ames: University of Iowa Press, 2003.
Shapiro, Henry D. *Appalachia on Our Mind: The Southern Mountains and Mountaineers in the American Consciousness, 1870–1920*. Chapel Hill: University of North Carolina Press, 1978.
Sicherman, Barbara. "Reading and Middle-Class Identity in Victorian America: Cultural Consumption, Conspicuous and Otherwise." In *Reading Acts: U.S. Readers' Interactions with Literature, 1800–1950*, edited by Barbara Ryan and Amy M. Thomas, 137–55. Knoxville: University of Tennessee Press, 2002.
Silber, Nina. *The Romance of Reunion: Northerners and the South, 1865–1900*. Chapel Hill: University of North Carolina Press, 1993.
———. "'What Does America Need So Much as Americans?': Race and Northern Reconciliation with Southern Appalachia, 1870–1900." In *Appalachians and Race: The Mountain South from Slavery to Segregation*, edited by John Inscoe, 245–58. Lexington: University Press of Kentucky, 2001.
Smith, Barbara Ellen. "De-gradations of Whiteness: Appalachia and the Complexities of Race." *Journal of Appalachian Studies* 10, nos. 1–2 (2004): 38–57.
Smith, Barbara Ellen, et al. "Appalachian Identity: A Roundtable Discussion," *Appalachian Journal* 38, no. 1 (2010): 56–76.
Smith, Barbara Hernstein. "Contingencies of Value." *Critical Inquiry* 10, no. 1 (1984): 1–35.
Smith, Lee. "Raised to Leave." *Now and Then: The Appalachian Magazine*, Spring 2002, 20–23.
Soja, Edward. *Postmetropolis: Critical Studies of Cities and Regions*. Malden, MA: Blackwell, 2000.
———. *Postmodern Geographies: The Reassertion of Space in Critical Social Theory*. New York: Verso, 1989.
Spence, Eleanor B. "Collected Reminiscences of Mary N. Murfree." MA thesis, George Peabody College for Teachers, 1928.
Squires, Claire. "Fiction in the Marketplace: The Literary Novel and the Publishing Industry, 1990–2000." PhD diss., Oxford University, 2003.
———. *Marketing Literature: The Making of Contemporary Writing in Britain*. New York: Palgrave Macmillan, 2007.
Stanley, Talmage Apperson. "The Poco Field: Politics, Culture, and Place in Contemporary Appalachia." PhD diss., Emory University, 1996.
Thompson, Jane. *West of Everything: The Inner Life of Westerns*. New York: Oxford University Press, 1992.
Tompkins, Jane. *Sensational Designs: The Cultural Work of American Fiction, 1790–1860*. New York: Oxford University Press, 1985.

Trachtenberg, Alan. *The Incorporation of America: Culture and Society in the Gilded Age.* New York: Hill & Wang, 1982.
"The Trail of the Lonesome Pine Outdoor Drama." 2004 program. Commonwealth of Virginia's Official Outdoor Drama. (In possession of the author.)
"The Trail of the Lonesome Pine Outdoor Drama." Initial adaptation by Earl Hobson Smith. Directed by Jill Bergeron. Big Stone Gap, VA, 10 July 2004.
Tuttle, Bettie J. *John Fox, Jr.* Paris, KY: DAR, 1995. (Booklet in possession of the author.)
Upton, Dell. "'Authentic' Anxieties." In *Consuming Tradition, Manufacturing Heritage: Global Norms and Urban Forms in the Age of Tourism,* edited by AlSayyad Nezar, 298–306. New York: Routledge, 2001.
Webb, James. *Born Fighting: How the Scots-Irish Shaped America.* New York: Broadway, 2004.
———. "Day to Day." Interview with Noah Adams. National Public Radio, 6 October 2004.
Whisnant, David E. *All That Is Native and Fine: The Politics of Culture in an American Region.* Chapel Hill: University of North Carolina Press, 1983.
———. *Modernizing the Mountaineer: People, Power, and Planning in Appalachia.* Boone, NC: Appalachia Consortium, 1980. Reprint, Knoxville: University of Tennessee Press, 1994.
Wiebe, Robert H. *The Search for Order, 1877–1920.* New York: Hill & Wang, 1967.
Williams, Cratis. "The Southern Mountaineer in Fact and Fiction." *Appalachian Journal* 3 (1975–76): 8–61, 100–162, 186–261, 334–92.
Williams, John Alexander. *Appalachia: A History.* Chapel Hill: University of North Carolina Press, 2002.
———. "Counting Yesterday's People: Using Aggregate Data to Address the Problem of Appalachia's Boundaries." *Journal of Appalachian Studies* 2, no. 1 (1996): 3–27.
Williams, Raymond. *The Country and the City.* New York: Oxford University Press, 1973.
———. *Culture and Society: 1780–1950.* New York: Columbia University Press, 1983.
———. *Keywords: A Vocabulary of Culture and Society.* New York: Oxford University Press, 1983.
———. *Marxism and Literature.* New York: Oxford University Press, 1977.
———. *The Sociology of Culture.* New York: Schocken, 1981.
———. *Writing in Society.* London: Verso, 1983.
Williamson, J. W. *Hillbillyland: What the Movies Did to the Mountains and What the Mountains Did to the Movies.* Chapel Hill: University of North Carolina Press, 1995.
Willis, Susan. "A Literary Lesson in Historical Thinking." *Social Text* 3 (Fall 1980): 136–43.

Wilson, Darlene. "The Felicitous Convergence of Mythmaking and Capital Accumulation: John Fox Jr. and the Formation of An(Other) Almost-White American Underclass." *Journal of Appalachian Studies* 1, no. 1 (1995): 5–44.

———. Foreword to *Heart of the Hills*, by John Fox Jr., vii–xxviii. Lexington: University Press of Kentucky, 1996.

———. "A Judicious Combination of Incident and Psychology: John Fox Jr. and the Southern Mountaineer Motif." In *Confronting Appalachian Stereotypes: Back Talk from an American Region*, edited by Dwight B. Billings, Gurney Norman, and Katherine Ledford, 98–118. Lexington: University Press of Kentucky, 1999.

Wray, Matt. *Not Quite White: White Trash and the Boundaries of Whiteness*. Durham, NC: Duke University Press, 2006.

Wrobel, David M., and Michael Steiner. *Many Wests: Place, Culture and Regional Identity*. Lawrence: University Press of Kansas, 1997.

Yaeger, Patricia. *Dirt and Desire: Southern Women's Writing, 1930–1990*. Chicago: University of Chicago Press, 2000.

———, ed. *The Geography of Identity*. Ann Arbor: University of Michigan Press, ca. 1996.

York, Bill. *John Fox, Jr., Appalachian Author*. Jefferson, NC: McFarland, 2003.

Zaragoza, June. "To Edify or Entertain: The Fiction of Catherine Marshall." *Christianity and the Arts* 3, no. 3 (1996): 11–13.

Index

Page numbers in *italics* refer to illustrations or information in their captions.

Abner, Hattie, 104, 236
Adams, Noah, 307n18
"affirmed Appalachians," 182, 192–93, 197, 202, 203–4, 319n133
African Americans, 322n3
  Appalachian-set fiction and, 194, 315–16n94
  "community" and exclusion of, 226
  Great Migration of, as part of Southern Diaspora, 92, 111, 124, 145, 179, 194
  as interchangeable with poor whites, 170, 175, 176
  as local-color characters, 24, 320n144
  Moynihan Report and, 291n40
  nostalgia lacking in, 194
  post-WWII suburbanization and, 124
  as racial Others, 24, 25, 175, 226
  as readers, 194–95
  segregated migration and, 282n46
  in South, 170
  white racial innocence and, 16, 219
Agnes Scott College (Atlanta, GA), 136, 242, 244
agrarianism, 100–102, 104–5, 212, 213
Agricultural Adjustment Act, 279n22
Ahrens, Pat, 160
Akron (OH), 282n46
Aldrich, Lilian Woodman, 49, 50
Aldrich, Thomas Bailey, 27, 28, 29, 32, 33, 38–39, 41, 49, 50, 259n3, 262n37
Algonquin Books, 307n20
Alice Lloyd College (Pippa Passes, KY), 283n54

Allen, James Lane, 63, 65, 239, 284n67
Allnutt, Susan, 296n79
Almgren, Gunnar, 6, 90, 251n19
"almost-white," 220, 251n22
Alquist, Sheldon D., Jr., 167
Amazon.com, 177, 179, 184, 237–38, 247
American Folklife Preservation Act (1976), 306n10
Americanness, 8, 19, 112, 217, 221
ancestry, 111–12, 148–49
Anderson, Helena, 156, 174
Andy Griffith Show, The (TV program), 23
Angel, Sheila, 293n55
Anglo-Saxon supremacy, 38–39, 66, 67, 219, 262n35
Angus, Barbara, 300n122
anticonsumerism, 132
anti-hillbilly sentiments, 92
Anti-immigration League, 39, 262n37
anti-industrialism, 123
antimodernism, 56, 57, 58, 83, 85–86, 91
anti-urbanism, 123
"A-Playin' of Old Sledge at the Settlemint" (Murfree), 41
Appalachia
  as ancestral homeland, 16, 38, 109, 111–12, 122, 135, 145, 148–49, 182, 188, 225
  as Celtic, 220, 221, 224
  "Christy Country" vs., 292n43
  commodification of, 227–28
  as concept, 2–3, 249n2, 249–50n7, 250n11
  cosmopolitan readers from, 7–8, 209
  development in, 209

353

Appalachia *(cont.)*
  early settlers of, 142
  gendered role of, 37–38, 157
  geographic definition of, 3, 250n10, 324n22
  as home, 93, 109, 188, 191–93
  "iconic books" for, 177–78
  idealized, 7
  late 19th-century literary representations of, 254n47
  local-color writing in, 19
  marketability of, 180–81
  nationalization of, 255n54
  as Other, 254n45
  poverty in, 16, 23, 144, 291n40
  production/commodification of, 8, 91, 142, 227–28
  racial victimization of, 224–25, 324–25nn29–31
  regional scholarship on, 3 (*see also* Appalachian studies)
  resource exploitation in, 86, 209, 217
  romance with, 212, 216–27
  as safe, 134, 187, 192, 226
  as Scottish, 65–66, 138, 142, 145, 218, 220, 221
  small-town virtues in, 187, 188, 192–93
  the South vs., 16–17
  stereotypes about, 1–2, 13, 133, 212, 216, 249n2 (*see also* hillbillies; mountaineers)
  white migration from, 180 (*see also* migration)
  whiteness of (*see* whiteness; Appalachian ethnicity; mountaineers as American "folk"; mountaineers: British origins of)
  "Year of," 246, 258n73
  See also "affirmed Appalachians"; Authentic Appalachia; "charmed Appalachians"; "offended Appalachians"
Appalachia: A History of Mountains and People (TV documentary; 2009), 4

"Appalachia: Heritage and Harmony" (Smithsonian Folklife Festival), 220–22
Appalachian ethnicity, 5, 6, 39, 56, 65–66, 109, 142, 165, 180, 181, 214, 217, 218, 219–21, 224, 226, 227, 251n22
Appalachianization, 307n18
Appalachian Journal, 161
Appalachian literature, 218. *See also* literature
Appalachian music, 218. *See also* music
Appalachian Regional Commission, 250n10, 324n22
Appalachian-set fiction
  African American view of, 195
  authorship of, 8–11, 27–29
  best sellers, 93, 230–35
  as boring, 188
  decline of, during Progressive Era, 21–22, 131
  documentary accuracy and, 8, 10–11, 208–10
  functions of, 5–7, 214
  Gilded Age fears alleviated by, 4
  popularity of, 3, 17
  during post-WWII era, 22
  during Progressive Era, 20
  protagonists in, 205
  readers' desires and, 5–8
  reader identification with characters in, 84, 91, 95, 113, 118
  resurgence of, during Neo–Gilded Age, 24–25, 307n18
  Southern Diaspora and, 22, 92–93, 110
  as unmediated missives, 209
  use of term, 11
  during Vietnam War era, 23
Appalachian State University (NC), 161, 164, 298n102
Appalachian studies
  Arnow's fiction as viewed in, 90–91
  critical focus of, 211–12

Index   355

and Dickey, 161
Murfree's fiction as viewed in, 15, 30
rise of, 164
Appalachia on Our Mind (Shapiro), 2–3
Appalachia Service Project (ASP), 167
Applegate, Wesley, 165
Appleton's, 34, 261n24
Arab, 226
Arnow, Elizabeth, 119, 240
Arnow, Harold, 105–7, 108, 125
Arnow, Harriette Simpson, 9, 10, 93–94, *107*
  awards received by, 280n35
  biographical details, 91, 105–7, 125–26, 186, 287n94
  empathic qualities of, 277n8
  fan mail to, 90, 92–93, 96–97 *map*, 98–99 *map*
  fan responses to, 22
  homes of, 107, 125–26
  migration and, 10, 105–8
  migrant fans of, 92–93, 95, 112–19, 114–15 *map*, 116–17 *map*, 222
  mobility and, 107–8
  nonfiction works of, 240, 280n35
  novels of, 22, 280n35
  papers of, 240–41
  readership types, 14, 92–93, 94–95, 112
  readers' view of, as authentic, 91, 93, 104–9, *107*, 119, 186
  See also Dollmaker, The; Hunter's Horn
Asheville (NC), 190, 217–18, 234
Asians, 175–76
At Home in Mitford (Karon), 24
  Appalachian local-color themes in, 182, 184–85
  Appalachian setting of, 181
  as best seller, 184
  "charmed Appalachians" as readers of, 202
  as community fantasy novel, 225

  customer reviews of, 182, 184, 246–47, 312nn55, 58, 314n80, 315n87, 317n104, 319–20n140
  documentary accuracy and, 186
  dialect as used in, 206
  identity and sense of belonging in, 187–88, 195, 209
  idyllic small-town life and, 191–92, 195
  malapropisms in, 320n147
  marketing of, 183
  methodological considerations, 246–47
  "nostalgic cosmopolitans" as readers of, 195
  publication of, 183, 307n20
  quirky characters in, 205, 312n58, 319–20n140
  racism and, 192
  sense of authentic place as constructed in, 185, 186–87
  "touristic cosmopolitans" as readers of, 188–89, 190–92
Atlanta Film Festival, 158
Atlantic Monthly
  circulation of, under Howells, 260n16
  Deliverance excerpt published in, 244
  as highbrow outlet, 6, 31, 49
  Murfree short stories published in, 20, 27, 32, 34, 36, 49
Aubry, Timothy, 229
Auburn University, 283n59
Aunt Jane of Kentucky (Obenchain), 233
Austen, Jane, 55
Austin, Nellie, 124
Authentic Appalachia
  essentialist notions of, 8
  fan migration narratives and, 13–14
  Fox and, 63–65
  Neo–Gilded Age novels and, 187
  popular regional fiction and, 5–6
  readers' embrace of, 2, 182–83
  terms denoting, 142

authenticity
  Arnow and construction of, 91, 93, 104–9, *107*, 119
  authors and, 8–10
  confining effects of demands for, 282n45
  continued desire for, 250–51n13, 251n18
  crafts and, 277–78n10
  Dickey and construction of, 158
  Dickey and reader romance with, 153
  Fox and construction of, 62–65
  Frazier and construction of, 186
  House and construction of, 186
  Karon and construction of, 186–87
  local-color fiction and, 132, 252n27
  Marshall and construction of, 144, 166
  Murfree and construction of, 27–29, 33–37
  need to define, 250–51n13
  Neo–Gilded Age fiction and construction of, 185–87
  regional fiction and production of, 2–3, 5–6, 221
  romance of, 104, 142, 251n14
  Trigiani and construction of, 186–87
  unique nation idea and, 323n15
  See also Authentic Appalachia
authorship, 8–11, 27–29
autoethnography, 260n12

back-to-the-land movement, 132
Baldacci, David, 234
Ballantine, 183, 234, 307n20
Ballard, Sandra L., 277n8, 279n22
Baltimore Radical Book Fair (2010), 217
Baltimore Sun, 65, 304n3
Barber, Arthur William, 67
Barcus, Holly, 196, 209
Barnes and Noble, 24, 179, 246–47, 289n17, 305n5, 309n32
Barnhill, William A., 242–43

Batteau, Allen, 1, 255n58
Bauman, Zygmunt, 209–10
Baxter, Sylvester, 264n52
Bears of Egypt, Maine, The (Chute), 305–6n6
Belasco, Susan, 31, 260n16
Bendix, Regina, 250–51n13, 251n18
Berea College (Berea, KY), 65, 66, 68, 72, 105, 106, 233, 280n35
Berlant, Lauren, 120–21
Berry, Chad, 124, 125, 277n6, 278n19, 278–79n21, 279n26, 286–87n91, 287n99
Berubé, Michael, 253n41
Bestseller Index (Justice), 231, 232, 233–34
best-seller lists, 231–34, 327n11
best sellers, 21, 230
  Oprah Book Club and, 181, 305n4, 328–29n28
  use of term, 12
"Betrothal Ring, The" (Fox), 269n33
"Beverly Hillbillies" (proposed reality TV show), 224–25
Beverly Hillbillies (TV program), 23, 325n31
Beyond Ourselves (Marshall), 242
Big Stone Gap (Trigiani), 24–25
  "affirmed Appalachians" as readers of, 204
  Appalachian ethnicity in, 220
  Appalachian local-color themes in, 182, 185
  Appalachian setting of, 181
  as best seller, 184, 309n30
  "charmed Appalachians" as readers of, 202–3
  as community fantasy novel, 225
  customer reviews of, 182, 184, 246–47, 310n40, 316n99, 317n117, 318n130
  documentary accuracy and, 177–79, 185–96
  identity and sense of belonging in, 187–88, 209

Index 357

marketing of, 183
methodological considerations, 246–47
migrant fans of, 193–95, 196–99, 198–99 *map*
"nostalgic cosmopolitans" as readers of, 193–94, 195, 196–97
publication of, 307n20
sense of authentic place as constructed in, 185, 186–87
quirky characters in, 205
"touristic cosmopolitans" as readers of, 189
Big Stone Gap (VA), 63, *198–99 map*
Billings, Dwight B., 21, 265n4
Billy Graham Evangelistic Association, 170
Blair, Amy L., 11, 213, 229, 236, 251n20, 329n30
Blount, Roy, Jr., 297n95
Blowen, Michael, 174
Blowing Rock (NC), 186–87, 190, 195, 311n50
bluegrass music, 1, 4, 218, 222
Blue Ridge Mountains, 190, 202
Blue Ridge Parkway, 168–69, 299n107
Boger, Lorise, 20, 21, 233
Booklist, 186
Bookman, The, 230
Book-of-the-Month Club, 132, 149, 287–88n2
Book Review Digest, 240
Books-a-Million, 289n17
Boone, Daniel, 157
Boorman, John, 175
boosterism, 58
Booth, Edwin, 50
Borders Books and Music, 289n17
Born Fighting (Webb), 224
Bostick, E. D., 274n79
Boston Herald, 27, 28, 32, 48, 239, 259n3
Bourdieu, Pierre, 251n20, 253n35
Bradley, Marianne, 244
Bragg, Alice Faye, 177

Branscome, James, 325n31
Braselton, Al, 150, 303n156
Brewer, Judy, 166–67
Brewster, Fred, 80–81
Bridges of Madison County, The (Waller), 178
Bristol (TN/VA), 258n73
Bristol Sessions, 258n73
British Isles, mountain people's origins in, 142, 291n37
Brodhead, Richard H., 5–6, 11, 14, 15, 17–18, 31, 82, 259n11, 263–64n50
Bruce and Kirstin (Smithsonian Folklife Festival visitors), 211, 217–18, 220, 221, 222, 322n1
Brunn, Stanley, 196, 209
Bryson, Bill, 307n18
Buck, Charles Neville, 233
Budd, Sam, 270n43
Bugbee, James M., 50
Bullitt, Joshua F., 239–40, 270n43
Bullock, Florence Haxton, 280n30
Burch, S. S., 82
bureaucratization, 56, 73, 109
Burke, Fielding, 233
Burke, James Henry, 233
Burman, Ben Lucien, 233
Burnett, Frances Hodgson, 19, 40, 61
Burnette, Mrs. Clyde, 120, 280n32
Burnham, James Russell, 160
Bush, George W., 213
Butler, Deborah, 167
Butler, Rodger, 298n102
Byars, Betsy, 233
Byrd, Eva Malone, 239

Cable, George Washington, 19, 304n3
Cajuns, 19
Call of the Cumberlands (Buck), 233
Campbell, John C., 244, 250n10
Canant, Judith, 149, 166, 167
Candy, Edna, 123–24
capitalism, 25, 60, 61, 126, 133, 208, 228, 250n8, 281n44
Carleton, Reese, 239, 262n30

Carson, Jo, 181
Carson, Rachel, 132
Carter, Jimmy, 158
Cassell, R. L., 95, 118, 123
Castells, Manuel, 179–80, 218
Cather, Willa, 256n59
Caudill, Harry, 23, 291n40
Celebration (Disney idealized small town), 225
Celts, 220, 221, 224
Century Illustrated, 264n52
Century magazine, 252n27, 267n11
Chapman, Maristan, 233
Chapman, S. B., 82–83
"charmed Appalachians," 182, 192–93, 200–203
Chatooga River, 173
Cherokee Indians, 220
Chesnutt, Charles, 255n52
Chicago (IL), 120, 277n10, 285n75
Chosen Books, 138
Christianity Today, 136
Christian Women's Job Corp (Lee County, AL), 283n59
Christy (Marshall), 23, 93
 advertising for, 137, 139–42
 appeal of, 133
 as best seller, 213–14, 232, 233, 288–89n15, 289n22
 celebration of white folk in, 135–36
 city-to-country imagined movement in, 135–36
 as critique of suburban life, 135
 Deliverance compared to, 132–36, 165
 denouement lacking in, 171
 documentary accuracy and, 133, 144–45, 149
 fan mail about, 132–33, 134, 138–39, *140–41 map*, *146–47 map*, 213, 241–44, 293n49
 film/TV adaptations, 136, 287n1
 identity and sense of belonging in, 133–34, 145–49, 187
 imperialism and, 165
 influence of, 131, 136, 176
 marketing of, 143–44
 methodological considerations, 241–44
 migrant readers of, 145–48, *146–47 map*, 214
 missionary perspective in, 167–72, 288n6, 300nn125, 128
 popularity of, 132, 136, 138, 287n1, 288–89n15, 289n17
 power circulation promoted in, 134, 165
 print reviews of, 138
 publication of, 136
 reader needs met by, 132–36
 sense of authentic place as constructed in, 133, 142–45, 165, 166
 simplicity as virtue in, 142, 291–92n41
 tourist perspective in, 165–67, 172, *168–69 map*, 189
Christy, Choices of the Heart (TV program), 287n1
Christy, the Movie (film; 2000), 287n1
"Christy Country," 144, 167, 292n43
ChristyFest (Townsend, TN), 172
Chung, Haeja, 277n8
Chute, Carolyn, 305–6n6
Cincinnati (OH), 120, 125, 145
civil rights activism, 23, 134, 135, 175
Clark, Billy, 233
Clark, Dan, 157
Clark, James Beauchamp ("Champ"), 273n63
Clark, Thomas D., 271n52
class, social, 16, 84, 94, 120–21, 226, 255n52, 278–79n21
Clay, Cassius, 82
Clay, Francis, 71–72, 82
Clay's Quilt (House), 25
 "affirmed Appalachians" as readers of, 204
 Appalachian ethnicity in, 220
 Appalachian local-color themes in, 184

Index   359

Appalachian setting of, 181
as "Appalachian studies 101," 177, 179
as best seller, 184, 309n31
"charmed Appalachians" as readers of, 202
customer reviews of, 179, 182, 184, 246–47, 310–11n43, 313–14n71, 321n155
dialect as used in, 206
documentary accuracy and, 177–79
as "iconic book," 177
identity and sense of belonging in, 187–88, 208–9
marketing of, 183–84, 185–86
methodological considerations, 246–47
"offended Appalachians" as critics of, 207
print reviews of, 183, 186, 189
publication of, 307n20
quirky characters in, 205
sense of authentic place as constructed in, 185, 186, 187
"touristic cosmopolitans" as readers of, 189, 192, 193
Cleland, R. W., 72
Cleveland (OH), 145, 282n46
coal industry, 59–60, 102, 198, 207, 269n25, 292n43
Cold Mountain (film; 2003), *191*
Cold Mountain (Frazier), 4, 24, 217
"affirmed Appalachians" as readers of, 204
Appalachian local-color themes in, 182, 184
Appalachian setting of, 181
as "Appalachian studies 101," 177
as best seller, 178, 184
"charmed Appalachians" as readers of, 202
customer reviews of, 182, 184, 246–47, 312n60, 313n67, 316n96, 319n138, 320n144, 321n150
dialect as used in, 206

documentary accuracy and, 177–79, 182, 185
as "iconic book," 177
identity and sense of belonging in, 187–88
marketing of, 183–84
methodological considerations, 246–47
"nostalgic cosmopolitans" as readers of, 194–95, 199–200
"offended Appalachians" as critics of, 206–7
publication of, 181, 307n20
quirky characters in, 205–6
sense of authentic place as constructed in, 185–86, 186, 187
"touristic cosmopolitans" as readers of, 189–90, *190*
Cold Sassy Tree (Burns), 305n6
Colliers, 267n11
Collins, Jane L., 252–53n35
Colored People (Gates), 315n94
Columbia (SC) Record, 158
Columbus (OH), 145
commodification, 8, 91, 142, 208, 227–28
communities, gated, 225–26
community
defined, 251n19
"dream of" (Arnow), 90–92, 108, 109, 110–11, 124, 126–27
exclusionary aspects of, 225–26
identity and sense of belonging in, 180, 306n13 (*see also under specific works*)
imagined, and Appalachian-set fiction, 6, 91, 122, 214
imagined, of American nationalism, 21, 57, 109–10
in Neo–Gilded Age fiction, 187–88, 208–10, 180
readers' desires for, 119, 179–80, 218, 251n19
community fantasy novels, 225–26
compassion, 120–21
conformity, 135, 282n52

Confronting Appalachian Stereotypes (ed. Billings, Norman, and Ledford), 265n4
Connelly, William, 73, 78–80, 82, 236, 273nn69–70
consumerism, 92, 126, 128, 157, 158, 179, 196, 227
Cooke, Grace MacGowan, 61, 233
Cooke, John Esten, 19
corporatization, 3–4, 24, 179
cosmopolitan elites, 213
cosmopolitanism, 57, 194, 215, 252n29. *See also* "jaded cosmopolitans"; "nostalgic cosmopolitans"; "touristic cosmopolitans"
country music, 22, 258n73
Country of the Pointed Firs, The (Jewett), 18
"cowbirds," 200–201, 215
Craddock, Charles Egbert
  as Appalachian author, 20
  fan mail written to, 42–45, 46–47 map
  literary skills of, 304n3
  metropolitan elite reception of, 36–41, 45
  reader assumptions about, 27–29
  regional elite reception of, 42–49
  Thaxter's interest in, 263n46
  unveiling of, as Murfree, 33, 48, 258–59n1
  See also Murfree, Mary Noailles
crafts, 277–78n10
Crawford, Una M., 55, 56, 73, 78, 82, 85
Creason, Joe, 266n4
Critic, 34
critics, 12
cultural heritage revivals, 224
cultural studies, 253n41
Cultures of Letters (Brodhead), 31
Cumberland Mountains, 63, 122–23
Cunningham, Albert Benjamin, 233
Cunningham, Rodger, 265n3

Curtis, Mrs. Fowler, 113, 283n60
Cushing, Frank H., 49, 264n52
Custer, George A., 175
customer reviews, 179–80, 181, 229–30, 237–38, 246–47, 309n32, 319n133
  methodologies for interpreting, 237–38, 246–47, 309n32
  See also fan mail; *under specific authors; under specific titles*
customs, 142
Cyrus, Billy Ray, 4

Daily Worker (London), 282n50
"Dancin' Party at Harrison's Cove" (Murfree), 36
Dargan, Olive Tilford, 233
Daughters of the American Revolution, 83
Davis, Alma B., 149
Davis, Kenneth C., 327n16
Davis, Rebecca Harding, 19, 40
Davis, Richard Harding, 239
"Deceiver's Ever" (Fox), 269n33
Deephaven (Jewett), 230
Deliverance (Dickey), 23
  advertising for, 159
  appeal of, 133
  authorship of, 158–60, 161–64
  as best seller, 213–14, 232, 233, 294n60
  Christy compared to, 132–36, 165
  city-to-country imagined movement in, 135–36
  consequences of, 153, 175–76
  documentary accuracy and, 133
  fan mail about, 132–33, 134–35, 152–56, 213, 241, 244–46, 295n70
  hillbillies in, 214, 303n156
  identity and sense of belonging in, 133–34, 156, 158, 160–61
  influence of, 131
  outdoor enthusiasts as fans of, 172–73
  popularity of, 132, 149, 152, 294n60

Index   361

power circulation promoted in, 134,
    156, 158–61, 164, 165, 173–76
print reviews of, 151–52
publication of, 131, 244
racial equivalencies/reversals
    influencing, 303n152
reader needs met by, 132–36
sense of authentic places as
    constructed in, 133, 153, 156–60,
    175–76
setting of, 150–51
tourist perspective in, 165, 172–73,
    295n72, 302n145
transitional readers of, 162–63 *map*
Deliverance (film; 1972), 131,
    150–51, 157, 158, 164, 175–76,
    296–97n85, 315n94
DeMott, Benjamin, 151, 152
Denney, Ferne, 283n59
Detroit (MI), 106, 109, 118–19, 122,
    125, 282nn46–47
dialect, 12–13 17, 45, 48, 63, 68, 134,
    142, 160–61, 178–79, 182, 185,
    206, 209, 212, 254n47, 282n50
Dick, Joan Tuckerman, 152
Dickens, Hazel, 177
Dickey, James, 14, 131, *159*
    academics and, 161, 164
    awards received by, 298n102
    biographical details, 149–50,
        303n156
    detractors of, 133, 164, 173
    death of, 244
    fan mail to, 153, *154–55 map*,
        162–63 map
    fans of, 23, 295n70
    female fans of, 295–96n74
    marketing skills of, 133
    migrant fans of, 133–34, 160–61,
        162–63 map
    novels of, 23
    papers of, 244–46
    readers' view of, as authentic, 158
    racism and, 150
    as southern author, 161–64, 297n95

writing workshops of, 164
See also *Deliverance*
Dickey, James (father), 150
Dickey, Noel C., 164
Disney, 225
*Divine Secrets of the YA-YA
    Sisterhood, The* (Wells), 178
Dixon, Thomas, 66, 239
Dollmaker, The (Arnow), 22
    advertising for, *103*, 280–81n36
    agrarian life as portrayed in,
        100–102, 105, 213
    Appalachian local-color themes in,
        102
    as best seller, 90, 91, 127, 233,
        327n21
    compassion aroused by, 120–21
    consumer culture critiqued in, 102,
        110, 126
    documentary accuracy and, 105,
        281n38
    fan mail about, 92–93, 94–95,
        98–99 *map*, 240–41
    "Get Gertie home" response to, 111,
        122–27, 285n78
    identity and sense of belonging in,
        91, 109, 110–11, 112
    methodological considerations,
        240–41
    migrant fans of, 112–19, *116–17
        map*
    popularity of, 276n2
    power circulation promoted in,
        119–22
    print reviews of, 102, 106, *107*,
        109–10, 279n27, 281n38, 282n50
    publication of, 106, 124
    regional tensions in, 282n47
    rural industrialization in, 102
    sense of authentic place as
        constructed in, 104–108
    Southern Diaspora and, 89–90,
        126–27
    touristic perspectives, lack of, 91
    writing of, 287n94

Dollmaker, The (film; 1984), 106
Dorman, Robert, 256n61
Dream of Kings, A (Grubb), 234
Driscoll, Beth, 328n28
drug abuse, 207
Dudley, Charles, 244
"Dueling Banjos," 175
Duke, Basil, 72–73
Dunaway, Wilma, 16, 249n2
Dykeman, Wilma, 177

Eastern Kentucky Social Club (EKSC), 194, 315–16n94
East Tennessee State University, 161, 164, 298n102
Eco, Umberto, 177, 326n2
Ecology of a Cracker Childhood (Ray), 294n64
education, 207, 273n63
Egg and I, The (MacDonald), 278n16
Ehle, John, 233
80 Years of Bestsellers: 1895–1975 (Hackett and Burke), 233
"Electioneerin' on Big Injun Mounting" (Murfree), 263n38
Elizabethan customs, 142–43, 222, 244, 279n28
Elliott, Michael, 178, 180
Emerson, Ralph Waldo, 49, 326n2
Emory University (Atlanta, GA), 238, 244
English, 142
environmental movement, 132
Erskine Dale: Pioneer (E. Fox), 266n11
essentialism, 8
Ethnic Heritage Act (1974), 306n10
ethnicity. *See* Appalachian ethnicity
evangelism, 170, 288n6
Evensong (Godwin), 234
Exley, Fred, 152

Fair and Tender Ladies (L. Smith), 177, 231
fan-acquaintances, 12, 235, 241

fan mail
 analysis models, 329n30
 Appalachia as viewed in, 2
 methodologies for interpreting, 11–17, 31, 235–37
 print reviews and, 236
 of transitional readers, 59
 use of, in reception studies, 229–30
 use of term, 12, 235
 See also customer reviews; *under specific authors; specific titles*
Fannin County (GA), 150
fans
 migration narratives of, 13–14
 use of term, 12, 235
Far Appalachia (Adams), 307n18
farmland, ancestral, 109, 111–12, 122
Father's Melancholy Daughter (Godwin), 234
Federal Writers Project, 106
Feinberg, Benjamin, 1
feminist revisionist scholarship, 14–15, 30, 31
feminization, 29, 30, 37–38, 279n26
Fetterley, Judith, 14–15
feuding, 62, 80, 220, 267n12
Fible, Micajah, 265n3
Fields, Annie, 33
Fields, James T., 33
film
 Christy adapted for, 136, 287n1
 Fox novels made into, 57, 267n12
 local-color, 4
 Neo–Gilded Age regional fiction and, 178
 See also Deliverance (film; 1972); *Dollmaker, The* (film; 1984); *Cold Mountain* (film; 2003)
Fish, Stanley, 326n2
Fisher, Stephen, 322n3
Flagg, Fanny, 306n6
Flowering of the Cumberland (Arnow), 240, 280n35
Flynn, Michael, 157
Foght, Harold W., 271n51

folklore, 71, 84, 142
folk songs, 142
folkways, 182, 263–64n50
Fonda, Henry, 57
Foote, Stephanie, 5, 12–13, 18, 24, 228, 250n8, 252n27, 254n50, 304n2
Ford, Thomas, 250n10
Fox, Elizabeth, 266n11
Fox, John, Jr., 13, 64, 93, 244
  Appalachian whiteness in, 220
  biographical details, 57, 63–65, 84–85, 275nn86–87
  correspondence of, 265n3
  critics of, 56, 265n3
  elite connections of, 284n67
  fan mail to, 58, 74–75 *map*, 76–77 *map*
  fears of recrimination, 272n55
  films inspired by works of, 267n12
  hate mail received by, 68
  as imperialist, 270–71n45
  literary career of, 266–67n11, 269n33
  memorial function of, 82–83
  migrant readers of, 56–57, 72–78, 76–77 *map*, 86
  migration and, 84–85, 86
  novels of, 20–21, 22
  papers of, 239–40
  popularity of, 57, 255–56n58, 266n8
  readership types, 14, 56–57, 212
  readers' view of, as authentic, 63
  sense of authentic places as constructed by, 62–65, 187
  "scientific" speeches of, 269n30
  tourism encouraged by, 269n25
  See also Little Shepherd of Kingdom Come, The; Trail of the Lonesome Pine, The
Fox, John, Sr., 85, 275n86
Fox Family Papers, 239–40
Foxfire series, 16, 132, 150, 177, 287–88n2
Fox Memorial Library (Paris, KY), 83, 240, 271n52
Frankenburg, Ruth, 158, 160–61
Frank Leslie's Illustrated Weekly, 269n33

Fraser, Steve, 257n67
Frazier, Charles, 4, 24, 186, 311n45, 313n67. *See also Cold Mountain*
Freckles (Stratton-Porter), 329n30
Fried Green Tomatoes at the Whistle Stop Café (Flagg), 306n6
frontier, 16, 290–91n34. *See also* pioneers
Frost, William Goodell, 65, 66, 219, 250n10, 255n58, 272n54
Furman, Lucy, 233
Future Shock (Toffler), 287n2

Gabrio, Jane, 295–96n74
Gap Creek (Morgan), 235, 307n18
Garland, Hamlin, 9, 11, 19, 255n52, 304n3
Garrett, Ferne Denney, 283n59
Garten, Jeffrey, 257n67
Gary (IN), 282n46
Gates, Henry Louis, Jr., 315n94
Gates, William, Sr., 257n67
gays, 226
Gemeinschaft, 251n19
gender, 37–38, 279n26
gender bias, 28
genealogy, 111–12, 145
Gentry, Ira, 303n156
Gentry, Lucas, 303n156
Germans, 142
Gesellschaft, 251n19
"Get Gertie home" response, 89, 93, 111, 122–27, 285n78
Giboney, Susan, 171, 300n125
Gilded Age (ca. 1865–1890s), 12, 216
  best sellers during, 12
  fan types during, 14, 18
  local-color movement during, 3–4, 133, 214, 255n52, 305n5
  Neo–Gilded Age (1985–2008) compared to, 24, 179–80, 257n67
  publishing trends during, 178, 205, 214, 254n47
  text popularity/selection, 230
Giles, Janice Holt, 233

Girl of the Limberlost, A (Stratton-Porter), 329n30
Glazener, Nancy, 14, 15, 31, 259n8
globalization, 179, 218
Glyndon, William, 44
Godsey, Joyce, 172
Godwin, Gail, 234, 324n24, 328n25
Goin, Mary Elizabeth, 133, 288n6
Govan, Christine Noble, 233
Graham, Billy, 170
Grant, George K., 44
Grant, Ozro F., 123, 236, 286n89
Great Depression, 22, 92
Greater Chicago Food Depository, 285n75
Great Meadow, The (Roberts), 233
Great Migration of African Americans, 92, 110–11. *See also* Southern Diaspora
Great Smoky Mountains, 143–45, 165, 171, 261n25, 292n43
Green, Chris, 263n46
Green, Katherine, 122
Green, Michelle, 316n94
Green Acres (TV program), 325n31
Greeson, Jennifer Rae, 9–10, 252n30, 254n45, 270n42, 325n37
Gregory, James, 92
Griswold, Wendy, 7, 200–201, 215, 216
Grove/Atlantic, 307n20
Grubb, Davis, 234
Guarrarra, Rosanne, 290n29
Gutjahr, Paul, 229

Hackett, Alice Payne, 57, 230, 233, 266n10
Hall, Talt, 270n45
Halter, Marilyn, 133, 180, 227
Hannum, Alberta Pierson, 233
Hardin, Myra Reeves, 294n56
Harkins, Anthony, 23, 255n54, 287n99
Harlan County (KY), 315n94
Harlem Renaissance, 256n59

"'Harnt' That Walks Chilhowie, The" (Murfree), 51–52, 263n39
Harper's magazine, 152
Harper's Weekly, 56, 57, 267n11
Harriette Simpson Arnow Papers, 240–41
Harrington, Michael, 23
Harris, Joel Chandler, 19, 66
Harrison, Max, 148
Hart, Henry, 303n156
Harte, Brett, 19
Harvard University, 63, 84–85, 265n4, 275n87
Harvey, David, 256n59
Harvey, Stephen W., 122
Hatfield, Sharon, 83–84
Hawthorne, Nathaniel, 49
Hayes, C. Willard, 250n10
Heart of Darkness (Conrad), 303n156
Heart of the Hills (Fox), 22, 93, 266n11
Hee-Haw (TV program), 325n31
Hendrick, Mrs. Jackson, 72
Hendrix, Vicki, 148
Henes, Martha, 89, 111, 122, 283n54
Hergesheimer, Joseph, 233
heritage, 145
Hermanson, Suzanne, 143
Herring, Caroline, 177
Hickam, Homer, 234, 307n18
Hicks, Granville, 108, 281n44
Hidden America, A (TV documentary; 2009), 4
highbrow periodicals, 14, 45
highbrow readership, 6–7
  as Arnow readers, 213
  as Dickey readers, 174
  as Fox readers, 71
  as Murfree readers, 28–30
  use of term, 13
Highlanders, 90, 142
high middlebrow readership, 6–7
  Appalachia as source of distinctiveness for, 180
  as Fox readers, 57, 267n11

use of term, 13, 252–53n35
    during Vietnam War era, 23,
        132–36
Hill, Jane, 324n24
hillbillies
    Big Stone Gap and, 203
    in *Deliverance*, 156, 173–76,
        303n156
    Fox's portrayals of, 21
    identity and, 287n99
    media portrayals of, 22–23
    racial victimization of, 224–25
    southern out-migrants and, 158
    See also mountaineers
Hillbilly Doctor (Seifert), 233
Hillbilly: The Real Story (TV
    documentary; 2008), 4
Hills Beyond, The (Wolfe), 328n23
Hines, Frank, 283n61
Hines, John E., 160
Hispanic Americans, 238
History Channel, 4
Hobbs, Glenda, 90
Hobsbawm, Eric, 306n13
Holmes, Oliver Wendell, 33,
    258–59n1
Holt, Henry, 230, 254n47
Holt, Minnie, 118
homesickness, 23, 72–73, 84–86, 100,
    113, 122, 126–27, 135, 160–61,
    193–94, 196–97, 199, 266n6,
    275n87, 279n26
homogenization, 3–4, 18, 20, 179
Horse Whisperer, The (Evans), 178
Houghton Mifflin, 28, 36, 45
House, Silas, 25, 186, 207, 217,
    310n43. *See also Clay's Quilt*
Howard, June, 258n69, 305n5
Howard, Louise, 293n47
Howells, William Dean, 27, 32, 33,
    36, 39, 260n16, 263n38, 269n29
Hsiung, David, 2, 8, 13, 209, 251n19
Hsu, Hsuan L., 215, 217
Hunter's Horn (Arnow), 22
    advertising for, *101*, 110

agrarian life as portrayed in, 100,
    104–5, 213
as best seller, 90, 91, 127, 231–32,
    233, 327n21
compassion aroused by, 120–21
documentary accuracy and, 105
fan mail about, 94, 96–97 *map*,
    240–41
identity and sense of belonging in,
    109, 110–12
methodological considerations,
    240–41
migrant fans of, 113–19, *114–15
    map*, 280n32
popularity of, 118–19, 276nn2–4
power circulation promoted in,
    119–22
pre-WWII setting of, 280n30
print reviews of, 102, 106, *107*, 110,
    276–77n5, 279nn27–28, 280n30
publication of, 106
readership types, 95
rural industrialization in, 102
sense of authentic place as
    constructed in, 104–8
Southern Diaspora and, 89–90, 127,
    279n25
writing of, 125
Hurd, H. R. ("Rod"), 302n145
Hutchins, William J., 280n31
hypermasculinity, 151, 157, 175

Icy Sparks (Rubio), 235, 307n18
identity
    Arnow and construction of, 93, 109–19
    Christy and construction of,
        133–34, 145–49
    collective, 218
    community and, 180, 306n13
    Deliverance and construction of,
        132, 133–34, 156
    geographic history and, 72
    in Neo–Gilded Age, 180
    in Neo–Gilded Age fiction, 187–88,
        208–9, 214

identity *(cont.)*
  regional, production of, 211, 212–16, 228
  regional fiction and enabling of, 72, 83–84, 128–29, 133, 149, 220–21
  See also under specific works
Illinois, 213
immigration, 17, 29, 30, 38, 66, 179, 187, 226
imperialism
  Appalachia and, 4, 212, 214, 221, 226–27
  Arnow readers and, 119, 128–29
  Christy and, 23, 133–34, 176, 213–14
  Deliverance and, 23, 133–34, 173–76, 213–14
  Fox fiction and, 56, 66, 81, 86, 270–71n45
  Fox readers and, 21, 57, 67
  during Gilded Age, 4, 179
  high middlebrow readers and, 176
  Murfree readers and, 20, 29, 37–39
  nationally identified readers and, 67
  during Neo–Gilded Age, 4, 24, 179
  Otherness and, 270–71n45
  power circulation promoted in (*see under specific works*)
  regionalism and, 3–4
  South as subordinated territory, 270n42, 325n37
  transitional readers and, 57
  during Vietnam War era, 23, 174–75
income inequality, 4, 24, 179, 250n8, 255n52
Independent, 33, 61–62
Indiana, 213
industrialization, 73
  anti-industrialism, 123
  Arnow readers and, 280n30
  Authentic Appalachia and, 2
  Fox's fiction and, 21, 56, 58, 59–62, 67, 87
  during Gilded Age, 37
  high middlebrow readers and, 179
  local-color fiction and, 3, 17–18
  local culture as lost through, 179
  pastoral literature and, 17
  post-WWII decline in, 157
  rural, 48, 82–83, 102
  Southern Diaspora and, 92
  white middle-/upper classes and problems resulting from, 37
  during WWII, 109
Inness, Sherrie A., 260n12
"insiders"/"outsiders" dichotomy, 9, 10–11, 13, 15, 29, 30, 32, 49, 50–52, 53, 58, 86, 144, 193, 253n40
In the Brush (Pierson), 42
In the Tennessee Mountains (Murfree)
  Atlantic stories published in book form as, 20, 27, 36
  as best seller, 266n10
  fan mail about, 44–45, 46–47 *map*, 238–39
  local-color collections and, 39–40
  methodological considerations, 230, 238–39
  popularity of, 230
  print reviews of, 33, 239, 304n3
In Wildness Is the Preservation of the World (Thoreau), 132
Isaacs, James, 152
Iser, Wolfgang, 229, 326nn2–3
Islam, 176. *See also* Muslims

Jackson (KY), 68
Jacobson, Matthew Frye, 224, 324n29
"jaded cosmopolitans," 182, 188
James, William, 49
James Dickey Papers, 244–46
Jauss, Hans Robert, 229, 326n3
Jewett, Sarah Orne, 18, 19, 45, 230, 304n3
John C. Campbell Folk School (Brasstown, NC), 171
John J. Fox, Jr. Memorial Library (Paris, KY), 83, 240, 271n52

Johnson, Lyndon B., 175
Johnson, Mrs. Everdean, 121, 285n78
Johnson, Susan, 170–71
Johnson City (TN), 136, 202, 203
Jones, Grover, 267n12
Jones, Leah, 105
Julie (Marshall), 289n22
Jurca, Catherine, 10, 126, 135
Justice, Keith, 231, 232, 327n16

Kant, Kristin, 197, 250n11
Karabell, Zachary, 225–26
Karem, Jeff, 5, 8, 24, 282n45
Karon, Jan, 24, 181, 186–87, 311n50.
    See also At Home in Mitford
Keillor, Garrison, 24, 178, 305n5
Kennedy, John F., assassination of, 135
Kentucky
   Arnow's portrayals of life in, 22
   coal mining regions of, 207, 292n43
   elites in, 71, 93, 94, 284n67
   Fox fears of recrimination in, 272n55
   hillbilly stereotype and boosterism in, 21
   industrialization in, 280n30
   migrations from, 84–85 (*see also* Southern Diaspora)
   poverty in, 16, 207
   volunteerism in, 167
Kentucky Explorer, 265–66n4
Kentucky in American Letters (Townsend), 284n67
Kentucky Trace, The (Arnow), 280n35
Kentucky University, 273n63
Kephart, Horace, 68, 144, 255–56n58
Keyser (WV), 136
Kinfolks (G. Norman), 177
King, Lewis, 150, 303n156
Kingsolver, Barbara, 234, 307n18, 308n22
Kingsport (TN), 202–3
Knight of the Cumberland, A (Fox), 244
Knoll, Harry Harrison, 233
Koncos, Joyce, 290–91n34

Kovach, Janet, 152
Kribs, Phyllis McKishnie, 121, 285n77

Lacy, Adolph, 124
Ladies' Home Journal, 57, 267n11
LaHaye, Tim, 225
Laighton, Lucy, 44
Lake Wobegon (Keillor), 24, 178, 305n5
Lane, Ellen, 152, 236
Langston, Penny, 170
LaPler, Darlene, 156, 173, 296n79
Latham, George, 95
Latino, 226
Lea, Mary, 291n37
Lears, T. J. Jackson, 58
Leaving Home (Keillor), 305n5
Ledford, Katherine, 265n4
"Left Behind" novels (LaHaye), 225
lesbians, 226
LeSourd, Catherine Marshall. *See* Marshall, Catherine
LeSourd, Leonard, 138
Lewis, Claudine, 108, 123
Lewis, Sinclair, 62, 213, 329n30
Lexis Nexis Academic database, 234
Life magazine, 136
Lily (KY), 186
Limits to Growth, The (Meadows et al.), 157
Linn, Robert, 164
Lion publishers, 183, 307n20
Lippincott's magazine, 34–36
literacy rates, 21, 73, 121
literary capital, 263–64n50
Literary Guild of America, 149
literature
   Appalachian, vs. Appalachian-set fiction, 11
   commercial vs. literary, 251n20
   cosmopolitanism and authenticity in, 252n29
   ethnography and, 304n3
   Marxist view of, 281n44
   pastoral, 13, 17, 187

Little, Helen C., 119, 284n68
Little Shepherd of Kingdom Come, The (Fox)
  as best seller, 20, 57, 230
  dedication of, 73
  fan mail about, 72, 75, 76–77 *map*, 239, 273n63
  North vs. South in, 266n9
Lloyd, Alice, 283n54
local color
  in urban settings, 109, 304n2
  use of term, 12–13
local-color fiction
  appeal of, 18
  as authentic, 252n27
  authors of, 34, 259n8
  consequences of, 11, 14–15, 19, 30–31, 52, 120, 153, 175, 217, 228, 229, 255n52
  documentary accuracy and, 10–11, 28, 29 (*see also under specific works*)
  elite view of, 52, 71
  during Gilded Age, 255n52, 305n5
  "literary tourism" through, 49, 52
  paradox of, 5–6
  popularity of, 4
  print reviews of, 33–34
  during Progressive Era, 20–21
  publishers of, 10
  reader needs met by, 132
  regional fiction vs., 14–15, 253n40
  resurgence of, during Neo–Gilded Age, 22, 178–79, 180, 227–28, 258n69, 305n5
  women's use of, 260n12
  See also Appalachian-set fiction; regional fiction
local-color movement, 3–4, 7, 212
local culture, loss of, 48, 179
locally identified readers
  defined, 56
  Fox novels as viewed by, 67–70, 69, 86, 271n51
Loftin, Charles, 156–57

Logan, B. A., 71
London, Jack, 66
Lonely Crowd, The (Riesman), 282n52
Long, Elizabeth, 253n41
Look Homeward, Angel (Wolfe), 233, 327–28n23
Los Angeles Times, 122–23
Lost Cause rhetoric, 224
"Louisiana" (Burnett), 40, 61
Louisiana bayou region, local-color writing in, 3
Louisville Courier-Journal, 266n4
Lovely Bones, The (Sebold), 178
Lowenthal, David, 196
Luca, Elizabeth, 167, 291n40
"Luck of the Roaring Camp" (Harte), 19
Lutz, Catherine A., 252–53n35
Lutz, Tom, 22, 252n29, 253n40, 256nn59–60, 258n69, 304n3

MacDonald, Betty, 278n16
MacGowan, Alice, 233
MacKethan, Lucinda, 18
Macmillan Library News, 281n36
Macmillan Publishers, 106, 110, 276n3, 280–81n36
Madison County (NC) News Record, 271n51
Mailloux, Steven, 11, 13
Main Street (Lewis), 213, 329n30
Mali program (Smithsonian Folklife Festival), 221–22
"mallification," 224
Man Called Peter, A (Marshall), 138, 242, 289n22
Manchester Evening News, 282n50
Marsh, Carol, 161
Marshall, Catherine, 14, 93, 137
  biographical details, 136–38
  correspondence of, 241–44
  death of, 138, 243
  fans of, 23, 146–47 *map*, 168–69 *map*, 290nn26–27, 292–93n47

marketing skills of, 133, 139–42, 143–45
marriage of, 136–38, 289n20
mother of, as portrayed in *Christy*, 171–72
nonfiction works of, 138, 242, 289n22
pastoral novels of, 23, 289n22
prayer ministry established by, 289n21
research done by, 144, 292nn44–45, 293n47
See also Christy
Marshall, Peter, 136–38, 288n6, 289nn20–21, 301n135
Marshfield, Anne, 292n41
Martha Berry School (Rome, GA), 171
Marx, Karl, 281n44
masculinity, 37, 38, 151, 157, 175, 212, 220
  Murfree and, 27, 29, 36–37
mass culture, 179, 218
mass production, 135
materialism, 20, 123, 126, 192, 227
Matheney, W. P., 81
Mathews, Currie Duke, 73
Matt, Susan J., 113, 196, 266n6
Mayo, John C. C., 78–80
Mayo, Thomas J., 78
Mayor, Barbara, 302n145
McCarthy, Cormac, 233, 313n67
McClellan, David, 164
McCrumb, Sharyn, 234–35, 307n18, 321n160
McKishnie, Archie P., 285n77
McRoberts, Dianna, 144
media, 1, 22, 203
Melungeons, 220, 323n19
Memoirs of a Geisha (Golden), 306n6
methodology, 11–17
  customer reviews, 237–38
  fan mail, 235–37
  reception evidence, 235–47
  text popularity/selection, 230–35

metropolitan elites
  as Arnow readers, 92–93, 94, 110
  as Fox readers, 212
  as Marshall readers, 290n26
  as Murfree readers, 14, 20, 29, 31–32, 36–41, 45, 212
  rural desires of, 278n16
metropolitan readership, 7
Meyer, Catharine, 152
Michigan, 213
middlebrow readership, 267n11. *See also* high middlebrow readership
middle class, 61
  alienation experienced by, 58–59, 126
  anxieties of, 21
  as "charmed Appalachians," 202
  Fox and, 256n58
  Fox novels as viewed by, 73–80, 81, 82, 84–85, 266n8
  as Marshall readers, 138–39, 290n26
  during Progressive Era, 21
  rise of, 56, 82
Midland, The (magazine), 256n60
Midwest
  Americanness in, 16
  Appalachian activism in, 213
  Dickey readers in, 153
  local-color writing in, 3, 19, 178
  Marshall readers in, 139
  migrant shuttling between Appalachia and, 90, 277n6
  professionals from, as Arnow readers, 93, 94, 110, 120
  Southern Diaspora to, 95, 110–11, 118, 124, 126–27, 213, 282n46, 286–87n91
  whiteness in, 19
migrants, rural-to-urban, 22, 93, 94–95, 127, 160–61, 241
migrant readers
  of Arnow, 92–93, 95, 112–19, *114–15 map*, *116–17 map*, 222
  of *At Home in Mitford*, 190, 195

migrant readers *(cont.)*
  of *Big Stone Gap*, 193–95, 196–99, 198–99 *map*
  of *Cold Mountain*, 195, 199–200
  cowbirds, 200–201, 215
  of Dickey, 133–34, 160–61, 162–63 *map*
  of Fox, 56–57, 72–78, 76–77 *map*
  of Marshall, 133–34, 145–48, 146–47 *map*, 214
  movers, 215
  vs. stayers, 215
  See also transitional readers; "nostalgic cosmopolitans"; "charmed Appalachians"; Southern Diaspora
migration
  Arnow and, 10, 105–8
  class and, 278–79n21
  "cowbirds" and, 200–201, 215
  Fox and, 84–85
  as impermanent, 90, 277n6
  Murfree and, 34
  during Neo-Gilded Age, 179, 196
  during post–World War II era, 92, 283n53
  during Progressive era, 56–57, 72–78
  regional fiction and, 128–29, 214–15
  retirement and, 190
  as segregated, 282n46
  Southern out-migration, beginnings of, 251–52n24
  transitional readers and, 56–57, 73–78
  See also Southern Diaspora
Miller, Helen Topping, 233
Miller, Laura J., 231, 232, 327n16
Mills, Harry, 148
Milner Award, 280n35
Minetree, Harry, 303n152
missionary perspective, 7
  of Arnow readers, 121
  Christy and, 132, 134, 145, 167–72, 214
  Deliverance and, 132, 214

  of Marshall readers, 23, 139, 300nn125, 128
  of "nostalgic cosmopolitans," 195
  regional fiction and, 23
mobility, 8, 71, 84, 179–80, 283n53
mobility, upward, 8, 84, 126, 212–13
modernization, 4, 48, 71, 91, 250–51n13
Montvale Springs resort (TN), 261n25
moonshiners, 81, 143
Moon Women (Duncan), 177
Moore, Mrs. Delbert, 89, 95, 122, 236
Moore, Mrs. Horace, 149, 294n59
Moore, William Cabell, 265–66n4
Morgan, Robert, 235, 307n18
Mother and Two Daughters, A (Godwin), 234
Motion Picture magazine, 235
mountaineers
  as American "folk," 65–67, 92, 110, 142, 148, 156, 171, 178, 182, 201–2, 209, 212, 219, 221–22, 226–27, 323n17
  British origins of, 39, 65–66, 110, 142, 171, 220, 291n37
  "charmed Appalachians" and, 200
  in *Christy*, 23, 133–34, 139, 142, 143, 149, 170
  in *Deliverance*, 133–34, 153, 156, 164
  dialect of, 63
  Fox fan mail and, 78–80, 81
  Fox's portrayals of, 21, 56, 59, 62, 63, 65, 66–67, 70, 86, 87, 105, 265–66n4, 269n30
  interchangeability of, 23, 121, 128, 132, 156, 170, 174–75, 303n156
  language of, 292n45
  Murfree fan mail and, 43–44
  Murfree imagined by readers as, 28–29, 34, 37, 49, 105
  Murfree's portrayals of, 20, 32, 36, 38–39, 44
  popularization of, 20
  racial innocence of, 219–20

racialization/colonization of, 265n3
racial status of, 268n19
romantic notions of, 249n2
as stereotype, 17
in WPA photography, 22
See also hillbillies; pioneers
"Mountain Europa, A" (Fox), 220
Mountain Heritage Literary Festival, 177
Mountain Path, A (Arnow), 89, 105, 125, 276nn2–4
mountaintop-removal mining, 207, 217
mountain whites, use of term, 300n129
movers, 215
Moynihan Report, 291n40
multiculturalism, 24, 25, 181, 224, 306n10
Murfree, Fanny, 33, 49, 50, 238, 260n20, 261n25
Murfree, Mary Noailles, 9, 35, 50, 269n29
  admiring correspondence to, 29, 43, 42–45
  Appalachian studies view of, 15, 30, 50–52
  biographical details, 32, 34, 52, 65, 261n25
  correspondence of, 238–39
  feminist revisionist view of, 15, 30, 31, 50–52
  first literary endeavors of, 34–36
  first mountain stories by, 19, 261n24
  literary skills of, 28–29, 45
  literary success of, 7, 20
  literary workshop of, 34
  masculine persona cultivated by, 37–38, 108
  in New England literary circles, 49–50, 50
  popularity of, 230
  print reviews of, 41, 261–62n30, 262–63n38
  pseudonym used by, 20, 27–28, 36

reader reception of, 19–20, 31–32
readership types, 14, 20, 212
significance of, 255n54
total literary output of, 36
See also Craddock, Charles Egbert; *In the Tennessee Mountains*
music, 16, 208, 278n12
  Appalachian, 177, 218
  bluegrass 1, 4, 218, 222
  Christy and, 143, 144, 165, 292n42
  Clay's Quilt and, 184–85, 189
  Cold Mountain and, 184–85, 205
  country, 22, 258n73
  Deliverance and, 131, 156, 164
  festivals, 4
  folk, 133, 143, 144
  "white soul," 218, 220
Muslims, 25, 217, 226. *See also* Islam
Myers, Opal, 299n114

NASCAR, 307n18
Nation, 151
National Barn Dance (radio program), 277n10
nationalism, 4, 20, 29, 56, 57, 67, 71, 81, 86, 109, 128, 212
nationalization, 18, 48, 255n54
nationally identified readers
  Arnow novels as viewed by, 110
  defined, 56
  Fox novels as viewed by, 65–67, 70, 81–82, 85–86
  southern writers and, 252n30
National Society of the Sons of the American Revolution, 67
Native Americans, 16, 170, 274n79, 292n43. *See also* tribe; Zuni Indians
nativism, 4, 20, 29, 38–39
naturalism, 38
Neff, Elizabeth, 120
Negri, Madeline, 160
Neo–Gilded Age (1985–2008)
  Appalachian whiteness during, 220
  characteristics of, 4, 179, 218

Neo–Gilded Age *(cont.)*
  community fantasy novels during, 225–26
  fan types during, 14
  Gilded Age compared to, 179–80, 257n67
  local-color writing during, 4, 22, 24–25, 133, 178–79, 208, 227–28, 305n5
  regionalism during, 214, 258n69
  secondary characters as used during, 205
  text popularity/selection, 234–35
  use of term, 257n67
Nesom, Louis, 82
Neumeyer, Peter F., 302n150
New England
  Americanness in, 16
  local-color writing in, 3, 19, 178
  Murfree and literary circles of, 49–50
  whiteness in, 16
New Orleans, local-color writing in, 19
New South, 265n4
New Statesman, 152, 174–75
New Yorker, 191
New York Herald Tribune, 280n30, 281n38
New York Life, 269n33
New York Post, 279n28
New York Times, 21, 58, 90, 94, 105, 132, 136, 152, 184, 231–33, 234, 278n16, 279n27, 289n22, 305n5, 306n6, 309nn30–31, 327nn11, 16, 327–28n23
New York Times Saturday Review of Books, 61, 62, 151, 231, 276–77n5
Nielsen Bookscan, 232
Night Comes to the Cumberlands (Caudill), 23, 291n40
Norman, Dean, 173
Norman, Gurney, 265n4
North Carolina, 167, 186
Northeast
  Dickey readers in, 153
  Marshall readers in, 139
North Georgia State University, 161
Northwest, local-color writing in, 178
nostalgia, 6, 22, 25, 266n9
"nostalgic cosmopolitans," 182, 192–200
not-quite-white, 39, 165, 220, 224, 251n22

Oates, Joyce Carol, 90
Obenchain, Eliza C., 233
O Brother, Where Art Thou? (film; 2000), 307n18
October Sky (film; 1999), 234, 307n18
"offended Appalachians," 182, 206–7
Office of the Council of the Southern Mountains (Berea, KY), 171
Of Time and the River (Wolfe), 328n23
Ogle, Anna Mae, 144
Ohio, 213
Old Burnside (Arnow), 280n35
"old country, the," 142
One Foot in Eden (Rash), 177
"On Fannin County" (poem; Dickey), 150
On Horseback (Dudley), 244
"On Horseback to Kingdom Come" (Fox), 74–75 map, 76–77 map, 83, 239, 272nn55–56
Oprah Book Club, 181, 235, 305n4, 328–29n28
Other, the
  African Americans as, 25
  Appalachianness and, 222, 324n24
  fantasies of the South and, 254n45
  hillbillies as, 158, 175, 176, 197
  imperialism and, 270–71n45
  interchangeability and, 23, 121, 128, 132, 156, 170, 175–76, 303n156
  missionary perspective and, 195
Other America, The (Harrington), 23
Our Southern Highlanders (Kephart), 68, 144, 255–56n58

Outing, 267n11
Outlook, 62–63
"outsiders." *See* "insiders"/"outsiders" dichotomy
"overcivilization," 37
"Over on t'Other Mounting" (Murfree), 263n39

Page, Thomas Nelson, 63, 65, 66, 269n30
Palin, Sarah, 213
"Panther of Jolton's Ridge, The" (Murfree), 261n24
paperback fiction, market expansion in, 304–5n4, 327n16
Parchment of Leaves, A (House), 177
Paris (KY), 83, 85
Park, Allen Joe, 148
Parker, Rita, 80
pastoralism, 1, 23, 61, 87, 92–93, 100–109, *103,* 127, 132, 187, 194, 217
pastoral novels, 17
paternalism, 227
Peck, W. H., 44–45
Penguin, 307n20
Perfect Storm, The (Junger), 178
Philadelphia (PA) Anthropological Society, 63
Phillips, Carol, 144
Phillips, Jerry, 270–71n45
piano, 61
Pierson, Hamilton Wilcox, 42–44, *43*
pioneers, 16, 81–82, 109, 136, 142, 145, 156–57, 217
place, sense of, 5, 22, 72, 185, 187, 195–96, 211, 307–8n22
placelessness, 8, 84
Plant Life (Duncan), 177
Pledge of Allegiance, 288n6
pluralism, 182
popular literature, Appalachian stereotypes in, 1–2
popular religion, 134

Port Chester Record, 67
Porter, Horace, 37
Posnock, Ross, 9
post–World War II era, 4
  Arnow novels' popularity during, 131–32
  mobility during, 283n53
  religiosity during, 288n6
  suburbanization and nostalgia during, 22, 124
  text popularity/selection, 231–34
poverty, 16, 23, 121, 143, 144, 207, 249n2, 250n11, 291n40
power, circulation of, 5, 6–7, 91, 93, 119–22, 132, 173–76, 221
Power and the Glory, The (Cooke), 61
Prairie Home Companion, A, 24, 178
Pratt, Mary Louise, 260n12
Prayers of Peter Marshall, The (ed. Marshall), 289n22
primitive masculinity, 38
primitives, Appalachians as, 7, 8, 17, 23, 49, 60–63, 65, 80, 109, 132–34, 156, 165, 172–74, 214, 324n24
primitivism, 3, 128, 133, 134, 174–75
Prince, Gerald, 326n2
print culture, 57
Proctor Coal Company (Jellico, TN), 65, 85
Prodigal Summer (Kingsolver), 234, 307n18, 308n22
professionalization, 56, 59, 84
Progressive Era, 4
  best sellers during, 21
  characteristics of, 67
  literary regionalism decline during, 20, 21–22, 131
  text popularity/selection, 230–31
Prophet of the Great Smoky Mountains, The (Murfree), 32–33, 239
Proulx, Annie, 306n6
Pryse, Marjorie, 14–15

Publishers Weekly, 183, 184, 231–33, 266–67n11, 288–89n15, 289n22, 294n60, 328n23
Pulitzer Prize, 277n5

quaintness, 7, 18, 19, 25, 28, 44, 48, 49, 56, 68, 83, 95, 102, *103*, 104, 122, 142, 195, 201, 203, 227

racial diversity, 29
racial innocence, 16, 219, 219–20, 224
racialization, 39, 62, 65, 265n3
racial victimization, 224–25, 324–25nn29–31
racism, 39, 56, 150, 171, 192, 200, 212, 219–20, 221–22
radio, 277n10
Radway, Janice, 11, 251n20
railroads, 48, 81, 269n25
Raitz, Karl B., 250n10
Ramsay, L., 111–12
Random House, 307n20
Ray, Janeice (Janisse), 236, 294n64
Ray, Michael, 173
reader, hypothetical, 326nn2–3
reading, 6, 127
Reagan, Ronald, 24, 257n67
reception geographies, 13, 212, 213, 229
reception histories, 11, 13
reception studies, 15, 31, 229–30
reception theory, 229
red scare, 134
Reed, John Shelton, 324–25n30
regional elite
  as Arnow readers, 93, 94, 119–20, 284n67
  "charmed Appalachians" and, 196
  as Dickey readers, 158, 160
  Fox legacy promoted by, 83–84
  as Fox readers, 71–73, 78
  as Murfree readers, 14, 20, 29–30, 42–49
  popular regional fiction and, 6–7, 212
  as transitional readers, 71–73

regional fiction
  compassion aroused by, 120–21
  consequences of, 11, 14–15, 19, 30–31, 52, 120, 153, 175, 217, 228, 229, 255n52
  decline of, during Progressive Era, 20
  defined, 254n50
  documentary accuracy and, 10–11, 178, 193
  functions of, 4–8, 178, 211, 214, 220–21
  during Gilded Age, 255n52
  local-color fiction vs., 14–15, 253n40
  migration and, 214–15
  paperback market expansion and, 304–5n4
  popularity of, 3, 82, 216, 218
  as primer on region, 178
  reader needs met by, 91
  region/regional identity produced through, 215–16
  resurgence of, during Neo–Gilded Age, 24, 216, 305–6n6
  would-be writers of, 82
  See also Appalachian-set fiction; local-color fiction; identity, regional fiction and enabling of
regionalism
  capitalism and, 250n8
  defined, 18
  literary, 15, 214, 256n60
  local color vs., 12–13
  resurgence of, during Neo–Gilded Age, 214, 258n69
  as symptom of passing older America, 256n61
  whiteness and, 178
  See also regional fiction; local-color fiction
regionalist scholarship, 15
Reichert Powell, Douglas, 203, 210, 211, 216, 227, 307–8n22
religion, popular, 134

Remington, Frederic, 66
"revolt from the village" fiction, 213
Rich's Department Store (Atlanta, GA), *159*
Ricks, Christopher, 151
River of Earth (Still), 91, 177, 231
Roanoke (VA), 202
Robbins, Mrs. Royal E., 49
Roberts, Elizabeth Madox, 213, 233
Robison, Ina M., 142, 300n128
Rocket Boys (Hickam), 234, 307n18
Rogers, Linda, 156, 295n72
Roosevelt, Theodore, 38, 65, 66, 81, 239, 270n45
rootlessness, 128, 218
roots music festivals, 4
Roseanna McCoy (Hannum), 233
Rosewood Casket, The (McCrumb), 235
Royall, Ann Newport, 254n47
Rubinstein, Mrs. (*Christy* reader), 142
Rubio, Gwyn Hyman, 235, 307n18
Ruble, Mary, 166, 244
Ryan, Barbara, 229, 329n30

Saturday Review, 109, 152, 261–62n30, 277n5
Sawyer, Diane, 4
Schubert, Mrs. Carl D., 290n28
Schulze, Mildred, 120
Scotland, 142, 218, 220, 221, 293n49
Scots-Irish, 142, 171, 220, 224, 244, 279n28, 306n15
Scribner, Charles, III, 239, 267n12
Scribner's, 56, *69*, 81, 267n11
Secret Life of Bees, The (Kidd), 178
Seedtime on the Cumberland (Arnow), 240, 280n35
Segure, Chris, 302–3n151
Seifert, Elizabeth, 233
settlement school movement, 167
Shaker, Bonnie James, 262n35
Shapcott, Tom, 173–74
Shapiro, Henry D., 2–3, 7, 40, 126, 216, 222, 249–50n7, 265n3, 304n3, 323n17

Shapiro, Tricia, 322n12
Shepherd of the Hills (Wright), 20
She Walks These Hills (McCrumb), 321n160
Shipping News (Proulx), 306n6
Silber, Nina, 266n9
Silent Spring (Carson), 132
simplicity, 149, 189, 217, 291–92n41, 317n104
Sjoberg, Gidean, 251n19
Sky, Patrick, 160
slums, authenticity in, 109
Smith, Barbara Ellen, 220, 224, 322n3
Smith, Dee Ann, 170, 291n38
Smith, Francis Hopkinson, 239
Smith, Lee, 9, 177, 181, 231, 307n18
Smithsonian Folklife Festival (2003), 217–18, 220–22, 258n73
Snodgrass, Gertrude, 111, 120, 236–37, 285n75
Snow Falling on Cedars (Guterson), 178
Songcatcher, The (film; 2000), 4
Sons of the American Revolution, National Society of the, 67
South
  Appalachia vs., 16–17
  crafts from, 277–78n10
  Dickey readers in, 153
  fictional respresentations of, 9–10
  local-color writing in, 3, 19, 178
  Marshall readers in, 139
  as Other, 254n45
  out-migrant burials in, 278n19
  out-migration from, 251–52n24
  reader fantasies of, 254n45
  rural music, 258n73
  southern writings about, 252n30
  as subordinated territory, 270n42, 325n37
  whiteness in, 16–17, 19
Southeastern Kentucky Heritage Association, 316n94
Southern Diaspora, 22
  African Americans in, 194

Southern Diaspora *(cont.)*
　Arnow novels and, 89–90, 110–11, 118
　Christy and, 145–48, *146–47 map*
　descendants of, 180, 213, 214
　economic success through, 124, 126–27, 279n25, 286–87n91
　as impermanent, 90, 277n6
　migrant burial choices during, 278n19
　migrant "divided heart" during, 125
　migration levels, 179
　as segregated, 282n46
　use of term, 92
　white migration during, 180
Southern Family, A (Godwin), 234, 328n25
Southern Highlander and His Homeland, The (Campbell), 244
"Southern Mountaineer in Fact and Fiction, The" (C. Williams), 232
Southern Mountaineer in Literature, The (Boger), 233
Southern Renaissance, 256n59
southwestern humor tales, 254n47
Sowinski, Koni, 167
Spacek, Sissy, 4
Spain, Mildred, 293n47
Spanish-American War (1898), 270n45
Spence, Eleanor B., 239
Sports Illustrated, 297n95
Spragins, Joyce, 285n78
Squires, Claire, 328n27
standardization, 135
"Star in the Valley, The" (Murfree), 40
stayers, 215
Stegner, Wallace, 23, 131, 135
Stenerson, Margaret, 158
Stern, Dick, 156
Steward, Margaret, 166
Still, James, 91, 231
St. Louis Post Dispatch, 160
Stonewall Jackson Female Institute, 264n1
storytelling, 186

Stowell, Mrs. Charles, 113
Stratton-Porter, Gene, 329n30
Stribling, Thomas, 233
Strother, David Hunter, 254n47
Stuart, Jesse, 21–22, 213, 234, 278n16, 284n67
suburbanization, 22, 92, 109, 124, 135, 157, 282n52
Summer of the Swans (Byars), 233

Taft, William Howard, 66, 239
"Taking the Blue Ribbon at the County Fair" (Murfree), 261n24
Taps for Private Tussie (Stuart), 21–22, 234, 278n16
television, 4, 23, 287n1, 325n31
Tennessee
　poverty in, 16
　volunteerism in, 167
Tennessee Valley region, 277n6
terrorism, 187
Thaxter, Celia, 45, 263n46
Thomson, Rosemarie Garland, 264n52
Thoreau, Henry David, 132, 172
Thwaite, Anthony, 174–75, 176
Time of Man, The (Roberts), 233
Times (London), 176, 282n50, 325n30
To Live Again (Marshall), 242, 289n22
Tönnies, Ferdinand, 251n19
tourism/tourist perspective, 7
　Arnow and lack of, 91
　Appalachia and, 188, 189–90, 214, 218
　Christy and, 132, 134, 145, 165–67, 168–69 map
　Cold Mountain and, 189–90, *190*
　Deliverance and, 132, 134, 145, 172–73, *190*, 295n72, 302n145
　Fox novels and, 63, 80, 84, 269n25
　literary, 49, 52
　in Murfree stories, 39–40, 50
　during the Neo–Gilded Age, 188–90

nostalgic out-migrants and, 197
regional fiction and, 23, 188–90
tourist art, 197, 250n11
"touristic cosmopolitans," 182, 188–93, 197
Townsend, John Wilson, 119, 236, 273n69, 284n67
tradition, 142, 182
Trail of the Lonesome Pine, The (Fox), 21
  advertising for, 58
  as best seller, 20, 57, 230–31, 267n12
  contradictory progress stories in, 86–87
  documentary accuracy and, 56, 63, 84–85
  ethnicity in, 323n19
  fan mail about, 55, 59, 71, 75, 76–77 *map*, 239–40, 241
  identity and sense of belonging in, 55, 57, 68, 71, 73, 78, 80
  illustrations from, 79
  industrialization as portrayed in, 59–62, 67, 87
  locally identified readers of, 67–70, 69, 271n51
  methodological considerations, 230–31, 239–40
  mountain life as portrayed in, 208
  mountain residents racialized/colonized by, 265n3
  nationally identified readers of, 65–67, 70, 85–86
  popularity of, 55–56, 57–58, 73, 136, 266n10
  power circulation in, 56, 58, 61–62, 66–67, 71–71, 81–84
  print reviews of, 56, 58–59, 61–63, 67, 85
  publication of, 57
  reader identification with characters in, 73, 78–80, 79
  readership types, 14, 56–57, 212
  sense of authentic place as constructed in, 63, 65–67, 78, 80, 83
  tourism and, 63, 80, 84, 269n25

Trail of the Lonesome Pine, The (Fox), transitional readers of
  class variation among, 71
  defined, 56–57
  fan mail from, 59, 71, 76–77 *map*, 86
  middling-class, 73–80
  mobility and, 71, 73–78
  modernization and, 71
  regional/local elite as, 71–73, 78
travelogue tradition, 254n47
tribe, 62, 268n19, 328n25
Trigiani, Adriana, 24–25, 181, 186–87. *See also Big Stone Gap*
True, Johnnie Sue, 236, 290n28
Turner, Bill, 194
Turner, Frederick Jackson, 16
Tuttle, Bettie J., 240, 265–66n4, 275n86
Twain, Mark, 49

Ulack, Richard, 250n10
Uncle Remus, 320n144
unemployment, 207, 286n91
"Unguarded Gates" (Aldrich), 38–39
United Mine Workers, 170
United Nations, 258n73
United States, compulsory education in, 273n63
United States Agriculture Department, 250n10
United States Congress, 258n73
universalism, 256n59
University of Kentucky, 239
University of Kentucky Libraries, 240
University of Louisville, 105, 106
University of North Carolina (Asheville), 161
Upper Cuyahoga Association (OH), 173
urbanization, 73
  anti-urbanism, 123
  during Gilded Age, 37–38
  high middlebrow readers and, 179
  homesickness as result of, 266n6

urbanization *(cont.)*
  local-color fiction and, 3
  local culture as lost through, 179
  Murfree readers and, 20, 29, 30
  pastoral literature and, 17
  during Progressive Era, 266n6
  women and, 279n26
USA Today, 178, 184, 186, 234–35, 289n17

Van der Meulen, Sandra, 172, 301–2n138
Vaught, Rana, 283n60
Vedder, Henry C., 39, 262–63n38
Viet Cong, 135
Vietnam War, 174–75
Vietnam War era, 4
  Appalachian-set fiction during, 23
  popular language of, 291n40
  reader needs during, 134–35
  text popularity/selection, 231–34
Vintage, 307n20
Virginia, 16, 21, 272n55
Virginia Cavalcade, 265n4
Voiers, Lena Wells, 284n67
Voigt, Jon, 176, 296–97n85
volunteerism, 167
Volunteer Police Guard, 66
Von Brandenburg, EVB, 271–72n52
voyeurism, emotional, 296–97n85

Walk in the Woods, A (Bryson), 307n18
Wallace, Anne, 170
Wallace, Tom, 68, 271n52
Waller, Altina, 256n58
Waltons, The (TV program), 23
Waltons, The (Weverka), 233
Warfel, Sidney Ernestine, 123, 286n88
War on Poverty, 144
Warren, Robert Penn, 233
Washington (DC) Star, 61
Watt, Irene, 118
Watterson, Henry, 239

Web and the Rock, The (Wolfe), 328n23
Webb, Jim, 224, 306n15
Webber, Everett, 236
Weber, Alma, 123
Weedkiller's Daughter, The (Arnow), 280n35
Weinberg, Cindy, 290n34
Weissman, Freda, 284–85n72
Weissman, Irving, 120, 237, 284–85n72
Wellington Enterprise, 111
Wells, Diane, 166, 301n136
Wells, Lena, 284n67
West
  Dickey readers in, 153
  local-color writing in, 3, 19, 178
  Marshall readers in, 139
West, John Foster, 164, 298n103
Western Carolina University (NC), 161
Westmoreland, William, 175
West Virginia, 16, 292n43
Weverka, Robert, 233
White, Mary Jane, 120
Whitehead, Henry, 67
white nationalism, 86, 91–92, 109–10, 222
whiteness, 324n29
  Appalachian, 16–17, 19, 192, 212, 217, 219–20, 224–25, 226
  Authentic Appalachia and celebration of, 8
  Fox and, 81–82
  generic, fear of, 6, 158, 202, 214, 221–22, 224
  "nongeneric," 160–61
  regionalism and, 178
  transitional readers and, 81–82
  See also Appalachian ethnicity; mountaineers as American "folk"; "almost-white"; not-quite-white
white readership, cultural identity of, 6
Whitesburg (KY), 69

"white soul," 218, 220
"white trash," 17, 205–6
Wigginton, Eliot, 150
Wilcox, Craig J., 167, 300n122
Williams, Cratis, 232, 265n3
Williams, John Alexander, 250n10
Williams, Mariane, 121
Williams, Raymond, 10–11, 17, 180, 229
Williamson, Jerry Wayne, 256n59, 267n12
Willie Pearl (Green), 315–16n94
Willis, Meredith Sue, 181
Wilson, Darlene, 59, 220, 265nn3–4, 266n8, 267n12, 269n25, 270n45, 272n54, 323n19
Wilson, Janice Meredith. *See* Karon, Jan
Wilson, Robert Burns, 239
Winfrey, Oprah, 181, 305n4, 328–29n28
Winthrop College (SC), 161
Wise County (VA), 83–84
Wish You Well (Baldacci), 234
Wister, Owen, 66, 239
Witten, W. H., 82, 274n79
WLS (Chicago radio station), 277n10
Wolfe, Thomas, 196, 213, 233, 327–28n23
women
  as Dickey readers, 295–96n74
  local-color fiction as used by, 260n12
  as Marshall readers, 139
  reading group participation of, 305n4
Women's Board of Domestic Missions, 285n78
Wood, Sarah Catherine. *See* Marshall, Catherine
Woolson, Constance Fenimore, 19, 259n11
working class, 3, 8, 17, 95, 125, 201, 208, 281n44, 290n26
Works Progress Administration (WPA), 22

World Congress on Evangelism (Berlin; 1966), 170
World War I, 21, 165, 251–52n24, 256n59
World War II, 89, 92, 100, 109, 124, 165
Wright, Harold Bell, 20

"Yares of Black Mountain, The" (Davis), 40
"Year of Appalachia," 246, 258n73
Yohey, Jeanne, 167
York, Bill, 85, 275n87
You Can't Go Home Again (Wolfe), 328n23
Young, Jock, 306n13
Young Harris College (GA), 161
Youngstown (OH), 282n46
Youth's Companion, 36, 38, 262n35

Zada Mae, 322n12
Zaragoza, June, 288n6
Zavasky, Mrs. R. L., 301n135
Zinsser, Mrs. Hans, 112, 236
Zuefle, Mark, 249n2
Zuni Indians, 49–50, 264n52

www.ingramcontent.com/pod-product-compliance
Lightning Source LLC
Chambersburg PA
CBHW031751220426
43662CB00007B/354